GO MATH!

Middle School

Advanced 1

Edward B. Burger • Juli K. Dixon • Timothy D. Kanold
Matthew R. Larson • Steven J. Leinwand
Martha E. Sandoval-Martinez

2018 Edition

Copyright © by Houghton Mifflin Harcourt Publishing Company

Printed in the U.S.A.

ISBN 978-1-328-77293-0

9 10 11   0029   29 28 27 26 25 24 23

4500862249   B C D E F G

Authors

Edward B. Burger, Ph.D., is the president of Southwestern University, a former Francis Christopher Oakley Third Century Professor of Mathematics at Williams College, and a former vice provost at Baylor University. He has authored or coauthored more than sixty-five articles, books, and video series; delivered over five hundred addresses and workshops throughout the world; and made more than fifty radio and television appearances. He is a Fellow of the American Mathematical Society as well as having earned many national honors, including the Robert Foster Cherry Award for Great Teaching in 2010. In 2012, Microsoft Education named him a "Global Hero in Education."

Juli K. Dixon, Ph.D., is a Professor of Mathematics Education at the University of Central Florida. She has taught mathematics in urban schools at the elementary, middle, secondary, and post-secondary levels. She is an active researcher and speaker with numerous publications and conference presentations. Key areas of focus are deepening teachers' content knowledge and communicating and justifying mathematical ideas. She is a past chair of the NCTM Student Explorations in Mathematics Editorial Panel and member of the Board of Directors for the Association of Mathematics Teacher Educators.

Timothy D. Kanold, Ph.D., is an award-winning international educator, author, and consultant. He is a former superintendent and director of mathematics and science at Adlai E. Stevenson High School District 125 in Lincolnshire, Illinois. He is a past president of the National Council of Supervisors of Mathematics (NCSM) and the Council for the Presidential Awardees of Mathematics (CPAM). He has served on several writing and leadership commissions for NCTM during the past decade. He presents motivational professional development seminars with a focus on developing professional learning communities (PLC's) to improve the teaching, assessing, and learning of students. He has recently authored nationally recognized articles, books, and textbooks for mathematics education and school leadership, including *What Every Principal Needs to Know about the Teaching and Learning of Mathematics*.

Matthew R. Larson, Ph.D., is the president of the National Council of Teachers of Mathematics (2016-2018) and served on the Board of Directors for NCTM from 2010-2013. He is a past chair of NCTM's Research Committee and was a member of NCTM's Task Force on Linking Research and Practice. He is the author of several books on implementing the Common Core Standards for Mathematics. He has taught mathematics at the secondary and college levels and held an appointment as an honorary visiting associate professor at Teachers College, Columbia University.

Steven J. Leinwand is a Principal Research Analyst at the American Institutes for Research (AIR) in Washington, D.C., and has over 30 years in leadership positions in mathematics education. He is past president of the National Council of Supervisors of Mathematics and served on the NCTM Board of Directors. He is the author of numerous articles, books, and textbooks and has made countless presentations with topics including student achievement, reasoning, effective assessment, and successful implementation of standards.

Martha E. Sandoval-Martinez is a mathematics instructor at El Camino College in Torrance, California. She was previously a Math Specialist at the University of California at Davis and former instructor at Santa Ana College, Marymount College, and California State University, Long Beach. In her current and former positions, she has worked extensively to improve fundamental pre-algebra and algebra skills in students who have historically struggled with mathematics.

Program Reviewers

Sharon Brown
Instructional Staff Developer
Pinellas County Schools
St. Petersburg, FL

Maureen Carrion
Math Staff Developer
Brentwood UFSD
Brentwood, NY

Jackie Cruse
Math Coach
Ferrell GPA
Tampa, FL

Esser
Secondary Mathematics
Coordinator
Racine Unified School District
Racine

Donald r
Math Teac
Discovery M   ol
Orlando, Flo

Becky (Rebecca) Jones, M.Ed.
NBCT EA-Math
Orange County Public Schools
Orlando, FL

Sheila D.P. Lea, MSA
Ben L. Smith High School
Greensboro, NC

Toni Lwanga
Newell Barney Jr. High
Queen Creek Unified School District
Queen Creek, AZ

Tiffany J. Mack
Charles A. Lindbergh Middle School
Peoria District #150
Peoria, IL

Jean Sterner
Thurgood Marshall Fundamental
Middle School
Pinellas County Schools
St. Petersburg, FL

Mona Toncheff
Math Content Specialist
Phoenix Union High School District
Phoenix, AZ

Kevin Voepel
Mathematics & Professional
Development Coordinator
Ferguson-Florissant School District
Florissant, MO

UNIT 1 Numbers

MODULE 1 Integers

MODULE 2 Factors and Multiples

MODULE 3 Rational Numbers

UNIT  Number Operations

MODULE 4 Operations with Fractions

MODULE 5 Operations with Decimals

MODULE **6** Representing Ratios and Rates

MODULE **7** Applying Ratios and Rates

Houghton Mifflin Harcourt Publishing Company • Image Credits: (t) ©Anne-Marie Palmer/Alamy;
(b) ©Bravo/NBCUniversal/Getty Images

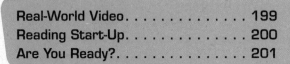

MODULE 8 Percents

UNIT 5 Equations and Inequalities

MODULE 11 Equations and Relationships

MODULE 12 Relationships in Two Variables

UNIT 6 Relationships in Geometry

MODULE 13 Area and Polygons

MODULE 14 Distance and Area in the Coordinate Plane

MODULE 15 Surface Area and Volume of Solids

UNIT 7 Measurement and Data

MODULE 16 Displaying, Analyzing, and Summarizing Data

UNIT 8 The Number System

MODULE 17 Adding and Subtracting Integers

MODULE 18 Multiplying and Dividing Integers

© Houghton Mifflin Harcourt Publishing Company • Image Credits: (t) ©Peter Haigh/Digital Vision/Getty Images; (b) ©wusuowei/Fotolia

MODULE 19 Rational Numbers

UNIT 9 Ratios and Proportional Relationships

MODULE 20 Rates and Proportionality

MODULE 21 Proportions and Percent

© Houghton Mifflin Harcourt Publishing Company • Image Credits: (t) ©OSO Media/Alamy Images

Mathematics Objectives

for *HMH Go Math* Advanced 1

Objective	Descriptor	Taught & Practiced
Unit 1 Numbers		
Module 1 Integers		
6.1.1.1	Students will identify an integer and its opposite.	Lesson 1.1: pp. 7–12
6.1.1.2	Students will compare and order integers.	Lesson 1.2: pp. 13–18
6.1.1.3	Students will find and use absolute value.	Lesson 1.3: pp. 19–24
Module 2 Factors and Multiples		
6.1.2.1	Students will find and use the greatest common factor of two whole numbers.	Lesson 2.1: pp. 31–36
6.1.2.2	Students will find and use the least common multiple of two numbers.	Lesson 2.2: pp. 37–40
Module 3 Rational Numbers		
6.1.3.1	Students will classify rational numbers.	Lesson 3.1: pp. 47–52
6.1.3.2	Students will identify opposites and absolute value of rational numbers.	Lesson 3.2: pp. 53–58
6.1.3.3	Students will compare and order rational numbers.	Lesson 3.3: pp. 59–64
Unit 2 Number Operations		
Module 4 Operations with Fractions		
6.2.4.1	Students will use the GCF and LCM when adding, subtracting, and multiplying fractions.	Lesson 4.1: pp. 79–84
6.2.4.2	Students will divide fractions.	Lesson 4.2: pp. 85–90
6.2.4.3	Students will divide mixed numbers.	Lesson 4.3: pp. 91–96
6.2.4.4	Students will solve word problems involving more than one fraction operation.	Lesson 4.4: pp. 97–100
Module 5 Operations with Decimals		
6.2.5.1	Students will divide multi-digit whole numbers.	Lesson 5.1: pp. 107–112
6.2.5.2	Students will add and subtract decimals.	Lesson 5.2: pp. 113–118
6.2.5.3	Students will multiply decimals.	Lesson 5.3: pp. 119–124
6.2.5.4	Students will divide decimals.	Lesson 5.4: pp. 125–130
6.2.5.5	Students will solve problems involving multiplication and division of fractions and decimals.	Lesson 5.5: pp. 131–134

Objective	Descriptor	Taught & Practiced
Unit 3 Proportionality: Ratios and Rates		
Module 6 Representing Ratios and Rates		
6.3.6.1	Students will use ratios to compare two quantities.	Lesson 6.1: pp. 149–154
6.3.6.2	Students will use rates to compare quantities.	Lesson 6.2: pp. 155–160
6.3.6.3	Students will use ratios and rates to make comparisons and predictions.	Lesson 6.3: pp. 161–166
Module 7 Applying Ratios and Rates		
6.3.7.1	Students will represent real-world problems involving ratios and rates with tables and graphs.	Lesson 7.1: pp. 173–178
6.3.7.2	Students will solve problems with proportions.	Lesson 7.2: pp. 179–184
6.3.7.3	Students will convert units within a measurement system.	Lesson 7.3: pp. 185–190
6.3.7.4	Students will use ratios and proportions to convert measurements.	Lesson 7.4: pp. 191–196
Module 8 Percents		
6.3.8.1	Students will write a ratio as a percent.	Lesson 8.1: pp. 203–208
6.3.8.2	Students will write equivalent percents, fractions, and decimals.	Lesson 8.2: pp. 209–214
6.3.8.3	Students will use percents to solve problems.	Lesson 8.3: pp. 215–222
Unit 4 Equivalent Expressions		
Module 9 Generating Equivalent Numerical Expressions		
6.4.9.1	Students will use exponents to represent numbers.	Lesson 9.1: pp. 237–242
6.4.9.2	Students will write the prime factorization of a number.	Lesson 9.2: pp. 243–248
6.4.9.3	Students will use the order of operations to simplify expressions with exponents.	Lesson 9.3: pp. 249–254
Module 10 Generating Equivalent Algebraic Expressions		
6.4.10.1	Students will model and write algebraic expressions.	Lesson 10.1: pp. 261–268
6.4.10.2	Students will use the order of operations to evaluate algebraic expressions.	Lesson 10.2: pp. 269–274
6.4.10.3	Students will identify and write equivalent expressions.	Lesson 10.3: pp. 275–282
Unit 5 Equations and Inequalities		
Module 11 Equations and Relationships		
6.5.11.1	Students will write equations and determine whether a number is a solution of an equation.	Lesson 11.1: pp. 297–302
6.5.11.2	Students will solve equations that contain addition or subtraction.	Lesson 11.2: pp. 303–310
6.5.11.3	Students will solve equations that contain multiplication or division.	Lesson 11.3: pp. 311–318
6.5.11.4	Students will use inequalities to represent real-world constraints or conditions.	Lesson 11.4: pp. 319–324

Objective	Descriptor	Taught & Practiced
Module 12 Relationships in Two Variables		
6.5.12.1	Students will locate and name points in the coordinate plane.	Lesson 12.1: pp. 331–336
6.5.12.2	Students will identify independent and dependent quantities from tables and graphs.	Lesson 12.2: pp. 337–344
6.5.12.3	Students will use an equation to show a relationship between two variables.	Lesson 12.3: pp. 345–350
6.5.12.4	Students will use verbal descriptions, tables, and graphs to represent algebraic relationships.	Lesson 12.4: pp. 351–356
Unit 6 Relationships in Geometry		
Module 13 Area and Polygons		
6.6.13.1	Students will find the areas of parallelograms, rhombuses, and trapezoids.	Lesson 13.1: pp. 371–376
6.6.13.2	Students will find the area of a triangle.	Lesson 13.2: pp. 377–382
6.6.13.3	Students will use equations to solve problems about area of rectangles, parallelograms, trapezoids, and triangles.	Lesson 13.3: pp. 383–388
6.6.13.4	Students will find the area of a polygon by breaking it into simpler shapes.	Lesson 13.4: pp. 389–394
Module 14 Distance and Area in the Coordinate Plane		
6.6.14.1	Students will use absolute value to find the distance between two points with the same x- or y-coordinates.	Lesson 14.1: pp. 401–406
6.6.14.2	Students will solve problems by drawing polygons in the coordinate plane.	Lesson 14.2: pp. 407–412
Module 15 Surface Area and Volume of Solids		
6.6.15.1	Students will use nets to find surface areas.	Lesson 15.1: pp. 419–424
6.6.15.2	Students will find the volume of a rectangular prism.	Lesson 15.2: pp. 425–430
6.6.15.3	Students will write equations to solve problems involving volume of rectangular prisms.	Lesson 15.3: pp. 431–434
Unit 7 Measurement and Data		
Module 16 Displaying, Analyzing, and Summarizing Data		
6.7.16.1	Students will use measures of center to describe a data set.	Lesson 16.1: pp. 449–454
6.7.16.2	Students will determine and use the mean absolute deviation of a set of data points.	Lesson 16.2: pp. 455–462
6.7.16.3	Students will use a box plot and measures of spread to describe a data set.	Lesson 16.3: pp. 463–468
6.7.16.4	Students will summarize and display numeric data.	Lesson 16.4: pp. 469–476
6.7.16.5	Students will display data in a histogram.	Lesson 16.5: pp. 477–482

Objective	Descriptor	Taught & Practiced
Unit 8 The Number System		
Module 17 Adding and Subtracting Integers		
7.1.1.1	Students will add integers with the same sign.	Lesson 17.1: pp. 495–500
7.1.1.2	Students will add integers with different signs.	Lesson 17.2: pp. 501–506
7.1.1.3	Students will subtract integers.	Lesson 17.3: pp. 507–512
7.1.1.4	Students will solve multistep problems involving addition and subtraction of integers.	Lesson 17.4: pp. 513–518
Module 18 Multiplying and Dividing Integers		
7.1.2.1	Students will multiply integers.	Lesson 18.1: pp. 525–530
7.1.2.2	Students will divide integers.	Lesson 18.2: pp. 531–536
7.1.2.3	Students will use integer operations to solve real-world problems.	Lesson 18.3: pp. 537–542
Module 19 Rational Numbers		
7.1.3.1	Students will convert a rational number to a decimal.	Lesson 19.1: pp. 549–554
7.1.3.2	Students will add rational numbers.	Lesson 19.2: pp. 555–562
7.1.3.3	Students will subtract rational numbers.	Lesson 19.3: pp. 563–570
7.1.3.4	Students will multiply rational numbers.	Lesson 19.4: pp. 571–576
7.1.3.5	Students will divide rational numbers.	Lesson 19.5: pp. 577–582
7.1.3.6	Students will use different forms of rational numbers and strategically choose tools to solve problems.	Lesson 19.6: pp. 583–588
Unit 9 Ratios and Proportional Relationships		
Module 20 Rates and Proportionality		
7.2.4.1	Students will find and use unit rates.	Lesson 20.1: pp. 605–610
7.2.4.2	Students will identify and represent proportional relationships.	Lesson 20.2: pp. 611–616
7.2.4.3	Students will use graphs to represent and analyze proportional relationships.	Lesson 20.3: pp. 617–622
Module 21 Proportions and Percent		
7.2.5.1	Students will use percents to describe change.	Lesson 21.1: pp. 629–634
7.2.5.2	Students will rewrite expressions to help solve markup and markdown problems.	Lesson 21.2: pp. 635–640
7.2.5.3	Students will use percents to solve problems.	Lesson 21.3: pp. 641–646

Process	Descriptor	Citations
MP Mathematical Processes		*The mathematical processes are integrated throughout the book. See, for example, the citations below.*
MP.1	**Problem Solving** Mathematically proficient students start by explaining to themselves the meaning of a problem and looking for entry points to its solution. They analyze givens, constraints, relationships, and goals. They make conjectures about the form and meaning of the solution and plan a solution pathway, rather than simply jumping into a solution attempt. They consider analogous problems and try special cases and simpler forms of the original problem in order to gain insight into its solution. They monitor and evaluate their progress and change course if necessary. Mathematically proficient students check their answers to problems using a different method, and they continually ask themselves, "Does this make sense?" and "Is my answer reasonable?" They understand the approaches of others to solving complex problems and identify correspondences between different approaches. Mathematically proficient students understand how mathematical ideas interconnect and build on one another to produce a coherent whole.	36, 97–98, 190, 268, 302, 376, 454, 588, 643
MP.2	**Abstract and Quantitative Reasoning** Mathematically proficient students make sense of quantities and their relationships in problem situations. They bring two complementary abilities to bear on problems involving quantitative relationships: the ability to decontextualize—to abstract a given situation and represent it symbolically and manipulate the representing symbols as if they have a life of their own, without necessarily attending to their referents—and the ability to contextualize, to pause as needed during the manipulation process in order to probe into the referents for the symbols involved. Quantitative reasoning entails habits of creating a coherent representation of the problem at hand; considering the units involved; attending to the meaning of quantities, not just how to compute them; and knowing and flexibly using different properties of operations and objects.	64, 90, 193, 254, 320, 382, 462, 582, 637

Process	Descriptor	Citations
MP.3	**Use and Evaluate Logical Reasoning** Mathematically proficient students understand and use stated assumptions, definitions, and previously established results in constructing arguments. They make conjectures and build a logical progression of statements to explore the truth of their conjectures. They analyze situations by breaking them into cases and recognize and use counterexamples. They organize their mathematical thinking, justify their conclusions and communicate them to others, and respond to the arguments of others. They reason inductively about data, making plausible arguments that take into account the context from which the data arose. Mathematically proficient students are also able to compare the effectiveness of two plausible arguments, distinguish correct logic or reasoning from that which is flawed, and—if there is a flaw in an argument—explain what it is. They justify whether a given statement is true always, sometimes, or never. Mathematically proficient students participate and collaborate in a mathematics community. They listen to or read the arguments of others, decide whether they make sense, and ask useful questions to clarify or improve the arguments.	24, 112, 208, 248, 318, 406, 468, 506, 622
MP.4	**Mathematical Modeling** Mathematically proficient students apply the mathematics they know to solve problems arising in everyday life, society, and the workplace using a variety of appropriate strategies. They create and use a variety of representations to solve problems and to organize and communicate mathematical ideas. Mathematically proficient students apply what they know and are comfortable making assumptions and approximations to simplify a complicated situation, realizing that these may need revision later. They are able to identify important quantities in a practical situation and map their relationships using such tools as diagrams, two-way tables, graphs, flowcharts and formulas. They analyze those relationships mathematically to draw conclusions. They routinely interpret their mathematical results in the context of the situation and reflect on whether the results make sense, possibly improving the model if it has not served its purpose.	17, 100, 215–216, 249, 324, 385, 468, 500, 610

Process	Descriptor	Citations
MP.5	**Use Mathematical Tools** Mathematically proficient students consider the available tools when solving a mathematical problem. These tools might include pencil and paper, models, a ruler, a protractor, a calculator, a spreadsheet, a computer algebra system, a statistical package, or dynamic geometry software. Mathematically proficient students are sufficiently familiar with tools appropriate for their grade or course to make sound decisions about when each of these tools might be helpful, recognizing both the insight to be gained and their limitations. Mathematically proficient students identify relevant external mathematical resources, such as digital content, and use them to pose or solve problems. They use technological tools to explore and deepen their understanding of concepts and to support the development of learning mathematics. They use technology to contribute to concept development, simulation, representation, reasoning, communication and problem solving.	8, 91, 185, 276, 303, 371, 458, 588, 635
MP.6	**Use Precise Mathematical Language** Mathematically proficient students communicate precisely to others. They use clear definitions, including correct mathematical language, in discussion with others and in their own reasoning. They state the meaning of the symbols they choose, including using the equal sign consistently and appropriately. They express solutions clearly and logically by using the appropriate mathematical terms and notation. They specify units of measure and label axes to clarify the correspondence with quantities in a problem. They calculate accurately and efficiently and check the validity of their results in the context of the problem. They express numerical answers with a degree of precision appropriate for the problem context.	13, 93, 214, 242, 336, 424, 452, 550, 616

Process	Descriptor	Citations
MP.7	**See Structure** Mathematically proficient students look closely to discern a pattern or structure. They step back for an overview and shift perspective. They recognize and use properties of operations and equality. They organize and classify geometric shapes based on their attributes. They see expressions, equations, and geometric figures as single objects or as being composed of several objects.	18, 97, 118, 146, 175, 214, 263–264, 283, 311, 349, 410, 430, 471, 588, 643
MP.8	**Generalize** Mathematically proficient students notice if calculations are repeated and look for general methods and shortcuts. They notice regularity in mathematical problems and their work to create a rule or formula. Mathematically proficient students maintain oversight of the process, while attending to the details as they solve a problem. They continually evaluate the reasonableness of their intermediate results.	19, 61, 125, 149, 152, 203–204, 237, 242, 265, 290, 310, 378, 407, 462, 588, 643

Succeeding with HMH Go Math

Actively participate in your learning with your write-in Student Edition. Explore concepts, take notes, answer questions, and complete your homework right in your textbook!

Explore Activities help you develop a deeper understanding of math concepts.

Essential Questions ensure that you know exactly what you are learning.

Scan QR codes with your smartphone or device to watch **Math On the Spot** tutorial videos for every example in the book!

Your Turn exercises check your understanding of new concepts.

Play strategy **Games and Activities** with classmates to practice using the concepts you have learned.

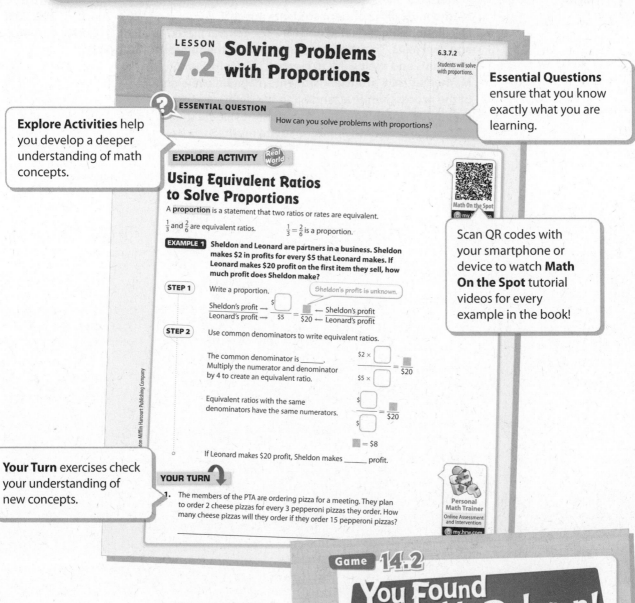

LESSON 7.2 Solving Problems with Proportions

6.3.7.2
Students will solve with proportions.

? ESSENTIAL QUESTION

How can you solve problems with proportions?

EXPLORE ACTIVITY Real World

Using Equivalent Ratios to Solve Proportions

A **proportion** is a statement that two ratios or rates are equivalent.

$\frac{1}{3}$ and $\frac{2}{6}$ are equivalent ratios. $\frac{1}{3} = \frac{2}{6}$ is a proportion.

EXAMPLE 1 Sheldon and Leonard are partners in a business. Sheldon makes $2 in profits for every $5 that Leonard makes. If Leonard makes $20 profit on the first item they sell, how much profit does Sheldon make?

STEP 1 Write a proportion.

Sheldon's profit is unknown.

Sheldon's profit → $\frac{\$\ }{\$5} = \frac{\ }{\$20}$ ← Sheldon's profit
Leonard's profit → ← Leonard's profit

STEP 2 Use common denominators to write equivalent ratios.

The common denominator is _____.
Multiply the numerator and denominator by 4 to create an equivalent ratio.

$\frac{\$2 \times \ }{\$5 \times \ } = \frac{\ }{\$20}$

Equivalent ratios with the same denominators have the same numerators.

$\frac{\$\ }{\$\ } = \frac{\ }{\$20}$

$\blacksquare = \$8$

If Leonard makes $20 profit, Sheldon makes _____ profit.

YOUR TURN

1. The members of the PTA are ordering pizza for a meeting. They plan to order 2 cheese pizzas for every 3 pepperoni pizzas they order. How many cheese pizzas will they order if they order 15 pepperoni pizzas?

Personal Math Trainer
Online Assessment and Intervention
my.hrw.com

Game 14.2

You Found My Polygon!

INSTRUCTIONS

Playing the Game

STEP 1 Sitting so that you and your opponent cannot see each other's work, draw copies of the polygons shown below on your Hiding Ground coordinate plane. Draw one polygon in each quadrant. You can place vertices on an axis, but all vertices must have integer coordinates. You can draw a polygon so that it is rotated from the position shown. For example, you can draw the rectangle rotated so that it is oriented vertically. You cannot, however, change the size of any polygon.

For example, your opponent draws the polygons on his or her Hiding Ground coordinate plane in the positions shown.

Hiding Ground

STEP 2 To play the game, alternate turns, keeping your coordinate plane hidden from your opponent's view. Begin your turn by calling out an ordered

© Houghton Mifflin Harcourt Publishing Company

© Houghton Mifflin Harcourt Publishing Company

Reading Start-Up

Visualize Vocabulary

Use the ✔ words to complete the graphic. You may put more than one word in each box.

Review concepts you will need to know before beginning each module.

```
┌──────────────┐          ┌──────────────┐
│    0.25      │          │   3/4, 3:4   │
└──────────────┘          └──────────────┘

         ┌────────────────────────────────┐
         │ Reviewing Fractions and Decimals │
         └────────────────────────────────┘

┌──────────────┐          ┌──────────────┐
│  2/3 = 6/9   │          │  4/8 → 1/2   │
└──────────────┘          └──────────────┘
```

Vocabulary

Review Words
✔ decimal (decimal)
✔ equivalent fractions (fracciones equivalentes)
denominator (denominador)
✔ fraction (fracción)
mixed number (número mixto)
numerator (numerador)
✔ ratio (razón)
✔ simplest form (mínima expresión)

Preview Words
equivalent decimals (decimales equivalentes)
model (modelo)
percent (porcentaje)
proportional reasoning (razonamiento proporcional)

Understand Vocabulary

Match the term on the left to the correct expression on the right.

1. percent   A. A ratio that compares a number to 100.

2. model   B. Decimals that name the same amount.

3. equivalent   C. Something that represents another thing.
   decimals

Active Reading

Pyramid Before beginning the module, create a pyramid to help you organize what you learn. Label one side "Decimals," one side "Fractions," and the other side "Percents." As you study the module, write important vocabulary and other notes on the appropriate side.

Get vocabulary, language, and note-taking support throughout the book.

Are YOU Ready?

Complete these exercises to review skills you will need for this module.

Personal Math Trainer — Online Assessment and Intervention

Simplify Fractions

EXAMPLE Simplify $\frac{15}{24}$.

15: 1, ③, 5, 15 → List all the factors of the numerator and denominator.
24: 1, 2, ③, 4, 6, 8, 12, 24 → Circle the greatest common factor (GCF).
$\frac{15 \div 3}{24 \div 3} = \frac{5}{8}$ → Divide the numerator and denominator by the GCF.

Write each fraction in simplest form.

1. $\frac{6}{9}$ 2. $\frac{4}{10}$ 3. $\frac{15}{20}$ 4. $\frac{20}{24}$

5. $\frac{16}{56}$ 6. $\frac{45}{72}$ 7. $\frac{18}{60}$ 8. $\frac{32}{72}$

Write Equivalent Fractions

EXAMPLE $\frac{6}{8} = \frac{6 \times 2}{8 \times 2}$ → Multiply the numerator and denominator by the same number to find an equivalent fraction.
$= \frac{12}{16}$

$\frac{6}{8} = \frac{6 \div 2}{8 \div 2}$ → Divide the numerator and denominator by the same number to find an equivalent fraction.
$= \frac{3}{4}$

Write the equivalent fraction.

9. $\frac{12}{15} = \frac{\square}{5}$ 10. $\frac{5}{6} = \frac{\square}{30}$ 11. $\frac{16}{24} = \frac{4}{\square}$ 12. $\frac{3}{9} = \frac{\square}{21}$

13. $\frac{15}{40} = \frac{\square}{8}$ 14. $\frac{18}{30} = \frac{\square}{10}$ 15. $\frac{48}{64} = \frac{12}{\square}$ 16. $\frac{2}{7} = \frac{18}{\square}$

Find out if you have mastered the concepts you learned in each module.

MODULE QUIZ

Ready to Go On?

Personal Math Trainer — Online Assessment and Intervention — my.hrw.com

4.1 Applying GCF and LCM to Fraction Operations

Solve.

1. $\frac{4}{5} \times \frac{3}{4}$ _____   2. $\frac{5}{7} \times \frac{9}{10}$ _____

3. $\frac{3}{8} + 2\frac{1}{2}$ _____   4. $1\frac{3}{5} - \frac{5}{6}$ _____

4.2 Dividing Fractions

Divide.

5. $\frac{1}{3} \div \frac{7}{9}$ _____   6. $\frac{1}{3} \div \frac{5}{8}$ _____

7. Luci cuts a board that is $\frac{3}{4}$ yard long into pieces that are $\frac{3}{8}$ yard long. How many pieces does she cut? _____

4.3 Dividing Mixed Numbers

Divide.

8. $3\frac{1}{3} \div \frac{2}{3}$ _____   9. $1\frac{7}{8} \div 2\frac{2}{5}$ _____

10. $4\frac{1}{4} \div 4\frac{1}{2}$ _____   11. $8\frac{1}{3} \div 4\frac{2}{7}$ _____

4.4 Solving Multistep Problems with Fractions and Mixed Numbers

12. Jamal hiked on two trails. The first trail was $5\frac{1}{3}$ miles long, and the second trail was $1\frac{3}{4}$ times as long as the first trail. How many miles did Jamal hike? _____

? ESSENTIAL QUESTION

13. Describe a real-world situation that is modeled by dividing two fractions or mixed numbers.

_____

_____

_____

Apply new skills and concepts to solve real-world problems in Unit Performance Tasks and Careers in Math activities.

Unit 2 Performance Tasks

1. **CAREERS IN MATH** **Chef** Chef Alonso is creating a recipe called Spicy Italian Chicken with the following ingredients: $\frac{3}{4}$ pound chicken, $2\frac{1}{2}$ cups tomato sauce, 1 teaspoon oregano, and $\frac{1}{3}$ teaspoon of his special hot sauce.

   a. Chef Alonso wants each serving of the dish to include $\frac{1}{2}$ pound of chicken. How many $\frac{1}{2}$ pound servings does this recipe make?

   _____

   b. What is the number Chef Alonso should multiply the amount of chicken by so that the recipe will make 2 full servings, each with $\frac{1}{2}$ pound of chicken?

   _____

   c. Use the multiplier you found in part **b** to find the amount of all the ingredients in the new recipe.

   _____

   d. Chef Alonso only has three measuring spoons: 1 teaspoon, $\frac{1}{2}$ teaspoon, and $\frac{1}{4}$ teaspoon. Can he measure the new amounts of oregano and hot sauce exactly? Explain why or why not.

   _____

2. Amira is painting a rectangular banner $2\frac{1}{4}$ yards wide on a wall in the cafeteria. The banner will have a blue background. Amira has enough blue paint to cover $1\frac{1}{2}$ square yards of wall.

   a. Find the height of the banner if Amira uses all of the blue paint. Show your work.

   _____

   b. The school colors are blue and yellow, so Amira wants to add yellow rectangles on the left and right sides of the blue rectangle. The yellow rectangles will each be $\frac{3}{4}$ yard wide and the same height as the blue rectangle. What will be the total area of the two yellow rectangles? Explain how you found your answer.

   _____

   c. What are the dimensions of the banner plus yellow rectangles? What is the total area? Show your work.

GO DIGITAL

my.hrw.com

Enhance Your Learning!

Interactive Student Editions provide additional multimedia resources to enhance your learning. You can enter in answers, watch videos, explore concepts with virtual manipulatives, and get homework help!

 Real-World Videos show you how specific math topics can be used in all kinds of situations.

Math On the Spot video tutorials provide step-by-step instruction of the math concepts covered in each example.

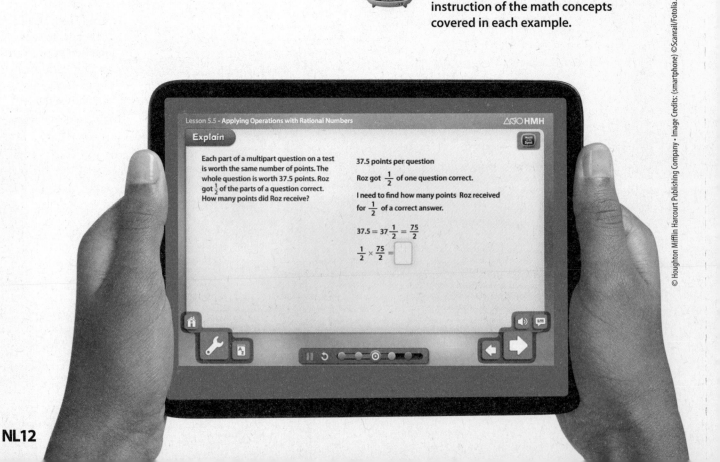

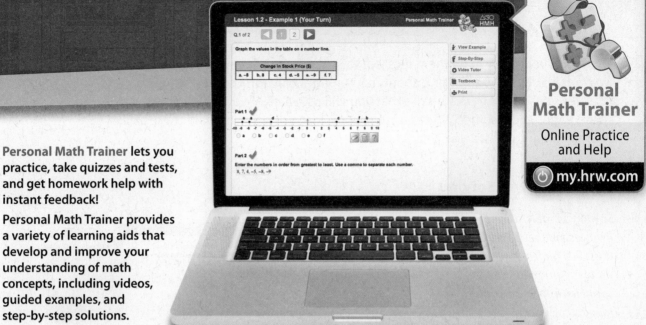

Personal Math Trainer lets you practice, take quizzes and tests, and get homework help with instant feedback!

Personal Math Trainer provides a variety of learning aids that develop and improve your understanding of math concepts, including videos, guided examples, and step-by-step solutions.

Personal Math Trainer

Online Practice and Help

my.hrw.com

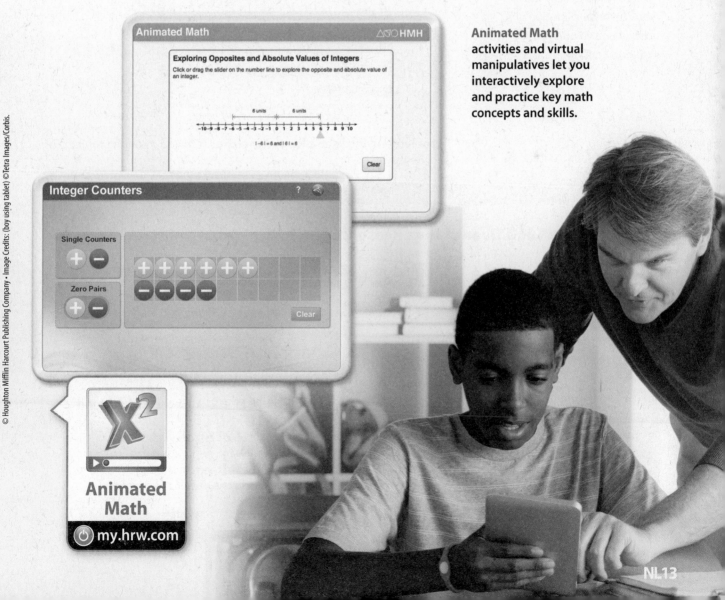

Animated Math activities and virtual manipulatives let you interactively explore and practice key math concepts and skills.

Animated Math

my.hrw.com

Mathematical Processes

The topics you study in mathematics will vary from year to year. However, the *way* you learn, study, and think about mathematics will not. The Mathematical Processes described here are skills that you will use in all of your math courses. These pages show some features of your book that will help you gain these skills and use them to master this year's topics.

MP.1 Problem Solving

Solving a problem often involves multiple steps. You must first understand the problem situation, analyze the given information, and identify the goal of the problem. Then you make a plan and implement that plan to solve the problem. Lastly, you check your solution and look back and analyze your solution method.

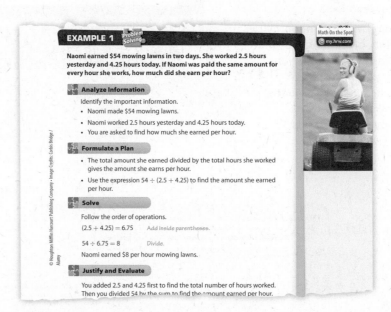

Problem-solving examples and exercises lead you through problem solving steps.

MP.2 Abstract and Quantitative Reasoning

When solving problems, you often need to represent a situation abstractly and work out a solution using a symbolic representation of the problem. At other times, you must refer back to the specific quantities the symbols represent in order to understand the meaning of your results.

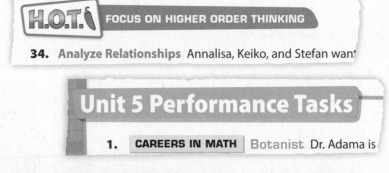

Focus on Higher Order Thinking exercises in every lesson and **Performance Tasks** in every unit require you to use logical reasoning, represent situations symbolically, use mathematical models to solve problems, and state your answers in terms of a problem context.

MP.3 Use and Evaluate Logical Reasoning

Mathematics provides a unique opportunity to develop your logical reasoning capacities. You can do this by expressing your thoughts and justifying your conclusions. Soon you will recognize and correct flaws in reasoning.

Reflect

1. **Critique Reasoning** Jo says she can find the percent equivalent multiplying the percent equivalent of $\frac{1}{4}$ by 3. How can you use bar model to support this claim?

? **ESSENTIAL QUESTION CHECK-IN**

Essential Question Check-in and **Reflect** in every lesson ask you to evaluate statements, explain relationships, apply mathematical principles, make conjectures, construct arguments, and justify your reasoning.

MP.4 Mathematical Modeling

You can use mathematics to solve problems in everyday life by learning how to represent real-world situations in mathematical terms.

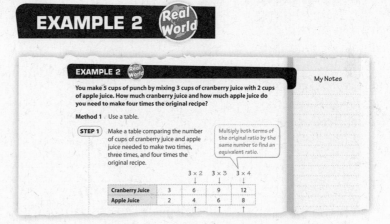

Real-world examples and **mathematical modeling** apply mathematics to other disciplines and real-world contexts such as science and business.

MP.5 Use Mathematical Tools

Knowing when and how to use mathematical tools, ranging from rulers and protractors to graphing calculators and computer software, is a valuable skill. Used properly, tools can both simplify problem-solving and give you a deeper understanding of mathematical concepts.

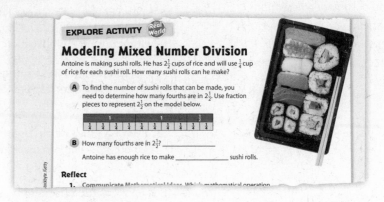

Exploration Activities in lessons use concrete and technological tools, such as manipulatives or graphing calculators, to explore mathematical concepts.

MP.6 Use Precise Mathematical Language

To communicate your reasoning and results to others, you must use mathematical terms, symbols, and units precisely and consistently. Defining terms clearly and labeling diagrams appropriately are essential for writing clear explanations.

31. Communicate Mathematical Ideas Write an example of an that cannot be simplified, and explain how you know that it simplified.

Precision refers not only to the correctness of calculations but also to the proper use of mathematical language and symbols. **Communicate Mathematical Ideas** exercises and **Key Vocabulary** highlighted for each module and unit help you learn and use the language of math to communicate mathematics precisely.

MP.7 See Structure

Recognizing patterns and similarities in the structure of varied problems can help you both to solve problems and to understand the underlying mathematical concepts.

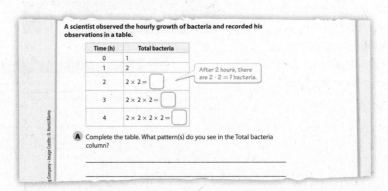

A scientist observed the hourly growth of bacteria and recorded his observations in a table.

Time (h)	Total bacteria
0	1
1	2
2	$2 \times 2 = $
3	$2 \times 2 \times 2 = $
4	$2 \times 2 \times 2 \times 2 = $

After 2 hours, there are $2 \cdot 2 = 7$ bacteria.

A Complete the table. What pattern(s) do you see in the Total bacteria column?

Throughout the lessons, you will observe regularity in mathematical structures in order to make generalizations and make connections between related problems. For example, you can use what you know about multiplication to understand how to use exponents.

MP.8 Generalize

As you do similar calculations repeatedly, you can discover general methods and shortcuts for solving problems.

46. Look for a Pattern Find the values of the powers in the follo pattern: $10^1, 10^2, 10^3, 10^4$…. Describe the pattern, and use it 10^6 without using multiplication.

25. Justify Reasoning Determine whether $3x + 12 + x$ is ec $4(3 + x)$. Use properties of operations to justify your ans

Reflect

8. Make a Conjecture Use the pattern in the table to make a c about how you can use multiplication to divide one fraction

You will look for repeated calculations and mathematical patterns in examples and exercises. Recognizing patterns can help you make generalizations and obtain a better understanding of the underlying mathematics.

Selected Response

1. Al used the expression $8 + 25 \times 2 - 45$ to find how many CDs he has. How many CDs does he have?

- Ⓐ 3
- Ⓒ 21
- Ⓑ 13
- Ⓓ 103

2. Jamie baked 24 biscuits. Her sister Mia ate 3 biscuits, and her brother David ate 2 biscuits. Which expression can Jamie use to find how many biscuits are left?

- Ⓐ $24 + (3 + 2)$
- Ⓒ $(24 - 3) + 2$
- Ⓑ $24 - (3 + 2)$
- Ⓓ $24 - (3 - 2)$

3. What is the unknown number in sequence 2 in the chart?

Sequence Number	1	2	3	5	7
Sequence 1	3	6	9	15	21
Sequence 2	15	30	45	75	?

- Ⓐ 63
- Ⓒ 105
- Ⓑ 90
- Ⓓ 150

4. Patel hopes to be one of the first fans to get into the stadium for the baseball game because the first 30,000 fans will receive a baseball cap. Which shows 30,000 as a whole number multiplied by a power of ten?

- Ⓐ 3×10^1
- Ⓒ 3×10^3
- Ⓑ 3×10^2
- Ⓓ 3×10^4

5. The Davis family pays $200,000 for a new house. They make a down payment that is $\frac{1}{10}$ of the price of the house. How much is the down payment?

- Ⓐ $20
- Ⓒ $2,000
- Ⓑ $200
- Ⓓ $20,000

6. Jackie found a rock that has a mass of 78.852 grams. What is the mass of the rock rounded to the nearest tenth?

- Ⓐ 78.85 grams
- Ⓒ 79 grams
- Ⓑ 78.9 grams
- Ⓓ 80 grams

7. A company manufactures 295 toy cars each day. How many toy cars does the company manufacture in 34 days?

- Ⓐ 3,065
- Ⓒ 10,065
- Ⓑ 7,610
- Ⓓ 10,030

8. There are 6 buses transporting students to a baseball game, with 32 students on each bus. Each row at the baseball stadium seats 8 students. If the students fill up all of the rows, how many rows of seats will the students need altogether?

- Ⓐ 22
- Ⓒ 24
- Ⓑ 23
- Ⓓ 1,536

9. The portions of a house that need to be heated can be modeled by one rectangular prism with a length of 45 feet, a width of 20 feet, and a height of 18 feet, and a second rectangular prism with a base area of 350 square feet and a height of 9 feet. What is the total volume?

- Ⓐ 12,500 cubic feet
- Ⓑ 16,200 cubic feet
- Ⓒ 16,550 cubic feet
- Ⓓ 19,350 cubic feet

10. Marci mailed 9 letters at the post office. Each letter weighed 3.5 ounces. What was the total weight of the letters?

  (A) 33.5 ounces   (C) 31.5 ounces

  (B) 32.5 ounces   (D) 27.5 ounces

11. Denise, Keith, and Tim live in the same neighborhood. Denise lives 0.3 mile from Keith. The distance that Tim and Keith live from each other is 0.2 times as great as the distance between Denise and Keith. How far from each other do Tim and Keith live?

  (A) 0.6 mile   (C) 0.1 mile

  (B) 0.5 mile   (D) 0.06 mile

12. Madison needs to buy enough meat to make 1,000 hamburgers for the company picnic. Each hamburger will weigh 0.25 pound. How many pounds of hamburger meat should Madison buy?

  (A) 2.5 pounds   (C) 250 pounds

  (B) 25 pounds   (D) 2,500 pounds

Mini-Tasks

13. Rayna wrote 260,980 as $(2 \times 100{,}000) + (6 \times 10{,}000) + (9 \times 1{,}000) + (8 \times 100)$. What error did Rayna make? Write the correct expanded form.

_____

_____

_____

_____

14. The highest scores at a gymnastics meet were 9.675, 9.25, 9.325, and 9.5. Write the scores in order from least to greatest.

_____

15. Ann and Joe's father donated $3 for every lap they swam in a swim-a-thon. Ann swam 21 laps, and Joe swam 15 laps. Use the Distributive Property to find the amount of money their father donated.

_____

_____

_____

_____

16. A grain of sand has a diameter of 0.049 millimeter. Write 0.049 in words.

_____

Performance Task

17. Jennifer has $12 to spend on lunch and the roller rink. Admission to the roller rink is $5.75. Jennifer estimates that she can buy a large drink and a turkey sandwich and still have enough money to get into the rink. Do you agree? Support your answer.

Sandwiches	Drinks
Tuna $3.95	Small $1.29
Turkey $4.85	Medium $1.59
Grilled Cheese $3.25	Large $1.79

_____

_____

_____

_____

Review Test

Personal Math Trainer

Online Assessment and Intervention

my.hrw.com

Selected Response

1. Charles bought $\frac{7}{8}$ foot of electrical wire and $\frac{5}{6}$ foot of copper wire for his science project. What is the least common denominator of the fractions?

   Ⓐ 14   Ⓒ 24

   Ⓑ 18   Ⓓ 48

2. Tom jogged $\frac{3}{5}$ mile on Monday and $\frac{2}{6}$ mile on Tuesday. How much farther did Tom jog on Monday than on Tuesday?

   Ⓐ $\frac{1}{30}$ mile   Ⓒ $\frac{8}{30}$ mile

   Ⓑ $\frac{3}{15}$ mile   Ⓓ $\frac{14}{15}$ mile

3. Three fences on a ranch measure $\frac{15}{16}$ mile, $\frac{7}{8}$ mile, and $\frac{7}{16}$ mile. Which is the best estimate of the total length of all three fences?

   Ⓐ $1\frac{1}{2}$ miles   Ⓒ $2\frac{1}{2}$ miles

   Ⓑ 2 miles   Ⓓ 3 miles

4. Lawrence bought $\frac{2}{3}$ pound of roast beef. He used $\frac{3}{4}$ of it to make a sandwich. How much roast beef did Lawrence use for his sandwich? You may use a model to help you solve the problem.

   Ⓐ $\frac{5}{12}$ pound   Ⓒ $\frac{5}{7}$ pound

   Ⓑ $\frac{1}{2}$ pound   Ⓓ $\frac{6}{7}$ pound

5. Sarah built a table using 6 pieces of wood that were each $3\frac{3}{4}$ inches wide. How wide was the table?

   Ⓐ $18\frac{1}{8}$ inches   Ⓒ $21\frac{1}{4}$ inches

   Ⓑ $18\frac{3}{4}$ inches   Ⓓ $22\frac{1}{2}$ inches

6. Vanessa made 6 sandwiches for a party and cut them all into fourths. How many $\frac{1}{4}$-sandwich pieces did she have?

   Ⓐ $1\frac{1}{2}$ Ⓒ 4

   Ⓑ $2\frac{1}{4}$ Ⓓ 24

7. Dr. Watson combines 400 mL of detergent, 800 mL of alcohol, and 1,500 mL of water. How many liters of solution does he have?

   Ⓐ 2.7 liters   Ⓒ 270 liters

   Ⓑ 27 liters   Ⓓ 2,700 liters

8. Give the most descriptive name for the figure.

   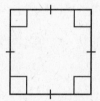

   Ⓐ square   Ⓒ parallelogram

   Ⓑ rectangle   Ⓓ rhombus

9. Find the volume of the rectangular prism.

   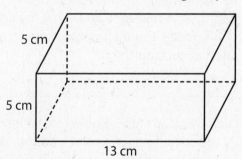

   5 cm, 5 cm, 13 cm

   Ⓐ 310 cm³   Ⓒ 325 cm³

   Ⓑ 184 cm³   Ⓓ 23 cm³

10. Which ordered pair describes the location of Point A?

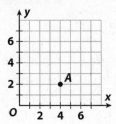

Ⓐ (0, 2) Ⓒ (4, 0)

Ⓑ (2, 4) Ⓓ (4, 2)

11. Which ordered pair describes the location of Point A?

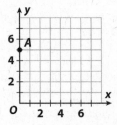

Ⓐ (0, 5) Ⓒ (5, 5)

Ⓑ (5, 0) Ⓓ (1, 5)

Mini-Tasks

12. When Bruce started bowling, he won $\frac{1}{4}$ of the games he played. Within six months, he was winning $\frac{7}{16}$ of his games. If he improves at the same rate, what fraction of his games should he expect to win after another six months?

_____

13. Gina wants to ship 3 books that weigh $2\frac{7}{16}$ pounds, $1\frac{7}{8}$ pounds and $\frac{1}{2}$ pound. The maximum weight she can ship is 6 pounds. Estimate to see if Gina can ship all 3 books. Explain your answer.

_____

_____

_____

14. How much trail mix will each person get if 5 people share $\frac{1}{2}$ pound of trail mix?

_____

15. Write a story to represent the division problem $6 \div \frac{1}{3}$.

_____

_____

_____

_____

16. What is the volume in cubic centimeters of the solid?

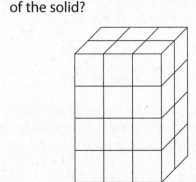

_____

Performance Task

17. Shia measured the thickness of some buttons. She graphed the results in a line plot.

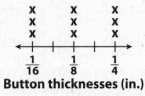

Button thicknesses (in.)

Part A: Suppose Shia makes a stack of all the buttons. How tall will the stack be?

_____

Part B: Suppose Shia wants the stack to be 2 inches high. How many buttons that are $\frac{1}{16}$ inch thick must be added to the stack of buttons?

_____

Benchmark Test

Selected Response

1. Suppose you have developed a scale that indicates the brightness of sunlight. Each category in the table is 9 times brighter than the category above it. For example, a day that is dazzling is 9 times brighter than a day that is radiant. How many times brighter is a dazzling day than an illuminated day?

Sunlight Intensity	
Category	**Brightness**
Dim	2
Illuminated	3
Radiant	4
Dazzling	5

Ⓐ 2 times brighter

Ⓑ 729 times brighter

Ⓒ 81 times brighter

Ⓓ 9 times brighter

2. Which group of numbers is in order from least to greatest?

Ⓐ 2.58, $2\frac{5}{8}$, 2.6, $2\frac{2}{3}$

Ⓑ $2\frac{2}{3}$, $2\frac{5}{8}$, 2.6, 2.58

Ⓒ $2\frac{5}{8}$, $2\frac{2}{3}$, 2.6, 2.58

Ⓓ 2.58, 2.6, $2\frac{5}{8}$, $2\frac{2}{3}$

3. Which temperature is coldest?

Ⓐ $-13\,°F$ Ⓒ $-20\,°F$

Ⓑ $20\,°F$ Ⓓ $13\,°F$

4. Patricia paid $385 for 5 nights at a hotel. Find the unit rate.

Ⓐ $\frac{\$77}{1\text{ night}}$ Ⓒ $\frac{\$385}{1\text{ night}}$

Ⓑ $\frac{\$154}{1\text{ night}}$ Ⓓ $\frac{\$39}{1\text{ night}}$

5. The fuel for a chain saw is a mix of oil and gasoline. The label says to mix 6 ounces of oil with 16 gallons of gasoline. How much oil would you use if you had 32 gallons of gasoline?

Ⓐ 3 ounces   Ⓒ 18 ounces

Ⓑ 12 ounces   Ⓓ 85.3 ounces

6. Lee is putting together fruit baskets for gifts. He has 18 apples, 24 pears, and 30 oranges. What is the greatest number of fruit baskets he can make if he uses all the fruit and each basket is the same?

Ⓐ 2 baskets   Ⓒ 4 baskets

Ⓑ 3 baskets   Ⓓ 6 baskets

7. It takes light about 134 milliseconds to travel the distance around Earth's Equator. How many seconds is this?

Ⓐ 0.000134 sec   Ⓒ 0.134 sec

Ⓑ 0.0134 sec   Ⓓ 1.34 sec

8. From the beginning of cross-country season to the end, Tisha reduced her time by 17%, Anchara reduced hers by $\frac{1}{6}$, Juanita reduced hers by $\frac{4}{25}$, and Julia reduced hers from 16:00 to 13:30. Who reduced her time by the greatest percent?

Ⓐ Tisha   Ⓒ Juanita

Ⓑ Anchara   Ⓓ Julia

9. A stack of blocks is 15.2 inches tall. If there are 10 blocks stacked one on top of the other, how tall is each block?

Ⓐ 1.62 inches   Ⓒ 1.72 inches

Ⓑ 1.52 inches   Ⓓ 5.2 inches

10. The ratio of students in Jaíme's class who have a dog or cat at home to those who don't is 12 : 8. What percent of the class do NOT have a dog or cat at home?

(A) $33\frac{1}{3}\%$ (C) 60%

(B) 40%   (D) $66\frac{2}{3}\%$

11. Ninety percent of a school's students, or 540 students, attended a school assembly. How many students are there at the school?

(A) 486 students   (C) 600 students

(B) 594 students   (D) 621 students

12. Find the quotient $9\frac{3}{5} \div \frac{8}{15}$.

(A) 2   (C) $16\frac{7}{8}$

(B) 18   (D) $18\frac{3}{4}$

13. Find the product 4.51×3.4.

(A) 153.34   (C) 7.91

(B) 1.5334   (D) 15.334

14. Jorge is building a table out of boards that are 3.75 inches wide. He wants the table to be at least 36 inches wide. What is the least number of boards he can use?

(A) 9   (C) 10

(B) 9.6   (D) 135

Mini-Tasks

15. Nikita is making spaghetti sauce and pizzas for a large party. Her spaghetti sauce recipe calls for $1\frac{3}{4}$ cups of tomato paste, and her pizza recipe uses $\frac{2}{3}$ cup of tomato paste per pizza. She will triple her spaghetti sauce recipe and make 6 pizzas. Write and evaluate an expression for how many $\frac{3}{4}$ cup cans of tomato paste she will need in all.

_____

_____

16. Explain how you can use multiplication to find the quotient $\frac{3}{4} \div \frac{3}{16}$. Then evaluate the expression.

_____

_____

17. A chef has 6 cups of berries and will use $\frac{2}{3}$ cup of berries for each serving of fruit salad. How many servings can be made?

_____

Performance Task

18. School A has 480 students and 16 classrooms. School B has 192 students and 12 classrooms.

Part A: What is the ratio of students to classrooms at School A?

Part B: What is the ratio of students to classrooms at School B?

Part C: How many students would have to transfer from School A to School B for the ratios of students to classrooms at both schools to be the same? Explain your reasoning.

_____

_____

_____

_____

_____

_____

_____

_____

_____

_____

Benchmark Test

Personal Math Trainer

Online Assessment and Intervention

my.hrw.com

Selected Response

1. Kahlil is recording a beat for a song that he is working on. He wants the length of the beat to be more than 10 seconds long. His friend tells him the beat needs to be 5 seconds longer than that to match the lyrics he has written.

   Write an inequality to represent the beat's length. Give three possible beat lengths that satisfy the inequality.

   Ⓐ $t > 5$; 16, 21, 22

   Ⓑ $t > 15$; 16, 21, 22

   Ⓒ $t < 15$; 4, 3, 2

   Ⓓ $t < 10$; 4, 3, 2

2. Write an expression for the missing value in the table.

Tom's Age	Kim's Age
10	13
11	14
12	15
a	?

   Ⓐ $a + 1$ Ⓒ $a + 3$

   Ⓑ $a + 15$ Ⓓ $a + 10$

3. What is the area of the polygon?

   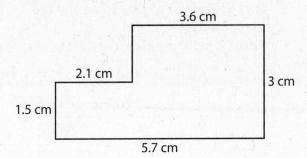

   3.6 cm

   2.1 cm

   3 cm

   1.5 cm

   5.7 cm

   Ⓐ 3.15 cm²   Ⓒ 13.95 cm²

   Ⓑ 10.8 cm²   Ⓓ 1395 cm²

4. Iris wants to buy two necklaces, one for her sister and one for herself. The necklace for her sister costs $42.00, and the necklace for herself costs $28.00. The sales tax on the purchases is 8%. Find the total cost of Iris's purchases, including sales tax. If necessary, round your answer to the nearest cent.

   Ⓐ $64.40   Ⓒ $75.60

   Ⓑ $5.60   Ⓓ $70.00

5. A rectangular box is $8\frac{1}{2}$ inches long, $5\frac{1}{4}$ inches wide, and 4 inches high. What is its volume?

   Ⓐ 160 cubic inches

   Ⓑ 168 cubic inches

   Ⓒ $178\frac{1}{2}$ cubic inches

   Ⓓ 180 cubic inches

6. Write the phrase as an algebraic expression.

   4 times the sum of a number and 20

   Ⓐ $20 \div y$ Ⓒ $4(y + 20)$

   Ⓑ $20 + y$ Ⓓ $4y - 20y$

7. Wilson bought gift cards for some lawyers and their assistants. Each lawyer got a gift card worth ℓ dollars. Each assistant got a gift card worth a dollars. There are 14 lawyers. Each lawyer has 3 assistants. The expression for the total cost of the gift cards is $14\ell + 42a$. Write an expression that is equivalent to the given expression.

   Ⓐ $14(\ell + 2a)$ Ⓒ $14(\ell + 42a)$

   Ⓑ $14(\ell + 3a)$ Ⓓ $42(\ell + 3a)$

8. At the beginning of the year, Jason had $120 in his savings account. Each month, he added $15 to his account. Write an expression for the amount of money in Jason's savings account each month. Then use the expression to find the amount of money in his account at the end of the year.

Month	January	February	March	m
Amount	$135	$150	$165	$?

Ⓐ $120 + 12m$; $264

Ⓑ $135 + 15m$; $315

Ⓒ $135 + m$; $147

Ⓓ $5m + 120$; $300

9. Which question is a statistical question?

Ⓐ What are the ages of schools in the school district?

Ⓑ How old is the middle school building?

Ⓒ How many classrooms are there in the elementary school building?

Ⓓ How many daily class periods are there in the high school?

10. Find the interquartile range for the data set: 10, 3, 8, 6, 9, 12, 13.

Ⓐ 12 Ⓒ 6

Ⓑ 8 Ⓓ 7

11. Which problem will have a negative integer as the solution?

Ⓐ $-4.6 \times (-7)$ Ⓒ $\frac{5}{9} - \frac{1}{3}$

Ⓑ $-7 + 9$ Ⓓ $-45 \div 5$

Mini-Tasks

12. Mike was in charge of collecting contributions for the Food Bank. He received contributions of $80, $70, $60, $40, and $80. Find the mean and the median of the contributions.

_____

13. One side of trapezoid is 10 inches. The side parallel to this is twice as long as this side. The height is half as long as the given side length. Find the area of the trapezoid.

_____

14. Find the perimeter of the rectangle with vertices at $R(-2, 3)$, $S(4, 3)$, $T(4, -1)$ and $U(-2, -1)$.

_____

15. Brian is ordering tickets online for a concert. The price of each ticket for the concert is t dollars. For online orders, there is an additional charge of $11 per ticket, and a service charge of $14 for the entire order. The cost for 7 tickets can be represented by the expression $7(t + 11) + 14$.

Write two expressions equivalent to the cost expression. Then, find the total cost of Brian's online order if the price of each ticket for this concert is $33.

_____

Performance Task

16. Jillian wants to find the surface area of a pyramid. The base is a square with with sides that are 4 inches long. The other faces are isosceles triangles. The ratio of the height of each triangle to its base is 3 : 2.

Part A: Give the base length and the height of each triangular face.

Part B: Find the combined area of the triangular faces.

Part C: Find the surface area of the pyramid.

_____

_____

_____

_____

UNIT 1
Numbers

MODULE 1
Integers

MODULE 2
Factors and Multiples

MODULE 3
Rational Numbers

CAREERS IN MATH

Climatologist A climatologist is a scientist who studies long-term trends in climate conditions. These scientists collect, evaluate, and interpret data and use mathematical models to study the dynamics of weather patterns and to understand and predict Earth's climate.

If you are interested in a career in climatology, you should study these mathematical subjects:
- Algebra
- Trigonometry
- Probability and Statistics
- Calculus

Research other careers that require the analysis of data and use of mathematical models.

Unit 1 Performance Task

At the end of the unit, check out how **climatologists** use math.

Vocabulary Preview

Use the puzzle to preview key vocabulary from this unit. Unscramble the circled letters within found words to answer the riddle at the bottom of the page.

```
E R Ⓘ N E Q U Ⓐ L I Ⓣ Y I L N
U S E R O J U J P Z Y M B Ⓔ M
L U E B P P H K F J A L G R Z
A M G Z M Y P G C R Y A R A D
Ⓥ K B E D U G O Ⓖ C Ⓣ K W G X
E D M F S L N A S I J J H Z C
Ⓣ B K H V M I L V I Q E L D R
U R Ⓘ M R Ⓓ I E Ⓐ Y T Z G K P
L V N T Ⓝ H N D Y N L E F T H
O X T N K Ⓤ K Q F X O A S T E
S R Ⓔ B M U N E V I T I S O P
B V G B D Z A F E A X Y Ⓣ Y A
A D Ⓔ P X N V I U B V S T A A
O R R V R R X I R G L V B U R
S X S M I Q V Y N L N P S S I
```

- Any number that can be written as a ratio of two integers. (Lesson 3.1)
- The greatest factor shared by two or more numbers. (Lesson 2.1)
- A diagram used to show the relationship between two sets or groups. (Lesson 3.1)
- A mathematical statement that shows two quantities are not equal. (Lesson 1.2)
- The set of all whole numbers and their opposites. (Lesson 1.1)
- The distance of a number from zero on the number line. (Lesson 1.3)
- Numbers less than zero. (Lesson 1.1)

Q: Why did the integer get a bad evaluation at work?

A: He had a ___ ___ ___ ___ ___ ___ ___ ___ ___ ___

___ ___ ___ ___ ___ ___ ___ ___ ___!

Integers

? ESSENTIAL QUESTION

How can you use integers to solve real-world problems?

Real-World Video

Integers can be used to describe the value of many things in the real world. The height of a mountain in feet may be a very great integer while the temperature in degrees Celsius at the top of that mountain may be a negative integer.

my.hrw.com

GO DIGITAL
my.hrw.com

my.hrw.com

Go digital with your write-in student edition, accessible on any device.

Math On the Spot

Scan with your smart phone to jump directly to the online edition, video tutor, and more.

Animated Math

Interactively explore key concepts to see how math works.

Personal Math Trainer

Get immediate feedback and help as you work through practice sets.

Reading Start-Up

Visualize Vocabulary

Use the ✔ words to complete the chart. Write the correct vocabulary word next to the symbol.

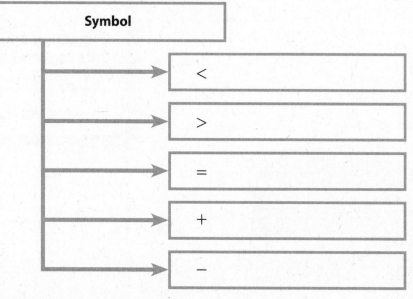

Symbol	
<	
>	
=	
+	
−	

Understand Vocabulary

Complete the sentences using the preview words.

1. An _____ is a statement that two quantities are not equal.

2. The set of all whole numbers and their opposites are _____.

3. Numbers greater than 0 are _____. Numbers less

   than 0 are _____.

Vocabulary

Review Words
- ✔ equal *(igual)*
- ✔ greater than *(más que)*
- ✔ less than *(menos que)*
- ✔ negative sign *(signo negativo)*
- number line *(recta numérica)*
- ✔ plus sign *(signo más)*
- symbol *(símbolo)*
- whole number *(número entero)*

Preview Words
- absolute value *(valor absoluto)*
- inequality *(desigualdad)*
- integers *(enteros)*
- negative numbers *(números negativos)*
- opposites *(opuestos)*
- positive numbers *(números positivos)*

Active Reading

Key-Term Fold Before beginning the module, create a key-term fold to help you learn the vocabulary in this module. Write the highlighted vocabulary words on one side of the flap. Write the definition for each word on the other side of the flap. Use the key-term fold to quiz yourself on the definitions in this module.

Are YOU Ready?

Complete these exercises to review skills you will need for this module.

Compare Whole Numbers

EXAMPLE

3,564 ⬤ 3,528	Compare digits in the thousands place: $3 = 3$
3,564 ⬤ 3,528	Compare digits in the hundreds place: $5 = 5$
3,564 > 3,528	Compare digits in the tens place: $6 > 2$

Compare. Write <, >, or =.

1. 471 ◯ 468   **2.** 5,005 ◯ 5,050   **3.** 398 ◯ 389

4. 10,973 ◯ 10,999   **5.** 8,471 ◯ 9,001   **6.** 108 ◯ 95

Order Whole Numbers

EXAMPLE

356, 348, 59, 416	Compare digits. Find the greatest number.
356, 348, 59, 416	Find the next greatest number.
356, 348, 59, 416	Find the next greatest number.
356, 348, 59, 416	Find the least number.
416 > 356 > 348 > 59	Order the numbers.

Order the numbers from greatest to least.

7. 156; 87; 177; 99

8. 591; 589; 603; 600

9. 2,650; 2,605; 3,056; 2,088

10. 1,037; 995; 10,415; 1,029

Locate Numbers on a Number Line

EXAMPLE

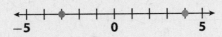

Graph +4 by starting at 0 and counting 4 units to the right. Graph −3 by starting at 0 and counting 3 units to the left.

Graph each number on the number line.

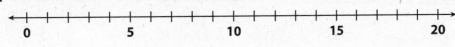

11. 12   **12.** 20   **13.** 2   **14.** 9

Complete these exercises to review skills you will need for this module.

Compare Whole Numbers

15. To compare the numbers 85,246 and 86,146, Kendra first compared the digits in the ones place, which are both 6. She then compared the digits in the tens place, which are both 4. Next, she compared the digits in the hundreds place. Since 2 > 1, Kendra determined that 85,246 > 86,146. Explain the error in Kendra's reasoning.

Order Whole Numbers

16. Five coworkers use the same fitness app, which monitors the number of minutes spent jogging. The table shows the time each person has spent jogging for the month of April. Order the numbers from greatest to least.

Coworker	Barry	Monique	Sinead	Divya	Roberto
Minutes Spent Jogging in April	1,515	1,920	192	1,020	298

Locate Numbers on a Number Line

17. Graph the numbers −6 and 8 on the number line. Explain how you determined where to graph each number.

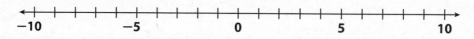

LESSON 1.1 Identifying Integers and Their Opposites

6.1.1.1
Students will identify an integer and its opposite.

? ESSENTIAL QUESTION

How do you identify an integer and its opposite?

EXPLORE ACTIVITY 1 *Real World*

Positive and Negative Numbers

Positive numbers are numbers greater than 0. Positive numbers can be written with or without a plus sign; for example, 3 is the same as +3. **Negative numbers** are numbers less than 0. Negative numbers must always be written with a negative sign.

> The number 0 is neither positive nor negative.

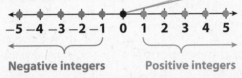

$-5\ -4\ -3\ -2\ -1\ \ 0\ \ 1\ \ 2\ \ 3\ \ 4\ \ 5$

Negative integers   **Positive integers**

The elevation of a location describes its height above or below sea level, which has elevation 0. Elevations below sea level are represented by negative numbers, and elevations above sea level are represented by positive numbers.

A The table shows the elevations of several locations in a state park. Graph the locations on the number line according to their elevations.

Location	Little Butte *A*	Cradle Creek *B*	Dinosaur Valley *C*	Mesa Ridge *D*	Juniper Trail *E*
Elevation (ft)	5	−5	−9	8	−3

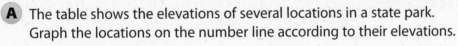

$-10\ -9\ -8\ -7\ -6\ -5\ -4\ -3\ -2\ -1\ \ 0\ \ 1\ \ 2\ \ 3\ \ 4\ \ 5\ \ 6\ \ 7\ \ 8\ \ 9\ \ 10$

B What point on the number line represents sea level? _____

C Which location is closest to sea level? How do you know?

_____

D Which two locations are the same distance from sea level? Are these locations above or below sea level?

_____

E Which location has the least elevation? How do you know?

_____

Reflect

1. **Analyze Relationships** Morning Glory Stream is 7 feet below sea level. What number represents the elevation of Morning Glory Stream?

   _____

2. **Multiple Representations** Explain how to graph the elevation of Morning Glory Stream on a number line.

   _____

EXPLORE ACTIVITY 2

Opposites

Two numbers are **opposites** if, on a number line, they are the same distance from 0 but on different sides of 0. For example, 5 and −5 are opposites. 0 is its own opposite.

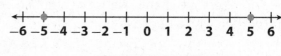

Integers are the set of all whole numbers and their opposites.

> Remember, the set of whole numbers is 0, 1, 2, 3, 4, 5, 6, …

On graph paper, use a ruler or straightedge to draw a number line. Label the number line with each integer from −10 to 10. Fold your number line in half so that the crease goes through 0. Numbers that line up after folding the number line are opposites.

A Use your number line to find the opposites of 7, −6, 1, and 9. _____

B How does your number line show that 0 is its own opposite?

   _____

C What is the opposite of the opposite of 3? _____

Reflect

3. **Justify Reasoning** Explain how your number line shows that 8 and −8 are opposites.

   _____

4. **Multiple Representations** Explain how to use your number line to find the opposite of the opposite of −6.

   _____

   _____

   _____

Integers and Opposites on a Number Line

Positive and negative numbers can be used to represent real-world quantities. For example, 3 can represent a temperature that is 3 °F above 0. −3 can represent a temperature that is 3 °F below 0. Both 3 and −3 are 3 units from 0.

Math On the Spot
my.hrw.com

EXAMPLE 1 Real World

My Notes

Sandy kept track of the weekly low temperature in her town for several weeks. The table shows the low temperature in °F for each week.

Week	Week 1	Week 2	Week 3	Week 4
Temperature (°F)	−1	3	−4	2

A Graph the temperature from Week 3 and its opposite on a number line. What do the numbers represent?

STEP 1 Graph the value from Week 3 on the number line.
The value from Week 3 is −4.
Graph a point 4 units below 0.

STEP 2 Graph the opposite of −4.
Graph a point 4 units above 0.

The opposite of −4 is 4.

−4 represents a temperature that is 4 °F below 0 and 4 represents a temperature that is 4 °F above 0.

B The value for Week 5 is the opposite of the opposite of the value from Week 1. What was the low temperature in Week 5?

STEP 1 Graph the value from Week 1 on the number line.
The value from Week 1 is −1.

STEP 2 Graph the opposite of −1.
The opposite of −1 is 1.

STEP 3 Graph the opposite of 1.
The opposite of 1 is −1.

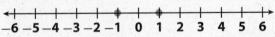

The opposite of the opposite of −1 is −1.
The low temperature in Week 5 was −1 °F.

Reflect

5. **Analyze Relationships** Explain how you can find the opposite of the opposite of any number without using a number line.

_____

© Houghton Mifflin Harcourt Publishing Company

YOUR TURN

Graph the opposite of the number shown on each number line.

6.
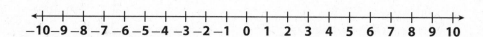
-10 -9 -8 -7 -6 -5 -4 -3 -2 -1 0 1 2 3 4 5 6 7 8 9 10

7.
-10 -9 -8 -7 -6 -5 -4 -3 -2 -1 0 1 2 3 4 5 6 7 8 9 10

Write the opposite of each number.

8. 10 _____   **9.** −5 _____   **10.** 0 _____

Math Talk
Mathematical Processes

Explain how you could use a number line to find the opposite of 8.

11. What is the opposite of the opposite of 6? _____

Guided Practice

1. Graph and label the following points on the number line.
(Explore Activity 1)

   a. −2   **b.** 9   **c.** −8   **d.** −9   **e.** 5   **f.** 8

-10 -9 -8 -7 -6 -5 -4 -3 -2 -1 0 1 2 3 4 5 6 7 8 9 10

Graph the opposite of the number shown on each number line.
(Explore Activity 2 and Example 1)

2.
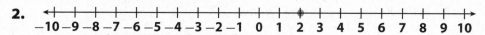
-10 -9 -8 -7 -6 -5 -4 -3 -2 -1 0 1 2 3 4 5 6 7 8 9 10

3.
-10 -9 -8 -7 -6 -5 -4 -3 -2 -1 0 1 2 3 4 5 6 7 8 9 10

4.
-10 -9 -8 -7 -6 -5 -4 -3 -2 -1 0 1 2 3 4 5 6 7 8 9 10

Write the opposite of each number. (Explore Activity 2 and Example 1)

5. 4 _____   **6.** −11 _____   **7.** 3 _____

8. −3 _____   **9.** 0 _____   **10.** 22 _____

? ESSENTIAL QUESTION CHECK-IN

11. Given an integer, how do you find its opposite?

_____

_____

1.1 Independent Practice

Personal
Math Trainer

Online
Assessment and
Intervention

my.hrw.com

12. Chemistry Atoms normally have an electric charge of 0. Certain conditions, such as static, can cause atoms to have a positive or a negative charge. Atoms with a positive or negative charge are called *ions*.

Ion	A	B	C	D	E
Charge	−3	+1	−2	+3	−1

a. Which ions have a negative charge?

_____

b. Which ions have charges that are opposites?

_____

c. Which ion's charge is not the opposite of another ion's charge?

_____

Name the integer that meets the given description.

13. the opposite of −17 _____

14. 4 units left of 0 _____

15. the opposite of the opposite of 2 _____

16. 15 units right of 0 _____

17. 12 units right of 0 _____

18. the opposite of −19 _____

19. Analyze Relationships Several wrestlers are trying to lose weight for a competition. Their change in weight since last week is shown in the chart.

Wrestler	Tino	Victor	Ramsey	Baxter	Luis
Weight Change (in pounds)	−2	6	2	5	−5

a. Did Victor lose or gain weight since last week? _____

b. Which wrestler's weight change is the opposite of Ramsey's? _____

c. Which wrestlers have lost weight since last week? _____

d. Frankie's weight change since last week was the opposite of Victor's.

What was Frankie's weight change? _____

e. Frankie's goal last week was to gain weight. Did he meet his goal? Explain.

_____

Find the distance between the given number and its opposite on a number line.

20. 6 _____

21. −2 _____

22. 0 _____

23. −7 _____

24. **What If?** Three contestants are competing on a trivia game show. The table shows their scores before the final question.

Contestant	Score Before Final Question
Timothy	−25
Shawna	18
Kaylynn	−14

a. How many points must Shawna earn for her score to be the opposite of Timothy's score before the final question?_____

b. Which person's score is closest to 0? _____

c. Who do you think is winning the game before the final question? Explain.

_____

 FOCUS ON HIGHER ORDER THINKING

25. **Communicate Mathematical Ideas** Which number is farther from 0 on a number line: −9 or 6? Explain your reasoning.

_____

_____

26. **Analyze Relationships** A number is *k* units to the left of 0 on the number line. Describe the location of its opposite.

_____

_____

27. **Critique Reasoning** Roberto says that the opposite of a certain integer is −5. Cindy concludes that the opposite of an integer is always negative. Explain Cindy's error.

_____

_____

_____

28. **Multiple Representations** Explain how to use a number line to find the opposites of the integers 3 units away from −7.

_____

_____

_____

Work Area

Comparing and Ordering Integers

6.1.1.2
Students will compare and order integers.

 ESSENTIAL QUESTION

How do you compare and order integers?

EXPLORE ACTIVITY

Comparing Positive and Negative Integers

The Westfield soccer league ranks its teams using a number called the "win/loss combined record." A team with more wins than losses will have a positive combined record, and a team with fewer wins than losses will have a negative combined record. The table shows the total win/loss combined record for each team at the end of the season.

Team	Sharks A	Jaguars B	Badgers C	Tigers D	Cougars E	Hawks F	Wolves G
Win/Loss Combined Record	0	4	−4	−6	2	−2	6

A Graph the win/loss combined record for each team on the number line.

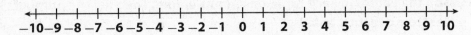

−10 −9 −8 −7 −6 −5 −4 −3 −2 −1 0 1 2 3 4 5 6 7 8 9 10

B Which team had the best record in the league? How do you know?

_____

C Which team had the worst record? How do you know?

_____

Reflect

1. Analyze Relationships Explain what the data tell you about the win/loss records of the teams in the league.

_____

_____

_____

_____

Ordering Positive and Negative Integers

When you read a number line from left to right, the numbers are in order from least to greatest.

EXAMPLE 1

Fred recorded the following golf scores during his first week at the golf academy. In golf, the player with the lowest score wins the game.

Day	Mon	Tues	Wed	Thurs	Fri	Sat	Sun
Score	4	−2	3	−5	−1	0	−3

Graph Fred's scores on the number line, and then list the numbers in order from least to greatest.

STEP 1   Graph the scores on the number line.

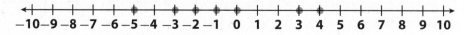

STEP 2   Read from left to right to list the scores in order from least to greatest.

The scores listed from least to greatest are −5, −3, −2, −1, 0, 3, 4.

YOUR TURN

Graph the values in each table on a number line. Then list the numbers in order from greatest to least.

2.

Change in Stock Price ($)					
−5	4	0	−3	−6	2

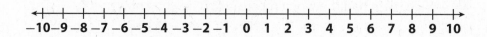

_____

3.

Elevation (meters)							
9	−1	−6	2	−10	0	5	8

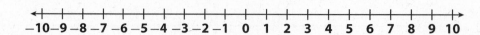

_____

Writing Inequalities

An **inequality** is a statement that two quantities are not equal. The symbols < and > are used to write inequalities.

- The symbol > means "is greater than."
- The symbol < means "is less than."

You can use a number line to help write an inequality.

EXAMPLE 2

A In 2005, Austin, Texas, received 51 inches in annual precipitation. In 2009, the city received 36 inches in annual precipitation. In which year was there more precipitation?

Graph 51 and 36 on the number line.

20 24 28 32 36 40 44 48 52 56 60

- 51 is to the *right* of 36 on the number line.

  This means that 51 is **greater than** 36.

  Write the inequality as 51 > 36.

- 36 is to the *left* of 51 on the number line.

  This means that 36 is **less than** 51.

  Write the inequality as 36 < 51.

  There was more precipitation in 2005.

B Write two inequalities to compare −6 and 7.
−6 < 7; 7 > −6

C Write two inequalities to compare −9 and −4.
−4 > −9; −9 < −4

Math Talk
Mathematical Processes

Is there a greatest integer? Is there a greatest negative integer? Explain.

YOUR TURN

Compare. Write > or <. Use the number line to help you.

4. −10 ◯ −2   **5.** −6 ◯ 6   **6.** −7 ◯ −8

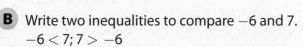
−10 −9 −8 −7 −6 −5 −4 −3 −2 −1 0 1 2 3 4 5 6 7 8 9 10

7. Write two inequalities to compare −2 and −18. _____

8. Write two inequalities to compare 39 and −39. _____

1a. Graph the temperature for each city on the number line. (Explore Activity)

City	A	B	C	D	E
Temperature (°F)	−9	10	−2	0	4

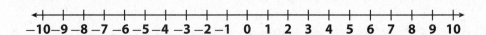

$$-10\ -9\ -8\ -7\ -6\ -5\ -4\ -3\ -2\ -1\ \ 0\ \ 1\ \ 2\ \ 3\ \ 4\ \ 5\ \ 6\ \ 7\ \ 8\ \ 9\ \ 10$$

b. Which city was coldest? _____

c. Which city was warmest? _____

List the numbers in order from least to greatest. (Example 1)

2. 4, −6, 0, 8, −9, 1, −3

_____

3. −65, 34, 7, −13, 55, 62, −7

_____

4. Write two inequalities to compare −17 and −22. _____

Compare. Write < or >. (Example 2)

5. −9 ◯ 2   **6.** 0 ◯ 6   **7.** 3 ◯ −7   **8.** 5 ◯ −10

9. −1 ◯ −3   **10.** −8 ◯ −4   **11.** −4 ◯ 1   **12.** −2 ◯ −6

13. Compare the temperatures for the following cities. Write < or >. (Example 2)

City	Alexandria	Redwood Falls	Grand Marais	Winona	International Falls
Average Temperature in March (°C)	−3	0	−2	2	−4

a. Alexandria and Winona _____

b. Redwood Falls and International Falls _____

? ESSENTIAL QUESTION CHECK-IN

14. How can you use a number line to compare and order numbers?

_____

_____

_____

1.2 Independent Practice

Personal
Math Trainer

Online
Assessment and
Intervention

my.hrw.com

15. **Multiple Representations** A hockey league tracks the plus-minus records for each player. A plus-minus record is the difference in even strength goals for and against the team when a player is on the ice. The following table lists the plus-minus values for several hockey players.

Player	A. Jones	B. Sutter	E. Simpson	L. Mays	R. Tomas	S. Klatt
Plus-minus	−8	4	9	−3	−4	3

a. Graph the values on the number line.

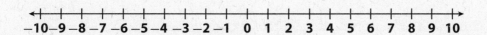

b. Which player has the best plus-minus record? _____

Astronomy The table lists the average surface temperature of some planets. Write an inequality to compare the temperatures of each pair of planets.

16. Uranus and Jupiter _____

17. Mercury and Mars _____

18. Arrange the planets in order of average surface temperature from greatest to least. _____

_____

Planet	Average Surface Temperature (°C)
Mercury	167
Uranus	−197
Neptune	−200
Earth	15
Mars	−65
Jupiter	−110

19. **Represent Real-World Problems** For a stock market project, five students each invested pretend money in one stock. They tracked gains and losses in the value of that stock for one week. In the following table, a gain is represented by a positive number and a loss is represented by a negative number.

Students	Andre	Bria	Carla	Daniel	Ethan
Gains and Losses ($)	7	−2	−5	2	4

Graph the students' results on the number line. Then list them in order from least to greatest.

a. Graph the values on the number line.

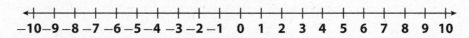

b. The results listed from least to greatest are _____.

Geography The table lists the lowest elevation for several countries. A negative number means the elevation is below sea level, and a positive number means the elevation is above sea level. Compare the lowest elevation for each pair of countries. Write $<$ or $>$.

Country	Lowest Elevation (feet)
Argentina	−344
Australia	−49
Czech Republic	377
Hungary	249
United States	−281

20. Argentina and the United States _____

21. Czech Republic and Hungary _____

22. Hungary and Argentina _____

23. Which country in the table has the lowest elevation? _____

24. **Analyze Relationships** There are three numbers a, b, and c, where $a > b$ and $b > c$. Describe the positions of the numbers on a number line.

_____

_____

_____

_____

 **FOCUS ON HIGHER ORDER THINKING**

25. **Critique Reasoning** At 9 A.M. the outside temperature was −3°F. By noon, the temperature was −12°F. Jorge said that it was getting warmer outside. Is he correct? Explain.

_____

26. **Problem Solving** Golf scores represent the number of strokes above or below par. A negative score means that you hit a number below par while a positive score means that you hit a number above par. The winner in golf has the lowest score. During a round of golf, Angela's score was −5 and Lisa's score was −8. Who won the game? Explain.

_____

27. **Look for a Pattern** Order −3, 5, 16, and −10 from least to greatest. Then order the same numbers from closest to zero to farthest from zero. Describe how your lists are similar. Would this be true if the numbers were −3, 5, −16 and −10?

_____

_____

_____

_____

Work Area

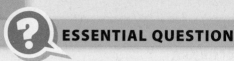

Constructing Number Lines

6.1.GF.1.2
Students will construct number lines.

? **ESSENTIAL QUESTION**

How do you create a number line to adequately display given values?

EXPLORE ACTIVITY 1

Intervals on the Number Line

Determine the numbering interval you should use to create tick marks on a number line to display the numbers 0.5, 2.5, 3.0, and 4.0.

A Since the values are decimals, the tick marks will represent _____.

B Look at the place value to determine the numbering interval. The decimals all go to the _____ place, so the numbering interval should be a multiple of _____.

C Numbering by _____ would take up too much room. Try using a multiple of 0.1, such as 0.5.

Since all of the values in the set are multiples of _____, using intervals of _____ displays the given values precisely.

Reflect

1. **Communicate Mathematical Ideas** Do all number lines need to display both positive and negative numbers? _____

_____

EXPLORE ACTIVITY 2

Constructing a Number Line

You can use number lines to display values. When you construct a number line, you need to consider many factors to make sure the number line displays the values clearly.

Construct a number line to display the numbers −1, 3, and 7.

A Circle the types of numbers that are included in the set above:

    Integers / Fractions / Decimals

B Since the numbers are all integers, you can count by ones. How many numbers are there when you count from −1 to 7? _____

C To make the number line easy to read, you need a tick mark for every number plus an extra tick mark on each end of the number line. Since the smallest number is −1, the number line should start on _____ The largest number is 7, so the number line should end with _____.

D To number from −2 to 8, how many tick marks do you need? _____

E Place 11 tick marks on the number line, keeping the spacing of the tick marks even. Then number the tick marks from −2 to 8.

←――――――――――――→

F On the number line, place a point on the corresponding tick mark for each of the given numbers.

Refle

2. **Analyze Relationships** How could interval size, or how you decide to label the tick marks, affect reading and interpreting the display?

_____

_____

_____

actice

ecide what numbering interval to use when labeling the number line for each set of numbers and explain your reasoning.

1. 0.60, 0.75, 0.80, 0.90 _____

_____

2. 25, 40, 50, 85 _____

_____

_____

3. How many tick marks do you need to display the numbers 2, 6, 10, 16, and 18 on a number line using an interval of 2? _____

_____

_____

4. Construct a number line to display the numbers −10, 0, 5, 15, and −5.

←――――――――――――→

? ESSENTIAL QUESTION

How do you find and use absolute value?

EXPLORE ACTIVITY 1

Finding Absolute Value

The **absolute value** of a number is the number's distance from 0 on a number line. For example, the absolute value of −3 is 3 because −3 is 3 units from 0. The absolute value of −3 is written |−3|.

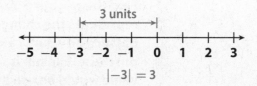

$|−3| = 3$

Because absolute value represents a distance, it is always nonnegative.

Graph the following numbers on the number line. Then use your number line to find each absolute value.

−7   5   7   −2   4   −4

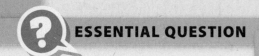

A |−7| = _____   **B** |5| = _____   **C** |7| = _____

D |−2| = _____   **E** |4| = _____   **F** |−4| = _____

Reflect

1. Analyze Relationships Which pairs of numbers have the same absolute value? How are these numbers related?

_____

_____

2. Justify Reasoning Negative numbers are less than positive numbers. Does this mean that the absolute value of a negative number must be less than the absolute value of a positive number? Explain.

_____

_____

_____

_____

Absolute Value In A Real-World Situation

In real-world situations, absolute values are often used instead of negative numbers. For example, if you use a $50 gift card to make a $25 purchase, the change in your gift card balance can be represented by −$25.

EXAMPLE 1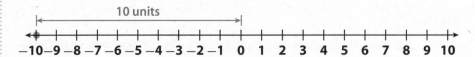

Jake uses his online music store gift card to buy an album of songs by his favorite band.

Find the negative number that represents the change in the balance on Jake's card after his purchase. Explain how absolute value would be used to express that number in this situation.

Music Online

Account Balance		$25.00
Cart	1 album	$10.00

STEP 1 Find the negative integer that represents the change in the balance.

−$10 *The balance decreased by $10, so use a negative number.*

_____

_____

Math Talk

Mathematical Processes

Explain why the price Jake paid for the album is represented by a negative number.

STEP 2 Use the number line to find the absolute value of −$10.

−10 is 10 units from 0 on the number line.

10 units

−10 −9 −8 −7 −6 −5 −4 −3 −2 −1 0 1 2 3 4 5 6 7 8 9 10

The absolute value of −$10 is $10, or $|-10| = 10$.

The balance on Jake's card decreased by $10.

Reflect

3. Communicate Mathematical Ideas Explain why the absolute value of a number will never be negative.

_____

_____

_____

1.3 Independent Practice

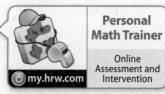

5. Financial Literacy Jacob earned $80 babysitting and deposited the money into his savings account. The next week he spent $85 on video games. Use integers to describe the weekly changes in Jacob's savings account balance.

_____

_____

6. Financial Literacy Sara's savings account balance changed by $34 one week and by −$67 the next week. Which amount represents the greatest

change? _____

7. Analyze Relationships Bertrand collects movie posters. The number of movie posters in his collection changes each month as he buys and sells posters. The table shows how many posters he bought or sold in the given months.

Month	January	February	March	April
Posters	Sold 20	Bought 12	Bought 22	Sold 28

a. Which months have changes that can be represented by positive numbers? Which months have changes that can be represented by negative numbers? Explain.

_____

_____

_____

_____

b. According to the table, in which month did the size of Bertrand's poster collection change the most? Use absolute value to explain your answer.

_____

_____

_____

8. Earth Science Death Valley has an elevation of −282 feet relative to sea level. Explain how to use absolute value to describe the elevation of Death Valley as a positive integer.

_____

_____

9. **Communicate Mathematical Ideas** Lisa and Alice are playing a game. Each player either receives or has to pay play money based on the result of their spin. The table lists how much a player receives or pays for various spins.

Red	Pay $5
Blue	Receive $4
Yellow	Pay $1
Green	Receive $3
Orange	Pay $2

    a. Express the amounts in the table as positive and negative numbers.

    _____

    b. Describe the change to Lisa's amount of money when the spinner lands on red.

    _____

    _____

10. **Financial Literacy** Sam's credit card balance is less than −$36. Does Sam owe more or less than $36? _____

11. **Financial Literacy** Emily spent $55 from her savings on a new dress. Explain how to describe the change in Emily's savings balance in two different ways.

_____

_____

_____

 **FOCUS ON HIGHER ORDER THINKING**

12. **Make a Conjecture** Can two different numbers have the same absolute value? If yes, give an example. If no, explain why not.

_____

13. **Communicate Mathematical Ideas** Does $-|-4| = |-(-4)|$? Justify your answer.

_____

14. **Critique Reasoning** Angelique says that finding the absolute value of a number is the same as finding the opposite of the number. For example, $|-5| = 5$. Explain her error.

_____

_____

_____

_____

Work Area

© Houghton Mifflin Harcourt Publishing Company

Ready to Go On?

Personal
Math Trainer

Online Assessment
and Intervention

my.hrw.com

1.1 Identifying Integers and Their Opposites

1. The table shows the elevations in feet of several locations around a coastal town. Graph and label the locations on the number line according to their elevations.

Location	Post Office *A*	Library *B*	Town Hall *C*	Laundromat *D*	Pet Store *E*
Elevation (feet)	8	−3	−9	3	1

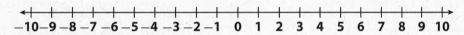

Write the opposite of each number.

2. −22 _____

3. 0 _____

1.2 Comparing and Ordering Integers

List the numbers in order from least to greatest.

4. −2, 8, −15, −5, 3, 1 _____

Compare. Write < or >.

5. −3 ◯ −15

6. 9 ◯ −10

1.3 Absolute Value

Graph each number on the number line. Then use your number line to find the absolute value of each number.

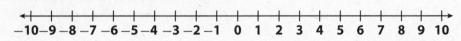

7. 2 _____

8. −8 _____

9. −5 _____

ESSENTIAL QUESTION

10. How can you use absolute value to represent a negative number in a real-world situation?

_____

_____

Personal Math Trainer

Online Assessment and Intervention

my.hrw.com

Selected Response

1. Which number line shows 2, 3, and −3?

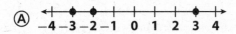

Ⓐ −4 −3 −2 −1 0 1 2 3 4

Ⓑ −4 −3 −2 −1 0 1 2 3 4

Ⓒ −4 −3 −2 −1 0 1 2 3 4

Ⓓ −4 −3 −2 −1 0 1 2 3 4

2. What is the opposite of −3?

Ⓐ 3   Ⓒ $-\frac{1}{3}$

Ⓑ 0   Ⓓ $\frac{1}{3}$

3. Darrel is currently 20 feet below sea level. Which correctly describes the opposite of Darrel's elevation?

Ⓐ 20 feet below sea level

Ⓑ 20 feet above sea level

Ⓒ 2 feet below sea level

Ⓓ At sea level

4. Which has the same absolute value as −55?

Ⓐ 0   Ⓒ 1

Ⓑ −1   Ⓓ 55

5. In Bangor it is −3 °F, in Fairbanks it is −12 °F, in Fargo it is −8 °F, and in Calgary it is −15 °F. In which city is it the coldest?

Ⓐ Bangor   Ⓒ Fargo

Ⓑ Fairbanks   Ⓓ Calgary

6. Which shows the integers in order from least to greatest?

Ⓐ 20, 6, −2, −13   Ⓒ −13, −2, 6, 20

Ⓑ −2, 6, −13, 20   Ⓓ 20, −13, 6, −2

7. How would you use a number line to put integers in order from greatest to least?

Ⓐ Graph the integers, then read them from left to right.

Ⓑ Graph the integers, then read them from right to left.

Ⓒ Graph the absolute values of the integers, then read them from left to right.

Ⓓ Graph the absolute values of the integers, then read them from right to left.

Mini-Task

8. The table shows the change in the amounts of money in several savings accounts over the past month.

Account	Change
A	$125
B	−$45
C	−$302
D	$108

a. List the dollar amounts in the order in which they would appear on a number line from left to right.

_____

b. In which savings account was the absolute value of the change the greatest? Describe the change in that account.

_____

c. In which account was the absolute value of the change the least?

_____

Factors and Multiples

? ESSENTIAL QUESTION

How can you use greatest common factors and least common multiples to solve real-world problems?

LESSON 2.1
Greatest Common Factor

LESSON 2.2
Least Common Multiple

Real-World Video

Organizers of banquets and other special events plan many things, including menus, seating arrangements, table decorations, and party favors. Factors and multiples can be helpful in this work.

ⓞ my.hrw.com

GO DIGITAL
my.hrw.com

my.hrw.com

Go digital with your write-in student edition, accessible on any device.

Math On the Spot

Scan with your smart phone to jump directly to the online edition, video tutor, and more.

Animated Math

Interactively explore key concepts to see how math works.

Personal Math Trainer

Get immediate feedback and help as you work through practice sets.

Reading Start-Up

Vocabulary

Review Words
- ✔ area *(área)*
- ✔ Distributive Property *(Propiedad distributiva)*
- ✔ factor *(factor)*
- ✔ multiple *(múltiplo)*
- ✔ product *(producto)*

Preview Words
- greatest common factor (GCF) *(máximo común divisor (MCD))*
- least common multiple (LCM) *(mínimo común múltiplo (m.c.m.))*

Visualize Vocabulary

Use the ✔ words to complete the graphic.

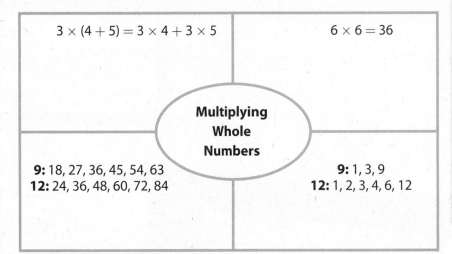

$3 \times (4 + 5) = 3 \times 4 + 3 \times 5$	$6 \times 6 = 36$
9: 18, 27, 36, 45, 54, 63 **12:** 24, 36, 48, 60, 72, 84	**9:** 1, 3, 9 **12:** 1, 2, 3, 4, 6, 12

Multiplying Whole Numbers

Understand Vocabulary

Complete the sentences below using the preview words.

1. Of all the whole numbers that divide evenly into two or more numbers, the one with the highest value is called the _____.

2. Of all the common products of two numbers, the one with the lowest value is called the _____.

Active Reading

Two-Panel Flip Chart Create a two-panel flip chart to help you understand the concepts in this module. Label one flap "Greatest Common Factor." Label the other flap "Least Common Multiple." As you study each lesson, write important ideas under the appropriate flap.

Are YOU Ready?

Complete these exercises to review skills you will need for this module.

Personal Math Trainer

Online Assessment and Intervention

my.hrw.com

Multiples

| EXAMPLE | 5×1 = 5 | 5×2 = 10 | 5×3 = 15 | 5×4 = 20 | 5×5 = 25 | To find the first five multiples of 5, multiply 5 by 1, 2, 3, 4, and 5. |

List the first five multiples of the number.

1. 7 _____

2. 11 _____

3. 15 _____

Factors

| EXAMPLE | $1 \times 12 = 12$ $2 \times 6 = 12$ $3 \times 4 = 12$ The factors of 12 are 1, 2, 3, 4, 6, 12. | To find the factors of 12, use multiplication facts of 12. Continue until pairs of factors repeat. |

Write all the factors of the number.

4. 24 _____

5. 36 _____

6. 45 _____

7. 32 _____

Multiplication Properties (Distributive)

| EXAMPLE | $7 \times 14 = 7 \times (10 + 4)$ $\quad = (7 \times 10) + (7 \times 4)$ $\quad = 70 + 28$ $\quad = 98$ | To multiply a number by a sum, multiply the number by each addend and add the products. |

Use the Distributive Property to find the product.

8. $8 \times 15 = 8 \times \left(\boxed{} + \boxed{} \right)$

$= \left(\boxed{} \times \boxed{} \right) + \left(\boxed{} \times \boxed{} \right)$

$= \boxed{} + \boxed{}$

$= \boxed{}$

9. $6 \times 17 = 6 \times \left(\boxed{} + \boxed{} \right)$

$= \left(\boxed{} \times \boxed{} \right) + \left(\boxed{} \times \boxed{} \right)$

$= \boxed{} + \boxed{}$

$= \boxed{}$

Complete these exercises to review skills you will need for this module.

Multiples

10. Hector plans to add $12 to his savings account at the end of each week. The table shows the total amount Hector has saved at the end of the first week. Complete the table to show how much Hector will have saved at the end of each week from Week 2 through Week 8.

Week	1	2	3	4	5	6	7	8
Total Savings	$12							

Factors

11. Felicia claims that all the factors of 60 are 1, 2, 3, 5, 6, 10, 12, 20, 30, and 60. Which factors of 60 did Felicia leave out? Explain how you found the factors.

Multiplication Properties (Distributive)

12. Tyrell wants to multiply 7×23. He starts by rewriting the problem as $7 \times (20 + 3)$.

    a. Explain how Tyrell can use the Distributive Property to rewrite the expression $7 \times (20 + 3)$.

    b. What is the product of 7 and 23?

Greatest Common Factor

6.1.2.1
Students will find and use the greatest common factor of two whole numbers.

? ESSENTIAL QUESTION

How can you find and use the greatest common factor of two whole numbers?

EXPLORE ACTIVITY 1 Real World

Understanding Common Factors

The **greatest common factor (GCF)** of two numbers is the greatest factor shared by those numbers.

A florist makes bouquets from 18 roses and 30 tulips. All the bouquets will include both roses and tulips. If all the bouquets are identical, what are the possible bouquets that can be made?

A Complete the tables to show the possible ways to divide each type of flower among the bouquets.

Roses

Number of Bouquets	1	2	3	6	9	18
Number of Roses in Each Bouquet	18	9				

Tulips

Number of Bouquets	1	2	3	5	6	10	15	30
Number of Tulips in Each Bouquet	30							

B Can the florist make five bouquets using all the flowers? Explain.

_____

C What are the common factors of 18 and 30? What do they represent?

_____

D What is the GCF of 18 and 30? _____

Reflect

1. **What If?** Suppose the florist has 18 roses and 36 tulips. What is the GCF of the numbers of roses and tulips? Explain.

_____

Finding the Greatest Common Factor

One way to find the GCF of two numbers is to list all of their factors. Then you can identify common factors and the GCF.

EXAMPLE 1

A baker has 24 sesame bagels and 36 plain bagels to put into boxes. Each box must have the same number of each type of bagel. What is the greatest number of boxes that the baker can make using all of the bagels? How many sesame bagels and how many plain bagels will be in each box?

STEP 1 List the factors of 24 and 36. Then circle the common factors.

> The baker can divide 24 sesame bagels into groups of 1, 2, 3, 4, 6, 8, 12, or 24.

Factors of 24: ① ② ③ ④ ⑥ 8 ⑫ 24

Factors of 36: ① ② ③ ④ ⑥ 9 ⑫ 18 36

STEP 2 Find the GCF of 24 and 36.

The GCF is 12. So, the greatest number of boxes that the baker can make is 12. There will be 2 sesame bagels in each box, because $24 \div 12 = 2$. There will be 3 plain bagels, because $36 \div 12 = 3$.

Reflect

2. **Critical Thinking** What is the GCF of two prime numbers? Give an example.

_____

YOUR TURN

Find the GCF of each pair of numbers.

3. 14 and 35 _____   4. 20 and 28 _____

5. The sixth-grade class is competing in the school field day. There are 32 girls and 40 boys who want to participate. Each team must have the same number of girls and the same number of boys. What is the greatest number of teams that can be formed? How many boys and how many girls will be on each team?

_____

Using the Distributive Property

You can use the Distributive Property to rewrite a sum of two or more numbers as a product of their GCF and a sum of numbers with no common factor. To understand how, you can use grid paper to draw area models of 45 and 60. Here are all the possible area models of 45.

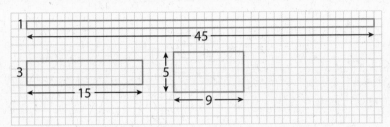

A What do the side lengths of the area models (1, 3, 5, 9, 15, and 45)

represent? _____

B On your own grid paper, show all of the possible area models of 60.

_____

C What side lengths do the area models of 45 and 60 have in common? What do the side lengths represent?

_____

D What is the greatest common side length? What does it represent?

_____

E Write 45 as a product of the GCF and another number. _____

Write 60 as a product of the GCF and another number. _____

F Use your answers above to rewrite 45 + 60.

$45 + 60 = 15 \times$ _____ $+ 15 \times$ _____

Use the Distributive Property and your answer above to write 45 + 60 as a product of the GCF and a sum of two numbers.

$15 \times$ _____ $+ 15 \times$ _____ $= 15 \times ($ _____ $+$ _____ $) = 15 \times 7$

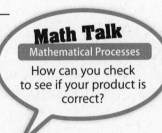

Math Talk
Mathematical Processes
How can you check to see if your product is correct?

Reflect

Write the sum of the numbers as the product of their GCF and another sum.

6. $27 + 18$ _____

7. $120 + 36$ _____

8. $9 + 35$ _____

1. Lee is sewing vests using 16 green buttons and 24 blue buttons. All the vests are identical, and all have both green and blue buttons. What are the possible numbers of vests Lee can make? What is the greatest number of vests Lee can make? (Explore Activity 1, Example 1)

List the factors of 16 and 24. Then circle the common factors.

Factors of 16:							
Factors of 24:							

What are the common factors of 16 and 24? _____

What are the possible numbers of vests Lee can make? _____

What is the GCF of 16 and 24? _____

What is the greatest number of vests Lee can make? _____

Write the sum of numbers as a product of their GCF and another sum.
(Explore Activity 2)

2. $36 + 45$

What is the GCF of 36 and 45? _____

Write each number as a product of the GCF and another number.
Then use the Distributive Property to rewrite the sum.

$$\left(\boxed{} \times \boxed{}\right) + \left(\boxed{} \times \boxed{}\right) = \left(\boxed{}\right) \times \left(\boxed{} + \boxed{}\right)$$

3. $75 + 90$

What is the GCF of 75 and 90? _____

Write each number as a product of the GCF and another number.
Then use the Distributive Property to rewrite the sum.

$$\left(\boxed{} \times \boxed{}\right) + \left(\boxed{} \times \boxed{}\right) = \left(\boxed{}\right) \times \left(\boxed{} + \boxed{}\right)$$

? **ESSENTIAL QUESTION CHECK-IN**

4. Describe how to find the GCF of two numbers.

_____

_____

2.1 Independent Practice

Personal Math Trainer

Online Assessment and Intervention

my.hrw.com

List the factors of each number.

5. 12 _____

6. 50 _____

7. 39 _____

8. 64 _____

Find the GCF of each pair of numbers.

9. 40 and 48 _____

10. 30 and 45 _____

11. 10 and 45 _____

12. 25 and 90 _____

13. 21 and 40 _____

14. 28 and 70 _____

15. 60 and 72 _____

16. 45 and 81 _____

17. 28 and 32 _____

18. 55 and 77 _____

19. Carlos is arranging books on shelves. He has 24 novels and 16 autobiographies. Each shelf will have the same numbers of novels and autobiographies. If Carlos must place all of the books on shelves, what are the possible numbers of shelves Carlos will use?

_____

20. The middle school band has 56 members. The high school band has 96 members. The bands are going to march one after the other in a parade. The director wants to arrange the bands into the same number of columns. What is the greatest number of columns in which the two bands can be arranged if each column has the same number of marchers? How many band members will be in each column?

_____

21. For football tryouts at a local school, 12 coaches and 42 players will split into groups. Each group will have the same numbers of coaches and players. What is the greatest number of groups that can be formed? How many coaches and players will be in each of these groups?

_____

22. Lola is placing appetizers on plates. She has 63 spring rolls and 84 cheese cubes. She wants to include both appetizers on each plate. Each plate must have the same numbers of spring rolls and cheese cubes. What is the greatest number of plates she can make using all of the appetizers? How many of each type of appetizer will be on each of these plates?

_____

Write the sum of the numbers as the product of their GCF and another sum.

23. $56 + 64$ _____

24. $48 + 14$ _____

25. $30 + 54$ _____

26. $24 + 40$ _____

27. $55 + 66$ _____

28. $49 + 63$ _____

29. $40 + 25$ _____

30. $63 + 15$ _____

31. Vocabulary Explain why the greatest common factor of two numbers is sometimes 1.

_____

_____

_____

 **FOCUS ON HIGHER ORDER THINKING**

Work Area

32. Communicate Mathematical Ideas Tasha believes that she can rewrite the difference $120 - 36$ as a product of the GCF of the two numbers and another difference. Is she correct? Explain your answer.

_____

_____

_____

33. Persevere in Problem Solving Explain how to find the greatest common factor of three numbers.

_____

_____

_____

_____

34. Critique Reasoning Xiao's teacher asked him to rewrite the sum $60 + 90$ as the product of the GCF of the two numbers and a sum. Xiao wrote $3(20 + 30)$. What mistake did Xiao make? How should he have written the sum?

_____

_____

_____

LESSON
2.2

6.1.2.2
Students will find and use the least common multiple of two numbers.

Least Common Multiple

ESSENTIAL QUESTION

How do you find and use the least common multiple of two numbers?

EXPLORE ACTIVITY Real World

Finding the Least Common Multiple

A multiple of a number is the product of the number and another number. For example, 9 is a multiple of the number 3. The **least common multiple (LCM)** of two or more numbers is the least number, other than zero, that is a multiple of all the numbers.

Ned is training for a biathlon. He will swim every sixth day and bicycle every eighth day. On what days will he both swim and bicycle?

A In the chart below, shade each day that Ned will swim. Circle each day Ned will bicycle.

1	2	3	4	5	6	7	8	9	10
11	12	13	14	15	16	17	18	19	20
21	22	23	24	25	26	27	28	29	30
31	32	33	34	35	36	37	38	39	40
41	42	43	44	45	46	47	48	49	50
51	52	53	54	55	56	57	58	59	60
61	62	63	64	65	66	67	68	69	70
71	72	73	74	75	76	77	78	79	80
81	82	83	84	85	86	87	88	89	90
91	92	93	94	95	96	97	98	99	100

B On what days will Ned both swim and bicycle? _____

The numbers of the days that Ned will swim and bicycle are common multiples of 6 and 8.

Reflect

1. **Interpret the Answer** What does the LCM represent in this situation?

_____

Applying the LCM

You can use the LCM of two whole numbers to solve problems.

EXAMPLE 1

A store is holding a promotion. Every third customer receives a free key chain, and every fourth customer receives a free magnet. Which customer will be the first to receive both a key chain and a magnet?

STEP 1 List the multiples of 3 and 4. Then circle the common multiples.

Multiples of 3: 3   6   9   (12)   15   18   21   (24)   27

Multiples of 4: 4   8   (12)   16   20   (24)   28   32   36

STEP 2 Find the LCM of 3 and 4.

The LCM is 12.

The first customer to get both a key chain and a magnet is the 12th customer.

Math Talk

Mathematical Processes

What steps do you take to list the multiples of a number?

Personal Math Trainer

Online Assessment and Intervention

© my.hrw.com

YOUR TURN

2. Find the LCM of 4 and 9 by listing the multiples. _____

   Multiples of 4: _____

   Multiples of 9: _____

Guided Practice

1. After every ninth visit to a restaurant you receive a free beverage. After every twelfth visit you receive a free appetizer. If you visit the restaurant 100 times, on which visits will you receive a free beverage and a free appetizer? At which visit will you first receive a free beverage and a free appetizer? (Explore Activity 1, Example 1)

   _____

? ESSENTIAL QUESTION CHECK-IN

2. What steps can you take to find the LCM of two numbers?

   _____

   _____

2.2 Independent Practice

Find the LCM of each pair of numbers.

3. 8 and 56 _____

4. 25 and 50 _____

5. 12 and 30 _____

6. 6 and 10 _____

7. 16 and 24 _____

8. 14 and 21 _____

9. 9 and 15 _____

10. 5 and 11 _____

11. During February, Kevin will water his ivy every third day, and water his cactus every fifth day.

    a. On which date will Kevin first water both plants together?

    _____

    b. Will Kevin water both plants together again in February? Explain.

    _____

    _____

12. **Vocabulary** Given any two numbers, which is greater, the LCM of the numbers or the GCF of the numbers? Why?

_____

_____

_____

Use the subway train schedule.

13. The red line and the blue line trains just arrived at the station. When will they next arrive at the station at the same time?

    In _____ minutes

14. The blue line and the yellow line trains just arrived at the station. When will they next arrive at the station at the same time?

    In _____ minutes

15. All three trains just arrived at the station. When will they next all arrive at the station at the same time?

    In _____ minutes

Train Schedule	
Train	**Arrives Every...**
Red line	8 minutes
Blue line	10 minutes
Yellow line	12 minutes

16. You buy a lily and an African violet on the same day. You are instructed to water the lily every fourth day and water the violet every seventh day after taking them home. What is the first day on which you will water both plants on the same day? How can you use this answer to determine each of the next days you will water both plants on the same day?

_____

_____

_____

H.O.T. **FOCUS ON HIGHER ORDER THINKING**

17. What is the LCM of two numbers if one number is a multiple of the other? Give an example.

_____

_____

18. What is the LCM of two numbers that have no common factors greater than 1? Give an example.

_____

_____

19. **Draw Conclusions** The least common multiple of two numbers is 60, and one of the numbers is 7 less than the other number. What are the numbers? Justify your answer.

_____

_____

_____

_____

20. **Communicate Mathematical Ideas** Describe how to find the least common multiple of three numbers. Give an example.

_____

_____

_____

_____

_____

_____

Work Area

Ready to Go On?

2.1 Greatest Common Factor

Find the GCF of each pair of numbers.

1. 20 and 32 _____

2. 24 and 56 _____

3. 36 and 90 _____

4. 45 and 75 _____

5. 28 girls and 32 boys volunteer to plant trees at a school. The principal divides the girls and boys into identical groups that have girls and boys in each group. What is the greatest number of groups the principal can make? _____

Write the sum of the numbers as the product of their GCF and another sum.

6. $32 + 20$ _____

7. $18 + 27$ _____

2.2 Least Common Multiple

Find the LCM of each pair of numbers.

8. 6 and 12 _____

9. 6 and 10 _____

10. 8 and 9 _____

11. 9 and 12 _____

12. Juanita runs every third day and swims every fifth day. If Juanita runs and swims today, in how many days will she run and swim again on the same day? _____

? ESSENTIAL QUESTION

13. What types of problems can be solved using the greatest common factor? What types of problems can be solved using the least common multiple?

_____

_____

_____

Selected Response

1. What is the least common multiple of 5 and 150?

- (A) 5
- (B) 50
- (C) 15
- (D) 150

2. Cy has 42 baseball cards and 70 football cards that he wants to group into packages. Each package will have the same number of cards, and each package will have the same numbers of baseball cards and football cards. How many packages will Cy make if he uses all of the cards?

- (A) 7
- (B) 10
- (C) 14
- (D) 21

3. During a promotional event, a sporting goods store gave a free T-shirt to every 8th customer and a free water bottle to every 10th customer. Which customer was the first to get a free T-shirt and a free water bottle?

- (A) the 10th customer
- (B) the 20th customer
- (C) the 40th customer
- (D) the 80th customer

4. The table below shows the positions relative to sea level of four divers.

Kareem	Li	Maria	Tara
−8 ft	−10 ft	−9 ft	−7 ft

Which diver is farthest from the surface?

- (A) Kareem
- (B) Li
- (C) Maria
- (D) Tara

5. What is the greatest common factor of 12 and 16?

- (A) 2
- (B) 4
- (C) 12
- (D) 48

6. Which expression is equivalent to $27 + 15$?

- (A) $9 \times (3 + 5)$
- (B) $3 \times (9 + 15)$
- (C) $9 \times (3 + 15)$
- (D) $3 \times (9 + 5)$

7. During a science experiment, the temperature of a solution in Beaker 1 was 5 degrees below zero. The temperature of a solution in Beaker 2 was the opposite of the temperature in Beaker 1. What was the temperature in Beaker 2?

- (A) −5 degrees
- (B) 0 degrees
- (C) 5 degrees
- (D) 10 degrees

Mini-Task

8. Tia is buying paper cups and plates. Cups come in packages of 12, and plates come in packages of 10. She wants to buy the same number of cups and plates, but plans to buy the least number of packages possible. How much should Tia expect to pay if each package of cups is $3 and each package of plates is $5? Explain.

_____

_____

_____

_____

_____

_____

Rational Numbers

ESSENTIAL QUESTION

How can you use rational numbers to solve real-world problems?

my.hrw.com

Real-World Video

In sports like baseball, coaches, analysts, and fans keep track of players' statistics such as batting averages, earned run averages, and runs batted in. These values are reported using rational numbers.

GO DIGITAL
my.hrw.com

my.hrw.com

Go digital with your write-in student edition, accessible on any device.

Math On the Spot

Scan with your smart phone to jump directly to the online edition, video tutor, and more.

Animated Math

Interactively explore key concepts to see how math works.

Personal Math Trainer

Get immediate feedback and help as you work through practice sets.

Reading Start-Up

Visualize Vocabulary

Use the ✔ words to complete the web. You may put more than one word in each box.

−15, −45, −60		25, 71, 102
	Integers	
−20 and 20		9

Vocabulary

Review Words

  absolute value *(valor absoluto)*

  decimal *(decimal)*

  dividend *(dividendo)*

  divisor *(divisor)*

  fraction *(fracción)*

  integers *(enteros)*

✔ negative numbers *(números negativos)*

✔ opposites *(opuestos)*

✔ positive numbers *(números positivos)*

✔ whole number *(número entero)*

Preview Words

  rational number *(número racional)*

  Venn diagram *(diagrama de Venn)*

Understand Vocabulary

Fill in each blank with the correct term from the preview words.

1. A _____ is any number that can be written as a ratio of two integers.

2. A _____ is used to show the relationships between groups.

Active Reading

Tri-Fold Before beginning the module, create a tri-fold to help you learn the concepts and vocabulary in this module. Fold the paper into three sections. Label the columns "What I Know," "What I Need to Know," and "What I Learned." Complete the first two columns before you read. After studying the module, complete the third column.

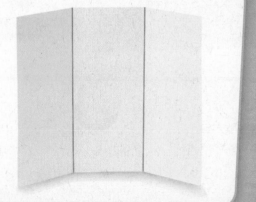

Are YOU Ready?

Complete these exercises to review skills you will need for this module.

Write an Improper Fraction as a Mixed Number

EXAMPLE
$\frac{11}{3} = \frac{3}{3} + \frac{3}{3} + \frac{3}{3} + \frac{2}{3}$ Write as a sum using names for one plus a proper fraction.
Write each name for one as one.

$= 1 + 1 + 1 + \frac{2}{3}$

$= 3 + \frac{2}{3}$ Add the ones.

$= 3\frac{2}{3}$ Write the mixed number.

Write each improper fraction as a mixed number.

1. $\frac{7}{2}$ _____ **2.** $\frac{12}{5}$ _____ **3.** $\frac{11}{7}$ _____ **4.** $\frac{15}{4}$ _____

Write a Mixed Number as an Improper Fraction

EXAMPLE
$3\frac{3}{4} = 1 + 1 + 1 + \frac{3}{4}$ Write the whole number as a sum of ones.

$= \frac{4}{4} + \frac{4}{4} + \frac{4}{4} + \frac{3}{4}$ Use the denominator of the fraction to write equivalent fractions for the ones.

$= \frac{15}{4}$ Add the numerators.

Write each mixed number as an improper fraction.

5. $2\frac{1}{2}$ _____ **6.** $4\frac{3}{5}$ _____ **7.** $3\frac{4}{9}$ _____ **8.** $2\frac{5}{7}$ _____

Compare and Order Decimals

EXAMPLE
Order from least to greatest: 7.32, 5.14, 5.16.
7.32 is greatest.
$5.14 < 5.16$
The order is 5.14, 5.16, 7.32.

Use place value to compare numbers, starting with ones, then tenths, then hundredths.

Compare the decimals.

9. 8.86 _____ 8.65   **10.** 0.732 _____ 0.75   **11.** 0.22 _____ 0.022

12. Order 0.98, 0.27, and 0.34 from greatest to least. _____

Complete these exercises to review skills you will need for this module.

Write an Improper Fraction as a Mixed Number

13. Liam determines that he needs $\frac{15}{4}$ cups of orange juice for a recipe. He has a 1-cup measuring cup. Show how to write $\frac{15}{4}$ as a mixed number and explain how he can measure out the correct amount of juice.

Write a Mixed Number as an Improper Fraction

14. Jin needs to write the mixed number $5\frac{3}{5}$ as an improper fraction. Show how he can write the improper fraction. Explain each step.

Compare and Order Decimals

15. An athlete is practicing for a shot put competition. On Monday, his best throw was 18.3 meters. On Wednesday, his best throw was 16.82 meters. On Friday, his best throw was 18.35 meters. Order the distances from least to greatest.

Classifying Rational Numbers

6.1.3.1
Students will classify rational numbers.

? ESSENTIAL QUESTION

How can you classify rational numbers?

EXPLORE ACTIVITY

Representing Division as a Fraction

Alicia and her friends Brittany, Kenji, and Ellis are taking a pottery class. The four friends have to share 3 blocks of clay. How much clay will each of them receive if they divide the 3 blocks evenly?

A The top faces of the 3 blocks of clay can be represented by squares. Use the model to show the part of each block that each friend will receive. Explain.

_____

_____

B Each piece of one square is equal to what fraction of a block of clay?

_____

C Explain how to arrange the pieces to model the amount of clay each person gets. Sketch the model.

Alicia   Brittany   Kenji   Ellis

_____

D What fraction of a square does each person's pieces cover? Explain.

_____

_____

E How much clay will each person receive?

_____

F **Multiple Representations** How does this situation represent division?

_____

_____

Reflect

1. Communicate Mathematical Ideas $3 \div 4$ can be written $\frac{3}{4}$. How are the dividend and divisor of a division expression related to the parts of a fraction?

_____

_____

2. Analyze Relationships How could you represent the division as a fraction if 5 people shared 2 blocks? if 6 people shared 5 blocks?

_____

Math On the Spot

my.hrw.com

Rational Numbers

A **rational number** is any number that can be written as $\frac{a}{b}$, where a and b are integers and $b \neq 0$.

EXAMPLE 1

Write each rational number as $\frac{a}{b}$.

Math Talk

Mathematical Processes

What division is represented by the fraction $\frac{34}{1}$?

A $3\frac{2}{5}$ Convert the mixed number to a fraction greater than 1. $3\frac{2}{5} = \frac{17}{5}$

B 0.6 The decimal is six tenths. Write as a fraction. $0.6 = \frac{6}{10}$

C 34 Write the whole number as a fraction with a denominator of 1. $34 = \frac{34}{1}$

D -7 Write the integer as a fraction with a denominator of 1. $-7 = \frac{-7}{1}$

YOUR TURN

Personal Math Trainer

Online Assessment and Intervention

my.hrw.com

Write each rational number as $\frac{a}{b}$.

3. -15 _____   **4.** 0.31 _____

5. $4\frac{5}{9}$ _____   **6.** 62 _____

Classifying Rational Numbers

A **Venn diagram** is a visual representation used to show the relationships between groups. The Venn diagram below shows how rational numbers, integers, and whole numbers are related.

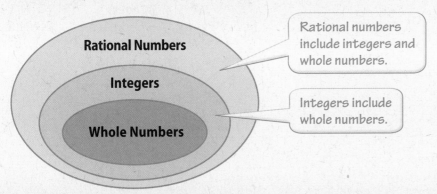

Rational numbers include integers and whole numbers.

Integers include whole numbers.

EXAMPLE 2

My Notes

Place each number in the Venn diagram. Then classify each number by indicating in which set or sets each number belongs.

```
Rational Numbers
0.35                    3/4
        Integers
   −3
          75
       Whole Numbers
```

A 75   The number 75 belongs in the sets of whole numbers, integers, and rational numbers.

B −3   The number −3 belongs in the sets of integers and rational numbers.

C $\frac{3}{4}$ The number $\frac{3}{4}$ belongs in the set of rational numbers.

D 0.35   The number 0.35 belongs in the set of rational numbers.

Reflect

7. Analyze Relationships Name two integers that are not also whole numbers.

_____

8. Analyze Relationships Describe how the Venn diagram models the relationship between rational numbers, integers, and whole numbers.

_____

_____

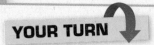

Place each number in the Venn diagram. Then classify each number by indicating in which set or sets it belongs.

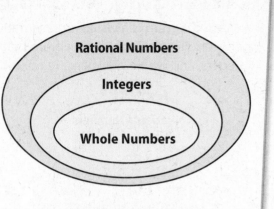

Rational Numbers

Integers

Whole Numbers

9. 14.1 _____

10. $7\frac{1}{5}$ _____

11. −8 _____

12. 101 _____

Guided Practice

1. Sarah and four friends are decorating picture frames with ribbon. They have 4 rolls of ribbon to share evenly. (Explore Activity 1)

   a. How does this situation represent division?

   _____

   b. How much ribbon does each person receive? _____

Write each rational number in the form $\frac{a}{b}$, where a and b are integers. (Example 1)

2. 0.7 _____

3. −29 _____

4. $8\frac{1}{3}$ _____

Place each number in the Venn diagram. Then classify each number by indicating in which set or sets each number belongs. (Example 2)

5. −15 _____

6. $5\frac{10}{11}$ _____

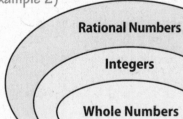

Rational Numbers

Integers

Whole Numbers

? **ESSENTIAL QUESTION CHECK-IN**

7. How is a rational number that is not an integer different from a rational number that is an integer?

_____

_____

_____

3.1 Independent Practice

List two numbers that fit each description. Then write the numbers in the appropriate location on the Venn diagram.

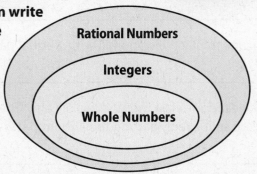

Rational Numbers

Integers

Whole Numbers

8. Integers that are not whole numbers

_____

9. Rational numbers that are not integers

_____

10. **Multistep** A nature club is having its weekly hike. The table shows how many pieces of fruit and bottles of water each member of the club brought to share.

Member	Pieces of Fruit	Bottles of Water
Baxter	3	5
Hendrick	2	2
Mary	4	3
Kendra	5	7

a. If the hikers want to share the fruit evenly, how many pieces should each person receive?

_____

b. Which hikers received more fruit than they brought on the hike?

_____

c. The hikers want to share their water evenly so that each member has the same amount. How much water does each hiker receive?

_____

11. Sherman has 3 cats and 2 dogs. He wants to buy a toy for each of his pets. Sherman has $22 to spend on pet toys. How much can he spend on each pet? Write your answer as a fraction and as an amount in dollars and cents.

_____

12. A group of 5 friends are sharing 2 pounds of trail mix. Write a division problem and a fraction to represent this situation.

_____

13. **Vocabulary** A _____ diagram can represent set relationships visually.

Financial Literacy **For 14–16, use the table. The table shows Jason's utility bills for one month. Write a fraction to represent the division in each situation. Then classify each result by indicating the set or sets to which it belongs.**

March Bills	
Water	$35
Gas	$14
Electric	$108

14. Jason and his 3 roommates share the cost of the electric bill evenly.

_____

15. Jason plans to pay the water bill with 2 equal payments.

_____

16. Jason owes $15 for last month's gas bill also. The total amount of the two gas bills is split evenly among the 4 roommates.

_____

17. Lynn has a watering can that holds 16 cups of water, and she fills it half full. Then she waters her 15 plants so that each plant gets the same amount of water. How many cups of water will each plant get?

_____

_____

 **FOCUS ON HIGHER ORDER THINKING**

18. Critique Reasoning DaMarcus says the number $\frac{24}{6}$ belongs only to the set of rational numbers. Explain his error.

_____

_____

_____

_____

19. Analyze Relationships Explain how the Venn diagrams in this lesson show that all integers and all whole numbers are rational numbers.

_____

_____

_____

_____

20. Critical Thinking Is it possible for a number to be a rational number that is not an integer but is a whole number? Explain.

_____

_____

Work Area

LESSON 3.2 Identifying Opposites and Absolute Value of Rational Numbers

6.1.3.2
Students will identify opposites and absolute value of rational numbers.

? ESSENTIAL QUESTION

How do you identify opposites and absolute value of rational numbers?

EXPLORE ACTIVITY

Positive and Negative Rational Numbers

Recall that positive numbers are greater than 0. They are located to the right of 0 on a number line. Negative numbers are less than 0. They are located to the left of 0 on a number line.

Water levels with respect to sea level, which has elevation 0, may be measured at beach tidal basins. Water levels below sea level are represented by negative numbers.

A The table shows the water level at a tidal basin at different times during a day. Graph the level for each time on the number line.

Time	4 A.M. A	8 A.M. B	Noon C	4 P.M. D	8 P.M. E
Level (ft)	3.5	2.5	−0.5	−2.5	0.5

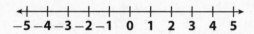

B How did you know where to graph −0.5? _____

C At what time or times is the level closest to sea level? How do you know?

_____

D Which point is located halfway between −3 and −2? _____

E Which point is the same distance from 0 as *D*? _____

Reflect

1. **Communicate Mathematical Ideas** How would you graph −2.25? Would it be left or right of point *D*?

_____

Rational Numbers and Opposites on a Number Line

You can find the opposites of rational numbers the same way you found the opposites of integers. Two rational numbers are opposites if they are the same distance from 0 but on different sides of 0.

$2\frac{3}{4}$ and $-2\frac{3}{4}$ are opposites.

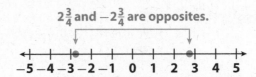

$$-5 \quad -4 \quad -3 \quad -2 \quad -1 \quad 0 \quad 1 \quad 2 \quad 3 \quad 4 \quad 5$$

EXAMPLE 1

Until June 24, 1997, the New York Stock Exchange priced the value of a share of stock in eighths, such as $\$27\frac{1}{8}$ or at $\$41\frac{3}{4}$. The change in value of a share of stock from day to day was also represented in eighths as a positive or negative number.

The table shows the change in value of a stock over two days. Graph the change in stock value for Wednesday and its opposite on a number line.

Day	Tuesday	Wednesday
Change in value ($)	$1\frac{5}{8}$	$-4\frac{1}{4}$

STEP 1 Graph the change in stock value for Wednesday on the number line.

The change in value for Wednesday is $-4\frac{1}{4}$.

Graph a point $4\frac{1}{4}$ units below 0.

STEP 2 Graph the opposite of $-4\frac{1}{4}$.

The opposite of $-4\frac{1}{4}$ is the same distance from 0 but on the other side of 0.

The opposite of $-4\frac{1}{4}$ is $4\frac{1}{4}$.

The opposite of the change in stock value for Wednesday is $4\frac{1}{4}$.

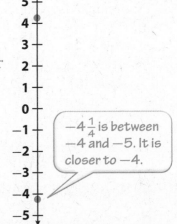

$-4\frac{1}{4}$ is between -4 and -5. It is closer to -4.

YOUR TURN

2. What are the opposites of 7, −3.5, 2.25, and $9\frac{1}{3}$?

Absolute Values of Rational Numbers

You can also find the absolute value of a rational number the same way you found the absolute value of an integer. The absolute value of a rational number is the number's distance from 0 on the number line.

Math On the Spot
my.hrw.com

EXAMPLE 2

The table shows the average low temperatures in January in one location during a five-year span. Find the absolute value of the average January low temperature in 2009.

Year	2008	2009	2010	2011	2012
Temperature (°C)	−3.2	−5.4	−0.8	3.8	−2

STEP 1 Graph the 2009 average January low temperature.

The 2009 average January low is −5.4 °C.
Graph a point 5.4 units below 0.

STEP 2 Find the absolute value of −5.4.

−5.4 is 5.4 units from 0.

$|-5.4| = 5.4$

My Notes

Reflect

3. **Communicate Mathematical Ideas** What is the absolute value of the average January low temperature in 2011? How do you know?

_____

_____

Math Talk
Mathematical Processes

How do you know where to graph −5.4?

YOUR TURN

Graph each number on the number line. Then use your number line to find each absolute value.

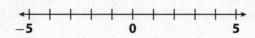

4. $-4.5; |-4.5| = $ _____

5. $1\frac{1}{2}; \left|1\frac{1}{2}\right| = $ _____

6. $4; |4| = $ _____

7. $-3\frac{1}{4}; \left|-3\frac{1}{4}\right| = $ _____

Personal Math Trainer

Online Assessment and Intervention

my.hrw.com

© Houghton Mifflin Harcourt Publishing Company

Graph each number and its opposite on a number line. (Explore Activity and Example 1)

1. −2.8

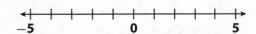

2. 4.3

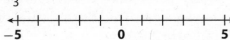

3. −3$\frac{4}{5}$

4. 1$\frac{1}{3}$

Find the opposite of each number. (Example 1)

5. 3.78 _____

6. −7$\frac{5}{12}$ _____

7. 0 _____

8. 4.2 _____

9. 12.1 _____

10. 2.6 _____

11. **Vocabulary** Explain why 2.15 and −2.15 are opposites. (Example 1)

_____

_____

Find the absolute value of each number. (Example 2)

12. 5.23 _____

13. −4$\frac{2}{11}$ _____

14. 0 _____

15. −6$\frac{3}{5}$ _____

16. −2.12 _____

17. 8.2 _____

? ESSENTIAL QUESTION CHECK-IN

18. How do you identify the opposite and the absolute value of a rational number?

_____

_____

_____

_____

3.2 Independent Practice

Personal
Math Trainer

Online
Assessment and
Intervention

my.hrw.com

19. **Financial Literacy** A store's balance sheet represents the amounts customers owe as negative numbers and credits to customers as positive numbers.

Customer	Girardi	Lewis	Stein	Yuan	Wenner
Balance ($)	−85.23	20.44	−116.33	13.50	−9.85

   a. Write the opposite of each customer's balance.

   _____

   _____

   b. Mr. Yuan wants to use his credit to pay off the full amount that another customer owes. Which customer's balance does Mr. Yuan

   have enough money to pay off? _____

   c. Which customer's balance would be farthest from 0 on a number line? Explain.

   _____

   _____

20. **Multistep** Trina and Jessie went on a vacation to Hawaii. Trina went scuba diving and reached an elevation of −85.6 meters, which is below sea level. Jessie went hang-gliding and reached an altitude of 87.9 meters, which is above sea level.

   a. Who is closer to the surface of the ocean? Explain.

   _____

   b. Trina wants to hang-glide at the same number of meters above sea level as she scuba-dived below sea level. Will she fly higher than Jessie did? Explain.

   _____

   _____

21. **Critical Thinking** Carlos finds the absolute value of −5.3, and then finds the opposite of his answer. Jason finds the opposite of −5.3, and then finds the absolute value of his answer. Whose final value is greater? Explain.

   _____

   _____

   _____

22. **Explain the Error** Two students are playing a math game. The object of the game is to make the least possible number by arranging the given digits inside absolute value bars on a card. In the first round, each player will use the digits 3, 5, and 7 to fill in the card.

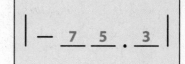

a. One student arranges the numbers on the card as shown. What was this student's mistake?

_____

_____

_____

b. What is the least possible number the card can show? _____

 FOCUS ON HIGHER ORDER THINKING

23. **Analyze Relationships** If you plot the point −8.85 on a number line, would you place it to the left or right of −8.8? Explain.

_____

_____

24. **Make a Conjecture** If the absolute value of a negative number is 2.78, what is the distance on the number line between the number and its absolute value? Explain your answer.

_____

_____

25. **Multiple Representations** The deepest point in the Indian Ocean is the Java Trench, which is 25,344 feet below sea level. Elevations below sea level are represented by negative numbers.

a. Write the elevation of the Java Trench. _____

b. A mile is 5,280 feet. Between which two integers is the elevation in miles? _____

c. Graph the elevation of the Java Trench in miles.

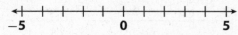

26. **Draw Conclusions** A number and its absolute value are equal. If you subtract 2 from the number, the new number and its absolute value are <u>not</u> equal. What do you know about the number? What is a possible number that satisfies these conditions?

_____

_____

Work Area

Magnitude Madness

INSTRUCTIONS

STEP 1 Get a game card from your teacher. Cards contain either a number or a real-world situation. Search the room to find the person with the real-world situation or number that matches your card.

−1.5

The interest rate dropped 1.5%.

STEP 2 Once you and your partner have found each other, fill in a row of your table using the information from your cards.

Number	Absolute Value (Magnitude)	Distance From 0 on the Number Line	Real-World Situation
−1.5	1.5	1.5	The interest rate dropped 1.5%.

STEP 3 Plot the number on the appropriate number line below your table. Make sure your number line graph agrees with your partner's graph.

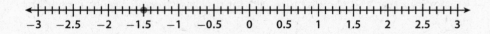

STEP 4 Turn your cards back in to your teacher, who will shuffle them and then give each of you a new card so that you may repeat Steps 1–3.

STEP 5 Once you have filled in all the rows in your table, answer the Reflect questions.

Value	Absolute Value (Magnitude)	Distance From 0 on the Number Line	Real-World Situation

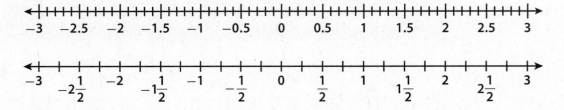

Reflect

1. What relationship do you see between the absolute value (magnitude) of a number and the distance of that number from 0 on a number line?

2. What relationship do you see between a number and its absolute value (magnitude)?

Compare and Order

? ESSENTIAL QUESTION

What strategies can you use to compare and order fractions and decimals?

EXPLORE ACTIVITY 1

Equivalent Fractions

You can order fractions by rewriting the fractions with a common denominator, then plotting them on a number line.

Four students are running a race and trying to reach a goal time. The table shows the students' times in relation to the goal time. Order the time differences from least to greatest.

Student	A	B	C	D
Time Difference	$\frac{10}{16}$	$-\frac{1}{4}$	$\frac{3}{2}$	$\frac{3}{8}$

A Write the fractions as equivalent fractions with a common denominator of 8.

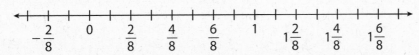

$\frac{10}{16} = \dfrac{\square}{\square}$ $-\frac{1}{4} = -\dfrac{\square}{\square}$ $\frac{3}{2} = \frac{12}{8} = \square \dfrac{\square}{\square}$ $\frac{3}{8} = \frac{3}{8}$

B Plot the fractions on the number line.

$-\frac{2}{8}$ 0 $\frac{2}{8}$ $\frac{4}{8}$ $\frac{6}{8}$ 1 $1\frac{2}{8}$ $1\frac{4}{8}$ $1\frac{6}{8}$

C Use the relative positions of the points on the number line to write the fractions in order from least to greatest.

Since _____ is the fraction furthest to the left, it has the least value. Reading

left to right, _____ is the next fraction, then _____, then _____.

_____ < _____ < _____ < _____

D When writing the fractions in order, be sure to use the original forms of the fractions given at the beginning of the problem. The time differences from

least to greatest are _____, _____, _____, and _____.

Reflect

1. **Justify Reasoning** Is 8 the only common denominator that could have been used?

_____

_____

Ordering Rational Numbers

You can order decimals by plotting them on a number line.

Order −0.2, 0.15, 0.4, −0.35, and 0.55 from greatest to least.

A Plot the decimals on the number line.

B Use the relative positions of the points on the number line to write the decimals in order from greatest to least.

Since _____ is closest to the top of the number line, it has the

greatest value.

Reading from the top down, _____ is the next decimal,

then _____, then _____, then _____.

The decimals in order from greatest to least are _____, _____,

_____, _____, and _____.

```
0.6
0.5
0.4
0.3
0.2
0.1
0
−0.1
−0.2
−0.3
−0.4
```

Practice

Order the numbers from least to greatest using the number line.

1. $-\dfrac{9}{2}$, $1\dfrac{5}{10}$, 4, and $-3\dfrac{1}{4}$

_____

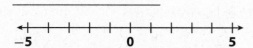

2. −2.5, 1.25, 4, and −3.25

_____

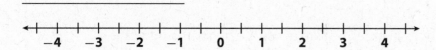

3. Order $\dfrac{1}{4}$, $1\dfrac{1}{2}$, $\dfrac{5}{8}$, $\dfrac{3}{16}$ from least to greatest using a number line.

_____

Comparing and Ordering Rational Numbers

6.1.3.3
Students will compare and order rational numbers.

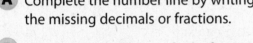

ESSENTIAL QUESTION

How do you compare and order rational numbers?

EXPLORE ACTIVITY

Equivalent Fractions and Decimals

Fractions and decimals that represent the same value are *equivalent*. The number line shows equivalent fractions and decimals from 0 to 1.

A Complete the number line by writing the missing decimals or fractions.

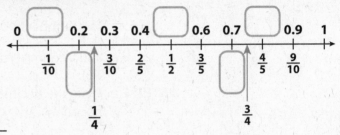

B Use the number line to find a fraction that is equivalent to 0.25. Explain.

_____

_____

C Explain how to use a number line to find a decimal equivalent to $1\frac{7}{10}$.

_____

_____

_____

D Use the number line to complete each statement.

0.2 = _____   _____ = $\frac{3}{10}$ 0.75 = _____   1.25 = _____

Reflect

1. **Communicate Mathematical Ideas** How does a number line represent equivalent fractions and decimals?

_____

_____

2. Name a decimal between 0.4 and 0.5.

_____

Ordering Fractions and Decimals

You can order fractions and decimals by rewriting the fractions as equivalent decimals or by rewriting the decimals as equivalent fractions.

EXAMPLE 1

A Order 0.2, $\frac{3}{4}$, 0.8, $\frac{1}{2}$, $\frac{1}{4}$, and 0.4 from least to greatest.

STEP 1 Write the fractions as equivalent decimals.

$$\frac{1}{4} = 0.25 \qquad \frac{1}{2} = 0.5 \qquad \frac{3}{4} = 0.75$$

STEP 2 Use the number line to write the decimals in order.

```
0   0.1  0.2  0.3  0.4  0.5  0.6  0.7  0.8  0.9   1
```

$$0.2 < 0.25 < 0.4 < 0.5 < 0.75 < 0.8$$

The numbers from least to greatest are 0.2, $\frac{1}{4}$, 0.4, $\frac{1}{2}$, $\frac{3}{4}$, 0.8.

B Order $\frac{1}{12}$, $\frac{2}{3}$, and 0.35 from least to greatest.

STEP 1 Write the decimal as an equivalent fraction.

$$0.35 = \frac{35}{100} = \frac{7}{20}$$

> 60 is a multiple of the denominators of all three fractions.

STEP 2 Find equivalent fractions with 60 as the common denominator.

$$\frac{1}{12} \xrightarrow{\times 5} \frac{5}{60} \qquad \frac{2}{3} \xrightarrow{\times 20} \frac{40}{60} \qquad \frac{7}{20} \xrightarrow{\times 3} \frac{21}{60}$$

STEP 3 Order fractions with common denominators by comparing the numerators.

$$5 < 21 < 40$$

The fractions in order from least to greatest are $\frac{5}{60}$, $\frac{21}{60}$, $\frac{40}{60}$.

The numbers in order from least to greatest are $\frac{1}{12}$, 0.35, and $\frac{2}{3}$.

YOUR TURN

Order the fractions and decimals from least to greatest.

3. 0.85, $\frac{3}{5}$, 0.15, $\frac{7}{10}$ _____

Ordering Rational Numbers

You can use a number line to order positive and negative rational numbers.

Math On the Spot
my.hrw.com

EXAMPLE 2

Five friends completed a triathlon that included a 3-mile run, a 12-mile bike ride, and a $\frac{1}{2}$-mile swim. To compare their running times they created a table that shows the difference between each person's time and the average time, with negative numbers representing times less than the average.

Runner	John	Sue	Anna	Mike	Tom
Time above or below average (minutes)	$\frac{1}{2}$	1.4	$-1\frac{1}{4}$	-2.0	1.95

Order the numbers from greatest to least.

STEP 1 Write the fractions as equivalent decimals.

$$\frac{1}{2} = 0.5 \qquad -1\frac{1}{4} = -1.25$$

STEP 2 Use the number line to write the decimals in order.

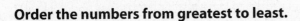

★ Average Time

$$1.95 > 1.4 > 0.5 > -1.25 > -2.0$$

The numbers in order from greatest to least are 1.95, 1.4, $\frac{1}{2}$, $-1\frac{1}{4}$, -2.0.

Math Talk
Mathematical Processes

Who was the fastest runner? Explain.

Reflect

4. **Communicate Mathematical Ideas** Describe a different way to order the numbers.

_____

_____

_____

YOUR TURN

5. To compare their bike times, the friends created a table that shows the difference between each person's time and the average bike time. Order the bike times from least to greatest.

Biker	John	Sue	Anna	Mike	Tom
Time above or below average (minutes)	-1.8	1	$1\frac{2}{5}$	$1\frac{9}{10}$	-1.25

Personal Math Trainer

Online Assessment and Intervention

my.hrw.com

Guided Practice

Find the equivalent fraction or decimal for each number.
(Explore Activity 1)

1. $0.6 =$ _____

2. $\frac{1}{4} =$ _____

3. $0.9 =$ _____

4. $0.1 =$ _____

5. $\frac{3}{10} =$ _____

6. $1.4 =$ _____

7. $\frac{4}{5} =$ _____

8. $0.4 =$ _____

9. $\frac{6}{8} =$ _____

Use the number line to order the fractions and decimals from least to greatest. (Example 1)

10. $0.75, \frac{1}{2}, 0.4,$ and $\frac{1}{5}$

0 0.1 0.2 0.3 0.4 0.5 0.6 0.7 0.8 0.9 1

_____

11. The table shows the lengths of fish caught by three friends at the lake last weekend. Write the lengths in order from greatest to least. (Example 1)

_____

Lengths of Fish (cm)		
Emma	**Anne**	**Emily**
12.7	$12\frac{3}{5}$	$12\frac{3}{4}$

List the fractions and decimals in order from least to greatest.
(Example 1, Example 2)

12. $2.3, 2\frac{4}{5}, 2.6$

_____

13. $0.5, \frac{3}{16}, 0.75, \frac{5}{48}$

_____

14. $0.5, \frac{1}{5}, 0.35, \frac{12}{25}, \frac{4}{5}$

_____

15. $\frac{3}{4}, -\frac{7}{10}, -\frac{3}{4}, \frac{8}{10}$

_____

16. $-\frac{3}{8}, \frac{5}{16}, -0.65, \frac{2}{4}$

_____

17. $-2.3, -2\frac{4}{5}, -2.6$

_____

18. $-0.6, -\frac{5}{8}, -\frac{7}{12} -0.72$

_____

19. $1.45, 1\frac{1}{2}, 1\frac{1}{3}, 1.2$

_____

20. $-0.3, 0.5, 0.55, -0.35$

_____

❓ ESSENTIAL QUESTION CHECK-IN

21. Explain how to compare 0.7 and $\frac{5}{8}$.

_____

_____

_____

3.3 Independent Practice

Personal
Math Trainer

Online
Assessment and
Intervention

my.hrw.com

22. Rosa and Albert receive the same amount of allowance each week. The table shows what part of their allowance they each spent on video games and pizza.

	Video games	Pizza
Rosa	0.4	$\frac{2}{5}$
Albert	$\frac{1}{2}$	0.25

   a. Who spent more of their allowance on video games? Write an inequality to compare the portion spent on video games.

   _____

   b. Who spent more of their allowance on pizza? Write an inequality to compare the portion spent on pizza.

   _____

   c. **Draw Conclusions** Who spent the greater part of their total allowance? How do you know?

   _____

   _____

23. A group of friends is collecting aluminum for a recycling drive. Each person who donates at least 4.25 pounds of aluminum receives a free movie coupon. The weight of each person's donation is shown in the table.

	Brenda	Claire	Jim	Micah	Peter
Weight (lb)	4.3	5.5	$6\frac{1}{6}$	$\frac{15}{4}$	$4\frac{3}{8}$

   a. Order the weights of the donations from greatest to least.

   _____

   b. Which of the friends will receive a free movie coupon? Which will not?

   _____

   c. **What If?** Would the person with the smallest donation win a movie coupon if he or she had collected $\frac{1}{2}$ pound more of aluminum? Explain.

   _____

   _____

   _____

24. Last week, several gas stations in a neighborhood all charged the same price for a gallon of gas. The table below shows how much gas prices have changed from last week to this week.

Gas Station	Gas and Go	Samson Gas	Star Gas	Corner Store	Tip Top Shop
Change from last week (in cents)	-6.6	5.8	$-6\frac{3}{4}$	$\frac{27}{5}$	$-5\frac{5}{8}$

a. Order the numbers in the table from least to greatest.

_____

b. Which gas station has the cheapest gas this week? _____

c. **Critical Thinking** Which gas station changed their price the least this week?

_____

 **FOCUS ON HIGHER ORDER THINKING**

25. **Analyze Relationships** Explain how you would order from least to greatest three numbers that include a positive number, a negative number, and zero.

_____

_____

_____

26. **Critique Reasoning** Luke is making pancakes. The recipe calls for 0.5 quart of milk and 2.5 cups of flour. He has $\frac{3}{8}$ quart of milk and $\frac{18}{8}$ cups of flour. Luke makes the recipe with the milk and flour that he has. Explain his error.

_____

_____

_____

27. **Communicate Mathematical Ideas** If you know the order from least to greatest of 5 negative rational numbers, how can you use that information to order the absolute values of those numbers from least to greatest? Explain.

_____

_____

_____

_____

_____

Work Area

Ready to Go On?

Personal Math Trainer

Online Assessment and Intervention

my.hrw.com

3.1 Classifying Rational Numbers

1. Five friends divide three bags of apples equally between them. Write the division represented in this situation as a fraction. _____

Write each rational number in the form $\frac{a}{b}$, where a and b are integers.

2. $5\frac{1}{6}$ _____

3. -12 _____

Determine if each number is a whole number, integer, or rational number. Include all sets to which each number belongs.

4. -12 _____

5. $\frac{7}{8}$ _____

3.2 Identifying Opposites and Absolute Value of Rational Numbers

6. Graph -3, $1\frac{3}{4}$, -0.5, and 3 on the number line.

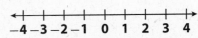

7. Find the opposite of $\frac{1}{3}$ and of $-\frac{7}{12}$. _____

8. Find the absolute value of 9.8 and of $-\frac{10}{3}$. _____

3.3 Comparing and Ordering Rational Numbers

9. Over the last week, the daily low temperatures in degrees Fahrenheit have been -4, 6.2, $18\frac{1}{2}$, -5.9, 21, $-\frac{1}{4}$, and 1.75. List these numbers in order from greatest to least.

_____

 **ESSENTIAL QUESTION**

10. How can you order rational numbers from least to greatest?

_____

_____

Assessment Readiness

Personal Math Trainer

Online Assessment and Intervention

my.hrw.com

Selected Response

1. Suki split five dog treats equally among her six dogs. Which fraction represents this division?

Ⓐ $\frac{6}{5}$ of a treat   Ⓒ $\frac{1}{5}$ of a treat

Ⓑ $\frac{5}{6}$ of a treat   Ⓓ $\frac{1}{6}$ of a treat

2. Which set or sets does the number 15 belong to?

Ⓐ whole numbers only

Ⓑ rational numbers only

Ⓒ integers and rational numbers only

Ⓓ whole numbers, integers, and rational numbers

3. Which of the following statements about rational numbers is correct?

Ⓐ All rational numbers are also whole numbers.

Ⓑ All rational numbers are also integers.

Ⓒ All rational numbers can be written in the form $\frac{a}{b}$, where a and b are integers and $b \neq 0$.

Ⓓ Rational numbers cannot be negative.

4. Which of the following shows the numbers in order from least to greatest?

Ⓐ $-\frac{1}{5}, -\frac{2}{3}, 2, 0.4$

Ⓑ $2, -\frac{2}{3}, 0.4, -\frac{1}{5}$

Ⓒ $-\frac{2}{3}, 0.4, -\frac{1}{5}, 2$

Ⓓ $-\frac{2}{3}, -\frac{1}{5}, 0.4, 2$

5. What is the absolute value of -12.5?

Ⓐ 12.5   Ⓒ -1

Ⓑ 1   Ⓓ -12.5

6. Which number line shows $-\frac{1}{4}$ and its opposite?

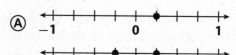

7. Horatio climbed to the top of a ladder that is 10 feet high. Which number is the opposite of the number that represents Horatio's height?

Ⓐ -10 Ⓒ 0

Ⓑ 10   Ⓓ $\frac{1}{10}$

Mini-Task

8. The table shows the heights in feet of several students in Mrs. Patel's class.

Name	Height (ft)
Olivia	$5\frac{1}{4}$
James	5.5
Carmela	4.9
Feng	5

a. Write each height in the form $\frac{a}{b}$.

_____

b. List the heights in order from greatest to least.

_____

MODULE 1 Integers

? ESSENTIAL QUESTION

How can you use integers to solve real-world problems?

EXAMPLE 1

James recorded the temperature at noon in Fairbanks, Alaska, over a week in January.

Day	Mon	Tues	Wed	Thurs	Fri
Temperature	3	2	7	−3	−1

Graph the temperatures on the number line, and then list the numbers in order from least to greatest.

Graph the temperatures on the number line.

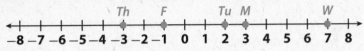

Read from left to right to list the temperatures in order from least to greatest.

The temperatures listed from least to greatest are −3, −1, 2, 3, 7.

EXAMPLE 2

Graph −4, 0, 2, and −1 on the number line. Then use the number line to find each absolute value.

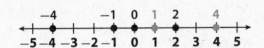

A number and its opposite are the same distance from 0 on the number line. The absolute value of a negative number is its opposite.

$|-4| = 4$ $|0| = 0$ $|2| = 2$ $|-1| = 1$

EXERCISES

1. Graph 7, −2, 5, 1, and −1 on the number line. (Lesson 1.1)

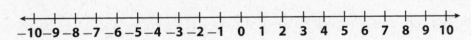

List the numbers from least to greatest. (Lesson 1.2)

2. 4, 0, −2, 3 _____

3. −3, −5, 2, −2 _____

Compare using < or >. (Lesson 1.2)

4. 4 ◯ 1   **5.** −2 ◯ 2   **6.** −3 ◯ −5   **7.** −7 ◯ 2

Find the opposite and absolute value of each number. (Lessons 1.1, 1.3)

8. 6 _____   **9.** −2 _____

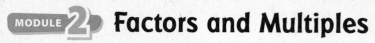 **Factors and Multiples**

Key Vocabulary

greatest common factor
(GCF) *(máximo común divisor (MCD))*

least common multiple
(LCM) *(mínimo común múltiplo (mcm))*

? ESSENTIAL QUESTION

How do you find and use the greatest common factor of two whole numbers? How do you find and use the least common multiple of two numbers?

EXAMPLE 1

Use the Distributive Property to rewrite $32 + 24$ as a product of their greatest common factor and another number.

A. List the factors of 24 and 32. Circle the common factors.

24: ① ② 3 ④ 6 ⑧ 12 24

32: ① ② ④ ⑧ 16 32

B. Rewrite each number as a product of the GCF and another number.

24: 8×3 **32:** 8×4

C. Use the Distributive Property and your answer above to rewrite $32 + 24$ using the GCF and another number.

$32 + 24 = 8 \times 3 + 8 \times 4$

$32 + 24 = 8 \times (3 + 4)$

$32 + 24 = 8 \times 7$

EXAMPLE 2

On Saturday, every 8th customer at Adam's Bagels will get a free coffee. Every 12th customer will get a free bagel. Which customer will be the first to get a free coffee and a free bagel?

A. List the first several multiples of 8 and 12. Circle the common multiples.

8: 8   16 ㉔ 32   40 ㊽

12: 12 ㉔ 36 ㊽

B. Find the LCM of 8 and 12.

The LCM is 24. The 24th customer will be the first to get a free coffee and a free bagel.

EXERCISES

1. Find the GCF of 49 and 63 (Lesson 2.1) _____

Rewrite each sum as a product of the GCF of the addends and another number. (Lesson 2.1)

2. $15 + 45 =$ _____   **3.** $9 + 27 =$ _____

4. Find the LCM of 9 and 6 (Lesson 2.2) _____

68 Unit 1

MODULE **3** **Rational Numbers**

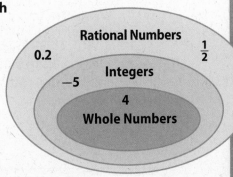

Key Vocabulary

rational number (*número racional*)

Venn diagram (*diagrama de Venn*)

? **ESSENTIAL QUESTION**

How can you use rational numbers to solve real-world problems?

EXAMPLE 1

Use the Venn diagram to determine in which set or sets each number belongs.

A. $\frac{1}{2}$ belongs in the set of rational numbers.

B. -5 belongs in the sets of integers and rational numbers.

C. 4 belongs in the sets of whole numbers, integers, and rational numbers.

D. 0.2 belongs in the set of rational numbers.

EXAMPLE 2

Order $\frac{2}{5}$, 0.2, and $\frac{4}{15}$ from greatest to least.

Write the decimal as an equivalent fraction. $0.2 = \frac{2}{10} = \frac{1}{5}$

Find equivalent fractions with 15 as the common denominator.

$$\frac{2 \times 3}{5 \times 3} = \frac{6}{15} \qquad \frac{1 \times 3}{5 \times 3} = \frac{3}{15} \qquad \frac{4}{15} = \frac{4}{15}$$

Order fractions with common denominators by comparing the numerators.

$$6 > 4 > 3 \qquad \frac{6}{15} > \frac{4}{15} > \frac{3}{15}$$

The numbers in order from greatest to least are, $\frac{2}{5}$, $\frac{4}{15}$, and 0.2.

EXERCISES

Classify each number by indicating in which set or sets it belongs.
(Lesson 3.1)

1. 8 _____

2. 0.25 _____

Find the absolute value of each rational number. (Lesson 3.2)

3. |3.7| _____   **4.** $\left|-\frac{2}{3}\right|$ _____

Graph each set of numbers on the number line and order the numbers from greatest to least. (Lessons 3.1, 3.3)

5. $-0.5, -1, -\frac{1}{4}, 0$

```
←+--+--+--+--+--+--+--+--+--+--+--+--+--+--+--+--+--+→
 -1.5        -1          -0.5         0          0.5
```

_____

1. **CAREERS IN MATH** Climatologist Each year a tree is alive, it adds a layer of growth, called a tree ring, between its core and its bark. A climatologist measures the width of tree rings of a particular tree for different years:

Year	1900	1910	1920	1930	1940
Width of ring (in mm)	$\frac{14}{25}$	$\frac{29}{50}$	$\frac{53}{100}$	$\frac{13}{20}$	$\frac{3}{5}$

The average temperature during the growing season is directly related to the width of the ring, with a greater width corresponding to a higher average temperature.

a. List the years in order of increasing ring width.

_____

b. Which year was hottest? How do you know?

_____

c. Which year was coldest? How do you know?

_____

2. A parking garage has floors above and below ground level. For a scavenger hunt, Gaia's friends are given a list of objects they need to find on the third and fourth level below ground, the first and fourth level above ground, and ground level.

a. If ground level is 0 and the first level above ground is 1, which integers can you use to represent the other levels where objects are hidden? Explain your reasoning.

_____

_____

b. Graph the set of numbers on the number line.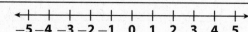

c. Gaia wants to start at the lowest level and work her way up. List the levels in the order that Gaia will search them.

_____

d. If she takes the stairs, how many flights of stairs will she have to climb? How do you know?

_____

_____

Personal Math Trainer

Online Assessment and Intervention

my.hrw.com

Selected Response

1. What is the opposite of −9?

Ⓐ 9

Ⓑ $-\frac{1}{9}$

Ⓒ 0

Ⓓ $\frac{1}{9}$

2. Kyle is currently 60 feet above sea level. Which correctly describes the opposite of Kyle's elevation?

Ⓐ 60 feet below sea level

Ⓑ 60 feet above sea level

Ⓒ 6 feet below sea level

Ⓓ At sea level

3. What is the absolute value of 27?

Ⓐ −27

Ⓑ 0

Ⓒ 3

Ⓓ 27

4. In Albany it is −4°F, in Chicago it is −14°F, in Minneapolis it is −11°F, and in Toronto it is −13°F. In which city is it the coldest?

Ⓐ Albany

Ⓑ Chicago

Ⓒ Minneapolis

Ⓓ Toronto

5. Which shows the integers in order from greatest to least?

Ⓐ 18, 4, 3, −2, −15

Ⓑ −2, 3, 4, −15, 18

Ⓒ −15, −2, 3, 4, 18

Ⓓ 18, −15, 4, 3, −2

6. Joanna split three pitchers of water equally among her eight plants. What fraction of a pitcher did each plant get?

Ⓐ $\frac{1}{8}$ of a pitcher

Ⓑ $\frac{1}{3}$ of a pitcher

Ⓒ $\frac{3}{8}$ of a pitcher

Ⓓ $\frac{8}{3}$ of a pitcher

7. Which set or sets does the number −22 belong to?

Ⓐ Whole numbers only

Ⓑ Rational numbers only

Ⓒ Integers and rational numbers only

Ⓓ Whole numbers, integers, and rational numbers

8. Carlos swam to the bottom of a pool that is 12 feet deep. What is the opposite of Carlos's elevation relative to the surface?

Ⓐ −12 feet Ⓒ 12 feet

Ⓑ 0 feet Ⓓ $\frac{1}{12}$ foot

9. Which number line shows $\frac{1}{3}$ and its opposite?

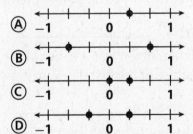

10. Which of the following shows the numbers in order from least to greatest?

Ⓐ $-\frac{2}{3}, -\frac{3}{4}, 0.7, 0$

Ⓑ $0.7, 0, -\frac{2}{3}, -\frac{3}{4}$

Ⓒ $-\frac{2}{3}, -\frac{3}{4}, 0, 0.7$

Ⓓ $-\frac{3}{4}, -\frac{2}{3}, 0, 0.7$

11. Which number line shows an integer and its opposite?

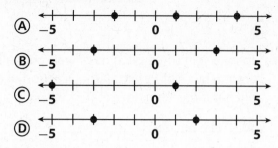

12. Which is another way to write $42 + 63$?

Ⓐ $7 \times (6 + 7)$ Ⓒ $7 \times 6 \times 9$

Ⓑ 7×15 Ⓓ $7 + 6 + 9$

13. What is the LCM of 9 and 15?

Ⓐ 30   Ⓒ 90

Ⓑ 45   Ⓓ 135

14. What is the GCF of 40 and 72?

Ⓐ 2   Ⓒ 8

Ⓑ 4   Ⓓ 12

Mini-Task

15. Stella is recording temperatures every day for 5 days. On the first day, Stella recorded a temperature of 0 °F.

a. On the second day, the temperature was 3 °F above the temperature on the first day. What was the temperature on the

second day? _____

b. On the third day, it was 4 °F below the temperature of the first day. What was

the temperature? _____

c. The temperature on the fourth day was the opposite of the temperature on the second day. What was the temperature?

_____

d. The temperature on the fifth day was the absolute value of the temperature on the fourth day. What was the

temperature? _____

e. Write the temperatures in order from

least to greatest. _____

f. What is the difference in temperature between the coldest day and the

warmest day? _____

16. Marco is making mosaic garden stones using red, yellow, and blue tiles. He has 45 red tiles, 90 blue tiles, and 75 yellow tiles. Each stone must have the same number of each color tile. What is the greatest number

of stones Marco can make? _____

a. How many of each color tile will Marco use in each stone?

_____

b. How can Marco use the GCF to find out how many tiles he has in all?

_____

_____

_____

_____

_____

UNIT 2

Number Operations

MODULE **4**
Operations with Fractions

MODULE **5**
Operations with Decimals

CAREERS IN MATH

Chef The role of a chef is diverse and can include planning menus, overseeing food preparation, training staff, and ordering and purchasing food items. Chefs use mathematics when scaling recipes as well as in budgeting and financial planning.

If you are interested in a career as a chef, you should study these mathematical subjects:
- Basic Math
- Business Math

Research other careers that require the use of scaling quantities, and financial planning.

Unit 2 Performance Task

At the end of the unit, check out how **chefs** use math.

© Houghton Mifflin Harcourt Publishing Company • Image Credits: ©Corbis

Use the puzzle to preview key vocabulary from this unit. Unscramble the circled letters to answer the riddle at the bottom of the page.

1. **ISROPCALCER**

2. **INERADRME**

3. **RENNOOAIDTM**

4. **DXMIE RUBMEN**

5. **NEIDIDDV**

6. **DRVIOSI**

1. Two numbers whose product is one. (Lesson 4.2)
2. The whole number left over when you divide and the divisor doesn't divide the dividend evenly. (Lesson 5.1)
3. The part of a fraction that represents how many parts the whole is divided into. (Lesson 4.1)
4. A number that is a combination of a whole number and a fraction. (Lesson 4.3)
5. The amount that you want to divide in a division problem. (Lesson 5.4)
6. The number you divide by in a division problem. (Lesson 5.4)

Q: Decimals always win in arguments with fractions. What do decimals have that fractions don't?

A: __ __ __ __ __ __!

Operations with Fractions

? ESSENTIAL QUESTION

How can you use operations with fractions to solve real-world problems?

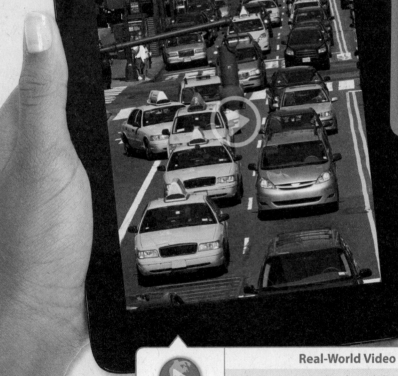

Real-World Video

To find your average rate of speed, divide the distance you traveled by the time you traveled. If you ride in a taxi and drive $\frac{1}{2}$ mile in $\frac{1}{4}$ hour, your rate was 2 mi/h which may mean you were in heavy traffic.

⊙ my.hrw.com

GO DIGITAL
my.hrw.com

my.hrw.com

Go digital with your write-in student edition, accessible on any device.

Math On the Spot

Scan with your smart phone to jump directly to the online edition, video tutor, and more.

Animated Math

Interactively explore key concepts to see how math works.

Personal Math Trainer

Get immediate feedback and help as you work through practice sets.

Reading Start-Up

© Houghton Mifflin Harcourt Publishing Company

Vocabulary

Review Words
- area (*área*)
- ✔ denominator (*denominador*)
- ✔ fraction (*fracción*)
- greatest common factor (GCF) (*máximo común divisor (MCD)*)
- least common multiple (LCM) (*mínimo común múltiplo (m.c.m.)*)
- length (*longitud*)
- ✔ numerator (*numerador*)
- product (*producto*)
- width (*ancho*)

Preview Words
- mixed number (*número mixto*)
- order of operations (*orden de las operaciones*)
- reciprocals (*recíprocos*)

Visualize Vocabulary

Use the ✔ words to complete the triangle. Write the review word that fits the description in each section of the triangle.

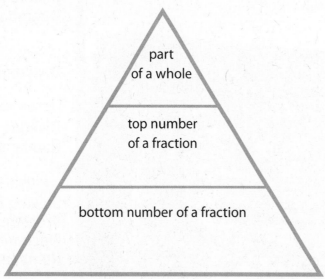

part of a whole

top number of a fraction

bottom number of a fraction

Understand Vocabulary

In each grouping, select the choice that is described by the given vocabulary word.

1. reciprocals   Ⓐ 1:15   Ⓑ $\frac{3}{4} \div \frac{1}{6}$ Ⓒ $\frac{3}{5}$ and $\frac{5}{3}$

2. mixed number   Ⓐ $\frac{1}{3} - \frac{1}{5}$ Ⓑ $3\frac{1}{2}$ Ⓒ -5

3. order of operations   Ⓐ $5 - 3 + 2 = 0$ Ⓑ $5 - 3 + 2 = 4$ Ⓒ $5 - 3 + 2 = 6$

Active Reading

Layered Book Before beginning the module, create a layered book to help you learn the concepts in this module. Label each flap with lesson titles. As you study each lesson, write important ideas, such as vocabulary and processes, under the appropriate flap. Refer to your finished layered book as you work on exercises from this module.

Are YOU Ready?

Complete these exercises to review skills you will need for this module.

Write an Improper Fraction as a Mixed Number

EXAMPLE $\frac{13}{5} = \frac{5}{5} + \frac{5}{5} + \frac{3}{5}$ Write as a sum using names for one plus a proper fraction.

$= 1 + 1 + \frac{3}{5}$ Write each name for one as one.

$= 2 + \frac{3}{5}$ Add the ones.

$= 2\frac{3}{5}$ Write the mixed number.

Write each improper fraction as a mixed number.

1. $\frac{9}{4}$ _____   **2.** $\frac{8}{3}$ _____   **3.** $\frac{23}{6}$ _____   **4.** $\frac{11}{2}$ _____

5. $\frac{17}{5}$ _____   **6.** $\frac{15}{8}$ _____   **7.** $\frac{33}{10}$ _____   **8.** $\frac{29}{12}$ _____

Multiplication Facts

EXAMPLE $7 \times 6 = $ ▢   Use a related fact you know.

$6 \times 6 = 36$

Think: $7 \times 6 = (6 \times 6) + 6$

$= 36 + 6$

$= 42$

$7 \times 6 = 42$

Multiply.

9. 6×5 _____   **10.** 8×9 _____   **11.** 10×11 _____   **12.** 7×8 _____

13. 9×7 _____   **14.** 8×6 _____   **15.** 9×11 _____   **16.** 11×12 _____

Division Facts

EXAMPLE $63 \div 7 = $ ▢   Think: 7 times what number equals 63?

$7 \times 9 = 63$

$63 \div 7 = 9$ So, $63 \div 7 = 9$.

Divide.

17. $35 \div 7$ _____   **18.** $56 \div 8$ _____   **19.** $28 \div 7$ _____   **20.** $48 \div 8$ _____

21. $36 \div 4$ _____   **22.** $45 \div 9$ _____   **23.** $72 \div 8$ _____   **24.** $40 \div 5$ _____

Complete these exercises to review skills you will need for this module.

Write an Improper Fraction as a Mixed Number

25. A store sells a gas can that can hold $\frac{35}{8}$ gallons of gasoline. What is the volume of the gas can in gallons, expressed as a mixed number? Show your work.

Multiplication Facts

26. A nursery is selling all houseplants for $12 each. Alexandra bought 5 houseplants. Use a multiplication fact to determine the total cost of the plants she bought.

Division Facts

27. Monica and Sasheer want to divide $42 \div 6$. Monica knows that $6 + 36 = 42$, so she says that $42 \div 6 = 36$. Sasheer knows that $6 \times 7 = 42$, so she says that $42 \div 6 = 7$. Whose reasoning is correct? Explain.

Applying GCF and LCM to Fraction Operations

6.2.4.1
Students will use the GCF and LCM when adding, subtracting, and multiplying fractions.

? **ESSENTIAL QUESTION**

How do you use the GCF and LCM when adding, subtracting, and multiplying fractions?

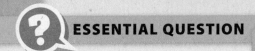

Multiplying Fractions

To multiply two fractions you first multiply the numerators and then multiply the denominators.

$$\frac{\text{numerator} \times \text{numerator}}{\text{denominator} \times \text{denominator}} = \frac{\text{numerator}}{\text{denominator}}$$

The resulting product needs to be written in simplest form. Below are two methods for making sure that the product of two fractions is in simplest form.

EXAMPLE 1 **Multiply. Write the product in simplest form.**

A $\frac{1}{3} \times \frac{3}{5}$

Write the problem as a single fraction.
Multiply numerators. Multiply denominators.

$\frac{1}{3} \times \frac{3}{5} = \frac{1 \times 3}{3 \times 5} = \frac{\boxed{}}{\boxed{}}$

Simplify by dividing by the GCF.
The GCF of 3 and 15 is _____.

$\dfrac{3 \div \boxed{}}{15 \div \boxed{}}$

Write the answer in simplest form.

$\dfrac{\boxed{}}{\boxed{}}$

B $\frac{6}{7} \times \frac{2}{3}$

Write the problem as a single fraction.

$\frac{6}{7} \times \frac{2}{3} = \dfrac{\boxed{}}{\boxed{}}$

The 6 in the numerator and the 3 in the denominator have a GCF of _____. Divide 6 and 3 by 3 and write the quotients in the boxes.

$\dfrac{\boxed{}\,6 \times 2}{7 \times 3\,\boxed{}}$

Use the quotients from the previous steps to multiply the numerators and denominators.

$\dfrac{\boxed{} \times 2}{7 \times \boxed{}} = \dfrac{\boxed{}}{\boxed{}}$

YOUR TURN

Multiply. Write each product in simplest form.

1. $\frac{1}{6} \times \frac{3}{5}$ _____

2. $\frac{3}{4} \times \frac{7}{9}$ _____

3. $\frac{3}{7} \times \frac{2}{3}$ _____

4. $\frac{4}{5} \times \frac{2}{7}$ _____

5. $\frac{7}{10} \times \frac{8}{21}$ _____

6. $\frac{6}{7} \times \frac{1}{6}$ _____

Math On the Spot

⏻ my.hrw.com

Multiplying Fractions and Whole Numbers

To multiply a fraction by a whole number, you rewrite the whole number as a fraction and multiply the two fractions. Remember to use the GCF to write the product in simplest form.

EXAMPLE 2

A class has 18 students. The teacher asks how many students in the class have pets and finds $\frac{5}{9}$ of the students have pets. How many students have pets?

STEP 1 Estimate the product. Multiply the whole number by the nearest benchmark fraction.

$\frac{5}{9}$ is close to $\frac{1}{2}$, so multiply $\frac{1}{2}$ times 18.

$\frac{1}{2} \times 18 = 9$

STEP 2 Multiply. Write the product in simplest form.

> You can write $\frac{5}{9}$ times 18 three ways.
>
> $\frac{5}{9} \times 18$ $\frac{5}{9} \cdot 18$ $\frac{5}{9}(18)$

$\frac{5}{9} \times 18$

$\frac{5}{9} \times 18 = \frac{5}{9} \times \frac{18}{1}$ Rewrite 18 as a fraction.

$= \frac{5 \times \overset{2}{\cancel{18}}}{\cancel{9} \times 1}$ Simplify before multiplying using the GCF.

$= \frac{5 \times 2}{1 \times 1}$ Multiply numerators. Multiply denominators.

$= \frac{10}{1} = 10$ Simplify by writing as a whole number.

10 students have pets.

Math Talk

Mathematical Processes

How can you check to see if the answer is correct?

Reflect

7. **Analyze Relationships** Is the product of a fraction less than 1 and a whole number greater than or less than the whole number? Explain.

_____

_____

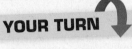

Multiply. Write each product in simplest form.

8. $\frac{5}{8} \times 24$ _____

9. $\frac{3}{5} \times 20$ _____

10. $\frac{1}{3} \times 8$ _____

11. $\frac{1}{4} \times 14$ _____

12. $3\frac{7}{10} \times 7$ _____

13. $2\frac{3}{10} \times 10$ _____

Personal Math Trainer

Online Assessment and Intervention

my.hrw.com

Adding and Subtracting Fractions

You have learned that to add or subtract two fractions, you can rewrite the fractions so they have the same denominator. You can use the least common multiple of the denominators of the fractions to rewrite the fractions.

Math On the Spot

my.hrw.com

EXAMPLE 3

Add $\frac{8}{15} + \frac{1}{6}$. Write the sum in simplest form.

My Notes

STEP 1 Rewrite the fractions as equivalent fractions. Use the LCM of the denominators as the new denominator.

$$\frac{8}{15} \rightarrow \frac{8 \times 2}{15 \times 2} \rightarrow \frac{16}{30}$$ *The LCM of 15 and 6 is 30.*

$$\frac{1}{6} \rightarrow \frac{1 \times 5}{6 \times 5} \rightarrow \frac{5}{30}$$

STEP 2 Add the numerators of the equivalent fractions. Then simplify.

$$\frac{16}{30} + \frac{5}{30} = \frac{21}{30}$$

$$= \frac{21 \div 3}{30 \div 3}$$ *Simplify by dividing by the GCF.*
The GCF of 21 and 30 is 3.

$$= \frac{7}{10}$$

Reflect

14. Can you also use the LCM of the denominators of the fractions to rewrite the difference $\frac{8}{15} - \frac{1}{6}$? What is the difference?

_____

YOUR TURN

Add or subtract. Write each sum or difference in simplest form.

15. $\frac{5}{14} + \frac{1}{6}$ _____

16. $\frac{5}{12} - \frac{3}{20}$ _____

17. $\frac{5}{12} - \frac{3}{8}$ _____

18. $1\frac{3}{10} + \frac{1}{4}$ _____

19. $\frac{2}{3} + 6\frac{1}{5}$ _____

20. $3\frac{1}{6} - \frac{1}{7}$ _____

Guided Practice

Multiply. Write each product in simplest form. (Explore Activity Example 1)

1. $\frac{1}{2} \times \frac{5}{8}$ _____

2. $\frac{3}{5} \times \frac{5}{9}$ _____

3. $\frac{3}{8} \times \frac{2}{5}$ _____

4. $2\frac{3}{8} \times 16$ _____

5. $1\frac{4}{5} \times \frac{5}{12}$ _____

6. $1\frac{2}{10} \times 5$ _____

Find each amount. (Example 2)

7. $\frac{1}{4}$ of 12 bottles of water = _____ bottles

8. $\frac{2}{3}$ of 24 bananas = _____ bananas

9. $\frac{3}{5}$ of $40 restaurant bill = $ _____

10. $\frac{5}{6}$ of 18 pencils = _____ pencils

Add or subtract. Write each sum or difference in simplest form.

11. $\frac{3}{8} + \frac{5}{24}$ _____

12. $\frac{1}{20} + \frac{5}{12}$ _____

13. $\frac{9}{20} - \frac{1}{4}$ _____

14. $\frac{9}{10} - \frac{3}{14}$ _____

15. $3\frac{3}{8} + \frac{5}{12}$ _____

16. $5\frac{7}{10} - \frac{5}{18}$ _____

? ESSENTIAL QUESTION CHECK-IN

17. How can knowing the GCF and LCM help you when you add, subtract, and multiply fractions?

_____

_____

_____

_____

4.1 Independent Practice

Personal Math Trainer

Online Assessment and Intervention

my.hrw.com

Solve. Write each answer in simplest form.

18. Erin buys a bag of peanuts that weighs $\frac{3}{4}$ of a pound. Later that week, the bag is $\frac{2}{3}$ full. How much does the bag of peanuts weigh now? Show your work.

_____

_____

19. Multistep Marianne buys 16 bags of potting soil that comes in $\frac{5}{8}$-pound bags.

a. How many pounds of potting soil does Marianne buy?

_____

_____

b. If Marianne's father calls and says he needs 13 pounds of potting soil, how many additional bags should she buy?

_____

_____

20. Music Two fifths of the instruments in the marching band are brass, one third are percussion, and the rest are woodwinds.

a. What fraction of the band is woodwinds?

_____

b. One half of the woodwinds are clarinets. What fraction of the band is clarinets?

_____

c. One eighth of the brass instruments are tubas. If there are 240 instruments in the band, how many are tubas?

_____

21. Marcial found a recipe for fruit salad that he wanted to try to make for his birthday party. He decided to triple the recipe.

Fruit Salad

$3\frac{1}{2}$ cups thinly sliced rhubarb

15 seedless grapes, halved

$\frac{1}{2}$ orange, sectioned

10 fresh strawberries, halved

$\frac{3}{5}$ apple, cored and diced

$\frac{2}{3}$ peach, sliced

1 plum, pitted and sliced

$\frac{1}{4}$ cup fresh blueberries

a. What are the new amounts for the oranges, apples, blueberries, and peaches?

_____

_____

_____

b. Communicate Mathematical Ideas The amount of rhubarb in the original recipe is $3\frac{1}{2}$ cups. Using what you know of whole numbers and what you know of fractions, explain how you could triple that mixed number.

_____

_____

_____

_____

22. One container holds $1\frac{7}{8}$ quarts of water and a second container holds $5\frac{3}{4}$ quarts of water. How many more quarts of water does the second container hold than the first container?

_____

23. Each of 15 students will give a $1\frac{1}{2}$-minute speech in English class.

a. How long will it take to give the speeches? _____

b. If the teacher begins recording on a digital camera with an hour available, is there enough time to record everyone if she gives a 15-minute introduction at the beginning of class and every student takes a minute to get ready? Explain.

_____

_____

_____

c. How much time is left on the digital camera? _____

24. **Represent Real-World Problems** Kate wants to buy a new bicycle from a sporting goods store. The bicycle she wants normally sells for $360. The store has a sale where all bicycles cost $\frac{5}{6}$ of the regular price. What is the sale price of the bicycle?

_____

25. **Error Analysis** To find the product $\frac{3}{7} \times \frac{4}{9}$, Cameron simplified $\frac{3}{7}$ to $\frac{1}{7}$ and then multiplied the fractions $\frac{1}{7}$ and $\frac{4}{9}$ to find the product $\frac{4}{63}$. What is Cameron's error?

_____

_____

_____

26. **Justify Reasoning** To multiply a whole number by a fraction, you can first write the whole number as a fraction by placing the whole number in the numerator and 1 in the denominator. Does following this step change the product? Explain.

_____

_____

_____

Work Area

Transforming Equations

6.2.GF.4.1

Students will transform division equations into multiplication equations.

? ESSENTIAL QUESTION

How can you transform a division equation into a multiplication equation?

EXPLORE ACTIVITY

Dividing Fractions

Division and multiplication are opposite, or inverse, operations. A division equation can be rewritten as a multiplication equation using the concept of fact families.

Rewrite $\frac{3}{5} \div \frac{2}{5} = \frac{3}{2}$ as a multiplication equation.

A What is the dividend? _____ This will be the product, or answer, in the multiplication equation. Write the product in the last set of boxes.

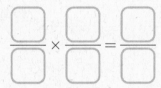

B What is the quotient, or answer, in the division equation? _____ This will become one of the two factors in the multiplication equation. Write the quotient in the first set of boxes.

C What is the divisor? _____ This will become the other factor in the multiplication equation. Write the divisor in the second set of boxes.

Reflect

1. **Analyze** How does the multiplication equation compare to the corresponding division equation?

_____

_____

_____

Rewriting Division as Multiplication

You can rewrite a division expression as a multiplication expression by changing the order of the terms.

EXAMPLE

Rewrite $\frac{5}{8} \div \frac{7}{8} = \frac{5}{7}$ as a multiplication problem.

STEP 1 The dividend becomes the product, or answer, in the multiplication equation.

STEP 2 The divisor becomes one of the factors in the multiplication equation.

STEP 3 The quotient becomes the other factor in the multiplication equation.

$$\frac{5}{8} \div \frac{7}{8} = \frac{5}{7}$$

$$\frac{5}{7} \times \frac{7}{8} = \frac{5}{8}$$

Practice

Complete the table below by using the completed equation to fill in the missing fraction in the incomplete equation.

	Division	Multiplication
1.	$\frac{7}{4} \div \frac{6}{12} = \frac{7}{2}$	$\frac{7}{2} \times \frac{6}{12} = \dfrac{\boxed{}}{\boxed{}}$
2.	$\frac{1}{3} \div \frac{3}{9} = 1$	$1 \times \dfrac{\boxed{}}{\boxed{}} = \frac{1}{3}$
3.	$\frac{4}{8} \div \frac{9}{2} = \frac{1}{9}$	$\dfrac{\boxed{}}{\boxed{}} \times \frac{9}{2} = \frac{4}{8}$
4.	$\dfrac{\boxed{}}{\boxed{}} \div \frac{8}{9} = \frac{9}{56}$	$\frac{9}{56} \times \frac{8}{9} = \frac{1}{7}$
5.	$\frac{9}{5} \div \dfrac{\boxed{}}{\boxed{}} = \frac{9}{10}$	$\frac{9}{10} \times \frac{10}{5} = \frac{9}{5}$
6.	$\frac{7}{1} \div \frac{4}{3} = \dfrac{\boxed{}}{\boxed{}}$	$\frac{21}{4} \times \frac{4}{3} = \frac{7}{1}$

6.2.GR.4.2
Students will model fraction division.

Modeling Fraction Division

? **ESSENTIAL QUESTION**

How can you model fraction division?

EXPLORE ACTIVITY

Modeling Division

Just like division of whole numbers, one method of solving a division problem with fractions is to make a model.

Model the division expression and find the quotient.

$15 \div 3$

A To model 15, draw 15 dots.

⬤ ⬤ ⬤ ⬤ ⬤
⬤ ⬤ ⬤ ⬤ ⬤
⬤ ⬤ ⬤ ⬤ ⬤

B To model dividing by 3, circle groups of _____ in the model above.

C How many circles did you draw? _____

Therefore, $15 \div 3 =$ _____.

Reflect

1. **Make a Conjecture** Using the Explore Activity above, make a conjecture about how to model a fraction division problem.

_____

_____

_____

Using Models to Divide Mixed Fractions

You can use a model to show division with mixed fractions the same way you modeled division with whole numbers.

Model the division expression and find the quotient.

$3\frac{1}{3} \div \frac{2}{3}$

STEP 1 Model the dividend. To model $3\frac{1}{3}$ draw four rectangles of equal size. Then shade $3\frac{1}{3}$ of the rectangles.

STEP 2 Circle groups of $\frac{2}{3}$, which is groups of two $\frac{1}{3}$-pieces.

There are 5 groups of $\frac{2}{3}$. So, $3\frac{1}{3} \div \frac{2}{3} = 5$.

Practice

Model each fraction division expression, then find the quotient.

1. $2\frac{2}{4} \div \frac{2}{4} =$ _____   ☐☐☐☐ ☐☐☐☐ ☐☐☐☐

2. $\frac{4}{6} \div \frac{1}{6} =$ _____   ☐☐☐☐☐☐

3. $\frac{8}{2} \div \frac{1}{2} =$ _____   ☐☐ ☐☐ ☐☐ ☐☐

ESSENTIAL QUESTION

How do you divide fractions?

EXPLORE ACTIVITY 1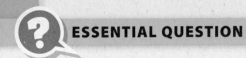

Modeling Fraction Division

In some division problems, you may know a number of groups and need to find how many or how much are in each group. In other division problems, you may know how many there are in each group and need to find the number of groups.

A You have $\frac{3}{4}$ cup of salsa for making burritos. Each burrito requires $\frac{1}{8}$ cup of salsa. How many burritos can you make?

To find the number of burritos that can be made, you need to determine how many $\frac{1}{8}$-cup servings are in $\frac{3}{4}$ cup. Use the diagram. How many eighths

are there in $\frac{3}{4}$? _____

You have enough salsa to make _____ burritos.

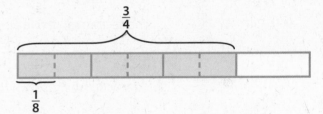

B Five people share $\frac{1}{2}$ pound of cheese equally. How much cheese does each person receive?

To find how much cheese each person receives, you need to determine how

much is in each of _____ parts.

How much is in each part? _____

Each person will receive _____ pound.

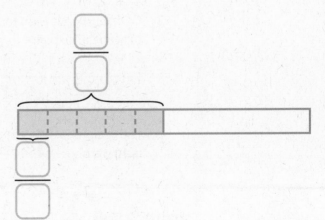

Reflect

1. Write the division shown by each model.

© Houghton Mifflin Harcourt Publishing Company

Reciprocals

Another way to divide fractions is to use *reciprocals*. Two numbers whose product is 1 are **reciprocals**.

$$\frac{3}{4} \times \frac{4}{3} = \frac{12}{12} = 1 \qquad \frac{3}{4} \text{ and } \frac{4}{3} \text{ are reciprocals.}$$

To find the reciprocal of a fraction, switch the numerator and denominator.

$$\frac{\text{numerator}}{\text{denominator}} \cdot \frac{\text{denominator}}{\text{numerator}} = 1$$

EXAMPLE 1

Find the reciprocal of each number.

A $\frac{2}{9}$ ⤬ $\frac{9}{2}$ Switch the numerator and denominator.

The reciprocal of $\frac{2}{9}$ is $\frac{9}{2}$.

B $\frac{1}{8}$ ⤬ $\frac{8}{1}$ Switch the numerator and denominator.

The reciprocal of $\frac{1}{8}$ is $\frac{8}{1}$, or 8.

C 5

$5 = \frac{5}{1}$ Rewrite as a fraction.

$\frac{5}{1}$ ⤬ $\frac{1}{5}$ Switch the numerator and the denominator.

The reciprocal of 5 is $\frac{1}{5}$.

Math Talk

Mathematical Processes

How can you check that the reciprocal in **A** is correct?

Reflect

2. Is any number its own reciprocal? If so, what number(s)? Justify your answer.

_____

3. **Communicate Mathematical Ideas** Does every number have a reciprocal? Explain.

_____

_____

4. The reciprocal of a whole number is a fraction with _____ in the numerator.

© Houghton Mifflin Harcourt Publishing Company

Personal Math Trainer

Online Assessment and Intervention

my.hrw.com

YOUR TURN

Find the reciprocal of each number.

5. $\frac{7}{8}$ _____   **6.** 9 _____   **7.** $\frac{1}{11}$ _____

Using Reciprocals to Find Equivalent Values

A Complete the table below.

Division	Multiplication
$\frac{6}{7} \div \frac{2}{7} = 3$	$\frac{6}{7} \times \frac{7}{2} =$
$\frac{5}{8} \div \frac{3}{8} = \frac{5}{3}$	$\frac{5}{8} \times \frac{8}{3} =$
$\frac{1}{6} \div \frac{5}{6} = \frac{1}{5}$	$\frac{1}{6} \times \frac{6}{5} =$
$\frac{1}{4} \div \frac{1}{3} = \frac{3}{4}$	$\frac{1}{4} \times \frac{3}{1} =$

B How does each multiplication problem compare to its corresponding division problem?

_____

_____

_____

C How does the answer to each multiplication problem compare to the answer to its corresponding division problem?

_____

_____

Reflect

8. Make a Conjecture Use the pattern in the table to make a conjecture about how you can use multiplication to divide one fraction by another.

_____

_____

_____

9. Write a division problem and a corresponding multiplication problem like those in the table. Assuming your conjecture in **8** is correct, what is the answer to your division problem?

_____

_____

Using Reciprocals to Divide Fractions

Dividing by a fraction is equivalent to multiplying by its reciprocal.

$$\frac{1}{5} \div \frac{1}{4} = \frac{4}{5} \qquad \frac{1}{5} \times \frac{4}{1} = \frac{4}{5}$$

EXAMPLE 2

Divide $\frac{5}{9} \div \frac{2}{3}$. Write the quotient in simplest form.

STEP 1 Rewrite as multiplication, using the reciprocal of the divisor.

$$\frac{5}{9} \div \frac{2}{3} = \frac{5}{9} \times \frac{3}{2} \qquad \text{The reciprocal of } \frac{2}{3} \text{ is } \frac{3}{2}.$$

STEP 2 Multiply and simplify.

$$\frac{5}{9} \times \frac{3}{2} = \frac{15}{18} \qquad \text{Multiply the numerators. Multiply the denominators}$$

$$= \frac{5}{6} \qquad \text{Write the answer in simplest form.}$$

$$\frac{5}{9} \div \frac{2}{3} = \frac{5}{6} \qquad \boxed{\frac{15 \div 3}{18 \div 3} = \frac{5}{6}}$$

YOUR TURN

Divide.

10. $\frac{9}{10} \div \frac{2}{5} = $ _____

11. $\frac{9}{10} \div \frac{3}{5} = $ _____

Guided Practice

Find the reciprocal of each fraction. (Example 1)

1. $\frac{2}{5}$ _____

2. $\frac{1}{9}$ _____

3. $\frac{10}{3}$ _____

Divide. (Explore 1, Explore 2, and Example 2)

4. $\frac{4}{3} \div \frac{5}{3} = $ _____

5. $\frac{3}{10} \div \frac{4}{5} = $ _____

6. $\frac{1}{2} \div \frac{2}{5} = $ _____

 ESSENTIAL QUESTION CHECK-IN

7. How do you divide fractions?

_____

4.2 Independent Practice

Personal
Math Trainer

my.hrw.com

Online
Assessment and
Intervention

8. Alison has $\frac{1}{2}$ cup of yogurt for making fruit parfaits. Each parfait requires $\frac{1}{8}$ cup of yogurt. How many parfaits can she make?

_____

9. A team of runners is needed to run a $\frac{1}{4}$-mile relay race. If each runner must run $\frac{1}{16}$ mile, how many runners will be needed?

_____

10. Trevor paints $\frac{1}{6}$ of the fence surrounding his farm each day. How many days will it take him to paint $\frac{3}{4}$ of the fence?

_____

11. Six people share $\frac{3}{5}$ pound of peanuts equally. What fraction of a pound of peanuts does each person receive?

_____

12. **Biology** If one honeybee makes $\frac{1}{12}$ teaspoon of honey during its lifetime, how many honeybees are needed to make $\frac{1}{2}$ teaspoon of honey?

_____

13. Jackson wants to divide a $\frac{3}{4}$-pound box of trail mix into small bags. Each of the bags will hold $\frac{1}{12}$ pound of trail mix. How many bags of trail mix can Jackson fill?

_____

14. A pitcher contains $\frac{2}{3}$ quart of lemonade. If an equal amount of lemonade is poured into each of 6 glasses, how much lemonade will each glass contain?

_____

15. How many tenths are there in $\frac{4}{5}$?

_____

16. You make a large bowl of salad to share with your friends. Your brother eats $\frac{1}{3}$ of it before they come over.

a. You want to divide the leftover salad evenly among six friends. What expression describes the situation? Explain.

_____

_____

_____

b. What fractional portion of the original bowl of salad does each friend receive?

_____

_____

_____

Work Area

17. **Interpret the Answer** The length of a ribbon is $\frac{3}{4}$ meter. Sun Yi needs pieces measuring $\frac{1}{3}$ meter for an art project. What is the greatest number of pieces measuring $\frac{1}{3}$ meter that can be cut from the ribbon? How much ribbon will be left after Sun Yi cuts the ribbon? Explain your reasoning.

_____

_____

_____

18. **Represent Real-World Problems** Liam has $\frac{9}{10}$ gallon of paint for painting the birdhouses he sells at the craft fair. Each birdhouse requires $\frac{1}{20}$ gallon of paint. How many birdhouses can Liam paint? Show your work.

_____

_____

19. **Justify Reasoning** When Kaitlin divided a fraction by $\frac{1}{2}$, the result was a mixed number. Was the original fraction less than or greater than $\frac{1}{2}$? Explain your reasoning.

_____

_____

_____

20. **Communicate Mathematical Ideas** The reciprocal of a fraction less than 1 is always a fraction greater than 1. Why is this?

_____

_____

_____

_____

21. **Make a Prediction** Susan divides the fraction $\frac{5}{8}$ by $\frac{1}{16}$. Her friend Robyn divides $\frac{5}{8}$ by $\frac{1}{32}$. Predict which person will get the greater quotient. Explain and check your prediction.

_____

_____

_____

Real-World Division

6.2.GF.4.2

Students will write and solve real-world division equations with fractions.

 ESSENTIAL QUESTION

How do fraction division equations relate to the real world?

EXPLORE ACTIVITY

Using Division in a Real-World Situation

When you are given a division problem, you can create a real-world situation to help understand what is going on in the problem. Any fractional amounts in the problem must make sense in the real-world situation.

Write a real-world situation for each division equation.

A $\frac{2}{3} \div 3 = \frac{2}{9}$

The equation represents the number of 3s you can divide $\frac{2}{3}$ into, which is $\frac{2}{9}$.

A can of paint that is $\dfrac{\square}{\square}$ full is shared by $\square$ people. Each person

gets $\dfrac{\square}{\square}$ of the can of paint.

B $6\frac{1}{3} \div \frac{2}{3} = 9\frac{1}{2}$

The equation represents the number of $\frac{2}{3}$ s you can divide $6\frac{1}{3}$ into,

which is $\square\dfrac{\square}{\square}$.

Marie is filling flower vases with water. She has a pitcher that holds

$\dfrac{\square}{\square}$ cups of water, and puts $\dfrac{\square}{\square}$ cup in each vase. Marie can fill

$\dfrac{\square}{\square}$ vases.

Complete the real-world situation for each division equation.

1. $\frac{3}{4} \div \frac{1}{2} = 1\frac{1}{2}$

It takes $\frac{\square}{\square}$ hour to build a birdhouse. If John works for $\frac{\square}{\square}$ hour today,

he can build $\square\frac{\square}{\square}$ birdhouses.

2. $1\frac{7}{8} \div \frac{3}{16} = 10$

Tom has a bottle of juice that contains $\square\frac{\square}{\square}$ quarts and is pouring

$\frac{\square}{\square}$-quart servings. He can pour $\square$ servings.

Write a real-world situation for each division equation.

3. $12\frac{2}{6} \div \frac{1}{3} = 37$

_____

_____

_____

4. $\frac{5}{4} \div \frac{1}{2} = 2\frac{1}{2}$

_____

_____

Fracto!

© Houghton Mifflin Harcourt Publishing Company

INSTRUCTIONS

Playing the Game

STEP 1   One student or the teacher is the caller, and gets the caller cards. Each caller card contains a fraction problem and its answer.

$$\frac{4}{9} - \frac{2}{9}$$

$$\frac{2}{9}$$

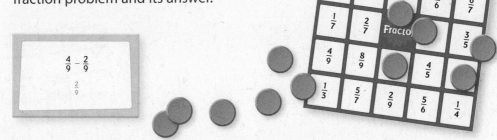

STEP 2   Each player gets a *Fracto!* board and 20–25 counters. The center is a free space. Players should cover the center square before play begins.

STEP 3   On each turn, the caller reads aloud a problem to the players. The caller does not read the answer aloud.

STEP 4   Solve the problem read by the caller. Then search for the answer on your *Fracto!* board. If the answer is on your board, cover it with a counter.

$$\frac{4}{9} - \frac{2}{9} = \frac{2}{9}$$

STEP 5   The caller places the card in a discard pile. Play continues until there is a winner.

Winning the Game

A player who covers five squares in a row horizontally, vertically, or diagonally says, "Fracto!" The caller uses the cards in the discard pile to check that this player has calculated correctly. If so, that player is the winner. If not, play continues until someone else says, "Fracto!"

© Houghton Mifflin Harcourt Publishing Company

LESSON 4.3
Dividing Mixed Numbers

6.2.4.3
Students will divide mixed numbers.

? ESSENTIAL QUESTION

How do you divide mixed numbers?

EXPLORE ACTIVITY

Modeling Mixed Number Division

Antoine is making sushi rolls. He has $2\frac{1}{2}$ cups of rice and will use $\frac{1}{4}$ cup of rice for each sushi roll. How many sushi rolls can he make?

A To find the number of sushi rolls that can be made, you need to determine how many fourths are in $2\frac{1}{2}$. Use fraction pieces to represent $2\frac{1}{2}$ on the model below.

1				1				$\frac{1}{2}$	
$\frac{1}{4}$	$\frac{1}{4}$	$\frac{1}{4}$	$\frac{1}{4}$	$\frac{1}{4}$	$\frac{1}{4}$	$\frac{1}{4}$	$\frac{1}{4}$	$\frac{1}{4}$	$\frac{1}{4}$

B How many fourths are in $2\frac{1}{2}$? _____

Antoine has enough rice to make _____ sushi rolls.

Reflect

1. **Communicate Mathematical Ideas** Which mathematical operation could you use to find the number of sushi rolls that Antoine can make? Explain.

   _____

   _____

2. **Multiple Representations** Write the division shown by the model.

   _____

3. **What If?** Suppose Antoine instead uses $\frac{1}{8}$ cup of rice for each sushi roll. How would his model change? How many rolls can he make? Explain.

   _____

   _____

   _____

© Houghton Mifflin Harcourt Publishing Company • Image Credits: Stockbyte /Getty Images

Lesson 4.3 **91**

Using Reciprocals to Divide Mixed Numbers

Dividing by a fraction is equivalent to multiplying by its reciprocal. You can use this fact to divide mixed numbers. First rewrite the mixed numbers as fractions greater than 1. Then multiply the dividend by the reciprocal of the divisor.

EXAMPLE 1 Real World

My Notes

One serving of Harold's favorite cereal contains $1\frac{2}{5}$ ounces. How many servings are in a $17\frac{1}{2}$-ounce box?

STEP 1 Write a division statement to represent the situation.

$$17\frac{1}{2} \div 1\frac{2}{5}$$

> You need to find how many groups of $1\frac{2}{5}$ are in $17\frac{1}{2}$.

STEP 2 Rewrite the mixed numbers as fractions greater than 1.

$$17\frac{1}{2} \div 1\frac{2}{5} = \frac{35}{2} \div \frac{7}{5}$$

STEP 3 Rewrite the problem as multiplication using the reciprocal of the divisor.

$$\frac{35}{2} \div \frac{7}{5} = \frac{35}{2} \times \frac{5}{7}$$ The reciprocal of $\frac{7}{5}$ is $\frac{5}{7}$.

STEP 4 Multiply.

$$\frac{35}{2} \times \frac{5}{7} = \frac{\overset{5}{35}}{2} \times \frac{5}{\underset{1}{7}}$$ Simplify first using the GCF.

$$= \frac{5 \times 5}{2 \times 1}$$ Multiply numerators. Multiply denominators.

$$= \frac{25}{2}, \text{ or } 12\frac{1}{2}$$ Write the result as a mixed number.

There are $12\frac{1}{2}$ servings of cereal in the box.

Reflect

4. **Analyze Relationships** Explain how can you check the answer.

_____

_____

5. **What If?** Harold serves himself $1\frac{1}{2}$-ounces servings of cereal each morning. How many servings does he get from a box of his favorite cereal? Show your work.

_____

© Houghton Mifflin Harcourt Publishing Company

YOUR TURN

6. Sheila has $10\frac{1}{2}$ pounds of potato salad. She wants to divide the potato salad into containers, each of which holds $1\frac{1}{4}$ pounds. How many containers does she need? Explain.

_____

Solving Problems Involving Area

Recall that to find the area of a rectangle, you multiply length × width. If you know the area and only one dimension, you can divide the area by the known dimension to find the other dimension.

Math On the Spot

my.hrw.com

EXAMPLE 2 Real World

The area of a rectangular sandbox is $56\frac{2}{3}$ square feet. The length of the sandbox is $8\frac{1}{2}$ feet. What is the width?

STEP 1 Write the situation as a division problem.

$$56\frac{2}{3} \div 8\frac{1}{2}$$

STEP 2 Rewrite the mixed numbers as fractions greater than 1.

$$56\frac{2}{3} \div 8\frac{1}{2} = \frac{170}{3} \div \frac{17}{2}$$

STEP 3 Rewrite the problem as multiplication using the reciprocal of the divisor.

$$\frac{170}{3} \div \frac{17}{2} = \frac{170}{3} \times \frac{2}{17}$$

$$= \frac{\overset{10}{\cancel{170}} \times 2}{3 \times \underset{1}{\cancel{17}}} \quad \text{Multiply numerators. Multiply denominators.}$$

$$= \frac{20}{3}, \text{ or } 6\frac{2}{3} \quad \text{Simplify and write as a mixed number.}$$

The width of the sandbox is $6\frac{2}{3}$ feet.

> ### Math Talk
> **Mathematical Processes**
>
> Explain how to find the length of a rectangle when you know the area and the width.

Reflect

7. **Check for Reasonableness** How can you determine if your answer is reasonable?

_____

_____

_____

_____

Personal Math Trainer

Online Assessment and Intervention

my.hrw.com

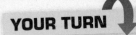

YOUR TURN

8. The area of a rectangular patio is $12\frac{3}{8}$ square meters. The width of the patio is $2\frac{3}{4}$ meters. What is the length? _____

9. The area of a rectangular rug is $14\frac{1}{12}$ square yards. The length of the rug is $4\frac{1}{3}$ yards. What is the width? _____

Guided Practice

Divide. Write each answer in simplest form. (Explore Activity and Example 1)

1. $4\frac{1}{4} \div \frac{3}{4}$

$$\frac{\boxed{}}{4} \div \frac{3}{4} =$$

$$\frac{\boxed{}}{4} \times \frac{\boxed{}}{\boxed{}} =$$

_____

2. $1\frac{1}{2} \div 2\frac{1}{4}$

$$\frac{\boxed{}}{2} \div \frac{\boxed{}}{4} =$$

$$\frac{\boxed{}}{2} \times \frac{\boxed{}}{\boxed{}} =$$

_____

3. $4 \div 1\frac{1}{8} = $ _____

4. $3\frac{1}{5} \div 1\frac{1}{7} = $ _____

5. $8\frac{1}{3} \div 2\frac{1}{2} = $ _____

6. $15\frac{1}{3} \div 3\frac{5}{6} = $ _____

Write each situation as a division problem. Then solve. (Example 2)

7. A sandbox has an area of 26 square feet, and the length is $5\frac{1}{2}$ feet. What is the width of the sandbox? _____

8. Mr. Webster is buying carpet for an exercise room in his basement. The room will have an area of 230 square feet. The width of the room is $12\frac{1}{2}$ feet. What is the length? _____

? ESSENTIAL QUESTION CHECK-IN

9. How does dividing mixed numbers compare with dividing fractions?

_____

_____

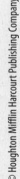

© Houghton Mifflin Harcourt Publishing Company

94 Unit 2

4.3 Independent Practice

10. Jeremy has $4\frac{1}{2}$ cups of iced tea. He wants to divide the tea into $\frac{3}{4}$-cup servings. Use the model to find the number of servings he can make.

_____

11. A ribbon is $3\frac{2}{3}$ yards long. Mae needs to cut the ribbon into pieces that are $\frac{2}{3}$ yard long. Use the model to find the number of pieces she can cut.

_____

12. Dao has $2\frac{3}{8}$ pounds of hamburger meat. He is making $\frac{1}{4}$-pound hamburgers. Does Dao have enough meat to make 10 hamburgers? Explain.

_____

_____

13. **Multistep** Zoey made $5\frac{1}{2}$ cups of trail mix for a camping trip. She wants to divide the trail mix into $\frac{3}{4}$-cup servings.

   a. Ten people are going on the camping trip. Can Zoey make enough $\frac{3}{4}$-cup servings so that each person on the trip has one serving?

   _____

   b. What size would the servings need to be for everyone to have a serving? Explain.

   _____

   c. If Zoey decides to use the $\frac{3}{4}$-cup servings, how much more trail mix will she need? Explain.

   _____

   _____

14. The area of a rectangular picture frame is $30\frac{1}{3}$ square inches. The length of the frame is $6\frac{1}{2}$ inches. Find the width of the frame.

_____

15. The area of a rectangular mirror is $11\frac{11}{16}$ square feet. The width of the mirror is $2\frac{3}{4}$ feet. If there is a 5 foot tall space on the wall to hang the mirror, will it fit? Explain.

_____

16. Ramon has a rope that is $25\frac{1}{2}$ feet long. He wants to cut it into 6 pieces that are equal in length. How long will each piece be?

_____

17. Eleanor and Max used two rectangular wooden boards to make a set for the school play. One board was 6 feet long, and the other was $5\frac{1}{2}$ feet long. The two boards had equal widths. The total area of the set was $60\frac{3}{8}$ square feet. What was the width?

_____

 **FOCUS ON HIGHER ORDER THINKING**

Work Area

18. **Draw Conclusions** Micah divided $11\frac{2}{3}$ by $2\frac{5}{6}$ and got $4\frac{2}{17}$ for an answer. Does his answer seem reasonable? Explain your thinking. Then check Micah's answer.

_____

_____

_____

_____

_____

19. **Explain the Error** To divide $14\frac{2}{3} \div 2\frac{3}{4}$, Erik multiplied $14\frac{2}{3} \times \frac{4}{3}$. Explain Erik's error.

_____

_____

_____

20. **Analyze Relationships** Explain how you can find the missing number in $3\frac{4}{5} \div \blacksquare = 2\frac{5}{7}$. Then find the missing number.

_____

_____

_____

Solving Multistep Problems with Fractions and Mixed Numbers

6.2.4.4

Students will solve word problems involving more than one fraction operation.

ESSENTIAL QUESTION

How can you solve word problems involving more than one fraction operation?

 EXPLORE ACTIVITY Problem Solving

Solving Rational Number Problems

Sometimes more than one operation will be needed to solve a multistep problem. You can use parentheses to group different operations. Recall that according to the **order of operations,** you perform operations in parentheses first.

EXAMPLE 1 Jon is cooking enough lentils for lentil barley soup and lentil salad. The soup recipe calls for $\frac{3}{4}$ cup of dried lentils. The salad recipe calls for $1\frac{1}{2}$ cups of dried lentils. Jon has a $\frac{1}{8}$-cup scoop. How many scoops of dried lentils will Jon need to have enough for the soup and the salad?

Analyze Information

Identify the important information.

- Jon needs _____ cup of dried lentils for soup and _____ cups for salad.

- Jon has a _____ cup scoop.

- You need to find the total number of _____ he needs.

Formulate a Plan

You can use the expression $\left(\frac{3}{4} + 1\frac{1}{2}\right) \div \frac{1}{8}$ to find the number of scoops of dried lentils Jon will need for the soup and the salad.

Solve

Follow the order of operations.

$$\frac{3}{4} + 1\frac{1}{2} = \frac{3}{4} + \frac{3}{2}$$

Perform the operations in parentheses first.

$$= \frac{3}{4} + \frac{\boxed{}}{4}$$

Find the total amount of dried lentils Jon will need.

$$= \frac{\boxed{}}{\boxed{}} = \boxed{}\frac{\boxed{}}{\boxed{}}$$

Math On the Spot
my.hrw.com

Jon needs _____ cups of dried lentils for both the soup and the salad.

To find how many $\frac{1}{8}$-cup scoops he
needs, divide the total amount
of dried lentils into groups of _____.

$$2\frac{1}{4} \div \frac{1}{8} = \frac{9}{4} \div \frac{\boxed{}}{\boxed{}}$$

$$= \frac{9}{4} \times \frac{\boxed{}}{\boxed{}}$$

Jon will need 18 scoops of dried lentils to have
enough for both the lentil barley soup and the
lentil salad.

$$= \frac{9 \times 8}{4 \times 1}$$

$$= \frac{18}{1} = 18$$

 **Justify and Evaluate**

You added _____ cups and _____ cups first to find the total number

of cups of lentils. Then you divided the sum by _____ to find the
number of $\frac{1}{8}$-cup scoops.

Personal Math Trainer

Online Assessment
and Intervention

⏻ my.hrw.com

YOUR TURN

1. Before conducting some experiments, a scientist mixes
   $\frac{1}{2}$ gram of Substance A with $\frac{3}{4}$ gram of Substance B. If
   the scientist uses $\frac{1}{8}$ gram of the mixture for each
   experiment, how many experiments can be conducted? _____

Guided Practice

1. An art student uses a roll of wallpaper to decorate two gift boxes. The
   student will use $1\frac{1}{3}$ yards of paper for one box and $\frac{5}{6}$ yard of paper for the
   other box. The paper must be cut into pieces that are $\frac{1}{6}$ yard long. How
   many pieces will the student cut to use for the gift boxes? (Explore Activity _____
   Example 1)

 ESSENTIAL QUESTION CHECK-IN

2. How can you solve a multistep problem that involves fractions?

_____

4.4 Independent Practice

Personal Math Trainer

my.hrw.com

Online Assessment and Intervention

3. Naomi has earned $54 mowing lawns the past two days. She worked $2\frac{1}{2}$ hours yesterday and $4\frac{1}{4}$ hours today. If Naomi is paid the same amount for every hour she works, how much does she earn per hour to mow lawns?

_____

4. An art teacher has $1\frac{1}{2}$ pounds of red clay and $\frac{3}{4}$ pound of yellow clay. The teacher mixes the red clay and yellow clay together. Each student in the class needs $\frac{1}{8}$ pound of the clay mixture to finish the assigned art project for the class. How many students can get enough clay to finish the project?

_____

5. A hairstylist schedules $\frac{1}{4}$ hour to trim a customer's hair and $\frac{1}{6}$ hour to style the customer's hair. The hairstylist plans to work $3\frac{1}{3}$ hours each day for 5 days each week. How many appointments can the hairstylist schedule each week if each customer must be trimmed and styled?

_____

6. A picture framer has a thin board $10\frac{1}{12}$ feet long. The framer notices that $2\frac{3}{8}$ feet of the board is scratched and cannot be used. The rest of the board will be used to make small picture frames. Each picture frame needs $1\frac{2}{3}$ feet of the board. At most, how many complete picture frames can be made?

_____

7. Jim's backyard is a rectangle that is $15\frac{5}{6}$ yards long and $10\frac{2}{5}$ yards wide. Jim buys sod in pieces that are $1\frac{1}{3}$ yards long and $1\frac{1}{3}$ yards wide. How many pieces of sod will Jim need to buy to cover his backyard with sod?

_____

8. Eva wants to make two pieces of pottery. She needs $\frac{3}{5}$ pound of clay for one piece and $\frac{7}{10}$ pound of clay for the other piece. She has three bags of clay that weigh $\frac{4}{5}$ pound each. How many bags of clay will Eva need to make both pieces of pottery? How many pounds of clay will she have left over?

_____

9. Mark wants to paint a mural. He has $1\frac{1}{3}$ gallons of yellow paint, $1\frac{1}{4}$ gallons of green paint, and $\frac{7}{8}$ gallon of blue paint. Mark plans to use $\frac{3}{4}$ gallon of each paint color. How many gallons of paint will he have left after painting the mural?

_____

10. Trina works after school and on weekends. She always works three days each week. This week she worked $2\frac{3}{4}$ hours on Monday, $3\frac{3}{5}$ hours on Friday, and $5\frac{1}{2}$ hours on Saturday. Next week she plans to work the same number of hours as this week, but will work for the same number of hours each day. How many hours will she work on each day?

_____

 **FOCUS ON HIGHER ORDER THINKING**

Work Area

11. Represent Real-World Problems Describe a real-world problem that can be solved using the expression $29 \div \left(\frac{3}{8} + \frac{5}{6}\right)$. Find the answer in the context of the situation.

_____

_____

_____

_____

12. Justify Reasoning Indira and Jean begin their hike at 10 a.m. one morning. They plan to hike from the $2\frac{2}{5}$-mile marker to the $8\frac{1}{10}$-mile marker along the trail. They plan to hike at an average speed of 3 miles per hour. Will they reach the $8\frac{1}{10}$-mile marker by noon? Explain your reasoning.

_____

_____

_____

_____

13. Multiple Representations You are measuring walnuts for banana-walnut oatmeal and a spinach and walnut salad. You need $\frac{3}{8}$ cup of walnuts for the oatmeal and $\frac{3}{4}$ cup of walnuts for the salad. You have a $\frac{1}{4}$-cup scoop. Describe two different ways to find how many scoops of walnuts you will need.

_____

_____

_____

_____

Ready to Go On?

Personal Math Trainer
Online Assessment and Intervention

⏻ my.hrw.com

4.1 Applying GCF and LCM to Fraction Operations

Solve.

1. $\frac{4}{5} \times \frac{3}{4}$ _____

2. $\frac{5}{7} \times \frac{9}{10}$ _____

3. $\frac{3}{8} + 2\frac{1}{2}$ _____

4. $1\frac{3}{5} - \frac{5}{6}$ _____

4.2 Dividing Fractions

Divide.

5. $\frac{1}{3} \div \frac{7}{9}$ _____

6. $\frac{1}{3} \div \frac{5}{8}$ _____

7. Luci cuts a board that is $\frac{3}{4}$ yard long into pieces that are $\frac{3}{8}$ yard long. How many pieces does she cut? _____

4.3 Dividing Mixed Numbers

Divide.

8. $3\frac{1}{3} \div \frac{2}{3}$ _____

9. $1\frac{7}{8} \div 2\frac{2}{5}$ _____

10. $4\frac{1}{4} \div 4\frac{1}{2}$ _____

11. $8\frac{1}{3} \div 4\frac{2}{7}$ _____

4.4 Solving Multistep Problems with Fractions and Mixed Numbers

12. Jamal hiked on two trails. The first trail was $5\frac{1}{3}$ miles long, and the second trail was $1\frac{3}{4}$ times as long as the first trail. How many miles did Jamal hike? _____

 ESSENTIAL QUESTION

13. Describe a real-world situation that is modeled by dividing two fractions or mixed numbers.

_____

_____

_____

Assessment Readiness

Selected Response

1. Two sides of a rectangular fence are $5\frac{5}{8}$ feet long. The other two sides are $6\frac{1}{4}$ feet long. What is the perimeter?

Ⓐ $11\frac{7}{8}$ feet   Ⓑ 13 feet

Ⓒ $23\frac{3}{4}$ feet   Ⓓ $35\frac{5}{32}$ feet

2. Which shows the GCF of 18 and 24 with $\frac{18}{24}$ in simplest form?

Ⓐ GCF: 3; $\frac{3}{4}$

Ⓑ GCF: 3; $\frac{6}{8}$

Ⓒ GCF: 6; $\frac{3}{4}$

Ⓓ GCF: 6; $\frac{6}{8}$

3. A jar contains 133 pennies. A bigger jar contains $1\frac{2}{7}$ times as many pennies. What is the value of the pennies in the bigger jar?

Ⓐ $1.49   Ⓑ $1.52

Ⓒ $1.68   Ⓓ $1.71

4. Which of these is the same as $\frac{3}{5} \div \frac{4}{7}$?

Ⓐ $\frac{3}{5} \div \frac{7}{4}$

Ⓑ $\frac{4}{7} \div \frac{3}{5}$

Ⓒ $\frac{3}{5} \times \frac{4}{7}$

Ⓓ $\frac{3}{5} \times \frac{7}{4}$

5. Andy has $6\frac{2}{3}$ cups of juice. How many $\frac{2}{3}$-cup servings can he pour?

Ⓐ $4\frac{4}{9}$ Ⓑ 6

Ⓒ 7   Ⓓ 10

6. What is the reciprocal of $3\frac{3}{7}$?

Ⓐ $\frac{7}{24}$ Ⓑ $\frac{3}{7}$

Ⓒ $\frac{7}{3}$ Ⓓ $\frac{24}{7}$

7. A rectangular patio has a length of $12\frac{1}{2}$ feet and an area of $103\frac{1}{8}$ square feet. What is the width of the patio?

Ⓐ $4\frac{1}{8}$ feet

Ⓑ $8\frac{1}{4}$ feet

Ⓒ $16\frac{1}{2}$ feet

Ⓓ 33 feet

8. Which number is greater than the absolute value of $-\frac{3}{8}$?

Ⓐ $-\frac{5}{8}$

Ⓑ $-\frac{1}{8}$

Ⓒ $\frac{1}{4}$

Ⓓ 0.5

Mini-Task

9. Jodi is cutting out pieces of paper that measure $8\frac{1}{2}$ inches by 11 inches from a larger sheet of paper that has an area of 1,000 square inches

a. What is the area of each piece of paper that Jodi is cutting out?

_____

b. What is the greatest possible number of pieces of paper that Jodi can cut out of the larger sheet?

_____

Operations with Decimals

ESSENTIAL QUESTION

How can you use operations with decimals to solve real-world problems?

Real-World Video

The gravitational force on Earth's moon is less than the gravitational force on Earth. You can calculate your weight on the moon by multiplying your weight on Earth by a decimal.

⏻ my.hrw.com

GO DIGITAL
my.hrw.com

my.hrw.com

Go digital with your write-in student edition, accessible on any device.

Math On the Spot

Scan with your smart phone to jump directly to the online edition, video tutor, and more.

Animated Math

Interactively explore key concepts to see how math works.

Personal Math Trainer

Get immediate feedback and help as you work through practice sets.

Reading Start-Up

© Houghton Mifflin Harcourt Publishing Company

Visualize Vocabulary

Use the ✔ words to complete the chart. You may put more than one word in each section.

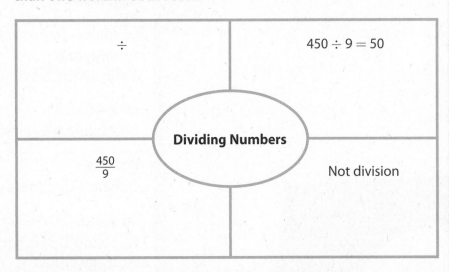

÷	450 ÷ 9 = 50
Dividing Numbers	
$\frac{450}{9}$	Not division

Vocabulary

Review Words

decimal *(decimal)*
✔ denominator *(denominador)*
divide *(dividir)*
✔ dividend *(dividendo)*
✔ divisor *(divisor)*
✔ fraction bar *(barra de fracciones)*
✔ multiply *(multiplicar)*
✔ numerator *(numerador)*
✔ operation *(operación)*
✔ product *(producto)*
✔ quotient *(cociente)*
✔ rational number *(número racional)*
✔ symbol *(símbolo)*
whole number *(número entero)*

Understand Vocabulary

Match the term on the left to the definition on the right.

1. divide
2. denominator
3. quotient
4. numerator

A. The bottom number in a fraction.

B. The top number in a fraction.

C. To split into equal groups.

D. The answer in a division problem.

Active Reading

Booklet Before beginning the module, create a booklet to help you learn the concepts in this module. Write the main idea of each lesson on its own page of the booklet. As you study each lesson, record examples that illustrate the main idea and make note of important details. Refer to your finished booklet as you work on assignments and study for tests.

Are YOU Ready?

Complete these exercises to review skills you will need for this module.

Represent Decimals

EXAMPLE

Think: 1 square = 1 of 100 equal parts
$= \frac{1}{100}$, or 0.01

10 squares = 10 of 100 equal parts
$= \frac{1}{10}$, or 0.1

So, 20 squares represent 2×0.1, or 0.2.

Write the decimal represented by the shaded square.

1.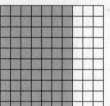

2.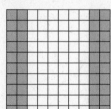

3.

4.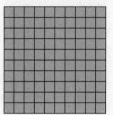

_____ _____ _____ _____

Multiply Decimals by Powers of 10

EXAMPLE 6.574×100 Count the zeros in 100: 2 zeros.

$6.574 \times 100 = 657.4$ Move the decimal point 2 places to the right.

Find the product.

5. 0.49×10 _____   **6.** $25.34 \times 1{,}000$ _____   **7.** 87×100 _____

Words for Operations

EXAMPLE   Write a numerical expression for the product of 5 and 9.   Think: *Product* means "to multiply."

5×9 Write 5 times 9.

Write a numerical expression for the word expression.

8. 20 decreased by 8 _____   **9.** the quotient of 14 and 7 _____

10. the difference between 72 and 16 _____   **11.** the sum of 19 and 3 _____

Complete these exercises to review skills you will need for this module.

Represent Decimals

12. A floor has a tile pattern 10 tiles wide and 10 tiles long as shown below. What part of the floor, written as a decimal, has colored tiles? Explain.

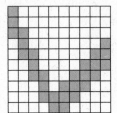

Multiply Decimals by Powers of 10

13. Two restaurants are having promotional events. The Sandwich Shop is giving away 1,000 bumper stickers that cost the restaurant $0.79 each. The Burrito Palace is giving away 100 T-shirts that cost the restaurant $7.75 each. How much did each restaurant spend on its promotion?

Words for Operations

14. Jonathan thinks that the quotient of 48 and 12 can be written as $48 + 12$. Explain Jonathan's error, and determine the correct numerical expression.

Dividing Whole Numbers

6.2.5.1
Students will divide multi-digit whole numbers.

ESSENTIAL QUESTION

How do you divide multi-digit whole numbers?

EXPLORE ACTIVITY

Estimating Quotients

You can use estimation to predict the quotient of multi-digit whole numbers.

A local zoo had a total of 98,464 visitors last year. The zoo was open every day except for three holidays. On average, about how many visitors did the zoo have each day?

$$\overset{\text{quotient}}{\text{divisor}\,\overline{)\,\text{dividend}}}$$

A To estimate the average number of visitors per day, you can divide the total number of visitors by the number of days. To estimate the quotient, first estimate the dividend by rounding the number of visitors to the nearest ten thousand.

98,464 rounded to the nearest ten thousand is _____.

B There were 365 days last year. How many

days was the petting zoo open? _____

C Estimate the divisor by rounding the number of days that the zoo was open to the nearest hundred.

_____ rounded to the nearest hundred is _____.

D Estimate the quotient. _____ ÷ _____ = _____

The average number of visitors per day last year was about _____.

Reflect

1. How can you check that your quotient is correct?

_____

_____

2. **Critical Thinking** Do you think that your estimate is greater than or less than the actual answer? Explain.

_____

Using Long Division

The exact average number of visitors per day at the zoo in the Explore Activity is the quotient of 98,464 and 362. You can use long division to find this quotient.

EXAMPLE 1

A local zoo had a total of 98,464 visitors last year. The zoo was open every day except three holidays? On average, how many visitors did the zoo have each day?

Math Talk
Mathematical Processes

How does the estimate from the Explore Activity compare to the actual average number of visitors per day?

STEP 1 362 is greater than 9 and 98, so divide 984 by 362. Place the first digit in the quotient in the hundreds place. Multiply 2 by 362 and place the product under 984. Subtract.

$$
\begin{array}{r}
2 \\
362\overline{)\,98{,}464} \\
-72\,4 \\
\hline
26\,0
\end{array}
$$

STEP 2 Bring down the tens digit. Divide 2,606 by 362. Multiply 7 by 362 and place the product under 2,606. Subtract.

$$
\begin{array}{r}
27 \\
362\overline{)\,98{,}464} \\
-72\,4\downarrow \\
\hline
26\,06 \\
-25\,34 \\
\hline
72
\end{array}
$$

STEP 3 Bring down the ones digit. Divide the ones.

$$
\begin{array}{r}
272 \\
362\overline{)\,98{,}464} \\
-72\,4 \\
\hline
26\,06 \\
-25\,34\downarrow \\
\hline
724 \\
-724 \\
\hline
0
\end{array}
$$

The average number of visitors per day last year was 272.

YOUR TURN

Find each quotient.

3. 34,989 ÷ 321 _____   **4.** 73,375 ÷ 125 _____

Dividing with a Remainder

Suppose you and your friend want to divide 9 polished rocks between you so that you each get the same number of polished rocks. You will each get 4 rocks with 1 rock left over. You can say that the quotient $9 \div 2$ has a remainder of 1.

EXAMPLE 2

Callie has 1,850 books. She must pack them into boxes to ship to a bookstore. Each box holds 12 books. How many boxes will she need to pack all of the books?

Divide 1,850 by 12.

```
        154 R2
  12) 1,850
      -12
       65
      -60
       50
      -48
        2
```

The quotient is 154, remainder 2. You can write 154 R2.

Reflect

5. **Interpret the Answer** What does the remainder mean in this situation?

_____

_____

6. **Interpret the Answer** How many boxes does Callie need to pack the books? Explain.

_____

_____

My Notes

YOUR TURN

Divide.

7. $5,796 \div 25$ _____

8. $67)\overline{3,098}$ _____

9. A museum gift shop manager wants to put 1,578 polished rocks into small bags to sell as souvenirs. If the shop manager wants to put 15 rocks in each bag, how many complete bags can be filled? How

   many rocks will be left over? _____

© Houghton Mifflin Harcourt Publishing Company

1. Estimate: 31,969 ÷ 488 (Explore Activity)

Round the numbers and then divide.

31,969 ÷ 488 = _____ ÷ _____ = _____

Divide. (Example 1, Example 2)

2. 3,072 ÷ 32 = _____

3. 4,539 ÷ 51 = _____

4. 9,317 ÷ 95 = _____

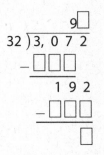

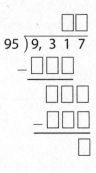

5. 2,226 ÷ 53 = _____

6. Divide 4,514 by 74. _____

7. 3,493 ÷ 37 = _____

8. 2,001 ÷ 83 = _____

9. 39,751 ÷ 313 = _____

10. 35,506 ÷ 438 = _____

11. During a food drive, a local middle school collected 8,982 canned food items. Each of the 28 classrooms that participated in the drive donated about the same number of items. Estimate the number of items each classroom donated. (Explore Activity)

_____

12. A theater has 1,120 seats in 35 equal rows. How many seats are in each row? (Example 1)

_____

13. There are 1,012 souvenir paperweights that need to be packed in boxes. Each box will hold 12 paperweights. How many boxes will be needed? (Example 2)

_____

❓ ESSENTIAL QUESTION CHECK-IN

14. What steps do you take to divide multi-digit whole numbers?

_____

_____

_____

_____

5.1 Independent Practice

Personal
Math Trainer

Online
Assessment and
Intervention

my.hrw.com

Divide.

15. 44,756 ÷ 167 = _____

16. 87,628 ÷ 931 = _____

17. 66,253 ÷ 317 = _____

18. 76,255 ÷ 309 = _____

19. 50,779 ÷ 590 = _____

20. 97,156 ÷ 107 = _____

21. 216,016 ÷ 368 = _____

22. 107,609 ÷ 72 = _____

23. Emilio has 8,450 trees to plant in rows on his tree farm. He will plant 125 trees per row. How many full rows of trees will he have? Explain.

_____

_____

24. Camilla makes and sells jewelry. She has 8,160 silver beads and 2,880 black beads to make necklaces. Each necklace will contain 85 silver beads

and 30 black beads. How many necklaces can she make? _____

25. During a promotional weekend, a state fair gives a free admission to every 175th person who enters the fair. On Saturday, there were 6,742 people attending the fair. On Sunday, there were 5,487 people attending the fair. How many people received a free admission over the two days?

_____

26. How is the quotient 80,000 ÷ 2,000 different from the quotient 80,000 ÷ 200 or 80,000 ÷ 20?

_____

_____

27. Given that 9,554 ÷ 562 = 17, how can you find the quotient 95,540 ÷ 562?

_____

_____

28. **Earth Science** The diameter of the Moon is about 3,476 kilometers. The distance from Earth to the Moon is about 384,400 kilometers. About how many moons could be lined up in a row between Earth and the Moon? Round to the nearest whole number.

_____

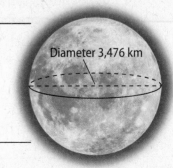

Diameter 3,476 km

29. Vocabulary Explain how you could check the answer to a division question in which there is a remainder.

_____

_____

_____

30. Yolanda is buying a car with a base price of $16,750. She must also pay the options, fees, and taxes shown. The car dealership will give her 48 months to pay off the entire amount. Yolanda can only afford to pay $395 each month. Will she be able to buy the car? Explain.

Jackson Auto Dealer		
4-door sedan		
	base price	**$16,750**
	options	$ 500
	fees	$ 370
	taxes	$ 1,425

_____

_____

_____

_____

H.O.T. FOCUS ON HIGHER ORDER THINKING

31. Check for Reasonableness Is 40 a reasonable estimate of a quotient for 78,114 ÷ 192? Explain your reasoning.

_____

_____

32. Critique Reasoning Harrison predicted that the actual quotient for 57,872 ÷ 305 will be less than the estimate 60,000 ÷ 300 = 200. Is Harrison correct? Explain how Harrison arrived at his prediction (without dividing the actual numbers).

_____

_____

_____

33. Make a Prediction In preparation for a storm, the town council buys 13,750 pounds of sand to fill sandbags. Volunteers are trying to decide whether to fill bags that can hold 25 pounds of sand or bags that can hold 50 pounds of sand. Will they have more or fewer sandbags if they fill the 25-pound bags? How many more or fewer? Explain your reasoning.

_____

_____

_____

Work Area

Adding and Subtracting Decimals

6.2.5.2

Students will add and subtract decimals.

? ESSENTIAL QUESTION

How do you add and subtract decimals?

EXPLORE ACTIVITY

Modeling Decimal Addition

You have probably used decimal grids to model decimals. For example, the decimal 0.25, or $\frac{25}{100}$, can be modeled by shading 25 squares in a 10×10 grid. You can also use decimal grids to add decimal values.

A chemist combines 0.17 mL of water and 0.49 mL of hydrogen peroxide in a beaker. How much total liquid is in the beaker?

A How many grid squares should you shade to represent 0.17 mL of water? Why?

_____

B How many grid squares should you shade to represent 0.49 mL of hydrogen peroxide?

_____

C Use the grid at the right to model the addition. Use one color for 0.17 mL of water and another color for 0.49 mL of hydrogen peroxide.

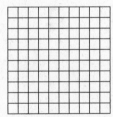

D How much total liquid is in the beaker? 0.17 + 0.49 = _____ mL

Reflect

Multiple Representations **Show how to shade each grid to represent the sum. Then find the sum.**

1. 0.24 + 0.71 = _____

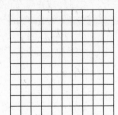

2. 0.08 + 0.65 = _____

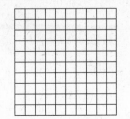

Adding Decimals

Adding decimals is similar to adding whole numbers. First align the numbers by place value. Start adding at the right and regroup when necessary. Bring down the decimal point into your answer.

EXAMPLE 1

Susan rode her bicycle 3.12 miles on Monday and 4.7 miles on Tuesday. How many miles did she ride in all?

STEP 1 Align the decimal points.

STEP 2 Add zeros as placeholders when necessary.

	3	.	1	2
+	4	.	7	0
	7	.	8	2

STEP 3 Add from right to left.

Susan rode 7.82 miles in all.

STEP 4 Use estimation to check that the answer is reasonable. Round each decimal to the nearest whole number.

$$\begin{array}{ccc} 3.12 & \longrightarrow & 3 \\ + 4.70 & \longrightarrow & + 5 \\ \hline 7.82 & & 8 \end{array}$$

Since 8 is close to 7.82, the answer is reasonable.

Reflect

3. Why can you rewrite 4.7 as 4.70?

_____

_____

4. Why is it important to align the decimal points when adding?

_____

_____

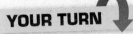

Add.

5. $0.42 + 0.27 =$ _____

6. $0.61 + 0.329 =$ _____

7. $3.25 + 4.6 =$ _____

8. $17.27 + 3.88 =$ _____

© Houghton Mifflin Harcourt Publishing Company • Image Credits: Jacek Chabraszewski / Shutterstock

Subtracting Decimals

The procedure for subtracting decimals is similar to the procedure for adding decimals.

Math On the Spot
⏻ my.hrw.com

EXAMPLE 2 Real World

A Mia is 160.2 centimeters tall. Rosa is 165.1 centimeters tall. How much taller is Rosa than Mia?

STEP 1 Align the decimal points.

STEP 2 Add zeros as placeholders when necessary.

STEP 3 Subtract from right to left, regrouping when necessary.

			4		1
	1	6	5̷	.	1̷
−	1	6	0	.	2
			4	.	9

Rosa is 4.9 centimeters taller than Mia.

To check that your answer is reasonable, you can estimate. Round each decimal to the nearest whole number.

$$\begin{array}{ccc} 165.1 & \longrightarrow & 165 \\ -\ 160.2 & \longrightarrow & -\ 160 \\ \hline 4.9 & & 5 \end{array}$$

Since 5 is close to 4.9, the answer is reasonable.

B Matthew throws a discus 58.7 meters. Zachary throws the discus 56.12 meters. How much farther did Matthew throw the discus?

STEP 1 Align the decimal points.

STEP 2 Add zeros as placeholders when necessary.

STEP 3 Subtract from right to left, regrouping when necessary.

			6	10
	5	8	.	7̷	0̷
−	5	6	.	1	2
		2	.	5	8

Matthew threw the discus 2.58 meters farther than Zachary.

To check that your answer is reasonable, you can estimate. Round each decimal to the nearest whole number.

$$\begin{array}{ccc} 58.7 & \longrightarrow & 59 \\ -\ 56.12 & \longrightarrow & -\ 56 \\ \hline 2.58 & & 3 \end{array}$$

Since 3 is close to 2.58, the answer is reasonable.

Math Talk
Mathematical Processes

How can you check a subtraction problem?

My Notes

© Houghton Mifflin Harcourt Publishing Company

Guided Practice

Shade the grid to find each sum. (Explore Activity)

1. 0.72 + 0.19 = _____

2. 0.38 + 0.4 = _____

Add. Check that your answer is reasonable. (Example 1)

3. 54.87 ⟶ 55
   + 7.48 ⟶ + 7

4. 2.19 ⟶ ☐
   + 34.92 ⟶ + ☐

5. 0.215 ⟶ ☐
   + 3.74 ⟶ + ☐

Subtract. Check that your answer is reasonable. (Example 2)

6. 9.73 ⟶ 10
   − 7.16 ⟶ − 7

7. 18.419 ⟶ ☐
   − 6.47 ⟶ − ☐

8. 5.006 ⟶ ☐
   − 3.2 ⟶ − ☐

Add or subtract. (Example 1, Example 2)

9. 17.2 + 12.9 = _____

10. 28.341 + 37.5 = _____

11. 25.36 − 2.004 = _____

12. 15.52 − 8.17 = _____

13. 25.68 + 12 = _____

14. 150.25 − 78 = _____

15. Perry connects a blue garden hose and a green garden hose to make one long hose. The blue hose is 16.5 feet. The green hose is 14.75 feet. How long is the combined hose? (Example 1) _____

16. Keisha has $20.08 in her purse. She buys a book for $8.72. How much does she have left? (Example 2) _____

? ESSENTIAL QUESTION CHECK-IN

17. How is adding and subtracting decimals similar to adding and subtracting whole numbers?

_____

_____

5.2 Independent Practice

Personal Math Trainer

Online Assessment and Intervention

my.hrw.com

Add or subtract.

18. 28.6 − 0.975 = _____

19. 5.6 − 0.105 = _____

20. 7.03 + 33.006 = _____

21. 57.42 + 4 + 1.602 = _____

22. 2.25 + 65.47 + 2.333 = _____

23. 18.419 − 6.47 = _____

24. 83 − 12.76 = _____

25. 102.01 − 95.602 = _____

26. **Multiple Representations** Ursula wrote the sum 5.815 + 6.021 as a sum of two mixed numbers.

   a. What sum did she write? _____

   b. Compare the sum of the mixed numbers to the sum of the decimals. _____

Use the café menu to answer 27–29.

27. Stephen and Jahmya are having lunch. Stephen buys a garden salad, a veggie burger, and lemonade. Jahmya buys a fruit salad, a toasted cheese sandwich, and a bottle of water. Whose lunch cost more? How much more?

_____

28. Jahmya wants to leave $1.75 as a tip for her server. She has a $20 bill. How much change should she receive after paying for her food and leaving a tip?

_____

29. **What If?** In addition to his meal, Stephen orders a fruit salad for take-out, and wants to leave $2.25 as a tip for his server. He has a $10 bill and a $5 bill. How much change should he receive after paying for his lunch, the fruit salad, and the tip?

_____

30. A carpenter who is installing cabinets uses thin pieces of material called shims to fill gaps. The carpenter uses four shims to fill a gap that is 1.2 centimeters wide. Three of the shims are 0.75 centimeter, 0.125 centimeter, and 0.09 centimeter wide. What is the width of the fourth shim?

_____

Café Menu

Garden Salad **$2.29**
Fruit Salad **$2.89**

Veggie Burger **$4.75**
Toasted Cheese Sandwich **$4.59**

Bottle of Water **$1.39**
Lemonade **$1.29**

31. A CD of classical guitar music contains 5 songs. The length of each song is shown in the table.

Track 1	Track 2	Track 3	Track 4	Track 5
6.5 minutes	8 minutes	3.93 minutes	4.1 minutes	5.05 minutes

a. Between each song is a 0.05-minute break. How long does it take to listen to the CD from the beginning of the first song

to the end of the last song? _____

b. **What If?** Juan wants to buy the CD from an Internet music site. He downloads the CD onto a disc that can hold up to 60 minutes of music. How many more minutes of music can he still buy after

downloading the CD? _____

H.O.T. FOCUS ON HIGHER ORDER THINKING

Work Area

32. **Analyze Relationships** Use the decimals 2.47, 9.57, and 7.1 to write two different addition facts and two different subtraction facts.

_____

_____

33. **Communicate Mathematical Ideas** The Commutative Property of Addition states that you can change the order of addends in a sum. The Associative Property of Addition states that you can change the grouping of addends in a sum. Use an example to show how the Commutative Property of Addition and the Associative Property of Addition apply to adding decimals.

_____

_____

_____

_____

_____

34. **Critique Reasoning** Indira predicts that the actual difference of $19 - 7.82$ will be greater than the estimate of $19 - 8 = 11$. Is Indira correct? Explain how Indira might have arrived at that prediction without subtracting the actual numbers.

_____

_____

_____

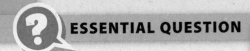

ESSENTIAL QUESTION

How do you multiply decimals?

EXPLORE ACTIVITY

Modeling Decimal Multiplication

Use decimal grids or area models to find each product.

A **0.3 × 0.5**

0.3 × 0.5 represents 0.3 of 0.5. Shade 5 *rows* of the decimal grid to represent 0.5.

Shade 0.3 of each 0.1 that is already shaded

to represent 0.3 of _____.

_____ square(s) are double-shaded.

This represents _____ hundredth(s), or 0.15.

0.3 × 0.5 = _____

B **3.2 × 2.1**

Use an area model. In the model, the large squares represent wholes, the small rectangles along the right and lower edges represent tenths, and the small squares at the lower right represent hundredths. The model is 3 and 2 tenths units long, and 2 and 1 tenth unit wide.

The area of the model is

_____ whole(s) + _____ tenth(s) + _____ hundredth(s) square units.

3.2 × 2.1 = _____

Reflect

1. **Analyze Relationships** How are the products 2.1 × 3.2 and 21 × 32 alike? How are they different?

_____

_____

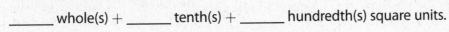

Multiplying Decimals

To multiply decimals, first multiply as you would with whole numbers. Then place the decimal point in the product. The number of decimal places in the product equals the sum of the number of decimal places in the factors.

EXAMPLE 1

Delia bought 3.8 pounds of peppers. The peppers cost $1.99 per pound. What was the total cost of Delia's peppers?

$$
\begin{array}{r}
1.99 \\
\times\ 3.8 \\
\hline
1592 \\
+\ 5970 \\
\hline
7.562
\end{array}
$$

← 2 decimal places
← + 1 decimal place

← 3 decimal places

The peppers cost $7.56.

> Round the answer to hundredths to show a dollar amount.

Reflect

2. **Communicate Mathematical Ideas** How can you use estimation to check that you have placed the decimal point correctly in your product?

_____

_____

_____

_____

_____

YOUR TURN

Multiply.

3.   12.6 ← ☐ decimal place(s)

   × 15.3 ← + ☐ decimal place(s)
   ――――――
      378

   ☐

   ☐

   + ☐

   ☐ ← ☐ decimal place(s)

4.   9.76 ← ☐ decimal place(s)

   × 0.46 ← + ☐ decimal place(s)
   ――――――

   ☐

   ☐

   + ☐

   ☐ ← ☐ decimal place(s)

Estimating to Check Reasonableness

In Example 1, you used estimation to check whether the decimal point was placed correctly in the product. You can also use estimation to check that your answer is reasonable.

EXAMPLE 2

Blades of grass grow 3.75 inches per month. If the grass continues to grow at this rate, how much will the grass grow in 6.25 months?

$$
\begin{array}{r}
3.75 \quad \leftarrow \quad \text{2 decimal places} \\
\times\ 6.25 \quad \leftarrow + \ \text{2 decimal places} \\
\hline
1875 \\
7500 \\
+\ 225000 \\
\hline
23.4375 \quad \leftarrow \quad \text{4 decimal places}
\end{array}
$$

The grass will grow 23.4375 inches in 6.25 months.

Estimate to check whether your answer is reasonable.

Round 3.75 to the nearest whole number. _____

Round 6.25 to the nearest whole number. _____

Multiply the whole numbers. _____ × _____ = 24

The answer is reasonable because 24 is close to 23.4375.

YOUR TURN

Multiply.

5.
$$
\begin{array}{r}
7.14 \\
\times\ 6.78 \\
\hline
5712
\end{array}
$$

▢
▢
+ ▢

6.
$$
\begin{array}{r}
11.49 \\
\times\ 8.27 \\
\end{array}
$$

▢
▢
▢
+ ▢

7. Rico bicycles at an average speed of 15.5 miles per hour.

   What distance will Rico bicycle in 2.4 hours? _____ miles

8. Use estimation to show that your answer to **7** is reasonable.

   _____

Personal
Math Trainer
Online Assessment
and Intervention
my.hrw.com

1. Use the grid to multiply 0.4 × 0.7.
   (Explore Activity)

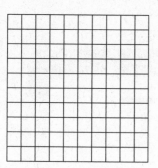

0.4 × 0.7 = _____

2. Draw an area model to multiply 1.1 × 2.4.
   (Explore Activity)

1.1 × 2.4 = _____

Multiply. (Example 1 and Example 2)

3. 0.18 × 0.06 = _____

4. 35.15 × 3.7 = _____

5. 0.96 × 0.12 = _____

6. 62.19 × 32.5 = _____

7. 3.4 × 4.37 = _____

8. 3.762 × 0.66 = _____

9. Chan Hee bought 3.4 pounds of coffee that cost $6.95 per pound.

   How much did he spend on coffee? $_____

10. Adita earns $9.40 per hour working at an animal shelter.

    How much money will she earn for 18.5 hours of work? $_____

Catherine tracked her gas purchases for one month.

11. How much did Catherine spend on gas in week 2?

    $_____

12. How much more did she spend in week 4 than

    in week 1? $_____

Week	Gallons	Cost per gallon ($)
1	10.4	2.65
2	11.5	2.54
3	9.72	2.75
4	10.6	2.70

? ESSENTIAL QUESTION CHECK-IN

13. How can you check the answer to a decimal multiplication problem?

    _____

    _____

5.3 Independent Practice

Personal Math Trainer

Online Assessment and Intervention

my.hrw.com

Make a reasonable estimate for each situation.

14. A gallon of water weighs 8.354 pounds. Simon uses 11.81 gallons of water while taking a shower. About how many pounds of water did Simon use?

_____

15. A snail moves at a speed of 2.394 inches per minute. If the snail keeps moving at this rate, about how many inches will it travel in 7.489 minutes?

_____

16. Tricia's garden is 9.87 meters long and 1.09 meters wide. What is the area of her garden?

_____

Kaylynn and Amanda both work at the same store. The table shows how much each person earns, and the number of hours each person works in a week.

	Wage	Hours worked per week
Kaylynn	$8.75 per hour	37.5
Amanda	$10.25 per hour	30.5

17. Estimate how much Kaylynn earns in a week.

_____

18. Estimate how much Amanda earns in a week.

_____

19. Calculate the exact difference between Kaylynn and Amanda's weekly salaries.

_____

20. Victoria's printer can print 8.804 pages in one minute. If Victoria prints pages for 0.903 minutes, about how many pages will she have?

_____

A taxi charges a flat fee of $4.00 plus $2.25 per mile.

21. How much will it cost to travel 8.7 miles? _____

22. **Multistep** How much will the taxi driver earn if he takes one passenger 4.8 miles and another passenger 7.3 miles? Explain your process.

_____

_____

_____

Kay goes for several bike rides one week. The table shows her speed and the number of hours spent per ride.

	Speed (in miles per hour)	Hours Spent on Bike
Monday	8.2	4.25
Tuesday	9.6	3.1
Wednesday	11.1	2.8
Thursday	10.75	1.9
Friday	8.8	3.75

23. How many miles did Kay bike on Thursday? _____

24. On which day did Kay bike a whole number of miles? _____

25. What is the difference in miles between Kay's longest bike ride and her shortest bike ride? _____

26. **Check for Reasonableness** Kay estimates that Wednesday's ride was about 3 miles longer than Tuesday's ride. Is her estimate reasonable? Explain.

_____

_____

_____

_____

 **FOCUS ON HIGHER ORDER THINKING**

27. **Explain the Error** To estimate the product 3.48 × 7.33, Marisa multiplied 4 × 8 to get 32. Explain how she can make a closer estimate.

_____

28. **Represent Real-World Problems** A jeweler buys gold jewelry and resells the gold to a refinery. The jeweler buys gold for $1,235.55 per ounce, and then resells it for $1,376.44 per ounce. How much profit does the jeweler make from buying and reselling 73.5 ounces of gold?

_____

29. **Problem Solving** To find the weight of the gold in a 22 karat gold object, multiply the object's weight by 0.917. To find the weight of the gold in an 14 karat gold object, multiply the object's weight by 0.583. A 22 karat gold statue and a 14 karat gold statue both weigh 73.5 ounces. Which one contains more gold? How much more gold does it contain?

_____

Work Area

LESSON
5.4 Dividing Decimals

? ESSENTIAL QUESTION

How do you divide decimals?

EXPLORE ACTIVITY

Modeling Decimal Division

Use decimal grids to find each quotient.

A $6.39 \div 3$

Shade grids to model 6.39. Separate the model into 3 equal groups.

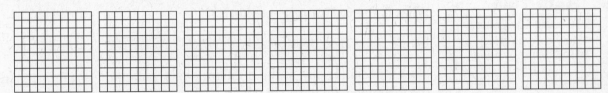

How many are in each group? _____

$6.39 \div 3 =$ _____

B $6.39 \div 2.13$

Shade grids to model 6.39. Separate the model into groups of 2.13.

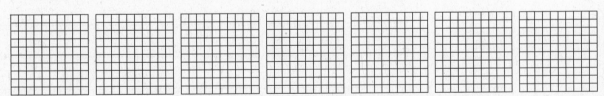

How many groups do you have? _____

$6.39 \div 2.13 =$ _____

Reflect

1. **Multiple Representations** When using models to divide decimals, when might you want to use grids divided into tenths instead of hundredths?

_____

_____

Math On the Spot

my.hrw.com

Dividing Decimals by Whole Numbers

Dividing decimals is similar to dividing whole numbers. When you divide a decimal by a whole number, the placement of the decimal point in the quotient is determined by the placement of the decimal in the dividend.

EXAMPLE 1

My Notes

A A high school track is 9.76 meters wide. It is divided into 8 lanes of equal width for track and field events. How wide is each lane?

Divide using long division as with whole numbers.

Place a decimal point in the quotient directly above the decimal point in the dividend.

Each lane is 1.22 meters wide.

$$
\begin{array}{r}
1.22 \\
8{\overline{\smash{)}\,9.76}} \\
\underline{-8} \\
1\ 7 \\
\underline{-1\ 6} \\
16 \\
\underline{-16} \\
0
\end{array}
$$

Math Talk

Mathematical Processes

How can you check to see that the answer is correct?

B Aerobics classes cost $153.86 for 14 sessions. What is the fee for one session?

Divide using long division as with whole numbers.

Place a decimal point in the quotient directly above the decimal point in the dividend.

The fee for one aerobics class is $10.99.

$$
\begin{array}{r}
10.99 \\
14{\overline{\smash{)}\,153.86}} \\
\underline{-14} \\
13 \\
\underline{-0} \\
13\ 8 \\
\underline{-12\ 6} \\
1\ 26 \\
\underline{-126} \\
0
\end{array}
$$

Reflect

2. **Check for Reasonableness** How can you estimate to check that your quotient in **A** is reasonable?

_____

_____

_____

_____

Personal Math Trainer

Online Assessment and Intervention

my.hrw.com

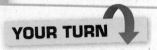

Divide.

3. $5{\overline{\smash{)}\,9.75}}$

4. $7{\overline{\smash{)}\,6.44}}$

Dividing a Decimal by a Decimal

When dividing a decimal by a decimal, first change the divisor to a whole number by multiplying by a power of 10. Then multiply the dividend by the same power of 10.

Math On the Spot
my.hrw.com

EXAMPLE 2

A **Ella uses 0.5 pound of raspberries in each raspberry cake that she makes. How many cakes can Ella make with 3.25 pounds of raspberries?**

STEP 1 The divisor has one decimal place, so multiply both the dividend and the divisor by 10 so that the divisor is a whole number.

$$0.5\overline{)3.25} \qquad 0.5\overline{)3.25}$$

$$0.5 \times 10 = 5$$

$$3.25 \times 10 = 32.5$$

Ella can make 6 cakes.

STEP 2 Divide.

```
      6.5
  5)32.5
    -30
      2 5
     -2 5
        0
```

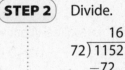
Math Talk
Mathematical Processes

The number of cakes Ella can make is not equal to the quotient. Why not?

B **Anthony spent $11.52 for some pens that were on sale for $0.72 each. How many pens did Anthony buy?**

STEP 1 The divisor has two decimal places, so multiply both the dividend and the divisor by 100 so that the divisor is a whole number.

$$0.72\overline{)11.52} \qquad 0.72\overline{)11.52}$$

$$0.72 \times 100 = 72$$

$$11.52 \times 100 = 1152$$

Anthony bought 16 pens.

STEP 2 Divide.

```
      16
 72)1152
   -72
    432
   -432
      0
```

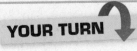
YOUR TURN

Divide.

5. $0.5\overline{)4.25}$ **6.** $0.84\overline{)15.12}$

Personal Math Trainer
Online Assessment and Intervention
my.hrw.com

Divide. (Explore Activity, Examples 1 and 2)

1. $4 \overline{)29.5}$ _____

2. $3.1 \overline{)10.261}$ _____

3. $2.4 \overline{)16.8}$ _____

4. $0.96 \overline{)0.144}$ _____

5. $38.5 \div 0.5 =$ _____

6. $23.85 \div 9 =$ _____

7. $5.6372 \div 0.17 =$ _____

8. $8.19 \div 4.2 =$ _____

9. $66.5 \div 3.5 =$ _____

10. $0.234 \div 0.78 =$ _____

11. $78.74 \div 12.7 =$ _____

12. $36.45 \div 0.09 =$ _____

13. $90 \div 0.36 =$ _____

14. $18.88 \div 1.6 =$ _____

15. Corrine has 9.6 pounds of trail mix to divide into 12 bags. How many pounds of trail mix will go in each bag? _____

16. Michael paid $11.48 for sliced cheese at the deli counter. The cheese cost $3.28 per pound. How much cheese did Michael buy? _____

17. A four-person relay team completed a race in 72.4 seconds. On average, what was each runner's time? _____

18. Elizabeth has a piece of ribbon that is 4.5 meters long. She wants to cut it into pieces that are 0.25 meter long. How many pieces of ribbon will she have? _____

19. Lisa paid $43.95 for 16.1 gallons of gasoline. What was the cost per gallon, rounded to the nearest hundredth? _____

20. One inch is equivalent to 2.54 centimeters. How many inches are there in 50.8 centimeters? _____

? ESSENTIAL QUESTION CHECK-IN

21. When you are dividing two decimals, how can you check whether you have divided the decimals correctly?

_____

_____

_____

_____

5.4 Independent Practice

Personal
Math Trainer

Online
Assessment and
Intervention

my.hrw.com

Use the table for 22 and 23.

Custom Printing Costs				
Quantity	25	50	75	100
Mugs	$107.25	$195.51	$261.75	$329.00
T-shirts	$237.50	$441.00	$637.50	$829.00

22. What is the price per mug for 25 coffee mugs? _____

23. Find the price per T-shirt for 75 T-shirts. _____

A movie rental website charges $5.00 per month for membership and $1.25 per movie.

24. How many movies did Andrew rent this month if this month's bill was $16.25? _____

25. Marissa has $18.50 this month to spend on movie rentals.

   a. How many movies can she view this month? _____

   b. **Critique Reasoning** Marisa thinks she can afford 11 movies in one month. What mistake could she be making?

   _____

   _____

Victoria went shopping for ingredients to make a stew. The table shows the weight and the cost of each of the ingredients that she bought.

Ingredient	Weight (in pounds)	Cost
Potatoes	6.3	$7.56
Carrots	8.5	$15.30
Beef	4	$9.56
Bell peppers	2.50	$1.25

26. What is the price for one pound of bell peppers? _____

27. Which ingredient costs the most per pound? _____

28. **What If?** If carrots were $0.50 less per pound, how much would Victoria have paid for 8.5 pounds of carrots? _____

29. Brenda is planning her birthday party. She wants to have 10.92 liters of punch, 6.5 gallons of ice cream, 3.9 pounds of fudge, and 25 guests at the birthday party.

    a. Brenda and each guest drink the same amount of punch. How many liters of punch will each person drink? _____

    b. Brenda and each guest eat the same amount of ice cream. How many gallons of ice cream will each person eat? _____

    c. Brenda and each guest eat the same amount of fudge. How many pounds of fudge will each person eat? _____

To make costumes for a play, Cassidy needs yellow and white fabric that she will cut into strips. The table shows how many yards of each fabric she needs, and how much she will pay for those yards.

Fabric	Yards	Cost
Yellow	12.8	$86.40
White	9.5	$45.60

30. Which costs more per yard, the yellow fabric or the white fabric? _____

31. Cassidy wants to cut the yellow fabric into strips that are 0.3 yards wide. How many strips of yellow fabric can Cassidy make? _____

H.O.T. **FOCUS ON HIGHER ORDER THINKING**

32. Problem Solving Eight friends purchase various supplies for a camping trip and agree to share the total cost equally. They spend $85.43 on food, $32.75 on water, and $239.66 on other items. How much does each person owe? _____

33. Analyze Relationships Constance is saving money to buy a new bicycle that costs $195.75. She already has $40 saved and plans to save $8 each week. How many weeks will it take her to save enough money to purchase the bicycle? _____

34. Represent Real-World Problems A grocery store sells twelve bottles of water for $13.80. A convenience store sells ten bottles of water for $11.80. Which store has the better buy? Explain.

_____

_____

_____

Applying Operations with Rational Numbers

6.2.5.5
Students will solve problems involving multiplication and division of fractions and decimals.

? ESSENTIAL QUESTION

How can you solve problems involving multiplication and division of fractions and decimals?

EXPLORE ACTIVITY Problem Solving

Interpreting a Word Problem

When you solve a word problem involving rational numbers, you often need to think about the problem to decide which operations to use.

EXAMPLE 1 **Naomi earned $54 mowing lawns in two days. She worked 2.5 hours yesterday and 4.25 hours today. If Naomi was paid the same amount for every hour she works, how much did she earn per hour?**

⬚ Analyze Information

Identify the important information.

- Naomi made _____ mowing lawns.
- Naomi worked _____ hours yesterday and _____ hours today.
- You are asked to find _____.

⬚ Formulate a Plan

- The total amount she earned divided by the total hours she worked gives the amount she earned per hour.
- Use the expression $54 \div (2.5 + 4.25)$ to find the amount she earned per hour.

⬚ Solve

Follow the order of operations.

Add inside parentheses. $(2.5 + 4.25) =$ _____

Divide. $54 \div 6.75 =$ _____

Naomi earned _____ per hour mowing lawns.

⬚ Justify and Evaluate

You added _____ and _____ first to find the total number of hours worked.
Then you divided _____ by the sum to find the amount earned per hour.

1. Casey buys 6.2 yards of blue fabric and 5.4 yards of red fabric. If the blue and red fabric cost the same amount per yard, and Casey pays $58 for all of the fabric, what is the cost per yard?

_____

Converting Fractions and Decimals to Solve Problems

Recall that you can use a number line to find equivalent fractions and decimals. If a fraction and a decimal are equivalent, they are represented by the same point on a number line.

EXAMPLE 2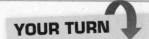

Each part of a multipart question on a test is worth the same number of points. The whole question is worth 37.5 points. Roz got $\frac{1}{2}$ of the parts of a question correct. How many points did Roz receive?

Solution 1

STEP 1 Convert the decimal to a fraction greater than 1.

$$\frac{1}{2} \times 37.5 = \frac{1}{2} \times \frac{75}{2} \qquad \textit{Write } 37.5 \textit{ as } 37\frac{1}{2}, \textit{ or } \frac{75}{2}.$$

STEP 2 Multiply. Write the product in simplest form.

$$\frac{1}{2} \times \frac{75}{2} = \frac{75}{4} = 18\frac{3}{4} \qquad \textit{Roz received } 18\frac{3}{4} \textit{ points.}$$

Solution 2

STEP 1 Convert the fraction to a decimal.

$$\frac{1}{2} \times 37.5 = 0.5 \times 37.5$$

STEP 2 Multiply.

$$0.5 \times 37.5 = 18.75 \qquad \textit{Roz received } 18.75 \textit{ points.}$$

Math Talk

Mathematical Processes

Do the solutions give the same result? Explain.

2. The bill for a pizza was $14.50. Charles paid for $\frac{3}{5}$ of the bill. Show two ways to find how much he paid.

_____

© Houghton Mifflin Harcourt Publishing Company

5.5 Guided Practice

1. Bob and Cheryl are taking a road trip that is 188.3 miles. Bob drove $\frac{5}{7}$ of the total distance. How many miles did Bob drive? (Explore Activity Example 1) _____

2. The winner of a raffle will receive $\frac{3}{4}$ of the $530.40 raised from raffle ticket sales. How much money will the winner get? (Example 2) _____

5.5 Independent Practice

Personal Math Trainer

Online Assessment and Intervention

my.hrw.com

3. Chanasia has 8.75 gallons of paint. She wants to use $\frac{2}{5}$ of the paint to paint her living room. How many gallons of paint will Chanasia use?

_____

4. Harold bought 3 pounds of red apples and 4.2 pounds of green apples from a grocery store, where both kinds of apples are $1.75 a pound. How much did Harold spend on apples?

_____

Samuel and Jason sell cans to a recycling center that pays $0.40 per pound of cans. The table shows the number of pounds of cans that they sold for several days.

Day	Samuel's cans (pounds)	Jason's cans (pounds)
Monday	16.2	11.5
Tuesday	11.8	10.7
Wednesday	12.5	7.1

5. Samuel wants to use his earnings from Monday and Tuesday to buy some batteries that cost $5.60 each. How many batteries can Samuel buy? Show your work.

_____

6. Jason wants to use his earnings from Monday and Tuesday for online movie rentals. The movies cost $2.96 each to rent. How many movies can Jason rent? Show your work.

_____

7. **Multistep** Samuel and Jason spend $\frac{3}{4}$ of their combined earnings from Wednesday to buy a gift. How much do they spend? Is there enough left over from Wednesday's earnings to buy a card that costs $3.25? Explain.

_____

_____

8. Multiple Representations Give an example of a problem that could be solved using the expression $9.5 \times (8 + 12.5)$. Solve your problem.

_____

_____

_____

_____

Tony and Alice are trying to reduce the amount of television they watch. For every hour they watch television, they have to put $2.50 into savings. The table shows how many hours of television Tony and Alice have watched in the past two months.

	Hours watched in February	Hours watched in March
Tony	35.4	18.2
Alice	21.8	26.6

9. Tony wants to use his savings at the end of March to buy video games. The games cost $35.75 each. How many games can Tony buy?

_____

10. Alice wants to use her savings at the end of the two months to buy concert tickets. If the tickets cost $17.50 each, how many can she buy?

_____

H.O.T. FOCUS ON HIGHER ORDER THINKING

Work Area

11. Represent Real-World Problems A caterer prepares three times as many pizzas as she usually prepares for a large party. The caterer usually prepares 5 pizzas. The caterer also estimates that each party guest will eat $\frac{1}{3}$ of a pizza. Write an expression that represents this situation. How many party guests will the pizzas serve?

_____

Nadia charges $7.50 an hour for babysitting. She babysits 18.5 hours the first week of the month and 20 hours the second week of the month.

12. Explain the Error To find her total earnings for those two weeks, Nadia writes $7.5 \times 18.5 + 20 = \$158.75$. Explain her error. Show the correct solution.

_____

_____

_____

13. What If? Suppose Nadia raises her rate by $0.75 an hour. How many hours would she need to work to earn the same amount of money she made in the first two weeks of the month? Explain.

_____

© Houghton Mifflin Harcourt Publishing Company • Image Credits:

Ready to Go On?

5.1 Dividing Whole Numbers

1. Landon is building new bookshelves for his bookstore's new mystery section. Each shelf can hold 34 books. There are 1,265 mystery books. How many shelves will he need to build? _____

5.2 Adding and Subtracting Decimals

2. On Saturday Keisha ran 3.218 kilometers. On Sunday she ran 2.41 kilometers. How much farther did she run on Saturday than on Sunday? _____

5.3 Multiplying Decimals

3. Marta walked at 3.9 miles per hour for 0.72 hours. How far did she walk? _____

Multiply.

4. 0.07×1.22 _____   **5.** 4.7×2.65 _____

5.4 Dividing Decimals

Divide.

6. $64 \div 0.4$ _____   **7.** $4.7398 \div 0.26$ _____

8. $26.73 \div 9$ _____   **9.** $4 \div 3.2$ _____

5.5 Applying Multiplication and Division of Rational Numbers

10. Doors for the small cabinets are 11.5 inches long. Doors for the large cabinets are 2.3 times as long as the doors for the small cabinets. How many large doors can be cut from a board that is $10\frac{1}{2}$ feet long? _____

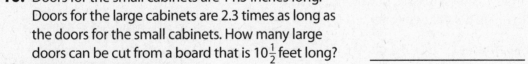

ESSENTIAL QUESTION

11. Describe a real-world situation that could be modeled by dividing two rational numbers.

_____

_____

Assessment Readiness

Selected Response

1. Delia has 493 stamps in her stamp collection. She can put 16 stamps on each page of an album. How many pages can she fill completely?

Ⓐ 30 pages   Ⓒ 31 pages

Ⓑ 32 pages   Ⓓ 33 pages

2. Sumeet uses 0.4 gallon of gasoline each hour mowing lawns. How much gas does he use in 4.2 hours?

Ⓐ 1.68 gallons

Ⓑ 3.8 gallons

Ⓒ 13 gallons

Ⓓ 16 gallons

3. Sharon spent $3.45 on sunflower seeds. The price of sunflower seeds is $0.89 per pound. How many pounds of sunflower seeds did Sharon buy?

Ⓐ 3.07 pounds

Ⓑ 3.88 pounds

Ⓒ 4.15 pounds

Ⓓ 4.34 pounds

4. How many 0.4-liter glasses of water does it take to fill up a 3.4-liter pitcher?

Ⓐ 1.36 glasses   Ⓒ 8.2 glasses

Ⓑ 3.8 glasses   Ⓓ 8.5 glasses

5. Each paper clip is $\frac{3}{4}$ of an inch long and costs $0.02. Exactly enough paper clips are laid end to end to have a total length of 36 inches. What is the total cost of these paper clips?

Ⓐ $0.36   Ⓒ $0.96

Ⓑ $0.54   Ⓓ $1.20

6. Nelson Middle School raised $19,950 on ticket sales for its carnival fundraiser last year at $15 per ticket. If the school sells the same number of tickets this year but charges $20 per ticket, how much money will the school make?

Ⓐ $20,600   Ⓒ $26,600

Ⓑ $21,600   Ⓓ $30,600

7. Keri walks her dog every morning. The length of the walk is 0.55 kilometer on each weekday. On each weekend day, the walk is 1.4 times as long as a walk on a weekday. How many kilometers does Keri walk in one week?

Ⓐ 2.75 kilometers

Ⓑ 3.85 kilometers

Ⓒ 4.29 kilometers

Ⓓ 5.39 kilometers

Mini-Task

8. To prepare for a wedding, Aiden bought 60 candles. He paid $0.37 for each candle. His sister bought 170 candles at a sale where she paid $0.05 less for each candle than Aiden did.

a. How much did Aiden spend on candles?

_____

b. How much did Aiden's sister spend on candles?

_____

c. Who spent more on candles? How much more?

_____

Study Guide Review

Key Vocabulary
reciprocals (recíprocos)

? ESSENTIAL QUESTION

How can you use operations with fractions to solve real-world problems?

EXAMPLE 1

Add.

$\frac{7}{9} + \frac{5}{12}$ The LCM of 9 and 12 is 36.

$\frac{7 \times 4}{9 \times 4} + \frac{5 \times 3}{12 \times 3}$ Use the LCM to make fractions with common denominators.

$\frac{28}{36} + \frac{15}{36} = \frac{43}{36}$ Simplify.

$\frac{43}{36} = 1\frac{7}{36}$

Subtract.

$\frac{9}{10} - \frac{5}{6}$ The LCM of 10 and 6 is 30.

$\frac{9 \times 3}{10 \times 3} - \frac{5 \times 5}{6 \times 5}$ Use the LCM to make fractions with common denominators.

$\frac{27}{30} - \frac{25}{30} = \frac{2}{30}$ Simplify.

$\frac{2}{30} = \frac{1}{15}$

EXAMPLE 2

Multiply.

A. $\frac{4}{5} \times \frac{1}{8}$

$\frac{4 \times 1}{5 \times 8} = \frac{4}{40}$ Multiply numerators.
Multiply denominators.

$\frac{4 \div 4}{40 \div 4} = \frac{1}{10}$ Simplify by dividing by the GCF.

B. $2\frac{1}{4} \times \frac{1}{5}$

$\frac{9}{4} \times \frac{1}{5}$ Rewrite the mixed number as a fraction greater than 1.

$\frac{9 \times 1}{4 \times 5} = \frac{9}{20}$ Multiply numerators.
Multiply denominators.

EXAMPLE 3

Divide.

A. $\frac{2}{7} \div \frac{1}{2}$

$\frac{2}{7} \times \frac{2}{1}$ Rewrite the problem as multiplication using the reciprocal of the second fraction.

$\frac{2 \times 2}{7 \times 1} = \frac{4}{7}$ Multiply numerators.
Multiply denominators.

B. $2\frac{1}{3} \div 1\frac{3}{4}$

$\frac{7}{3} \div \frac{7}{4}$ Write both mixed numbers as improper fractions.

$\frac{{}^1\cancel{7} \times 4}{3 \times \cancel{7}_1} = \frac{4}{3}$ Multiply by the reciprocal of the second fraction.

$1\frac{1}{3}$ Simplify: $\frac{4}{3} = 1\frac{1}{3}$

EXERCISES

Add. Write the answer in simplest form. (Lesson 4.1)

1. $\frac{3}{8} + \frac{4}{5}$ _____

2. $1\frac{9}{10} + \frac{3}{4}$ _____

3. $\frac{2}{8} + \frac{6}{12}$ _____

Subtract. Write the answer in simplest form. (Lesson 4.1)

4. $1\frac{3}{7} - \frac{4}{5}$ _____

5. $\frac{7}{8} - \frac{5}{12}$ _____

6. $3\frac{5}{10} - \frac{4}{8}$ _____

Multiply. Write the answer in simplest form. (Lesson 4.1)

7. $\frac{1}{7} \times \frac{4}{5}$ _____

8. $\frac{5}{6} \times \frac{2}{3}$ _____

9. $\frac{3}{7} \times \frac{14}{15}$ _____

10. $1\frac{1}{3} \times \frac{5}{8}$ _____

11. $1\frac{2}{9} \times 1\frac{1}{2}$ _____

12. $2\frac{1}{7} \times 3\frac{2}{3}$ _____

Divide. Write the answer in simplest form. (Lessons 4.2, 4.3)

13. $\frac{3}{7} \div \frac{2}{3}$ _____

14. $\frac{1}{8} \div \frac{3}{4}$ _____

15. $1\frac{1}{5} \div \frac{1}{4}$ _____

16. On his twelfth birthday, Ben was $4\frac{3}{4}$ feet tall. On his thirteenth birthday, Ben was $5\frac{3}{8}$ feet tall. How much did Ben grow between his twelfth and thirteenth birthdays? (Lesson 4.1)

_____

17. Ron had 20 apples. He used $\frac{2}{5}$ of the apples to make pies. How many apples did Ron use for pies? (Lesson 4.4)

_____

18. The area of a rectangular garden is $38\frac{1}{4}$ square meters. The width of the garden is $4\frac{1}{2}$ meters. Find the length of the garden. (Lesson 4.4)

_____

MODULE 5

Operations with Decimals

Key Vocabulary
order of operations (orden de las operaciones)

? ESSENTIAL QUESTION

How can you use operations with decimals to solve real-world problems?

EXAMPLE 1

To prepare for a race, Lloyd ran every day for two weeks. He ran a total of 67,592 meters. Lloyd ran the same distance every day. He took a two-day rest and then started running again. The first day after his rest, he ran the same distance plus 1,607.87 meters more. How far did Lloyd run that day?

Step 1 Divide to see how far Lloyd ran every day during the two weeks.

$$\begin{array}{r} 4,828 \\ 14\overline{)67,592} \end{array}$$

Lloyd ran 4,828 meters a day.

Step 2 Add 1,607.87 to 4,828 to find out how far Lloyd ran the first day after his rest.

$$\begin{array}{r} 1,607.87 \\ + 4,828.00 \\ \hline 6,435.87 \end{array}$$

Lloyd ran 6,435.87 meters that day.

© Houghton Mifflin Harcourt Publishing Company

EXAMPLE 2

Rebecca bought 2.5 pounds of red apples. The apples cost $0.98 per pound. What was the total cost of Rebecca's apples?

$$
\begin{array}{r}
2.5 \quad \leftarrow \quad \text{1 decimal place} \\
\times\ .98 \quad \leftarrow\ +\text{2 decimal places} \\
\hline
200 \\
+\ 2250 \\
\hline
2.450 \quad \leftarrow \quad \text{3 decimal places}
\end{array}
$$

The apples cost $2.45.

EXAMPLE 3

Rashid spent $37.29 on gas for his car. Gas was $3.39 per gallon. How many gallons did Rashid purchase?

Step 1 The divisor has two decimal places, so multiply both the dividend and the divisor by 100 so that the divisor is a whole number:

$$3.39\overline{)37.29} \qquad 339\overline{)3729}$$

Step 2 Divide:

$$
\begin{array}{r}
11 \\
339\overline{)3729} \\
-339 \\
\hline
339 \\
-339 \\
\hline
0
\end{array}
$$

Rashid purchased 11 gallons of gas.

EXERCISES

Add. (Lesson 5.2)

1. $12.24 + 3.9$ _____

2. $0.986 + 0.342$ _____

3. $2.479 + 0.31$ _____

Subtract. (Lesson 5.2)

4. $6.19 - 3.05$ _____

5. $7.285 - 0.975$ _____

6. $14.31 - 13.41$ _____

Multiply. (Lesson 5.3)

7. $\begin{array}{r} 12 \\ \times 0.4 \end{array}$ _____

8. $\begin{array}{r} 0.15 \\ \times\ 9.1 \end{array}$ _____

9. $\begin{array}{r} 3.12 \\ \times 0.25 \end{array}$ _____

Divide. (Lessons 5.1, 5.4)

10. $78,974 \div 21$ _____

11. $19,975 \div 25$ _____

12. $67,396 \div 123$ _____

13. $5\overline{)64.5}$ _____

14. $0.6\overline{)25.2}$ _____

15. $2.1\overline{)36.75}$ _____

16. A pound of rice crackers costs $2.88. Matthew purchased $\frac{1}{4}$ pound of crackers. How much did he pay for the crackers? (Lesson 5.5) _____

Unit 2 Performance Tasks

1. **CAREERS IN MATH**   **Chef**   Chef Alonso is creating a recipe called Spicy Italian Chicken with the following ingredients: $\frac{3}{4}$ pound chicken, $2\frac{1}{2}$ cups tomato sauce, 1 teaspoon oregano, and $\frac{1}{2}$ teaspoon of his special hot sauce.

   a. Chef Alonso wants each serving of the dish to include $\frac{1}{2}$ pound of chicken. How many $\frac{1}{2}$ pound servings does this recipe make?

   _____

   b. What is the number Chef Alonso should multiply the amount of chicken by so that the recipe will make 2 full servings, each with $\frac{1}{2}$ pound of chicken?

   _____

   c. Use the multiplier you found in part **b** to find the amount of all the ingredients in the new recipe.

   _____

   d. Chef Alonso only has three measuring spoons: 1 teaspoon, $\frac{1}{2}$ teaspoon, and $\frac{1}{4}$ teaspoon. Can he measure the new amounts of oregano and hot sauce exactly? Explain why or why not.

   _____

   _____

2. Amira is painting a rectangular banner $2\frac{1}{4}$ yards wide on a wall in the cafeteria. The banner will have a blue background. Amira has enough blue paint to cover $1\frac{1}{2}$ square yards of wall.

   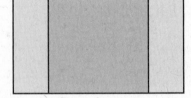

   a. Find the height of the banner if Amira uses all of the blue paint. Show your work.

   _____

   b. The school colors are blue and yellow, so Amira wants to add yellow rectangles on the left and right sides of the blue rectangle. The yellow rectangles will each be $\frac{3}{4}$ yard wide and the same height as the blue rectangle. What will be the total area of the two yellow rectangles? Explain how you found your answer.

   _____

   _____

   c. What are the dimensions of the banner plus yellow rectangles? What is the total area? Show your work.

   _____

   _____

Assessment Readiness

Selected Response

1. Each paper clip is $\frac{7}{8}$ of an inch long and costs $0.03. Exactly enough paper clips are laid end to end to have a total length of 56 inches. What is the total cost of these paper clips?

   Ⓐ $0.49   Ⓒ $1.47

   Ⓑ $0.64   Ⓓ $1.92

2. Which of these is the same as $\frac{8}{9} \div \frac{2}{3}$?

   Ⓐ $\frac{8}{9} \div \frac{3}{2}$ Ⓒ $\frac{8}{9} \times \frac{2}{3}$

   Ⓑ $\frac{2}{3} \div \frac{8}{9}$ Ⓓ $\frac{8}{9} \times \frac{3}{2}$

3. A rectangular tabletop has a length of $4\frac{3}{4}$ feet and an area of $11\frac{7}{8}$ square feet. What is the width of the tabletop?

   Ⓐ $1\frac{1}{16}$ feet

   Ⓑ $2\frac{1}{2}$ feet

   Ⓒ $4\frac{1}{4}$ feet

   Ⓓ $8\frac{1}{2}$ feet

4. Dorothy types 120 words per minute. How many words does Dorothy type in 1.75 minutes?

   Ⓐ 150 words

   Ⓑ 180 words

   Ⓒ 200 words

   Ⓓ 210 words

5. What is the opposite of 17?

   Ⓐ -17

   Ⓑ $-\frac{1}{17}$

   Ⓒ $\frac{1}{17}$

   Ⓓ 17

6. What is the absolute value of -36?

   Ⓐ -36

   Ⓑ 0

   Ⓒ 6

   Ⓓ 36

7. Noelle has $\frac{5}{6}$ of a yard of purple ribbon and $\frac{9}{10}$ of a yard of pink ribbon. How much ribbon does she have altogether?

   Ⓐ $1\frac{11}{15}$ yards   Ⓒ $2\frac{1}{5}$ yards

   Ⓑ $1\frac{4}{5}$ yards   Ⓓ $1\frac{14}{16}$ yards

8. Apples are on sale for $1.20 a pound. Logan bought $\frac{3}{4}$ of a pound. How much money did he spend on apples?

   Ⓐ $0.75   Ⓒ $0.90

   Ⓑ $0.80   Ⓓ $1.00

9. Samantha bought 4.5 pounds of pears. Each pound cost $1.68. How much did Samantha spend in all?

   Ⓐ $7.52   Ⓒ $8.40

   Ⓑ $7.56   Ⓓ $75.60

10. Gillian earns $7.50 an hour babysitting on the weekends. Last week she babysat for 2.2 hours on Saturday and 3.5 hours on Sunday. How much did Gillian earn?

    Ⓐ $4.25   Ⓒ $42.75

    Ⓑ $40.25   Ⓓ $427.50

11. Luis made some trail mix. He mixed $4\frac{2}{3}$ cups of popcorn, $1\frac{1}{4}$ cups of peanuts, $1\frac{1}{3}$ cups of raisins, and $\frac{3}{4}$ cup of sunflower seeds. He gave 5 of his friends an equal amount of trail mix each. How much did each friend get?

    Ⓐ $1\frac{3}{5}$ cups   Ⓒ $1\frac{3}{4}$ cups

    Ⓑ $1\frac{2}{3}$ cups   Ⓓ 2 cups

12. Emily cycled 20.25 miles over 4 days last week. She cycled the same amount each day. How many miles did Emily cycle each day to the nearest hundredth?

Ⓐ 5.01 miles   Ⓒ 5.60 miles

Ⓑ 5.06 miles   Ⓓ 5.65 miles

13. Landon drove 103.5 miles on Tuesday, 320.75 miles on Wednesday, and 186.30 miles on Thursday. How far did Landon drive all three days combined?

Ⓐ 61.55 miles   Ⓒ 610.55 miles

Ⓑ 610.055 miles   Ⓓ 6,105.5 miles

Mini Task

14. Carl earns \$3.25 per hour walking his neighbor's dogs. He walks them $\frac{1}{3}$ of an hour in the morning and $\frac{1}{2}$ of an hour in the afternoon.

a. How much time does Carl spend dog walking every day?

_____

b. How much time does Carl spend dog walking in a week?

_____

c. Ten minutes is equal to $\frac{1}{6}$ of an hour. How many minutes does Carl work dog walking each week?

_____

d. How much money does Carl earn each week?

_____

15. The city zoo had an equal number of visitors on Saturday and Sunday. In all, 32,096 people visited the zoo that weekend. How many visited each day?

_____

a. On Saturday, $\frac{1}{8}$ of the people who visited were senior citizens, $\frac{1}{8}$ were infants, $\frac{1}{4}$ were children, and $\frac{1}{2}$ were adults. How many of each group visited the zoo on Saturday?

Senior Citizens: _____

Infants: _____

Children: _____

Adults: _____

b. On Sunday, $\frac{1}{16}$ of the people who visited were senior citizens, $\frac{3}{16}$ were infants, $\frac{3}{8}$ were children, and $\frac{3}{8}$ were adults. How many of each group visited the zoo on Sunday?

Senior Citizens: _____

Infants: _____

Children: _____

Adults: _____

c. The chart shows how much each type of ticket costs.

Type of Ticket	Cost
Infants	Free
Children Over 2	$4.50
Adults	$7.25
Senior Citizens	$5.75

d. How much money did the zoo make on Saturday? Show your work.

_____

_____

_____

e. How much did the zoo make on Sunday?

_____

_____

_____

_____

Proportionality: Ratios and Rates

CAREERS IN MATH

Residential Builder A residential builder, also called a homebuilder, specializes in the construction of residences that range from single-family custom homes to buildings that contain multiple housing units, such as apartments and condominiums. Residential builders use math in numerous ways, such as blueprint reading, measuring and scaling, using ratios and rates to calculate the amounts of different building materials needed, and estimating costs for jobs.

If you are interested in a career as a residential builder, you should study these mathematical subjects:

- Algebra
- Geometry
- Business Math
- Technical Math

Research other careers that require using ratios and rates, and measuring and scaling.

Unit 3 Performance Task

At the end of the unit, check out how **residential builders** use math.

Vocabulary Preview

Use the puzzle to preview key vocabulary from this unit. Unscramble the circled letters within found words to answer the riddle at the bottom of the page.

Down

1. A rate that describes how much smaller or larger the scale drawing is than the real object. (Lesson 7.2)

4. A comparison by division of two quantities (Lesson 6.1)

5. Ratio of two quantities that have different units. (Lesson 6.2)

Across

1. Drawing that uses a scale to make an object proportionally smaller or larger than the real object. (Lesson 7.2)

2. A rate in which the second quantity is one unit. (Lesson 6.2)

3. A fraction that compares two equivalent measurements. (Lesson 7.3)

6. An equation that states two ratios are equivalent. (Lesson 7.2)

Q: Why was the draftsman excited that the raffle prize was a weighing device?

A: It was a ___ ___ ___ ___ ___ – ___ ___ ___ ___ ___ ___ ___!

Representing Ratios and Rates

ESSENTIAL QUESTION

How can you use ratios and rates to solve real-world problems?

Real-World Video

Scientists studying sand structures determined that the perfect sand and water mixture is equal to 1 bucket of water for every 100 buckets of sand. This recipe can be written as the ratio $\frac{1}{100}$.

ⓜ my.hrw.com

GO DIGITAL

my.hrw.com

my.hrw.com

Go digital with your write-in student edition, accessible on any device.

Math On the Spot

Scan with your smart phone to jump directly to the online edition, video tutor, and more.

Animated Math

Interactively explore key concepts to see how math works.

Personal Math Trainer

Get immediate feedback and help as you work through practice sets.

Reading Start-Up

Visualize Vocabulary

Use the ✔ words to complete the chart. Choose the review words that describe multiplication and division.

Understanding Multiplication and Division		
Symbol	**Operation**	**Term for the answer**
×		
÷		

Understand Vocabulary

Match the term on the left to the definition on the right.

1. rate

2. ratio

3. unit rate

4. equivalent ratios

A. Rate in which the second quantity is one unit.

B. Comparison of two quantities by division.

C. Ratios that name the same comparison.

D. Ratio of two quantities that have different units.

Active Reading

Two-Panel Flip Chart Create a two-panel flip chart, to help you understand the concepts in this module. Label one flap "Ratios" and the other flap "Rates." As you study each lesson, write important ideas under the appropriate flap. Include information about unit rates and any sample equations that will help you remember the concepts when you look back at your notes.

Are YOU Ready?

Complete these exercises to review skills you will need for this module.

Simplify Fractions

EXAMPLE   Simplify $\frac{15}{24}$.

15: 1, ③, 5, 15
24: 1, 2, ③, 4, 6, 8, 12, 24

$\frac{15 \div 3}{24 \div 3} = \frac{5}{8}$

List all the factors of the numerator and denominator.

Circle the greatest common factor (GCF).

Divide the numerator and denominator by the GCF.

Write each fraction in simplest form.

1. $\frac{6}{9}$ _____

2. $\frac{4}{10}$ _____

3. $\frac{15}{20}$ _____

4. $\frac{20}{24}$ _____

5. $\frac{16}{56}$ _____

6. $\frac{45}{72}$ _____

7. $\frac{18}{60}$ _____

8. $\frac{32}{72}$ _____

Write Equivalent Fractions

EXAMPLE $\frac{6}{8} = \frac{6 \times 2}{8 \times 2}$ Multiply the numerator and denominator by the same number to find an equivalent fraction.

$= \frac{12}{16}$

$\frac{6}{8} = \frac{6 \div 2}{8 \div 2}$ Divide the numerator and denominator by the same number to find an equivalent fraction.

$= \frac{3}{4}$

Write the equivalent fraction.

9. $\frac{12}{15} = \frac{\square}{5}$

10. $\frac{5}{6} = \frac{\square}{30}$

11. $\frac{16}{24} = \frac{4}{\square}$

12. $\frac{3}{9} = \frac{21}{\square}$

13. $\frac{15}{40} = \frac{\square}{8}$

14. $\frac{18}{30} = \frac{\square}{10}$

15. $\frac{48}{64} = \frac{12}{\square}$

16. $\frac{2}{7} = \frac{18}{\square}$

Complete these exercises to review skills you will need for this module.

Simplify Fractions

17. When a fraction cannot be simplified, what must be true about the greatest common factor of the numerator and denominator?

18. Ernesto's bus arrived 51 minutes after he got to the bus stop. Determine what fraction of an hour Ernesto spent waiting for the bus. Write the fraction in simplest form.

Write Equivalent Fractions

19. Lina wants to find the least common denominator of $\frac{4}{32}$ and $\frac{5}{8}$ so that she can add the fractions. What is the least common denominator? Rewrite the fractions with a common denominator. Explain your reasoning.

20. Write equivalent fractions for $\frac{3}{4}$, $\frac{10}{24}$, and $\frac{5}{6}$ so that each one has a denominator of 12. Then order the original fractions from least to greatest.

6.1 Ratios

6.3.6.1

Students will use ratios to compare two quantities.

? ESSENTIAL QUESTION

How do you use ratios to compare two quantities?

EXPLORE ACTIVITY

Representing Ratios with Models

A **ratio** is a comparison of two quantities. It shows how many times as great one quantity is than another.

For example, the ratio of star-shaped beads to moon-shaped beads in a bracelet is 3 to 1.

A Write the ratio of moon beads to star beads.   _____

B Write the ratio of moon beads to all the beads.   _____

C If the bracelet has 2 moon beads, how many star beads does it have? _____

D If the bracelet has 9 star beads, how many moon beads does it have?
How do you know?

_____

_____

_____

Reflect

1. **Make a Prediction** Write a rule that you can use to find the number of star beads in a bracelet when you know the number of moon beads. Then write a rule that you can use to find the number of moon beads when you know the number of star beads.

_____

_____

_____

2. **Make a Prediction** Write a rule that you can use to find the total number of beads in a bracelet when you know the number of moon beads.

_____

Math On the Spot

my.hrw.com

Writing Ratios

The numbers in a ratio are called *terms*. A ratio can be written in several different ways.

| 5 dogs to 3 cats | 5 to 3 | 5:3 | $\frac{5}{3}$ |

A ratio can compare a part to a part, a part to the whole, or the whole to a part.

EXAMPLE 1

A Write the ratio of comedies to dramas in three different ways.

part to part

8:3 $\frac{8}{3}$ 8 comedies to 3 dramas

Sam's Video Collection	
Comedies	8
Dramas	3
Cartoons	2
Science Fiction	1

B Write the ratio of dramas to total videos in three different ways.

part to whole

3:14 $\frac{3}{14}$ 3 dramas to 14 total videos

> The total number of videos is $8 + 3 + 2 + 1 = 14$.

Math Talk
Mathematical Processes

What is the ratio of videos that are dramas to videos that are not dramas? Is this a part to part or part to whole ratio?

Reflect

3. **Analyze Relationships** Describe the relationship between the drama videos and the science fiction videos.

_____

_____

4. **Analyze Relationships** The ratio of floor seats to balcony seats in a theater is 20:1. Does this theater have more floor seats or more balcony seats? How do you know?

_____

Personal Math Trainer

Online Assessment and Intervention

my.hrw.com

YOUR TURN

Write each ratio in three different ways.

5. bagel chips to peanuts _____

6. total party mix to pretzels _____

7. cheese crackers to peanuts _____

Party Mix Makes 8 cups
3 cups pretzels
3 cups bagel chips
1 cup cheese crackers
1 cup peanuts

© Houghton Mifflin Harcourt Publishing Company

Equivalent Ratios

Equivalent ratios are ratios that name the same comparison. You can find equivalent ratios by using a table or by multiplying or dividing both terms of a ratio by the same number. So, equivalent ratios have a multiplicative relationship.

Math On the Spot
my.hrw.com

A ratio with terms that have no common factors is said to be in simplest form.

EXAMPLE 2

You make 5 cups of punch by mixing 3 cups of cranberry juice with 2 cups of apple juice. How much cranberry juice and how much apple juice do you need to make four times the original recipe?

Method 1   Use a table.

STEP 1   Make a table comparing the number of cups of cranberry juice and apple juice needed to make two times, three times, and four times the original recipe.

> Multiply both terms of the original ratio by the same number to find an equivalent ratio.

$$3 \times 2 \quad 3 \times 3 \quad 3 \times 4$$

Cranberry Juice	3	6	9	12
Apple Juice	2	4	6	8

$$2 \times 2 \quad 2 \times 3 \quad 2 \times 4$$

STEP 2   Write the original ratio and the ratio that shows the amount of cranberry juice and apple juice needed to make four times the original recipe.

$$\frac{3}{2} = \frac{12}{8}$$

You will need 12 cups of cranberry juice and 8 cups of apple juice.

Method 2   Multiply both terms of the ratio by the same number.

STEP 1   Write the original ratio in fraction form.

$$\frac{3}{2}$$

STEP 2   Multiply the numerator and denominator by the same number.

To make four times the original recipe, multiply by 4.

$$\frac{3}{2} \quad \overset{\times 4}{\underset{\times 4}{}} \quad \frac{12}{8}$$

To make four times the original recipe, you will need 12 cups of cranberry juice and 8 cups of apple juice.

Math Talk
Mathematical Processes

The ratio of apple juice to grape juice in a recipe is 8 cups to 10 cups. What is this ratio in simplest form? Explain.

YOUR TURN

Write three ratios equivalent to the given ratio.

8. $\frac{8}{10}$ _____

9. $\frac{5}{2}$ _____

Guided Practice

The number of dogs compared to the number of cats in an apartment complex is represented by the model shown. (Explore Activity)

1. Write a ratio that compares the number of dogs to the number of cats. _____

2. If there are 15 cats in the apartment complex, how many dogs are there?

   15 ÷ _____ **=** _____ **dogs**

3. How many cats are there if there are 5 dogs in the apartment complex?

   5 × _____ **=** _____ **cats**

4. The only pets in the apartment complex are cats and dogs. If there are 10 dogs, how many *pets* are there? _____

The contents of Dana's box of muffins are shown. Write each ratio in three different ways. (Example 1)

5. banana nut muffins to corn muffins _____

6. corn muffins to total muffins _____

Dana's Dozen Muffins
5 corn
4 bran
2 banana nut
1 blueberry

Vocabulary Write three equivalent ratios for the given ratio. Circle the simplest form of the ratio. (Example 2)

7. $\frac{10}{12}$ _____

8. $\frac{14}{2}$ _____

9. $\frac{4}{7}$ _____

? **ESSENTIAL QUESTION CHECK-IN**

10. Use an example to describe the multiplicative relationship between two equivalent ratios.

_____

_____

6.1 Independent Practice

Write three ratios equivalent to the ratio described in each situation.

11. The ratio of cups of water to cups of milk in a recipe is 1 to 3.

_____

12. The ratio of boys to girls on the bus is $\frac{20}{15}$.

_____

13. In each bouquet of flowers, there are 4 roses and 6 white carnations. Complete the table to find how many roses and carnations there are in 4 bouquets of flowers.

Roses	4			
Carnations	6			

_____

14. Ed is using the recipe shown to make fruit salad. He wants to use 30 diced strawberries in his fruit salad. How many bananas, apples, and pears should Ed use in his fruit salad?

_____

Fruit Salad Recipe
4 bananas, diced
3 apples, diced
6 pears, diced
10 strawberries, diced

15. A collector has 120 movie posters and 100 band posters. She wants to sell 24 movie posters but still have her poster collection maintain the same ratio of 120:100. If she sells 24 movie posters, how many band posters should she sell? Explain.

_____

_____

_____

16. Bob needs to mix 2 cups of orange juice concentrate with 3.5 cups of water to make orange juice. Bob has 6 cups of concentrate. How much orange juice can he make? _____

17. **Multistep** The ratio of North American butterflies to South American butterflies at a butterfly park is 5:3. The ratio of South American butterflies to European butterflies is 3:2. There are 30 North American butterflies at the butterfly park.

a. How many South American butterflies are there? _____

b. How many European butterflies are there? _____

18. Sinea and Ren are going to the carnival next week. The table shows the amount that each person spent on snacks, games, and souvenirs the last time they went to the carnival.

	Snacks	Games	Souvenirs
Sinea	$5	$8	$12
Ren	$10	$8	$20

a. Sinea wants to spend money using the same ratios as on her last trip to the carnival. If she spends $26 on games, how much will she spend on souvenirs? _____

b. Ren wants to spend money using the same ratios as on his last trip to the carnival. If he spends $5 on souvenirs, how much will he spend on snacks? _____

c. **What If?** Suppose Sinea and Ren each spend $40 on snacks, and each person spends money using the same ratios as on their last trip. Who spends more on souvenirs? Explain.

_____

_____

_____

 FOCUS ON HIGHER ORDER THINKING

19. **Multiple Representations** The diagram compares the ratio of girls in the chorus to boys in the chorus. What is the ratio of girls to boys? If there are 50 students in the chorus, how many are girls and how many are boys?

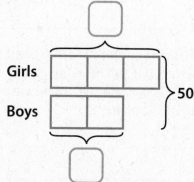

_____

20. **Analyze Relationships** How is the process of finding equivalent ratios like the process of finding equivalent fractions?

_____

_____

21. **Explain the Error** Tina says that 6:8 is equivalent to 36:64. What did Tina do wrong?

_____

_____

R·A·T·I·O

Playing the Game

STEP 1 To begin, place one of the sliders in the "1" position on the shaded slide row and the other in the "1" position on the unshaded slide row.

STEP 2 Move one slider to a new position so that the slide rows form a ratio that is illustrated by an open space on the gameboard, and place a game piece on the space. You may not reduce a ratio to create an equivalent ratio.

For example, assume that the previous turn ended with the slider on 2 for the shaded number and 4 for the unshaded number to form the ratio 2:4. On this turn, a player moves the unshaded slider to 3 to form the ratio 2:3.

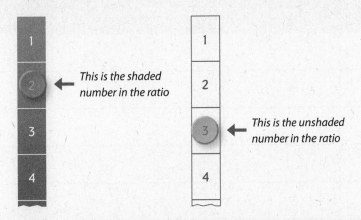

This is the shaded number in the ratio

This is the unshaded number in the ratio

STEP 3 Record the ratio in your table. You can write the comparison as unshaded to shaded, shaded to unshaded, unshaded:shaded, shaded:unshaded, $\frac{\text{unshaded}}{\text{shaded}}$, or $\frac{\text{shaded}}{\text{unshaded}}$.

Round	Comparison	Ratio
1	shaded:unshaded	2:3

STEP 4 Alternate turns with your opponent.

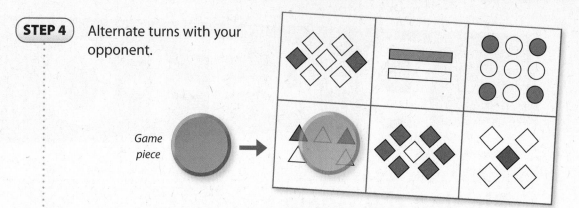

Game piece

STEP 5 You must move exactly one slider on each turn, and you must try to form a ratio whose illustration is not yet covered with a game piece, even if doing so may give your opponent an advantage. Even if you cannot form a new ratio by moving only one slider, you must move one slider before your opponent's turn.

Winning the Game

The first player to claim four spaces in a row, either horizontally, vertically, or diagonally, wins.

Round	Comparison	Ratio
1		
2		
3		
4		
5		
6		
7		
8		
9		
10		

? **ESSENTIAL QUESTION**

How do you use rates to compare quantities?

EXPLORE ACTIVITY Real World

Using Rates to Compare Prices

A **rate** is a comparison of two quantities that have different units.

Chris drove 107 miles in two hours. This can be expressed as the rate shown at the right. Notice that the units are different: miles and hours.

The rate is $\frac{107 \text{ miles}}{2 \text{ hours}}$.

Shana is at the grocery store comparing two brands of juice. Brand A costs $3.84 for a 16-ounce bottle. Brand B costs $4.50 for a 25-ounce bottle.

To compare the costs, Shana must compare prices for equal amounts of juice. How can she do this?

A Complete the tables.

Brand A	
Ounces	Price ($)
16	3.84
8	1.92
4	
2	
1	

÷ 2 (applied between rows) ÷ 2

Brand B	
Ounces	Price ($)
25	4.50
5	
1	

÷ 5 (applied between rows) ÷ 5

B Brand A costs $ _____ per ounce. Brand B costs $ _____ per ounce.

C Which brand is the better buy? Why? _____

Reflect

1. **Analyze Relationships** Describe another method to compare the costs.

_____

_____

Calculating Unit Rates

A **unit rate** is a rate in which the second quantity is one unit. When the first quantity in a unit rate is an amount of money, the unit rate is sometimes called a *unit price* or *unit cost*.

EXAMPLE 1

A Gerald pays $90 for 6 yoga classes. What is the cost per class?

Use the information in the problem to write a rate: $\dfrac{\$90}{6\ \text{classes}}$

To find the unit rate, divide both quantities in the rate by the same number so that the second quantity is 1.

Gerald's yoga classes cost $15 per class.

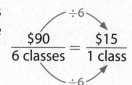

$$\dfrac{\$90}{6\ \text{classes}} = \dfrac{\$15}{1\ \text{class}}$$

B The cost of 2 cartons of milk is $5.50. What is the unit price?

The unit price is $2.75 per carton of milk.

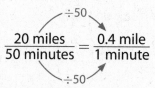

$$\dfrac{\$5.50}{2\ \text{cartons}} = \dfrac{\$2.75}{1\ \text{carton}}$$

C A cruise ship travels 20 miles in 50 minutes. How far does the ship travel per minute?

The ship travels 0.4 mile per minute.

$$\dfrac{20\ \text{miles}}{50\ \text{minutes}} = \dfrac{0.4\ \text{mile}}{1\ \text{minute}}$$

> The first quantity in a unit rate can be less than 1.

Reflect

2. **Multiple Representations** Explain how you could use a diagram like the one shown below to find the unit rate in **A**. Then complete the diagram to find the unit rate.

_____

_____

_____

_____

$90

6 yoga classes

1 yoga class

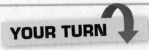

3. There are 156 players on 13 teams. How many players are on each

team? _____ players per team

Personal Math Trainer
Online Assessment and Intervention
⏻ my.hrw.com

Math On the Spot
⏻ my.hrw.com

Problem Solving with Unit Rates

You can solve rate problems by using a unit rate or by using equivalent rates.

EXAMPLE 2

At a summer camp, the campers are divided into groups. Each group has 16 campers and 2 cabins. How many cabins are needed for 112 campers?

Method 1   Find the unit rate. How many campers per cabin?

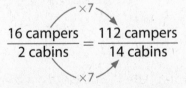

$$\frac{16 \text{ campers}}{2 \text{ cabins}} = \frac{8 \text{ campers}}{1 \text{ cabin}}$$

Divide to find the unit rate.

There are 8 campers per cabin.

$$\frac{112 \text{ campers}}{8 \text{ campers per cabin}} = 14 \text{ cabins}$$

Divide to find the number of cabins.

Method 2   Use equivalent rates.

$$\frac{16 \text{ campers}}{2 \text{ cabins}} = \frac{112 \text{ campers}}{14 \text{ cabins}}$$

The camp needs 14 cabins.

Check Use a diagram to check the unit rate if there are 16 campers in 2 cabins. Then, use the unit rate to check if 14 cabins is a reasonable number for 112 campers.

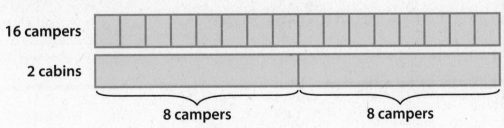

16 campers

2 cabins

8 campers   8 campers

The unit rate of 8 campers per cabin is reasonable. You can multiply 14 cabins by 8 campers per cabin to find that there would be enough room for 112 campers.

Animated Math
⏻ my.hrw.com

YOUR TURN

4. Petra jogs 3 miles in 27 minutes. At this rate, how long would it take her to jog 5 miles? Show your work.

_____

_____

Guided Practice

Mason's favorite brand of peanut butter is available in two sizes. Each size and its price are shown in the table. Use the table for 1 and 2. (Explore Activity)

1. What is the unit rate for each size of peanut butter?

   Regular: $ _____ per ounce

   Family size: $ _____ per ounce

	Size (oz)	Price ($)
Regular	16	3.36
Family Size	40	7.60

2. Which size is the better buy? _____

3. Martin charges $10 for every 5 bags of leaves he rakes. Last weekend, he raked 24 bags of leaves. How much money did he earn? (Example 1)

   _____ for 24 bags of leaves

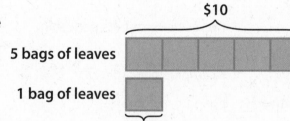

$10

5 bags of leaves

1 bag of leaves

Find the unit rate. (Example 1)

4. Lisa walked 48 blocks in 3 hours.

   _____ blocks per hour

5. Gordon types 1,800 words in 25 minutes.

   _____ words per minute

6. A particular frozen yogurt has 75 calories in 2 ounces. How many calories are in 8 ounces of the yogurt? (Example 2)   _____

7. The cost of 10 oranges is $1. What is the cost of 5 dozen oranges? (Example 2)   _____

? ESSENTIAL QUESTION CHECK-IN

8. How can you use a rate to compare the costs of two boxes of cereal that are different sizes?

   _____

   _____

6.2 Independent Practice

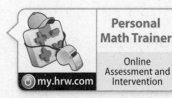

Personal Math Trainer

Online Assessment and Intervention

my.hrw.com

Taryn and Alastair both mow lawns. Each charges a flat fee to mow a lawn. The table shows the number of lawns mowed in the past week, the time spent mowing lawns, and the money earned.

	Number of Lawns Mowed	Time Spent Mowing Lawns (in hours)	Money Earned
Taryn	9	7.5	$112.50
Alastair	7	5	$122.50

9. How much does Taryn charge to mow a lawn? _____

10. How much does Alastair charge to mow a lawn? _____

11. Who earns more per hour, Taryn or Alastair? _____

12. **What If?** If Taryn and Alastair want to earn an additional $735 each, how many additional hours will each spend mowing lawns? Assume each mows at the rate shown in the table and charges by the hour. Explain.

_____

_____

_____

13. **Multistep** Tomas makes balloon sculptures at a circus. In 180 minutes, he uses 252 balloons to make 36 identical balloon sculptures.

   a. How many minutes does it take to make one balloon sculpture? How many balloons are used in one sculpture?

   _____

   b. What is Tomas's unit rate for balloons used per minute?

   _____

   c. Complete the diagram to find out how many balloons he will use in 10 minutes.

____ **balloons**

Balloons per minute

10 minutes

____ **balloons**

14. Abby can buy an 8-pound bag of dog food for $7.40 or a 4-pound bag of the same dog food for $5.38. Which is the better buy?

_____

15. A bakery offers a sale price of $3.50 for 4 muffins. What is the price per dozen?

_____

16. Mrs. Jacobsen wants to order toy instruments to give as prizes to her music students. The table shows the prices for various order sizes.

	25 items	50 items	80 items
Whistles	$21.25	$36.00	$60.00
Kazoos	$10.00	$18.50	$27.20

   a. What is the difference between the highest unit price for whistles and the lowest unit price for whistles?

_____

   b. What is the highest unit price per kazoo?

_____

   c. **Persevere in Problem Solving** If Mrs. Jacobsen wants to buy the item with the lowest unit price, what item should she order and how many of that item should she order?

_____

 FOCUS ON HIGHER ORDER THINKING

Work Area

17. **Draw Conclusions** There are 2.54 centimeters in 1 inch. How many centimeters are there in 1 foot? in 1 yard? Explain your reasoning.

_____

_____

_____

18. **Critique Reasoning** A 2-pound box of spaghetti costs $2.50. Philip says that the unit cost is $\frac{2}{2.50} = \$0.80$ per pound. Explain his error.

_____

_____

_____

19. **Look for a Pattern** A grocery store sells three different quantities of sugar. A 1-pound bag costs $1.10, a 2-pound bag costs $1.98, and a 3-pound bag costs $2.85. Describe how the unit cost changes as the quantity of sugar increases.

_____

_____

_____

_____

Using Ratios and Rates to Solve Problems

6.3.6.3

Students will use ratios and rates to make comparisons and predictions.

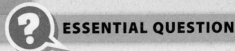

ESSENTIAL QUESTION

How can you use ratios and rates to make comparisons and predictions?

EXPLORE ACTIVITY 1

Using Tables to Compare Ratios

Anna's recipe for lemonade calls for 2 cups of lemonade concentrate and 3 cups of water. Bailey's recipe calls for 3 cups of lemonade concentrate and 5 cups of water.

A In Anna's recipe, the ratio of concentrate to water is _____.
Use equivalent ratios to complete the table.

$$2 \times 2 \qquad 2 \times \boxed{} \qquad 2 \times \boxed{}$$

Concentrate (c)	2	4		
Water (c)	3		9	15

$$3 \times 2 \qquad 3 \times 3 \qquad 3 \times 5$$

B In Bailey's recipe, the ratio of concentrate to water is _____
Use equivalent ratios to complete the table.

$$3 \times 3 \qquad 3 \times 4 \qquad 3 \times \boxed{}$$

Concentrate (c)	3	9	12	
Water (c)	5			25

$$5 \times 3 \qquad 5 \times \boxed{} \qquad 5 \times \boxed{}$$

C Find two columns, one in each table, in which the amount of water is the same. Circle these two columns.

D Whose recipe makes stronger lemonade? How do you know?

_____

_____

E Compare the ratios: $\dfrac{10}{15} \bigcirc \dfrac{9}{15}$ $\qquad \dfrac{2}{3} \bigcirc \dfrac{3}{5}$

Reflect

1. Analyze Relationships Suppose each person pours herself one cup of the lemonade she made. How much concentrate is in each person's cup? How do you know?

_____

_____

_____

Comparing Ratios

You can use equivalent ratios to solve real-world problems.

EXAMPLE 1

A fruit and nut bar recipe calls for 4 cups of chopped nuts and 6 cups of dried fruit. When Tonya made a batch of these bars, she used 6 cups of chopped nuts and 9 cups of dried fruit. Did Tonya use the correct ratio of nuts to fruit?

STEP 1 Find the ratio of nuts to fruit in the recipe.

$\frac{4}{6}$ *4 cups of nuts to 6 cups of fruit*

STEP 2 Find the ratio of nuts to fruit that Tonya used.

$\frac{6}{9}$ *6 cups of nuts to 9 cups of fruit*

> *18 is a multiple of 6 and 9, so find equivalent ratios with 18 in the second term.*

STEP 3 Find equivalent ratios that have the same second term.

$$\frac{4}{6} = \frac{12}{18} \qquad \frac{6}{9} = \frac{12}{18}$$
$$\times 3 \qquad\qquad \times 2$$

$$\frac{12}{18} = \frac{12}{18}$$

The ratios $\frac{4}{6}$ and $\frac{6}{9}$ are equivalent. So, Tonya used the same ratio of nuts to fruit that was given in the recipe.

Math Talk

Mathematical Processes

Explain how you compare two ratios to check if they are equivalent.

YOUR TURN

2. In the science club, there are 2 sixth-graders for every 3 seventh-graders. At this year's science fair, there were 7 projects by sixth-graders for every 12 projects by seventh-graders. Is the ratio of sixth-graders to seventh-graders in the science club equivalent to the ratio of science fair projects by sixth-graders to projects by seventh-graders? Explain.

_____

Using Rates to Make Predictions

You can represent rates on a double number line to make predictions.

Janet drives from Clarkson to Humbolt in 2 hours. Suppose Janet drives for 10 hours. If she maintains the same driving rate, can she drive more than 600 miles? Justify your answer.

Clarkson   112 miles   Humbolt

The double number line shows the number of miles Janet drives in various amounts of time.

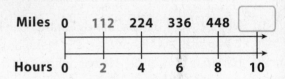

| Miles | 0 | 112 | 224 | 336 | 448 | |
| Hours | 0 | 2 | 4 | 6 | 8 | 10 |

A Explain how Janet's rate for two hours is represented on the double number line.

_____

_____

B Describe the relationship between Janet's rate for two hours and the other rates shown on the double number line.

_____

_____

C Complete the number line.

D At this rate, can Janet drive more than 600 miles in 10 hours? Explain.

_____

Reflect

3. In fifteen minutes, Lena can finish 2 math homework problems. How many math problems can she finish in 75 minutes? Use a double number line to find the answer.

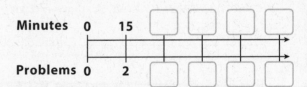

| Minutes | 0 | 15 | | | | |
| Problems | 0 | 2 | | | | |

_____

4. How is using a double number line similar to finding equivalent ratios?

_____

1. Celeste is making fruit baskets for her service club to take to a local hospital. The directions say to fill the boxes using 5 apples for every 6 oranges. Celeste is filling her baskets with 2 apples for every 3 oranges. (Explore Activity 1)

a. Complete the tables to find equivalent ratios.

Apples	5		
Oranges	6		

Apples	2		
Oranges	3		

b. Compare the ratios. Is Celeste using the correct ratio of apples to oranges?

_____

_____

2. Neha used 4 bananas and 5 oranges in her fruit salad. Daniel used 7 bananas and 9 oranges. Did Neha and Daniel use the same ratio of bananas to oranges? If not, who used the greater ratio of bananas to oranges? (Example 1)

_____

_____

3. Tim is a first grader and reads 28 words per minute. Assuming he maintains the same rate, use the double number line to find how many words he can read in 5 minutes. (Explore Activity 2)

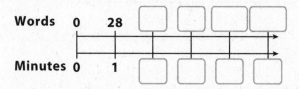

_____

4. A cafeteria sells 30 drinks every 15 minutes. Predict how many drinks the cafeteria sells every hour. (Explore Activity 2)

_____

? ESSENTIAL QUESTION CHECK-IN

5. Explain how to compare two ratios.

_____

_____

6.3 Independent Practice

6. Gina's art teacher mixes 9 pints of yellow paint with 6 pints of blue paint to create green paint. Gina mixes 4 pints of yellow paint with 3 pints of blue paint. Did Gina use the same ratio of yellow paint to blue paint instructed by her teacher? Explain.

_____

_____

7. The Suarez family paid $15.75 for 3 movie tickets. How much would they have paid for 12 tickets? _____

8. A grocery store sells snacks by weight. A six-ounce bag of mixed nuts costs $3.60. Predict the cost of a two-ounce bag. _____

9. The Martin family's truck gets an average of 25 miles per gallon. Predict how many miles they can drive using 7 gallons of gas. _____

10. Multistep The table shows two cell phone plans that offer free minutes for each given number of paid minutes used. Pablo has Plan A and Sam has Plan B.

a. What is Pablo's ratio of free to paid minutes?

_____

b. What is Sam's ratio of free to paid minutes?

_____

	Cell Phone Plans	
	Plan A	Plan B
Free minutes	2	8
Paid minutes	10	25

c. Does Pablo's cell phone plan offer the same ratio of free to paid minutes as Sam's? Explain.

_____

_____

11. Consumer Math A store has apples on sale for $3.00 for 2 pounds. How many pounds of apples can you buy for $9? If an apple is approximately 5 ounces, how many apples can you buy for $9? Explain your reasoning.

_____

_____

_____

_____

12. Science Grass can grow up to six inches in a week depending on temperature, humidity, and time of year. At this rate, how tall will grass grow in 24 days?

_____

13. A town in east Texas received 10 inches of rain in two weeks. If it kept raining at this rate for a 31-day month, how much rain did the town receive?

_____

14. One patterned blue fabric sells for $15.00 every two yards, and another sells for $37.50 every 5 yards. Do these fabrics have the same unit cost? Explain.

_____

H.O.T. FOCUS ON HIGHER ORDER THINKING

Work Area

15. Problem Solving Complete each ratio table.

	12	18	24
4.5			18

80.8	40.4		10.1
	512	256	

16. Represent Real-World Problems Write a real-world problem that compares the ratios 5 to 9 and 12 to 15.

_____

_____

_____

_____

17. Analyze Relationships Explain how you can be sure that all the rates you have written on a double number line are correct.

_____

_____

_____

_____

18. Paul can choose to be paid $50 for a job, or he can be paid $12.50 per hour. Under what circumstances should he choose the hourly wage? Explain.

_____

_____

_____

Ready to Go On?

Personal Math Trainer

Online Assessment and Intervention

my.hrw.com

6.1 Ratios

Use the table to find each ratio.

1. white socks to brown socks _____

2. blue socks to nonblue socks _____

3. black socks to all of the socks _____

Color of socks	white	black	blue	brown
Number of socks	8	6	4	5

4. Find two ratios equivalent to the ratio in Exercise 1.

_____

6.2 Rates

Find each rate.

5. Earl runs 75 meters in 30 seconds. How many meters does Earl run per second? _____

6. The cost of 3 scarves is $26.25. What is the unit price? _____

6.3 Using Ratios and Rates to Solve Problems

7. Danny charges $35 for 3 hours of swimming lessons. Martin charges $24 for 2 hours of swimming lessons. Who offers a better deal? _____

8. There are 32 female performers in a dance recital. The ratio of men to women is 3:8. How many men are in the dance recital? _____

? **ESSENTIAL QUESTION**

9. How can you use ratios and rates to solve problems?

_____

_____

_____

_____

Assessment Readiness

Personal
Math Trainer

Online
Assessment and
Intervention

my.hrw.com

Selected Response

1. Which ratio is **not** equivalent to the other three?

(A) $\frac{2}{3}$ (C) $\frac{12}{15}$

(B) $\frac{6}{9}$ (D) $\frac{18}{27}$

2. A lifeguard received 15 hours of first aid training and 10 hours of cardiopulmonary resuscitation (CPR) training. What is the ratio of hours of CPR training to hours of first aid training?

(A) 15:10   (C) 10:15

(B) 15:25   (D) 25:15

3. Jerry bought 4 DVDs for $25.20. What was the unit rate?

(A) $3.15   (C) $6.30

(B) $4.20   (D) $8.40

4. There are 1,920 fence posts used in a 12-kilometer stretch of fence. How many fence posts are used in 1 kilometer of fence?

(A) 150   (C) 155

(B) 160   (D) 180

5. Sheila can ride her bicycle 6,000 meters in 15 minutes. How far can she ride her bicycle in 2 minutes?

(A) 400 meters   (C) 800 meters

(B) 600 meters   (D) 1,000 meters

6. Lennon has a checking account. He withdrew $130.47 from an ATM Tuesday. Wednesday he deposited $240.93. Friday he wrote a check for $56.02. What was the total change in Lennon's account?

(A) $-73.21   (C) $166.48

(B) $54.44   (D) $315.38

7. Cheyenne is making a recipe that uses 5 cups of beans and 2 cups of carrots. Which combination below uses the same ratio of beans to carrots?

(A) 10 cups of beans and 3 cups of carrots

(B) 10 cups of beans and 4 cups of carrots

(C) 12 cups of beans and 4 cups of carrots

(D) 12 cups of beans and 5 cups of carrots

8. $\frac{5}{8}$ of the 64 musicians in a music contest are guitarists. Some of the guitarists play jazz solos, and the rest play classical solos. The ratio of the number of guitarists playing jazz solos to the total number of guitarists in the contest is 1:4. How many guitarists play classical solos in the contest?

(A) 10   (C) 16

(B) 30   (D) 48

Mini-Task

9. Mikaela is competing in a race in which she both runs and rides a bicycle. She runs 5 kilometers in 0.5 hour and rides her bicycle 20 kilometers in 0.8 hour.

a. At the rate given, how many kilometers can Mikaela run in 1 hour?

_____

b. At the rate given, how many kilometers can Mikaela bike in 1 hour?

_____

c. If Mikaela runs for 1 hour and bikes for 1 hour at the rates given, how far will she travel?

_____

Applying Ratios and Rates

ESSENTIAL QUESTION

How can you use ratios and rates to solve real-world problems?

Real-World Video

Chefs use lots of measurements when preparing meals. If a chef needs more or less of a dish, he can use ratios to scale the recipe up or down. Using proportional reasoning, the chef keeps the ratios of all ingredients constant.

my.hrw.com

GO DIGITAL
my.hrw.com

my.hrw.com

Go digital with your write-in student edition, accessible on any device.

Math On the Spot

Scan with your smart phone to jump directly to the online edition, video tutor, and more.

Animated Math

Interactively explore key concepts to see how math works.

Personal Math Trainer

Get immediate feedback and help as you work through practice sets.

Reading Start-Up

Visualize Vocabulary

Use the ✔ words to complete the graphic.

Comparing Unit Rates

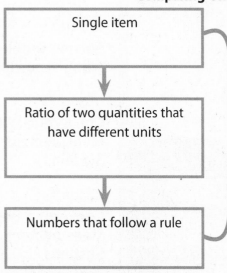

Single item

↓

Ratio of two quantities that have different units

↓

Numbers that follow a rule

Rate in which the second quantity is one unit

Understand Vocabulary

Complete the sentences using the preview words.

1. A _____ is a rate that compares two equivalent measurements.

2. In a scale drawing, the _____ describes how the dimensions in the actual object compare to the dimensions in the drawing.

Active Reading

Tri-Fold Before beginning the module, create a tri-fold to help you learn the concepts and vocabulary in this module. Fold the paper into three sections. Label one column "Rates and Ratios," the second column "Proportions," and the third column "Converting Measurements." Complete the tri-fold with important vocabulary, examples, and notes as you read the module.

Are YOU Ready?

Complete these exercises to review skills you will need for this module.

Graph Ordered Pairs (First Quadrant)

EXAMPLE

To graph A(2, 7), start at the origin.
Move 2 units right.
Then move 7 units up.
Graph point A(2, 7).

Graph each ordered pair on the coordinate plane above.

1. $B(9, 6)$ **2.** $C(0, 2)$ **3.** $D(6, 10)$ **4.** $E(3, 4)$

Write Equivalent Fractions

EXAMPLE $\frac{14}{21} = \frac{14 \times 2}{21 \times 2} = \frac{28}{42}$ Multiply the numerator and denominator by the same number to find an equivalent fraction.

$\frac{14}{21} = \frac{14 \div 7}{21 \div 7} = \frac{2}{3}$ **Divide** the numerator and denominator by the same number to find an equivalent fraction.

Write the equivalent fraction.

5. $\frac{6}{8} = \frac{\boxed{}}{32}$ **6.** $\frac{4}{6} = \frac{\boxed{}}{12}$ **7.** $\frac{1}{8} = \frac{\boxed{}}{56}$ **8.** $\frac{9}{12} = \frac{\boxed{}}{4}$

9. $\frac{5}{9} = \frac{25}{\boxed{}}$ **10.** $\frac{5}{6} = \frac{20}{\boxed{}}$ **11.** $\frac{36}{45} = \frac{12}{\boxed{}}$ **12.** $\frac{20}{36} = \frac{10}{\boxed{}}$

Multiples

EXAMPLE   List the first five multiples of 4.

$4 \times 1 = 4$
$4 \times 2 = 8$ Multiply 4 by the numbers 1, 2,
$4 \times 3 = 12$ 3, 4, and 5.
$4 \times 4 = 16$
$4 \times 5 = 20$

List the next four multiples of each number.

13. 3 _____   **14.** 7 _____   **15.** 8 _____

Complete these exercises to review skills you will need for this module.

Graph Ordered Pairs (First Quadrant)

16. Ori is graphing the points $M(3, 4)$ and $N(2, 1)$. To graph point M, he starts at the origin and then moves 3 units right and 4 units up. To graph point N, he starts at point M and then moves 2 units right and 1 unit up. Describe the error Ori made while graphing, and graph any incorrect points in the correct position.

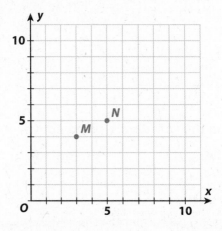

Write Equivalent Fractions

17. Margo thinks that $\frac{2}{3}$ has no equivalent fractions because no integer other than 1 evenly divides both 2 and 3. Is Margo's reasoning correct? Explain.

Multiples

18. The first 4 multiples of a number are 13, 26, 39, and 52. Describe how to find the next 4 multiples of the same number.

LESSON
7.1

6.3.7.1
Students will represent real-world problems involving ratios and rates with tables and graphs.

Ratios, Rates, Tables, and Graphs

ESSENTIAL QUESTION

How can you represent real-world problems involving ratios and rates with tables and graphs?

EXPLORE ACTIVITY 1

Finding Ratios from Tables

Students in Mr. Webster's science classes are doing an experiment that requires 250 milliliters of distilled water for every 5 milliliters of ammonia. The table shows the amount of distilled water needed for various amounts of ammonia.

Ammonia (mL)	2	3	3.5		5
Distilled water (mL)	100			200	250

A Use the numbers in the first column of the table to write a ratio of distilled water to ammonia. _____

B How much distilled water is used for 1 milliliter of ammonia? _____

Use your answer to write another ratio of distilled water to ammonia.

_____

C The ratios in **A** and **B** are

D How can you use your answer to **B** to find the amount of distilled water to add to a given amount of ammonia?

_____

_____

Math Talk
Mathematical Processes

Is the relationship between the amount of ammonia and the amount of distilled water additive or multiplicative? Explain.

E Complete the table. What are the equivalent ratios shown in the table?

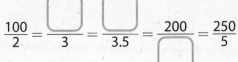

Reflect

1. **Look for a Pattern** When the amount of ammonia increases

by 1 milliliter, the amount of distilled water increases by _____

milliliters. So 6 milliliters of ammonia requires _____ milliliters of distilled water.

Graphing with Ratios

A Copy the table from Explore Activity 1 that shows the amounts of ammonia and distilled water.

Ammonia (mL)	2	3	3.5		5
Distilled water (mL)	100			200	250

B Write the information in the table as ordered pairs. Use the amount of ammonia as the *x*-coordinates and the amount of distilled water as the *y*-coordinates.

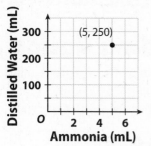

(2, _____) (3, _____), (3.5, _____), (_____, 200), (5, 250)

Graph the ordered pairs. Because fractions and decimals can represent amounts of chemicals, connect the points.

Describe your graph. _____

C For each ordered pair that you graphed, write the ratio of the

y-coordinate to the *x*-coordinate. _____

D The ratio of distilled water to ammonia is $\dfrac{\boxed{}}{1}$. How are the ratios in

C related to this ratio? _____

E The point (2.5, 125) is on the graph but not in the table. The ratio of the

y-coordinate to the *x*-coordinate is _____. How is this ratio related to

the ratios in **C** and **D**? _____

2.5 milliliters of ammonia requires _____ milliliters of distilled water.

F **Conjecture** What do you think is true for every point on the graph?

_____

_____

Reflect

2. **Communicate Mathematical Ideas** How can you use the graph to find the amount of distilled water to use for 4.5 milliliters of ammonia?

_____

_____

Representing Rates with Tables and Graphs

You can use tables and graphs to represent real-world problems involving equivalent rates.

Math On the Spot
my.hrw.com

EXAMPLE 1

The Webster family is taking an express train to Washington, D.C. The train travels at a constant speed and makes the trip in 2 hours.

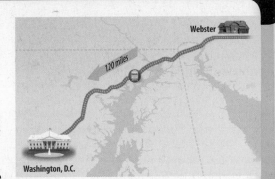

A Make a table to show the distance the train travels in various amounts of time.

STEP 1 Write a ratio of distance to time to find the rate.

$$\frac{\text{distance}}{\text{time}} = \frac{120 \text{ miles}}{2 \text{ hours}} = \frac{60 \text{ miles}}{1 \text{ hour}} = 60 \text{ miles per hour}$$

STEP 2 Use the unit rate to make a table.

Time (h)	2	3	3.5	4	5
Distance (mi)	120	180	210	240	300

B Graph the information from the table.

STEP 1 Write ordered pairs. Use Time as the x-coordinates and Distance as the y-coordinates.

(2, 120), (3, 180), (3.5, 210), (4, 240), (5, 300)

STEP 2 Graph the ordered pairs and connect the points.

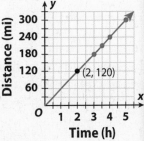

X²
Animated Math
my.hrw.com

YOUR TURN

3. A shower uses 12 gallons of water in 3 minutes. Complete the table and graph.

Time (min)	2	3	3.5		6.5
Water used (gal)				20	

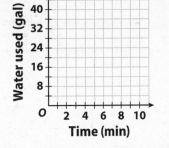

Personal Math Trainer
Online Assessment and Intervention
my.hrw.com

© Houghton Mifflin Harcourt Publishing Company

1. The ratio of oxygen atoms to sulfur atoms in sulfur dioxide is always the same. The table shows the numbers of atoms in different quantities of sulfur dioxide. Complete the table. (Explore Activity 1)

Sulfur atoms	6	9	21	
Oxygen atoms	12			54

What are the equivalent ratios shown in the table?

_____

2. Use the table in Exercise 1 to graph the relationship between sulfur atoms and oxygen atoms. (Explore Activity 2)

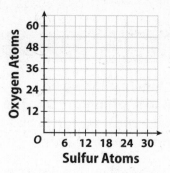

3. Stickers are made with the same ratio of width to length. A sticker 2 inches wide has a length of 4 inches. Complete the table. (Explore Activity 1)

Width (in.)	2	4	7	
Length (in.)				16

What are the equivalent ratios shown in the table?

_____

4. Graph the relationship between the width and the length of the stickers from Exercise 3. (Explore Activity 2)

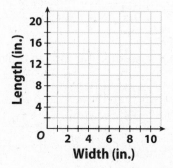

5. Five boxes of candles contain a total of 60 candles. Each box holds the same number of candles. Complete the table and graph the relationship. (Example 1)

Boxes	5	8	
Candles			120

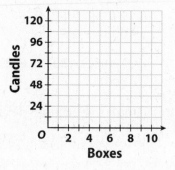

? **ESSENTIAL QUESTION CHECK-IN**

6. How do you represent real-world problems involving ratios and rates with tables and graphs?

_____

_____

_____

_____

7.1 Independent Practice

Personal Math Trainer

Online Assessment and Intervention

my.hrw.com

The table shows information about the number of sweatshirts sold and the money collected at a fundraiser for school athletic programs. For Exercises 7–12, use the table.

Sweatshirts sold	3	5	8		12
Money collected ($)	60			180	

7. Find the rate of money collected per sweatshirt sold. Show your work.

_____

_____

8. Use the unit rate to complete the table.

9. Explain how to graph information from the table.

_____

_____

_____

_____

10. Write the information in the table as ordered pairs. Graph the relationship from the table.

_____

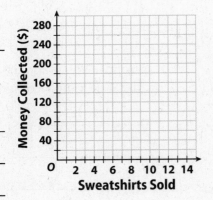

11. **What If?** How much money would be collected if 24 sweatshirts were sold? Show your work.

_____

_____

_____

12. **Analyze Relationships** Does the point (5.5, 110) make sense in this context? Explain.

_____

_____

_____

13. Communicate Mathematical Ideas The table shows the distance Randy drove on one day of her vacation. Find the distance Randy would have gone if she had driven for one more hour at the same rate. Explain how you solved the problem.

Time (h)	1	2	3	4	5
Distance (mi)	55	110	165	220	275

_____

_____

Use the graph for Exercises 14–15.

14. Analyze Relationships How many weeks correspond to 56 days? Explain.

_____

15. Represent Real-World Problems What is a real-life relationship that might be described by the graph?

_____

_____

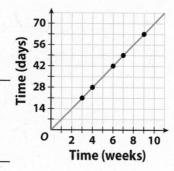

H.O.T. **FOCUS ON HIGHER ORDER THINKING**

16. Make a Conjecture Complete the table. Then find the rates $\frac{distance}{time}$ and $\frac{time}{distance}$.

Time (min)	1	2	5	
Distance (m)			25	100

$\frac{distance}{time}$ = _____

$\frac{time}{distance}$ = _____

a. Are the $\frac{time}{distance}$ rates equivalent? Explain.

_____

b. Suppose you graph the points (time, distance) and your friend graphs (distance, time). How will your graphs be different?

_____

_____

_____

17. Communicate Mathematical Ideas To graph a rate or ratio from a table, how do you determine the scales to use on each axis?

_____

_____

_____

178 Unit 3

? ESSENTIAL QUESTION

How can you solve problems with proportions?

EXPLORE ACTIVITY (Real World)

Math On the Spot
my.hrw.com

Using Equivalent Ratios to Solve Proportions

A **proportion** is a statement that two ratios or rates are equivalent.

$\frac{1}{3}$ and $\frac{2}{6}$ are equivalent ratios. $\frac{1}{3} = \frac{2}{6}$ is a proportion.

EXAMPLE 1 Sheldon and Leonard are partners in a business. Sheldon makes $2 in profits for every $5 that Leonard makes. If Leonard makes $20 profit on the first item they sell, how much profit does Sheldon make?

STEP 1 Write a proportion.

Sheldon's profit is unknown.

$$\text{Sheldon's profit} \rightarrow \frac{\$\boxed{}}{\$5} = \frac{\blacksquare}{\$20} \leftarrow \text{Sheldon's profit}$$
$$\text{Leonard's profit} \rightarrow \qquad\qquad\qquad \leftarrow \text{Leonard's profit}$$

STEP 2 Use common denominators to write equivalent ratios.

The common denominator is _____.
Multiply the numerator and denominator by 4 to create an equivalent ratio.

$$\frac{\$2 \times \boxed{}}{\$5 \times \boxed{}} = \frac{\blacksquare}{\$20}$$

Equivalent ratios with the same denominators have the same numerators.

$$\frac{\$\boxed{}}{\$\boxed{}} = \frac{\blacksquare}{\$20}$$

$$\blacksquare = \$8$$

If Leonard makes $20 profit, Sheldon makes _____ profit.

YOUR TURN

1. The members of the PTA are ordering pizza for a meeting. They plan to order 2 cheese pizzas for every 3 pepperoni pizzas they order. How many cheese pizzas will they order if they order 15 pepperoni pizzas?

Personal Math Trainer
Online Assessment and Intervention
my.hrw.com

Using Unit Rates to Solve Proportions

You can also use equivalent rates to solve proportions. Finding a unit rate may help you write equivalent rates.

EXAMPLE 2 Real World

The distance Ali runs in 36 minutes is shown on the pedometer. At this rate, how far could he run in 60 minutes?

STEP 1 Write a proportion.

$$\underset{\text{distance}}{\overset{\text{time}}{}} \longrightarrow \frac{36 \text{ minutes}}{3 \text{ miles}} = \frac{60 \text{ minutes}}{\blacksquare \text{ miles}} \longleftarrow \underset{\text{distance}}{\overset{\text{time}}{}}$$

60 is not a multiple of 36. So, there is no whole number by which you can multiply 3 miles to find ■.

STEP 2 Find the unit rate of the rate you know.

> You know that Ali runs 3 miles in 36 minutes.

$$\frac{36 \div 3}{3 \div 3} = \frac{12}{1}$$

The unit rate is 12 minutes per 1 mile.

STEP 3 Use the unit rate to write an equivalent rate that compares 60 miles to an unknown number of minutes.

Think: You can multiply $12 \times 5 = 60$. So multiply the denominator by the same number.

Math Talk

Mathematical Processes

Compare the fractions $\frac{36}{3}$ and $\frac{60}{5}$ using $<$, $>$ or $=$. Explain.

$$\frac{12 \times 5}{1 \times 5} = \frac{60}{\blacksquare}$$

$$\frac{60}{5} = \frac{60}{\blacksquare}$$

Equivalent rates with the same numerators have the same denominators.

$$\blacksquare = 5 \text{ miles}$$

At this rate, Ali can run 5 miles in 60 minutes.

YOUR TURN

2. Ms. Reynold's sprinkler system has 9 stations that water all the parts of her front and back lawn. Each station runs for an equal amount of time. If it takes 48 minutes for the first 4 stations to water, how long does it take to water all parts of her lawn? _____

Using Proportional Relationships to Find Distance on a Map

A **scale drawing** is a drawing of a real object that is proportionally smaller or larger than the real object. A **scale** describes how the dimensions in the objects compare.

A map is a scale drawing. The measurements on a map are in proportion to the actual distances. If 1 inch on a map equals an actual distance of 2 miles, the scale is 1 inch = 2 miles. You can write a scale as a rate to solve problems.

Math On the Spot
my.hrw.com

EXAMPLE 3

The distance between two schools on Lehigh Avenue is shown on the map. What is the actual distance between the schools?

STEP 1 Write a proportion.

$$\frac{2 \text{ miles}}{1 \text{ inch}} = \frac{\boxed{} \text{ miles}}{3 \text{ inches}}$$

Write the scale as a unit rate.

Scale: 1 inch = 2 miles

STEP 2 Write an equivalent rate to find the missing number.

$$\frac{2 \text{ miles} \times 3}{1 \text{ inch} \times 3} = \frac{6 \text{ miles}}{3 \text{ inches}}$$

So, in Step 1, the missing number is 6.

The actual distance between the two schools is 6 miles.

YOUR TURN

3. The distance between Sandville and Lewiston is shown on the map. What is the actual distance between the towns?

_____

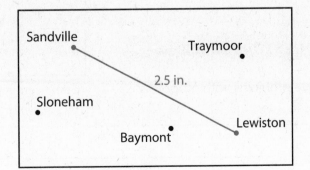

Scale: 1 inch = 20 miles

Personal Math Trainer
Online Assessment and Intervention
my.hrw.com

Find the unknown value in each proportion. (Explore Activity Example 1)

1. $\dfrac{3}{5} = \dfrac{\blacksquare}{30}$

$\dfrac{3 \times \bigcirc}{5 \times \bigcirc} = \dfrac{\bigcirc}{30}$

2. $\dfrac{4}{10} = \dfrac{\blacksquare}{5}$

$\dfrac{4 \div \bigcirc}{10 \div \bigcirc} = \dfrac{\bigcirc}{5}$

Solve using equivalent ratios. (Explore Activity Example 1)

3. Leila and Jo are two of the partners in a business. Leila makes $3 in profits for every $4 that Jo makes. If Jo makes $60 profit on the first item they sell, how much profit does Leila make? _____

4. Hendrick wants to enlarge a photo that is 4 inches wide and 6 inches tall. The enlarged photo keeps the same ratio. How tall is the enlarged photo if it is 12 inches wide? _____

Solve using unit rates. (Example 2)

5. A person on a moving sidewalk travels 21 feet in 7 seconds. The moving sidewalk has a length of 180 feet. How long will it take to move from one end of the sidewalk to the other?

_____

6. In a repeating musical pattern, there are 56 beats in 7 measures. How many measures are there in 104 beats?

_____

7. Contestants in a dance-a-thon rest for the same amount of time every hour. A couple rests for 25 minutes in 5 hours. How long did they rest in 8 hours?

_____

8. Frances gets 6 paychecks in 12 weeks. How many paychecks does she get in 52 weeks?

_____

9. What is the actual distance between Gendet and Montrose? (Example 3)

_____

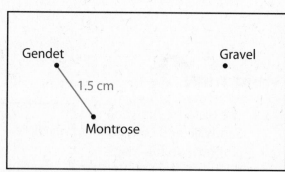

Scale: 1 centimeter = 16 kilometers

? ESSENTIAL QUESTION CHECK-IN

10. How do you solve problems with proportions?

_____

_____

_____

7.2 Independent Practice

Personal
Math Trainer

Online
Assessment and
my.hrw.com   Intervention

11. The scale of the map is missing. The actual distance from Liberty to West Quall is 72 miles, and it is 6 inches on the map.

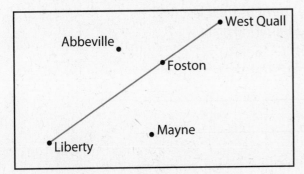

a. What is the scale of the map?

_____

b. Foston is between Liberty and West Quall and is 4 inches from Liberty on the map. How far is Foston from West Quall?

_____

12. A punch recipe says to mix 4 cups pineapple juice, 8 cups orange juice, and 12 cups seltzer in order to make 18 servings of punch.

a. How many cups of each ingredient do you need to make 108 cups of punch?

_____ cups pineapple juice

_____ cups orange juice

_____ cups seltzer

b. How many servings can be made from 108 cups of punch? _____

c. For every cup of seltzer you use, how much orange juice do you use?

_____

13. On an airplane, there are two seats on the left side in each row and three seats on the right side. There are 90 seats on the right side of the plane.

a. How many seats are on the left side of the plane? _____

b. How many seats are there altogether? _____

14. Carrie and Krystal are taking a road trip from Greenville to North Valley. Each person has her own map, and the scales on the maps are different.

a. On Carrie's map, Greenville and North Valley are 4.5 inches apart. The scale on her map is 1 inch = 20 miles. How far is Greenville from North Valley?

_____

b. The scale on Krystal's map is 1 inch = 18 miles. How far apart are Greenville and North Valley on Krystal's map?

_____

15. Multistep A machine can produce 27 inches of ribbon every 3 minutes. How many feet of ribbon can the machine make in one hour? Explain.

_____

_____

_____

_____

_____

Marta, Loribeth, and Ira all have bicycles. The table shows the number of miles of each rider's last bike ride, as well as the time it took each rider to complete the ride.

	Distance of Last Ride (in miles)	Time Spent on Last Bike Ride (in minutes)
Marta	8	80
Loribeth	6	42
Ira	15	75

16. What is Marta's unit rate, in minutes per mile? _____

17. Whose speed was the fastest on their last bike ride? _____

18. If all three riders travel for 3.5 hours at the same speed as their last ride, how many total miles will the 3 riders travel altogether? Explain.

_____

_____

_____

_____

19. Critique Reasoning Jason watched a caterpillar move 10 feet in 2 minutes. Jason says that the caterpillar's unit rate is 0.2 feet per minute. Is Jason correct? Explain.

_____

_____

 FOCUS ON HIGHER ORDER THINKING

Work Area

20. Analyze Relationships If the number in the numerator of a unit rate is 1, what does this indicate about the equivalent unit rates? Give an example.

_____

_____

21. Multiple Representations A boat travels at a constant speed. After 20 minutes, the boat has traveled 2.5 miles. The boat travels a total of 10 miles to a bridge.

a. Graph the relationship between the distance the boat travels and the time it takes.

b. How long does it take the boat to reach the bridge? Explain how you found it.

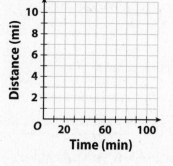

_____

_____

_____

_____

How Fast Can You Go?

A circus has set up an obstacle course race. The animals participating in the race are a horse, a camel, a polar bear, and an elephant. You and your classmates have been chosen to help the animals through the obstacle course. Your goal is to have your animal reach the corner diagonally opposite your starting corner in as little total time as possible.

INSTRUCTIONS

Playing the Game

STEP 1 Choose an animal token and place it on a red or blue triangle on the obstacle course. More than one player can start at the same location. On the obstacle course, each pathway represents a type of terrain: grass, snow, stone, or sand. The terrain pathways are connected by rock resting areas.

STEP 2 On your first turn, move your animal's token across the corner terrain pathway, stopping when the animal reaches a square rock resting area. You may choose which direction your animal travels, but only one player's token may stop on a given rock resting area at a time.

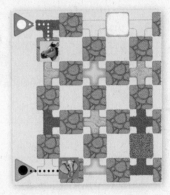

STEP 3 Fill in your table for Turn 1 with the terrain type and your animal's traveling rate on that terrain. Do not include the stone resting area.

STEP 4 An animal travels 80 meters to cross each terrain pathway, no matter the direction. Using this fact and your animal's traveling rate on the terrain, write a proportion describing the total time *t* (in seconds) it takes your animal to cross the pathway(s). Then solve the proportion to find the animal's travel time for the turn.

HORSE		
Grass		4 meters per second
Snow		5 meters per second
Stone		10 meters per second
Sand		2 meters per second

Animal: HORSE

Turn	Terrain Type	Rate	Proportion	Time Traveled
1	Grass	4 meters per second	$\frac{80}{t} = \frac{4}{1}$	20 seconds

STEP 5 Continue taking turns in a clockwise direction, each time choosing which terrain pathway(s) your animal will cross. If two alike terrain pathways are separated by a square terrain resting area, both terrain pathways can be crossed in one turn. The square terrain resting area is not calculated in the distance traveled.

STEP 6 Play ends when all players' animals have reached their opposite corners. When play ends, find the total time your animal took to cross the obstacle course.

Winning the Game

The player whose animal goes from one corner to the diagonally opposite corner in the least amount of time is the winner.

Animal:

Turn	Terrain Type	Rate	Proportion	Time Traveled
1				
2				
3				
4				
5				
6				
7				
8				
TOTAL				

LESSON 7.3

6.3.7.3
Students will convert units within a measurement system.

Converting Within Measurement Systems

How do you convert units within a measurement system?

EXPLORE ACTIVITY

Using a Model to Convert Units

The two most common systems of measurement are the customary system and the metric system. You can use a model to convert from one unit to another within the same measurement system.

STEP 1 Use the model to complete each statement below.

1 yard = 3 feet

2 yards = _____ feet

3 yards = _____ feet

4 yards = _____ feet

STEP 2 Rewrite your answers as ratios.

$$\dfrac{\boxed{}\text{ feet}}{2\text{ yards}} = \dfrac{3\text{ feet}}{1\text{ yard}} \qquad \dfrac{\boxed{}\text{ feet}}{3\text{ yards}} = \dfrac{3\text{ feet}}{1\text{ yard}} \qquad \dfrac{\boxed{}\text{ feet}}{4\text{ yards}} = \dfrac{3\text{ feet}}{1\text{ yard}}$$

Since 1 yard = 3 feet, the ratio of feet to yards in any measurement is always $\frac{3}{1}$. This means any ratio forming a proportion with $\frac{3}{1}$ can represent a ratio of feet to yards.

$\frac{3}{1} = \frac{12}{4}$ so 12 feet = _____ yards. $\frac{3}{1} = \frac{54}{18}$ so _____ feet = 18 yards.

Reflect

1. **Communicate Mathematical Ideas** How could you draw a model to show the relationship between feet and inches?

_____

_____

_____

Converting Units Using Proportions and Unit Rates

You can use ratios and proportions to convert both customary and metric units. Use the table below to convert from one unit to another within the same measurement system.

Customary Measurements		
Length	**Weight**	**Capacity**
1 ft = 12 in. 1 yd = 36 in. 1 yd = 3 ft 1 mi = 5,280 ft 1 mi = 1,760 yd	1 lb = 16 oz 1 T = 2,000 lb	1 c = 8 fl oz 1 pt = 2 c 1 qt = 2 pt 1 qt = 4 c 1 gal = 4 qt
Metric Measurements		
Length	**Mass**	**Capacity**
1 km = 1,000 m 1 m = 100 cm 1 cm = 10 mm	1 kg = 1,000 g 1 g = 1,000 mg	1 L = 1,000 mL

EXAMPLE 1

A What is the weight of a 3-pound human brain in ounces?

Use a proportion to convert 3 pounds to ounces.

Use $\frac{16 \text{ ounces}}{1 \text{ pound}}$ to convert pounds to ounces.

STEP 1 Write a proportion.

$$\frac{16 \text{ ounces}}{1 \text{ pound}} = \frac{\blacksquare \text{ ounces}}{3 \text{ pounds}}$$

STEP 2 Use common denominators to write equivalent ratios.

$$\frac{16 \times 3}{1 \times 3} = \frac{\blacksquare}{3} \qquad \text{3 is a common denominator.}$$

$$\frac{48}{3} = \frac{\blacksquare}{3} \qquad \text{Equivalent rates with the same denominators have the same numerators.}$$

$$\blacksquare = 48 \text{ ounces}$$

The weight is 48 ounces.

B A moderate amount of daily sodium consumption is 2,000 milligrams. What is this mass in grams?

Use a proportion to convert 2,000 milligrams to grams.

Use $\frac{1,000 \text{ mg}}{1 \text{ g}}$ to convert milligrams to grams.

STEP 1 Write a proportion.

$$\frac{1{,}000 \text{ mg}}{1 \text{ g}} = \frac{2{,}000 \text{ mg}}{\blacksquare \text{ g}}$$

STEP 2 Write equivalent ratios.

Think: You can multiply 1,000 × 2 = 2,000. So multiply the denominator by the same number.

$$\frac{1{,}000 \times 2}{1 \times 2} = \frac{2{,}000}{\blacksquare}$$

$$\frac{2{,}000}{2} = \frac{2{,}000}{\blacksquare}$$

Equivalent ratios with the same numerators have the same denominators.

$$\blacksquare = 2 \text{ grams}$$

The mass is 2 grams.

Math Talk
Mathematical Processes

How would you convert 3 liters to milliliters?

YOUR TURN

2. The height of a doorway is 2 yards. What is the height of the doorway in inches? _____

Personal Math Trainer

Online Assessment and Intervention

⏻ my.hrw.com

Converting Units by Using Conversion Factors

Another way to convert measurements is by using a conversion factor. A **conversion factor** is a ratio comparing two equivalent measurements.

Math On the Spot

⏻ my.hrw.com

EXAMPLE 2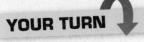

Elena wants to buy 2 gallons of milk but can only find quart containers for sale. How many quarts does she need?

You are converting to quarts from gallons.

STEP 1 Find the conversion factor.

Write 4 quarts = 1 gallon as a ratio: $\frac{4 \text{ quarts}}{1 \text{ gallon}}$

STEP 2 Multiply the given measurement by the conversion factor.

$$2 \text{ gallons} \cdot \frac{4 \text{ quarts}}{1 \text{ gallon}} = \blacksquare \text{ quarts}$$

$$2 \text{ gallons} \cdot \frac{4 \text{ quarts}}{1 \text{ gallon}} = 8 \text{ quarts} \quad \textit{Cancel the common unit.}$$

Elena needs 8 quarts of milk.

3. An oak tree is planted when it is 250 centimeters tall. What is this height in meters? _____

Guided Practice

Use the model below to complete each statement. (Explore Activity 1)

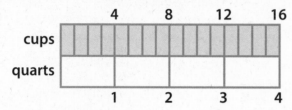

1. $\frac{4}{1} = \frac{12}{3}$, so 12 cups = _____ quarts

2. $\frac{4}{1} = \frac{48}{12}$, so _____ cups = 12 quarts

Use ratios and proportions to solve. (Example 1)

3. Mary Catherine makes 2 gallons of punch for her party. How many cups of punch did she make?

_____

4. An African elephant weighs 6 tons. What is the weight of the elephant in pounds?

_____

5. The distance from Jason's house to school is 0.5 kilometer. What is this distance in meters?

_____

6. The mass of a moon rock is 3.5 kilograms. What is the mass of the moon rock in grams?

_____

Use a conversion factor to solve. (Example 2)

7. 1.75 grams $\cdot \frac{1,000 \text{ mg}}{1 \text{ g}} =$ _____

8. 27 millimeters $\cdot \frac{1 \text{ cm}}{10 \text{ mm}} =$ _____

9. A package weighs 96 ounces. What is the weight of the package in pounds?

_____

10. A jet flies at an altitude of 52,800 feet. What is the height of the jet in miles?

_____

? ESSENTIAL QUESTION CHECK-IN

11. How do you convert units within a measurement system?

_____

_____

7.3 Independent Practice

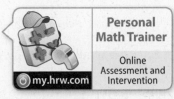

Personal Math Trainer

Online Assessment and Intervention

my.hrw.com

12. What is a conversion factor that you can use to convert gallons to pints? How did you find it?

_____

13. Three friends each have some ribbon. Carol has 42 inches of ribbon, Tino has 2.5 feet of ribbon, and Baxter has 1.5 yards of ribbon. Express the total length of ribbon the three friends have in inches, feet and yards.

_____ inches = _____ feet = _____ yards

14. Suzanna wants to measure a board, but she doesn't have a ruler to measure with. However, she does have several copies of a book that she knows is 17 centimeters tall.

   a. Suzanna lays the books end to end and finds that the board is the same length as 21 books. How many centimeters long is the board?

   _____

   b. Suzanna needs a board that is at least 3.5 meters long. Is the board long enough? Explain.

   _____

   _____

Sheldon needs to buy 8 gallons of ice cream for a family reunion. The table shows the prices for different sizes of two brands of ice cream.

	Price of small size	**Price of large size**
Cold Farms	$2.50 for 1 pint	$4.50 for 1 quart
Cone Dreams	$4.25 for 1 quart	$9.50 for 1 gallon

15. Which size container of Cold Farm ice cream is the better deal for Sheldon? Explain.

_____

_____

_____

16. **Multistep** Which size and brand of ice cream is the best deal?

_____

17. In Beijing in 2008, the Women's 3,000 meter Steeplechase became an Olympic event. What is this distance in kilometers? _____

18. How would you convert 5 feet 6 inches to inches? _____

_____

London 2012

H.O.T. **FOCUS ON HIGHER ORDER THINKING**

19. **Analyze Relationships** A Class 4 truck weighs between 14,000 and 16,000 pounds.

a. What is the weight range in tons? _____

b. If the weight of a Class 4 truck is increased by 2 tons, will it still be classified as a Class 4 truck? Explain.

_____

_____

20. **Persevere in Problem Solving** A football field is shown at right.

a. What are the dimensions of a football field in feet?

_____

$53\frac{1}{3}$ yd

120 yd

b. A chalk line is placed around the perimeter of the football field. What is the length of this line in feet?

_____

c. About how many laps around the perimeter of the field would equal 1 mile? Explain.

_____

_____

21. **Look for a Pattern** What is the result if you multiply a number of cups by $\frac{8 \text{ fl oz}}{1 \text{ cup}}$ and then multiply the result by $\frac{1 \text{ cup}}{8 \text{ fl oz}}$? Give an example.

_____

_____

22. **Make a Conjecture** 1 hour = 3,600 seconds and 1 mile = 5,280 feet. Make a conjecture about how you could convert a speed of 15 miles per hour to feet per second. Then convert.

_____

_____

_____

Work Area

Converting Between Measurement Systems

6.3.7.4
Students will use ratios and proportions to convert measurements.

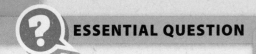

? ESSENTIAL QUESTION

How can you use ratios and proportions to convert measurements?

EXPLORE ACTIVITY Real World

Converting Inches to Centimeters

Measurements are used when determining the length, weight, or capacity of an object. The two most common systems of measurement are the *customary system* and the *metric system*.

The table shows equivalencies between the customary and metric systems. You can use these equivalencies to convert a measurement in one system to a measurement in the other system.

Length	Weight/Mass	Capacity
1 inch = 2.54 centimeters	1 ounce ≈ 28.4 grams	1 fluid ounce ≈ 29.6 milliliters
1 foot ≈ 0.305 meter	1 pound ≈ 0.454 kilogram	1 quart ≈ 0.946 liter
1 yard ≈ 0.914 meter		1 gallon ≈ 3.79 liters
1 mile ≈ 1.61 kilometers		

Most conversions are approximate, as indicated by the symbol ≈.

The length of a sheet of paper is 11 inches. What is this length in centimeters?

A You can use a bar diagram to solve this problem. Each part represents 1 inch.

1 inch = _____ centimeter(s)

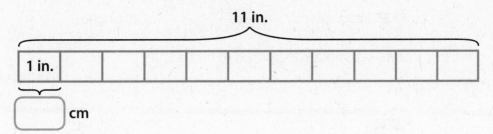

11 in.

| 1 in. | | | | | | | | | | |

_____ cm

B How does the diagram help you solve the problem?

_____

C 11 inches = _____ centimeters

Reflect

1. **Communicate Mathematical Ideas** Suppose you wanted to use a diagram to convert ounces to grams. Which unit would the parts in your diagram represent?

_____

_____

Math On the Spot

my.hrw.com

Using Conversion Factors

Another way to convert measurements is by using a ratio called a *conversion factor*. A **conversion factor** is a ratio of two equivalent measurements. Since the two measurements in a conversion factor are equivalent, a conversion factor is equal to 1.

EXAMPLE 1

While lifting weights, John adds 11.35 kilograms to his bar. About how many pounds does he add to his bar?

STEP 1 Find the conversion factor.

1 pound ≈ 0.454 kilogram

Write the conversion factor as a ratio: $\dfrac{1 \text{ pound}}{0.454 \text{ kilogram}}$

STEP 2 Convert the given measurement.

kilograms	×	conversion factor	=	pounds

11.35 kilograms × $\dfrac{1 \text{ pound}}{0.454 \text{ kilogram}}$ ≈ 25 pounds

John adds about 25 pounds to his bar.

Personal Math Trainer

Online Assessment and Intervention

my.hrw.com

YOUR TURN

2. 6 quarts ≈ _____ liters

3. 14 feet ≈ _____ meters

4. 255.6 grams ≈ _____ ounces

5. 7 liters ≈ _____ quarts

Using Proportions to Convert Measurements

You can also convert a measurement from one unit to another by using a proportion. First write the conversion factor as a ratio, then multiply by a form of 1 to generate an equivalent ratio. Recall that two equal ratios form a proportion.

Math On the Spot

⊙ my.hrw.com

Proportions: $\dfrac{3 \text{ inches}}{2 \text{ feet}} = \dfrac{6 \text{ inches}}{4 \text{ feet}}$ $\dfrac{5}{10} = \dfrac{1}{2}$

EXAMPLE 2

My Notes

Bob's driveway is 45 feet long by 18 feet wide. He plans to pave the entire driveway. The asphalt paving costs $24 per square meter. What will be the total cost of the paving?

45 ft

18 ft

STEP 1 First find the dimensions of the driveway in meters.

Convert each measurement to meters.
Use 1 foot ≈ 0.305 meter.

$$\dfrac{1 \text{ foot}}{0.305 \text{ meter}} \overset{\times\,45}{\underset{\times\,45}{=}} \dfrac{45 \text{ feet}}{13.725 \text{ meters}}$$

Length ≈ 13.725 meters

$$\dfrac{1 \text{ foot}}{0.305 \text{ meter}} \overset{\times\,18}{\underset{\times\,18}{=}} \dfrac{18 \text{ feet}}{5.49 \text{ meters}}$$

Width ≈ 5.49 meters

> The length and width are approximate because the conversion between feet and meters is approximate.

STEP 2 Find the area in square meters.

Area = length × width

   = 13.725 × 5.49

   = 75.35 square meters

Math Talk
Mathematical Processes

How much does the paving cost per square foot? Explain.

STEP 3 Now find the total cost of the paving.

square meters × cost per square meter = total cost
   75.35   × $24   = $1,808.40

Reflect

6. **Error Analysis** Yolanda found the area of Bob's driveway in square meters as shown. Explain why Yolanda's answer is incorrect.

Area = 45 × 18 = 810 square feet

810 square feet × $\dfrac{0.305 \text{ meter}}{1 \text{ foot}}$ ≈ 247.1 square meters

_____

_____

YOUR TURN

7. A flower bed is 2 meters wide and 3 meters long. What is the area of the flower bed in square feet? Round your converted dimensions and your final answer to the nearest hundredth.

_____ square feet

Guided Practice

Complete each diagram to solve the problem. (Explore Activity)

1. Kate ran 5 miles. How far did she run in kilometers?

5 miles = _____ kilometers

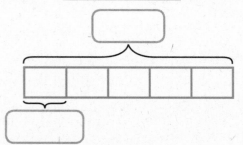

2. Alex filled a 5-gallon jug with water. How many liters of water are in the container?

5 gallons ≈ _____ liters

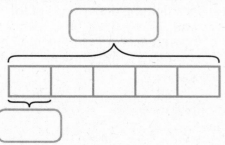

Use a conversion factor to convert each measurement. (Example 1 and 2)

3. A ruler is 12 inches long. What is the length of this ruler in centimeters?

_____ centimeters

4. A kitten weighs 4 pounds. What is the approximate mass of the kitten in kilograms?

_____ kilograms

Use a proportion to convert each measurement. (Example 2)

5. 20 yards ≈ _____ meters

6. 12 ounces ≈ _____ grams

7. 5 quarts ≈ _____ liters

8. 400 meters ≈ _____ yards

9. 10 liters ≈ _____ gallons

10. 137.25 meters ≈ _____ feet

11. 165 centimeters ≈ _____ inches

12. 10,000 kilometers ≈ _____ miles

? ESSENTIAL QUESTION CHECK-IN

13. Write a proportion that you can use to convert 60 inches to centimeters.

_____

7.4 Independent Practice

Personal Math Trainer

Online Assessment and Intervention

my.hrw.com

Tell which measure is greater.

14. Six feet or two meters _____

15. One inch or one centimeter _____

16. One yard or one meter _____

17. One mile or one kilometer _____

18. One ounce or one gram _____

19. One quart or one liter _____

20. 10 pounds or 10 kilograms _____

21. Four liters or one gallon _____

22. Two miles or three kilometers _____

23. What is the limit in kilograms?

weight limit for checked baggage: 50 pounds

24. What is the speed limit in miles per hour?

25. Which container holds more, a half-gallon milk jug or a 2-liter juice bottle?

_____

26. The label on a can of lemonade gives the volume as 12 fl oz, or 355 mL. Verify that these two measurements are nearly equivalent.

_____

27. The mass of a textbook is about 1.25 kilograms. About how many pounds is this?

_____

28. **Critique Reasoning** Michael estimated his mass as 8 kilograms. Is his estimate reasonable? Justify your answer.

_____

29. Your mother bought a three-liter bottle of water. When she got home, she discovered a small leak in the bottom and asked you to find a container to transfer the water into. All you could find were two half-gallon jugs.

a. Will your containers hold all of the water?

_____

_____

_____

b. **What If?** Suppose an entire liter of water leaked out in the car. In that case, would you be able to fit all of the remaining water into one of the half-gallon jugs?

_____

_____

_____

30. The track team ran a mile and a quarter during their practice.

How many kilometers did the team run? _____

31. A countertop is 16 feet long and 3 feet wide.

    a. What is the area of the countertop in square meters? _____

    b. Tile costs $28 per square meter. How much will it cost to cover the

    countertop with new tile? $ _____

32. At a school picnic, your teacher asks you to mark a field every ten yards so students can play football. The teacher accidentally gave you a meter stick instead of a yard stick. How far apart in meters should you mark the lines if you still want them to be in the right places?

_____

33. You weigh a gallon of 2% milk in science class and learn that it is approximately 8.4 pounds. You pass the milk to the next group, and then realize that your teacher wanted an answer in kilograms, not pounds. Explain how you can adjust your answer without weighing the milk again. Then give the weight in kilograms.

_____

H.O.T. FOCUS ON HIGHER ORDER THINKING

34. Analyze Relationships Annalisa, Keiko, and Stefan want to compare their heights. Annalisa is 64 inches tall. Stefan tells her, "I'm about 7.5 centimeters taller than you." Keiko knows she is 1.5 inches shorter than Stefan. Give the heights of all three people in both inches and centimeters to the nearest half unit.

_____

_____

_____

35. Communicate Mathematical Ideas Mikhael wanted to rewrite the conversion factor "1 yard ≈ 0.914 meter" to create a conversion factor to convert meters to yards. He wrote "1 meter ≈ _____." "Tell how Mikhael should finish his conversion, and explain how you know.

_____

_____

_____

Ready to Go On?

Personal Math Trainer

Online Assessment and Intervention

⏻ my.hrw.com

7.1 Ratios, Rates, Tables, and Graphs

1. Charlie runs laps around a track. The table shows how long it takes him to run different numbers of laps. How long would it take Charlie to run 5 laps?

Number of Laps	2	4	6	8	10
Time (min)	10	20	30	40	50

_____

7.2 Solving Proportionality Problems

2. Emily is entering a bicycle race for charity. Her mother pledges $0.40 for every 0.25 mile she bikes. If Emily bikes 15 miles, how much will her

mother donate? _____

3. Rob is saving to buy a new MP3 player. For every $15 he earns babysitting, he saves $6. On Saturday, Rob earned $75 babysitting.

How much money did he save? _____

7.3 Within Measurement Systems

Convert each measurement.

4. 18 meters = _____ centimeters

5. 5 pounds = _____ ounces

6. 6 quarts = _____ fluid ounces

7. 9 liters = _____ milliliters

7.4 Converting Between Measurement Systems

Convert each measurement.

8. 5 inches = _____ centimeters

9. 198.9 grams ≈ _____ ounces

10. 8 gallons ≈ _____ liters

11. 12 feet ≈ _____ meters

? ESSENTIAL QUESTION

12. Write a real-world problem that could be solved using a proportion.

_____

_____

_____

Personal Math Trainer

my.hrw.com

Online Assessment and Intervention

Selected Response

1. The graph below represents the distance Manuel walks over several hours.

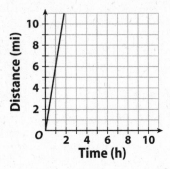

Which is an ordered pair on the line?

Ⓐ (2.5, 14)   Ⓒ (2.25, 12)

Ⓑ (1.25, 5)   Ⓓ (1.5, 9)

2. Jonah's house and his grandparents' house are 8,046.72 meters apart. What is this distance in miles?

Ⓐ 4 miles   Ⓒ 7 miles

Ⓑ 5 miles   Ⓓ 8 miles

3. Megan is making bracelets to sell to earn money for the local animal shelter. It takes her $\frac{1}{4}$ hour to pick out all the beads and $\frac{1}{10}$ hour to string them. This week, she only has $5\frac{1}{4}$ hours to make bracelets. How many bracelets will Megan be able to make?

Ⓐ 10 bracelets   Ⓒ 15 bracelets

Ⓑ 12 bracelets   Ⓓ 21 bracelets

4. Rosa can run 4 miles in 56 minutes. How many miles does Rosa run if she runs for 42 minutes?

Ⓐ 2 miles   Ⓒ 3.5 miles

Ⓑ 3 miles   Ⓓ 5 miles

5. The table below shows the number of petals and leaves for different numbers of flowers.

Petals	5	10	15	20
Leaves	2	4	6	8

How many petals are present when there are 12 leaves?

Ⓐ 25 petals   Ⓒ 35 petals

Ⓑ 30 petals   Ⓓ 36 petals

6. A recipe calls for 3 cups of sugar and 9 cups of water. How many cups of water should be used with 2 cups of sugar?

Ⓐ 3 cups   Ⓒ 6 cups

Ⓑ 4 cups   Ⓓ 8 cups

Mini-Task

7. The unlabeled graph shows the relationship between two customary units of measure. Only two pairs of units can be represented by the graph.

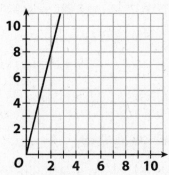

a. Determine the possible pairs of units.

_____

_____

b. Describe the relationship for each pair.

_____

_____

Percents

? **ESSENTIAL QUESTION**

How can you use percents to solve real-world problems?

Real-World Video

When you eat at a restaurant, your bill will include sales tax for most items. It is customary to add a tip for your server in many restaurants. Both taxes and tips are calculated as a percent of the bill.

my.hrw.com

GO DIGITAL
my.hrw.com

my.hrw.com

Go digital with your write-in student edition, accessible on any device.

Math On the Spot

Scan with your smart phone to jump directly to the online edition, video tutor, and more.

Animated Math

Interactively explore key concepts to see how math works.

Personal Math Trainer

Get immediate feedback and help as you work through practice sets.

Reading Start-Up

Visualize Vocabulary

Use the ✔ words to complete the graphic. You may put more than one word in each box.

```
┌─────────────────┐        ┌─────────────────┐
│      0.25       │        │   3/4,  3:4     │
└─────────────────┘        └─────────────────┘
         \                        /
          ┌───────────────────────────┐
          │ Reviewing Fractions and   │
          │        Decimals           │
          └───────────────────────────┘
         /                        \
┌─────────────────┐        ┌─────────────────┐
│   2/3 = 6/9     │        │  4/8 → 1/2      │
└─────────────────┘        └─────────────────┘
```

Understand Vocabulary

Match the term on the left to the correct expression on the right.

1. percent

2. model

3. equivalent decimals

A. A ratio that compares a number to 100.

B. Decimals that name the same amount.

C. Something that represents another thing.

Active Reading

Pyramid Before beginning the module, create a pyramid to help you organize what you learn. Label one side "Decimals," one side "Fractions," and the other side "Percents." As you study the module, write important vocabulary and other notes on the appropriate side.

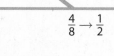

Vocabulary

Review Words
✔ decimal (decimal)
✔ equivalent fractions (fracciones equivalentes)
denominator (denominador)
✔ fraction (fracción)
mixed number (número mixto)
numerator (numerador)
✔ ratio (razón)
✔ simplest form (mínima expresión)

Preview Words
equivalent decimals (decimales equivalentes)
model (modelo)
percent (porcentaje)
proportional reasoning (razonamiento proporcional)

Are YOU Ready?

Complete these exercises to review skills you will need for this module.

Personal Math Trainer

Online Assessment and Intervention

⏻ my.hrw.com

Write Equivalent Fractions

EXAMPLE $\dfrac{9}{12} = \dfrac{9 \times 4}{12 \times 4} = \dfrac{36}{48}$ Multiply the numerator and denominator by the same number to find an equivalent fraction.

$\dfrac{9}{12} = \dfrac{9 \div 3}{12 \div 3} = \dfrac{3}{4}$ Divide the numerator and denominator by the same number to find an equivalent fraction.

Write the equivalent fraction.

1. $\dfrac{9}{18} = \dfrac{\boxed{}}{6}$

2. $\dfrac{4}{6} = \dfrac{\boxed{}}{18}$

3. $\dfrac{25}{30} = \dfrac{5}{\boxed{}}$

4. $\dfrac{12}{15} = \dfrac{36}{\boxed{}}$

5. $\dfrac{15}{24} = \dfrac{\boxed{}}{8}$

6. $\dfrac{24}{32} = \dfrac{\boxed{}}{8}$

7. $\dfrac{50}{60} = \dfrac{10}{\boxed{}}$

8. $\dfrac{5}{9} = \dfrac{20}{\boxed{}}$

Multiply Fractions

EXAMPLE $\dfrac{5}{12} \times \dfrac{3}{10} = \dfrac{{}^1\cancel{5}}{\cancel{12}_4} \times \dfrac{{}^1\cancel{3}}{\cancel{10}_2}$ Divide by the common factors.

$= \dfrac{1}{8}$ Simplify.

Multiply. Write each product in simplest form.

9. $\dfrac{3}{8} \times \dfrac{4}{11} =$ _____

10. $\dfrac{8}{15} \times \dfrac{5}{6} =$ _____

11. $\dfrac{7}{12} \times \dfrac{3}{14} =$ _____

12. $\dfrac{9}{20} \times \dfrac{4}{5} =$ _____

13. $\dfrac{7}{10} \times \dfrac{20}{21} =$ _____

14. $\dfrac{8}{18} \times \dfrac{9}{20} =$ _____

Decimal Operations (Multiplication)

EXAMPLE $\begin{array}{r} 1.6 \\ \times\,0.3 \\ \hline 0.48 \end{array}$ Multiply as you would with whole numbers.

Count the total number of decimal places in the factors.

Place the decimal point that number of places in the product.

Multiply.

15. 20×0.25 _____

16. 0.3×16.99 _____

17. 0.2×75 _____

18. 5.5×1.1 _____

19. 11.99×0.8 _____

20. 7.25×0.5 _____

21. 4×0.75 _____

22. 0.15×12.50 _____

23. 6.5×0.7 _____

Complete these exercises to review skills you will need for this module.

Write Equivalent Fractions

24. Anat and Jeremy are meeting at a restaurant. Anat lives $\frac{2}{3}$ mile from the restaurant, and Jeremy lives $\frac{5}{6}$ mile from the restaurant. Which pair of fractions is equivalent to the distances Anat and Jeremy live from the restaurant? Choose all that apply.

Ⓐ $\frac{9}{12}$ and $\frac{10}{12}$　　　Ⓑ $\frac{12}{18}$ and $\frac{15}{18}$　　　Ⓒ $\frac{16}{24}$ and $\frac{21}{24}$　　　Ⓓ $\frac{28}{42}$ and $\frac{35}{42}$

Multiply Fractions

25. An artist has collected $\frac{15}{16}$ pound of seashells. He wants to give away $\frac{8}{21}$ of the total weight of the seashells. How many pounds of seashells does the artist want to give away? Show your work, and write the answer in simplest form.

Decimal Operations (Multiplication)

26. Blueridge Supplies sells gravel for $12.75 per cubic yard, and Westview Landscaping sells gravel for $9.50 per cubic yard. Complete the table by determining the cost at each store for 15 cubic yards of gravel and 6.8 cubic yards of gravel.

	Blueridge Supplies $12.75 per cubic yard	Westview Landscaping $9.50 per cubic yard
15 cubic yards of gravel		
6.8 cubic yards of gravel		

ESSENTIAL QUESTION

How can you write a ratio as a percent?

EXPLORE ACTIVITY 1 Real World

Using a Grid to Model Percents

A **percent** is a ratio that compares a number to 100. The symbol % is used to show a percent.

17% is equivalent to

- $\frac{17}{100}$
- 17 to 100
- 17:100

The free-throw ratios for three basketball players are shown.

Player 1: $\frac{17}{25}$ Player 2: $\frac{33}{50}$ Player 3: $\frac{14}{20}$

A Rewrite each ratio as a number compared to 100. Then shade the grid to represent the free-throw ratio.

Player 1: $\frac{17}{25} = \frac{\boxed{}}{100}$ Player 2: $\frac{33}{50} = \frac{\boxed{}}{100}$ Player 3: $\frac{14}{20} = \frac{\boxed{}}{100}$

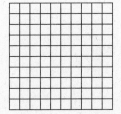   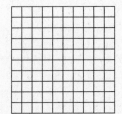   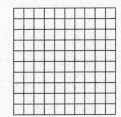

B Which player has the greatest free-throw ratio? _____

How is this shown on the grids? _____

C Use a percent to describe each player's free-throw ratio. Write the percents in order from least to greatest.

_____

_____

D How did you determine how many squares to shade on each grid?

_____

_____

Connecting Fractions and Percents

You can use a percent bar model to model a ratio expressed as a fraction and to find an equivalent percent.

A Use a percent bar model to find an equivalent percent for $\frac{1}{4}$.

Draw a model to represent 100 and divide it into fourths. Shade $\frac{1}{4}$.

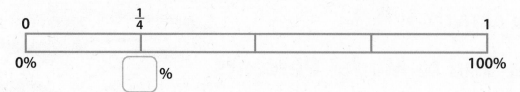

$\frac{1}{4}$ of 100 = 25, so $\frac{1}{4}$ of 100% = _____

Tell which operation you can use to find $\frac{1}{4}$ of 100.

Then find $\frac{1}{4}$ of 100%. _____

B Use a percent bar model to find an equivalent percent for $\frac{1}{3}$.

Draw a model and divide it into thirds. Shade $\frac{1}{3}$.

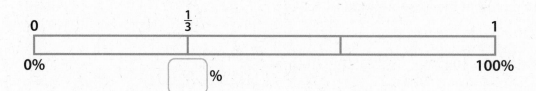

$\frac{1}{3}$ of 100 = $33\frac{1}{3}$, so $\frac{1}{3}$ of 100% = _____ %

Tell which operation you can use to find $\frac{1}{3}$ of 100.

Then find $\frac{1}{3}$ of 100%. _____

Reflect

1. **Critique Reasoning** Jo says she can find the percent equivalent of $\frac{3}{4}$ by multiplying the percent equivalent of $\frac{1}{4}$ by 3. How can you use a percent bar model to support this claim?

_____

_____

_____

Using Benchmarks and Proportional Reasoning

Math On the Spot
my.hrw.com

You can use certain *benchmark* percents to write other percents and to estimate fractions.

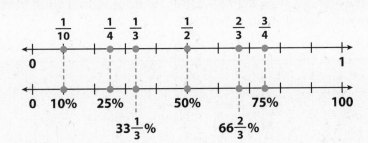

EXAMPLE 1

A Find an equivalent percent for $\frac{3}{10}$.

STEP 1 Write $\frac{3}{10}$ as a multiple of a benchmark fraction.

$$\frac{3}{10} = 3 \cdot \frac{1}{10}$$ Think: $\frac{3}{10} = \frac{1}{10} + \frac{1}{10} + \frac{1}{10}$

STEP 2 Find an equivalent percent for $\frac{1}{10}$.

$$\frac{1}{10} = 10\%$$ Use the number lines to find the equivalent percent for $\frac{1}{10}$.

STEP 3 Multiply.

$$\frac{3}{10} = 3 \cdot \frac{1}{10} = 3 \cdot 10\% = 30\%$$

> **Math Talk**
> Mathematical Processes
>
> Explain how you could use equivalent ratios to write $\frac{3}{10}$ as a percent.

B 76% of the students at a middle school bring their own lunch. About what fraction of the students bring their own lunch?

STEP 1 Note that 76% is close to the benchmark 75%.

STEP 2 Find a fraction equivalent for 75%:

$$75\% = \frac{3}{4}$$

About $\frac{3}{4}$ of the students bring their own lunch.

YOUR TURN

Use a benchmark to find an equivalent percent for each fraction.

2. $\frac{9}{10}$ _____

3. $\frac{2}{5}$ _____

4. 64% of the animals at an animal shelter are dogs. About what fraction of the animals at the shelter are dogs?

_____

Guided Practice

1. Shade the grid to represent the ratio $\frac{9}{25}$. Then find a percent equivalent to the given ratio. (Explore Activity 1)

$$\frac{9 \times \boxed{}}{25 \times \boxed{}} = \frac{\boxed{}}{100} = \underline{}$$

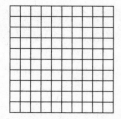

2. Use the percent bar model to find the missing percent. (Explore Activity 2)

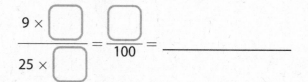

0     $\frac{1}{5}$ 1

0%   100%

$\boxed{}$ %

Identify a benchmark you can use to find an equivalent percent for each ratio. Then find the equivalent percent. (Example 1)

3. $\frac{6}{10}$ Benchmark: $\dfrac{1}{\boxed{}}$

4. $\frac{2}{4}$ Benchmark: $\dfrac{\boxed{}}{4}$

5. $\frac{4}{5}$ Benchmark: $\dfrac{\boxed{}}{5}$

_____   _____   _____

6. 41% of the students at an art college want to be graphic designers. About what fraction of the students want to be graphic designers? (Example 1)

_____

? ESSENTIAL QUESTION CHECK-IN

7. How do you write a ratio as a percent?

_____

_____

8.1 Independent Practice

Shade the grid to represent the ratio. Then find the missing number.

8. $\dfrac{23}{50} = \dfrac{\boxed{}}{100}$

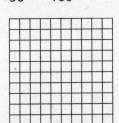

9. $\dfrac{11}{20} = \dfrac{\boxed{}}{100}$

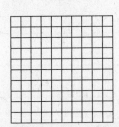

10. Mark wants to use a grid like the ones in Exercises 1 and 2 to model the percent equivalent of the fraction $\frac{2}{3}$. How many grid squares should he shade? What percent would his model show?

_____

11. The ratios of saves for a baseball pitcher to the number of save opportunities are given for three relief pitchers: $\frac{9}{10}, \frac{4}{5}, \frac{17}{20}$. Write each ratio as a percent. Order the percents from least to greatest.

_____

Circle the greater quantity.

12. $\frac{1}{3}$ of a box of Corn Krinkles

50% of a box of Corn Krinkles

13. 30% of your minutes are used up

$\frac{1}{4}$ of your minutes are used up

14. **Multiple Representations** Explain how you could write 35% as the sum of two benchmark percents or as a multiple of a percent.

_____

15. Use the percent bar model to find the missing percent.

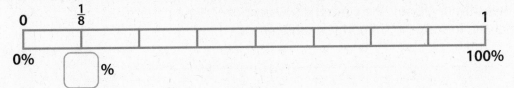

16. Multistep Carl buys songs and downloads them to his computer. The bar graph shows the numbers of each type of song he downloaded last year.

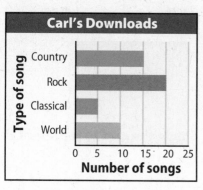

Carl's Downloads

a. What is the total number of songs Carl downloaded last year?

_____

b. What fraction of the songs were country? Find the fraction for each type of song. Write each fraction in simplest form and give its percent equivalent.

_____

_____

_____

_____

H.O.T. **FOCUS ON HIGHER ORDER THINKING**

17. Critique Reasoning Marcus bought a booklet of tickets to use at the amusement park. He used 50% of the tickets on rides, $\frac{1}{3}$ of the tickets on video games, and the rest of the tickets in the batting cage. Marcus says he used 10% of the tickets in the batting cage. Do you agree? Explain.

_____

_____

_____

_____

Work Area

18. Look for a Pattern Complete the table.

Fraction	$\frac{1}{5}$	$\frac{2}{5}$	$\frac{3}{5}$	$\frac{4}{5}$	$\frac{5}{5}$	$\frac{6}{5}$
Percent	20%					

a. Analyze Relationships What is true when the numerator and denominator of the fraction are equal? What is true when the numerator is greater than the denominator?

_____

_____

b. Justify Reasoning What is the percent equivalent of $\frac{3}{2}$? Use a pattern like the one in the table to support your answer.

_____

_____

Percents, Fractions, and Decimals

6.3.8.2
Students will write equivalent percents, fractions, and decimals.

? ESSENTIAL QUESTION

How can you write equivalent percents, fractions, and decimals?

EXPLORE ACTIVITY

Writing Percents as Decimals and Fractions

You can write a percent as an equivalent fraction or as an equivalent decimal. Equivalent percents, decimals, and fractions all represent equal parts of the same whole.

EXAMPLE 1 **Lorenzo spends 35% of his budget on rent for his apartment. Write this percent as a fraction and as a decimal.**

STEP 1 Write the percent as a fraction in simplest form.

Percent means _____. $35\% = \dfrac{\boxed{}}{100}$

Simplify the fraction. $\dfrac{35}{100} = \dfrac{7}{\boxed{}}$

$\div 5$ ... $\div 5$

Math On the Spot
my.hrw.com

STEP 2 Write the percent as a decimal.

Write the decimal equivalent of $\dfrac{35}{100}$. $\dfrac{35}{100} =$ _____

So, 35% written as a fraction in simplest form is $\boxed{}$ and written as a decimal is _____.

YOUR TURN

Write each percent as a fraction and as a decimal.

1. 15% _____
2. 48% _____
3. 80% _____
4. 75% _____
5. 36% _____
6. 40% _____

Personal Math Trainer
Online Assessment and Intervention
my.hrw.com

© Houghton Mifflin Harcourt Publishing Company

Modeling Decimal, Fraction, and Percent Equivalencies

Using models can help you understand how decimals, fractions, and percents are related.

A Model 0.78 by shading a 10-by-10 grid.

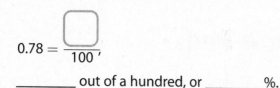

$0.78 = \dfrac{\boxed{}}{100},$

_____ out of a hundred, or _____%.

B Model 1.42 by shading 10-by-10 grids.

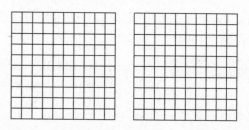

$1.42 = \dfrac{\boxed{}}{100} + \dfrac{\boxed{}}{100} = \dfrac{\boxed{}}{100} = 1\dfrac{\boxed{}}{100}.$

$1.42 = 100\% + \underline{}\% = \underline{}\%$

C Model 125% by shading 10-by-10 grids.

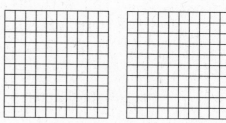

The model shows $100\% + \underline{}\% = 125\%$.

$125\% =$ the decimal _____.

$125\% = \dfrac{\boxed{}}{100} + \dfrac{\boxed{}}{100} = \dfrac{\boxed{}}{100} = 1\dfrac{\boxed{}}{100} = 1\dfrac{\boxed{}}{\boxed{}}.$

Reflect

7. **Multiple Representations** What decimal, fraction, and percent equivalencies are shown in each model? Explain.

a. _____

_____

_____

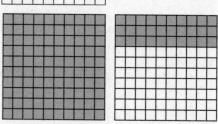

b. _____

_____

Writing Fractions as Decimals and Percents

You can write some fractions as percents by writing an equivalent fraction with a denominator of 100. This method is useful when the fraction has a denominator that is a factor or a multiple of 100. If a fraction does not have a denominator that is a factor or multiple of 100, you can use long division.

Math On the Spot

my.hrw.com

EXAMPLE 2

A 96 out of 200 animals treated by a veterinarian are horses. Write $\frac{96}{200}$ as a decimal and as a percent.

> Notice that the denominator is a multiple of 100.

STEP 1 Write an equivalent fraction with a denominator of 100.

$$\frac{96}{200} = \frac{48}{100}$$ *Divide both the numerator and denominator by 2.*

STEP 2 Write the decimal equivalent.

$$\frac{48}{100} = 0.48$$

STEP 3 Write the percent equivalent.

$$\frac{48}{100} = 48\%$$ *Percent means per 100.*

> Notice that the denominator is not a factor or multiple of 100.

B $\frac{1}{8}$ of the animals treated by the veterinarian are dogs. Write $\frac{1}{8}$ as a decimal and as a percent.

STEP 1 Use long division to divide the numerator by the denominator.

$$\frac{1}{8} = 8)\overline{1.000} \quad \begin{array}{r} 0.125 \\ \hline \end{array}$$

```
        0.125
  8)1.000
   − 8
   ─────
     20
    −16
   ─────
     40
    −40
   ─────
      0
```

Add a decimal point and zeros to the right of the numerator as needed.

The decimal equivalent of $\frac{1}{8}$ is 0.125.

STEP 2 Write the decimal as a percent.

$$0.125 = \frac{125}{1,000}$$ *Write the fraction equivalent of the decimal.*

$$\frac{125}{1,000} \overset{\div 10}{\underset{\div 10}{=}} \frac{12.5}{100}$$ *Write an equivalent fraction with a denominator of 100.*

$$\frac{12.5}{100} = 12.5\%$$ *Write as a percent.*

The percent equivalent of $\frac{1}{8}$ is 12.5%.

YOUR TURN

Write each fraction as a decimal and as a percent.

8. $\frac{9}{25}$ _____

9. $\frac{7}{8}$ _____

Guided Practice

1. Helene spends 12% of her budget on transportation expenses. Write this percent as a fraction and as a decimal. (Explore Activity Example 1)

_____

Model the decimal. Then write percent and fraction equivalents.
(Explore Activity 2)

2. 0.53

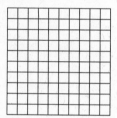

_____

3. 1.07

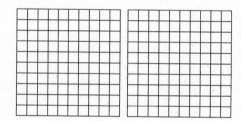

_____

Write each fraction as a decimal and as a percent. (Example 2)

4. $\frac{7}{20}$ of the packages _____

5. $\frac{3}{8}$ of a pie _____

? **ESSENTIAL QUESTION CHECK-IN**

6. How does the definition of *percent* help you write fraction and decimal equivalents?

_____

_____

_____

_____

_____

8.2 Independent Practice

Write each percent as a fraction and as a decimal.

7. 72% full

8. 25% successes

9. 500% increase

_____

_____

_____

10. 5% tax

11. 37% profit

12. 165% improvement

_____

_____

_____

Write each fraction as a decimal and as a percent.

13. $\frac{5}{8}$ of an inch

14. $\frac{258}{300}$ of the contestants

15. $\frac{350}{100}$ of the revenue

_____

_____

_____

16. The poster shows how many of its games the football team has won so far. Express this information as a fraction, a percent, and as a decimal.

17. Justine answered 68 questions correctly on an 80-question test. Express this amount as a fraction, percent, and decimal.

GO TEAM!

12 out of 15 wins!

_____

_____

Each diagram is made of smaller, identical pieces. Tell how many pieces you would shade to model the given percent.

18. 75% _____

19. 25% _____

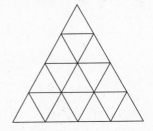

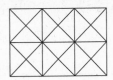

20. Multiple Representations At Brian's Bookstore, 0.3 of the shelves hold mysteries, 25% of the shelves hold travel books, and $\frac{7}{20}$ of the shelves hold children's books. Which type of book covers the most shelf space in the store? Explain how you arrived at your answer.

_____

_____

H.O.T. FOCUS ON HIGHER ORDER THINKING

21. Critical Thinking A newspaper article reports the results of an election between two candidates. The article says that Smith received 60% of the votes and that Murphy received $\frac{1}{3}$ of the votes. A reader writes in to complain that the article cannot be accurate. What reason might the reader have to say this?

_____

_____

_____

22. Represent Real-World Problems Evan budgets $2,000 a month to spend on living expenses for his family. Complete the table to express the portion spent on each cost as a percent, fraction, and decimal.

	Food: $500	Rent: $1,200	Transportation: $300
Fraction			
Percent			
Decimal			

23. Communicate Mathematical Ideas Find the sum of each row in the table. Explain why these sums make sense.

_____

_____

_____

24. Explain the Error Your friend says that 14.5% is equivalent to the decimal 14.5. Explain why your friend is incorrect by comparing the fractional equivalents of 14.5% and 14.5.

_____

_____

Triple Equivalence

Playing the Game

STEP 1 Complete the Percent, Decimal, and Fraction columns of your table, so that the three entries in each row are equivalent, making sure fractions are written in simplest form. Do not enter your name. When the group is finished, check each other's work.

Percent	Decimal	Fraction	Player Name
52%	0.52	$\frac{13}{25}$	

STEP 2 Shuffle the game cards, and deal five cards to each player. Place the remainder of the deck face-down in the middle of the group for all to reach. Players take turns, proceeding clockwise. When it is your turn, ask any other player for a specific card that is equivalent to a card currently in your hand. If the player has the card you asked for, he or she must hand you the card. If the player does not have the card, draw the top card from the deck to end your turn.

For example, Player 1 has the 52% card, and asks Player 2 for the 0.52 card. Player 2 has the 0.52 card, and passes it to Player 1.

STEP 3 When a triple is gathered by a single player, the player places the three cards face-up. Then, all group members write the player's name in the Player Name column for the corresponding row in their table.

Percent	Decimal	Fraction	Player Name
52%	0.52	$\frac{13}{25}$	Player 1

STEP 4 If at any time you run out of cards, immediately draw three cards from the top of the deck. If there are fewer than three cards, draw the remaining card(s). Play continues without drawing until all triples are formed.

Winning the Game

The player with the most triples in the table at the end of the game wins.

Percent	Decimal	Fraction	Player Name
	0.05		
10%			
	0.15		
		$\frac{1}{5}$	
	0.25		
		$\frac{7}{20}$	
40%			
		$\frac{21}{50}$	
50%			
	0.55		
60%			
		$\frac{3}{4}$	
	0.8		
90%			
		$\frac{19}{20}$	
		$\frac{5}{5}$	

LESSON 8.3 Solving Percent Problems

6.3.8.3

Students will use percents to solve problems.

 ESSENTIAL QUESTION

How do you use percents to solve problems?

EXPLORE ACTIVITY Real World

Modeling a Percent Problem

You can use a model to solve a percent problem.

A sports store received a shipment of 400 baseball gloves. 30% were left-handed. How many left-handed gloves were in the shipment?

A Use the diagram to solve this problem.

30% means 30 out of _____.

There were _____ left-handed gloves
for every 100 baseball gloves.

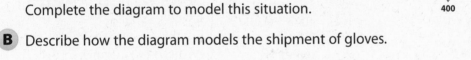

Complete the diagram to model this situation.

B Describe how the diagram models the shipment of gloves.

_____

_____

_____

C Explain how you can use the diagram to find the total number of
left-handed gloves in the shipment.

_____

D Use a bar model to solve this problem. The bar represents 100%, or the
entire shipment of 400 gloves. The bar is divided into 10 equal parts.
Complete the labels along the bottom of the bar.

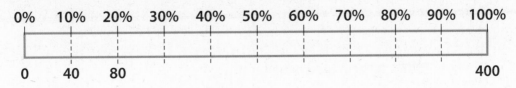

© Houghton Mifflin Harcourt Publishing Company • Image Credits: ©Photodisc/
Getty Images

Lesson 8.3 **215**

Reflect

1. **Justify Reasoning** How did you determine the labels along the bottom of the bar model in Step D?

_____

_____

2. **Communicate Mathematical Ideas** How can you use the bar model to find the number of left-handed gloves?

_____

Math On the Spot

ⓑ my.hrw.com

Finding a Percent of a Number

A percent is equivalent to the ratio of a part to a whole. To find a percent of a number, you can write a ratio to represent the percent, and find an equivalent ratio that compares the part to the whole.

To find 30% of 400, you can use:

> The word *of* indicates multiplication.

Proportional Reasoning

$$\frac{30}{100} = \frac{?}{400} \quad \begin{matrix} \leftarrow\text{part} \\ \leftarrow\text{whole} \end{matrix}$$

$$= \frac{120}{400}$$

(×4 arrows around the proportion)

Multiplication

$$30\% \text{ of } 400 = \frac{30}{100} \text{ of } 400$$

$$= \frac{30}{100} \times 400$$

$$= 120$$

EXAMPLE 1

A Use proportional reasoning to find 28% of 25.

Math Talk
Mathematical Processes

Could you also use the proportion $\frac{28}{100} = \frac{?}{25}$ to find 28% of 25? Explain.

STEP 1 Write a proportion comparing the percent to the ratio of part to whole.

$$\frac{?}{25} = \frac{28}{100}$$

Notice that 25 is a factor of 100.

STEP 2 Find the multiplication factor.

$$\begin{matrix} \text{part} \rightarrow \\ \text{whole} \rightarrow \end{matrix} \frac{?}{25} = \frac{28}{100}$$

(×4 arrows)

Since 25 · 4 = 100, find what number times 4 equals 28.

STEP 3 Find the numerator.

$$\frac{7}{25} = \frac{28}{100}$$

Since 4 · 7 = 28, 28% of 25 = 7.

28% of 25 is 7.

B Multiply by a fraction to find 35% of 60.

STEP 1 Write the percent as a fraction.

$$35\% \text{ of } 60 = \frac{35}{100} \text{ of } 60$$

STEP 2 Multiply.

$$\frac{35}{100} \text{ of } 60 = \frac{35}{100} \times 60$$

$$= \frac{2,100}{100}$$

$$= 21 \quad \text{Simplify.}$$

35% of 60 is 21.

C Multiply by a decimal to find 5% of 180.

STEP 1 Write the percent as a decimal.

$$5\% = \frac{5}{100} = 0.05$$

STEP 2 Multiply.

$$180 \times 0.05 = 9$$

5% of 180 is 9.

Animated Math

my.hrw.com

Reflect

3. **Analyze Relationships** In **B**, the percent is 35%. What is the part and what is the whole?

_____

_____

4. **Communicate Mathematical Ideas** Explain how to use proportional reasoning to find 35% of 600.

_____

_____

_____

_____

_____

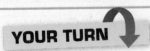 **YOUR TURN**

Find the percent of each number.

5. 38% of 50 _____ 6. 27% of 300 _____ 7. 60% of 75 _____

Personal Math Trainer

Online Assessment and Intervention

my.hrw.com

Find a Percent Given a Part and a Whole

You can use proportional reasoning to solve problems in which you need to find a percent.

EXAMPLE 2 Real World

The school principal spent $2,000 to buy some new computer equipment. Of this money, $120 was used to buy some new keyboards. What percent of the money was spent on keyboards?

STEP 1 Since you want to know the part of the money spent on keyboards, compare the part to the whole.

part → $120
whole → $2,000

STEP 2 Write a proportion comparing the percent to the ratio of part to whole.

part → $\dfrac{?}{100} = \dfrac{120}{2,000}$ ← part
whole → ← whole

STEP 3 Find the multiplication factor.

$\dfrac{?}{100} = \dfrac{120}{2,000}$ ×20

Since $100 \times 20 = 2,000$, find what number times 20 equals 120.

STEP 4 Find the numerator.

$\dfrac{6}{100} = \dfrac{120}{2,000}$

Since $20 \times 6 = 120$, the percent is 6%.

The principal spent 6% of the money on keyboards.

Reflect

8. **Communicate Mathematical Ideas** Write 57% as a ratio. Which part of the ratio represents the part and which part represents the whole? Explain.

_____

_____

_____

YOUR TURN

9. Out of the 25 students in Mrs. Green's class, 19 have a pet. What percent of the students in Mrs. Green's class have a pet? _____

Finding a Whole Given a Part and a Percent

You can use proportional reasoning to solve problems in which you know a part and a percent and need to find the whole.

Math On the Spot
my.hrw.com

EXAMPLE 3

Twelve of the students in the school choir like to sing solos. These 12 students make up 24% of the choir. How many students are in the choir?

STEP 1 Since you want to know the total number of students in the choir, compare the part to the whole.

part → 12
whole → $\frac{12}{?}$

STEP 2 Write a proportion comparing the percent to the ratio of part to whole.

part → $\frac{12}{?} = \frac{24}{100}$ ← part
whole →   ← whole

You know that 12 students represent 24%.

STEP 3 Find the multiplication factor.

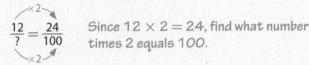

$\frac{12}{?} = \frac{24}{100}$ Since $12 \times 2 = 24$, find what number times 2 equals 100.

STEP 4 Find the denominator.

$\frac{12}{50} = \frac{24}{100}$ Since $50 \times 2 = 100$, the denominator is 50.

There are 50 students in the choir.

Math Talk
Mathematical Processes

Suppose 10 more students join the choir. None of them are soloists. What percent are soloists now?

Reflect

10. **Check for Reasonableness** In Example 3, 24% is close to 25%. How could you use this fact to check that 50 is a reasonable number for the total number of students in the choir?

_____

_____

_____

_____

YOUR TURN

11. 6 is 30% of _____.

12. 15% of _____ is 75.

Personal Math Trainer
Online Assessment and Intervention
my.hrw.com

1. A store has 300 televisions on order, and 80% are high definition. How many televisions on order are high definition? Use the bar model and complete the bottom of the bar. (Explore Activity)

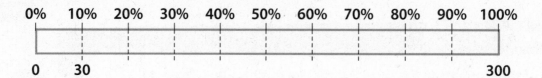

0%   10%   20%   30%   40%   50%   60%   70%   80%   90%   100%

0   30   300

2. Use proportional reasoning to find 65% of 200. (Example 1)

part → $\dfrac{\boxed{}}{100}$ = $\dfrac{?}{\boxed{}}$ ← part ← whole

65% of 200 is _____.

3. Use multiplication to find 5% of 180. (Example 1)

$\dfrac{5}{100}$ of 180 = $\dfrac{5}{100}$ $\boxed{}$ 180

= $\dfrac{\boxed{}}{100}$ = $\boxed{}$

5% of 180 is _____.

4. Alana spent $21 of her $300 paycheck on a gift. What percent of her paycheck was spent on the gift? (Example 2)

part → $\dfrac{?}{\boxed{}}$ = $\dfrac{\$\boxed{}}{\$\boxed{}}$ ← part ← whole

Alana spent _____ of her paycheck on the gift.

5. At Pizza Pi, 9% of the pizzas made last week had extra cheese. If 27 pizzas had extra cheese, how many pizzas in all were made last week? (Example 3)

part → $\dfrac{\boxed{}}{100}$ = $\dfrac{27}{?}$ ← part ← whole

There were _____ pizzas made last week.

? ESSENTIAL QUESTION CHECK-IN

6. How can you use proportional reasoning to solve problems involving percent?

_____

_____

_____

_____

8.3 Independent Practice

Find the percent of each number.

7. 64% of 75 tiles

_____

8. 20% of 70 plants

_____

9. 32% of 25 pages

_____

10. 85% of 40 e-mails

_____

11. 72% of 350 friends

_____

12. 5% of 220 files

_____

Complete each sentence.

13. 4 students is _____ % of 20 students.

14. 2 doctors is _____ % of 25 doctors.

15. _____ % of 50 shirts is 35 shirts.

16. _____ % of 200 miles is 150 miles.

17. 4% of _____ days is 56 days.

18. 60 minutes is 20% of _____ minutes.

19. 80% of_____ games is 32 games.

20. 360 kilometers is 24% of _____ kilometers.

21. 75% of _____ peaches is 15 peaches.

22. 9 stores is 3% of _____ stores.

23. At a shelter, 15% of the dogs are puppies. There are 60 dogs at the shelter.

How many are puppies? _____ puppies

24. Carl has 200 songs on his MP3 player. Of these songs, 24 are country songs. What percent of

Carl's songs are country songs? _____

25. **Consumer Math** The sales tax in the town where Amanda lives is 7%. Amanda paid $35 in sales tax on a new stereo. What was

the price of the stereo? _____

26. **Financial Literacy** Ashton is saving money to buy a new bike. He needs $120 but has only saved 60% so far. How much more money

does Ashton need to buy the scooter? _____

27. **Consumer Math** Monica paid sales tax of $1.50 when she bought a new bike helmet. If the sales tax rate was 5%, how much did the store charge

for the helmet before tax? _____

28. Use the circle graph to determine how many hours per day Becky spends on each activity.

School: _____ hours

Eating: _____ hours

Sleep: _____ hours

Homework: _____ hours

Free time: _____ hours

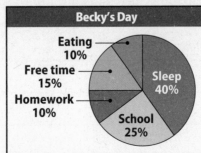

Becky's Day

Eating 10%
Free time 15%
Homework 10%
Sleep 40%
School 25%

Work Area

29. Multistep Marc ordered a rug. He gave a deposit of 30% of the cost and will pay the rest when the rug is delivered. If the deposit was $75, how much more does Marc owe? Explain how you found your answer.

_____

_____

_____

_____

_____

30. Earth Science Your weight on different planets is affected by gravity. An object that weighs 150 pounds on Earth weighs only 56.55 pounds on Mars. The same object weighs only 24.9 pounds on the Moon.

a. What percent of an object's Earth weight is its weight on Mars and on the Moon?

_____

b. Suppose x represents an object's weight on Earth. Write two expressions: one that you can use to find the object's weight on Mars and another that you can use to write the object's weight on the Moon.

_____

c. The space suit Neil Armstrong wore when he stepped on the Moon for the first time weighed about 180 pounds on Earth. How much did it weigh on the Moon?

_____

d. What If? If you could travel to Jupiter, your weight would be 236.4% of your Earth weight. How much would Neil Armstrong's space suit weigh on Jupiter?

_____

31. Explain the Error Your friend used the proportion $\frac{25}{100} = \frac{50}{?}$ to find 25% of 50 and says that the answer is 200. Explain why your friend is incorrect and find the correct answer.

_____

_____

_____

_____

Ready to Go On?

Personal Math Trainer

Online Assessment and Intervention

⏻ my.hrw.com

8.1 Understanding Percent

Shade the grid and write the equivalent percent for each fraction.

1. $\frac{19}{50}$ _____

2. $\frac{13}{20}$ _____

8.2 Percents, Fractions, and Decimals

Write each number in two equivalent forms.

3. $\frac{3}{5}$ _____

4. 62.5% _____

5. 0.24 _____

6. $\frac{31}{50}$ _____

7. Selma spent $\frac{7}{10}$ of her allowance on a new backpack. What percent of her allowance did she spend? _____

8.3 Solving Percent Problems

Complete each sentence.

8. 12 is 30% of _____.

9. 45% of 20 is _____.

10. 18 is _____ % of 30.

11. 56 is 80% of _____.

12. A pack of cinnamon-scented pencils sells for $4.00. What is the sales tax rate if the total cost of the pencils is $4.32? _____

 **ESSENTIAL QUESTION**

13. How can you solve problems involving percents?

_____

_____

_____

Selected Response

1. What percent does this shaded grid represent?

(A) 42%

(B) 48%

(C) 52%

(D) 58%

2. Which expression is **not** equal to one fourth of 52?

(A) 0.25 · 52

(B) 4% of 52

(C) 52 ÷ 4

(D) $\frac{52}{4}$

3. Approximately $\frac{4}{5}$ of U.S. homeowners have a cell phone. What percent of homeowners do **not** have a cell phone?

(A) 20%

(B) 45%

(C) 55%

(D) 80%

4. The ratio of rock music to total CDs that Ella owns is $\frac{25}{40}$. Paolo has 50 rock music CDs. The ratio of rock music to total CDs in his collection is equivalent to the ratio of rock music to total CDs in Ella's collection. How many CDs do they own?

(A) 65

(C) 120

(B) 80

(D) 130

5. Gabriel saves 40% of his monthly paycheck for college. He earned $270 last month. How much money did Gabriel save for college?

(A) $96

(C) $162

(B) $108

(D) $180

6. Forty children from an after-school club went to the matinee. This is 25% of the children in the club. How many children are in the club?

(A) 10

(C) 200

(B) 160

(D) 900

7. Dominic answered 43 of the 50 questions on his spelling test correctly. Which decimal represents the fraction of problems he answered incorrectly?

(A) 0.07

(C) 0.86

(B) 0.14

(D) 0.93

Mini-Task

8. Jen bought some sesame bagels and some plain bagels. The ratio of the number of sesame bagels to the number of plain bagels is 1 : 3.

   a. What fraction of the bagels are plain?

   _____

   b. What percent of the bagels are plain?

   _____

   c. If Jill bought 2 dozen bagels, how many of each type of bagel did she buy?

   _____

Study Guide Review

MODULE **6** **Representing Ratios and Rates**

Key Vocabulary
equivalent ratios *(razones equivalentes)*
rate *(tasa)*
ratio *(razón)*
unit rate *(tasa unitaria)*

 ESSENTIAL QUESTION

How can you use ratios and rates to solve real-world problems?

EXAMPLE 1

Tina pays $45.50 for 13 boxes of wheat crackers. What is the unit price?

$$\frac{\$45.50}{13 \text{ boxes}} = \frac{\$3.50}{1 \text{ box}}$$

The unit price is $3.50 per box of crackers.

EXAMPLE 2

A trail mix recipe calls for 3 cups of raisins and 4 cups of peanuts. Mitt made trail mix for a party and used 5 cups of raisins and 6 cups of peanuts. Did Mitt use the correct ratio of raisins to peanuts?

$$\frac{3 \text{ cups of raisins}}{4 \text{ cups of peanuts}}$$

The ratio of raisins to peanuts in the recipe is $\frac{3}{4}$.

$$\frac{5 \text{ cups of raisins}}{6 \text{ cups of peanuts}}$$

Mitt used a ratio of $\frac{5}{6}$.

$$\frac{3}{4} \times \frac{3}{3} = \frac{9}{12} \qquad \frac{5}{6} \times \frac{2}{2} = \frac{10}{12} \qquad \frac{9}{12} < \frac{10}{12}$$

Mitt used a higher ratio of raisins to peanuts in his trail mix.

EXERCISES

Write three equivalent ratios for each ratio. (Lesson 6.1)

1. $\frac{18}{6}$ _____ **2.** $\frac{5}{45}$ _____ **3.** $\frac{3}{5}$ _____

4. To make a dark orange color, Ron mixes 3 ounces of red paint with 2 ounces of yellow paint. Write the ratio of red paint to yellow paint three ways. (Lesson 6.1) _____

5. A box of a dozen fruit tarts costs $15.00. What is the cost of one fruit tart?

(Lesson 6.2) _____

Compare the ratios. (Lesson 6.3)

6. $\frac{2}{5}$ ◯ $\frac{3}{4}$ **7.** $\frac{9}{2}$ ◯ $\frac{10}{7}$ **8.** $\frac{2}{11}$ ◯ $\frac{3}{12}$ **9.** $\frac{6}{7}$ ◯ $\frac{8}{9}$

Applying Ratios and Rates

Key Vocabulary

conversion factor *(factor de conversión)*

proportion *(proporción)*

scale *(escala)*

scale drawing *(dibujo a escala)*

? **ESSENTIAL QUESTION**

How can you use ratios and rates to solve real-world problems?

EXAMPLE 1

A. **Jessica earns $5 for each dog she walks. Complete the table, describe the rule, and tell whether the relationship is additive or multiplicative. Then graph the ordered pairs on a coordinate plane.**

Number of dogs	1	2	3	4	5
Profit ($)	5	10	15	20	25

Jessica's profit is the number of dogs walked multiplied by $5. The relationship is multiplicative.

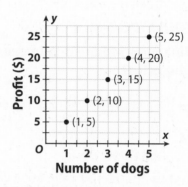

B. **A veterinarian tells Lee that his dog should have a 35 centimeter collar. What is this measurement in inches?**

Use the conversion factor 1 inch = 2.54 centimeters, written as the rate $\frac{1 \text{ in.}}{2.54 \text{ cm}}$.

$35 \text{ cm} \cdot \frac{1 \text{ in.}}{2.54 \text{ cm}} \approx 13.78$

The collar should be about 14 inches.

EXERCISES

1. Thaddeus already has $5 saved. He wants to save more to buy a book. Complete the table, and graph the ordered pairs on the coordinate graph. (Lessons 7.1, 7.2)

New savings	4	6	8	10
Total savings	9			

2. There are 2 hydrogen atoms and 1 oxygen atom in a water molecule. Complete the table, and list the equivalent ratios shown on the table. (Lessons 7.1, 7.2)

Hydrogen atoms	8		16	20
Oxygen atoms		6		

_____

3. Sam can solve 30 multiplication problems in 2 minutes. How many can he solve in 20 minutes? (Lesson 7.3)

_____

4. A male Chihuahua weighs 5 pounds. How many ounces does he weigh? (Lesson 7.4)

_____

 **Percents**

? ESSENTIAL QUESTION

How can you use percents to solve real-world problems?

EXAMPLE 1

Find an equivalent percent for $\frac{7}{10}$.

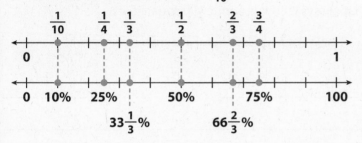

$$\frac{7}{10} = 7 \cdot \frac{1}{10} \qquad \frac{7}{10} = 7 \cdot 10\% \qquad \frac{7}{10} = 70\%$$

Find an equivalent percent for $\frac{1}{5}$.

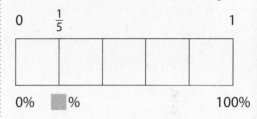

$\frac{1}{5}$ of $100 = 20$, so $\frac{1}{5}$ of $100\% = 20\%$

$\frac{1}{5} = 20\%$

EXAMPLE 2

Thirteen of the 50 states in the United States do not touch the ocean. Write $\frac{13}{50}$ as a decimal and a percent.

$$\frac{13}{50} = \frac{26}{100} \qquad \frac{26}{100} = 0.26 \qquad 0.26 = 26\% \qquad \frac{13}{50} = 0.26 = 26\%$$

EXAMPLE 3

Buckner put \$60 of his \$400 paycheck into his savings account. Find the percent of his paycheck that Buckner saved.

$$\frac{60}{400} = \frac{?}{100} \qquad \frac{60 \div 4}{400 \div 4} = \frac{15}{100} \qquad$$ Buckner saved 15% of his paycheck.

EXERCISES

Write each fraction as a decimal and a percent. (Lessons 8.1, 8.2)

1. $\frac{3}{4}$ _____

2. $\frac{7}{20}$ _____

3. $\frac{8}{5}$ _____

Complete each statement. (Lessons 8.1, 8.2)

4. 25% of 200 is _____.

5. 16 is _____ of 20.

6. 21 is 70% of _____.

7. 42 of the 150 employees at Carlo's Car Repair wear contact lenses. What percent of the employees wear

contact lenses? (Lesson 8.3) _____

8. Last week at Best Bargain, 75% of the computers sold were laptops. If 340 computers were sold last week,

how many were laptops? (Lesson 8.3) _____

Unit 3 Performance Tasks

1. **CAREERS IN MATH** Residential Builder Kaylee, a residential builder, is working on a paint budget for a custom-designed home she is building. A gallon of paint costs $38.50, and its label says it covers about 350 square feet.

a. Explain how to calculate the cost of paint per square foot. Find this value. Show your work.

_____

_____

b. Kaylee measured the room she wants to paint and calculated a total area of 825 square feet. If the paint is only available in one-gallon cans, how many cans of paint should she buy? Justify your answer.

_____

_____

2. Davette wants to buy flannel sheets. She reads that a weight of at least 190 grams per square meter is considered high quality.

a. Davette finds a sheet that has a weight of 920 grams for 5 square meters. Does this sheet satisfy the requirement for high-quality sheets? If not, what should the weight be for 5 square meters? Explain.

_____

b. Davette finds 3 more options for flannel sheets:

   Option 1: 1,100 g of flannel in 6 square meters, $45

   Option 2: 1,260 g of flannel in 6.6 square meters, $42

   Option 3: 1,300 g of flannel in 6.5 square meters, $52

She would like to buy the sheet that meets her requirements for high quality and has the lowest price per square meter. Which option should she buy? Justify your answer.

_____

_____

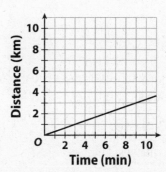
Selected Response

1. The deepest part of a swimming pool is 12 feet deep. The shallowest part of the pool is 3 feet deep. What is the ratio of the depth of the deepest part of the pool to the depth of the shallowest part of the pool?

Ⓐ 4:1

Ⓑ 12:15

Ⓒ 1:4

Ⓓ 15:12

2. How many centimeters are in 15 meters?

Ⓐ 0.15 centimeters

Ⓑ 1.5 centimeters

Ⓒ 150 centimeters

Ⓓ 1,500 centimeters

3. Barbara can walk 3,200 meters in 24 minutes. How far can she walk in 3 minutes?

Ⓐ 320 meters

Ⓑ 400 meters

Ⓒ 640 meters

Ⓓ 720 meters

4. The table below shows the number of windows and panes of glass in the windows.

Windows	2	3	4	5
Panes	12	18	24	30

Which represents the number of panes?

Ⓐ windows × 5

Ⓑ windows × 6

Ⓒ windows + 10

Ⓓ windows + 15

5. The graph below represents Donovan's speed while riding his bike.

Which would be an ordered pair on the line?

Ⓐ (1, 3)

Ⓑ (2, 2)

Ⓒ (6, 4)

Ⓓ (9, 3)

Hot Tip! Read the graph or diagram as closely as you read the actual test question. These visual aids contain important information.

6. Which percent does this shaded grid represent?

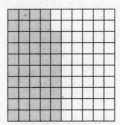

Ⓐ 42%

Ⓑ 48%

Ⓒ 52%

Ⓓ 58%

7. Ivan saves 20% of his monthly paycheck for music equipment. He earned $335 last month. How much money did Ivan save for music equipment?

Ⓐ $65

Ⓑ $67

Ⓒ $70

Ⓓ $75

8. How many 0.6-liter glasses can you fill up with a 4.5-liter pitcher?

Ⓐ 1.33 glasses

Ⓑ 3.9 glasses

Ⓒ 7.3 glasses

Ⓓ 7.5 glasses

9. Which shows the integers in order from greatest to least?

Ⓐ 22, 8, 7, 2, −11

Ⓑ 2, 7, 8, −11, 22

Ⓒ −11, 2, 7, 8, 22

Ⓓ 22, −11, 8, 7, 2

10. How do you convert 15 feet to centimeters?

Ⓐ Multiply 15 ft by $\frac{1\,ft}{12\,in.}$ and $\frac{2.54\,cm}{1\,in.}$.

Ⓑ Multiply 15 ft by $\frac{1\,ft}{12\,in.}$ and $\frac{1\,in.}{2.54\,cm}$.

Ⓒ Multiply 15 ft by $\frac{12\,in.}{1\,ft}$ and $\frac{2.54\,cm}{1\,in.}$.

Ⓓ Multiply 15 ft by $\frac{12\,in.}{1\,ft}$ and $\frac{1\,cm}{2.54\,in.}$.

Mini Task

11. Claire and Malia are training for a race.

a. Claire runs 10 km in 1 hour. How many kilometers does she run in half an hour? in $2\frac{1}{2}$ hours?

_____

b. Malia runs 5 miles in 1 hour. How many miles does she run in half an hour? in $2\frac{1}{2}$ hours?

_____

c. On Tuesday, Claire and Malia both ran for $2\frac{1}{2}$ hours. Who ran the farther distance?

_____

12. A department store is having a sale.

a. Malcolm bought 6 bowls for $13.20. What is the unit rate?

_____

b. The store is having a promotion. For every 8 glasses you buy, you get 3 free plates. Malcolm got 9 free plates. How many glasses did he buy?

_____

c. The unit rate of the glasses was $1.80 per glass. How much did Malcolm spend on glasses?

_____

13. A recipe calls for 6 cups of water and 4 cups of flour.

a. What is the ratio of water to flour?

_____

b. If the recipe is increased to use 6 cups of flour, how much water should be used?

_____

c. If the recipe is decreased to use 2 cups of water, how much flour should be used?

_____

UNIT 4
Equivalent Expressions

Generating Equivalent Numerical Expressions

MODULE 10
Generating Equivalent Algebraic Expressions

CAREERS IN MATH

Freelance Computer Programmer
A computer programmer translates commands into code, a language that a computer understands. Programmers work on a variety of tasks, from creating computer games to testing software. A freelance programmer doesn't work for a specific company; this gives the freelancer more flexibility with his or her work schedule. Computer programmers use mathematical logic when writing or altering code.

If you are interested in a career as a computer programmer, you should study these mathematical subjects:
- Algebra
- Geometry
- Trigonometry
- Calculus
- Discrete Math

Research other careers that require the understanding of mathematical logic.

Unit 4 Performance Task

At the end of the unit, check out how a **freelance computer programmer** uses math.

Light   Camera   Fly   Rotate   Cruise   View

© Houghton Mifflin Harcourt Publishing Company • Image Credits: ©berCPC/Alamy

Vocabulary Preview

Use the puzzle to preview key vocabulary from this unit. Unscramble the letters to create a key vocabulary term. Use the circled letters to answer the riddle at the bottom of the page.

1. **TEPNNEOX**

2. **EBSA**

3. **EPROW**

4. **RERDO FO SONPEOIRAT**

5. **CALIAGERB ENOXSPSRIE**

6. **ELTGNAVAIU**

7. **ELKI SEMRT**

8. **BVLIAREA**

1. Tells how many times the base appears in the expression. (Lesson 9.1)
2. A number that is multiplied. (Lesson 9.1)
3. The number formed by repeated multiplication by the same factor. (Lesson 9.1)
4. The rules which tell which calculations are done before others in an expression. (Lesson 9.3)
5. An expression that contains one or more variables. (Lesson 10.1)
6. Substituting a number for a variable in an expression and solving. (Lesson 10.2)
7. Terms with the same variables. (Lesson 10.3)
8. A letter or symbol used to represent an unknown number. (Lesson 10.1)

Q: Why does *n* always change its mind?

A: Because it's ___ ___ ___ ___ ___ ___!

Generating Equivalent Numerical Expressions

? ESSENTIAL QUESTION

How can you generate equivalent numerical expressions and use them to solve real-world problems?

Real-World Video

Assume that you post a video on the internet. Two of your friends view it, then two friends of each of those view it, and so on. The number of views is growing exponentially. Sometimes we say the video went viral.

my.hrw.com

GO DIGITAL
my.hrw.com

my.hrw.com

Go digital with your write-in student edition, accessible on any device.

Math On the Spot

Scan with your smart phone to jump directly to the online edition, video tutor, and more.

Animated Math

Interactively explore key concepts to see how math works.

Personal Math Trainer

Get immediate feedback and help as you work through practice sets.

Reading Start-Up

© Houghton Mifflin Harcourt Publishing Company

Vocabulary

Review Words
- ✔ factor *(factor)*
- factor tree *(árbol de factores)*
- ✔ integers *(entero)*
- ✔ numerical expression *(expresión numérica)*
- ✔ operations *(operaciones)*
- ✔ prime factorization *(factorización prima)*
- repeated multiplication *(multiplicación repetida)*
- simplified expression *(expresión simplificada)*

Preview Words
- base *(base)*
- exponent *(exponente)*
- order of operations *(orden de las operaciones)*
- power *(potencia)*

Visualize Vocabulary

Use the ✔ words to complete the graphic. You may put more than one word in each box.

Reviewing Factorization

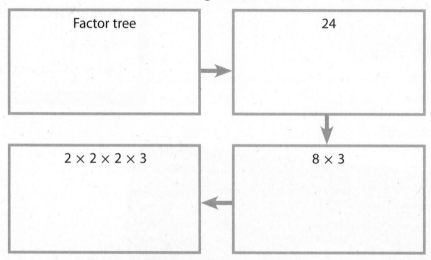

| Factor tree | → | 24 |

| 2 × 2 × 2 × 3 | ← | 8 × 3 |

Understand Vocabulary

Complete the sentences using the preview words.

1. A number that is formed by repeated multiplication by the same factor is a _____ .

2. A rule for simplifying expressions is _____ .

3. The _____ is a number that is multiplied. The number that indicates how many times this number is used as a factor is the _____ .

Active Reading

Three-Panel Flip Chart Before beginning the module, create a three-panel flip chart to help you organize what you learn. Label each flap with one of the lesson titles from this module. As you study each lesson, write important ideas like vocabulary, properties, and formulas under the appropriate flap.

Are YOU Ready?

Complete these exercises to review skills you will need for this module.

Whole Number Operations

EXAMPLE 270×83

$$
\begin{array}{r}
270 \\
\times\ 83 \\
\hline
810 \\
+21{,}600 \\
\hline
22{,}410
\end{array}
$$

$\leftarrow\ 3 \times 270$
$\leftarrow\ 80 \times 270$
$\leftarrow\ (3 \times 270) + (80 \times 270)$

Find the product.

1. 992×16 **2.** 578×27 **3.** 839×65 **4.** 367×23

_____   _____   _____   _____

Use Repeated Multiplication

EXAMPLE $5 \times 5 \times 5 \times 5$ Multiply the first two factors.

$25\ \times 5$ Multiply the result by the next factor.

$125\ \times 5$ Multiply that result by the next factor.

625 Continue until there are no more factors to multiply.

Find the product.

5. $7 \times 7 \times 7$ **6.** $3 \times 3 \times 3 \times 3$ **7.** $6 \times 6 \times 6 \times 6 \times 6$ **8.** $2 \times 2 \times 2 \times 2 \times 2 \times 2$

_____   _____   _____   _____

Division Facts

EXAMPLE $54 \div 9 = \blacksquare$ Think: 9 times what number equals 54?
$9 \times 6 = 54$

$54 \div 9 = 6$ So, $54 \div 9 = 6$.

Divide.

9. $20 \div 4$ **10.** $21 \div 7$ **11.** $42 \div 7$ **12.** $56 \div 8$

_____   _____   _____   _____

Are YOU Ready? *(cont'd)*

Complete these exercises to review skills you will need for this module.

Whole Number Operations

13. Joseph's last 13 paychecks were each $485 after taxes. How much money did Joseph make after taxes during this time?

Use Repeated Multiplication

14. Cameron has a clear container in the shape of a cube. Each edge is 9 centimeters long. He found the volume of the container in cubic centimeters by multiplying the edge length by itself 3 times. What is the volume of the container in cubic centimeters?

15. Leah multiplied the number 2 by itself 4 times ($2 \times 2 \times 2 \times 2$). Deshon multiplied the number 4 by itself 2 times (4×4). Which product is greater? Explain.

Division Facts

16. Yolanda was pouring glasses of juice for brunch. She used a 48-ounce bottle of apple juice to fill 8 glasses equally, and she used a 35-ounce bottle of orange juice to fill 7 glasses equally. Which contained more juice, a glass of apple juice or a glass of orange juice? Explain.

How do you use exponents to represent numbers?

EXPLORE ACTIVITY

Identifying Repeated Multiplication

A real-world problem may involve repeatedly multiplying a factor by itself.

A scientist observed the hourly growth of bacteria and recorded his observations in a table.

Time (h)	Total bacteria
0	1
1	2
2	$2 \times 2 = \boxed{}$
3	$2 \times 2 \times 2 = \boxed{}$
4	$2 \times 2 \times 2 \times 2 = \boxed{}$

> After 2 hours, there are $2 \cdot 2 = ?$ bacteria.

A Complete the table. What pattern(s) do you see in the Total bacteria column?

_____

_____

B Complete each statement.

At 2 hours, the total is equal to the product of two 2s.

At 3 hours, the total is equal to the product of _____ 2s.

At 4 hours, the total is equal to the product of _____ 2s.

Reflect

1. Communicate Mathematical Ideas How is the time, in hours, related to the number of times 2 is used as a factor?

_____

_____

Using Exponents

A number that is formed by repeated multiplication of the same factor is called a **power**. You can use an *exponent* and a *base* to write a power. For example, 7^3 means the product of three 7s:

$$7^3 = 7 \times 7 \times 7$$

The **base** is the number that is multiplied.

The **exponent** tells how many times the base appears in the expression.

Power	How to read the power
6^2	6 squared, 6 to the power of 2, 6 raised to the 2nd power
7^3	7 cubed, 7 to the power of 3, 7 raised to the 3rd power
9^4	9 to the power of 4, 9 raised to 4th power

EXAMPLE 1

Use an exponent to write each expression.

A $3 \times 3 \times 3 \times 3 \times 3$

Find the base, or the number being multiplied. The base is 3.

Find the exponent by counting the number of 3s being multiplied. The exponent is 5.

$$\underbrace{3 \times 3 \times 3 \times 3 \times 3}_{5 \text{ factors of } 3} = 3^5$$

B $\frac{4}{5} \times \frac{4}{5} \times \frac{4}{5} \times \frac{4}{5}$

Find the base, or the number being multiplied. The base is $\frac{4}{5}$.

Find the exponent by counting the number of times $\frac{4}{5}$ appears in the expression. The exponent is 4.

$$\underbrace{\frac{4}{5} \times \frac{4}{5} \times \frac{4}{5} \times \frac{4}{5}}_{4 \text{ factors of } \frac{4}{5}} = \left(\frac{4}{5}\right)^4$$

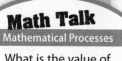

Math Talk

Mathematical Processes

What is the value of a number raised to the power of 1?

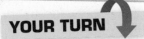

YOUR TURN

Use exponents to write each expression.

2. $4 \times 4 \times 4$ _____

3. 6 _____

4. $\frac{1}{8} \times \frac{1}{8}$ _____

5. $5 \times 5 \times 5 \times 5 \times 5 \times 5$ _____

© Houghton Mifflin Harcourt Publishing Company

Finding the Value of a Power

To find the value of a power, remember that the exponent indicates how many times to use the base as a factor.

> ### Property of Zero as an Exponent
>
> The value of any nonzero number raised to the power of 0 is 1.
>
> **Example:** $5^0 = 1$

EXAMPLE 2

Find the value of each power.

A 10^4

Identify the base and the exponent.
The base is 10, and the exponent is 4.

Evaluate: $10^4 = 10 \times 10 \times 10 \times 10 = 10,000$

B 0.4^3

Identify the base and the exponent.
The base is 0.4, and the exponent is 3.

Evaluate: $0.4^3 = 0.4 \times 0.4 \times 0.4 = 0.064$

C $\left(\frac{3}{5}\right)^0$

Identify the base and the exponent.
The base is $\frac{3}{5}$, and the exponent is 0.

Evaluate.
$\left(\frac{3}{5}\right)^0 = 1$ *Any number raised to the power of 0 is 1.*

D $\left(\frac{2}{3}\right)^2$

Identify the base and the exponent.
The base is $\frac{2}{3}$, and the exponent is 2.

Evaluate.
$\left(\frac{2}{3}\right)^2 = \left(\frac{2}{3}\right) \times \left(\frac{2}{3}\right) = \frac{4}{9}$

> **Math Talk**
> **Mathematical Processes**
>
> Is the value of 2^3 the same as the value of 3^2? Explain.

YOUR TURN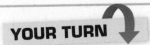

Find the value of each power.

6. 3^4 _____   **7.** $(1)^9$ _____   **8.** $\left(\frac{2}{5}\right)^3$ _____   **9.** 12^2 _____

Guided Practice

1. Complete the table. (Explore Activity 1)

Exponential form	Product	Simplified product
5^1	5	5
5^2	5×5	
5^3		125
	$5 \times 5 \times 5 \times 5$	
5^5		

Use an exponent to write each expression. (Example 1)

2. $6 \times 6 \times 6$ ______

__ factors of 6

3. $10 \times 10 \times 10 \times 10 \times 10 \times 10 \times 10$ ______

4. $\frac{3}{4} \times \frac{3}{4} \times \frac{3}{4} \times \frac{3}{4} \times \frac{3}{4}$ ______

5. $\frac{7}{9} \times \frac{7}{9} \times \frac{7}{9} \times \frac{7}{9} \times \frac{7}{9} \times \frac{7}{9} \times \frac{7}{9} \times \frac{7}{9}$ ______

Find the value of each power. (Example 2)

6. 8^3 ______

7. 7^4 ______

8. 10^3 ______

9. $\left(\frac{1}{4}\right)^2$ ______

10. $\left(\frac{1}{3}\right)^3$ ______

11. $\left(\frac{6}{7}\right)^2$ ______

12. 0.8^2 ______

13. 0.5^3 ______

14. 1.1^2 ______

15. 8^0 ______

16. 12^1 ______

17. $\left(\frac{1}{2}\right)^0$ ______

18. $(13)^2$ ______

19. $\left(\frac{2}{5}\right)^2$ ______

20. 0.9^2 ______

ESSENTIAL QUESTION CHECK-IN

21. How do you use an exponent to represent a number such as 16?

______

______

______

______

______

9.1 Independent Practice

Write the missing exponent.

22. $100 = 10^{\boxed{}}$

23. $8 = 2^{\boxed{}}$

24. $25 = 5^{\boxed{}}$

25. $27 = 3^{\boxed{}}$

26. $\dfrac{1}{169} = \left(\dfrac{1}{13}\right)^{\boxed{}}$

27. $14 = 14^{\boxed{}}$

28. $32 = 2^{\boxed{}}$

29. $\dfrac{64}{81} = \left(\dfrac{8}{9}\right)^{\boxed{}}$

Write the missing base.

30. $1{,}000 = \boxed{}^{3}$

31. $256 = \boxed{}^{4}$

32. $16 = \boxed{}^{4}$

33. $9 = \boxed{}^{2}$

34. $\dfrac{1}{9} = \left(\boxed{}\right)^{2}$

35. $64 = \boxed{}^{2}$

36. $\dfrac{9}{16} = \left(\boxed{}\right)^{2}$

37. $729 = \boxed{}^{3}$

For Exercises 38–42, write the answer with and without using an exponent.

38. Hadley's softball team has a phone tree in case a game is canceled. The coach calls 3 players. Then each of those players calls 3 players, and so on. How many players will be notified during the third round of calls?

_____

39. Tim is reading a book. On Monday he reads 3 pages. On each day after that, he reads 3 times the number of pages that he read on the previous day. How many pages does he read on Thursday?

_____

40. The square tile shown has a side length of 10.5 inches. What power can you write to represent the area of the tile? Write the power as an expression with a base and an exponent, and then find the area of the square.

_____

41. Antonia is saving for a video game. On the first day, she saves two dollars in her piggy bank. Each day after that, she doubles the number of dollars she saved on the previous day. How many dollars does she save on the sixth day?

_____

42. A certain colony of bacteria triples in length every 10 minutes. Its length is now 1 millimeter. How long will it be in 40 minutes?

_____

43. Which power can you write to represent the volume of the cube shown? Write the power as an expression with a base and an exponent, and then find the volume of the cube.

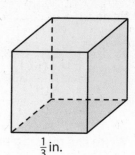

$\frac{1}{3}$ in.

_____

44. Write a power represented with a positive base and a positive exponent whose value is less than the base.

_____

Work Area

45. Communicate Mathematical Ideas What is the value of 1 raised to the power of any exponent? What is the value of 0 raised to the power of any nonnegative nonzero exponent? Explain.

_____

_____

_____

_____

46. Look for a Pattern Find the values of the powers in the following pattern: 10^1, 10^2, 10^3, 10^4.... Describe the pattern, and use it to evaluate 10^6 without using multiplication.

_____

_____

_____

_____

47. Critical Thinking Some numbers can be written as powers of different bases. For example, $81 = 9^2$ and $81 = 3^4$. Write the number 64 using three different bases.

_____

48. Justify Reasoning Oman said that it is impossible to raise a number to the power of 2 and get a value less than the original number. Do you agree with Oman? Justify your reasoning.

_____

_____

_____

LESSON
9.2 Prime Factorization

6.4.9.2
Students will write the prime factorization of a number.

ESSENTIAL QUESTION

How do you write the prime factorization of a number?

EXPLORE ACTIVITY

Finding Factors of a Number

Whole numbers that are multiplied to find a product are called factors of that product. A number is divisible by its factors. For example, 4 and 2 are factors of 8 because $4 \cdot 2 = 8$, and 8 is divisible by 4 and by 2.

Math On the Spot
my.hrw.com

EXAMPLE 1 **Ana wants to build a rectangular garden with an area of 24 square feet. What are the possible whole number lengths and widths of the garden?**

STEP 1 Recall that area = length · width. For Ana's garden,
_____ ft² = length · width.

STEP 2 List the factors of 24 in pairs. List each pair only once.

$24 = 1 \cdot$ _____ $24 = 3 \cdot$ _____

$24 = 2 \cdot$ _____ $24 = 4 \cdot$ _____

> $4 \cdot 6 = 6 \cdot 4$, so you only list $4 \cdot 6$.

You can also use a diagram to show the factor pairs.

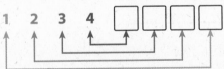

1   2   3   4   ▢ ▢ ▢ ▢

The factors of 24 are: 1, 2, 3, _____.

STEP 3 The possible lengths and widths are:

Length (ft)	24	12	8	6
Width (ft)				

YOUR TURN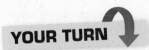

List all the factors of each number.

1. 21 _____

2. 37 _____

3. 42 _____

4. 30 _____

Personal Math Trainer

Online Assessment and Intervention

my.hrw.com

Finding the Prime Factorization of a Number

Animated Math

my.hrw.com

The prime factorization of a number is the number written as the product of its prime factors. For example, the prime factors of 12 are 3, 2, and 2.

The prime factorization of 12 is $2 \cdot 3 \cdot 2$ or $2^2 \cdot 3$.

> Use exponents to show repeated factors.

Use a factor tree to find the prime factorization of 240.

A List the factor pairs of 240.

240

$\cdot$ 48

_____

_____

B Choose any factor pair to begin the tree. If a number in this pair is prime, circle it. If a number in the pair can be written as a product of two factors, draw additional branches and write the factors.

C Continue adding branches until the factors at the ends of the branches are prime numbers.

D Write the prime factorization of 240.

_____

Then write the prime factorization using exponents.

_____

Reflect

240

5. What If? What will the factor tree for 240 look like if you start the tree with a different factor pair? Check your prediction by creating another factor tree for 240 that starts with a different factor pair.

_____

_____

_____

_____

Using a Ladder Diagram

A ladder diagram is another way to find the prime factorization of a number.

Use a ladder diagram to find the prime factorization of 132.

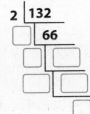

A Write 132 in the top "step" of the ladder. Choose a prime factor of 132 to write next to the step with 132. Choose 2. Divide 132 by 2 and write the quotient 66 in the next step of the ladder.

B Now choose a prime factor of 66. Write the prime factor next to the step with 66. Divide 66 by that prime factor and write the quotient in the next step of the ladder.

C Keep choosing prime factors, dividing, and adding to the ladder until you get a quotient of 1.

D What are the prime factors of 132? How can you tell from the ladder diagram?

_____

_____

E Write the prime factorization of 132 using exponents.

_____

Reflect

6. Complete a factor tree and a ladder diagram to find the prime factorization of 54.

54
⋏

7. **Communicate Mathematical Ideas** If one person uses a ladder diagram and another uses a factor tree to write a prime factorization, will they get the same result? Explain.

_____

_____

Use a diagram to list the factor pairs of each number. (Explore Activity Example 1)

1. 18

2. 52

_____

_____

3. Karl needs to build a stage that has an area of 72 square feet. The length of the stage should be longer than the width. What are the possible whole number measurements for the length and width of the stage? (Explore Activity Example 1)

Complete the table with possible measurements of the stage.

Length	72				
Width		2			

Use a factor tree to find the prime factorization of each number.
(Explore Activity 2)

4. 402

5. 36

_____

_____

Use a ladder diagram to find the prime factorization of each number.
(Explore Activity 3)

6. 64

7. 27

_____

_____

? ESSENTIAL QUESTION CHECK-IN

8. Tell how you know when you have found the prime factorization of a number.

_____

_____

9.2 Independent Practice

Personal
Math Trainer

Online
Assessment and
Intervention

my.hrw.com

9. Multiple Representations Use the grid to draw three different rectangles so that each has an area of 12 square units and they all have different widths. What are the dimensions of the rectangles?

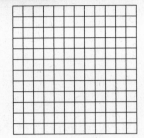

_____

_____

10. Brandon has 32 stamps. He wants to display the stamps in rows, with the same number of stamps in each row. How many different ways can he display the stamps? Explain.

_____

_____

_____

11. Communicate Mathematical Ideas How is finding the factors of a number different from finding the prime factorization of a number?

_____

_____

_____

_____

Find the prime factorization of each number.

12. 891 _____   **13.** 504 _____

14. 23 _____   **15.** 230 _____

16. The number 2 is chosen to begin a ladder diagram to find the prime factorization of 66. What other numbers could have been used to start the ladder diagram for 66? How does starting with a different number change the diagram?

_____

_____

_____

17. Critical Thinking List five numbers that have 3, 5, and 7 as prime factors.

_____

18. In a game, you draw a card with three consecutive numbers on it. You can choose one of the numbers and find the sum of its prime factors. Then you can move that many spaces. You draw a card with the numbers 25, 26, 27. Which number should you choose if you want to move as many spaces as possible? Explain.

_____

_____

_____

_____

19. **Explain the Error** When asked to write the prime factorization of the number 27, a student wrote $9 \cdot 3$. Explain the error and write the correct answer.

_____

 FOCUS ON HIGHER ORDER THINKING

20. **Communicate Mathematical Ideas** Explain why it is possible to draw more than two different rectangles with an area of 36 square units, but it is not possible to draw more than two different rectangles with an area of 15 square units. The sides of the rectangles are whole numbers.

_____

_____

_____

21. **Critique Reasoning** Alice wants to find all the prime factors of the number you get when you multiply $17 \cdot 11 \cdot 13 \cdot 7$. She thinks she has to use a calculator to perform all the multiplications and then find the prime factorization of the resulting number. Do you agree? Why or why not?

_____

_____

_____

22. **Look for a Pattern** Ryan wrote the prime factorizations shown below. If he continues this pattern, what prime factorization will he show for the number one million? What prime factorization will he show for one billion?

$10 = 5 \cdot 2$

$100 = 5^2 \cdot 2^2$

$1{,}000 = 5^3 \cdot 2^3 = 1{,}000$

_____

Work Area

LESSON

9.3 Order of Operations

6.4.9.3

Students will use the order of operations to simplify expressions with exponents.

 ESSENTIAL QUESTION

How do you use the order of operations to simplify expressions with exponents?

 **EXPLORE ACTIVITY** Real World

Exploring the Order of Operations

Order of Operations

1. Perform operations in parentheses.

2. Find the value of numbers with exponents.

3. Multiply or divide from left to right.

4. Add or subtract from left to right.

Amy and three friends launch a new website. Each friend e-mails the web address to three new friends. These new friends forward the web address to three more friends. If no one receives the e-mail more than once, how many people will receive the web address in the second wave of e-mails?

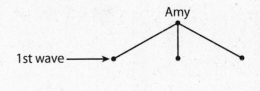

Amy

1st wave →

2nd wave →

A Use a diagram to model the situation for Amy. Each dot represents one e-mail. Complete the diagram to show the second wave.

B Complete the table to show how many e-mails are sent in each wave of Amy's diagram.

Wave	Number of e-mails	Power of 3
1st		
2nd		

C Amy is just one of four friends initiating the first wave of e-mails. Write an expression for the total number of e-mails sent in the 2nd wave.

number of people × number of e-mails in 2nd wave written as a power

 × ☐

D Identify the computation that should be done first to simplify the expression in **C**. Then simplify the expression.

Multiply 4 and 3 / Find the value of 3^2

The value of the expression is 4 × _____ = _____.

Reflect

1. In **B**, why does it makes sense to write the numbers of e-mails as powers? What is the pattern for the number of e-mails in each wave for Amy?

_____

_____

_____

Math On the Spot
⏻ my.hrw.com

Simplifying Numerical Expressions

A numerical expression is an expression involving numbers and operations. You can use the order of operations to simplify numerical expressions.

EXAMPLE 1

Simplify each expression.

A $5 + 18 \div 3^2$

$$5 + 18 \div 3^2 = 5 + 18 \div 9 \qquad \text{Evaluate } 3^2.$$
$$= 5 + 2 \qquad \text{Divide.}$$
$$= 7 \qquad \text{Add.}$$

B $21 + \frac{3^2}{3}$

$$21 + \frac{3^2}{3} = 21 + \frac{9}{3} \qquad \text{Evaluate } 3^2.$$
$$= 21 + 3 \qquad \text{Divide.}$$
$$= 24 \qquad \text{Add.}$$

C $6 \times 2^3 \div 3 + 1$

$$6 \times 2^3 \div 3 + 1 = 6 \times 8 \div 3 + 1 \qquad \text{Evaluate } 2^3.$$
$$= 48 \div 3 + 1 \qquad \text{Multiply.}$$
$$= 16 + 1 \qquad \text{Divide.}$$
$$= 17 \qquad \text{Add.}$$

Personal Math Trainer

Online Assessment and Intervention

⏻ my.hrw.com

YOUR TURN

Simplify each expression using the order of operations.

2. $7 + 15 \times 9^2 =$ _____

3. $220 - 450 \div 3^2 =$ _____

Using Exponents with Grouping Symbols

Remember to perform operations inside parentheses first when you simplify expressions.

Math On the Spot
my.hrw.com

EXAMPLE 2

Simplify each expression using the order of operations.

A $4 \times (9 \div 3)^2$

$4 \times (9 \div 3)^2 = 4 \times 3^2$	Perform operations inside parentheses.
$= 4 \times 9$	Evaluate 3^2.
$= 36$	Multiply.

B $5^3 + (12 - 2)^2$

$5^3 + (12 - 2)^2 = 5^3 + 10^2$	Perform operations inside parentheses.
$= 125 + 100$	Evaluate powers.
$= 225$	Add.

C $8 + \dfrac{(12 - 8)^2}{2}$

$8 + \dfrac{(12 - 8)^2}{2} = 8 + \dfrac{4^2}{2}$	Perform operations inside parentheses.
$= 8 + \dfrac{16}{2}$	Evaluate 4^2.
$= 8 + 8$	Divide.
$= 16$	Add.

Reflect

4. **Critique Reasoning** John wants to simplify the expression $(5 + 3)^2$. As a first step, he writes $5^2 + 3^2$. Will he get the correct value for the expression? If not, what should he do to simplify the expression?

_____

_____

_____

YOUR TURN

Simplify each expression using the order of operations.

5. $5 \times (20 \div 4)^2 = $ _____

6. $8^2 - (5 + 2)^2 = $ _____

7. $7 - \dfrac{(63 \div 9)^2}{7} = $ _____

Personal Math Trainer

Online Assessment and Intervention

my.hrw.com

1. In a video game, a guppy that escapes a net turns into three goldfish. Each goldfish can turn into two betta fish. Each betta fish can turn into two angelfish. Complete the diagram and write the number of fish at each stage. Write and evaluate an expression for the number of angelfish that can be formed from one guppy. (Explore Activity)

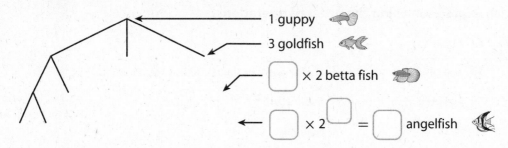

1 guppy

3 goldfish

☐ × 2 betta fish

☐ × 2^☐ = ☐ angelfish

_____

Complete to simplify each expression. (Examples 1 and 2)

2. $89 - 4^2 \times 4 + 12 = 89 - \underline{\hspace{1cm}} \times 4 + 12$

   $= 89 - \underline{\hspace{1cm}} + 12$

   $= \underline{\hspace{1cm}} + 12$

   $= \underline{\hspace{1cm}}$

3. $6 \times (36 \div 12)^2 + 8 = 6 \times (\underline{\hspace{1cm}})^2 + 8$

   $= 6 \times \underline{\hspace{1cm}} + 8$

   $= \underline{\hspace{1cm}} + 8$

   $= \underline{\hspace{1cm}}$

4. $12 \times \left(\dfrac{(4 + 2)^2}{4} \right) - 7 = 12 \times \left(\dfrac{(\boxed{})^2}{4} \right) - 7$

   $= 12 \times \left(\dfrac{\boxed{}}{4} \right) - 7$

   $= 12 \times \underline{\hspace{1cm}} - 7$

   $= \underline{\hspace{1cm}} - 7$

   $= \underline{\hspace{1cm}}$

5. $320 \div \left(\dfrac{(11 - 9)^3}{2} \right) \times 8 = 320 \div \left(\dfrac{(\boxed{})^3}{2} \right) \times 8$

   $= 320 \div \left(\dfrac{\boxed{}}{2} \right) \times 8$

   $= 320 \div \underline{\hspace{1cm}} \times 8$

   $= \underline{\hspace{1cm}} \times 8$

   $= \underline{\hspace{1cm}}$

? ESSENTIAL QUESTION CHECK-IN

6. How do you use the order of operations to simplify expressions with exponents?

   _____

   _____

   _____

9.3 Independent Practice

Simplify each expression using the order of operations.

7. $5 \times 2 + 3^2$ _____

8. $15 - 7 \times 2 + 2^3$ _____

9. $(11 - 8)^3 - 2 \times 6$ _____

10. $6 + 3(13 - 2) - 5^2$ _____

11. $12 + \dfrac{9^2}{3}$ _____

12. $\dfrac{8 + 6^2}{11} + 7 \times 2$ _____

13. **Explain the Error** Jay simplified the expression $3 \times (3 + 12 \div 3) - 4$. For his first step, he added $3 + 12$ to get 15. What was Jay's error? Find the correct answer.

_____

_____

14. **Multistep** A clothing store has the sign shown in the shop window. Pani sees the sign and wants to buy 3 shirts and 2 pairs of jeans. The cost of each shirt before the discount is $12, and the cost of each pair of jeans is $19 before the discount.

SALE Today ONLY $3 off every purchase!

a. Write and simplify an expression to find the amount Pani pays if a $3 discount is applied to her total.

_____

b. Pani says she should get a $3 discount on the price of each shirt and a $3 discount on the price of each pair of jeans. Write and simplify an expression to find the amount she would pay if this is true.

_____

c. **Analyze Relationships** Why are the amounts Pani pays in **a** and **b** different?

_____

_____

d. If you were the shop owner, how would you change the sign? Explain.

_____

_____

_____

_____

15. Ellen is playing a video game in which she captures butterflies. There are 3 butterflies onscreen, but the number of butterflies doubles every minute. After 4 minutes, she was able to capture 7 of the butterflies.

a. Look for a Pattern Write an expression for the number of butterflies after 4 minutes. Use a power of 2 in your answer.

_____

b. Write an expression for the number of butterflies remaining after Ellen captured the 7 butterflies. Simplify the expression.

_____

16. Show how to write, evaluate and simplify an expression to represent and solve this problem: Jeff and his friend each text four classmates about a concert. Each classmate then texts four students from another school about the concert. If no one receives the message more than once, how many students from the other school receive a text about the concert?

_____

© Houghton Mifflin Harcourt Publishing Company • Image Credits: imagebroker/Alamy

 **FOCUS ON HIGHER ORDER THINKING**

Work Area

17. Geometry The figure shown is a rectangle. The green shape in the figure is a square. The blue and white shapes are rectangles, and the area of the blue rectangle is 24 square inches.

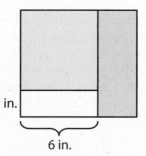

2 in.

6 in.

a. Write an expression for the area of the entire figure that includes an exponent. Then find the area.

_____

b. Find the dimensions of the entire figure.

_____

18. Explain the Error Rob and Lila try to simplify $18 \times 4^2 + (9 - 3)^2$. Rob simplifies the expression and gets 360. Lila simplifies it and gets 324. Which student is correct? What error did the other student make?

_____

_____

_____

19. Persevere in Problem Solving Use parentheses to make this statement true: $8 \times 4 - 2 \times 3 + 8 \div 2 = 25$

_____

Goooaaalll!

Playing the Game

STEP 1 Start with the first goal in the table. Roll all four number cubes and write the results in the Numbers column of your table. Each player should complete a roll before the next step.

STEP 2 On scratch paper, use the numbers you rolled to create a numerical expression whose value is as close as possible to the goal number. You may use the four operations (addition, subtraction, multiplication, and division), write a number as an exponent, or group two numbers using parentheses. You may not use any of these more than once for any goal number, but you may use parentheses to indicate multiplication in addition to using a multiplication symbol. The expression $2(3 \times 4)^2$ is an acceptable expression.

For example, if 1, 2, 4, and 5 are rolled, write and evaluate numerical expressions on scratch paper to find one whose value is as close as possible to the Goal number.

$$5 \times 2(4 - 1) = 30 \qquad 5(2 + 1) + 4 = 19 \qquad 4^2 + 5 - 1 = 20$$
$$1(2^4 + 5) = 21 \qquad 5^2 - 4 + 1 = 22 \qquad 5(4 + 1) - 2 = 23$$

STEP 3 Write both the expression that you chose and its value in your table. Then find the distance from the value of your expression to the goal, and write it in the table. Remember, the distance between two numbers on a number line is the absolute value of the difference of the numbers. For example,

$$|25 - 23| = 2$$

Goal	Numbers	Expression	Value	Distance from Goal
25	1, 2, 4, 5	$5(4 + 1) - 2$	23	2

STEP 4 Repeat Steps 1–3 for each of the remaining goals.

STEP 5 After you have completed all rows of the table, find the total of the Distance from Goal column and write it in the table.

Winning the Game

The winner of the game is the player with the lowest total in the Distance from Goal column.

Goal	Numbers	Expression	Value	Distance from Goal
87				
92				
58				
75				
65				
15				
40				
130				
27				
225				
TOTAL:				

Ready to Go On?

Personal Math Trainer

Online Assessment and Intervention

my.hrw.com

9.1 Exponents

Find the value of each power.

1. 7^3 _____

2. 9^2 _____

3. $\left(\frac{7}{9}\right)^2$ _____

4. $\left(\frac{1}{2}\right)^6$ _____

5. $\left(\frac{2}{3}\right)^3$ _____

6. $\left(\frac{1}{3}\right)^4$ _____

7. 12^0 _____

8. 1.4^2 _____

9.2 Prime Factorization

Find the factors of each number.

9. 96 _____

10. 120 _____

Find the prime factorization of each number.

11. 58 _____

12. 212 _____

13. 2,800 _____

14. 900 _____

9.3 Order of Operations

Simplify each expression using the order of operations.

15. $(21 - 3) \div 3^2$ _____

16. $7^2 \times (6 \div 3)$ _____

17. $17 + 15 \div 3 - 2^4$ _____

18. $(8 + 56) \div 4 - 3^2$ _____

19. The nature park has a pride of 7 adult lions and 4 cubs. The adults eat 6 pounds of meat each day and the cubs eat 3 pounds. Simplify $7 \times 6 + 4 \times 3$ to find the amount of meat consumed each day by the lions. _____

 ESSENTIAL QUESTION

20. How do you use numerical expressions to solve real-world problems?

_____

_____

_____

_____

MODULE 9 MIXED REVIEW
Assessment Readiness

Personal
Math Trainer

Online
Assessment and
Intervention

my.hrw.com

Selected Response

1. Which expression has a value that is less than the base of that expression?

Ⓐ 2^3

Ⓑ $\left(\frac{5}{6}\right)^2$

Ⓒ 3^2

Ⓓ 4^4

2. After the game the coach bought 9 chicken meals for $5 each and 15 burger meals for $6 each. What percent of the total amount the coach spent was used for the chicken meals?

Ⓐ $33\frac{1}{3}\%$

Ⓑ 45%

Ⓒ $66\frac{2}{3}\%$

Ⓓ 90%

3. Which operation should you perform first when you simplify $175 - (8 + 45 \div 3) \times 7$?

Ⓐ addition

Ⓑ division

Ⓒ multiplication

Ⓓ subtraction

4. For a game, three people are chosen in the first round. Each of those people chooses 3 people in the second round, and so on. How many people are chosen in the sixth round?

Ⓐ 18

Ⓑ 216

Ⓒ 243

Ⓓ 729

5. Which expression shows the prime factorization of 100?

Ⓐ $2^2 \times 5^2$

Ⓒ 10^{10}

Ⓑ 10×10

Ⓓ $2 \times 5 \times 10$

6. Which number has only two factors?

Ⓐ 21

Ⓒ 25

Ⓑ 23

Ⓓ 27

7. Which expression is equivalent to $3.6 \times 3.6 \times 3.6 \times 3.6$?

Ⓐ 3.6×4

Ⓒ $3^4 \times 6^4$

Ⓑ 36^3

Ⓓ 3.6^4

8. Which expression gives the prime factorization of 80?

Ⓐ $2^4 \times 10$

Ⓑ $2 \times 5 \times 8$

Ⓒ $2^3 \times 5$

Ⓓ $2^4 \times 5$

Mini-Task

9. George wants to put carpeting in a rectangular living room and a square bedroom. The length and width of the living room is 12 feet by 18 feet. One side of the square bedroom is 13 feet. It will cost $3.50 per square foot to carpet the rooms.

a. Write an expression that can be used to find the total amount George will pay for carpeting.

_____

b. Evaluate the expression. How much will George pay for the carpeting?

_____

Generating Equivalent Algebraic Expressions

ESSENTIAL QUESTION

How can you generate equivalent algebraic expressions and use them to solve real-world problems?

LESSON 10.1
Modeling and Writing Expressions

LESSON 10.2
Evaluating Expressions

LESSON 10.3
Generating Equivalent Expressions

Real-World Video

Carpenters use formulas to calculate a project's materials supply. Sometimes formulas can be written in different forms. The perimeter of a rectangle can be written as $P = 2(l + w)$ or $P = 2l + 2w$.

my.hrw.com

GO DIGITAL

my.hrw.com

my.hrw.com

Go digital with your write-in student edition, accessible on any device.

Math On the Spot

Scan with your smart phone to jump directly to the online edition, video tutor, and more.

Animated Math

Interactively explore key concepts to see how math works.

Personal Math Trainer

Get immediate feedback and help as you work through practice sets.

Reading Start-Up

Vocabulary

Review Words
- base *(base)*
- exponent *(exponente)*
- numerical expression *(expresión numérica)*
- operations *(operaciones)*
- order of operations *(orden de las operaciones)*

Preview Words
- algebraic expression *(expresión algebraica)*
- coefficient *(coeficiente)*
- constant *(constante)*
- equivalent expression *(expresión equivalente)*
- evaluating *(evaluar)*
- like terms *(términos semejantes)*
- term *(término, en una expresión)*
- variable *(variable)*

Visualize Vocabulary

Use the review words to complete the graphic. You may put more than one word in each oval.

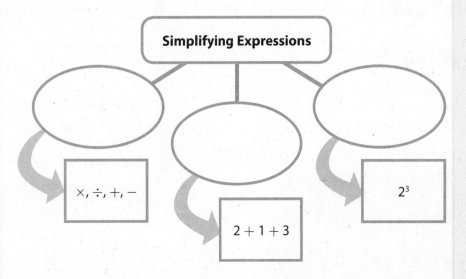

Understand Vocabulary

Complete the sentences using the preview words.

1. An expression that contains at least one variable is an

   _____ .

2. A part of an expression that is added or subtracted is a _____ .

3. A _____ is a specific number whose value does not change.

Active Reading

Key-Term Fold Before beginning the module, create a key-term fold to help you learn the vocabulary in this module. Write the highlighted vocabulary words on one side of the flap. Write the definition for each word on the other side of the flap. Use the key-term fold to quiz yourself on the definitions used in this module.

Are YOU Ready?

Complete these exercises to review skills you will need for this module.

Use of Parentheses

EXAMPLE $(6 + 4) \times (3 + 8 + 1) = 10 \times 12$ Do the operations inside parentheses first.

$= 120$ Multiply.

Evaluate.

1. $11 + (20 - 13)$ _____

2. $(10 - 7) - (14 - 12)$ _____

3. $(4 + 17) - (16 - 9)$ _____

4. $(23 - 15) - (18 - 13)$ _____

5. $8 \times (4 + 5 + 7)$ _____

6. $(2 + 3) \times (11 - 5)$ _____

Words for Operations

EXAMPLE   Write a numerical expression for the quotient of 20 and 5.   Think: *Quotient* means to divide.

$20 \div 5$ Write 20 divided by 5.

Write a numerical expression for the word expression.

7. the difference between 42 and 19 _____

8. the product of 7 and 12 _____

9. 30 more than 20 _____

10. 100 decreased by 77 _____

Evaluate Expressions

EXAMPLE   Evaluate $2(5) - 3^2$.

$2(5) - 3^2 = 2(5) - 9$ Evaluate exponents.

$= 10 - 9$ Multiply.

$= 1$ Subtract.

Evaluate the expression.

11. $3(8) - 15$ _____

12. $4(12) + 11$ _____

13. $3(7) - 4(2)$ _____

14. $4(2 + 3) - 12$ _____

15. $9(14 - 5) - 42$ _____

16. $7(8) - 5(8)$ _____

Complete these exercises to review skills you will need for this module.

Use of Parentheses

17. Kira took a quiz in which the questions were worth 5 points each. There were 12 questions in the first part and 4 questions in the second part. Evaluate the expression $5 \times (12 + 4)$ to find the total number of points that were possible for the quiz.

Words for Operations

18. How are the numerical expressions for "22 more than 45" and for "45 more than 22" different? How are they alike?

Evaluate Expressions

19. To find the area of a square that has a side length of 4 units, you can square the number 4. The expression $(4 + 3)^2$ gives the area of the square if the side lengths are increased by 3 units. How much greater is the area of the new square than the area of the original square? Explain your reasoning.

Modeling and Writing Expressions

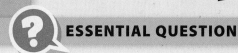

? **ESSENTIAL QUESTION**

How can you model and write algebraic expressions?

EXPLORE ACTIVITY

Math On the Spot
my.hrw.com

Writing Algebraic Expressions

An **algebraic expression** is an expression that contains one or more variables and may also contain operation symbols, such as + or −.

A **variable** is a letter or symbol used to represent an unknown or unspecified number. The value of a variable may change.

A **constant** is a specific number whose value does not change.

> 150 is a constant and y is a variable.

Algebraic Expressions	x $w + n$ $150 + y$

In algebraic expressions, multiplication and division are usually written without the symbols $\times$ and $\div$.

- Write $3 \times n$ as $3n$, $3 \cdot n$, or $n \cdot 3$.
- Write $3 \div n$ as $\frac{3}{n}$.

There are several different ways to describe expressions with words.

Operation	Addition	Subtraction	Multiplication	Division
Words	• added to • plus • sum • more than	• subtracted from • minus • difference • less than	• times • multiplied by • product • groups of	• divided by • divided into • quotient

EXAMPLE 1 Complete each statement.

A Write each phrase as an algebraic expression.

The sum of 7 and x

The operation is _____.   The algebraic expression is _____.

The quotient of z and 3

The operation is _____.   The algebraic expression is $\frac{\square}{\square}$.

B Write a phrase for each expression.

11x   The operation is _____.

Phrase: _____

8 − y   The operation is _____.

Phrase: _____

YOUR TURN

Write each phrase as an algebraic expression.

1. n times 7 _____   **2.** 4 minus y _____   **3.** 13 added to x _____

Write a phrase for each expression.

4. $\frac{x}{12}$ _____

5. 10y _____

6. c + 3 _____

Personal
Math Trainer

Online Assessment
and Intervention

⊙ my.hrw.com

Math On the Spot

⊙ my.hrw.com

Modeling Algebraic Expressions

Algebraic expressions can also be represented with models.

EXAMPLE 2

Use a bar model to represent each expression.

A 7 + x   Combine 7 and x.

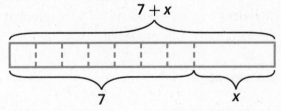

B $\frac{z}{3}$ Divide z into 3 equal parts.

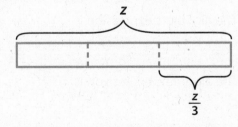

YOUR TURN

Draw a bar model to represent each expression.

7. $t - 2$

8. $4y$

Comparing Expressions Using Models

Algebraic expressions are *equivalent* if they are equal for all values of the variable. For example, $x + 2$ and $x + 1 + 1$ are equivalent.

EXAMPLE 3

Math On the Spot
⏻ my.hrw.com

Katriana and Andrew started the day with the same amount of money. Katriana spent 5 dollars on lunch. Andrew spent 3 dollars on lunch and 2 dollars on a snack after school. Do Katriana and Andrew have the same amount of money left?

My Notes

STEP 1   Write an algebraic expression to represent the money Katriana has left. Represent the expression with a model.

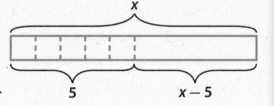

$x - 5$

> The variable represents the amount of money both Katriana and Andrew have at the beginning of the day.

STEP 2   Write an algebraic expression to represent the money Andrew has left. Represent the expression with a model.

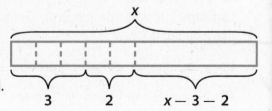

$x - 3 - 2$

STEP 3   Compare the models.

The models are equivalent, so the expressions are equivalent.

Andrew and Katriana have the same amount of money left.

YOUR TURN

9. On a math quiz, Tina scored 3 points more than Julia. Juan scored 2 points more than Julia and earned 2 points in extra credit. Write an expression and draw a bar model to represent Tina's score and Juan's score. Did Tina and Juan make the same grade on the quiz? Explain.

Modeling Real-World Situations

You can use expressions to represent real-world situations.

EXAMPLE 4

A Tickets to the water park cost $53 per person. Write an expression to show the total cost of tickets for a group of people.

A group of is a clue to multiply. The ticket price of $53 is a constant. The number of people who need tickets is a variable.

Use x for the number of people.

The algebraic expression for the total cost of tickets is $53x$.

B Genise has some savings. After babysitting, she adds $75 to her savings. How much money has Genise saved?

Adds is a clue to use addition. The $75 Genise added to her savings is a constant. The amount of money Genise had saved before is unknown, so use a variable.

Use y for Genise's savings before she adds the babysitting money.

The algebraic expression for Genise's total savings is $y + 75$.

Math Talk

Mathematical Processes

How do you know what operation to use to find the amount each niece receives?

YOUR TURN

10. Helen divides up some money to give equally to her four nieces. If d represents the total amount, write an expression to represent how much money each niece receives. _____

Write each phrase as an algebraic expression. (Explore Activity Example 1)

1. 3 less than y _____

2. The product of 2 and p _____

Write a phrase for each algebraic expression.
(Explore Activity Example 1)

3. $y + 12$ _____

4. $\frac{p}{10}$ 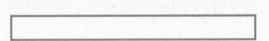 _____

5. Draw a bar model to represent the expression $m \div 4$. (Example 2)

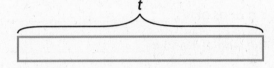

At 6 p.m., the temperature in Phoenix, AZ, t, is the same as the temperature in Tucson, AZ. By 9 p.m., the temperature in Phoenix has dropped 2 degrees and in Tucson it has dropped 4 degrees. By 11 p.m., the temperature in Phoenix has dropped another 3 degrees. (Example 3)

6. Represent each city's temperature at 11 p.m. with an algebraic expression and a bar model.

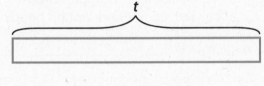

_____ _____

7. Are the expressions that represent the temperatures in the two cities equivalent? Justify your answer.

_____

_____

8. Noelle bought some boxes of water bottles for a picnic. Each box contained 24 bottles of water. If c is the number of boxes, write an expression to show how many bottles of water Noelle bought. (Example 4)

_____

 ESSENTIAL QUESTION CHECK-IN

9. Give an example of a real-world situation that could be represented by an algebraic expression.

_____

_____

10.1 Independent Practice

Personal Math Trainer

my.hrw.com

Online Assessment and Intervention

10. Write an algebraic expression with the constant 7 and the variable y.

_____

Write each phrase as an algebraic expression.

11. n divided by 8 _____

12. p multiplied by 4 _____

13. b plus 14 _____

14. 90 times x _____

15. a take away 16 _____

16. k less than 24 _____

17. 3 groups of w _____

18. the sum of 1 and q _____

19. the quotient of 13 and z _____

20. c added to 45 _____

21. 8 less than w _____

Write a phrase in words for each algebraic expression.

22. $m + 83$ _____

23. $42s$ _____

24. $\dfrac{9}{d}$ _____

25. $t - 29$ _____

26. $2 + g$ _____

27. $11x$ _____

28. $\dfrac{h}{12}$ _____

29. $5 - k$ _____

Sarah and Noah work at Read On Bookstore and get paid the same hourly wage. The table shows their work schedule for last week.

Read On Bookstore Work Schedule (hours)			
	Monday	**Tuesday**	**Wednesday**
Sarah	5	3	
Noah			8

30. Write an expression that represents Sarah's total pay last week. Represent her hourly wage with w. _____

31. Write an expression that represents Noah's total pay last week. Represent his hourly wage with w. _____

32. Are the expressions equivalent? Did Sarah and Noah earn the same amount last week? Use models to justify your answer.

_____

33. Mia buys 3 gallons of gas that costs d dollars per gallon. Bob buys g gallons of gas that costs $3 per gallon.

a. Write an expression for the amount Mia pays for gas. _____

b. Write an expression for the amount Bob pays for gas. _____

c. What do the numeral and the variable represent in each expression?

_____

_____

_____

_____

34. The student council is asking people to donate money for the new park outside the school. Everyone who makes the suggested donation amount will be given a bracelet. If everyone donates the suggested amount, and *b* bracelets are given away, what algebraic expression represents the total amount collected in donations?

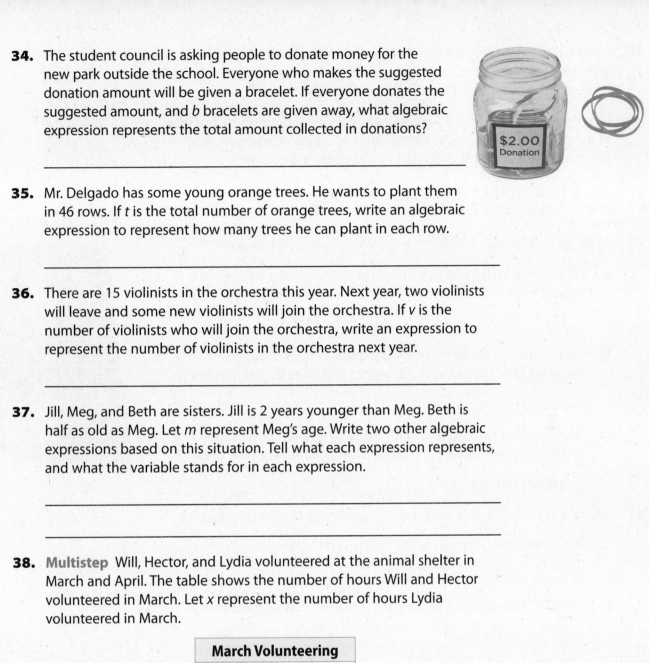

_____

35. Mr. Delgado has some young orange trees. He wants to plant them in 46 rows. If *t* is the total number of orange trees, write an algebraic expression to represent how many trees he can plant in each row.

_____

36. There are 15 violinists in the orchestra this year. Next year, two violinists will leave and some new violinists will join the orchestra. If *v* is the number of violinists who will join the orchestra, write an expression to represent the number of violinists in the orchestra next year.

_____

37. Jill, Meg, and Beth are sisters. Jill is 2 years younger than Meg. Beth is half as old as Meg. Let *m* represent Meg's age. Write two other algebraic expressions based on this situation. Tell what each expression represents, and what the variable stands for in each expression.

_____

_____

38. **Multistep** Will, Hector, and Lydia volunteered at the animal shelter in March and April. The table shows the number of hours Will and Hector volunteered in March. Let *x* represent the number of hours Lydia volunteered in March.

March Volunteering	
Will	3 hours
Hector	5 hours

a. Will's volunteer hours in April were equal to his March volunteer hours plus Lydia's March volunteer hours. Write an expression to represent Will's volunteer hours in April. _____

b. Hector's volunteer hours in April were equal to 2 hours less than his March volunteer hours plus Lydia's March volunteer hours. Write an expression to represent Hector's volunteer hours in April. _____

c. Did Will and Hector volunteer the same number of hours in April?

Explain. _____

39. The town of Rayburn received 6 more inches of snow than the town of Greenville. Let *g* represent the amount of snow in Greenville. Write an algebraic expression to represent the amount of snow in Rayburn. _____

40. Abby baked 48 dinner rolls and divided them evenly into bags. Let b represent the number of bags. Write an algebraic expression to represent the number of dinner rolls in each bag.

_____

41. Eli is driving at a speed of 55 miles per hour. Let h represent the number of hours that Eli drives at this speed. Write an algebraic expression to represent the number of miles that Eli travels during this time.

_____

 FOCUS ON HIGHER ORDER THINKING

42. Multistep Bob's Bagels offers two breakfast options, as shown.

   a. Let x represent the number of customers who order coffee and a bagel. How much money will Bob's Bagels make from these orders?

   _____

   b. Let y represent the number of customers who order tea and a breakfast sandwich. How much money will Bob's Bagels make from

   these orders? _____

   c. Write an algebraic expression for the total amount Bob's Bagels will make from all the coffee and bagel orders and from all the tea and

   breakfast sandwich orders. _____

43. Represent Real-World Problems The number of shoes in a closet is s.

   a. How many pairs of shoes are in the closet? Explain.

   _____

   b. What If? Suppose one of the pairs is missing a shoe. How many

   shoes are in the closet? _____

44. Problem Solving Write an expression that has three terms, two different

variables, and one constant. _____

45. Represent Real-World Problems Describe a situation that can be modeled by the expression $x - 8$.

_____

_____

46. Critique Reasoning Ricardo says that the expression $y + 4$ is equivalent to the expression $1y + 4$. Is he correct? Explain.

_____

_____

_____

Work Area

Evaluating Expressions

6.4.10.2

Students will use the order of operations to evaluate algebraic expressions.

? ESSENTIAL QUESTION

How can you use the order of operations to evaluate algebraic expressions?

EXPLORE ACTIVITY

Evaluating Expressions

Recall that an algebraic expression contains one or more variables. You can substitute a number for that variable and then find the value of the expression. This is called **evaluating** the expression.

Math On the Spot
my.hrw.com

EXAMPLE 1 Evaluate each expression for the given value of the variable.

A $x - 9$; $x = 15$

Substitute 15 for x.

⬜ $- 9$

Subtract.

⬜

When $x =$ _____, $x - 9 =$ _____.

B $\frac{16}{n}$; $n = 8$

Substitute 8 for n.

$\dfrac{16}{⬜}$

Divide.

⬜

When $n =$ _____, $\frac{16}{n} =$ _____.

C $0.5y$; $y = 1.4$

Substitute 1.4 for y.

$0.5\left(⬜\right)$

Multiply.

⬜

When $y =$ _____, $0.5y =$ _____.

D $6k$; $k = \frac{1}{3}$ (Hint: Think of 6 as $\frac{6}{1}$.)

Substitute $\frac{1}{3}$ for k.

$6\left(\dfrac{⬜}{⬜}\right)$

Multiply.

⬜

When $k =$ _____, $6k =$ _____.

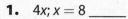

YOUR TURN

Evaluate each expression for the given value of the variable.

1. $4x; x = 8$ _____   **2.** $6.5 - n; n = 1.8$ _____   **3.** $\frac{m}{6}; m = 18$ _____

Math On the Spot

⏻ my.hrw.com

Using the Order of Operations

Expressions may have more than one operation or more than one variable. To evaluate these expressions, substitute the given value for each variable and then use the order of operations.

EXAMPLE 2

Evaluate each expression for the given value of the variable.

A $4(x - 4); x = 7$

$4(7 - 4)$	Substitute 7 for x.
$4(3)$	Subtract inside the parentheses.
12	Multiply.

When $x = 7$, $4(x - 4) = 12$.

B $4x - 4; x = 7$

$4(7) - 4$	Substitute 7 for x.
$28 - 4$	Multiply.
24	Subtract.

When $x = 7$, $4x - 4 = 24$.

C $w - x + y; w = 6, x = 5, y = 3$

$(6) - (5) + (3)$	Substitute 6 for w, 5 for x, and 3 for y.
$1 + 3$	Subtract.
4	Add.

When $w = 6, x = 5, y = 3$, $w - x + y = 4$.

> **Math Talk**
> Mathematical Processes
>
> Is $w - x + y$ equivalent to $w - y + x$? Explain any difference in the order the math operations are performed.

D $x^2 - x; x = 9$

$(9)^2 - (9)$	Substitute 9 for each x.
$81 - 9$	Evaluate exponents.
72	Subtract.

When $x = 9$, $x^2 - x = 72$.

Evaluate each expression for $n = 5$.

4. $3(n + 1)$ _____   **5.** $4(n - 4) + 14$ _____   **6.** $6n + n^2$ _____

Evaluate each expression for $a = 3$, $b = 4$, and $c = 6$.

7. $ab - c$ _____   **8.** $bc + 5a$ _____   **9.** $a^3 - (b + c)$ _____

Evaluating Real-World Expressions

You can evaluate expressions to solve real-world problems.

EXAMPLE 3 (Real World)

The expression $1.8c + 32$ gives the temperature in degrees Fahrenheit for a given temperature in degrees Celsius c. Find the temperature in degrees Fahrenheit that is equivalent to 30 °C.

STEP 1 Find the value of c.

$c = 30 °C$

STEP 2 Substitute the value into the expression.

$1.8c + 32$

$1.8(30) + 32$ Substitute 30 for c.

$54 + 32$ Multiply.

86 Add.

86 °F is equivalent to 30 °C.

YOUR TURN

10. The expression $6x^2$ gives the surface area of a cube, and the expression x^3 gives the volume of a cube, where x is the length of one side of the cube. Find the surface area and the volume of a cube with a side length of 2 m.

$S =$ _____ m^2; $V =$ _____ m^3

11. The expression $60m$ gives the number of seconds in m minutes. How many seconds are there in 7 minutes?

_____ seconds

Evaluate each expression for the given value(s) of the variable(s).
(Explore Activity Example 1 and Example 2)

1. $x - 7; x = 23$ _____

2. $3a - b; a = 4, b = 6$ _____

3. $\frac{8}{t}; t = 4$ _____

4. $9 + m; m = 1.5$ _____

5. $\frac{1}{2}w + 2; w = \frac{1}{9}$ _____

6. $5(6.2 + z); z = 3.8$ _____

7. The table shows the prices for games in Bella's soccer league. Her parents and grandmother attended a soccer game. How much did they spend if they all went together in one car? (Example 3)

Women's Soccer Game Prices	
Student tickets	$6
Nonstudent tickets	$12
Parking	$5

a. Write an expression that represents the cost of one carful of nonstudent soccer fans. Use x as the number of people who rode in the car and attended the game.

_____ is an expression that represents the cost of one carful of nonstudent soccer fans.

b. Since there are three attendees, evaluate the expression $12x + 5$ for $x = 3$.

$12(\_\_\_) + 5 = \_\_\_\_\_ + 5 = \_\_\_\_\_$

The family spent _____ to attend the game.

8. Stan wants to add trim all around the edge of a rectangular tablecloth that measures 5 feet long by 7 feet wide. The perimeter of the rectangular tablecloth is twice the length added to twice the width. How much trim does Stan need to buy? (Example 3)

a. Write an expression that represents the perimeter of the rectangular tablecloth. Let l represent the length of the tablecloth and w represent its width. The expression would be _____.

b. Evaluate the expression $P = 2w + 2l$ for $l = 5$ and $w = 7$.

$2(\_\_\_\_\_) + 2(\_\_\_\_\_) = 14 + \_\_\_\_\_ = \_\_\_\_\_$

Stan bought _____ of trim to sew onto the tablecloth.

? ESSENTIAL QUESTION CHECK-IN

9. How do you know the correct order in which to evaluate algebraic expressions?

_____

_____

10.2 Independent Practice

Personal
Math Trainer

Online
Assessment and
Intervention

my.hrw.com

10. The table shows ticket prices at the Movie 16 theater. Let a represent the number of adult tickets, c the number of children's tickets, and s the number of senior citizen tickets.

Movie 16 Ticket Prices	
Adults	$8.75
Children	$6.50
Seniors	$6.50

a. Write an expression for the total cost of tickets.

_____

_____

b. The Andrews family bought 2 adult tickets, 3 children's tickets, and 1 senior ticket. Evaluate your expression in part a to find the total cost of the tickets.

_____

_____

c. The Spencer family bought 4 adult tickets and 2 children's tickets. Did they spend the same as the Andrews family? Explain.

_____

11. The area of a triangular sail is given by the expression $\frac{1}{2}bh$, where b is the length of the base and h is the height. What is the area of a triangular sail in a model sailboat when $b = 12$ inches and $h = 7$ inches?

$A =$ _____ in.^{2}

12. Ramon wants to balance his checking account. He has $2,340 in the account. He writes a check for $140. He deposits a check for $268. How much does Ramon have left

in his checking account? _____

13. **Look for a Pattern** Evaluate the expression $6x - x^2$ for $x = 0, 1, 2, 3, 4, 5,$ and 6. Use your results to fill in the table and describe any pattern that you see.

x	0	1	2	3	4	5	6
$6x - x^2$							

_____

_____

_____

_____

_____

_____

_____

14. The kinetic energy (in joules) of a moving object can be calculated from the expression $\frac{1}{2}mv^2$, where m is the mass of the object in kilograms and v is its speed in meters per second. Find the kinetic energy of a 0.145-kg baseball that is thrown at a speed of 40 meters per second.

$E =$ _____ joules

15. The area of a square is given by x^2, where x is the length of one side. Mary's original garden was in the shape of a square. She has decided to double the area of her garden. Write an expression that represents the area of Mary's new garden. Evaluate the expression if the side length of Mary's original garden was 8 feet.

_____

_____

16. The volume of a pyramid with a square base is given by the expression $\frac{1}{3}s^2h$, where s is the length of a side of the base and h is the height. Find the volume of a pyramid with a square base of side length 24 feet and a height of 30 feet.

_____

Work Area

17. Draw Conclusions Consider the expressions $3x(x-2)+2$ and $2x^2 + 3x - 12$.

a. Evaluate each expression for $x = 2$ and for $x = 7$. Based on your results, do you know whether the two expressions are equivalent? Explain.

_____

_____

_____

_____

_____

b. Evaluate each expression for $x = 5$. Based on your results, do you know whether the two expressions are equivalent? Explain.

_____

_____

_____

_____

_____

18. Critique Reasoning Marjorie evaluated the expression $3x + 2$ for $x = 5$ as shown:

$$3x + 2 = 35 + 2 = 37$$

What was Marjorie's mistake? What is the correct value of $3x + 2$ for $x = 5$?

_____

_____

_____

Evaluate This!

Playing the Game

STEP 1 Shuffle the game cards and place them in a pile face-down. Choose a game piece, and choose which player will go first.

STEP 2 On your first turn, place your game piece on the Start space and draw a game card.

$$x - 7$$
$$x = 13$$

STEP 3 If the card is an expression card, substitute the given value (input) into the expression and evaluate it to find the result (output). Use a row in the table to record your work. Move the game piece the number of spaces given by the output. You may ask other players for help evaluating an expression, if needed.

Complete the table as shown:

Expression	Input	Substitution (Show your work.)	Output
$x - 7$	$x = 13$	$13 - 7$	6

For this example, your game piece would move forward 6 spaces.

STEP 4 If the card has directions instead of an expression, follow the directions.

STEP 5 Follow the directions given in a space on the gameboard only if you land on that space by an exact count.

STEP 6 Play continues clockwise.

Winning the Game

The first player to reach the End space wins. You do not have to reach the End space by an exact count.

Expression	Input	Substitution (Show your work.)	Output

Generating Equivalent Expressions

6.4.10.3

Students will identify and write equivalent expressions.

? ESSENTIAL QUESTION

How can you identify and write equivalent expressions?

EXPLORE ACTIVITY 1

Identifying Equivalent Expressions

One way to test whether two expressions might be equivalent is to evaluate them for the same value of the variable.

Match the expressions in List A with their equivalent expressions in List B.

List A	List B
$5x + 65$	$5x + 1$
$5(x + 1)$	$5x + 5$
$1 + 5x$	$5(13 + x)$

A Evaluate each of the expressions in the lists for $x = 3$.

List A	List B
$5(3) + 65 = \boxed{}$	$5(3) + 1 = \boxed{}$
$5(3 + 1) = \boxed{}$	$5(3) + 5 = \boxed{}$
$1 + 5(3) = \boxed{}$	$5(13 + 3) = \boxed{}$

B Which pair(s) of expressions have the same value for $x = 3$?

_____

_____

C How could you further test whether the expressions in each pair are equivalent?

_____

D Do you think the expressions in each pair are equivalent? Why or why not?

_____

_____

Reflect

1. **Error Analysis** Lisa evaluated the expressions $2x$ and x^2 for $x = 2$ and found that both expressions were equal to 4. Lisa concluded that $2x$ and x^2 are equivalent expressions. How could you show Lisa that she is incorrect?

_____

_____

EXPLORE ACTIVITY 2

Modeling Equivalent Expressions

You can also use models to determine if two expressions are equivalent. *Algebra tiles* are one way to model expressions.

Algebra Tiles

 = 1

 = x

Determine if the expression $3(x + 2)$ is equivalent to $3x + 6$.

A Model each expression using algebra tiles.

$3(x + 2)$ $3x + 6$

B The model for $3(x + 2)$ has _____ x tiles and _____ 1 tiles.

The model for $3x + 6$ has _____ x tiles and _____ 1 tiles.

C Is the expression $3(x + 2)$ equivalent to $3x + 6$? Explain.

_____

_____

Reflect

2. Use algebra tiles to determine if $2(x + 3)$ is equivalent to $2x + 3$. Explain your answer.

_____

_____

Writing Equivalent Expressions Using Properties

Math On the Spot
my.hrw.com

Properties of operations can be used to identify equivalent expressions.

Properties of Operations	Examples
Commutative Property of Addition: When adding, changing the order of the numbers does not change the sum.	$3 + 4 = 4 + 3$
Commutative Property of Multiplication: When multiplying, changing the order of the numbers does not change the product.	$2 \times 4 = 4 \times 2$
Associative Property of Addition: When adding more than two numbers, the grouping of the numbers does not change the sum.	$(3 + 4) + 5 = 3 + (4 + 5)$
Associative Property of Multiplication: When multiplying more than two numbers, the grouping of the numbers does not change the product.	$(2 \times 4) \times 3 = 2 \times (4 \times 3)$
Distributive Property: Multiplying a number by a sum or difference is the same as multiplying by each number in the sum or difference and then adding or subtracting.	$6(2 + 4) = 6(2) + 6(4)$ $8(5 - 3) = 8(5) - 8(3)$
Identity Property of Addition: Adding zero to a number does not change its value.	$9 + 0 = 9$
Identity Property of Multiplication: Multiplying a number by one does not change its value.	$1 \times 7 = 7$

EXAMPLE 1

Use a property to write an expression that is equivalent to $x + 3$.

The operation in the expression is addition.

You can use the Commutative Property of Addition to write an equivalent expression: $x + 3 = 3 + x$.

YOUR TURN

For each expression, use a property to write an equivalent expression. Tell which property you used.

3. $(ab)c = $ _____

4. $3y + 4y = $ _____

5. 6×7 _____

Personal Math Trainer
Online Assessment and Intervention
my.hrw.com

Identifying Equivalent Expressions Using Properties

EXAMPLE 2

Use the properties of operations to determine if the expressions are equivalent.

A $3(x - 2)$; $3x - 6$

$3(x - 2) = 3x - 6$ Distributive Property

$3(x - 2)$ and $3x - 6$ are equivalent expressions.

B $2 + x$; $\frac{1}{2}(4 + x)$

$$\frac{1}{2}(x + 4) = \frac{1}{2}x + 2$$ Distributive Property

$$= 2 + \frac{1}{2}x$$ Commutative Property

$2 + x$ does not equal $2 + \frac{1}{2}x$.

They are not equivalent expressions.

YOUR TURN

Use the properties of operations to determine if the expressions are equivalent.

6. $6x - 8$; $2(3x - 5)$

_____

_____

7. $2 - 2 + 5x$; $5x$

_____

_____

8. Jamal bought 2 packs of stickers and 8 individual stickers. Use x to represent the number of stickers in a pack of stickers and write an expression to represent the number of stickers Jamal bought. Is the expression equivalent to $2(4 + x)$? Check your answer with algebra tile models.

_____

_____

Generating Equivalent Expressions

Parts of an algebraic expression		
terms	The parts of the expression that are separated by + or − signs	$12 + 3y^2 + 4x + 2y^2 + 4$
coefficients	Numbers that are multiplied by at least one variable	$12 + 3y^2 + 4x + 2y^2 + 4$
like terms	Terms with the same variable(s) raised to the same power(s)	$12 + 3y^2 + 4x + 2y^2 + 4$

When an expression contains like terms, you can use properties to combine the like terms and write an equivalent expression.

EXAMPLE 3

Combine like terms.

A $6x^2 - 4x^2$ ⟶ ⎡ $6x^2$ and $4x^2$ are like terms. ⎤

$6x^2 - 4x^2 = x^2(6 - 4)$ Distributive Property

$\qquad = x^2(2)$ Subtract inside the parentheses.

$\qquad = 2x^2$ Commutative Property of Multiplication

$6x^2 - 4x^2 = 2x^2$

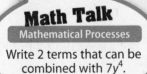

Math Talk

Mathematical Processes

Write 2 terms that can be combined with $7y^4$.

B $3a + 2(b + 5a)$

$3a + 2(b + 5a) = 3a + 2b + 2(5a)$ Distributive Property

$\qquad = 3a + 2b + (2 \cdot 5)a$ Associative Property of Multiplication

$\qquad = 3a + 2b + 10a$ Multiply 2 and 5.

$\qquad = 3a + 10a + 2b$ Commutative Property of Addition

$\qquad = (3 + 10)a + 2b$ Distributive Property

$\qquad = 13a + 2b$ Add inside the parentheses.

$3a + 2(b + 5a) = 13a + 2b$

C $y + 11x + 7y - 7x$ ⟶ ⎡ y and $7y$ are like terms; $11x$ and $7x$ are like terms. ⎤

$y + 11x + 7y - 7x = y + 7y + 11x - 7x$ Commutative Property

$\qquad = (1 + 7)y + (11 - 7)x$ Distributive Property

$\qquad = 8y + 4x$ Simplify inside parentheses.

$y + 11x + 7y - 7x = 8y + 4x$

YOUR TURN

Combine like terms.

9. $8y - 3y =$ _____

10. $6x^2 + 4(x^2 - 1) =$ _____

11. $4a^5 - 2a^5 + 4b + b =$

_____

12. $8m + 14 - 12 + 4n =$

_____

Guided Practice

1. Evaluate each of the expressions in the list for $y = 5$. Then, draw lines to match the expressions in List A with their equivalent expressions in List B. (Explore Activity 1)

List A

$4 + 4y =$ _____

$4(y - 1) =$ _____

$4y + 1 =$ _____

List B

$4y - 4 =$ _____

$4(y + 1) =$ _____

$1 + 4y =$ _____

2. Determine if the expressions are equivalent by comparing the models. (Explore Activity 2) _____

$x + 4$ $2(x + 2)$

For each expression, use a property to write an equivalent expression. Tell which property you used. (Example 1)

3. $ab =$ _____

_____

4. $5(3x - 2) =$ _____

_____

Use the properties of operations to determine if each pair of expressions is equivalent. (Example 2)

5. $\frac{1}{2}(4 - 2x); 2 - 2x$ _____

6. $\frac{1}{2}(6x - 2); 3 - x$ _____

Combine like terms. (Example 3)

7. $32y + 12y =$ _____

8. $12 + 3x - x - 12 =$ _____

? ESSENTIAL QUESTION CHECK-IN

9. Describe two ways to write equivalent algebraic expressions.

_____

_____

10.3 Independent Practice

Personal
Math Trainer

Online
Assessment and
Intervention

my.hrw.com

**For each expression, use a property to write an equivalent expression.
Tell which property you used.**

10. $cd = $ _____

11. $x + 13 = $ _____

12. $4(2x - 3) = $ _____

13. $2 + (a + b) = $ _____

14. Draw algebra tile models to prove that $4 + 8x$ and $4(2x + 1)$ are equivalent.

_____   _____

Combine like terms.

15. $7x^4 - 5x^4 = $ _____

16. $32y + 5y = $ _____

17. $6b + 7b - 10 = $ _____

18. $2x + 3x + 4 = $ _____

19. $y + 4 + 3(y + 2) = $ _____

20. $7a^2 - a^2 + 16 = $ _____

21. $3y^2 + 3(4y^2 - 2) = $ _____

22. $z^2 + z + 4z^3 + 4z^2 = $ _____

23. $0.5(x^4 - 3) + 12 = $ _____

24. $\frac{1}{4}(16 + 4p) = $ _____

25. **Justify Reasoning** Determine whether $3x + 12 + x$ is equivalent to $4(3 + x)$. Use properties of operations to justify your answer.

_____

_____

26. William earns $13 an hour working at a movie theater. Last week he worked h hours at the concession stand and three times as many hours at the ticket counter. Write and simplify an expression for the amount of money William earned last week.

_____

27. Multiple Representations Use the information in the table to write and simplify an expression to find the total weight of the medals won by the top medal-winning nations in the 2012 London Olympic Games. The three types of medals have different weights.

2012 Summer Olympics			
	Gold	Silver	Bronze
United States	46	29	29
China	38	27	23
Great Britain	29	17	19

_____

_____

Write an expression for the perimeters of each given figure. Simplify the expression.

28. _____   **29.** _____

$3x - 1$ mm

6 mm   6 mm

$3x - 1$ mm

10.2 in.

$x + 4$ in. $x + 4$ in.

$x + 4$ in. $x + 4$ in.

10.2 in.

H.O.T.   **FOCUS ON HIGHER ORDER THINKING**

30. Problem Solving Examine the algebra tile model.

a. Write two equivalent expressions for the model. _____

b. **What If?** Suppose a third row of tiles identical to the ones above is added to the model. How does that change the two expressions?

_____

31. Communicate Mathematical Ideas Write an example of an expression that cannot be simplified, and explain how you know that it cannot be simplified.

_____

32. Problem Solving Write an expression that is equivalent to $8(2y + 4)$ that can be simplified.

_____

Houghton Mifflin Harcourt Publishing Company • Image Credits: ©Comstock/Jupiterimages/Getty Images

Work Area

Going Further 10.3

Equivalent Expressions

6.4.GF.10.3
Students will determine if two expressions are equivalent.

? ESSENTIAL QUESTION

How can you determine if two expressions are equivalent?

EXPLORE ACTIVITY

Substituting to Determine Equivalence

Expressions can be equivalent for all values or only when specific values are used. To determine if expressions are equivalent when given a specific value, substitute the value into the expressions and evaluate the expressions.

Substitute the given value into the expressions to determine if they are equivalent for the given value. Explain your reasoning.

A $13h + 39h$ and $13h + 13(3h)$ when $h = 4$

	$13h + 39h$		$13h + 13(3h)$
Substitute.	$13(\_\_) + 39(\_\_)$	Substitute.	$13(\_\_) + 13(3 \times \_\_)$
Multiply.	$\_\_\_\_ + \_\_\_\_\_$	Multiply.	$\_\_\_\_ + 13(\_\_\_)$
Add.	$\_\_\_\_\_$	Multiply.	$\_\_\_\_ + \_\_\_\_\_$
		Add.	$\_\_\_\_\_$

The two expressions ⎢ **are / are not** ⎥ equivalent when $h = 4$. When 4 is substituted

in $13h + 39h$, the result is _____. When 4 is substituted in $13h + 13(3h)$, the result

is _____.

B $3(p + 6) - 4$ and $3p + 2^2$ when $p = 5$

	$3(p + 6) - 4$		$3p + 2^2$
Substitute 5 for p.	$3(\_\_\_\_ + 6) - 4$	Substitute 5 for p.	$3(\_\_\_\_) + 2^2$
Add.	$3(\_\_\_) - 4$	Evaluate the exponent.	$3(\_\_\_) + (\_\_\_)$
Multiply.	$\_\_\_\_ - 4$	Multiply.	$\_\_\_\_ + \_\_\_$
Subtract.	$\_\_\_\_$	Add.	$\_\_\_\_$

The two expressions ⎢ **are / are not** ⎥ equivalent for $p = 5$. When 5 is substituted in

$3(p + 6) - 4$, the result is ____. When 5 is substituted in $3p + 2^2$, the result is ____.

Simplifying To Determine Equivalence

You can determine if two expressions are equivalent by simplifying the expressions.

EXAMPLE

Determine if the expressions are equivalent. Justify your reasoning.

A $4a + 4(6a + 7b) + 7b$ and $(4a + 5b)7$

$4a + 4(6a + 7b) + 7b$		$(4a + 5b)7$	
$4a + 4(6a) + 4(7b) + 7b$	Distributive Property	$7(4a + 5b)$	Commutative Proper
$4a + 24a + 28b + 7b$	Multiply.	$7(4a) + 7(5b)$	Distributive Propert
$28a + 35b$	Combine like terms.	$28a + 35b$	Multiply.

The expressions are equivalent.

B $3b^3 + 8 - 2c - b^3 + 6c$ and $2(2b^3 + 4c) + 8$

$3b^3 + 8 - 2c - b^3 + 6c$		$2(2b^3 + 4c) + 8$	
$3b^3 - b^3 - 2c + 6c + 8$	Commutative Property	$4b^3 + 8c + 8$	Distributive Prope
$2b^3 + 4c + 8$	Combine like terms.		

The expressions are not equivalent.

Practice

Determine if the expressions are equivalent for the given value. Explain your reasoning.

1. $\dfrac{p + p}{2}$ and $2p - 6$ when $p = 6$

_____

_____

2. $7(2m + 4)$ and $10m + 4m + 14$ when $m = 3$

_____

_____

Determine if the expressions are equivalent by simplifying. Justify your answer.

3. $2(4x^2 + 4) + 10x^2 + 1$ and $6(x^2 + 1) + 12x^2 + 3$

_____

4. $5(x + 2) + 4 + 10x$ and $8x - 9 + 8x + 23$

_____

_____

Ready to Go On?

Personal Math Trainer

Online Assessment and Intervention

⏻ my.hrw.com

10.1 Modeling and Writing Expressions

Write each phrase as an algebraic expression.

1. p divided by 6 _____

2. 65 less than j _____

3. the sum of 185 and h _____

4. the product of 16 and g _____

5. Let x represent the number of television show episodes that are taped in a season. Write an expression for the number of episodes taped in

4 seasons. _____

10.2 Evaluating Expressions

Evaluate each expression for the given value of the variable.

6. $8p$; $p = 9$ _____

7. $11 + r$; $r = 7$ _____

8. $4(d + 7)$; $d = -2$ _____

9. $\frac{60}{m}$; $m = 5$ _____

10. To find the area of a triangle, you can use the expression $b \times h \div 2$, where b is the base of the triangle and h is its height. What is the area of

a triangle with a base of 6 and a height of 8? _____

10.3 Generating Equivalent Expressions

11. Draw lines to match the expressions in List A with their equivalent expressions in List B.

List A	List B
$7x + 14$	$7(1 + x)$
$7 + 7x$	$7x - 7$
$7(x - 1)$	$7(x + 2)$

? ESSENTIAL QUESTION

12. How can you solve problems involving equivalent expressions?

_____

_____

_____

_____

Assessment Readiness

Personal
Math Trainer

Online
Assessment and
Intervention

my.hrw.com

Selected Response

1. Which expression represents the product of 83 and x?

   (A) $83 + x$

   (B) $83 \div x$

   (C) $83x$

   (D) $83 - x$

2. Which phrase describes the algebraic expression $\frac{r}{9}$?

   (A) the product of r and 9

   (B) the quotient of r and 9

   (C) 9 less than r

   (D) r more than 9

3. Rhonda was organizing photos in a photo album. She took 60 photos and divided them evenly among p pages. Which algebraic expression represents the number of photos on each page?

   (A) $p - 60$ (C) $\frac{p}{60}$

   (B) $60 - p$ (D) $\frac{60}{p}$

4. Using the algebraic expression $4n + 6$, what is the greatest whole-number value of n that will give you a result less than 100?

   (A) 22   (C) 24

   (B) 23   (D) 25

5. Evaluate $7w - 14$ for $w = 9$.

   (A) 2

   (B) 18

   (C) 49

   (D) 77

6. Katie has read 32% of a book. If she has read 80 pages, how many more pages does Katie have left to read?

   (A) 40

   (B) 170

   (C) 200

   (D) 250

7. The expression $12(x + 4)$ represents the total number of CDs Mei bought in April and May at $12 each. Which property is applied to write the equivalent expression $12x + 48$?

   (A) Associative Property of Addition

   (B) Associative Property of Multiplication

   (C) Commutative Property of Multiplication

   (D) Distributive Property

Mini-Task

8. You can convert a temperature given in degrees Celsius to a Fahrenheit temperature by using the expression $9x \div 5 + 32$, where x is the Celsius temperature.

   a. Water freezes when the temperature is 0 °C. At what Fahrenheit temperature does water freeze? _____

   b. Water boils at 100 °C. At what temperature does water boil in degrees Fahrenheit? _____

   c. The temperature of some water is 15 °C. What is the Fahrenheit temperature? _____

MODULE 9 ## Generating Equivalent Numerical Expressions

? ESSENTIAL QUESTION

How can you generate equivalent numerical expressions and use them to solve real-world problems?

EXAMPLE 1

Find the value of each power.

A. 0.9^2

$0.9^2 = 0.9 \times 0.9 = 0.81$

B. 18^0

Any number raised to the power of 0 is 1.

$18^0 = 1$

C. $\left(\frac{1}{4}\right)^4$

$\left(\frac{1}{4}\right)^4 = \left(\frac{1}{4}\right)\left(\frac{1}{4}\right)\left(\frac{1}{4}\right)\left(\frac{1}{4}\right) = \frac{1}{256}$

EXAMPLE 2

Find the prime factorization of 60.

$$\begin{array}{r} 2\,|\,\underline{60} \\ 2\,|\,\underline{30} \\ 3\,|\,\underline{15} \\ 5\,|\,\underline{5} \\ 1 \end{array}$$

$60 = 2 \times 2 \times 3 \times 5$

$60 = 2^2 \times 3 \times 5$

The prime factorization of 60 is $2^2 \times 3 \times 5$.

EXAMPLE 3

Simplify each expression.

A. $4 \times (2^3 + 5)$

$= 4 \times (8 + 5)$ $2^3 = 8$

$= 4 \times 13$ Add.

$= 52$ Multiply.

B. $27 \div 3^2 \times 6$

$= 27 \div 9 \times 6$ $3^2 = 9$

$= 3 \times 6$ Divide.

$= 18$ Multiply.

EXERCISES

Use an exponent to write each expression. (Lesson 9.1)

1. 3.6×3.6 _____

2. $9 \times 9 \times 9 \times 9$ _____

3. $\frac{4}{5} \times \frac{4}{5} \times \frac{4}{5}$ _____

Find the value of each power. (Lesson 9.1)

4. 12^0 _____   **5.** 13^2 _____   **6.** $\left(\frac{2}{7}\right)^3$ _____

7. 0.4^2 _____   **8.** $\left(\frac{4}{9}\right)^1$ _____   **9.** 0.7^3 _____

Find the prime factorization of each number. (Lesson 9.2)

10. 75 _____   **11.** 29 _____   **12.** 168 _____

13. Eduardo is building a sandbox that has an area of 84 square feet. What are the possible whole number measurements for the length and width of the sandbox? (Lesson 9.2)

_____

Simplify each expression. (Lesson 9.3)

14. $2 \times 5^2 - (4 + 1)$ _____   **15.** $\dfrac{22 - (3^2 + 4)}{12 \div 4}$ _____

 **MODULE 10**   # Generating Equivalent Algebraic Expressions

© Houghton Mifflin Harcourt Publishing Company

Key Vocabulary
algebraic expression
   (expresión algebraica)
coefficients *(coeficiente)*
constant *(contante)*
equivalent expressions
   (expresión equivalente)
evaluating *(evaluar)*
term *(término (en una expresión))*

? ESSENTIAL QUESTION

How can you generate equivalent algebraic expressions and use them to solve real-world problems?

EXAMPLE 1

Evaluate each expression for the given values of the variables.

A. $2(x^2 - 9)$; $x = 5$

$2(5^2 - 9)$ $5^2 = 25$

$= 2(16)$ Subtract.

$= 32$ Multiply.

When $x = 5$, $2(x^2 - 9) = 32$.

B. $w + y^2 + 3w$; $w = 2$, $y = 6$

$2 + 6^2 + 3(2)$ $6^2 = 36$

$= 2 + 36 + 6$ Multiply.

$= 44$ Add.

When $w = 2$ and $y = 6$, $w + y^2 + 3w = 44$.

EXAMPLE 2

Determine whether the algebraic expressions are equivalent:
$5(x + 2)$ **and** $10 + 5x$.

$5(x + 2) = 5x + 10$ Distributive Property

$= 10 + 5x$ Commutative Property

$5(x + 2)$ is equal to $10 + 5x$. They are equivalent expressions.

EXERCISES

Write each phrase as an algebraic expression. (Lesson 10.1)

1. x subtracted from 15 _____

2. 12 divided by t _____

3. 4 groups of y _____

4. the sum of z and 7 _____

Write a phrase for each algebraic expression. (Lesson 10.1)

5. $8p$ _____

6. $s + 7$ _____

Evaluate each expression for the given values of the variables.
(Lesson 10.2)

7. $8z + 3; z = 8$ _____

8. $3(7 + x^2); x = 2$ _____

9. $s - 5t + s^2; s = 4, t = -1$ _____

10. $x - y^3; x = -7, y = 3$ _____

11. The expression $\frac{1}{2}(h)(b_1 + b_2)$ gives the area of a trapezoid, with b_1 and b_2 representing the two base lengths of a trapezoid and h representing the height. Find the area of a trapezoid with base lengths 4 in. and 6 in. and a height of 8 in. (Lesson 10.2)   _____

Determine if the expressions are equivalent. (Lesson 10.3)

12. $7 + 7x; 7\left(x + \frac{1}{7}\right)$ _____

13. $2.5(3 + x); 2.5x + 7.5$ _____

Combine like terms. (Lesson 10.3)

14. $3m - 6 + m^2 - 5m + 1$ _____

15. $7x + 4(2x - 6)$ _____

16. $b^2 + 3 + 2b^2 + 4 - 7$ _____

17. $3(p + 5) - 8 + 11p$ _____

Unit 4 Performance Tasks

1. **CAREERS IN MATH** | Freelance Computer Programmer

   Antonio is a freelance computer programmer. In his work, he often uses the power of 2^n to find the number of ways bits (or units of information) can be arranged. The n often stands for the number of bits.

   a. Antonio is working on programming a new video game called *Millie's Quest*. In the game, the main character, Millie, collects golden keys to help her in her quest. Antonio wants to write a formula to show that Millie can collect one less key than the highest number of bits that can be arranged in the system. What formula can he use?

   _____

   b. If Antonio is working with a 16-bit system, how many golden keys can Millie collect?

   _____

   c. Antonio is also working on a new spreadsheet program. The program takes up 14 bytes of memory. If each byte is equal to 8 bits, how many bits is Antonio's program? Show your work.

   _____

2. Hannah just bought a new camera. In January she took 14 pictures. The number of pictures she took doubled each month for three months.

   a. How many pictures did Hannah take in March? Write and solve an expression with an exponent to show how many pictures she took.

   _____

   b. In April, Hanna took half the number of pictures she took in March. Her brother Jack thinks she took the same number of pictures in April that she did in February. Hanna knew he was incorrect. Write and solve an expression to show why Hannah is right.

   _____

   _____

Assessment Readiness

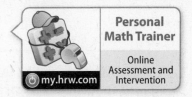

Personal Math Trainer

Online Assessment and Intervention

my.hrw.com

Selected Response

1. Which expression is equivalent to $2.3 \times 2.3 \times 2.3 \times 2.3 \times 2.3$?

   Ⓐ 2.3×5

   Ⓑ 23^5

   Ⓒ $2^5 \times 3^5$

   Ⓓ 2.3^5

2. Which operation should you perform first when you simplify $63 - (2 + 54 \times 6) \div 5$?

   Ⓐ addition

   Ⓑ division

   Ⓒ multiplication

   Ⓓ subtraction

3. Sheena was organizing items in a scrapbook. She took 25 photos and divided them evenly between p pages. Which algebraic expression represents the number of photos on each page?

   Ⓐ $p - 25$

   Ⓑ $25 - p$

   Ⓒ $\frac{p}{25}$

   Ⓓ $\frac{25}{p}$

4. Which is another way to write $7 \times 7 \times 7 \times 7$?

   Ⓐ 7^4

   Ⓑ $7(4)$

   Ⓒ 28

   Ⓓ 4^7

5. Angela earns x dollars an hour. On Friday, she worked 6 hours. On Saturday, she worked 8 hours. Which expression shows how much she earned both days?

   Ⓐ $6x + 8$

   Ⓑ $8x \times 6x$

   Ⓒ $(6 + 8)x$

   Ⓓ $\frac{6 + 8}{x}$

6. Marcus is doing a science experiment in which he measures the rate at which bacteria multiply. Every 15 seconds, the bacteria double in number. If there are 10 bacteria now, how many will there be in 2 minutes?

   Ⓐ 160 bacteria

   Ⓑ 256 bacteria

   Ⓒ 1,280 bacteria

   Ⓓ 2,560 bacteria

7. The prime factorization of which number is $2^5 \times 5$?

   Ⓐ 50

   Ⓑ 125

   Ⓒ 160

   Ⓓ 500

8. Which expression has a value of 36 when $x = 4$ and $y = 7$?

   Ⓐ $2xy$

   Ⓑ $2x + 4y$

   Ⓒ $6y - x$

   Ⓓ $12x - 2y$

9. What should you do first to simplify the expression $(4^3 + 9) \div 76 + 5$?

   (A) Add 4 and 9.

   (B) Add 76 and 5.

   (C) Multiply $4 \times 4 \times 4$.

   (D) Divide $(4^3 + 9)$ by 76.

10. Which ratio is equivalent to 4:10?

    (A) $\frac{2}{5}$

    (B) $\frac{8}{10}$

    (C) $\frac{12}{16}$

    (D) $\frac{16}{10}$

11. Travis and Paula went to lunch. Travis ordered a sandwich for $7.50, and Paula ordered a burger for $5.25. After lunch, they left a 15% tip for their waiter. How much money did they spend altogether?

    (A) $12.75

    (B) $14.66

    (C) $15.95

    (D) $16.00

12. Which shows the following numbers in order from greatest to least?

    $$1.5, \frac{2}{4}, \frac{4}{2}, 1.05$$

    (A) $\frac{4}{2}$, 1.5, 1.05, $\frac{2}{4}$

    (B) 1.05, 1.5, $\frac{2}{4}$, $\frac{4}{2}$

    (C) $\frac{4}{2}$, $\frac{2}{4}$, 1.5, 1.05

    (D) 1.05, $\frac{4}{2}$, $\frac{2}{4}$, 1.5

Mini-Tasks

13. For every bag of trail mix the local Scout Guide troop sells, they earn $0.45.

    a. Write an expression to represent this situation.

    _____

    b. Sarah sold 52 bags of trail mix. How much did she earn for her troop?

    _____

    c. Let x represent the total number of bags of trail mix sold by Sarah's troop. Write an expression to show what percentage of bags Sarah sold.

    _____

14. Robert is replacing sod in two square-shaped areas of his backyard. One side of the first area is 7.5 feet. One side of the other area is 5.7 feet. The sod costs y dollars per square foot.

    a. Write an expression to show how much Robert will spend on sod.

    _____

    b. If the sod costs $3.25 per square foot, about how much will Robert spend to put sod down in both areas of his backyard? Round to the nearest dollar.

    _____

15. Jose wants to find how many gallons of water he needs to fill his cube-shaped aquarium. One side of his aquarium is 4 feet long.

    a. Write and solve an expression to find the volume of Jose's aquarium.

    _____

    b. One cubic foot is equal to 7.48 gallons of water. How many gallons of water does Jose need to fill his aquarium? Round to the nearest gallon.

    _____

Equations and Inequalities

CAREERS IN MATH

Botanist A botanist is a biologist who studies plants. Botanists use math to analyze data and create models of biological organisms and systems. They use these models to make predictions. They also use statistics to determine correlations. If you are interested in a career in botany, you should study these mathematical subjects:

- Algebra
- Trigonometry
- Probability and Statistics
- Calculus

Research other careers that require the analysis of data and use of mathematical models.

Unit 5 Performance Task

At the end of the unit, check out how **botanists** use math.

© Houghton Mifflin Harcourt Publishing Company • Image Credits: Andy Sotiriou/ Photodisc/Getty Images

Vocabulary Preview

Use the puzzle to preview key vocabulary from this unit. Unscramble the circled letters within found words to answer the riddle at the bottom of the page.

- A word that describes a variable that depends on another variable. (Lesson 12.2)
- A value of the variable that makes the equation true. (Lesson 11.1)
- The numbers in an ordered pair. (Lesson 12.1)
- The point where the axes intersect to form the coordinate plane. (Lesson 12.1)
- One of the four regions into which the x- and y-axes divide the coordinate plane. (Lesson 12.1)
- The two number lines that intersect at right angles to form a coordinate plane. (Lesson 12.1)

Q: Why did the paper rip when the student tried to stretch out the horizontal axis of his graph?

A: Too much ___ – ___ ___ ___ ___ ___ ___ ___ !

Equations and Relationships

 ESSENTIAL QUESTION

How can you use equations and relationships to solve real-world problems?

Real-World Video

Suppose a world weightlifting record is w pounds. To find how many more pounds m must be lifted to set a new record of n pounds, you can use the equation $n = w + m$.

my.hrw.com

 GO DIGITAL

my.hrw.com

 my.hrw.com

Go digital with your write-in student edition, accessible on any device.

 Math On the Spot

Scan with your smart phone to jump directly to the online edition, video tutor, and more.

 Animated Math

Interactively explore key concepts to see how math works.

 Personal Math Trainer

Get immediate feedback and help as you work through practice sets.

Reading Start-Up

Visualize Vocabulary

Use the ✔ words to complete the graphic.

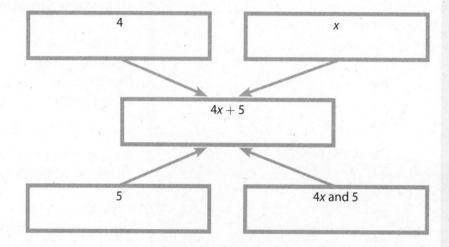

4		x

$$4x + 5$$

5		4x and 5

Understand Vocabulary

Match the term on the left to the correct expression on the right.

1. algebraic expression

2. equation

3. solution

A. A mathematical statement that two expressions are equal.

B. A value of the variable that makes the statement true.

C. A mathematical statement that includes one or more variables.

Vocabulary

Review Words

✔ algebraic expression (*expresión algebraica*)

✔ coefficient (*coeficiente*)

✔ constant (*constante*)

   equivalent expression (*expresión equivalente*)

   evaluating (*evaluar*)

   like terms (*términos semejantes*)

✔ term (*término, en una expresión*)

✔ variable (*variable*)

Preview Words

   equation (*ecuación*)

   properties of operations (*propiedades de las operaciones*)

   solution (*solución*)

Active Reading

Booklet Before beginning the module, create a booklet to help you learn the concepts in this module. Write the main idea of each lesson on each page of the booklet. As you study each lesson, write important details that support the main idea, such as vocabulary and formulas. Refer to your finished booklet as you work on assignments and study for tests.

Are YOU Ready?

Complete these exercises to review skills you will need for this module.

Evaluate Expressions

EXAMPLE   Evaluate $8(3+2) - 5^2$

$8(3+2) - 5^2 = 8(5) - 5^2$ Perform operations inside parentheses first.

$= 8(5) - 25$ Evaluate exponents.

$= 40 - 25$ Multiply.

$= 15$ Subtract.

Evaluate the expression.

1. $4(5 + 6) - 15$ _____

2. $8(2 + 4) + 16$ _____

3. $3(14 - 7) - 16$ _____

4. $6(8 - 3) + 3(7 - 4)$ _____

5. $10(6 - 5) - 3(9 - 6)$ _____

6. $7(4 + 5 + 2) - 6(3 + 5)$ _____

7. $2(8 + 3) + 4^2$ _____

8. $7(14 - 8) - 6^2$ _____

9. $8(2 + 1)^2 - 4^2$ _____

Connect Words and Equations

EXAMPLE   The product of a number and 4 is 32.

The product of x and 4 is 32.   Represent the unknown with a variable.

$4 \times x$ is 32.   Determine the operation.

$4 \times x = 32.$ Determine the placement of the equal sign.

Write an algebraic equation for the word sentence.

10. A number increased by 7.9 is 8.3. _____

11. 17 is the sum of a number and 6. _____

12. The quotient of a number and 8 is 4. _____

13. 81 is three times a number. _____

14. The difference between 31 and a number is 7. _____

15. Eight less than a number is 19. _____

Complete these exercises to review skills you will need for this module.

Evaluate Expressions

16. Which expressions have the same value? Choose all that apply.

    Ⓐ $7(5 + 3) - 2^2$ Ⓑ $[(7)(5)] + (3 - 2)^2$ Ⓒ $(7)(5) + (3 - 2)^2$ Ⓓ $7(5) + 3 - 2^2$

17. Regina evaluated the expression $(2 + 3 \times 4)^2 - 11$ as follows.

$$(2 + 3 \times 4)^2 - 11 = (5 \times 4)^2 - 11$$
$$= (20)^2 - 11$$
$$= 400 - 11$$
$$= 389$$

Is she correct? If so, explain each step. If not, explain her error and correct her work.

Connect Words and Equations

18. A decade is 10 years. Ian wants to write an algebraic equation for the year that was a decade before 2016. What equation can he use?

19. Consider the two statements below.

The _____ of 2 and a number is 10.
The _____ of a number and 2 is 10.

  a. If the word "sum" is inserted in both blanks, what equations are obtained? Are the expressions on the left side of the equations equivalent? Explain.

  b. If the word "difference" is inserted in both blanks, what equations are obtained? Are the expressions on the left side of the equations equivalent? Explain.

Writing Equations to Represent Situations

6.5.11.1

Students will write equations and determine whether a number is a solution of an equation.

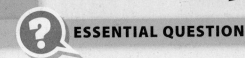

? ESSENTIAL QUESTION

How do you write equations and determine whether a number is a solution of an equation?

EXPLORE ACTIVITY

Determining Whether Values Are Solutions

Math On the Spot

my.hrw.com

An **equation** is a mathematical statement that two *expressions* are equal. An equation may or may not contain variables. For an equation that has a variable, a **solution** of the equation is a value of the variable that makes the equation true.

> An expression represents a single value.

> An equation represents a relationship between two values.

	Expression	**Equation**
Numerical	$5 + 4$	$5 + 4 = 9$
Words	a number *plus* 4	A number *plus* 4 *is* 9.
Algebraic	$n + 4$	$n + 4 = 9$

> An equation relates two expressions using symbols for *is* or *equals*.

EXAMPLE 1 Determine whether the given value is a solution of the equation.

A $x + 9 = 15; x = 6$

Substitute 6 for x. $\boxed{} + 9 \overset{?}{=} 15$

Add. $\boxed{} \overset{?}{=} 15$

6 is/is not a solution of $x + 9 = 15$.

B $\frac{y}{4} = 32; y = 8$

Substitute 8 for y. $\dfrac{\boxed{}}{4} \overset{?}{=} 32$

Divide. $\boxed{} \overset{?}{=} 32$

8 is/is not a solution of $\frac{y}{4} = 32$.

C $8x = 72; x = 9$

Substitute 9 for x. $8\left(\boxed{}\right) \overset{?}{=} 72$

Multiply. $\boxed{} \overset{?}{=} 72$

9 is/is not a solution of $8x = 72$.

EXPLORE ACTIVITY *(cont'd)*

YOUR TURN

Determine whether the given value is a solution of the equation.

1. $11 = n + 6; n = 5$

2. $y - 6 = 24; y = 18$

3. $\frac{x}{9} = 4; x = 36$

4. $15t = 100; t = 6$

Personal Math Trainer

Online Assessment and Intervention

ⓞ my.hrw.com

Math On the Spot

ⓞ my.hrw.com

Writing Equations to Represent Situations

You can represent some real-world situations with an equation. Making a model first can help you organize the information.

EXAMPLE 2

Mark scored 17 points for the home team in a basketball game. His teammates as a group scored p points. Write an equation to represent this situation.

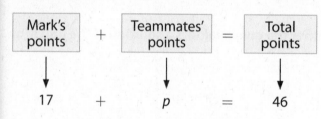

YOUR TURN

Write an equation to represent each situation.

5. Marilyn has a fish tank that contains 38 fish. There are 9 goldfish and f other fish.

6. Juanita has 102 beads to make n necklaces. Each necklace will have 17 beads.

7. Craig is c years old. His 12-year-old sister Kaitlin is 3 years younger than Craig.

8. Kim rented skates for h hours. The rental fee was $2 per hour and she paid a total of $8.

Personal Math Trainer

Online Assessment and Intervention

ⓞ my.hrw.com

Writing an Equation and Checking Solutions

You can substitute a given value for the variable in a real-world equation to check if that value makes sense for the situation.

Math On the Spot
⊙ my.hrw.com

EXAMPLE 3

Sarah used a gift card to buy $47 worth of groceries. Now she has $18 left on her gift card. Write an equation to represent this situation. Use your equation to determine whether Sarah had $65 or $59 on the gift card before buying groceries.

STEP 1 Write a word equation based on the situation.

| Amount on card | − | Amount spent | = | Amount left on card |

STEP 2 Rewrite the equation using a variable for the unknown quantity and the given values for the known quantities.

Let *x* be the amount on the card.

| Amount on card | − | Amount spent | = | Amount left on card |

$$x \quad - \quad 47 \quad = \quad 18$$

> The amount spent and the amount left on the card are the known quantities. Substitute those values in the equation.

STEP 3 Substitute 65 and 59 for *x* to see which equation is true.

$$x - 47 = 18 \qquad x - 47 = 18$$
$$65 - 47 \overset{?}{=} 18 \qquad 59 - 47 \overset{?}{=} 18$$
$$18 \overset{?}{=} 18 \qquad 12 \overset{?}{=} 18$$

The amount on Sarah's gift card before she bought groceries was $65.

Animated Math
⊙ my.hrw.com

Reflect

9. **What If?** Suppose Sarah has $12 left on her gift card. How would this change the equation and the final answer?

_____

_____

10. On Saturday morning, Owen earned $24. By the end of the afternoon he had earned a total of $62. Write an equation represent the situation. Determine whether Owen earned $38 or $31 on Saturday afternoon.

_____

Personal Math Trainer

Online Assessment and Intervention

⊙ my.hrw.com

Determine whether the given value is a solution of the equation. (Explore Activity Example 1)

1. $23 = x - 9; x = 14$ _____

$23 \stackrel{?}{=} \boxed{} - 9$

$23 \stackrel{?}{=} \boxed{}$

2. $\frac{n}{13} = 4; n = 52$ _____

$\frac{\boxed{}}{13} \stackrel{?}{=} 4$

$\boxed{} \stackrel{?}{=} 4$

3. $14 + x = 46; x = 32$ _____

4. $17y = 85; y = 5$ _____

5. $25 = \frac{k}{5}; k = 5$ _____

6. $2.5n = 45; n = 18$ _____

7. $21 = m + 9; m = 11$ _____

8. $21 - h = 15; h = 6$ _____

9. $d - 4 = 19; d = 15$ _____

10. $5 + x = 47; x = 52$ _____

11. $w - 9 = 0; w = 9$ _____

12. $5q = 31; q = 13$ _____

13. Each floor of a hotel has r rooms. On 8 floors, there are a total of 256 rooms. Write an equation to represent this situation. (Example 2)

Number		Number of rooms		
_____	×	_____	=	_____

_____

14. In the school band, there are 5 trumpet players and f flute players. There are twice as many flute players as there are trumpet players. Write an equation to represent this situation. (Example 2)

_____

15. Pedro bought 8 tickets to a basketball game. He paid a total of $208. Write an equation to determine whether each ticket cost $26 or $28. (Example 3)

_____

16. The high temperature was 92 °F. This was 24 °F higher than the overnight low temperature. Write an equation to determine whether the low temperature was 62 °F or 68 °F. (Example 3)

_____

? ESSENTIAL QUESTION CHECK-IN

17. Tell how you can determine whether a number is a solution of an equation.

_____

_____

11.1 Independent Practice

18. Andy is one-fourth as old as his grandfather, who is 76 years old. Write an equation to determine whether Andy is 19 or 22 years old.

_____

19. A sleeping bag weighs 8 pounds. Your backpack and sleeping bag together weigh 31 pounds. Write an equation to determine whether the backpack without the sleeping bag weighs 25 or 23 pounds.

_____

20. Halfway through a bus route, 23 students have been dropped off and 48 students remain on the bus. Write an equation to determine whether there are 61 or 71 students on the bus at the beginning of the route.

_____

21. Write an equation that involves multiplication, contains a variable, and has a solution of 5. Then write another equation that has the same solution and includes the same variable and numbers but uses division.

_____

_____

22. **Vocabulary** How are expressions and equations different?

_____

_____

_____

_____

23. **Multistep** Alan has partially completed a table showing the distances between his town, Greenville, and two other towns.

Distance between Greenville and Nearby Towns (miles)	
Parker	29
Hadley	?

a. The distance between Hadley and Greenville is 13 miles less than the distance between Parker and Greenville. Write two equations that compare the distance between Hadley and Greenville and the distance between Parker and Greenville. Tell what your variable represents.

_____

_____

b. Alan says the distance from Hadley to Greenville is 16 miles. Is he correct? Explain.

_____

_____

24. **Explain the Error** A problem states that Ursula earns $9 per hour. To write an expression that tells how much money Ursula earns for h hours, Joshua wrote $\frac{9}{h}$. Sarah wrote $9h$. Whose expression is correct and why?

_____

_____

_____

25. Communicate Mathematical Ideas A dog weighs 44 pounds and the veterinarian thinks it needs to lose 7 pounds. Mikala wrote the equation $x + 7 = 44$ to represent the situation. Kirk wrote the equation $44 - x = 7$. Which equation is correct? Can you write another equation that represents the situation?

_____

_____

26. Multiple Representations The table shows the ages of Cindy and her dad.

Dad's Age	Cindy's Age
28 years old	2 years old
36 years old	10 years old
?	18 years old

a. Write an equation that relates Cindy's age to her dad's age when Cindy is 18. Tell what the variable represents.

_____

b. Determine if 42 is a solution to the equation. Show your work.

_____

c. Explain the meaning of your answer in part **b**.

_____

 **FOCUS ON HIGHER ORDER THINKING**

Work Area

27. Critical Thinking In the school band, there are 4 trumpet players and f flute players. The total number of trumpet and flute players is 12. Are there twice as many flute players as trumpet players? Explain.

_____

_____

28. Problem Solving Ronald paid $162 for 6 tickets to a basketball game. During the game he noticed that his friend paid $130 for 5 tickets. The price of each ticket was $26. Was Ronald overcharged? Explain.

_____

_____

29. Communicate Mathematical Ideas Tariq said you can write an equation by setting an expression equal to itself. Would an equation like this be true? Explain.

_____

_____

_____

6.5.GF.11.1
Students will identify parts of and write expressions and equations.

Expressions and Equations

ESSENTIAL QUESTION How can you identify parts of equations and expressions using mathematical terms?

EXPLORE ACTIVITY

Using Vocabulary

Match the term on the left to the correct expression on the right.

1. sum _____
2. term _____
3. product _____
4. factor _____
5. quotient _____
6. coefficient _____
7. difference _____

A. a number that is multiplied by the variable in an algebraic expression

B. a number that is multiplied by another number to get a product

C. the result of subtracting one number from another

D. a part of an expression that is added to or subtracted from another part of an expression

E. the result when two or more numbers are multiplied

F. the result when one number is divided by another

G. the result when two or more numbers are added

Understanding an Expression

An expression represents mathematical operations using signs and symbols. Expressions can also be written with words. There is usually more than one way to describe an expression.

EXAMPLE 1

Describe each expression using the vocabulary from the Explore Activity. Examine each part of the expression and the expression as a whole.

A $5(3 + 7)$

$3 + 7$ the sum of 3 and 7

$5(3 + 7)$ the product of 5 and the sum of 3 and 7

B $4u \div 2$

$4u$ the product of the factors u and 4

$4u \div 2$ the quotient of the terms 4 times u and 2

Writing a Multi-Step Equation

You can solve real-world problems by writing an equation.

EXAMPLE 2

Write an equation to represent the real-world situation. Show how the parts of the equation match the real-world situation.

A A plumber charges a $25 service fee plus an additional hourly rate of $85. What is the total cost of hiring the plumber?

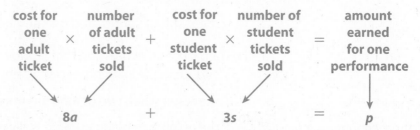

B A school theater group sells both adult and student tickets for each play it puts on. Adult tickets cost $8 each and student tickets cost $3 each. How much will the theater group earn for one performance?

cost for one adult ticket	×	number of adult tickets sold	+	cost for one student ticket	×	number of student tickets sold	=	amount earned for one performance
8a			+			3s	=	p

Practice

Describe each expression using the terms *sum, difference, product, quotient, factor, term,* and *coefficient*.

1. $\frac{c}{5} + 10$

_____

2. $3f - 7$

_____

Write an equation to represent the real-world situation. Show how the parts of the equation match the real-world situation.

3. An amusement park charges an entrance fee of $7.50 plus $2.50 per ride. Calculate the amount spent at the amusement park in one day for five students if all students ride the rides together.

Getting Ready

Addition Equations

6.5.GR.11.2

Students will solve addition equations using balance scales.

? **ESSENTIAL QUESTION**

How can you model solving an addition equation?

EXPLORE ACTIVITY 1

Looking for Patterns

A simple equation can sometimes be solved just by noticing patterns and equivalent values.

A **Determine the value of x in the equation $x + 2x = 2x + 5$.**

Circle the term repeated on both sides of the equation. $x + 2x = 2x + 5$

The variable x will have the same value everywhere it appears in the equation, so $2x$ on the left side will have the same value as $2x$ on the right side. Rewrite the equation with $2x$ removed from both sides.

$$x = \underline{\hspace{1cm}}$$

B **Determine the value of $4t$ in the equation $4t + 3t = 3t + 8$.**

Circle the term repeated on both sides of the equation. $4t + 3t = 3t + 8$

The variable t will have the same value everywhere it appears in the equation, so $3t$ on the left side will have the same value as $3t$ on the right side. Rewrite the equation with $3t$ removed from both sides.

$$4t = \underline{\hspace{1cm}}$$

Reflect

1. **Analyze Relationships** Identify the terms that could be removed from both sides of the equation. Explain your reasoning. $5g + 15 = 2g + 5g$

_____

_____

_____

2. **Analyze Relationships** Would you be able to use this method for determining the value of $3x$ in the equation $3x + 6x = 5x + 15$? Explain.

_____

_____

Modeling Equations

When solving an addition equation, you can model the equation on a balance scale. For the equation to remain true, both sides must remain equal, or be the same "weight." If you take something from one side, you must take the same thing from the opposite side.

Solve $x + 3 = 8$.

A Model the equation on a balance scale. For this lesson the variable will be represented by a triangle and 1 will be represented by a square. The left side of the equation is already represented on the scale. Represent the right side by drawing eight squares on the right side of the scale.

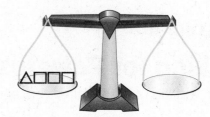

B Cross out shapes that appear on both sides of the scale. Make sure you keep the scale balanced by crossing out an equal number of the same shape on each side of the scale.

C Use the remaining shapes from the scale to determine the value of one triangle.

There are _____ squares that have not been crossed out, so the solution is $x =$ _____.

Reflect

3. Justify Reasoning Why do you need to remove an equal number of the same shape from each side of the scale?

_____

_____

_____

_____

Find the value of the variable in each equation.

1. Determine the value of x in the equation $x + 5x = 5x + 7$.

$x =$ _____

2. Determine the value of $4p$ in the equation $4p + 2p = 2p + 3$.

$4p =$ _____

3. Can you determine the value of y in the equation $2y + y = 5y + 7$ by removing a term from each side? Why or why not?

_____

_____

_____

Solve each equation by crossing out an equal number of the same shape on each side of the scale. Write the solution in the space provided.

4. $7 = p + 6$

$p =$ _____

5. $b + 4 = 10$

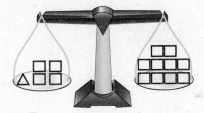

$b =$ _____

6. $2 + c = 5$

$c =$ _____

7. $x + 1 = 2$

$x =$ _____

Solve each equation by modeling the equation on the blank scale and crossing out an equal number of the same shape on each side. Write the solution in the space provided.

8. $x + 3 = 5$

$x =$ _____

9. $9 = c + 5$

$c =$ _____

10. $6 = z + 1$

$z =$ _____

11. $t + 4 = 5$

$t =$ _____

Solve each equation. Write the solution in the space provided.

12. $x + 20 = 27$ $x =$ _____

13. $17 + r = 30$ $r =$ _____

14. $45 = m + 22$ $m =$ _____

15. $32 = 15 + p$ $p =$ _____

Addition and Subtraction Equations

? ESSENTIAL QUESTION

How do you solve equations that contain addition or subtraction?

EXPLORE ACTIVITY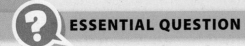

Modeling Equations

A puppy weighed 6 ounces at birth. After two weeks, the puppy weighed 14 ounces. How much weight did the puppy gain?

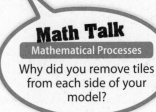

Let *x* represent the number of ounces gained.

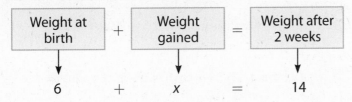

| Weight at birth | + | Weight gained | = | Weight after 2 weeks |

$$6 \quad + \quad x \quad = \quad 14$$

To answer this question, you can solve the equation $6 + x = 14$.

Algebra tiles can model some equations. An equation mat represents the two sides of an equation. To solve the equation, remove the same number of tiles from both sides of the mat until the *x* tile is by itself on one side.

A Model $6 + x = 14$.

B How many 1 tiles must you remove on the left side so that the *x* tile is by itself? _____
Cross out these tiles on the equation mat.

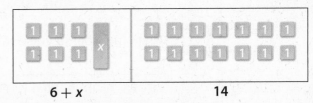

$6 + x$ 14

C Whenever you remove tiles from one side of the mat, you must remove the same number of tiles from the other side of the mat. Cross out the tiles that should be removed on the right side of the mat.

D How many tiles remain on the right side of the mat? _____
This is the solution of the equation.

The puppy gained _____ ounces.

> **Math Talk**
> Mathematical Processes
>
> Why did you remove tiles from each side of your model?

Reflect

1. **Communicate Mathematical Ideas** How do you know when the model shows the final solution? How do you read the solution?

_____

_____

Using Subtraction to Solve Equations

Removing the same number of tiles from each side of an equation mat models subtracting the same number from both sides of an equation.

Subtraction Property of Equality

You can subtract the same number from both sides of an equation, and the two sides will remain equal.

When an equation contains addition, solve by subtracting the same number from both sides.

EXAMPLE 1

Solve the equation $a + 15 = 26$. Graph the solution on a number line.

$a + 15 = 26$ Notice that the number 15 is added to a.

$$\begin{array}{rcl} a + 15 &=& 26 \\ -15 & & -15 \\ \hline a &=& 11 \end{array}$$ Subtract 15 from both sides of the equation.

Check: $a + 15 = 26$

$11 + 15 \overset{?}{=} 26$ Substitute 11 for a.

$26 \overset{?}{=} 26$ Add on the left side.

Graph the solution on a number line.

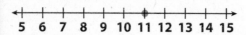

5 6 7 8 9 10 11 12 13 14 15

Reflect

2. **Communicate Mathematical Ideas** How do you decide which number to subtract from both sides?

_____

_____

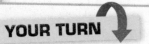

3. Solve the equation $5 = w + 1.5$.

   Graph the solution on a number line.

   -5 -4 -3 -2 -1 0 1 2 3 4 5

   $w =$ _____

Using Addition to Solve Equations

When an equation contains subtraction, solve by adding the same number to both sides.

Math On the Spot

⏻ my.hrw.com

> ### Addition Property of Equality
>
> You can add the same number to both sides of an equation, and the two sides will remain equal.

EXAMPLE 2

Solve the equation $y - 21 = 18$. Graph the solution on a number line.

$y - 21 = 18$ Notice that the number 21 is subtracted from y.

$$\begin{array}{rl} y - 21 = & 18 \\ \underline{+21 \quad +21} & \\ y \quad = & 39 \end{array}$$ Add 21 to both sides of the equation.

Check: $y - 21 = 18$

$39 - 21 \overset{?}{=} 18$ Substitute 39 for y.

$18 \overset{?}{=} 18$ Subtract.

Graph the solution on a number line.

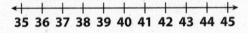

35 36 37 38 39 40 41 42 43 44 45

Reflect

4. **Communicate Mathematical Ideas** How do you know whether to add on both sides or subtract on both sides when solving an equation?

_____

_____

_____

YOUR TURN

5. Solve the equation $h - \frac{1}{2} = \frac{3}{4}$.

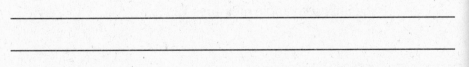

Graph the solution on a number line.

$h = $ _____

Personal Math Trainer

Online Assessment and Intervention

⏻ my.hrw.com

Solving Equations that Represent Geometric Concepts

You can write equations to represent geometric relationships.

Recall that a straight line has an angle measure of 180°. Two angles whose measures have a sum of 180° are called supplementary angles. Two angles whose measures have a sum of 90° are called complementary angles.

EXAMPLE 3

Find the measure of the unknown angle.

STEP 1 Write the information in the boxes.

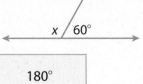

| Unknown angle | + | 60° | = | 180° |

STEP 2 Write a description to represent the model. Include a question for the unknown angle.

The sum of an unknown angle and a 60° angle is 180°. What is the measure of the unknown angle?

STEP 3 Write an equation.

$x + 60° = 180°$

STEP 4 Solve the equation.

$$x + \quad 60° = 180°$$
$$\underline{\quad -60° \quad -60°}$$
$$x \quad\quad = 120°$$

Subtract 60 from each side.

The unknown angle measures 120°.

The final answer includes units of degrees.

YOUR TURN

6. Write and solve an equation to find the measure of the unknown angle.

_____

7. Write and solve an equation to find the complement of an angle that measures 42°.

_____

Writing Real-World Problems for a Given Equation

You can write a real-world problem for a given equation. Examine each number and mathematical operation in the equation.

EXAMPLE 4

Write a real-world problem for the equation 21.79 + x = 25. Then solve the equation.

$21.79 + x = 25$

STEP 1 Examine each part of the equation.

x is the unknown or quantity we are looking for.

21.79 is added to x.

$= 25$ means that after adding 21.79 and x, the result is 25.

STEP 2 Write a real-world situation that involves *adding* two quantities.

Joshua wants to buy his mother flowers and a card for Mother's Day. Joshua has $25 to spend and selects roses for $21.79. How much can he spend on a card?

Math Talk
Mathematical Processes

How is the question in a real-world problem related to its equation?

STEP 3 Solve the equation.

$$
\begin{array}{r}
21.79 + x = 25 \\
-21.79 \quad\quad -21.79 \\
\hline
x = 3.21
\end{array}
$$

The final answer includes units of money in dollars.

Joshua can spend $3.21 on a Mother's Day card.

Reflect

8. **What If?** How might the real-world problem change if the equation was $x - 21.79 = 25$ and you still used roses for 21.79?

_____

_____

_____

YOUR TURN

9. Write a real-world problem for the equation $x - 100 = 40$. Then solve the equation.

_____

Personal Math Trainer

Online Assessment and Intervention

my.hrw.com

1. A total of 14 guests attended a birthday party. Three friends stayed after the party to help clean up. How many left when the party ended? (Explore Activity)

   a. Let x represent the _____

   b.
Number that		Number that		

   $+$ $=$

   _____ $+$ _____ $=$ _____

   c. Draw algebra tiles to model the equation.

   _____ friends left when the party ended.

Solve each equation. Graph the solution on a number line. (Examples 1 and 2)

2. $2 = x - 3$ $x =$ _____

   $$-5 \ -4 \ -3 \ -2 \ -1 \ \ 0 \ \ 1 \ \ 2 \ \ 3 \ \ 4 \ \ 5$$

3. $s + 12.5 = 14$ $s =$ _____

   $$-5 \ -4 \ -3 \ -2 \ -1 \ \ 0 \ \ 1 \ \ 2 \ \ 3 \ \ 4 \ \ 5$$

Solve each equation. (Examples 1 and 2)

4. $h + 6.9 = 11.4$

   $h =$ _____

5. $82 + p = 122$

   $p =$ _____

6. $n + \frac{1}{2} = \frac{7}{4}$

   $n =$ _____

7. Write and solve an equation to find the measure of the unknown angle. (Example 3)

   _____

   $45°$ \ x

8. Write a real-world problem for the equation $x - 75 = 200$. Then solve the equation. (Example 4)

   _____

? ESSENTIAL QUESTION CHECK-IN

9. How do you solve equations that contain addition or subtraction?

   _____

   _____

   _____

© Houghton Mifflin Harcourt Publishing Company

11.2 Independent Practice

Personal Math Trainer

Online Assessment and Intervention

my.hrw.com

Write and solve an equation to answer each question.

10. A wildlife reserve had 8 elephant calves born during the summer and now has 31 total elephants. How many elephants were in the reserve before summer began?

_____

_____

11. My sister is 14 years old. My brother says that his age minus twelve is equal to my sister's age. How old is my brother?

_____

_____

12. Kim bought a poster that cost $8.95 and some colored pencils. The total cost was $21.35. How much did the colored pencils cost?

_____

_____

13. The Acme Car Company sold 37 vehicles in June. How many compact cars were sold in June?

Acme Car Company — June Sales	
Type of car	**Number sold**
SUV	8
Compact	?

_____

_____

14. Sandra wants to buy a new MP3 player that is on sale for $95. She has saved $73. How much more money does she need?

_____

_____

15. Ronald spent $123.45 on school clothes. He counted his money and discovered that he had $36.55 left. How much money did he originally have?

_____

_____

16. Brita withdrew $225 from her bank account. After her withdrawal, there was $548 left in Brita's account. How much money did Brita have in her account before the withdrawal?

_____

_____

17. Represent Real-World Problems Write a real-world situation that can be represented by $15 + c = 17.50$. Then solve the equation and describe what your answer represents for the problem situation.

_____

_____

_____

_____

18. Critique Reasoning Paula solved the equation $7 + x = 10$ and got 17, but she is not certain if she got the correct answer. How could you explain Paula's mistake to her?

_____

_____

_____

_____

_____

Work Area

19. Multistep A grocery store is having a sale this week. If you buy a 5-pound bag of apples for the regular price, you can get another bag for $1.49. If you buy a 5-pound bag of oranges at the regular price, you can get another bag for $2.49.

Grocery Prices	
	Regular price
5-pound bag of apples	$2.99
5-pound bag of oranges	$3.99

a. Write an equation to find the discount for each situation using *a* for the amount of the discount for apples and *r* for the amount of the discount for oranges.

_____

b. Which fruit has a greater discount? Explain.

_____

_____

20. Critical Thinking An orchestra has twice as many woodwind instruments as brass instruments. There are a total of 150 brass and woodwind instruments.

a. Write two different addition equations that describe this situation. Use *w* for woodwinds and *b* for brass.

_____

b. How many woodwinds and how many brass instruments satisfy the given information?

_____

21. Look for a Pattern Assume the following: $a + 1 = 2, b + 10 = 20,$ $c + 100 = 200, d + 1{,}000 = 2{,}000, \ldots$

a. Solve each equation for each variable.

_____

b. What pattern do you notice between the variables?

_____

c. What would be the value of *g* if the pattern continues?

_____

Multiplication Equations

6.5.GR.11.3
Students will solve
multiplication equations
using balance scales.

? **ESSENTIAL QUESTION**

How can you model solving a multiplication equation?

EXPLORE ACTIVITY 1

Modeling Equations

When solving a multiplication equation, you can model the equation on a balance scale.

Solve $3x = 9$.

A Model the equation on a balance scale. For this lesson the variable will be represented by a triangle and 1 will be represented by a square. The left side of the equation is already represented on the scale. Represent the right side by drawing nine squares on the right side of the scale.

B Place the triangles in a single column. Place one square across from each triangle. Continue placing squares across from the triangles until all nine squares have been used.

C Circle each of the groups created above. Each group should have one triangle on the left side of the scale and three squares on the right side.

How many squares are equal to one triangle? _____

$x =$ _____

Reflect

1. **What if?** Suppose the equation were $3x = 15$. How many squares would be grouped with each triangle? Why?

_____

_____

© Houghton Mifflin Harcourt Publishing Company

Balancing Equations

When balancing equations, the first step is to place all triangles and squares on the scale.

Solve $8 = 2g$.

A Model the equation on a balance scale. Represent the left side by drawing eight squares on the left side of the scale. Represent the right side by drawing two triangles on the right side of the scale.

B Place the triangles in a single column. Place one square across from each triangle. Continue placing squares across from the triangles until all eight squares have been used.

C Circle each of the groups created above. Each group should have one triangle on the right side of the scale and four squares on the left side.

How many squares are equal to one triangle? _____

$g =$ _____

Reflect

2. **What If?** Which steps from Explore Activity 1 and Explore Activity 2 could you combine?

_____

_____

_____

Solving Equations

When solving equations on a balance scale, make sure each row has one triangle and an equal number of squares.

EXAMPLE

Solve the equation by modeling on the scale provided. Place triangles on one side of the scale and squares on the other. Write the solution in the space provided.

$4w = 4$

STEP 1 Draw four triangles on the left side of the scale to represent $4w$. Draw 4 squares on the right side of the scale to represent 4.

STEP 2 Place the triangles in a single column. Place one square across from each triangle until all squares have been used.

STEP 3 Circle each of the groups created above.

$w = 1$

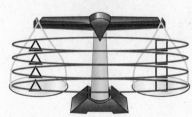

Practice

Solve each equation by circling each triangle and the corresponding group of squares. Write the solution in the space provided.

1. $4x = 16$

$x = $ _____

2. $8 = 4b$

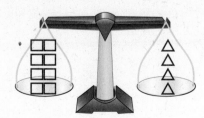

$b = $ _____

Solve each equation by modeling on the scale provided. Group the squares on the empty side of the scale based on the number of triangles provided. Circle each triangle and the corresponding groups of squares. Write the solution in the space provided.

3. $3f = 3$

$f = \underline{\hphantom{xxxx}}$

4. $5x = 10$

$x = \underline{\hphantom{xxxx}}$

Solve each equation by modeling on the scale provided. Place triangles on one side of the scale and squares on the other. Write the solution in the space provided.

5. $2y = 6$

$y = \underline{\hphantom{xxxx}}$

6. $12 = 3c$

$c = \underline{\hphantom{xxxx}}$

7. $6 = 3r$

$r = \underline{\hphantom{xxxx}}$

8. $2p = 4$

$p = \underline{\hphantom{xxxx}}$

LESSON
11.3 Multiplication and Division Equations

6.5.11.3
Students will solve equations that contain multiplication or division.

ESSENTIAL QUESTION

How do you solve equations that contain multiplication or division?

EXPLORE ACTIVITY

Modeling Equations

Deanna has a cookie recipe that requires 12 eggs to make 3 batches of cookies. How many eggs are needed per batch of cookies?

Let x represent the number of eggs needed per batch.

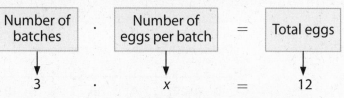

To answer this question, you can use algebra tiles to solve $3x = 12$.

A Model $3x = 12$.

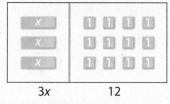

$3x$ 12

B There are 3 x tiles, so draw circles to separate the tiles into 3 equal groups. One group has been circled for you.

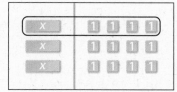

Math Talk
Mathematical Processes

Why is the solution to the equation the number of tiles in each group?

C How many 1 tiles are in each group? _____
This is the solution of the equation.

_____ eggs are needed per batch of cookies.

Reflect

1. **Look for a Pattern** Why does it make sense to arrange the twelve 1 tiles in 3 rows of 4 instead of any other arrangement of twelve 1 tiles, such as 2 rows of 6?

_____

Using Division to Solve Equations

Separating the tiles on both sides of an equation mat into an equal number of groups models dividing both sides of an equation by the same number.

> **Division Property of Equality**
>
> You can divide both sides of an equation by the same nonzero number, and the two sides will remain equal.

When an equation contains multiplication, solve by dividing both sides of the equation by the same nonzero number.

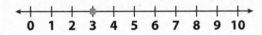

EXAMPLE 1

Solve each equation. Graph the solution on a number line.

A $9a = 54$

$9a = 54$ Notice that 9 is multiplied by a.

$\dfrac{9a}{9} = \dfrac{54}{9}$ Divide both sides of the equation by 9.

$a = 6$

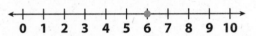

Check: $9a = 54$

$9(6) \overset{?}{=} 54$ Substitute 6 for a.

$54 \overset{?}{=} 54$ Multiply on the left side.

B $18 = 6d$

$18 = 6d$ Notice that 6 is multiplied by d.

$\dfrac{18}{6} = \dfrac{6d}{6}$ Divide both sides of the equation by 6.

$3 = d$

Check: $18 = 6d$

$18 \overset{?}{=} 6(3)$ Substitute 3 for d.

$18 \overset{?}{=} 18$ Multiply on the right side.

My Notes

YOUR TURN

Solve the equation $3x = 21$. Graph the solution on a number line.

2. $x =$ _____

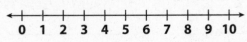

Using Multiplication to Solve Equations

When an equation contains division, solve by multiplying both sides of the equation by the same number.

Math On the Spot

my.hrw.com

> **Multiplication Property of Equality**
>
> You can multiply both sides of an equation by the same number, and the two sides will remain equal.

EXAMPLE 2

Solve each equation. Graph the solution on a number line.

A $\frac{x}{5} = 10$

$\frac{x}{5} = 10$ Notice that x is divided by the number 5.

$5 \cdot \frac{x}{5} = 5 \cdot 10$ Multiply both sides of the equation by 5.

$x = 50$

Number line: 0 10 20 30 40 50 60 70 (point at 50)

Check: $\frac{x}{5} = 10$

$\frac{50}{5} \stackrel{?}{=} 10$ Substitute 50 for x.

$10 \stackrel{?}{=} 10$ Divide on the left side.

B $15 = \frac{r}{2}$

$15 = \frac{r}{2}$ Notice that r is divided by the number 2.

$2 \cdot 15 = 2 \cdot \frac{r}{2}$ Multiply both sides of the equation by 2.

$30 = r$

Number line: 0 5 10 15 20 25 30 35 40 45 50 (point at 30)

Check: $15 = \frac{r}{2}$

$15 \stackrel{?}{=} \frac{30}{2}$ Substitute 30 for r.

$15 \stackrel{?}{=} 15$ Divide on the right side.

Math Talk
Mathematical Processes

How is solving a multiplication equation similar to solving a division equation? How is it different?

© Houghton Mifflin Harcourt Publishing Company

YOUR TURN

Solve the equation $\frac{y}{9} = 1$. Graph the solution on a number line.

3. $\frac{y}{9} = 1$

$y = \underline{\hspace{2cm}}$

Number line: 0 1 2 3 4 5 6 7 8 9 10

Personal Math Trainer

Online Assessment and Intervention

my.hrw.com

Using Equations to Solve Problems

You can use equations to solve real-world problems.

EXAMPLE 3 Problem Solving

Juanita is scrapbooking. She usually completes about 9 pages per hour. One night last week she completed pages 23 through 47 in 2.5 hours. Did she work at her average rate?

Analyze Information

Identify the important information.

- Worked for 2.5 hours
- Starting page: 23   Ending page: 47
- Scrapbooking rate: 9 pages per hour

Formulate a Plan

- Solve an equation to find the number of pages Juanita can expect to complete.
- Compare the number of pages Juanita can expect to complete with the number of pages she actually completed.

Solve

Let n represent the number of pages Juanita can expect to complete in 2.5 hours if she works at her average rate of 9 pages per hour.

Write an equation.

$$\frac{n}{2.5} = 9 \qquad \text{Write the equation.}$$

$$2.5 \cdot \frac{n}{2.5} = 2.5 \cdot 9 \qquad \text{Multiply both sides by 2.5.}$$

$$n = 22.5$$

Juanita can expect to complete 22.5 pages in 2.5 hours.

Juanita completed pages 23 through 47, a total of 25 pages. Because $25 > 22.5$, she worked faster than her expected rate.

Justify and Evaluate

You used an equation to find the number of pages Juanita could expect to complete in 2.5 hours if she worked at her average rate. You found that she could complete 22.5 pages.

Since 22.5 pages is less than the 25 pages Juanita completed, she worked faster than her average rate.

The answer makes sense, because Juanita completed 25 pages in 2.5 hours, which is equivalent to a rate of 10 pages in 1 hour. Since $10 > 9$, you know that she worked faster than her average rate.

My Notes

YOUR TURN

4. Roberto is dividing his baseball cards equally among himself, his brother, and his 3 friends. Roberto was left with 9 cards. How many cards did Roberto give away? Write and solve an equation to solve the problem.

_____

_____

Writing Real-World Problems

You can write a real-world problem for a given equation.

EXAMPLE 4

Write a real-world problem for the equation 8x = 72. Then solve the problem.

STEP 1 Examine each part of the equation.

x is the unknown value you want to find.

8 is multiplied by *x*.

= 72 means that after multiplying 8 and *x*, the result is 72.

STEP 2 Write a real-world situation that involves multiplying two quantities.

A hot air balloon flew at 8 miles per hour. Write and solve a multiplication equation to find out how many hours the balloon traveled if it covered a distance of 72 miles.

STEP 3 Use the equation to solve the problem.

$8x = 72$

$\dfrac{8x}{8} = \dfrac{72}{8}$ *Divide both sides by 8.*

$x = 9$

The balloon traveled for 9 hours.

YOUR TURN

5. Write a real-world problem for the equation $11x = 385$. Then solve the problem.

_____

_____

1. Caroline ran 15 miles in 5 days. She ran the same distance each day. Write and solve an equation to determine the number of miles she ran each day. (Explore Activity)

   a. Let *x* represent the _____.

   b.
   | Number of | · | Number of | | = | |

   _____ · _____ = _____

   c. Draw algebra tiles to model the equation.

   Caroline ran _____ miles each day.

   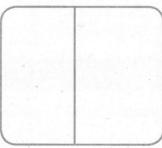

Solve each equation. Graph the solution on a number line.
(Examples 1 and 2)

2. $x \div 3 = 3$; $x =$ _____

   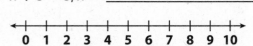

3. $4x = 32$; $x =$ _____

   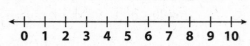

4. The area of the rectangle shown is 24 square inches. How much longer is its length than its width? (Example 3)

   _____

   _____

   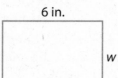

   6 in.

   w

5. Write a real-world problem for the equation $15w = 45$. Then solve the problem. (Example 4)

   _____

   _____

? ESSENTIAL QUESTION CHECK-IN

6. How do you solve equations that contain multiplication or division?

   _____

   _____

   _____

11.3 Independent Practice

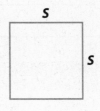

Personal Math Trainer
Online Assessment and Intervention
my.hrw.com

In 7–13, write and solve an equation to answer each question.

7. Jorge baked cookies for his math class's end-of-year party. There are 28 people in Jorge's math class including Jorge and his teacher. Jorge baked enough cookies for everyone to get 3 cookies each. How many cookies did Jorge bake?

_____

8. Sam divided a rectangle into 8 congruent rectangles that each have the area shown. What is the area of the rectangle before Sam divided it?

Area = 5 cm²		

_____

9. Carmen participated in a read-a-thon. Mr. Cole pledged $4.00 per book and gave Carmen $44. How many books did Carmen read?

_____

10. Lee drove 420 miles and used 15 gallons of gasoline. How many miles did Lee's car travel per gallon of gasoline?

_____

11. On some days, Melvin commutes 3.5 hours per day to the city for business meetings. Last week he commuted for a total of 14 hours. How many days did he commute to the city?

_____

12. Dharmesh has a square garden with a perimeter of 132 feet. Is the area of the garden greater than 1,000 square feet?

s

s

_____

_____

_____

_____

13. Ingrid walked her dog and washed her car. The time she spent walking her dog was one-fourth the time it took her to wash her car. It took Ingrid 14 minutes to walk the dog. How long did it take Ingrid to wash her car?

_____

14. **Representing Real-World Problems** Write and solve a problem involving money that can be solved with a multiplication equation.

_____

_____

_____

_____

_____

15. Representing Real-World Problems Write and solve a problem involving money that can be solved with a division equation and has a solution of 1,350.

H.O.T. FOCUS ON HIGHER ORDER THINKING

Work Area

16. Communicating Mathematical Ideas Explain why $7 \cdot \frac{x}{7} = x$. How does your answer help you solve a division equation such as $\frac{x}{7} = 2$?

17. Critical Thinking A number tripled and tripled again is 729. What is the number? Show your work.

18. Multistep Andre has 4 times as many model cars as Peter, and Peter has one-third as many model cars as Jade. Andre has 36 model cars.

a. Write and solve an equation to find how many model cars Peter has.

b. Using your answer from part **a**, write and solve an equation to find how many model cars Jade has.

19. Persevere in Problem Solving The area of a rectangle is 42 square inches and one side is 12 inches long. Find the perimeter of the rectangle. Show your work.

What is the Value?

Playing the Game

STEP 1 One student or the teacher is the caller, and gets the caller cards. Each caller card contains a fraction problem and its answer.

STEP 2 Each player gets a gameboard and 20–25 counters. The center is a free space. Players should cover the center square before play begins.

STEP 3 On each turn, the caller reads aloud a problem to the players. The caller does not read the answer aloud.

STEP 4 Solve the problem read by the caller. Then search in the correct variable column for the answer on your gameboard. If the answer is on your gameboard, cover it with a counter.

$$A - 5 = 0$$
$$A = 5$$

STEP 5 The caller places the card in a discard pile. Play continues until there is a winner.

$$5V = 25$$
$$V = 5$$

Winning the Game

A player who covers five squares in a row horizontally, vertically, or diagonally says, "What is the value?" The caller uses the cards in the discard pile to check that this player has calculated correctly. If so, that player is the winner. If not, play continues until someone else says, "What is the value?"

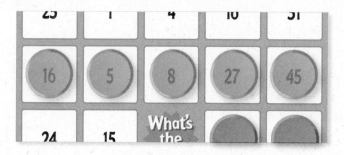

11.4 Writing Inequalities

6.5.11.4

Students will use inequalities to represent real-world constraints or conditions.

? ESSENTIAL QUESTION

How can you use inequalities to represent real-world constraints or conditions?

EXPLORE ACTIVITY

Using Inequalities to Describe Quantities

You can use inequality symbols with variables to describe quantities that can have many values.

Symbol	Meaning	Word Phrases
$<$	Is less than	Fewer than, below
$>$	Is greater than	More than, above
$\leq$	Is less than or equal to	At most, no more than
$\geq$	Is greater than or equal to	At least, no less than

A The lowest temperature ever recorded in Florida was $-2\,°F$. Graph this temperature on the number line.

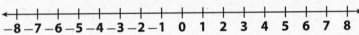

$$-8\ -7\ -6\ -5\ -4\ -3\ -2\ -1\ \ 0\ \ 1\ \ 2\ \ 3\ \ 4\ \ 5\ \ 6\ \ 7\ \ 8$$

B The temperatures $0\,°F$, $3\,°F$, $6\,°F$, $5\,°F$, and $-1\,°F$ have also been recorded in Florida. Graph these temperatures on the number line.

C How do the temperatures in **B** compare to -2? How can you see this relationship on the number line?

_____

_____

D How many other numbers have the same relationship to -2 as the temperatures in **B** ? Give some examples.

_____

E Suppose you could graph all of the possible answers to **D** on a number line. What would the graph look like?

_____

F Let x represent all the possible answers to **D** .

Complete this inequality: x ☐ -2

Graphing the Solutions of an Inequality

A **solution of an inequality** that contains a variable is any value of the variable that makes the inequality true. For example, 7 is a solution of $x > -2$, since $7 > -2$ is a true statement.

EXAMPLE 1

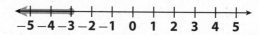

Graph the solutions of each inequality. Check the solutions.

A $y \leq -3$

> **STEP 1** Draw a solid circle at -3 to show that -3 is a solution.

> **STEP 2** Shade the number line to the left of -3 to show that numbers less than -3 are solutions.
>
> *Use a solid circle for an inequality that uses $\geq$ or $\leq$.*

> **STEP 3** Check your solution.
>
> Choose a number that is on the shaded section of the number line, such as -4. Substitute -4 for y.
>
> $-4 \leq -3$ -4 is less than -3, so -4 is a solution.

Math Talk

Mathematical Processes

Is $-4\frac{1}{4}$ a solution of $y \leq -3$? Is -5.6?

B $1 < m$

> **STEP 1** Draw an empty circle at 1 to show that 1 is not a solution.

> **STEP 2** Shade the number line to the right of 1 to show that numbers greater than 1 are solutions.
>
> *Use an open circle for an inequality that uses $>$ or $<$.*

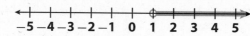

> **STEP 3** Check your answer.
> Substitute 2 for m.
> $1 < 2$ 1 is less than 2, so 2 is a solution.

Reflect

1. **Critique Reasoning** Inez says you can rewrite $1 < m$ as $m > 1$. Do you agree?

2. **Analyze Relationships** How is $x < 5$ different from $x \leq 5$?

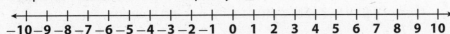

YOUR TURN

3. Graph the solution of the inequality $t \leq -4$.

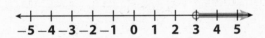

Writing Inequalities

You can write an inequality to model the relationship between an algebraic expression and a number. You can also write inequalities to represent certain real-world situations.

EXAMPLE 2 (Real World)

A Write an inequality that represents the phrase *the sum of y and 2 is greater than 5*. Draw a graph to represent the inequality.

STEP 1 Write the inequality.

The sum of y and 2 is greater than 5.

$$y + 2 \qquad > \qquad 5$$

STEP 2 Graph the solution.

For $y + 2$ to have a value greater than 5, y must be a number greater than 3.

> Use an open circle at 3 and shade to the right of 3.

STEP 3 Check your solution by substituting a number greater than 3, such as 4, into the original inequality.

$4 + 2 > 5$ Substitute 4 for y.

$6 > 5$ 6 is greater than 5, so 4 is a solution.

B To test the temperature rating of a coat, a scientist keeps the temperature below 5 °C. Write and graph an inequality to represent this situation.

STEP 1 Write the inequality. Let *t* represent the temperature in the lab.

$t < 5$ The temperature must be less than 5 °C.

STEP 2 Graph the inequality.

My Notes

YOUR TURN

4. Write an inequality that represents the phrase *the sum of 1 and y is greater than or equal to 3* . Check to see if $y = 1$ is a solution.

_____

_____

Write and graph an inequality to represent each situation.

5. The temperature in February was at most 6 °F. _____

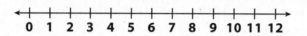

0 1 2 3 4 5 6 7 8 9 10 11 12

6. Each package must weigh more than 2 ounces. _____

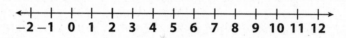

−2 −1 0 1 2 3 4 5 6 7 8 9 10 11 12

Guided Practice

1. Graph $1 \leq x$. Use the graph to determine which of these numbers are solutions of the inequality: −1, 3, 0, 1 (Explore Activity and Example 1)

_____

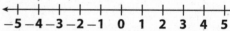

−5 −4 −3 −2 −1 0 1 2 3 4 5

2. Graph $-3 > z$. Check the graph using substitution. (Example 1)

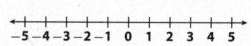

−5 −4 −3 −2 −1 0 1 2 3 4 5

3. Write an inequality that represents the phrase "the sum of 4 and *x* is greater than 6." Draw a graph that represents the inequality, and check your solution. (Example 2)

_____

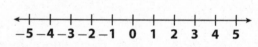

−5 −4 −3 −2 −1 0 1 2 3 4 5

4. During hibernation, a garter snake's body temperature never goes below 3 °C. Write and graph an inequality that represents this situation. (Example 2)

_____

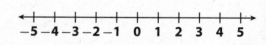

−5 −4 −3 −2 −1 0 1 2 3 4 5

❓ ESSENTIAL QUESTION CHECK-IN

5. Write an inequality to represent this situation: Nina wants to take at least $15 to the movies. How did you decide which inequality symbol to use?

_____

_____

11.4 Independent Practice

6. Which of the following numbers are solutions to $x \geq 0$?

$-5, 0.03, -1, 0, 1.5, -6, \frac{1}{2}$ _____

Graph each inequality.

7. $t \leq 8$

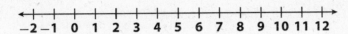

8. $-7 < h$

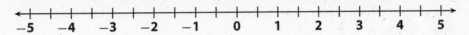

9. $x \geq -9$

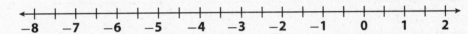

10. $n > 2.5$

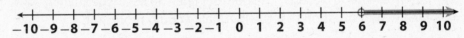

11. $-4\frac{1}{2} > x$

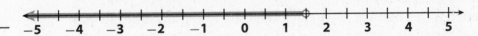

Write an inequality that matches the number line model.

12. _____

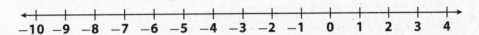

13. _____

14. _____

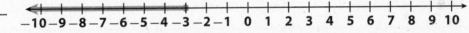

15. _____

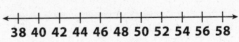

16. A child must be at least 48 inches tall to ride a roller coaster.

a. Write and graph an inequality to represent this situation.

38 40 42 44 46 48 50 52 54 56 58

_____

b. Can a child who is 46 inches tall ride the roller coaster? Explain.

_____

Write and graph an inequality to represent each situation.

17. The stock is worth at least $14.50. _____

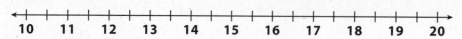

18. The temperature is less than 3.5°F. _____

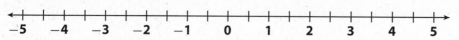

19. The goal of the fundraiser is to make more than $150. _____

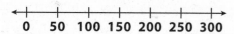

 **FOCUS ON HIGHER ORDER THINKING**

Work Area

20. Communicate Mathematical Ideas Explain how to graph the inequality $8 \geq y$.

_____

_____

_____

_____

21. Represent Real-World Problems The number line shows an inequality. Describe a real-world situation that the inequality could represent.

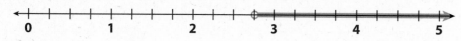

_____

22. Critique Reasoning Natasha is trying to represent the following situation with a number line model: There are fewer than 5 students in the cafeteria. She has come up with two possible representations, shown below. Which is the better representation, and why?

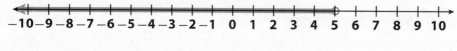

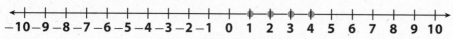

_____

_____

_____

_____

Ready to Go On?

Personal
Math Trainer
Online Assessment
and Intervention
⏻ my.hrw.com

11.1 Writing Equations to Represent Situations

Determine whether the given value is a solution of the equation.

1. $\frac{b}{12} = 5$; $b = 60$ _____

2. $7w = 87$; $w = 12$ _____

Write an equation to represent the situation.

3. The number of eggs in the refrigerator e decreased by 5 equals 18.

_____

11.2 Addition and Subtraction Equations

Solve each equation.

4. $r - 38 = 9$ _____

5. $h + 17 = 40$ _____

6. $n + 75 = 155$ _____

7. $q - 17 = 18$ _____

11.3 Multiplication and Division Equations

Solve each equation.

8. $8z = 112$ _____

9. $\frac{d}{14} = 7$ _____

10. $\frac{f}{28} = 24$ _____

11. $3a = 57$ _____

11.4 Writing Inequalities

Write an inequality to represent each situation, then graph the solutions.

12. There are fewer than 8 gallons of gas in the tank. _____

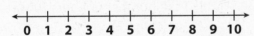

0 1 2 3 4 5 6 7 8 9 10

13. There are at least 3 slices of bread left in the bag. _____

0 1 2 3 4 5 6 7 8 9 10

? ESSENTIAL QUESTION

14. How can you solve problems involving equations that contain addition, subtraction, multiplication, or division?

_____

_____

Personal
Math Trainer

Online
Assessment and
Intervention

my.hrw.com

Selected Response

1. Kate has gone up to the chalkboard to do math problems 5 more times than Andre. Kate has gone up 11 times. Which equation represents this situation?

- Ⓐ $a - 11 = 5$
- Ⓑ $5a = 11$
- Ⓒ $a - 5 = 11$
- Ⓓ $a + 5 = 11$

2. For which equation is $y = 7$ a solution?

- Ⓐ $7y = 1$
- Ⓑ $18 = 11 + y$
- Ⓒ $y + 7 = 0$
- Ⓓ $\frac{y}{2} = 14$

3. Which is an equation?

- Ⓐ $17 + x$
- Ⓒ $20x = 200$
- Ⓑ $45 \div x$
- Ⓓ $90 - x$

4. The temperature never rose above 6 °F on Friday. Which number line could represent this situation?

Ⓐ

Ⓑ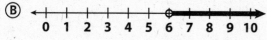

Ⓒ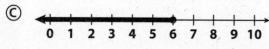

Ⓓ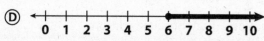

5. Becca hit 7 more home runs than Beverly. Becca hit 21 home runs. How many home runs did Beverly hit?

- Ⓐ 3
- Ⓒ 21
- Ⓑ 14
- Ⓓ 28

6. Jeordie spreads out a rectangular picnic blanket with an area of 42 square feet. Its width is 6 feet. Which equation could you use to find its length?

- Ⓐ $6x = 42$
- Ⓒ $\frac{6}{x} = 42$
- Ⓑ $42 - x = 6$
- Ⓓ $6 + x = 42$

7. What is a solution to the equation $6t = 114$?

- Ⓐ $t = 19$
- Ⓒ $t = 120$
- Ⓑ $t = 108$
- Ⓓ $t = 684$

8. The area of a rectangular deck is 680 square feet. The deck's width is 17 feet. What is its perimeter?

- Ⓐ 40 feet
- Ⓒ 114 feet
- Ⓑ 57 feet
- Ⓓ 228 feet

Mini-Task

9. Sylvia earns $7 per hour at her afterschool job. After working one week, she received a paycheck for $91.

a. Write and solve an equation to find the number of hours Sylvia worked to earn $91.

_____

b. The greatest number of hours Sylvia can work in any week is 15. Write an inequality to represent this statement.

_____

c. What is the greatest amount of money Sylvia can earn in one week?

_____

Relationships in Two Variables

ESSENTIAL QUESTION

How can you use relationships in two variables to solve real-world problems?

my.hrw.com

Real-World Video

A two-variable equation can represent an animal's distance over time. A graph can display the relationship between the variables. You can graph two or more animals' data to visually compare them.

GO DIGITAL
my.hrw.com

my.hrw.com

Go digital with your write-in student edition, accessible on any device.

Math On the Spot

Scan with your smart phone to jump directly to the online edition, video tutor, and more.

Animated Math

Interactively explore key concepts to see how math works.

Personal Math Trainer

Get immediate feedback and help as you work through practice sets.

Reading Start-Up

Visualize Vocabulary

Use the ✔ words to complete the chart.

Parts of the Algebraic Expression $14 + 3x$		
Definition	**Mathematical Representation**	**Review Word**
A specific number whose value does not change	14	
A number that is multiplied by a variable in an algebraic expression	3	
A letter or symbol used to represent an unknown	x	

Understand Vocabulary

Complete the sentences using the preview words.

1. The numbers in an ordered pair are _____.

2. A _____ is formed by two number lines that intersect at right angles.

Active Reading

Layered Book Before beginning the module, create a layered book to help you learn the concepts in this module. Label each flap with lesson titles from this module. As you study each lesson, write important ideas such as vocabulary and formulas under the appropriate flap. Refer to your finished layered book as you work on exercises from this module.

Vocabulary

Review Words

✔ coefficient *(coeficiente)*
✔ constant *(constante)*
　equation *(ecuación)*
　negative number *(número negativo)*
　positive number *(número positivo)*
　scale *(escala)*
✔ variable *(variable)*

Preview Words

　axes *(ejes)*
　coordinate plane *(plano cartesiano)*
　coordinates *(coordenadas)*
　dependent variable *(variable dependiente)*
　independent variable *(variable independiente)*
　ordered pair *(par ordenado)*
　origin *(origen)*
　quadrants *(cuadrante)*
　x-axis *(eje x)*
　x-coordinate *(coordenada x)*
　y-axis *(eje y)*
　y-coordinate *(coordenada y)*

Are YOU Ready?

Complete these exercises to review skills you will need for this module.

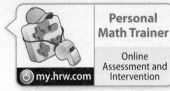

Personal
Math Trainer

Online
Assessment and
Intervention

my.hrw.com

Multiplication Facts

> **EXAMPLE** $8 \times 7 = $ ▇
>
> Use a related fact you know.
> $7 \times 7 = 49$
> Think: $8 \times 7 = (7 \times 7) + 7$
> $= 49 + 7$
> $= 56$

Multiply.

1. 7×6 _____ **2.** 10×9 _____ **3.** 13×12 _____ **4.** 8×9 _____

Write the rule for each table.

5.

x	1	2	3	4
y	7	14	21	28

_____

6.

x	1	2	3	4
y	7	8	9	10

_____

7.

x	1	2	3	4
y	5	10	15	20

_____

8.

x	0	4	8	12
y	0	2	4	6

_____

Graph Ordered Pairs (First Quadrant)

> **EXAMPLE**
>
>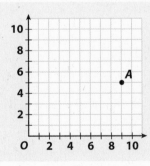
>
> Start at the origin.
> Move 9 units right.
> Then move 5 units up.
> Graph point A(9, 5).

Graph each point on the coordinate grid above.

9. $B\,(0, 8)$ **10.** $C\,(2, 3)$ **11.** $D\,(6, 7)$ **12.** $E\,(5, 0)$

Complete these exercises to review skills you will need for this module.

Multiplication Facts

13. Movie tickets at the Cineplex cost $9.00 per ticket. Erin buys 5 movie tickets for $45. Marcial buys 6 movie tickets. Use multiplication facts to determine the total cost of Marcial's movie tickets.

14. Write the rule for the table. Then complete the table using the rule. Explain how you found the missing value.

x	0	6	12	18	24
y	0	2	4	6	

Graph Ordered Pairs (First Quadrant)

15. On the coordinate grid below, graph only the points where y, the vertical distance from the origin, is greater than x, the horizontal distance from the origin.

$A(4, 4)$ $B(7, 4)$ $C(3, 5)$ $D(6, 0)$
$E(1, 2)$ $F(0, 3)$ $G(8, 7)$ $H(9, 10)$

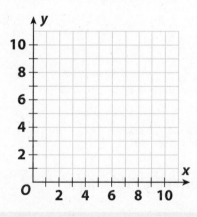

LESSON
12.1
Graphing on the Coordinate Plane

6.5.12.1
Students will locate and name points in the coordinate plane.

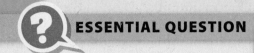

© Houghton Mifflin Harcourt Publishing Company

? ESSENTIAL QUESTION

How do you locate and name points in the coordinate plane?

EXPLORE ACTIVITY

Naming Points in the Coordinate Plane

A **coordinate plane** is formed by two number lines that intersect at right angles. The point of intersection is 0 on each number line.

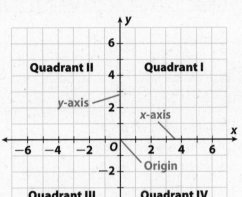

- The two number lines are called the **axes**.

- The horizontal axis is called the **x-axis**.

- The vertical axis is called the **y-axis**.

- The point where the axes intersect is called the **origin**.

- The two axes divide the coordinate plane into four **quadrants**.

An **ordered pair** is a pair of numbers that gives the location of a point on a coordinate plane. The first number tells how far to the right (positive) or left (negative) the point is located from the origin. The second number tells how far up (positive) or down (negative) the point is located from the origin.

The numbers in an ordered pair are called **coordinates**. The first number is the **x-coordinate** and the second number is the **y-coordinate**.

EXAMPLE 1 Identify the coordinates of each point. Name the quadrant where each point is located.

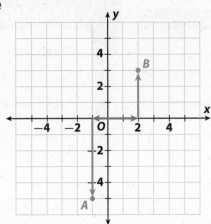

Point *A* is 1 unit _____ of the origin and 5 units _____.

It has *x*-coordinate _____ and *y*-coordinate _____, written

(____, ____). It is located in Quadrant _____.

Point *B* is 2 units _____ of the origin and 3 units _____.

It has *x*-coordinate _____ and *y*-coordinate _____, written

(____, ____). It is located in Quadrant _____.

Reflect

1. If both coordinates of a point are negative, in which quadrant is the point located? _____

2. Describe the coordinates of all points in Quadrant I.

   _____

3. **Communicate Mathematical Ideas** Explain why (−3, 5) represents a different location than (3, 5).

   _____

   _____

   _____

YOUR TURN

Identify the coordinates of each point. Name the quadrant where each point is located.

4. G _____

   E _____

5. F _____

   H _____

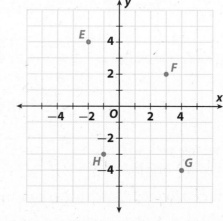

Personal Math Trainer

Online Assessment and Intervention

my.hrw.com

Math On the Spot

my.hrw.com

Graphing Points in the Coordinate Plane

Points that are located on the axes are not located in any quadrant. Points on the x-axis have a y-coordinate of 0, and points on the y-axis have an x-coordinate of 0.

EXAMPLE 2

Graph and label each point on the coordinate plane.
   $A(-5, 2), B(3, 1.5), C(0, -3)$

Point A is 5 units *left* and 2 units *up* from the origin.

Point B is 3 units *right* and 1.5 units *up* from the origin. Graph the point halfway between (3, 1) and (3, 2).

Point C is 3 units *down* from the origin. Graph the point on the y-axis.

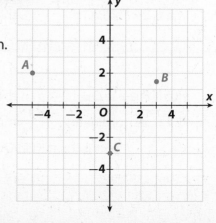

YOUR TURN

Graph and label each point on the coordinate plane.

6. $P(-4, 2)$

7. $Q(3, 2.5)$

8. $R(-4.5, -5)$

9. $S(4, -5)$

10. $T(-2.5, 0)$

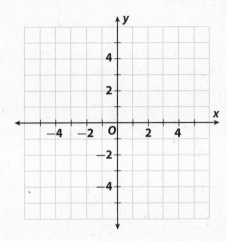

Reading Scales on Axes

The *scale* of an axis is the number of units that each grid line represents. So far, the graphs in this lesson have a scale of 1 unit, but graphs frequently use other units.

EXAMPLE 3

The graph shows the location of a city. It also shows the location of Gary's and Jen's houses. The scale on each axis represents miles.

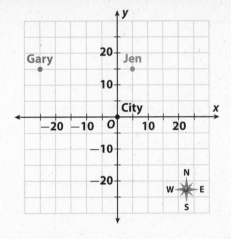

A Use the scale to describe Gary's location relative to the city.

Each grid square is 5 miles on a side.

Gary's house is at $(-25, 15)$, which is 25 miles west and 15 miles north of the city.

B Describe the location of Jen's house relative to Gary's house.

Jen's house is located 6 grid squares to the right of Gary's house. Since each grid square is 5 miles on a side, her house is $6 \cdot 5 = 30$ miles from Gary's.

Math Talk
Mathematical Processes

How are north, south, east, and west represented on the graph in Example 3?

YOUR TURN

Use the graph in the Example.

11. Ted lives 20 miles south and 20 miles west of the city represented on the graph in Example 3. His brother Ned lives 50 miles north of Ted's house. Give the coordinates of each brother's house.

_____

Identify the coordinates of each point in the coordinate plane. Name the quadrant where each point is located.
(Explore Activity Example 1)

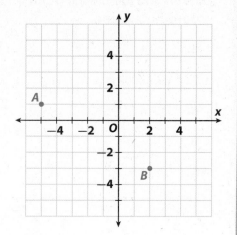

1. Point A is 5 units _____ of the origin and

1 unit _____ from the origin.

Its coordinates are _____. It is in quadrant _____.

2. Point B is _____ units right of the origin

and _____ units down from the origin.

Its coordinates are _____. It is in quadrant _____.

Graph and label each point on the coordinate plane above. (Example 2)

3. Point C at (−3.5, 3)

4. Point D at (5, 0)

For 5–7, use the coordinate plane shown. (Example 3)

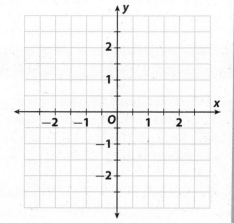

5. Describe the scale of the graph.

_____

6. Plot point A at $\left(-\frac{1}{2}, 2\right)$.

7. Plot point B at $\left(2\frac{1}{2}, -2\right)$.

8. **Vocabulary** Describe how an ordered pair represents a point on a coordinate plane. Include the terms x-coordinate, y-coordinate, and origin in your answer.

_____

_____

_____

_____

? ESSENTIAL QUESTION CHECK-IN

9. Give the coordinates of one point in each of the four quadrants, one point on the x-axis, and one point on the y-axis.

_____

_____

_____

12.1 Independent Practice

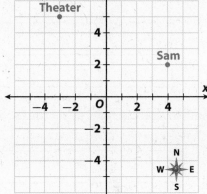

Personal Math Trainer

my.hrw.com

Online Assessment and Intervention

For 10–13, use the coordinate plane shown. Each unit represents 1 kilometer.

10. Write the ordered pairs that represent the location of Sam and the theater.

_____

11. Describe Sam's location relative to the theater.

_____

_____

12. Sam wants to meet his friend Beth at a restaurant before they go to the theater. The restaurant is 9 km south of the theater. Plot and label a point representing the restaurant. What are the coordinates of the point?

_____

13. Beth describes her current location: "I'm directly south of the theater, halfway to the restaurant." Plot and label a point representing Beth's location. What are the coordinates of the point?

_____

_____

For 14–15, use the coordinate plane shown.

14. Find the coordinates of points *T*, *U*, and *V*.

_____

15. Points *T*, *U*, and *V* are the vertices of a rectangle. Point *W* is the fourth vertex. Plot point *W* and give its coordinates.

_____

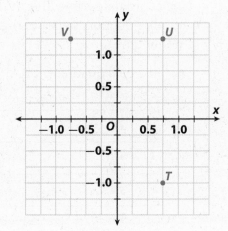

16. **Explain the Error** Janine tells her friend that ordered pairs that have an *x*-coordinate of 0 lie on the *x*-axis. She uses the origin as an example. Describe Janine's error. Use a counterexample to explain why Janine's statement is false.

_____

_____

_____

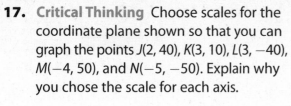

Work Area

17. Critical Thinking Choose scales for the coordinate plane shown so that you can graph the points $J(2, 40)$, $K(3, 10)$, $L(3, -40)$, $M(-4, 50)$, and $N(-5, -50)$. Explain why you chose the scale for each axis.

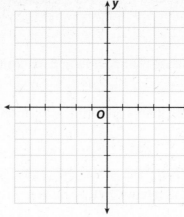

_____

_____

_____

_____

_____

_____

_____

18. Communicate Mathematical Ideas Edgar wants to plot the ordered pair $(1.8, -1.2)$ on a coordinate plane. On each axis, one grid square equals 0.1. Starting at the origin, how can Edgar find $(1.8, -1.2)$?

_____

_____

_____

19. Represent Real-World Problems Zach graphs some ordered pairs in the coordinate plane. The x-values of the ordered pairs represent the number of hours since noon, and the y-values represent the temperature at that time.

a. In which quadrants could Zach graph points? Explain your thinking.

_____

_____

_____

_____

_____

b. In what part of the world and at what time of year might Zach collect data so that the points he plots are in Quadrant IV?

_____

_____

Graphing Rational Numbers

6.5.GF.12.1
Students will locate and graph rational ordered pairs in the coordinate plane.

? ESSENTIAL QUESTION

How do you locate rational ordered pairs in the coordinate plane?

EXPLORE ACTIVITY

Identifying Points

Identify the coordinates of each point.

A From the origin, point A is _____

units left and _____ unit up.

Point A has x-coordinate $-1\frac{1}{4}$ and

y-coordinate $\frac{3}{4}$, written (▢ , ▢).

B From the origin, point B is _____

unit right and _____ units down.

Point B has x-coordinate $\frac{1}{2}$ and y-coordinate $-1\frac{1}{2}$, written (▢ , ▢).

Graphing Points

Ordered pairs with rational coordinates can be graphed in the coordinate plane using the same method as graphing ordered pairs with integer coordinates.

EXAMPLE

Graph and label each point on the coordinate plane.
G(−0.5, 0.6), H(0.4, 0.1), J(0.2, −0.9)

A Point G is 0.5 unit left and 0.6 unit up from the origin.

B Point H is 0.4 unit right and 0.1 unit up from the origin.

C Point J is 0.2 unit right and 0.9 unit down from the origin.

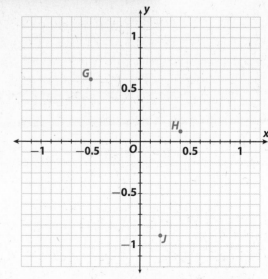

Identify the coordinates of each point.

1. C

_____

2. D

_____

3. E

_____

4. F

_____

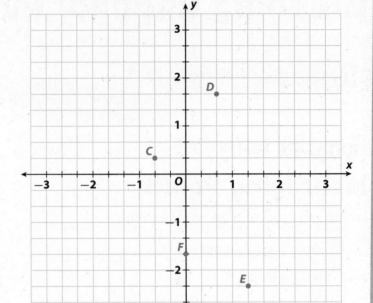

Graph and label each point on the coordinate plane.

5. P(−0.8, 0.5)

6. Q(0.4, 0.7)

7. R(0.3, −0.3)

8. S(0.8, −1)

9. T(−0.7, −0.6)

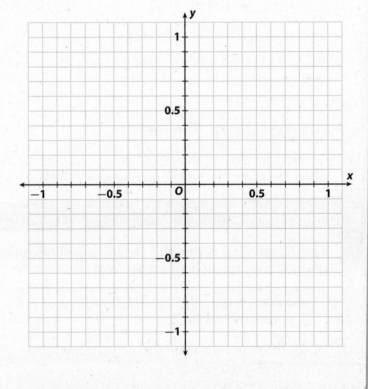

LESSON
12.2

6.5.12.2
Students will identify independent and dependent quantities from tables and graphs.

Independent and Dependent Variables in Tables and Graphs

? ESSENTIAL QUESTION

How can you identify independent and dependent quantities from tables and graphs?

EXPLORE ACTIVITY 1

Identifying Independent and Dependent Quantities from a Table

Many real-world situations involve two variable quantities in which one quantity depends on the other. The quantity that depends on the other quantity is called the **dependent variable**, and the quantity it depends on is called the **independent variable**.

A freight train moves at a constant speed. The distance y in miles that the train has traveled after x hours is shown in the table.

Time x (h)	0	1	2	3
Distance y (mi)	0	50	100	150

A What are the two quantities in this situation?

_____

Which of these quantities depends on the other?

_____

What is the independent variable? _____

What is the dependent variable? _____

B How far does the train travel each hour? _____

The relationship between the distance traveled by the train and the time in hours can be represented by an equation in two variables.

Distance traveled (miles)	=	Distance traveled per hour	·	Time (hours)
↓		↓		↓
y	=	50	·	x

Reflect

1. Analyze Relationships Describe how the value of the independent variable is related to the value of the dependent variable. Is the relationship additive or multiplicative?

_____

2. What are the units of the independent variable and of the dependent variable?

_____

_____

3. A rate is used in the equation. What is the rate?

_____

EXPLORE ACTIVITY 2

Identifying Independent and Dependent Variables from a Graph

In Explore Activity 1, you used a table to represent a relationship between an independent variable (time) and a dependent variable (distance). You can also use a graph to show this relationship.

An art teacher has 20 pounds of clay but wants to buy more clay for her class. The amount of clay *x* purchased by the teacher and the amount of clay *y* available for the class are shown on the graph.

A If the teacher buys 10 more pounds of clay, how many

pounds will be available for the art class? _____ lb

If the art class has a total of 50 pounds of clay available, how many pounds of clay did the teacher buy?

How can you use the graph to find this information?

_____

_____

_____

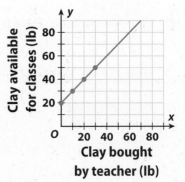

Clay Used in Art Class

Clay available for classes (lb) — y-axis: 20, 40, 60, 80

Clay bought by teacher (lb) — x-axis: 20, 40, 60, 80

B What are the two quantities in this situation?

_____

_____

Which of these quantities depends on the other?

_____

_____

What is the independent variable? _____

What is the dependent variable? _____

C The relationship between the amount of clay purchased by the teacher and the amount of clay available to the class can be represented by an equation in two variables.

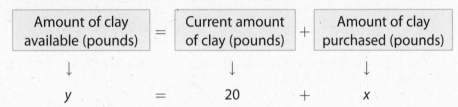

Amount of clay available (pounds)	=	Current amount of clay (pounds)	+	Amount of clay purchased (pounds)
↓		↓		↓
y	=	20	+	x

D Describe in words how the value of the independent variable is related to the value of the dependent variable.

_____

_____

Reflect

4. In this situation, the same units are used for the independent and dependent variables. How is this different from the situation involving the train in the first Explore?

_____

_____

5. **Analyze Relationships** Tell whether the relationship between the independent variable and the dependent variable is a multiplicative or an additive relationship.

_____

6. What are the units of the independent variable, and what are the units of the dependent variable?

independent variable: _____; dependent variable: _____

Describing Relationships Between Independent and Dependent Variables

Thinking about how one quantity depends on another helps you identify which quantity is the independent variable and which quantity is the dependent variable. In a graph, the independent variable is usually shown on the horizontal axis and the dependent variable on the vertical axis.

EXAMPLE 1

A The table shows a relationship between two variables, x and y. Describe a possible situation the table could represent. Describe the independent and dependent variables in the situation.

Independent variable, x	0	1	2	3
Dependent variable, y	10	11	12	13

As x increases by 1, y increases by 1. The relationship is additive. The value of y is always 10 units greater than the value of x.

The table could represent Jina's savings if she starts with $10 and adds $1 to her savings every day.

The independent variable, x, is the number of days she has been adding money to her savings.
The dependent variable, y, is her savings after x days.

B The graph shows a relationship between two variables. Describe a possible situation that the graph could represent. Describe the independent and dependent variables.

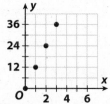

As x increases by 1, y increases by 12. The relationship is multiplicative. The value of y is always 12 times the value of x.

The graph could represent the number of eggs in cartons that each hold 12 eggs.

The independent variable, x, is the number of cartons.
The dependent variable, y, is the total number of eggs.

Reflect

7. What are other possible situations that the table and graph in the Examples could represent?

_____

_____

_____

_____

YOUR TURN

Describe real-world values that the variables could represent. Describe the relationship between the independent and dependent variables.

8.

x	0	1	2	3
y	15	16	17	18

_____

_____

_____

_____

9.

x	0	1	2	3	4
y	0	16	32	48	64

_____

_____

_____

_____

10.

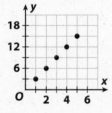

_____

_____

_____

_____

1. A boat rental shop rents paddleboats for a fee plus an additional cost per hour. The cost of renting for different numbers of hours is shown in the table.

Time (hours)	0	1	2	3
Cost ($)	10	11	12	13

What is the independent variable, and what is the dependent variable? How do you know? (Explore Activity 1)

_____

_____

_____

2. A car travels at a constant rate of 60 miles per hour. (Explore Activity 1)

Time x (h)	0	1	2	3
Distance y (mi)				

   a. Complete the table.

   b. What is the independent variable, and what is the dependent?

   _____

   _____

   c. Describe how the value of the independent variable is related to the value of the dependent variable.

   _____

Use the graph to answer the questions.

3. Describe in words how the value of the independent variable is related to the value of the dependent variable. (Explore Activity 2)

   _____

   _____

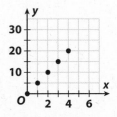

4. Describe a real-world situation that the graph could represent. (Example 1)

   _____

   _____

? ESSENTIAL QUESTION CHECK-IN

5. How can you identify the dependent and independent variables in a real-world situation modeled by a graph?

   _____

   _____

12.2 Independent Practice

Personal
Math Trainer
Online
Assessment and
Intervention
my.hrw.com

6. The graph shows the relationship between the hours a soccer team practiced after the season started and their total practice time for the year.

a. How many hours did the soccer team practice before the season began?

_____

b. What are the two quantities in this situation?

_____

_____

c. What are the dependent and independent variables?

_____

_____

d. Is the relationship between the variables additive or multiplicative? Explain.

_____

_____

e. **Analyze Relationships** Describe the relationship between the quantities in words.

_____

_____

7. **Multistep** Teresa is buying glitter markers to put in gift bags. The table shows the relationship between the number of gift bags and the number of glitter markers she needs to buy.

Number of gift bags, x	0	1	2	3
Number of markers, y	0	5	10	15

a. What is the dependent variable? _____

b. What is the independent variable? _____

c. Is the relationship additive or multiplicative? Explain.

_____

_____

d. Describe the relationship between the quantities in words.

_____

8. Ty borrowed $500 from his parents. The graph shows how much he owes them each month if he pays back a certain amount each month.

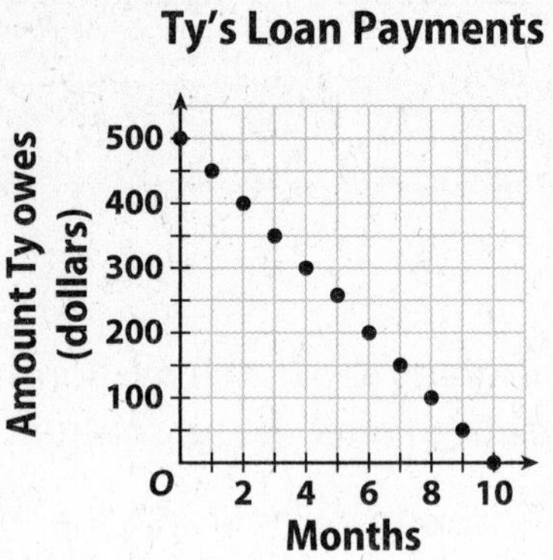

Ty's Loan Payments

a. Describe the relationship between the number of months and the amount Ty owes. Identify an independent and dependent variable and explain your thinking.

_____

_____

_____

_____

_____

b. How long will it take Ty to pay back his parents?

_____

H.O.T. FOCUS ON HIGHER ORDER THINKING

9. Error Analysis A discount store has a special: 8 cans of juice for a dollar. A shopper decides that since the number of cans purchased is 8 times the number of dollars spent, the cost is the independent variable and the number of cans is the dependent variable. Do you agree? Explain.

_____

_____

_____

_____

_____

10. Analyze Relationships Provide an example of a real-world relationship where there is no clear independent or dependent variable. Explain.

_____

_____

_____

_____

_____

_____

Work Area

Writing Equations from Tables

6.5.12.3

Students will use an equation to show a relationship between two variables.

ESSENTIAL QUESTION

How can you use an equation to show a relationship between two variables?

Writing an Equation to Represent a Real-World Relationship

Many real-world situations involve two variable quantities in which one quantity depends on the other. This type of relationship can be represented by a table. You can also use an equation to model the relationship.

The table shows how much Amanda earns for walking 1, 2, or 3 dogs. Use the table to determine how much Amanda earns per dog. Then write an equation that models the relationship between number of dogs walked and earnings. Use your equation to complete the table.

Dogs walked	1	2	3	5	10	20
Earnings	$8	$16	$24			

> For 1 dog, Amanda earns $1 \cdot 8 = \$8$.
> For 2 dogs, she earns $2 \cdot 8 = \$16$.

A For each column, compare the number of dogs walked and earnings. What is the pattern?

_____

_____

B Based on the pattern, Amanda earns $ _____ for each dog she walks.

C Write an equation that relates the number of dogs Amanda walks to the amount she earns. Let *e* represent earnings and *d* represent dogs.

_____

D Use your equation to complete the table for 5, 10, and 20 walked dogs.

E Amanda's earnings depend on _____.

Reflect

1. **What If?** If Amanda changed the amount earned per dog to $11, what equation could you write to model the relationship between number of

dogs walked and earnings? _____

Math On the Spot
my.hrw.com

Writing an Equation Based on a Table

The relationship between two variables where one variable depends on the other can be represented in a table or by an equation. An equation expresses the dependent variable in terms of the independent variable.

When there is no real-world situation to consider, we usually say *x* is the independent variable and *y* is the dependent variable. The value of *y* depends on the value of *x*.

Animated Math
my.hrw.com

EXAMPLE 1

Write an equation that expresses *y* in terms of *x*.

A

x	1	2	3	4	5
y	0.5	1	1.5	2	2.5

STEP 1 Compare the *x*- and *y*-values to find a pattern.

Each *y*-value is $\frac{1}{2}$, or 0.5 times, the corresponding *x*-value.

STEP 2 Use the pattern to write an equation expressing *y* in terms of *x*.

$$y = 0.5x$$

B

x	2	4	6	8	10
y	5	7	9	11	13

STEP 1 Compare the *x*- and *y*-values to find a pattern.

Each *y*-value is 3 more than the corresponding *x*-value.

STEP 2 Use the pattern to write an equation expressing *y* in terms of *x*.

$$y = x + 3$$

Math Talk
Mathematical Processes

How can you check that your equations are correct?

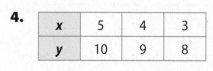 **YOUR TURN**

For each table, write an equation that expresses *y* in terms of *x*.

2.

x	12	11	10
y	10	9	8

_____

3.

x	10	12	14
y	25	30	35

_____

4.

x	5	4	3
y	10	9	8

_____

5.

x	0	1	2
y	0	2	4

_____

Personal Math Trainer

Online Assessment and Intervention

my.hrw.com

© Houghton Mifflin Harcourt Publishing Company

Using Tables and Equations to Solve Problems

You can use tables and equations to solve real-world problems.

Math On the Spot
my.hrw.com

EXAMPLE 2 Problem Solving

A certain percent of the sale price of paintings at a gallery will be donated to charity. The donation will be $50 if a painting sells for $200. The donation will be $75 if a painting sells for $300. Find the amount of the donation if a painting sells for $1,200.

 Analyze Information

You know the donation amount when the sale price of a painting is $200 and $300. You need to find the donation amount if a painting sells for $1,200.

 Formulate a Plan

You can make a table to help you determine the relationship between sale price and donation amount. Then you can write an equation that models the relationship. Use the equation to find the unknown donation amount.

 Solve

Make a table.

Sale price ($)	200	300
Donation amount ($)	50	75

One way to determine the relationship between sale price and donation amount is to find the percent.

$$\frac{50}{200} = \frac{50 \div 2}{200 \div 2} = \frac{25}{100} = 25\% \qquad \frac{75}{300} = \frac{75 \div 3}{300 \div 3} = \frac{25}{100} = 25\%$$

Write an equation. Let p represent the sale price of the painting. Let d represent the donation amount to charity.

The donation amount is equal to 25% of the sale price.

$$d = 0.25 \cdot p$$

p is the independent variable; its value does not depend on any other value. d is the dependent variable; its value depends on the price of the painting.

Find the donation amount when the sale price is $1,200.

$$d = 0.25 \cdot p$$

$$d = 0.25 \cdot 1,200 \qquad \textit{Substitute \$1,200 for the sale price of the painting.}$$

$$d = 300 \qquad \textit{Simplify to find the donation amount.}$$

When the sale price is $1,200, the donation to charity is $300.

 Justify and Evaluate

Substitute values from the table for p and d to check that they are solutions of the equation $d = 0.25 \cdot p$. Then check your answer of $300 by substituting for d and solving for p.

$d = 0.25 \cdot p$	$d = 0.25 \cdot p$	$d = 0.25 \cdot p$
$d = 0.25 \cdot 200$	$d = 0.25 \cdot 300$	$300 = 0.25 \cdot p$
$d = 50$ ✓	$d = 75$ ✓	$p = 1,200$ ✓

YOUR TURN

6. When Ryan is 10, his brother Kyle is 15. When Ryan is 16, Kyle will be 21. When Ryan is 21, Kyle will be 26. Write and solve an equation to find Kyle's age when Ryan is 52.

_____

Guided Practice

Write an equation to express *y* in terms of *x*. (Explore Activity, Example 1)

1.

x	10	20	30	40
y	6	16	26	36

_____

2.

x	0	1	2	3
y	0	4	8	12

_____

3.

x	4	6	8	10
y	7	9	11	13

_____

4.

x	12	24	36	48
y	2	4	6	8

_____

5. Jameson downloaded one digital song for $1.35, two digital songs for $2.70, and 5 digital songs for $6.75. Write and solve an equation to find the cost to download 25 digital songs. (Example 2)

Songs downloaded	1	2	5	10
Total cost ($)	1.35			

Number of songs = *n*; Cost = _____

The total cost of 25 songs is _____

? **ESSENTIAL QUESTION CHECK-IN**

6. Explain how to use a table to write an equation that represents the relationship in the table.

_____

_____

12.3 Independent Practice

Personal
Math Trainer

Online
Assessment and
Intervention

my.hrw.com

7. Vocabulary What does it mean for an equation to express y in terms of x?

_____

_____

_____

8. The length of a rectangle is 2 inches more than twice its width.

Write an equation relating the length l of the rectangle to its width w.

_____

9. Look for a Pattern Compare the y-values in the table to the corresponding x-values. What pattern do you see? How is this pattern used to write an equation that represents the relationship between the x- and y-values?

x	20	24	28	32
y	5	6	7	8

_____

_____

10. Explain the Error A student modeled the relationship in the table with the equation $x = 4y$. Explain the student's error. Write an equation that correctly models the relationship.

x	2	4	6	8
y	8	16	24	32

_____

_____

11. Multistep Marvin earns $8.25 per hour at his summer job. He wants to buy a video game system that costs $206.25.

a. Write an equation to model the relationship between number of hours worked h and amount earned e.

_____

b. Solve your equation to find the number of hours Marvin needs to work in order to afford the video game system.

_____

12. Communicate Mathematical Ideas For every hour that Noah studies, his test score goes up 3 points. Explain which is the independent variable and which is the dependent variable. Write an equation modeling the relationship between hours studied *h* and the increase in Noah's test score *s*.

_____

_____

_____

Work Area

13. Make a Conjecture Compare the *y*-values in the table to the corresponding *x*-values. Determine whether there is an additive relationship or a multiplicative relationship between *x* and *y*. If possible, write an equation modeling the relationship. If, not explain why.

x	1	3	5	7
y	3	6	8	21

_____

_____

14. Represent Real-World Problems Describe a real-world situation in which there is an additive or multiplicative relationship between two quantities. Make a table that includes at least three pairs of values. Then write an equation that models the relationship between the quantities.

_____

_____

_____

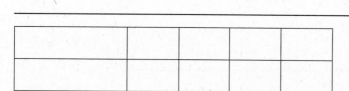

15. Critical Thinking Georgia knows that there is either an additive or multiplicative relationship between *x* and *y*. She only knows a single pair of data values. Explain whether Georgia has enough information to write an equation that models the relationship between *x* and *y*.

_____

_____

_____

_____

Equation Outpost

INSTRUCTIONS

Playing the Game

STEP 1 Each player in your group should have game pieces of a unique color. Take turns in a clockwise direction.

STEP 2 Draw a game card.

- If the card has one equation and one *x*-value (input), evaluate the equation for the given value. Then place a game piece on the corresponding *y*-value (output) on the gameboard.

$$y = 4 + 2x$$
$$x = 2$$

- If the card has multiple equations and/or multiple *x*-values, find all possible output values before choosing ONE space to cover on the gameboard. Sometimes, not all possible output values will be available on the gameboard, but at least one space will always be available for each card.

$$y = 2x + 1 \text{ for } x = 2$$
$$\text{or}$$
$$y = 2x - 1 \text{ for } x = 3$$

- Put a game piece on a FREE space only if you draw a card with instructions to use a FREE space.

$$y = 6 - x \text{ for } x = 1$$
AND
Place a new game piece on any available FREE space.

STEP 3 Fill out a row in your table for the equation and input you used.

Equation	Input	Substitution	Output
$y = 6 - x$	$x = 1$	$y = 6 - 1$	5

Winning the Game

A player wins by getting three of his or her game pieces in a row horizontally, vertically, or diagonally.

Equation	Input	Substitution	Output

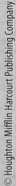

Representing Algebraic Relationships in Tables and Graphs

6.5.12.4

Students will use verbal descriptions, tables, and graphs to represent algebraic relationships.

? ESSENTIAL QUESTION

How can you use verbal descriptions, tables, and graphs to represent algebraic relationships?

EXPLORE ACTIVITY 1 Real World

Representing Algebraic Relationships

Angie's walking speed is 5 kilometers per hour, and May's is 4 kilometers per hour. Show how the distance each girl walks is related to time.

A For each girl, make a table comparing time and distance.

Time (h)	0	1	2	3	4
Angie's distance (km)	0	5	10		

> For every hour Angie walks, she travels 5 km.

Time (h)	0	1	2	3	4
May's distance (km)	0	4	8		

> For every hour May walks, she travels 4 km.

B For each girl, make a graph showing her distance *y* as it depends on time *x*. Plot points from the table and connect them with a line. Write an equation for each girl that relates distance *y* to time *x*.

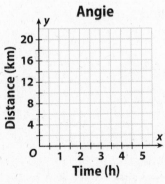

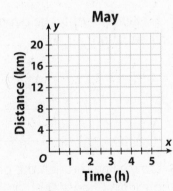

> **Math Talk**
> **Mathematical Processes**
> Why does it make sense to connect the points in each graph?

Angie's equation: _____

May's equation: _____

Reflect

1. **Analyze Relationships** How can you use the tables to determine which girl is walking faster? How can you use the graphs?

_____

_____

© Houghton Mifflin Harcourt Publishing Company

Writing an Equation from a Graph

Cherise pays the entrance fee to visit a museum, then buys souvenirs at the gift shop. The graph shows the relationship between the total amount she spends at the museum and the amount she spends at the gift shop. Write an equation to represent the relationship.

A Read the ordered pairs from the graph. Use them to complete a table comparing total spent y to amount spent at the gift shop x.

Gift shop amount ($)	0	5	10	15	
Total amount ($)	5	10			

B What is the pattern in the table?

_____

_____

C Write an equation that expresses the total amount spent, y, in terms of the amount spent at the gift shop, x.

_____

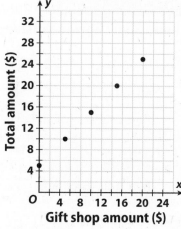

Reflect

2. Communicate Mathematical Ideas Identify the dependent and independent quantities in this situation.

_____

_____

_____

3. Multiple Representations Draw a line through the points on the graph. Find the point that represents Cherise spending $18 at the gift shop. Use this point to find the total she would spend if she spent $18 at the gift shop. Then use your equation from **C** to verify your answer.

_____

_____

Graphing an Equation

An ordered pair (x, y) that makes an equation like y = x + 1 true is called a **solution** of the equation. The graph of an equation represents all the ordered pairs that are solutions.

Math On the Spot

my.hrw.com

EXAMPLE 1

Graph each equation.

A y = x + 1

STEP 1 Make a table of values. Choose some values for x and use the equation to find the corresponding values for y.

STEP 2 Plot the ordered pairs from the table.

STEP 3 Draw a line through the plotted points to represent all of the ordered pair solutions of the equation.

x	x + 1 = y	(x, y)
1	1 + 1 = 2	(1, 2)
2	2 + 1 = 3	(2, 3)
3	3 + 1 = 4	(3, 4)
4	4 + 1 = 5	(4, 5)
5	5 + 1 = 6	(5, 6)

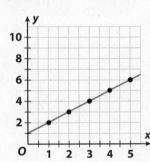

Math Talk

Mathematical Processes

Is the ordered pair (3.5, 4.5) a solution of the equation y = x + 1? Explain.

B y = 2x

STEP 1 Make a table of values. Choose some values for x and use the equation to find the corresponding values for y.

STEP 2 Plot the ordered pairs from the table.

STEP 3 Draw a line through the plotted points to represent all of the ordered pair solutions of the equation.

x	2x = y	(x, y)
1	2 × 1 = 2	(1, 2)
2	2 × 2 = 4	(2, 4)
3	2 × 3 = 6	(3, 6)
4	2 × 4 = 8	(4, 8)
5	2 × 5 = 10	(5, 10)

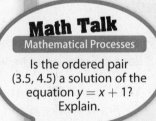

YOUR TURN

4. Graph $y = x + 2.5$.

x	$x + 2.5 = y$	(x, y)

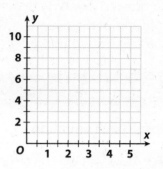

Guided Practice

Frank mows lawns in the summer to earn extra money. He can mow 3 lawns every hour he works. (Explore Activity 1 and Explore Activity 2)

1. Make a table to show the relationship between the number of hours Frank works, *x*, and the number of lawns he mows, *y*. Graph the relationship and write an equation. Label the axes of your graph.

Hours worked	Lawns mowed
0	
1	

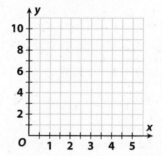

_____

Graph $y = 1.5x$. (Example 1)

2. Make a table to show the relationship.

x				
y				

3. Plot the points and draw a line through them.

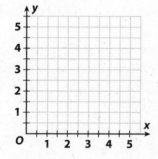

? **ESSENTIAL QUESTION CHECK-IN**

4. How can a table represent an algebraic relationship between two variables?

_____

_____

12.4 Independent Practice

Personal Math Trainer

my.hrw.com

Online Assessment and Intervention

Students at Mills Middle School are required to work a certain number of community service hours. The table shows the numbers of additional hours several students worked beyond their required hours, as well as the total numbers of hours worked.

5. Read the ordered pairs from the graph to make a table.

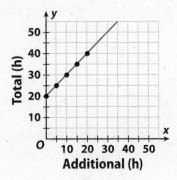

Additional hours					
Total hours					

6. Write an equation that expresses the total hours in terms of the additional hours.

_____

7. **Analyze Relationships** How many community service hours are students required to work? Explain.

_____

_____

Beth is using a map. Let *x* represent a distance in centimeters on the map. To find an actual distance *y* in kilometers, Beth uses the equation $y = 8x$.

8. Make a table comparing a distance on the map to the actual distance.

Map distance (cm)					
Actual distance (km)					

9. Make a graph that compares the map distance to the actual distance. Label the axes of the graph.

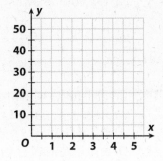

10. **Critical Thinking** The actual distance between Town A and Town B is 64 kilometers. What is the distance on Beth's map? Did you use the graph or the equation to find the answer? Why?

_____

_____

_____

_____

11. **Multistep** The equation $y = 9x$ represents the total cost y for x movie tickets. Label the axes of the graph.

a. Make a table and a graph to represent the relationship between x and y.

Number of tickets, x					
Total cost ($), y					

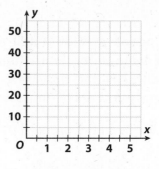

b. **Critical Thinking** In this situation, which quantity is dependent and which is independent? Justify your answer.

_____

_____

_____

c. **Multiple Representations** Eight friends want to go see a movie. Would you prefer to use an equation, a table, or a graph to find the cost of 8 movie tickets? Explain how you would use your chosen method to find the cost.

_____

_____

 **FOCUS ON HIGHER ORDER THINKING**

Work Area

12. **Critical Thinking** Suppose you graph $y = 5x$ and $y = x + 500$ on the same coordinate plane. Which line will be steeper? Why?

_____

_____

13. **Persevere in Problem Solving** Marcus plotted the points (0, 0), (6, 2), (18, 6), and (21, 7) on a graph. He wrote an equation for the relationship. Find another ordered pair that could be a solution of Marcus's equation. Justify your answer.

_____

_____

14. **Error Analysis** The cost of a personal pizza is $4. A drink costs $1. Anna wrote the equation $y = 4x + 1$ to represent the relationship between total cost y of buying x meals that include one personal pizza and one drink. Describe Anna's error and write the correct equation.

_____

_____

Ready to Go On?

Personal Math Trainer

Online Assessment and Intervention

 my.hrw.com

12.1 Graphing on the Coordinate Plane

Graph each point on the coordinate plane.

1. $A(-2, 4)$

2. $B(3, 5)$

3. $C(6, -4)$

4. $D(-3, -5)$

5. $E(7, 2)$

6. $F(-4, 6)$

12.2 Independent and Dependent Variables in Tables and Graphs

7. Jon buys packages of pens for $5 each. Identify the independent and dependent variables in the situation.

_____

12.3 Writing Equations from Tables

Write an equation that represents the data in the table.

8.

x	3	5	8	10
y	21	35	56	70

9.

x	5	10	15	20
y	17	22	27	32

_____   _____

12.4 Representing Algebraic Relationships in Tables and Graphs

Graph each equation.

10. $y = x + 3$

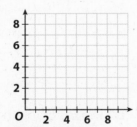

11. $y = 5x$

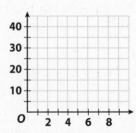

? ESSENTIAL QUESTION

12. How can you write an equation in two variables to solve a problem?

_____

_____

MODULE 12 MIXED REVIEW
Assessment Readiness

Personal
Math Trainer

my.hrw.com

Online
Assessment and
Intervention

Selected Response

1. What are the coordinates of point *G* on the coordinate grid below?

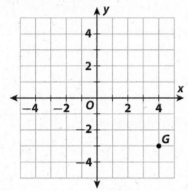

Ⓐ (4, 3)   Ⓒ (−4, 3)

Ⓑ (4, −3)   Ⓓ (−4, −3)

2. A point is located in quadrant II of a coordinate plane. Which of the following could be the coordinates of that point?

Ⓐ (−5, −7)   Ⓒ (−5, 7)

Ⓑ (5, 7)   Ⓓ (5, −7)

3. Matt had 5 library books. He checked 1 additional book out every week without returning any books. Which equation describes the number of books he has, *y*, after *x* weeks?

Ⓐ $y = 5x$ Ⓒ $y = 1 + 5x$

Ⓑ $y = 5 − x$ Ⓓ $y = 5 + x$

4. Stewart is playing a video game. He earns the same number of points for each prize he captures. He earned 1,200 points for 6 prizes, 2,000 points for 10 prizes, and 2,600 points for 13 prizes. Which is the dependent variable in the situation?

Ⓐ the number of prizes captured

Ⓑ the number of points earned

Ⓒ the number of hours

Ⓓ the number of prizes available

5. Which point is *not* on the graph of the equation $y = 10 + x$?

Ⓐ (0, 10)   Ⓒ (8, 2)

Ⓑ (3, 13)   Ⓓ (5, 15)

6. Amy gets paid by the hour. Her sister helps. As shown, Amy gives her sister part of her earnings. Which equation represents Amy's pay when her sister's pay is $13?

Amy's pay in dollars	10	20	30	40
Sister's pay in dollars	2	4	6	8

Ⓐ $y = \frac{13}{5}$ Ⓒ $5 = 13y$

Ⓑ $13 = \frac{x}{5}$ Ⓓ $13 = 5x$

Mini-Task

7. The table compares the ages, in years, of two cousins.

Ann's age, *x*	4	8	12
Tom's age, *y*	8	12	16

a. Write an equation that compares Tom's and Ann's ages.

_____

b. Draw a graph to represent the equation.

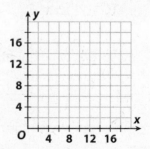

MODULE **11** ▶ **Equations and Relationships**

? ESSENTIAL QUESTION

How can you use equations and relationships to solve real-world problems?

EXAMPLE 1

Determine if the given value is a solution of the equation.

A. $r - 5 = 17; r = 12$

$12 - 5 \overset{?}{=} 17$ Substitute.

$7 \neq 17$

12 is not a solution of $r - 5 = 17$.

B. $\frac{x}{6} = 7; x = 42$

$\frac{42}{6} \overset{?}{=} 7$ Substitute.

$7 = 7$

42 is a solution of $\frac{x}{6} = 7$.

EXAMPLE 2

Solve each equation. Check your answer.

A. $y - 12 = 10$

$\underline{+12 \quad +12}$ Add 12 to both sides.

$y = 22$

Check: $22 - 12 \overset{?}{=} 10$ Substitute.

$10 = 10$

B. $5p = 30$

$\frac{5p}{5} = \frac{30}{5}$ Divide both sides by 5.

$p = 6$

Check: $5(6) \overset{?}{=} 30$ Substitute.

$30 = 30$

EXAMPLE 3

Write and graph an inequality to represent each situation.

A. There are at least 5 gallons of water in an aquarium.

$g \geq 5$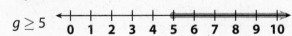

B. The temperature today will be less than 35 °F.

$t < 35$

EXERCISES

Determine whether the given value is a solution of the equation. (Lesson 11.1)

1. $7x = 14; x = 3$ _____

2. $y + 13 = 17; y = 4$ _____

Write an equation to represent the situation. (Lesson 11.1)

3. Don has three times as much money as his brother, who has $25. _____

4. There are *s* students enrolled in Mr. Rodriguez's class. There are

   6 students absent and 18 students present today. _____

Solve each equation. Check your answer. (Lessons 11.2, 11.3)

5. $p - 5 = 18$ _____   **6.** $9q = 18.9$ _____

7. $3.5 + x = 7$ _____   **8.** $\frac{2}{7} = 2x$ _____

9. Sonia used $12.50 to buy a new journal. She has $34.25 left in her
   savings account. How much money did Sonia have before she
   bought the journal? Write and solve an equation to solve

   the problem. (Lesson 11.2) _____

Write and graph an inequality to represent each situation.
(Lesson 11.4)

10. The company's stock is worth less than

   $2.50 per share. _____

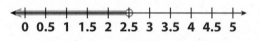

11. Tina got a haircut, and her hair is still at least

   15 inches long. _____

 **MODULE 12** **Relationships in Two Variables**

Key Vocabulary

axes *(ejes)*

coordinate plane *(plano cartesiano)*

coordinates *(coordenadas)*

ordered pair *(par ordenado)*

origin *(origen)*

quadrants *(cuadrantes)*

x-axis *(eje x)*

? ESSENTIAL QUESTION

How can you use relationships in two variables to solve real-world
problems?

EXAMPLE 1

**Graph the point (4, −2) and identify
the quadrant where it is located.**

(4, −2) is located 4 units
to the right of the origin and 2 units
down from the origin.

(4, −2) is in quadrant IV.

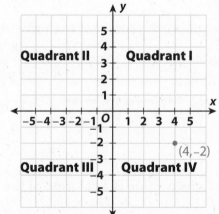

EXAMPLE 2

Tim is paid $8 more than the number of bags of peanuts he sells at the baseball stadium. The table shows the relationship between the money Tim earns and the number of bags of peanuts Tim sells. Identify the independent and dependent variables, and write an equation that represents the relationship.

Bags of peanuts, x	0	1	2	3
Money earned, y	8	9	10	11

The number of bags is the independent variable, and the money Tim earns is the dependent variable.

The equation $y = x + 8$ expresses the relationship between the number of bags Tim sells and the amount he earns.

EXERCISES

Graph and label each point on the coordinate plane. (Lesson 12.1)

1. $(4, 4)$

2. $(-3, -1)$

3. $(-1, 4)$

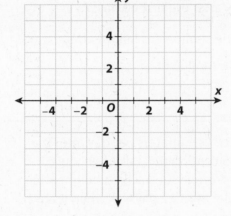

Use the graph to answer the questions. (Lesson 12.2)

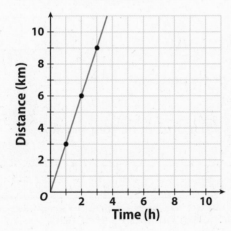

4. What is the independent variable? _____

5. What is the dependent variable? _____

6. Describe the relationship between the independent variable and the dependent variable.

_____

7. Use the data in the table to write an equation to express *y* in terms of *x*. Then graph the equation. (Lessons 12.3, 12.4)

x	0	1	2	3
y	4	5	6	7

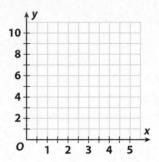

_____

Unit 5 Performance Tasks

1. **CAREERS IN MATH** Botanist Dr. Adama is a botanist. She measures the daily height of a particular variety of sunflower, Sunny Yellow, beginning when the sunflower is 60 days old. At 60 days, the height of the sunflower is 205 centimeters. Dr. Adama finds that the growth rate of this sunflower is 2 centimeters per day after the first 60 days.

  a. Write an expression to represent the sunflower's height after *d* days. _____

  b. How many days does it take for the sunflower to reach 235 centimeters? Show your work.

  _____

  c. The Suntracker grows at a rate of 2.5 centimeters per day after the first 60 days. If this sunflower is 195 centimeters tall when it is 60 days old, write an expression to represent Suntracker's height after *d* days. Which sunflower will be taller after 22 days, or when it is 82 days old? Explain how you found your answer.

  _____

  _____

2. Vernon practiced soccer $5\frac{3}{4}$ hours this week. He practiced $4\frac{1}{3}$ hours on weekdays and the rest over the weekend.

  a. Write an equation that represents the situation. Define your variable.

  _____

  _____

  b. What is the least common multiple of the denominators of $5\frac{3}{4}$ and $4\frac{1}{3}$? Show your work.

  _____

  c. Solve the equation and interpret the solution. Show your work.

  _____

  _____

Assessment Readiness

Personal
Math Trainer

Online
Assessment and
Intervention

my.hrw.com

1. Using the expression $7x = 3y$, if y is 35, what is x?

Ⓐ 15
Ⓑ 21
Ⓒ 35
Ⓓ 105

2. Bruce has 97 sports cards. 34 of them are football cards. Which equation can be used to find the number of sports cards y that are not football cards?

Ⓐ $97 + 34 = y$
Ⓑ $y + 97 = 34$
Ⓒ $34 + y = 97$
Ⓓ $y - 97 = 34$

3. The overnight temperature in Tampa never reached below 40 °F during November. Which inequality shows that?

Ⓐ $x < 40$
Ⓑ $x > 40$
Ⓒ $x = 40$
Ⓓ $x \geq 40$

4. Truman puts money into his savings account every time he gets paid. The table below shows how much he saves.

Amount Truman is paid	$15	$30	$45
Amount Truman saves	$1.50	$3	$4.50

Which of the following equations can be used to find the amount m Truman saves when he is paid $20?

Ⓐ $m = 20(0.10)$
Ⓒ $0.10m = 20$
Ⓑ $20m = 0.10$
Ⓓ $m = \frac{10}{20}$

5. No more than 7 copies of a newspaper are left in the newspaper rack. Which inequality represents this situation?

Ⓐ $n < 7$
Ⓑ $n \leq 7$
Ⓒ $n > 7$
Ⓓ $n \geq 7$

6. For which of the inequalities below is $v = 4$ a solution?

Ⓐ $v + 5 \geq 9$
Ⓑ $v + 5 > 9$
Ⓒ $v + 5 \leq 8$
Ⓓ $v + 5 < 8$

7. Sarah has read aloud in class 3 more times than Joel. Sarah has read 9 times. Which equation represents this situation?

Ⓐ $j - 9 = 3$
Ⓑ $3j = 9$
Ⓒ $j - 3 = 9$
Ⓓ $j + 3 = 9$

8. The number line below represents the solution to which inequality?

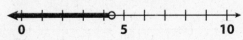

Ⓐ $m > 4.4$
Ⓑ $m > 5$
Ⓒ $m < 4.4$
Ⓓ $m < 4$

Hot Tip!

When possible, use logic to eliminate at least two answer choices.

9. Brian is playing a video game. He earns the same number of points for each star he picks up. He earned 2,400 points for 6 stars, 4,000 points for 10 stars, and 5,200 points for 13 stars. Which is the independent variable in the situation?

(A) the number of stars picked up

(B) the number of points earned

(C) the number of hours played

(D) the number of stars available

10. Which ratio is **not** equivalent to the other three?

(A) $\frac{2}{5}$ (C) $\frac{6}{15}$

(B) $\frac{12}{25}$ (D) $\frac{18}{45}$

11. One inch is about 2.54 centimeters. About how many centimeters is 4.5 inches?

(A) 1.8 centimeters

(B) 11.4 centimeters

(C) 13.7 centimeters

(D) 114 centimeters

Mini-Tasks

12. Dana, Neil, and Frank are siblings. Dana is the oldest.

a. Frank's age is one-fourth of Dana's age. Write an equation to represent Frank's age f if Dana's age is d years.

_____

b. Neil's age is one-half of the difference between Dana's and Frank's ages. Write an equation to represent Neil's age n in terms of Dana's age d.

_____

c. Use the equations to find Neil's and Frank's ages if Dana is 16 years old.

_____

_____

13. Jillian is participating in a book reading contest to raise funds for her local library. For every book Jillian reads, her mother pledged to make a donation.

a. The table shows how much Jillian's mother will donate. Find the pattern, and finish the table.

Books Jillian reads	3	5	7	
Money Jillian's mother donates	$15	$25		

b. Write an equation showing the pattern from the table. Identify the variables.

_____

_____

_____

c. Graph the equation.

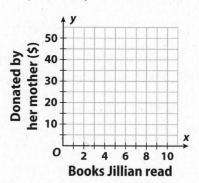

Relationships in Geometry

CAREERS IN MATH

Theater Set Construction A person who works in theater set construction works with the set designer to create scenery and needs technical precision when scaling and building sets based on the dimensions of the models.

If you are interested in a career in theater set construction, you should study these mathematical subjects:
- Geometry
- Algebra
- Trigonometry

Research other careers that require technical precision in scaling and building models.

Unit 6 Performance Task

At the end of the unit, check out how **theater set construction** workers use math.

Use the puzzle to preview key vocabulary from this unit. Unscramble the circled letters within found words to answer the riddle at the bottom of the page.

```
B Y W (P) R E V L P G E J Z V S
P Z O A V P R K L E B L F C U
D J M R Q W O E H Z B F Z O B
Z J W A (S) N B G L W W M C E M
K P O L G U I E G A G B Q S O
M N D L L R J V V E D J G H
Q E H E Q L I F G S (I) S G Q (R)
Q T W L Y V D Y A O P M C N Q
O S O O E K B Z Z C B U D P B
Q B L G S K U E N E E L G C N
F H F R T S P L E C S A S I A
W Q F A T A L V D I (M) A R Y P
H L G M R I X G D Z F W W E W
X Y K T V A U P L V V J P C A
Z J H L K Q C A P I Q A D J L
```

- A quadrilateral where opposite sides are congruent and parallel. (Lesson 13.1)
- A quadrilateral in which all sides are congruent and opposite sides are parallel. (Lesson 13.1)
- A quadrilateral with at least one pair of parallel sides. (Lesson 13.1)
- An arrangement of two-dimensional figures that can be folded to make a three-dimensional figure. (Lesson 15.1)
- A three-dimensional figure with a polygon base and where the other faces are triangles that all meet at a common vertex. (Lesson 15.1)
- The sum of the areas of the faces, or surfaces, of a three-dimensional figure. (Lesson 15.1)

Q: Where does a mathematician go when she commits a crime?

A: __ __ __ __ __ !

© Houghton Mifflin Harcourt Publishing Company

Area and Polygons

ESSENTIAL QUESTION

How can you find the area of an irregular polygon using area formulas?

Real-World Video

Quilting, painting, and other art forms use familiar geometric shapes, such as triangles and rectangles. To buy enough supplies for a project, you need to find or estimate the areas of each shape in the project.

⏻ my.hrw.com

GO DIGITAL

my.hrw.com

my.hrw.com

Go digital with your write-in student edition, accessible on any device.

Math On the Spot

Scan with your smart phone to jump directly to the online edition, video tutor, and more.

Animated Math

Interactively explore key concepts to see how math works.

Personal Math Trainer

Get immediate feedback and help as you work through practice sets.

Reading Start-Up

Visualize Vocabulary

Use the ✔ words to complete the graphic. You will put one word in each oval.

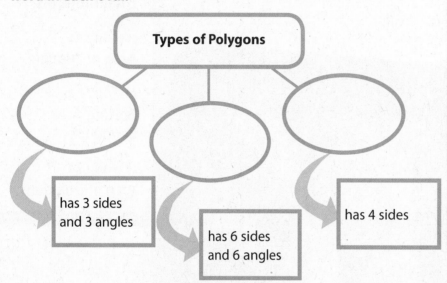

Types of Polygons

has 3 sides and 3 angles

has 6 sides and 6 angles

has 4 sides

Vocabulary

Review Words
✔ hexagon *(hexágono)*
✔ polygon *(polígono regular)*
  quadrilateral *(cuadrilátero)*
  rectangular prism *(prisma rectangular)*
  regular polygon *(polígono)*
  right triangle *(triángulo rectángulo)*
✔ triangle *(triángulo)*

Preview Words
  parallelogram *(paralelogramo)*
  rhombus *(rombo)*
  trapezoid *(trapecio)*

Understand Vocabulary

Match the term on the left to the correct expression on the right.

1. parallelogram

A. A quadrilateral in which all sides are congruent and opposite sides are parallel.

2. trapezoid

B. A quadrilateral in which opposite sides are parallel and congruent.

3. rhombus

C. A quadrilateral in which two sides are parallel.

Active Reading

Pyramid Before beginning the module, create a pyramid to help you organize what you learn. Label each side with one of the lesson titles from this module. As you study each lesson, write important ideas like vocabulary, properties, and formulas on the appropriate side.

Are YOU Ready?

Complete these exercises to review skills you will need for this module.

Inverse Operations

EXAMPLES

$7k = 35$ k is multiplied by 7.
$\dfrac{7k}{7} = \dfrac{35}{7}$ Use the inverse operation, division.
$k = 5$

$k + 7 = 9$ 7 is added to k.
$k + 7 - 7 = 9 - 7$ Use the inverse operation, subtraction.
$k = 2$

Solve each equation using the inverse operation.

1. $9p = 54$ _____   **2.** $m - 15 = 9$ _____   **3.** $\dfrac{b}{8} = 4$ _____   **4.** $z + 17 = 23$ _____

Metric Units

EXAMPLE

$6\text{ m} = \blacksquare\text{ cm}$ Multiply to go from a larger unit to a smaller unit.
$6\text{ m} = 600\text{ cm}$

$4{,}000\text{ mL} = \blacksquare\text{ L}$ Divide to go from a smaller unit to a larger unit.
$4{,}000\text{ mL} = 4\text{ L}$

Convert to the given units.

5. $64\text{ m} = $ _____ cm   **6.** $500\text{ g} = $ _____ kg   **7.** $4.6\text{ kL} = $ _____ L

Area of Squares and Rectangles

EXAMPLE

7 ft

4 ft

Find the area of the rectangle.
$A = bh$ Use the formula for the area of a rectangle. Substitute for base and height.
$= 7 \times 4$
$= 28$
The area is 28 square feet.

8. Find the area of a rectangle with a base of 5 feet and a height

of $9\frac{1}{2}$ feet _____

Complete these exercises to review skills you will need for this module.

Inverse Operations

9. Kayleigh solved the equation $24 = \frac{c}{12}$ as shown. What error did she make? Correct her work.

$$24 = \frac{c}{12}$$
$$\frac{c}{12} = 24$$
$$12\left(\frac{c}{12}\right) = \frac{24}{12}$$
$$c = 2$$

Metric Units

10. A track is 400 meters long. How long is the track in centimeters and in kilometers?

Areas of Squares and Rectangles

11. A rectangular card has a base of 12 centimeters and a height of 7.5 centimeters. Which would result in a greater area, increasing the base by 3.5 centimeters or increasing the height by 3.5 centimeters? Justify your answer.

LESSON
13.1

6.6.13.1

Students will find the areas of parallelograms, rhombuses, and trapezoids.

Area of Quadrilaterals

© Houghton Mifflin Harcourt Publishing Company

? ESSENTIAL QUESTION

How can you find the areas of parallelograms, rhombuses, and trapezoids?

EXPLORE ACTIVITY

Area of a Parallelogram

Recall that a rectangle is a special type of parallelogram.

A Draw a large parallelogram on grid paper. Cut out your parallelogram.

B Cut your parallelogram on the dashed line as shown. Then move the triangular piece to the other side of the parallelogram.

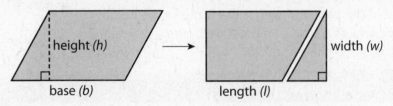

C What figure have you formed? _____

Does this figure have the same area as the parallelogram? _____

base of parallelogram = _____ of rectangle

height of parallelogram = _____ of rectangle

area of parallelogram = _____ of rectangle

What is the formula for the area of this figure? $A =$ _____

or _____

D What is the formula for the area of a parallelogram? $A =$ _____

> **Math Talk**
> **Mathematical Processes**
>
> How is the relationship between the length and width of a rectangle similar to the relationship between the base and height of a parallelogram?

Area of a Parallelogram

The area A of a parallelogram is the product of its base b and its height h.

$$A = bh$$

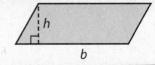

Reflect

1. Find the area of the parallelogram.

$A =$ _____

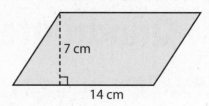

7 cm

14 cm

Math On the Spot

my.hrw.com

Finding the Area of a Trapezoid

To find the formula for the area of a trapezoid, notice that two copies of the same trapezoid fit together to form a parallelogram. Therefore, the area of the trapezoid is $\frac{1}{2}$ the area of the parallelogram.

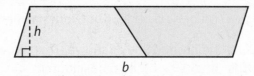

h

b

The height of the parallelogram is the same as the height of the trapezoid. The base of the parallelogram is the sum of the two bases of the trapezoid.

$$A = \quad b \quad \cdot h$$
$$\downarrow$$
$$A = (b_1 + b_2) \cdot h$$

Area of a Trapezoid

The area of a trapezoid is half its height multiplied by the sum of the lengths of its two bases.

$$A = \frac{1}{2}h(b_1 + b_2)$$

b_1

h

b_2

EXAMPLE 1 Real World

A section of a deck is in the shape of a trapezoid. What is the area of this section of the deck?

$b_1 = 17 \qquad b_2 = 39 \qquad h = 16$

Use the formula for area of a trapezoid.

$A = \frac{1}{2}h(b_1 + b_2)$

$= \frac{1}{2} \cdot 16(17 + 39)$ Substitute.

$= \frac{1}{2} \cdot 16(56)$ Add inside the parentheses.

$= 8 \cdot 56$ Multiply $\frac{1}{2}$ and 16.

$= 448$ square feet Multiply.

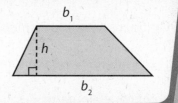

17 ft

16 ft

39 ft

Math Talk

Mathematical Processes

Does it matter which of the trapezoid's bases is substituted for b_1 and which is substituted for b_2? Why or why not?

Animated Math

my.hrw.com

YOUR TURN

2. Another section of the deck is also shaped like a trapezoid. For this section, the length of one base is 27 feet, and the length of the other base is 34 feet. The height is 12 feet. What is the area of this section of the deck? $A = $ _____ ft²

Math On the Spot

⏵ my.hrw.com

Finding the Area of a Rhombus

A **rhombus** is a quadrilateral in which all sides are congruent and opposite sides are parallel. A rhombus can be divided into four triangles that can then be rearranged into a rectangle.

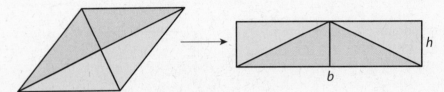

The base of the rectangle is the same length as one of the diagonals of the rhombus. The height of the rectangle is $\frac{1}{2}$ the length of the other diagonal.

$$A = b \cdot h$$
$$\downarrow \qquad \downarrow$$
$$A = d_1 \cdot \frac{1}{2}d_2$$

Area of a Rhombus

The area of a rhombus is half of the product of its two diagonals.

$$A = \frac{1}{2}d_1d_2$$

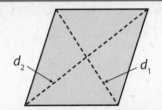

EXAMPLE 2 Real World

Cedric is constructing a kite in the shape of a rhombus. The spars of the kite measure 15 inches and 24 inches. How much fabric will Cedric need for the kite?

To determine the amount of fabric needed, find the area of the kite.

$$d_1 = 15 \qquad d_2 = 24$$

Use the formula for area of a rhombus.

$$A = \frac{1}{2}d_1d_2$$

$$= \frac{1}{2}(15)(24) \qquad \text{Substitute.}$$

$$= 180 \text{ square inches} \qquad \text{Multiply.}$$

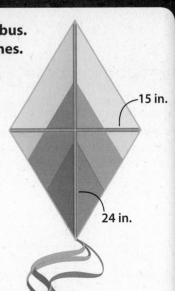

15 in.

24 in.

Lesson 13.1 **373**

YOUR TURN

Find the area of each rhombus.

3. $d_1 = 35$ m; $d_2 = 12$ m

   $A =$ _____ m²

4. $d_1 = 9.5$ in.; $d_2 = 14$ in.

   $A =$ _____ in²

5. $d_1 = 10$ m; $d_2 = 18$ m

   $A =$ _____ m²

6. $d_1 = 8\frac{1}{4}$ ft; $d_2 = 40$ ft

   $A =$ _____ ft²

Guided Practice

1. Find the area of the parallelogram. (Explore Activity)

   $A = bh$

   $= ($ _____ $)($ _____ $)$

   $=$ _____ in²

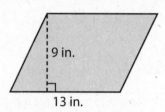

9 in.

13 in.

2. Find the area of the trapezoid. (Example 1)

   $A = \frac{1}{2}h(b_1 + b_2)$

   $= \frac{1}{2}\left(\bigcirc\right)\left(\bigcirc + \bigcirc\right)$

   $=$ _____ cm²

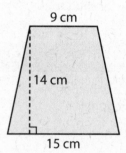

9 cm

14 cm

15 cm

3. Find the area of the rhombus. (Example 2)

   $A = \frac{1}{2}d_1d_2$

   $= \frac{1}{2}\left(\bigcirc\right)\left(\bigcirc\right)$

   $=$ _____ in²

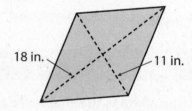

18 in.   11 in.

? ESSENTIAL QUESTION CHECK-IN

4. How can you find the areas of parallelograms, rhombuses, and trapezoids?

   _____

   _____

   _____

   _____

13.1 Independent Practice

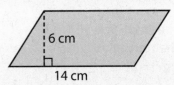

Personal Math Trainer

my.hrw.com   Online Assessment and Intervention

5. Find the area of the parallelogram.

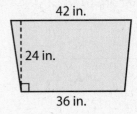

6 cm

14 cm

_____

6. What is the area of a parallelogram that has a base of $12\frac{3}{4}$ in. and a height of $2\frac{1}{2}$ in.?

_____

7. Find the area of the trapezoid.

42 in.

24 in.

36 in.

_____

8. The bases of a trapezoid are 11 meters and 14 meters. Its height is 10 meters. What is the area of the trapezoid?

_____

9. Find the area of the rhombus.

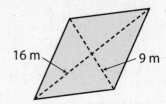

16 m   9 m

_____

10. The diagonals of a rhombus are 21 m and 32 m. What is the area of the rhombus?

_____

11. The seat of a bench is in the shape of a trapezoid with bases of 6 feet and 5 feet and a height of 1.5 feet. What is the area of the seat?

_____

12. A kite in the shape of a rhombus has diagonals that are 25 inches long and 15 inches long. What is the area of the kite?

_____

13. A window in the shape of a parallelogram has a base of 36 inches and a height of 45 inches. What is the area of the window?

_____

14. **Communicate Mathematical Ideas** Find the area of the figure. Explain how you found your answer.

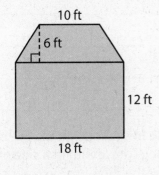

10 ft

6 ft

12 ft

18 ft

_____

_____

_____

_____

_____

_____

15. Multistep A parking space shaped like a parallelogram has a base of 17 feet and a height is 9 feet. A car parked in the space is 16 feet long and 6 feet wide. How much of the parking space is not covered by the car?

_____

 FOCUS ON HIGHER ORDER THINKING

Work Area

16. Critique Reasoning Simon says that to find the area of a trapezoid, you can multiply the height by the top base and the height by the bottom base. Then add the two products together and divide the sum by 2. Is Simon correct? Explain your answer.

_____

_____

_____

_____

17. Multistep The height of a trapezoid is 8 in. and its area is 96 in.^{2} One base of the trapezoid is 6 inches longer than the other base. What are the lengths of the bases? Explain how you found your answer.

_____

_____

_____

_____

_____

_____

18. Multiple Representations The diagonals of a rhombus are 12 in. and 16 in. long. The length of a side of the rhombus is 10 in. What is the height of the rhombus? Explain how you found your answer.

_____

_____

_____

_____

_____

_____

ESSENTIAL QUESTION

How do you find the area of a triangle?

EXPLORE ACTIVITY 1

Area of a Right Triangle

A Draw a large rectangle on grid paper.

What is the formula for the area of a rectangle? $A = $ _____

B Draw one diagonal of your rectangle.

The diagonal divides the rectangle into _____.

Each one represents _____ of the rectangle.

Use this information and the formula for area of a rectangle to

write a formula for the area of a right triangle. $A = $ _____

Reflect

1. **Communicate Mathematical Ideas** In the formula for the area
   of a right triangle, what do b and h represent?

   _____

EXPLORE ACTIVITY 2

Area of a Triangle

A Draw a large triangle on grid paper. Do not draw a right triangle.

B Cut out your triangle. Then trace around it to make a copy of
your triangle. Cut out the copy.

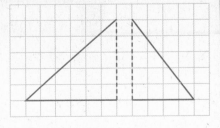

C Cut one of your triangles into two pieces by cutting through
one angle directly across to the opposite side. Now you have
three triangles — one large triangle and two smaller right
triangles.

When added together, the areas of the two smaller triangles

equal the _____ of the large triangle.

D Arrange the three triangles into a rectangle.

What fraction of the rectangle does the large

triangle represent? _____

The area of the rectangle is $A = bh$. What is the area

of the large triangle? $A =$ _____

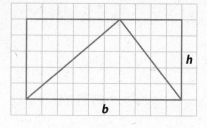

How does this formula compare to the formula for the area
of a right triangle that you found in Explore Activity 1?

_____

Reflect

2. **Communicate Mathematical Ideas** What type of angle is formed by
the base and height of a triangle?

_____

Finding the Area of a Triangle

Area of a Triangle

The area A of a triangle is half the product
of its base b and its height h.

$$A = \frac{1}{2} bh$$

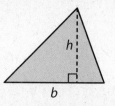

EXAMPLE 1

Find the area of each triangle.

A

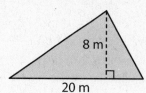

$b = 20$ meters $\qquad h = 8$ meters

$A = \frac{1}{2} bh$

$ = \frac{1}{2} (20 \text{ meters}) (8 \text{ meters})$ Substitute.

$ = 80$ square meters Multiply.

Find the area of each triangle.

B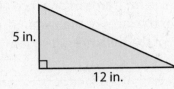

5 in.

12 in.

$b = 12$ inches $h = 5$ inches

$A = \frac{1}{2}bh$

$\quad = \frac{1}{2}(12 \text{ inches})(5 \text{ inches})$ Substitute.

$\quad = 30$ square inches   Multiply.

YOUR TURN

Find the area of the triangle.

3.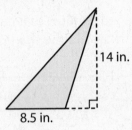

14 in.

8.5 in.

$A = \underline{\hspace{2cm}}$

Personal Math Trainer

Online Assessment and Intervention

🔵 my.hrw.com

Math Talk
Mathematical Processes

Why can you also write the formula for the area of a triangle as $A = \frac{bh}{2}$?

Math On the Spot

🔵 my.hrw.com

Problem Solving Using Area of Triangles

You can use the formula for the area of a triangle to solve real-world problems.

EXAMPLE 2 Real World

Each triangular face of the Pyramid of Peace in Kazakhstan is made up of 25 smaller equilateral triangles. These triangles have measurements as shown in the diagram. What is the area of one of the smaller equilateral triangles?

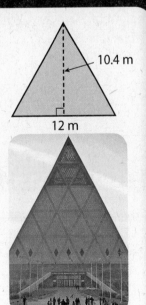

10.4 m

12 m

STEP 1 Identify the length of the base and the height of the triangle.

$b = 12$ m and $h = 10.4$ m

STEP 2 Use the formula to find the area of the triangle.

$A = \frac{1}{2}bh$ Substitute.

$\quad = \frac{1}{2}(12)(10.4)$ Multiply.

$\quad = 62.4$

The area of one small equilateral triangle is 62.4 m².

Lesson 13.2 **379**

Reflect

4. **Persevere in Problem Solving** What is the total area of one face of the pyramid? What is the total surface area of the faces of the pyramid, not counting the bottom? (Hint: the bottom of the pyramid is a square.)

_____

_____

_____

Personal Math Trainer

Online Assessment and Intervention

⏻ my.hrw.com

YOUR TURN

5. Amy needs to order a shade for a triangular-shaped window that has a base of 6 feet and a height of 4 feet. What is the area of the shade?

_____

Guided Practice

Find the area of each triangle. (Explore Activities 1 and 2, Example 1)

1.

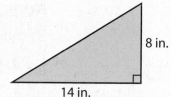

8 in.

14 in.

$A = \frac{1}{2}bh$

$= \frac{1}{2}(\underline{\hspace{1cm}})(\underline{\hspace{1cm}})$

$= \underline{\hspace{1cm}}$ in^2

2. A pennant in the shape of a triangle has a base of 12 inches and a height of 30 inches. What is the area of the pennant? (Example 2)

$A = \frac{1}{2}bh$

$= \frac{1}{2}(\underline{\hspace{1cm}})(\underline{\hspace{1cm}})$

$= \underline{\hspace{1cm}}$ in^2

GO COYOTES!

? **ESSENTIAL QUESTION CHECK-IN**

3. How do you find the area of a triangle?

_____

_____

_____

13.2 Independent Practice

Find the area of each triangle.

4.

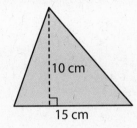

10 cm

15 cm

_____

5.

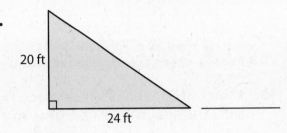

20 ft

24 ft

_____

6.

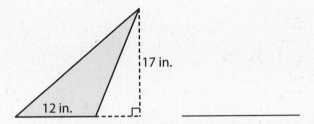

17 in.

12 in.

_____

7.

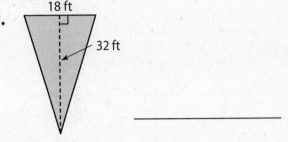

18 ft

32 ft

_____

8. What is the area of a triangle that has a base of $15\frac{1}{4}$ in. and a height of 18 in.?

_____

9. A right triangle has legs that are 11 in. and 13 in. long. What is the area of the triangle?

_____

10. A triangular plot of land has the dimensions shown in the diagram. What is the area of the land?

_____

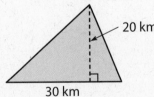

20 km

30 km

11. The front part of a tent has the dimensions shown in the diagram. What is the area of this part of the tent?

_____

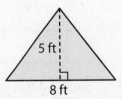

5 ft

8 ft

12. **Multistep** The sixth-grade art students are making a mosaic using tiles in the shape of right triangles. Each tile has leg measures of 3 centimeters and 5 centimeters. If there are 200 tiles in the mosaic, what is the area of the mosaic?

_____

13. **Critique Reasoning** Monica has a triangular piece of fabric. The height of the triangle is 15 inches and the triangle's base is 6 inches. Monica says that the area of the fabric is 90 in². What error did Monica make? Explain your answer.

_____

14. Multistep Wayne is going to paint the side of the house shown in the diagram. What is the area that will be painted? Explain how you found your answer.

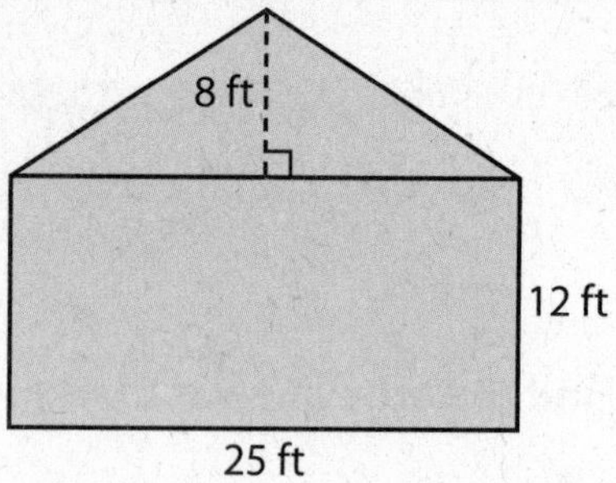

_____

_____

_____

8 ft

12 ft

25 ft

15. Communicate Mathematical Ideas Explain how the areas of a triangle and a parallelogram with the same base and height are related.

_____

_____

_____

_____

_____

16. Analyze Relationships A rectangle and a triangle have the same area. If their bases are the same lengths, how do their heights compare? Justify your answer.

_____

_____

_____

_____

_____

_____

_____

17. What If? A right triangle has an area of 18 square inches.

  a. If the triangle is an isosceles triangle, what are the lengths of the legs of the triangle?

  _____

  b. If the triangle is not an isosceles triangle, what are all the possible lengths of the legs, if the lengths are whole numbers?

  _____

Work Area

© Houghton Mifflin Harcourt Publishing Company

Solving Area Equations

6.6.13.3
Students will use equations to solve problems about area of rectangles, parallelograms, trapezoids, and triangles.

? ESSENTIAL QUESTION

How do you use equations to solve problems about area of rectangles, parallelograms, trapezoids, and triangles?

EXPLORE ACTIVITY

Math On the Spot
my.hrw.com

Problem Solving Using the Area of a Triangle

Recall that the formula for the area of a triangle is $A = \frac{1}{2}bh$. You can also use the formula to find missing dimensions if you know the area and one dimension.

EXAMPLE 1 The Hudson High School wrestling team just won the state tournament and has been awarded a triangular pennant to hang on the wall in the school gymnasium. The base of the pennant is 1.5 feet long. It has an area of 2.25 square feet. What is the height of the pennant?

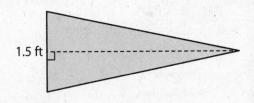

1.5 ft

Write the formula.

$$A = \boxed{}\ \boxed{}\ \boxed{}$$

Substitute the given values into the equation.

$$\boxed{} = \frac{1}{2}\left(\boxed{}\right)h$$

Multiply $\frac{1}{2}$ and 1.5.

$$2.25 = \boxed{}\,h$$

Divide both sides of the equation by _____.

$$\frac{2.25}{\boxed{}} = \frac{0.75h}{\boxed{}}$$

$$\boxed{} = h$$

The height of the pennant is _____ feet.

YOUR TURN

1. Renee is sewing a quilt whose pattern contains right triangles. Each quilt piece has a height of 6 in. and an area of 24 in².

   How long is the base of each quilt piece? _____

Personal Math Trainer

Online Assessment and Intervention

my.hrw.com

Math On the Spot

my.hrw.com

Writing Equations Using the Area of a Trapezoid

You can use the formula for area of a trapezoid to write an equation to solve a problem.

EXAMPLE 2

A garden in the shape of a trapezoid has an area of 44.4 square meters. One base is 4.3 meters long and the other base is 10.5 meters long. The height of the trapezoid is the width of the garden. How wide is the garden?

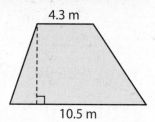

4.3 m

10.5 m

$$A = \frac{1}{2} h (b_1 + b_2)$$ Write the formula.

$$44.4 = \frac{1}{2} h (4.3 + 10.5)$$ Use the formula to write an equation.

$$44.4 = \frac{1}{2} h (14.8)$$ Add inside parentheses.

$$44.4 = 7.4 h$$ Multiply $\frac{1}{2}$ and 14.8.

$$\frac{44.4}{7.4} = \frac{7.4 h}{7.4}$$ Divide both sides of the equation by 7.4.

$$6 = h$$

The garden is 6 meters wide.

Math Talk

Mathematical Processes

How can you check that the answer is reasonable?

Reflect

2. **Communicate Mathematical Ideas** Explain why the first step after substituting is addition.

_____

_____

_____

_____

Personal Math Trainer

Online Assessment and Intervention

my.hrw.com

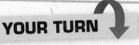**YOUR TURN**

3. The cross section of a water bin is shaped like a trapezoid. The bases of the trapezoid are 18 feet and 8 feet long. It has an area of 52 square feet. What is the height of the cross section?

_____

© Houghton Mifflin Harcourt Publishing Company

Solving Multistep Problems

You can write and solve equations that represent real-world problems related to relationships in geometry.

EXAMPLE 3 Problem Solving

John and Mary are using rolls of fabric to make a rectangular stage curtain for their class play. The rectangular piece of fabric on each roll measures 2.5 feet by 15 feet. If the area of the curtain is 200 square feet, what is the least number of rolls they need?

Analyze Information

Rewrite the question as a statement.

- Find the least number of rolls of fabric needed to cover an area of 200 ft^2.

List the important information.

- Each roll of fabric is a 2.5 foot by 15 foot rectangle.
- The area of the curtain is 200 square feet.

Formulate a Plan

Write an equation to find the area of each roll of fabric.

Use the area of the curtain and the area of each roll to write an equation to find the least number of rolls.

Solve

STEP 1 Write an equation to find the area of each roll of fabric.

$A = lw$

$A = 15 \cdot 2.5$

$A = 37.5 \text{ ft}^2$

STEP 2 Write an equation to find the least number of rolls.

$n = 200 \div 37.5$

$n = 5\frac{1}{3}$

STEP 3 The problem asks for the least number of rolls needed. Since 5 rolls will not be enough, they will need 6 rolls to make the curtain.

John and Mary will need 6 rolls of fabric to make the curtain.

Justify and Evaluate

The area of each roll is about 38 ft^2. Since 38 ft$^2 \cdot 6 = 228$ ft^2, the answer is reasonable.

YOUR TURN

4. A parallelogram-shaped field in a park needs sod. The parallelogram has a base of 21.5 meters and a height of 18 meters. The sod is sold in pallets of 50 square meters. How many pallets of sod are needed to fill the field?

_____

Guided Practice

1. A triangular bandana has an area of 70 square inches. The height of the triangle is $8\frac{3}{4}$ inches. Write and solve an equation to find the length of the base of the triangle. (Explore Activity Example 1)

_____

2. The top of a desk is shaped like a trapezoid. The bases of the trapezoid are 26.5 and 30 centimeters long. The area of the desk is 791 square centimeters. The height of the trapezoid is the width of the desk. Write and solve an equation to find the width of the desk. (Example 2)

_____

3. Taylor wants to paint his rectangular deck that is 42 feet long and 28 feet wide. A gallon of paint covers about 350 square feet. How many gallons of paint will Taylor need to cover the entire deck? (Example 3)

Write an equation to find the _____ of the deck.

Write and solve the equation.

Write an equation to find the _____.

Write and solve the equation.

Taylor will need _____ gallons of paint.

? ESSENTIAL QUESTION CHECK-IN

4. How do you use equations to solve problems about area of rectangles, parallelograms, trapezoids, and triangles?

_____

_____

13.3 Independent Practice

Personal Math Trainer

Online Assessment and Intervention

my.hrw.com

5. A window shaped like a parallelogram has an area of $18\frac{1}{3}$ square feet. The height of the window is $3\frac{1}{3}$ feet. How long is the base of the window?

_____

6. A triangular sail has a base length of 2.5 meters. The area of the sail is 3.75 square meters. How tall is the sail?

_____

7. A section in a stained glass window is shaped like a trapezoid. The top base is 4 centimeters and the bottom base is 2.5 centimeters long. If the area of the section of glass is 3.9 square centimeters, how tall is the section?

_____

8. Multistep Amelia wants to paint three walls in her family room. Two walls are 26 feet long by 9 feet wide. The other wall is 18 feet long by 9 feet wide.

a. What is the total area of the walls that Amelia wants to paint?

_____

b. Each gallon of paint covers about 250 square feet. How many gallons of paint should Amelia buy to paint the walls?

_____

9. Critical Thinking The area of a triangular block is 64 square inches. If the base of the triangle is twice the height, how long are the base and the height of the triangle?

_____

10. Multistep Alex needs to varnish the top and the bottom of a dozen rectangular wooden planks. The planks are 8 feet long and 3 feet wide. Each pint of varnish covers about 125 square feet and costs $3.50.

a. What is the total area that Alex needs to varnish?

_____

b. How much will it cost Alex to varnish all the wooden planks?

_____

11. Multistep Leia cuts congruent triangular patches with an area of 45 square centimeters from a rectangular piece of fabric that is 18 centimeters long and 10 centimeters wide. How many of the patches can Leia cut from 32 pieces of the fabric?

_____

12. Multistep A farmer needs to buy fertilizer for two fields. One field is shaped like a trapezoid, and the other is shaped like a triangle. The trapezoidal field has bases that are 35 and 48 yards and a height of 26 yards. The triangular field has the same height as the trapezoidal field and a base of 39 yards. Each bag of fertilizer covers 150 square yards. How many bags of fertilizer does the farmer need to buy?

_____

13. A tennis court for singles play is 78 feet long and 27 feet wide.

   a. The court for doubles play is 9 feet wider than the court for singles play. How much more area is covered by the tennis court used for doubles play?

   _____

   b. The junior court for players 8 and under is 36 feet long and 18 feet wide. How much more area is covered by the tennis court used for singles play?

   _____

   c. The court for players 10 and under is 18 feet shorter than the court for singles play. How much more area is covered by the tennis court used for singles play?

   _____

14. **Draw Conclusions** The cross section of a metal ingot is a trapezoid. The cross section has an area of 39 square centimeters. The top base of the cross section is 12 centimeters. The length of the bottom base is 2 centimeters greater than the top base. How tall is the metal ingot? Explain.

_____

_____

_____

 **FOCUS ON HIGHER ORDER THINKING**

15. **Analyze Relationships** A mirror is made of two congruent parallelograms as shown in the diagram. The parallelograms have a combined area of $9\frac{1}{3}$ square yards. The height of each parallelogram is $1\frac{1}{3}$ yards.

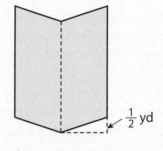

$\frac{1}{2}$ yd

   a. How long is the base of each parallelogram?

   _____

   b. What is the area of the smallest *rectangle* of wall that the mirror could fit on?

   _____

16. **Persevere in Problem Solving**
A watercolor painting is 20 inches long by 9 inches wide. Ramon makes a border around the watercolor painting by making a mat that adds 1 inch to each side of the length and the width. What is the area of the mat?

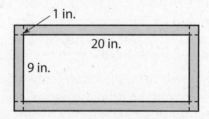

1 in.

20 in.

9 in.

_____

What is the Area?

INSTRUCTIONS

STEP 1 Shuffle the activity cards and place them in a pile face-down. Draw a card, which may contain a shape, the name of a shape, or a formula. Fill in the Shape and Area Formula columns in the table.

- If the card has a shape on it, write the most specific name for the shape and its area formula in the table.

- If the card has the name of a shape on it, write the name and its area formula in the table.

- If the card has an area formula on it, write the formula and the name of the shape whose area it describes.

$$A = \frac{1}{2} h(b_1 + b_2)$$

STEP 2 Roll a number cube once for each variable in the formula, and record the values in the Values column of the table.

Shape	Area Formula	Values	Calculations	Units	Area
Trapezoid	$A = \frac{1}{2} h(b_1 + b_2)$	$h = 3, b_1 = 6, b_2 = 2$		meters	

STEP 3 Use the values you rolled and the area formula to find the area of the shape. Show your work in the Calculations column of the table.

Shape	Area Formula	Values	Calculations	Units	Area
Trapezoid	$A = \frac{1}{2} h(b_1 + b_2)$	$h = 3$, $b_1 = 6$, $b_2 = 2$	$A = \frac{1}{2}(3)(6 + 2)$ $= \frac{1}{2}(3)(8) = 12$	meters	12 m²

STEP 4 Take turns, going clockwise, until all of the cards are used.

STEP 5 Trade tables with another student and check his or her work. Remember, the area of a square can be written as: $A = 4^2$ ft² or $A = 16$ ft².

Work Area

13.4 Area of Polygons

6.6.13.4

Students will find the area of a polygon by breaking it into simpler shapes.

? **ESSENTIAL QUESTION**

How can you find the area of a polygon by breaking it into simpler shapes?

EXPLORE ACTIVITY Real World

Finding Areas Using Tangrams

A tangram is a square that is divided into smaller shapes. The area of the small square is 1 square unit. Use a tangram to find the area of each of the other tangram pieces.

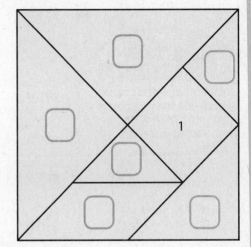

A Place one large triangle on top of the other large triangle. What is true about these two triangles? What does this mean about the areas of these two triangles?

_____

B Place the two small triangles on top of the square. What is the area of each small triangle? Write this area on the diagram.

_____

C Arrange the square and one of the small triangles as shown.

What is the combined area? _____

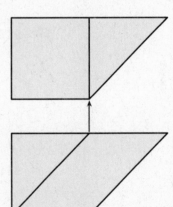

Place the parallelogram and the other small triangle on top of the combined square and triangle. What is the area of the parallelogram? Explain.

_____

_____

_____

_____

Reflect

1. **Critical Thinking** Complete the rest of the diagram by filling in the remaining areas. Explain how you found your answers.

_____

_____

Finding Areas of Polygons

You can find the areas of polygons by breaking the polygons into smaller shapes. Then you can apply area formulas you already know.

EXAMPLE 1

Find the area of each polygon.

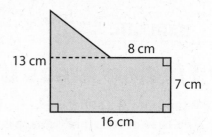

A **STEP 1** Draw a horizontal line segment on the diagram that divides the polygon into a rectangle and a triangle.

STEP 2 Find the area of the rectangle.

$A = bh = 16 \cdot 7 = \mathbf{112}$ square centimeters

STEP 3 Find the area of the triangle.

$b = 16 - 8 = 8$ $\qquad$ $h = 13 - 7 = 6$

$A = \frac{1}{2}bh = \frac{1}{2} \cdot 8 \cdot 6 = \mathbf{24}$ square centimeters

STEP 4 Add the areas from Steps 2 and 3 to find the total area.

$A = \mathbf{112} + \mathbf{24} = 136$ square centimeters

B **STEP 1** Extend the top edge and the right edge of the polygon to form a square with side length 60 feet. Find the area of this square.

$60 \cdot 60 = \mathbf{3600}$ square feet

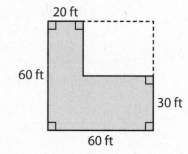

STEP 2 Notice that the square you drew has a rectangular "missing piece." Find the area of this missing piece.

$b = 60 - 20 = 40$ $\qquad$ $h = 60 - 30 = 30$

$A = bh = 40 \cdot 30 = \mathbf{1200}$ square feet

STEP 3 Subtract the area in Step 2 from the area in Step 1.

$A = \mathbf{3600} - \mathbf{1200} = 2400$ square feet

Reflect

2. Describe another way to find the area of the polygon in **B**.

_____

_____

YOUR TURN

Find the area of each polygon.

3.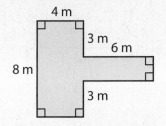

4 m
3 m
6 m
8 m
3 m

$A =$ _____ square meters

4.

18 in.
9 in.
18 in.   18 in.
36 in.

$A =$ _____ square inches

Solving Real-World Problems

You can apply the technique of dividing a shape into smaller shapes in problems that involve finding area.

Math On the Spot

my.hrw.com

EXAMPLE 2 Real World

The diagram shows the shape and dimensions of Teresa's rose garden.

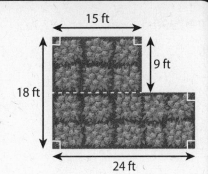

15 ft
9 ft
18 ft
24 ft

My Notes

A Find the area of the garden.

STEP 1 Draw a horizontal line segment on the diagram that divides the polygon into two rectangles, one on top of the other.

STEP 2 Find the area of the smaller (top) rectangle.

$A = bh = 15 \cdot 9 = \mathbf{135}$ square feet

STEP 3 Find the area of the larger (bottom) rectangle.

The base of the larger rectangle is 24 feet.

The height is $18 - 9 = 9$ feet.

$A = bh = 24 \cdot 9 = \mathbf{216}$ square feet

STEP 4 Add the areas from Steps 2 and 3 to find the total area.

$A = \mathbf{135} + \mathbf{216} = 351$ square feet

The area of the garden is 351 square feet.

B Teresa wants to buy mulch for her garden. One bag of mulch covers 12 square feet. How many bags will she need?

$\dfrac{351 \text{ square feet}}{12 \text{ square feet}} = 29.25$ *Divide to find the number of bags needed.*

Teresa will need to buy 30 bags of mulch.

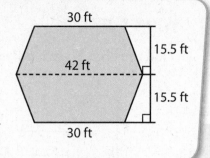

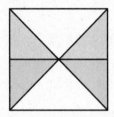

YOUR TURN

5. The diagram shows the floor plan of a hotel lobby. Carpet costs $3 per square foot. How much will it cost to carpet the lobby?

_____

30 ft

15.5 ft

42 ft

15.5 ft

30 ft

Guided Practice

1. In the diagram, the area of the large square is 1 square unit. Two diagonal segments divide the square into four equal-sized triangles. Two of these triangles are divided into smaller red and blue triangles that all have the same height and base length. Find the area of a red triangle. (Explore Activity)

_____

Find the area of each polygon. (Example 1)

2.

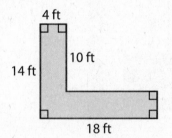

4 ft

10 ft

14 ft

18 ft

$A =$ _____ square feet

3.

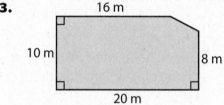

16 m

10 m

8 m

20 m

$A =$ _____ square meters

4. Jess is painting a giant arrow on a playground. Find the area of the giant arrow. If one can of paint covers 100 square feet, how many cans should Jess buy? (Example 2)

_____

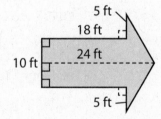

5 ft

18 ft

24 ft

10 ft

5 ft

? ESSENTIAL QUESTION CHECK-IN

5. How can you find the area of a polygon that is not one for which you know an area formula?

_____

_____

_____

13.4 Independent Practice

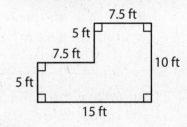

Personal Math Trainer

my.hrw.com Online Assessment and Intervention

6. Alice wants to put wall-to-wall carpeting in a small room with the floor plan shown.

a. Alice says she can find the area of the room by dividing the floor plan into two trapezoids. Show how she can divide the floor plan. Then find the area using her method.

_____

b. Describe another way to find the area.

_____

_____

c. How much will Alice pay for carpet that costs $4.50 per square foot?

_____

7. Hal's backyard has a patio, a walkway, and a garden.

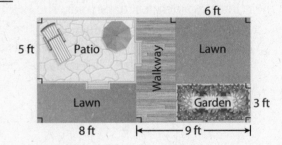

a. About what percent of the total area of Hal's backyard is the area taken up by the patio, walkway, and garden? Round to the nearest whole percent.

_____

b. One longer side of Hal's backyard lies next to the back of his house. Hal wants to build a fence that costs $9.75 per foot around the other three sides. How much will Hal spend on his new fence?

_____

8. The students in a furniture-making class make a tabletop shaped like the figure shown.

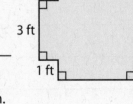

a. What is the area of the tabletop?

_____

b. One of the students wants to make a tabletop shaped like a right triangle. This tabletop will have the same area as the tabletop shown. What are a set of possible lengths for the sides of the tabletop that meet in a right angle? Explain.

_____

_____

_____

9. Multistep Cho is making banners shaped like triangles out of a rectangular piece of fabric. She cuts out two triangular banners as shown.

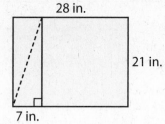

28 in.

21 in.

7 in.

a. What is the area of a triangular banner?

_____

b. What are the dimensions of the fabric left over after Cho cuts out the two banners?

_____

c. What is the maximum number of banners that Cho can cut out from the fabric? Will she use all the fabric?

_____

FOCUS ON HIGHER ORDER THINKING

10. Persevere in Problem Solving The base of a parallelogram is 8 units, and the height is 5 units. A segment divides the parallelogram into two identical trapezoids. The height of each trapezoid is 5 units. Draw the parallelogram and the two trapezoids on the grid shown. Then find the area of one of the trapezoids.

_____

11. Persevere in Problem Solving The figure shown is a square with a triangular hole cut into one side. The ratio of the height h of the triangle to a side length of the square is 7 to 8. The ratio of the base b of the triangle to the side length of the square is 1 to 2. If the area of the square is 64 square inches, what is the area of the shaded part of the square? Show your work.

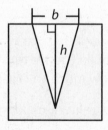

b

h

_____

_____

_____

_____

_____

_____

Ready to Go On?

13.1 Area of Quadrilaterals

1. Find the area of the figure.

_____

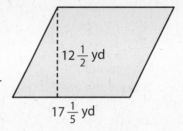

$12\frac{1}{2}$ yd

$17\frac{1}{5}$ yd

13.2 Area of Triangles

2. Find the area of the triangle.

_____

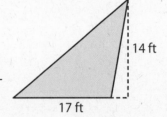

14 ft

17 ft

13.3 Solving Area Equations

3. A triangular pane of glass has a height of 30 inches and an area of 270 square inches. What is the length of the base of the pane?

_____

4. A tabletop in the shape of a trapezoid has an area of 6,550 square centimeters. Its longer base measures 115 centimeters, and the shorter base is 85 centimeters. What is the height?

_____

13.4 Area of Polygons

5. Find the area of the polygon.

_____ square centimeters

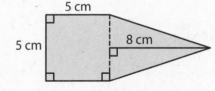

5 cm

5 cm

8 cm

 ESSENTIAL QUESTION

6. How can you find the area of an irregular polygon using area formulas?

_____

_____

_____

_____

MODULE 13 MIXED REVIEW

Assessment Readiness

Personal
Math Trainer

Online
Assessment and
Intervention

my.hrw.com

Selected Response

1. The lengths of the diagonals of the rhombus are given. What is the area of the rhombus?

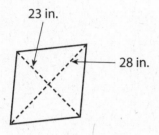

23 in.

28 in.

(A) 161 in²   (C) 644 in²

(B) 322 in²   (D) 966 in²

2. In the triangle below, the value of h is $\frac{3}{4}$ the side length that is labeled on the figure. What is the area of the triangle?

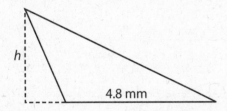

h

4.8 mm

(A) 3.6 mm²   (C) 8.64 mm²

(B) 6.4 mm²   (D) 17.28 mm²

3. Tim is designing a logo. The logo is a polygon whose shape is a square attached to an equilateral triangle. The square and the equilateral triangle have side lengths of 2 centimeters, and the equilateral triangle has a height of about 1.7 cm. Find the area of the logo.

(A) 1.7 cm²   (C) 5.7 cm²

(B) 4 cm²   (D) 7.4 cm²

4. The trapezoid below has an area of 1,575 cm².

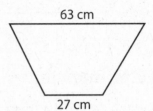

63 cm

27 cm

Which equation could you solve to find the height of the trapezoid?

(A) $45h = 1{,}575$ (C) $850.5h = 1{,}575$

(B) $90h = 1{,}575$ (D) $1{,}701h = 1{,}575$

Mini-Task

5. Cindy is designing a rectangular fountain in the middle of a courtyard. The rest of the courtyard will be covered in stone.

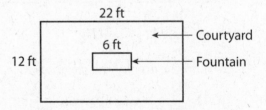

22 ft

12 ft

6 ft

Courtyard

Fountain

The part of the courtyard that will be covered in stone has an area of 246 square feet.

a. What is the width of the fountain?

_____

b. What fraction of the area of the courtyard will be occupied by the fountain?

_____

Distance and Area in the Coordinate Plane

ESSENTIAL QUESTION

What steps might you take to solve a polygon problem given the coordinates of its vertices?

Real-World Video

Many cities are designed on a grid. You can use the lengths of blocks to calculate perimeters and areas just like on a coordinate plane.

my.hrw.com

GO DIGITAL
my.hrw.com

my.hrw.com

Go digital with your write-in student edition, accessible on any device.

Math On the Spot

Scan with your smart phone to jump directly to the online edition, video tutor, and more.

Animated Math

Interactively explore key concepts to see how math works.

Personal Math Trainer

Get immediate feedback and help as you work through practice sets.

Reading Start-Up

Visualize Vocabulary

Use the ✔ words to complete the graphic.

Use the coordinates to find the distance from the origin on each	Add or subtract these to find the distance between two points on a coordinate plane

If a rectangle is formed, multiply base and height to find	If a shape is formed, add the sides to find

Vocabulary

Review Words
- ✔ absolute value *(valor absoluto)*
- ✔ area *(área)*
- ✔ axis *(eje)*
- coordinate plane *(plano cartesiano)*
- ✔ perimeter *(perímetro)*

Preview Words
- polygon *(polígono)*
- reflection *(reflexión)*
- vertex, vertices *(vértice, vértices)*

Understand Vocabulary

Complete the sentences using the preview words.

1. A corner of a rectangle is called a _____.

2. How an image would appear in a mirror is called a _____.

3. A two-dimensional shape with straight sides is

   a _____.

Active Reading

Two-Panel Flip Chart Create a two-panel flip chart to help you understand the concepts in Lesson 14.1. Label one flap "Reflection across the *x*-axis." Label the other flap "Reflection across the *y*-axis." Write important ideas about each type of reflection under the appropriate flap.

Are YOU Ready?

Complete these exercises to review skills you will need for this module.

Graph Ordered Pairs

EXAMPLE Find the coordinates for Point *A*.

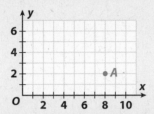

Start at *O*.
Count 8 units to the right and 2 units up from *O*.

The coordinates for Point *A* are (8, 2).

Write the ordered pair for each point shown on the graph.

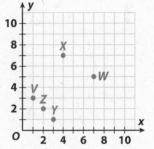

1. Point *V* _____

2. Point *W* _____

3. Point *X* _____

4. Point *Y* _____

5. Point *Z* _____

Identify Polygons

EXAMPLE Name the type of polygon.

Count the number of sides.
Compare the sides.
Compare the angles.

There are 4 congruent sides and angles. The shape is a rhombus.

Name each figure. Choose from hexagon, isosceles triangle, right triangle, and trapezoid.

6. _____

7. _____

Complete these exercises to review skills you will need for this module.

Graph Ordered Pairs

8. Find the coordinates of points A, B, C, and D. Then find the coordinates of a point E that will continue the visual pattern, and plot the point on the grid. Explain how you found it.

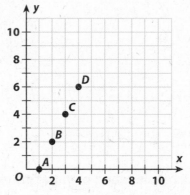

Identify Polygons

9. One leg of a right triangle is shown. Which point could be connected to points A and B to complete the right triangle? Justify your answer and complete the right triangle.

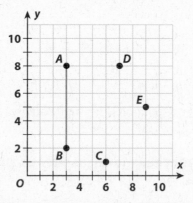

Distance in the Coordinate Plane

6.6.14.1

Students will use absolute value to find the distance between two points with the same *x*- or *y*-coordinates.

? ESSENTIAL QUESTION

How can you use absolute value to find the distance between two points with the same *x*- or *y*-coordinates?

EXPLORE ACTIVITY 1

Reflecting in the Coordinate Plane

A point on a coordinate plane can be *reflected* across an axis. The **reflection** is located on the opposite side of the axis, at the same distance from the axis.

Hold your paper up to the light if necessary to see the reflection.

Draw a coordinate plane on graph paper. Label both axes from −10 to 10.

A Graph (3, −2). Then fold your coordinate plane along the *y*-axis and find the reflection of (3, −2). Record the coordinates of the new point in the table.

B Unfold your coordinate plane. Then fold it along the *x*-axis and find the reflection of (3, −2). Record the coordinates of the new point in the table.

C Choose three additional points and repeat **A** and **B**.

Point	Reflected across *y*-axis	Reflected across *x*-axis
(3, −2)		

Reflect

1. What is the relationship between the coordinates of a point and the coordinates of its reflection across each axis?

_____

_____

_____

2. **Conjecture** A point is reflected across the *y*-axis. Then the reflected point is reflected across the *x*-axis. How will the coordinates of the final point be related to the coordinates of the original point?

_____

_____

Finding Distances in the Coordinate Plane

You can also use absolute values to find distances between two points that have the same x-coordinates or the same y-coordinates on a coordinate plane.

EXAMPLE 1

Find each distance.

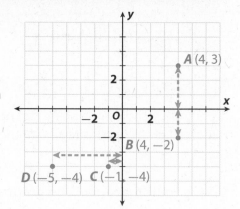

A What is the distance between point A and point B?

STEP 1 Find the distance between point A and the x-axis.

The y-coordinate is 3, so point A is $|3|$ units from the x-axis.

STEP 2 Find the distance between point B and the x-axis.

The y-coordinate of B is -2, so point B is $|-2| = 2$ units from the x-axis.

STEP 3 Find the sum of the distances.

Distance from A to $B = |3| + |-2| = 3 + 2 = 5$ units.

B What is the distance between point D and point C?

STEP 1 Find the distance between point D and the y-axis.

Point D is $|-5| = 5$ units from the y-axis.

STEP 2 Find the distance between point C and the y-axis.

Point C is $|-1| = 1$ unit from the y-axis.

STEP 3 Find the distance between C and D by finding this difference:

Distance of D from the y-axis $-$ distance of C from the y-axis

$|-5| - |-1| = 4$ units

YOUR TURN

Find the distance between each pair of points.

3. $E(-4, 7)$ and $F(5, 7)$ _____

4. $G(0, -5)$ and $H(0, -10)$ _____

© Houghton Mifflin Harcourt Publishing Company

Solving Distance Problems

You can solve problems using the distance between points on a grid.

EXAMPLE 2 · Problem Solving

The coordinate plane represents a map. Each grid unit represents 20 miles. A retail company has warehouses at $M(-70, 10)$ and $N(50, 10)$. How long does it take a truck that drives 40 miles per hour to travel from warehouse M to warehouse N?

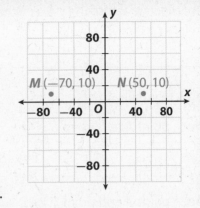

Analyze Information

Identify the important information.

- One warehouse is located at $M(-70, 10)$. The other is at $N(50, 10)$.
- A truck drives from M to N at a speed of 40 miles per hour.

Formulate a Plan

- Find the distance between M and N by adding the absolute values of the x-coordinates of the points.
- Find the time it takes the truck to drive this distance by using the relationship, distance = rate · time.

Solve

Add the absolute values of the x-coordinates to find the distance between point M and point N on the grid.

$$|-70| + |50| = 70 + 50 = 120$$

The warehouses are 120 miles apart.

The truck drives 120 miles at 40 mi/h. Because $120 = 40(3)$, it takes the truck 3 hours to travel from M to N.

Justify and Evaluate

You found the sum of the absolute values of the x-coordinates to find the horizontal distance on the grid. Then you used distance = rate · time to find the time it takes to drive that distance.

YOUR TURN

5. A store is located at $P(50, -30)$. How long will it take a truck driving at 50 miles per hour to drive from warehouse N to this store?

Personal Math Trainer

Online Assessment and Intervention

my.hrw.com

1. The point $(5, -2)$ is reflected across the x-axis. What are the coordinates of the reflection? (Explore Activity)

_____

2. The point $(-6, 8)$ is reflected across the y-axis. What are the coordinates of the reflection? (Explore Activity)

_____

Use the coordinate plane. (Example 1)

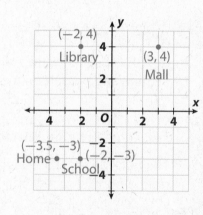

3. The distance between point A and point B is

$\left|\;\;\right| + \left|\;\;\right| = \bigcirc + \bigcirc = \bigcirc$ units.

4. The distance between point A and point C is

$\left|\;\;\right| - \left|\;\;\right| = \bigcirc - \bigcirc = \bigcirc$ units.

5. Plot the reflection of point C across the y-axis. What is the distance between point C and its reflection? _____

6. Plot the reflection of point A across the x-axis. What is the distance of the reflection from the x-axis? _____

Use the map shown. Each grid on the map represents 1 city block. (Example 2)

7. Yoko walks from the library to the mall. How many city blocks does she walk? _____

8. If Yoko walks 1 block in 3 minutes, how long does it take her to walk from the school to the library? How long does it take her to walk from home to school?

_____

? ESSENTIAL QUESTION CHECK-IN

9. How do you use absolute value to find the distance between two points that have the same x-coordinates but different y-coordinates?

_____

_____

_____

_____

14.1 Independent Practice

Personal Math Trainer

Online Assessment and Intervention

my.hrw.com

Use the coordinate plane.

10. Plot the reflection of point *A* across the *x*-axis. What are the coordinates of the reflection of point *A* across the *x*-axis? What is the distance between point *A* and its reflection?

_____

11. How can you plot the reflection of point *A* across the *y*-axis? Give the coordinates of the reflection across the *y*-axis, and tell how many units the reflection is from point *A*.

_____

_____

_____

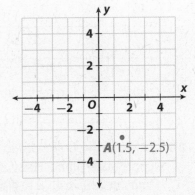

A(1.5, −2.5)

Find the coordinates of each point after the described reflection. Give the distance between each point and its reflection.

12. $R(-5, 8)$ is reflected across the *x*-axis. _____

13. $S(-7, -3)$ is reflected across the *y*-axis. _____

14. $T(8, 2)$ is reflected across the *x*-axis. _____

15. $U(2.4, -1)$ is reflected across the *y*-axis _____

Pedro uses a coordinate system to map the locations of some tourist locations in a large city. Each grid unit represents one mile.

16. The planetarium, which is not marked on the map, is halfway between the historic village and the science center. What are its coordinates?

_____

17. Pedro wants to walk from the historic village to the science center. Then he will walk from the science center to the museum. If he walks at a speed of $4\frac{1}{2}$ miles per hour, how long will it take him?

_____

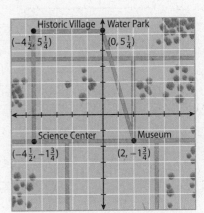

Historic Village
$(-4\frac{1}{2}, 5\frac{1}{4})$

Water Park
$(0, 5\frac{1}{4})$

Science Center
$(-4\frac{1}{2}, -1\frac{3}{4})$

Museum
$(2, -1\frac{3}{4})$

18. Pedro is staying at a hotel whose location is a reflection across the *x*-axis of the museum's location. What are the coordinates of the location of Pedro's hotel?

_____

Work Area

19. Communicate Mathematical Ideas Deirdre plotted a point D in Quadrant IV. After she reflected the point across an axis, the reflection was in Quadrant III. Give possible coordinates for point D and its reflection, and tell why you chose these coordinates.

_____

_____

_____

_____

20. Explain the Error Jason plotted the points $(4, 4)$ and $(-4, -4)$ on a coordinate plane. He says that the distance between the two points is 8 units because $|4| + |-4| = 8$. What mistake is Jason making?

_____

_____

_____

21. Look for a Pattern A point is reflected over the x-axis and then reflected again over the y-axis. Will the coordinates after these two reflections be the same or different if the point is first reflected over the y-axis and then over the x-axis? Use an example to support your answer.

_____

_____

_____

_____

_____

22. Explain the Error Bentley states that the distance between $R(-8, -3.5)$ and $S(-8, -12)$ is $|-12| + |-3.5| = 15.5$ units. Is Bentley correct? Explain your answer. If Bentley is not correct, explain how to find the correct distance between the points.

_____

_____

_____

_____

Polygons in the Coordinate Plane

6.6.14.2
Students will solve problems by drawing polygons in the coordinate plane.

? **ESSENTIAL QUESTION**

How can you solve problems by drawing polygons in the coordinate plane?

EXPLORE ACTIVITY *Real World*

Polygons in the Coordinate Plane

A **polygon** is a closed plane figure formed by three or more line segments that meet only at their endpoints. A **vertex** is the point where two sides of a polygon meet. The *vertices* of a polygon can be represented as ordered pairs, and the polygon can then be drawn in the coordinate plane.

Sheila wants to make a pattern of two different tile shapes on a floor. She first graphs the shapes on a coordinate plane.

A Plot these points to form one of the tile shapes:

A(3, 5), B(4, 6), C(5, 5), D(4, 4)

Connect the points in order.

The polygon formed is a(n) _____.

B Plot these points to form the other tile shape:

P(−5, 2), Q(−4, 3), R(0, 3), S(1, 2),

T(1, −2), U(0, −3), V(−4, −3), W(−5, −2)

Connect the points in order.

The polygon formed is a(n) _____.

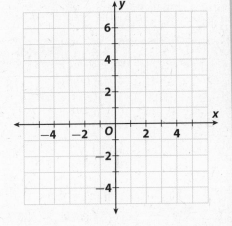

Reflect

1. How is the number of vertices related to the number of sides of the polygon and to the type of polygon? Give two examples.

_____

_____

_____

_____

Finding Perimeter in the Coordinate Plane

You can use what you know about finding lengths in the coordinate plane to find the perimeter of a polygon.

EXAMPLE 1

The grid shows the path Tommy followed when he walked from his home at (0, 0) to various locations and back home again. If each grid square represents one block, how many blocks did he walk?

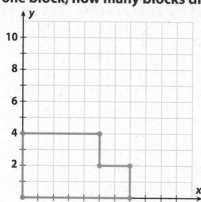

Home (0, 0)

Library (0, 4)

Park (5, 4)

Friend's house (5, 2)

Pond (7, 2)

Store (7, 0)

Math Talk
Mathematical Processes

How do you find the distance between two points in the same quadrant that have the same x-coordinate?

STEP 1 Find each distance. Each grid unit represents one block.

Tommy's home (0, 0) to the library (0, 4) is $|4| - 0 = 4 - 0 = 4$ blocks.

The library (0, 4) to the park (5, 4) is $|5| - 0 = 5 - 0 = 5$ blocks.

The park (5, 4) to Tommy's friend's house (5, 2) is $|4| - |2| = 4 - 2 = 2$ blocks.

Tommy's friend's house (5, 2) to the pond (7, 2) is $|7| - |5| = 7 - 5 = 2$ blocks.

The pond (7, 2) to the store (7, 0) is $|2| - 0 = 2 - 0 = 2$ blocks.

The store (7, 0) to Tommy's home (0, 0) is $|7| - 0 = 7 - 0 = 7$ blocks.

STEP 2 Find the sum of the distances.

Tommy walked $4 + 5 + 2 + 2 + 2 + 7 = 22$ blocks.

YOUR TURN

2. Suppose the next day Tommy walks from his home to the mall at (0, 8), and then walks to a movie theater at (7, 8). After leaving the theater Tommy walks to the store at (7, 0) before returning home.

   How far does he walk? _____ blocks

Finding Area in the Coordinate Plane

You can use familiar area formulas to find areas of polygons in the coordinate plane.

Math On the Spot
⊙ my.hrw.com

EXAMPLE 2 *Real World*

Caleb is planning a new deck for his house. He graphs the deck as polygon *ABCDEF* on a coordinate plane in which each grid unit represents one foot. The vertices of the polygon are *A*(1, 0), *B*(3, 2), *C*(3, 5), *D*(8, 5), *E*(8, 2), and *F*(6, 0). What is the area of Caleb's deck?

STEP 1 Graph the vertices, and connect them in order.

Draw a horizontal dashed line segment to divide the polygon into two quadrilaterals—a rectangle and a parallelogram.

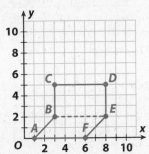

STEP 2 Find the area of the rectangle using the length of segment *BE* as the base *b* and the length of segment *BC* as the height *h*.

$b = |8| - |3| = 5$ feet $h = |5| - |2| = 3$ feet

$A = bh = 5 \cdot 3 = 15$ square feet

STEP 3 Find the area of the parallelogram using the length of segment *AF* as the base. Use the length of a segment from *F*(6, 0) to the point (6, 2) as the height *h*.

$b = |6| - |1| = 5$ feet $h = |2| - 0 = 2$ feet

$A = bh = 5 \cdot 2 = 10$ square feet

STEP 4 Add the areas to find the total area of the deck.

$A = 15 + 10 = 25$ square feet

YOUR TURN

3. The vertices of a polygon are *L*(1, 2), *M*(1, 6), *N*(7, 6), *O*(7, 2), *P*(5, 0), and *Q*(3, 0). Graph the polygon. Then find its area.

   $A =$ _____ square units

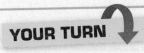

Personal Math Trainer
Online Assessment and Intervention
⊙ my.hrw.com

A gardener uses a coordinate grid to design a new garden. The gardener uses polygon *WXYZ* on the grid to represent the garden. The vertices of this polygon are *W*(3, 3), *X*(−3, 3), *Y*(−3, −3), and *Z*(3, −3). Each grid unit represents one yard.

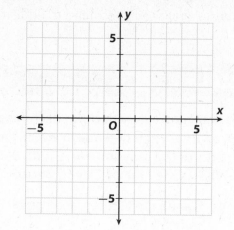

1. Graph the points, and connect them in order. What is the shape of the garden? (Explore Activity)

    _____

2. How much fencing will the gardener need to enclose the garden? (Example 1)

    Each side of the garden is _____ yards in length.

    The gardener will need _____ yards of fencing to enclose the garden.

3. What is the area of the garden? (Example 2)

    _____

4. A clothing designer makes letters for varsity jackets by graphing the letters as polygons on a coordinate plane. One of the letters is polygon *ABCDEF*. The vertices of this polygon are *A*(3, −2), *B*(3, −4), *C*(−3, −4), *D*(−3, 4), *E*(−1, 4), and *F*(−1, −2). Each grid unit represents one inch. Graph the points on the coordinate plane, and connect them in order. Identify the letter formed. Then find its area. (Example 2)

    _____

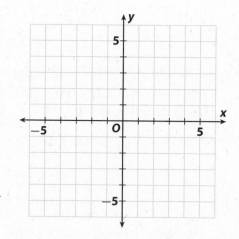

5. How can you use a coordinate plane to solve perimeter and area problems?

    _____

    _____

    _____

    _____

14.2 Independent Practice

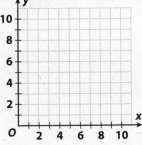

Personal Math Trainer

Online Assessment and Intervention

my.hrw.com

6. A graphic designer creates letters for wall art by first graphing the letters as polygons on a coordinate plane. One of the letters is polygon *MNOPQRSTUV* with vertices *M*(2, 1), *N*(2, 9), *O*(7, 9), *P*(7, 7), *Q*(4, 7), *R*(4, 6), *S*(6, 6), *T*(6, 4), *U*(4, 4), and *V*(4, 1). Each grid unit represents one inch.

a. Graph the points on the coordinate plane, and connect them in

order. What letter is formed? _____

b. The designer will use decorative tape to paint the outline of the

letter on a wall. How many inches of tape are needed? _____

c. How much space does the letter cover on the wall? _____

d. How did you find your answer to c? Use the name(s) of shapes in your answer.

_____

_____

7. Vocabulary The polygon shown is a regular polygon since all sides have equal length and all angles have equal measure.

a. The polygon is a regular _____.

b. What is the perimeter of the polygon? _____

c. A line can divide the figure into two identical four-sided polygons. Each polygon has two bases, and one base is twice the length of the other base. Identify the polygon, and give its perimeter.

_____

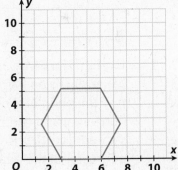

8. Jean wants to put furniture in her clubhouse. She drew a floor plan of the clubhouse, as shown. Each grid unit represents one foot.

a. Which polygon names the shape of the floor?

_____

b. How many feet of baseboard are needed to go around the entire clubhouse?

_____

c. How much carpet is needed for the clubhouse floor?

_____

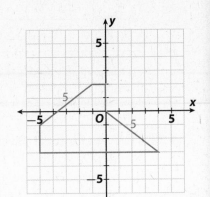

9. **Persevere in Problem Solving** To find the area of triangle *ABC*, Jen first drew a square around the figure. Two sides of the square passed through the points *B* and *C*. The other two sides met at point *A*. Draw Jen's square, and explain how you can use it to find the area of triangle *ABC*.

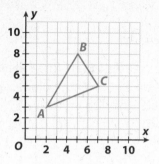

_____

_____

_____

_____

_____

10. **Communicate Mathematical Ideas** The coordinates $A(5, -2)$, $B(3, -1)$, $C(-4, -4)$, $D(-3, 8)$, and $E(-1, 4)$ form the vertices of a polygon when they are connected in order from *A* through *E*. Classify the polygon without plotting the points. Explain your answer.

_____

_____

_____

_____

11. **Explain the Error** Josh's teacher draws a regular octagon on a coordinate plane. One side has endpoints at (1, 5) and (4, 5). Josh says he can't find the perimeter of the octagon because he can only find lengths of horizontal and vertical segments. He says he can't find the lengths of the slanted sides of the octagon. What mistake is Josh making? What is the perimeter of the octagon?

_____

_____

_____

_____

12. **Critical Thinking** Give coordinates for the vertices of a triangle that could have an area of 35 square units. Prove that your triangle fits the description by finding its area.

_____

_____

You Found My Polygon!

Playing the Game

STEP 1 Sitting so that you and your opponent cannot see each other's work, draw copies of the polygons shown below on your Hiding Ground coordinate plane. Draw one polygon in each quadrant. You can place vertices on an axis, but all vertices must have integer coordinates. You can draw a polygon so that it is rotated from the position shown. For example, you can draw the rectangle rotated so that it is oriented vertically. You cannot, however, change the size of any polygon.

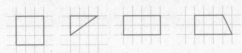

For example, your opponent draws the polygons on his or her Hiding Ground coordinate plane in the positions shown.

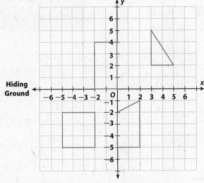

STEP 2 To play the game, alternate turns, keeping your coordinate plane hidden from your opponent's view. Begin your turn by calling out an ordered pair.

STEP 3 Your opponent must respond to the ordered pair you called out in one of four ways:

a. "That is a vertex of my (name of shape)." In this case, use a "V" to plot the point on your Opponent's Hiding Ground coordinate plane. Your opponent records the point on his or her Hiding Ground coordinate plane.

You Call Out	Opponent Responds	You Plot	Opponent Plots
(−2, 4)	That is a vertex of my rectangle.		

© Houghton Mifflin Harcourt Publishing Company

b. "That is on a side of my (name of shape)." In this case, use an "S" to plot the point on your Opponent's Hiding Ground coordinate plane. Your opponent records the point on his or her Hiding Ground coordinate plane.

You Call Out	Opponent Responds	You Plot	Opponent Plots
(−2, 2)	That is on a side of my rectangle.		

c. "That is inside of my (name of shape)." In this case, use an "I" to plot the point on your Opponent's Hiding Ground coordinate plane. Your opponent records the point on his or her Hiding Ground coordinate plane.

You Call Out	Opponent Responds	You Plot	Opponent Plots
(−3, −3)	That is inside of my square.		

d. "You missed my polygons." In this case, use a "•" to plot the point on your Opponent's Hiding Ground coordinate plane.

You Call Out	Opponent Responds	You Plot	Opponent Plots
(2, 2)	You missed my polygons.		Your opponent does not need to record this point.

STEP 4 When your turn ends, switch roles so that your opponent now calls out an ordered pair to you.

Winning the Game

A player has found an opponent's polygon when he or she has found all four vertices. The first player to find all of an opponent's polygons wins the game.

Ready to Go On?

14.1 Distance in the Coordinate Plane

1. Reflect *A* across the *x*-axis. Label the reflection as *N*, and give its coordinates on the graph.

2. Reflect *B* across the *x*-axis. Label the reflection as *M*, and give its coordinates on the graph.

3. The distance between *A* and *N* is _____.

4. Suppose the graph represents a map in which each grid unit equals 1 mile. If a school is located at *B* and a library is located at *N*, what is the distance

   between the school and the library? _____

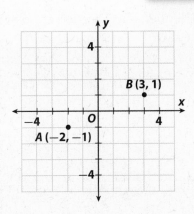

Find the coordinates of the point for each reflection.

5. (−5, 7) across the *x*-axis _____

6. (2, 5.5) across the *y*-axis _____

Find the distance between each pair of points.

7. (1, 1) and (1, −2) _____ units

8. (−2, 3) and (−4, 3) _____ units

14.2 Polygons in the Coordinate Plane

9. On the coordinate plane shown, each grid unit represents 10 feet. Polygon *QRST* has vertices *Q*(10, 20), *R*(−10, 20), *S*(−10, −10), and *T*(10, −10), and represents the floor plan of a room. Find the perimeter and area of the room.

   _____

   _____

 ESSENTIAL QUESTION

10. Suppose you are given the coordinates of the vertices of a polygon. What steps could you take to solve a problem involving the polygon's area?

    _____

    _____

    _____

MODULE 14 MIXED REVIEW

Assessment Readiness

Personal
Math Trainer

Online
Assessment and
Intervention

my.hrw.com

Selected Response

1. Which point is a reflection of point *R* across the *x*-axis?

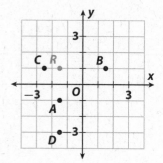

(A) Point *A*   (C) Point *C*

(B) Point *B*   (D) Point *D*

2. Which point is a reflection of (12, −8) across the *y*-axis on a coordinate plane?

(A) (−12, −8)   (C) (8, 12)

(B) (−8, 12)   (D) (12, 8)

3. What is the distance between points *J* and *L* on the grid?

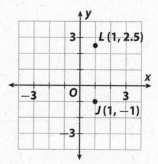

(A) 1.5 units   (C) 3 units

(B) 2 units   (D) 3.5 units

4. What is the greatest common factor of 12 and 30?

(A) 2   (C) 6

(B) 3   (D) 12

5. What is the distance between two points located at (−6, 2) and (−6, 8) on a coordinate plane?

(A) 4 units   (C) 10 units

(B) 6 units   (D) 12 units

6. Which is the sum of $\frac{1}{12} + \frac{3}{8}$?

(A) $\frac{1}{6}$ (C) $\frac{11}{48}$

(B) $\frac{1}{5}$ (D) $\frac{11}{24}$

Mini-Task

7. An artist is laying out the design for a wall hanging on a coordinate plane. She uses polygon *EFGH* with vertices *E*(4, 4), *F*(−4, 4), *G*(−4, −4), and *H*(4, −4) to represent the finished piece. Each unit on the grid represents two feet.

a. Plot the polygon on the grid, and classify its shape.

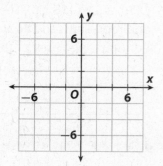

Name of Polygon: _____

b. How much area will the art cover on

a wall? _____

Surface Area and Volume of Solids

? ESSENTIAL QUESTION

How can a model help you to solve surface area and volume problems?

Real-World Video

Surface area and volume can be important considerations when constructing or repairing buildings or other structures.

my.hrw.com

GO DIGITAL
my.hrw.com

my.hrw.com

Go digital with your write-in student edition, accessible on any device.

Math On the Spot

Scan with your smart phone to jump directly to the online edition, video tutor, and more.

Animated Math

Interactively explore key concepts to see how math works.

Personal Math Trainer

Get immediate feedback and help as you work through practice sets.

415

Reading Start-Up

© Houghton Mifflin Harcourt Publishing Company

Visualize Vocabulary

Use review words to complete the graphic.

Shape	Area Formula
	$A = b \times \underline{\hspace{2cm}}$
	$A = \frac{1}{2} \times \underline{\hspace{2cm}} \times h$

Vocabulary

Review Words

- area *(área)*
- base *(base)*
- height *(altura)*
- rectangular prism *(prisma rectangular)*
- volume *(volumen)*

Preview Words

- net *(plantilla)*
- pyramid *(pirámide)*
- surface area *(área total)*

Understand Vocabulary

Complete the sentences using the preview words.

1. The total area of all the faces of a three-dimensional figure is

   called the _____.

2. A model that looks like an unfolded three-dimensional figure is a

   _____.

3. A three-dimensional shape with a polygon for a base and triangles

   for sides is a _____.

Active Reading

Booklet Before beginning the module, create a booklet to help you learn the concepts in this module. Write the main idea of each lesson on each page of the booklet. As you study each lesson, write important details that support the main idea, such as vocabulary and important steps in solving problems. Refer to your finished booklet as you work on assignments and study for tests.

Are YOU Ready?

Complete these exercises to review skills you will need for this module.

Use of Parentheses

EXAMPLE $\frac{1}{2}(14)(12 + 18) = \frac{1}{2}(14)(30)$ Perform operations inside parentheses first.

$= 7(30)$ Multiply left to right.

$= 210$ Multiply again.

Evaluate.

1. $\frac{1}{2}(3)(5 + 7)$ 2. $\frac{1}{2}(15)(13 + 17)$ 3. $\frac{1}{2}(10)(9.4 + 3.6)$ 4. $\frac{1}{2}(2.1)(3.5 + 5.7)$

_____   _____   _____   _____

Area of Squares, Rectangles, Triangles

EXAMPLE Find the area of the rectangle.

8 ft

3 ft

$A = bh$ Use the formula for area of a rectangle.

$= 8 \cdot 3$ Substitute for base and height.

$= 24$ Multiply.

Area equals 24 square feet.

Find the area of each figure.

5. a triangle with base 6 in. and height 3 in. _____

6. a square with sides of 7.6 m _____

7. a rectangle with length $3\frac{1}{4}$ ft and width $2\frac{1}{2}$ ft _____

8. a triangle with base 8.2 cm and height 5.1 cm _____

Complete these exercises to review skills you will need for this module.

Use of Parentheses

9. Use the expression $\frac{1}{2}(x + y)(h)$. Evaluate the expression for $x = 2$, $y = 5$, and $h = 8$ to find the area of the triangular region shown.

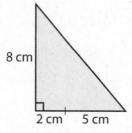

8 cm

2 cm   5 cm

Area of Squares, Rectangles, Triangles

10. Jeffrey made two triangular flags, each with a base of 12 centimeters and a height of 10 centimeters. To find the total area of the flags in square centimeters, he multiplied the base times the height of one flag. Did he find the correct total area? Justify your answer.

11. How would you find the area of a rectangle that has a length of 3 feet and a width of 6 inches? Explain. Then find the area.

Nets and Surface Area

6.6.15.1
Students will use nets to find surface areas.

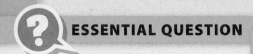

? ESSENTIAL QUESTION

How can you use nets to find surface areas?

EXPLORE ACTIVITY

Using a Net

A **net** is a two-dimensional pattern of shapes that can be folded into a three-dimensional figure. The shapes in the net become the faces of the three-dimensional figure.

A Copy each net on graph paper. Cut out each net along the blue lines.

Net A 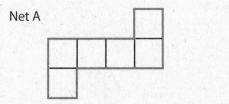   Net B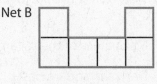

One of these nets can be folded along the black lines to make a cube.

Which net will NOT make a cube? _____

B On your graph paper, draw a different net that you think will make a cube. Confirm by cutting out and folding your net. Compare results with several of your classmates. How many different nets for a cube did

you and your classmates find? _____

Reflect

How do you know that each net cannot be folded into a cube without actually cutting and folding it?

1.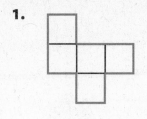

2.

_____   _____

_____   _____

3. What shapes will appear in a net for a rectangular prism that is not a cube? How many of these shapes will there be?

_____

Surface Area of a Pyramid

The **surface area** of a three-dimensional figure is the sum of the areas of its faces. A net can be helpful when finding surface area.

A **pyramid** is a three-dimensional figure whose base is a polygon and whose other faces are triangles that meet at a point. A pyramid is identified by the shape of its base.

EXAMPLE 1

Make a net of this square pyramid, and use the net to find the surface area.

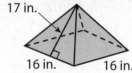

STEP 1 Make a net of the pyramid.

Draw the square base.

Draw a triangle on each side.

Label the dimensions.

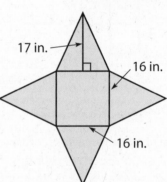

Math Talk

Mathematical Processes

How many surfaces does a triangular pyramid have? What shape are they?

STEP 2 Use the net to find the surface area.

There are four triangles with base 16 in. and height 17 in.

The area of the 4 triangles is $4 \times \frac{1}{2}(16)(17) = 544$ in^2.

The area of the base is $16 \times 16 = 256$ in^2.

The surface area is $544 + 256 = 800$ in^2.

YOUR TURN

4. Use a net to find the surface area of the pyramid.

_____

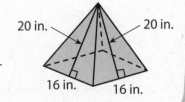

Surface Area of a Prism

A **prism** is a three-dimensional figure with two identical and parallel bases that are polygons. The other faces are rectangles. A prism is identified by the shape of its base.

Math On the Spot
my.hrw.com

EXAMPLE 2

A sculpture sits on pedestal in the shape of a square prism. The side lengths of a base of the prism are 3 feet. The height of the prism is 4 feet. The museum director wants to cover all but the underside of the pedestal with foil that costs $0.22 per square foot. How much will the foil cost?

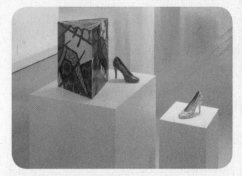

My Notes

STEP 1 Use a net to show the faces that will be covered with foil.

Draw the top.

Draw the faces of the prism that are connected to the top.

You don't need to include the bottom of the pedestal.

4 ft | Back | 4 ft — Right side
4 ft | 3 ft | 4 ft
3 ft | Top | 3 ft
Left side
3 ft | 4 ft
Front | 4 ft

STEP 2 Use the net to find the area that will be covered with foil.

Area of top = 3 · 3 = 9 ft²

The other four faces are identical.

Area of four faces = 4 · 3 · 4 = 48 ft²

Area to be covered = 9 + 48 = 57 ft²

STEP 3 Find the cost of the foil.

57 · $0.22 = $12.54

The foil will cost $12.54.

Reflect

5. Critical Thinking What shapes would you see in the net of a triangular prism?

_____

6. The figure shown is a triangular prism. How much would it cost to cover the bases and the other three faces with foil that costs $0.22 per square foot?

_____

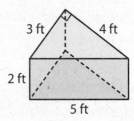

Guided Practice

A square pyramid is shown.

1. The figure has _____ square base and _____ triangular faces. (Explore Activity)

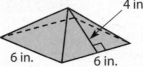

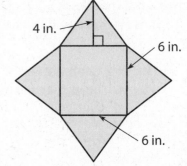

2. Find the surface area. (Example 1)

   The area of the base is _____ square inches.

   The area of the four faces is _____ square inches.

   The surface area is _____ square inches.

3. Yolanda makes wooden boxes for a crafts fair. She makes 100 boxes like the one shown, and she wants to paint all the outside faces. (Example 2)

   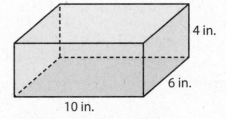

   a. Find the surface area of one box.

      _____

   b. Find the total surface area of 100 boxes.

      _____

   c. One can of paint will cover 14,000 square inches. How many cans of paint will Yolanda need to buy?

      _____

4. How is a net useful when finding the surface area of prisms and pyramids?

   _____

   _____

   _____

15.1 Independent Practice

Personal
Math Trainer

Online
Assessment and
Intervention

my.hrw.com

5. Use a net to find the surface area of the cereal box.

Total surface area: _____

Yoms

12 in.

8 in.   2 in.

6. Inez bought a shipping container at a packaging store. She measured the dimensions shown to the nearest tenth.

a. Sketch a net of the container, and label the dimensions.

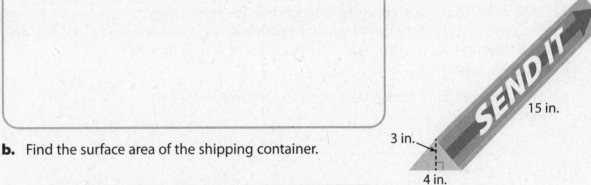

3.6 in.

SEND IT

15 in.

3 in.

4 in.

b. Find the surface area of the shipping container.

_____

7. Raj builds a side table in the shape of a cube. Each edge of the cube measures 20 inches. Raj wants to cover the top and four sides of the table with ceramic tiles. Each tile has an edge length of 5 inches. How many tiles will he need?

_____

8. Santana wants to cover a gift box shaped like a rectangular prism with foil. The foil costs $0.03 per square inch. Santana has a choice between Box A which is 8 inches long, 3 inches wide, and 6 inches high, and Box B which is 10 inches long, 3 inches wide, and 4 inches high. Which box will be less expensive to cover with foil, and by how much?

_____

9. **Vocabulary** Name a three-dimensional shape that has four triangular faces and one rectangular face. Name a three-dimensional shape that has three rectangular faces and two triangular faces.

_____

10. Victor wrapped the gift box shown with adhesive paper (with no overlaps). How much paper did he use?

_____

5 in.

6 in.

8 in.

11. Communicate Mathematical Ideas Describe how you approach a problem involving surface area. What do you do first? What are some strategies you can use?

_____

_____

_____

_____

_____

12. Persevere in Problem Solving A pedestal in a craft store is in the shape of a triangular prism. The bases are right triangles with side lengths of 12 centimeters, 16 centimeters, and 20 centimeters. The store owner wraps a piece of rectangular cloth around the pedestal, but does not cover the identical bases of the pedestal with cloth. The area of the cloth is 192 square centimeters.

a. What is the distance around the base of the pedestal? How do you know?

_____

_____

b. What is the height of the pedestal? How did you find your answer?

_____

_____

_____

13. Critique Reasoning Robert sketches two rectangular prisms, A and B. Prism A's side lengths are 5 centimeters, 6 centimeters, and 7 centimeters. Prism B's side lengths were twice those of prism A's: 10 centimeters, 12 centimeters, and 14 centimeters. Robert says the surface area of prism B is twice the surface area of prism A. Is he correct? If he is not, how many times as great as prism A's surface area is prism B's surface area? Show your work.

_____

_____

_____

_____

Work Area

Volume of Rectangular Prisms

? ESSENTIAL QUESTION

How do you find the volume of a rectangular prism?

EXPLORE ACTIVITY

Using Fractional Edge Lengths

A cube with edge length 1 unit and volume 1 cubic unit is filled with smaller cubes as shown.

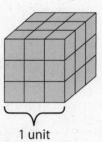

1 unit

A How many small cubes are there? _____

How does the combined volume of the small cubes compare to the volume of the large cube?

_____

Number of small cubes	·	Volume of one small cube	=	Volume of large cube
☐	·	?	=	☐

What is the volume of one small cube? _____ cubic unit(s)

B Each edge of the large cube contains _____ small cubes.

Number of small cubes per edge	·	Edge length of one small cube	=	Edge length of large cube
☐	·	?	=	☐

What is the edge length of one small cube? _____ unit(s)

C Complete:

Each small cube has edge length _____ unit(s) and

volume _____ cubic unit(s).

D The formula for volume of a cube with edge length ℓ is $V = \ell \cdot \ell \cdot \ell$, or $V = \ell^3$. Find the volume of one small cube using this formula.

$V =$ _____ = _____

Reflect

1. Several of the small cubes in the Explore Activity are arranged into a medium-sized cube as shown.

Show two different ways to find the volume of this cube.

_____

_____

_____

_____

Math On the Spot

⏻ my.hrw.com

Finding Volume

A rectangular prism has six faces. Any pair of opposite faces can be called the **bases** of the prism.

Volume of a Rectangular Prism

$V = \ell wh$, or $V = Bh$

(where B represents the area of the prism's base; $B = \ell w$)

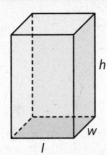

EXAMPLE 1

Find the volume of the rectangular prism.

$\ell = 3$ meters $w = 2\frac{1}{4}$ meters $h = 4\frac{1}{2}$ meters

$V = \ell wh$

$= 3 \cdot 2\frac{1}{4} \cdot 4\frac{1}{2}$

$= 3 \cdot \frac{9}{4} \cdot \frac{9}{2}$ Write each mixed number as an improper fraction. Multiply.

$= \frac{243}{8}$

$= 30\frac{3}{8}$ cubic meters   Write as a mixed number in simplest form.

Math Talk

Mathematical Processes

Can you also use the formula $V = Bh$ to find the volume? Does it matter which face you choose as the base?

[diagram labels: $4\frac{1}{2}$ m, $2\frac{1}{4}$ m, 3 m]

YOUR TURN

Find the volume of each rectangular prism.

2.

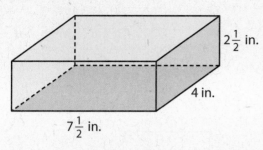

$2\frac{1}{2}$ in.

4 in.

$7\frac{1}{2}$ in.

3. length $= 5\frac{1}{4}$ inches

width $= 3\frac{1}{2}$ inches

height $= 3$ inches

_____   _____

Solving Volume Problems

When you solve a real-world problem involving the volume of a prism, you can choose to use either of the volume formulas you know.

EXAMPLE 2 Real World

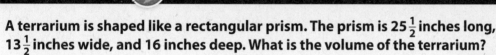

A terrarium is shaped like a rectangular prism. The prism is $25\frac{1}{2}$ inches long, $13\frac{1}{2}$ inches wide, and 16 inches deep. What is the volume of the terrarium?

STEP 1 Choose one side to be the base, and find its area.

$B = 25\frac{1}{2} \times 13\frac{1}{2}$ Use the $25\frac{1}{2}$-inch by $13\frac{1}{2}$-inch face as the base.

$= \frac{51}{2} \times \frac{27}{2}$

$= \frac{1,377}{4}$

> The area of the base is $\frac{1,377}{4}$ square inches. You need to perform another operation, so you don't need to write this value as a mixed number.

STEP 2 Find the volume.

$V = Bh$

$= \frac{1,377}{4} \times 16$ Substitute $\frac{1,377}{4}$ for B and 16 for h.

$= \frac{1,377}{\,_1 4} \times \frac{\cancel{16}^{\,4}}{1}$ Simplify before multiplying.

$= 5,508$

The volume of the terrarium is 5,508 cubic inches.

YOUR TURN

4. A rectangular swimming pool is 15 meters long, $10\frac{1}{2}$ meters wide, and $2\frac{1}{2}$ meters deep. What is its volume?

_____

A large cube is made up of smaller unit cubes as shown on the right. Each small cube has an edge length of $\frac{1}{2}$ unit. (Explore Activity)

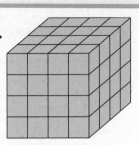

1. Each edge of the large cube is _____ units.

2. The volume of the large cube is _____ cubic units.

Find the volume of each prism. (Example 1)

3.

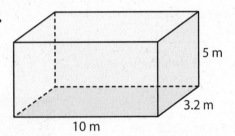

5 m

3.2 m

10 m

$V =$ _____ × _____ × _____

  = _____ cubic meters

4.

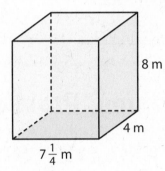

8 m

4 m

$7\frac{1}{4}$ m

$B =$ _____ × _____ = _____ m^2

$V =$ _____ cubic meters

5.

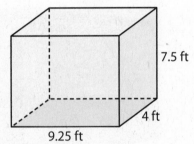

7.5 ft

4 ft

9.25 ft

$V =$ _____ cubic feet

6.

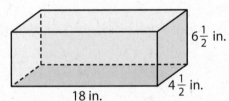

$6\frac{1}{2}$ in.

$4\frac{1}{2}$ in.

18 in.

$V =$ _____ cubic inches

7. A cereal box is $8\frac{1}{2}$ inches long, $3\frac{1}{2}$ inches wide, and 12 inches high.

   What is the volume of the box? (Example 2) _____

ESSENTIAL QUESTION CHECK-IN

8. Which two formulas can you use to find the volume of a rectangular prism? Why are these two formulas equivalent?

   _____

   _____

   _____

15.2 Independent Practice

Personal Math Trainer

Online Assessment and Intervention

my.hrw.com

9. A block of wood measures 4.5 inches by 3.5 inches by 7 inches. What is the volume of the block of wood?

_____

10. A restaurant buys a freezer in the shape of a rectangular prism. The dimensions of the freezer are shown. What is the volume of the freezer?

_____

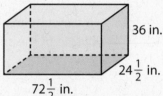

36 in.

$24\frac{1}{2}$ in.

$72\frac{1}{2}$ in.

11. Rectangular prism A measures 6 inches by 4 inches by 5 inches. Rectangular prism B's dimensions are twice those of prism A. Find the volume of each prism. How many times as great is prism B's volume as prism A's volume?

_____

12. Leticia has a small paper weight in the shape of a rectangular prism. The dimensions of the paper weight are shown. What is the volume of the paper weight?

_____

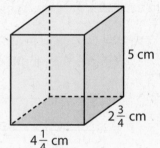

5 cm

$2\frac{3}{4}$ cm

$4\frac{1}{4}$ cm

13. A company is designing a juice box. The box is in the shape of a rectangular prism. The base of the box is $6\frac{1}{2}$ inches by $2\frac{1}{2}$ inches, and the box is 4 inches high. If juice fills 90% of the box's volume, find the volume of juice in the box.

_____

14. **Science** Density is the amount of mass in a certain volume of an object. To find the density in grams per cubic centimeter of a substance you can use this relationship:

$$\text{Density} = \frac{\text{mass in grams}}{\text{volume in cubic centimeters}}$$

A gold bar that is 16 centimeters by 2.5 centimeters by 5 centimeters has a density of 19.3 grams per cubic centimeter. What is the mass of the gold bar?

_____

15. A suitcase is a rectangular prism whose dimensions are $1\frac{1}{4}$ feet by $1\frac{3}{4}$ feet by $1\frac{1}{4}$ feet. Find the volume of the suitcase.

_____

16. The Smith family is moving and needs to decide on the size of the moving truck they should rent.

Inside Dimensions of Trucks			
Type	Length (ft)	Width (ft)	Height (ft)
Van	$10\frac{1}{2}$	6	6
Small Truck	12	8	$6\frac{3}{4}$
Large Truck	20	$8\frac{3}{4}$	$8\frac{1}{2}$

   a. A moving van rents for $94.50 per day, and a small truck rents for $162 per day. Based on the amount of space inside the van or truck, which is the better deal? Explain your answer.

   _____

   _____

   _____

   b. How much greater is the volume of the large truck than the volume of the small truck?

   _____

   c. The family estimates that they need about 1,100 cubic feet to move their belongings. What should they rent?

   _____

 FOCUS ON HIGHER ORDER THINKING

Work Area

17. **Persevere in Problem Solving** A cube has a volume of $\frac{1}{512}$ cubic meter. What is the length of each side of the cube? Explain your thinking.

   _____

   _____

18. **Communicate Mathematical Ideas** Think about two rectangular prisms, one labeled prism P and one labeled prism Q.

   a. Suppose the bases of the prisms have the same area, but the height of prism Q is twice the height of prism P. How do the volumes compare?

   _____

   b. Suppose the area of the base of prism Q is twice the area of the base of prism P. How do the volumes compare?

   _____

19. **Critical Thinking** The dimensions of a rectangular prism are $3\frac{1}{4}$ feet by $2\frac{1}{2}$ feet by 5 feet. Lee found the volume by multiplying $12\frac{1}{2}$ by $3\frac{1}{4}$. Lola found the volume by multiplying $16\frac{1}{4}$ by $2\frac{1}{2}$. Who is correct? Explain.

   _____

   _____

   _____

   _____

Solving Volume Equations

6.6.15.3

Students will write equations to solve problems involving volume of rectangular prisms.

? ESSENTIAL QUESTION

How do you write equations to solve problems involving volume of rectangular prisms?

EXPLORE ACTIVITY  *Real World*

Math On the Spot
⏻ my.hrw.com

Writing Equations Using the Volume of a Rectangular Prism

You can use the formula for the volume of a rectangular prism to write an equation. Then solve the equation to find missing measurements for a prism.

EXAMPLE 1 Samuel has an ant farm with a volume of 375 cubic inches. The width of the ant farm is 2.5 inches and the length is 15 inches. What is the height of Samuel's ant farm?

Write a formula. $\qquad$ $V = \ell \;\square\;\square$

Substitute the given values into the equation. $\quad \square = \square \cdot \square \cdot h$

Multiply 15 and 2.5. $\qquad 375 = \square\; h$

Divide both sides of the equation by _____ . $\qquad \dfrac{375}{\square} = \dfrac{37.5h}{\square}$

Simplify. $\qquad \square = h$

The height of the ant farm is _____ inches.

Reflect

1. **Communicate Mathematical Ideas** Explain how you would find the solution to Example 1 using the formula $V = Bh$.

_____

 **YOUR TURN**

2. Find the height of this rectangular prism, which has a volume of $\frac{15}{16}$ cubic feet.

_____

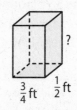
$\frac{3}{4}$ ft $\quad \frac{1}{2}$ ft

Personal Math Trainer

Online Assessment and Intervention

⏻ my.hrw.com

Solving Multistep Problems

One cubic foot of water equals approximately 7.5 gallons and weighs approximately 62.43 pounds.

EXAMPLE 2

The classroom aquarium holds 30 gallons of water. It is 0.8 feet wide and has a height of 2 feet. Find the length of the aquarium.

STEP 1 Find the volume of the classroom aquarium in cubic feet.

> Divide the total number of gallons by the unit rate to find the number of cubic feet.

$$\frac{30 \text{ gallons}}{7.5 \text{ gallons per cubic foot}} = 4 \text{ cubic feet}$$

STEP 2 Find the length of the aquarium.

$4 = \ell \cdot 0.8 \cdot 2$ Use the formula $V = \ell wh$ to write an equation.

$4 = \ell(1.6)$ Multiply.

$\dfrac{4}{1.6} = \dfrac{\ell(1.6)}{1.6}$ Divide both sides of the equation by 1.6.

$2.5 = \ell$

The length of the aquarium is 2.5 feet.

Math Talk
Mathematical Processes

How much does the water in the classroom aquarium weigh? Explain.

YOUR TURN

3. An aquarium holds 33.75 gallons of water. It has a length of 2 feet and a height of 1.5 feet. What is the width of the aquarium? _____

Guided Practice

1. Use an equation to find the width of the rectangular prism.
   (Explore Activity Example 1)

   _____

2. One clay brick weighs 5.76 pounds. The brick is 8 inches long and $2\frac{1}{4}$ inches wide. If the clay weighs 0.08 pounds per cubic inch, what is the volume of the brick? Find the height of the brick. (Example 2)

   _____

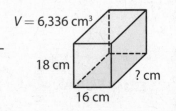

$V = 6{,}336 \text{ cm}^3$

18 cm

16 cm

? cm

15.3 Independent Practice

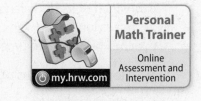
Personal Math Trainer

my.hrw.com

Online Assessment and Intervention

3. Jala has an aquarium in the shape of a rectangular prism with the dimensions shown. What is the height of the aquarium?

Height = _____

4. The area of the base of a rectangular juice box is $4\frac{1}{2}$ square inches. If the volume of the box is 18 cubic inches, how tall is the box?

Height = _____

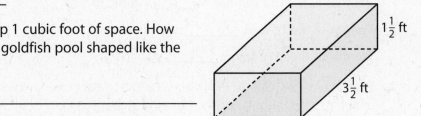

$V = 3{,}758.75$ cubic inches

?

12.5 in.

24.25 in.

5. A box of cereal is shaped like a rectangular prism. The box is 20 centimeters long and 30 centimeters high. Its volume is 3,600 cubic centimeters. Find the width of the box.

Width = _____

6. About 7.5 gallons of water fill up 1 cubic foot of space. How many gallons of water will fill a goldfish pool shaped like the prism shown?

_____

7. Physical Science A small bar of gold measures 40 mm by 25 mm by 2 mm. One cubic millimeter of gold weighs about 0.0005 ounce. Find the volume in cubic millimeters and the weight in ounces of this small bar of gold.

_____

_____

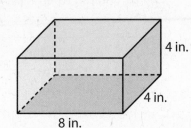

$1\frac{1}{2}$ ft

$3\frac{1}{2}$ ft

3 ft

8. History A typical stone on the lowest level of the Great Pyramid in Egypt was a rectangular prism 5 feet long by 5 feet high by 6 feet deep and weighed 15 tons. What was the volume of the average stone? How much did one cubic foot of this stone weigh?

_____

_____

9. Hank has cards that are 8 inches by 4 inches. A stack of these cards fits inside the box shown and uses up 32 cubic inches of volume. How tall is the stack of cards? What percent of the box's volume is taken up by the cards?

_____

4 in.

4 in.

8 in.

10. A freshwater fish is healthiest when there is at least 1 gallon of water for every inch of its body length. Roshel wants to put a goldfish that is about $2\frac{1}{2}$ inches long in her tank. Roshel's tank is 7 inches long, 5 inches wide, and 7 inches high. The volume of 1 gallon of water is about 231 cubic inches.

    a. How many gallons of water would Roshel need for the fish? _____

    b. What is the volume of Roshel's tank? _____

    c. Is her fish tank large enough for the fish? Explain. _____

    _____

Work Area

11. **Multistep** Larry has a clay brick that is 7 inches long, 3.5 inches wide, and 1.75 inches thick, the same size as the gold stored in Fort Knox in the form of gold bars. Find the volume of this brick. If the weight of the clay in the brick is 0.1 pound per cubic inch and the weight of the gold is 0.7 pound per cubic inch, find the weight of the brick and the gold bar. Round all answers the nearest tenth.

Volume of the brick or bar = _____ cubic inches

Weight of the brick = _____ pounds

Weight of the gold bar = _____ pounds

12. **Represent Real-World Problems** Luisa's toaster oven, which is in the shape of a rectangular prism, has a base that is 55 cm long by 40 cm wide. It is 30 cm high. Luisa wants to buy a different oven with the same volume but a smaller length, so it will fit better on her kitchen counter. What is a possible set of dimensions for this different oven?

_____

_____

_____

13. **Multiple Representations** Use the formula $V = Bh$ to write a different version of this formula that you could use to find the area of the base B of a rectangular prism if you know the height h and the volume V. Explain what you did to find this equation.

_____

_____

14. **Communicate Mathematical Ideas** The volume of a cube is 27 cubic inches. What is the length of an edge? Explain.

_____

Ready to Go On?

Personal Math Trainer
Online Assessment and Intervention
⏻ my.hrw.com

15.1 Nets and Surface Area

A square pyramid is shown sitting on its base.

1. Draw the net of the pyramid.

2. The surface area of the pyramid

is _____ square centimeters.

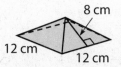

15.2 Volume of Rectangular Prisms

Find the volume of each rectangular prism.

3.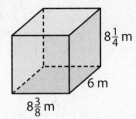

$8\frac{1}{4}$ m

6 m

$8\frac{3}{8}$ m

$V =$ _____ cubic meters

4.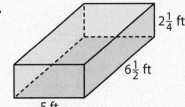

$2\frac{1}{4}$ ft

$6\frac{1}{2}$ ft

5 ft

$V =$ _____ cubic feet

15.3 Solving Volume Equations

Find the volume of each rectangular prism.

5. The volume inside a rectangular storage room is 2,025 cubic feet. The room is 9 feet high. Find the area of the floor. _____

6. An aquarium holds 11.25 cubic feet of water, and is 2.5 feet long and 1.5 feet wide. What is its depth? _____

? ESSENTIAL QUESTION

7. How can a model help you to solve surface area and volume problems?

_____

_____

_____

Selected Response

1. Indira is wrapping the box below. How much wrapping paper does she need?

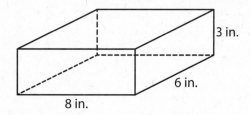

3 in.

6 in.

8 in.

  Ⓐ 34 in.²   Ⓒ 144 in.²

  Ⓑ 90 in.²   Ⓓ 180 in.²

2. Colin has an ice cube tray with 12 identical compartments. Each compartment is a prism that is 4 centimeters long, 3 centimeters wide, and 3 centimeters high. Given that 1 cubic centimeter holds 1 milliliter of water, how many milliliters of water can the tray hold?

  Ⓐ 36 mL   Ⓒ 432 mL

  Ⓑ 66 mL   Ⓓ 792 mL

3. A store manager set up a cardboard display to advertise a new brand of perfume. The display is a square pyramid whose base is 18 inches on each side. The height of each triangular face of the pyramid is 12 inches. How much cardboard was used to make the display?

  Ⓐ 516 in²   Ⓒ 756 in²

  Ⓑ 612 in²   Ⓓ 1,080 in²

4. Which expression is equivalent to $24 + 32$?

  Ⓐ $8 \times (3 + 4)$

  Ⓑ $8 \times (3 + 32)$

  Ⓒ $6 \times (4 + 32)$

  Ⓓ $6 \times (4 + 6)$

5. A bathtub in the shape of a rectangular prism is 5 feet long, $3\frac{1}{2}$ feet wide, and $4\frac{1}{4}$ feet high. How much water could the tub hold?

  Ⓐ $14\frac{7}{8}$ ft³   Ⓒ $74\frac{3}{8}$ ft³

  Ⓑ $25\frac{1}{2}$ ft³   Ⓓ $87\frac{1}{2}$ ft³

6. The point $(-1.5, 2)$ is reflected across the y-axis, What are the coordinates of the point after the reflection?

  Ⓐ $(-1.5, -2)$ Ⓒ $(2, -1.5)$

  Ⓑ $(1.5, 2)$ Ⓓ $(2, 1.5)$

Mini-Task

7. An cardboard box is open at one end and is shaped like a square prism missing one of its square bases. The volume of the prism is 810 cubic inches, and its height is 10 inches.

  a. What is the length of each side of

    the base? _____

  b. Draw a net of the box.

  c. How much cardboard is used for the box?

  _____

Study Guide Review

MODULE 13 · Area and Polygons

Key Vocabulary
parallelogram
(paralelogramo)
rhombus *(rombo)*
trapezoid *(trapecio)*

? ESSENTIAL QUESTION

How can you use area and volume equations to solve real-world problems?

EXAMPLE 1

Find the area of the trapezoid.

$A = \frac{1}{2}(h)(b_1 + b_2)$

$A = \frac{1}{2}(10)(7 + 4)$

$A = 55 \text{ in}^2$

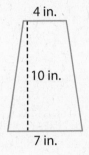

4 in.

10 in.

7 in.

EXAMPLE 2

Find the area of Jorge's backyard.

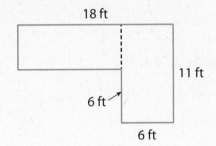

18 ft

11 ft

6 ft

6 ft

Find the area of the first rectangle.

$A = bh$

$A = 12(5)$

$A = 60 \text{ square feet}$

Find the area of the second rectangle.

$A = bh$

$A = 6(11)$

$A = 66 \text{ square feet}$

Total area of yard $= 60 + 66 = 126$ square feet

EXERCISES

Find the area of each figure. (Lessons 13.1, 13.2)

1.

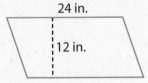

24 in.

12 in.

_____

2.

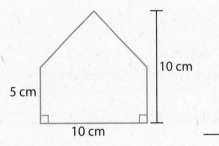

5 cm

10 cm

10 cm

_____

Find the missing measurement. (Lesson 13.3)

3.

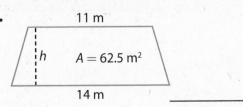

11 m

h $A = 62.5 \text{ m}^2$

14 m

_____

4.

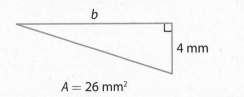

b

4 mm

$A = 26 \text{ mm}^2$

_____

Distance and Area in the Coordinate Plane

Key Vocabulary
polygon (*polígono*)
reflection (*reflexión*)
vertex, vertices (*vértice, vértices*)

? ESSENTIAL QUESTION

What steps might you take to solve a polygon problem given the coordinates of its vertices?

EXAMPLE 1

Find the distance between points *A* and *B* on the coordinate plane.

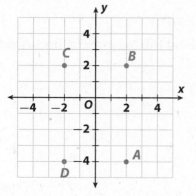

Find the distance between point *A* and the *x*-axis.

The *y*-coordinate is −4. The absolute value represents the distance.

$|-4| = 4$ The distance is 4 units.

Find the distance between point *B* and the *x*-axis.

The *y*-coordinate is 2. The distance is 2 units.

Add the two distances to find the distance between the two points.

$4 + 2 = 6$ The distance between points *A* and *B* is 6 units.

EXAMPLE 2

Find the area of the rectangle whose vertices are the points on the coordinate plane in Example 1.

Use the distance between points *A* and *B* in Example 1 as the height.

height = 6 units

Find the distance between points *A* and *D* and use it as the base.

Distance from *A* to $D = |-2| + 2 = 2 + 2 = 4$

base = 4 units

Find the area.

$A = bh = 4 \cdot 6 = 24$ square units

EXERCISES

Find the distance between the two points.

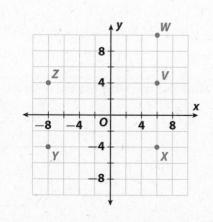

1. *Z* and *Y* _____

2. *X* and *Y* _____

3. *W* and *X* _____

4. Find the area of rectangle *XYZV*. _____

Surface Area and Volume of Solids

Key Vocabulary

net (plantilla)

pyramid (pirámide)

surface area (área total)

? ESSENTIAL QUESTION

How can a model help you solve surface area and volume problems?

EXAMPLE 1

Draw a net and find the surface area of the pyramid.

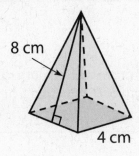

8 cm

4 cm

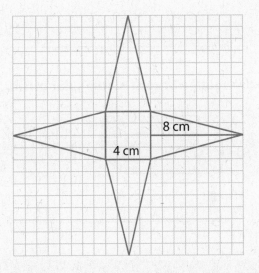

8 cm

4 cm

Find the area of the square base.

$A = bh$

$A = 4 \cdot 4$

$A = 16 \text{ cm}^2$

Find the area of one triangle and multiply by four.

$A = \frac{1}{2}bh$

$A = \frac{1}{2}(4 \cdot 8)$

$A = 16 \text{ cm}^2$

The area of the 4 triangles is $4 \cdot 16 = 64 \text{ cm}^2$.

The total surface area of the pyramid is $16 \text{ cm}^2 + 64 \text{ cm}^2 = 80 \text{ cm}^2$.

EXAMPLE 2

A cubic centimeter of gold weighs approximately 19.32 grams. Find the weight of a brick of gold that has a height of 6 centimeters, width of 3 centimeters, and length of 8 centimeters.

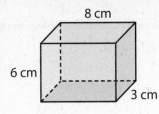

8 cm

6 cm

3 cm

$V = lwh$

$V = 8\,(3)\,(6)$

$V = 144 \text{ cm}^3$

The weight of the gold is 144×19.32 grams, which is 2,782.08 grams.

EXERCISES

Draw a net to find the surface area of each solid shape. (Lesson 15.1)

1.

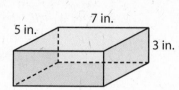

7 in.
5 in.
3 in.

_____

2.

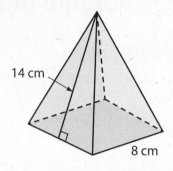

14 cm
8 cm

_____

Find the volume of each rectangular prism. (Lesson 15.2)

3.

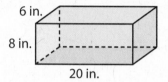

6 in.
8 in.
20 in.

_____

4. A rectangular prism with a width of 7 units, a length of 8 units, and a height of 2 units _____

Unit 6 Performance Tasks

1. | **CAREERS IN MATH** | Theater Set Construction Ahmed and Karina are building scenery of the Egyptian pyramids out of plywood for a community play. The pyramids are represented by triangles on a rectangular base. The diagram shows the measurements of the piece of scenery.

1 ft
1.5 ft
0.75 ft
1.5 ft
2 ft
1 ft
0.75 ft
5 ft

a. How many square feet of plywood is in the scenery? Show your work.

_____

_____

b. The pyramids (the triangles) will be painted gray, and the base (the rectangle) will be painted black. How much of each paint color will they use, if one quart covers 45 square feet? Only one side of the model needs to be painted, but two coats of paint will be needed. Show your work. Round to the nearest hundredth of a square foot.

_____

_____

_____

Assessment Readiness

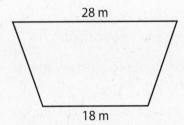

Personal
Math Trainer

Online
Assessment and
Intervention

my.hrw.com

Selected Response

1. Jessie has a piece of cardboard that is 8.5 inches by 11 inches. She makes a picture frame with the cardboard by cutting out a 4 inch by 4 inch square from the center of the cardboard. What is the area of the frame?

Ⓐ 16 in²   Ⓒ 93.5 in²

Ⓑ 77.5 in²   Ⓓ 118.5 in²

2. Jermaine is ordering a piece of glass in the shape of a trapezoid to create a patio table top. Each square foot of glass costs $25. The trapezoid has base lengths of 5 feet and 3 feet and a height of 4 feet. What is the cost of the glass?

Ⓐ $400   Ⓒ $800

Ⓑ $437.50   Ⓓ $1,500

3. What is the area of a trapezoid that has bases measuring 19 centimeters and 23 centimeters, and a height of 14 centimeters?

Ⓐ 105 square centimeters

Ⓑ 266 square centimeters

Ⓒ 294 square centimeters

Ⓓ 322 square centimeters

4. What is the area of the triangle shown below?

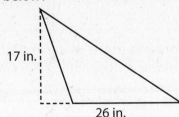

17 in.

26 in.

Ⓐ 110.5 square inches

Ⓑ 221 square inches

Ⓒ 442 square inches

Ⓓ 884 square inches

5. The trapezoid below has an area of 475 square meters.

28 m

18 m

Which equation could you solve to find the height of the trapezoid?

Ⓐ $23h = 475$

Ⓑ $252h = 475$

Ⓒ $46h = 475$

Ⓓ $504h = 475$

6. A rectangular prism has a volume of 1,500 cubic centimeters. It has a length of 34 centimeters and a width of 22 centimeters. Which equation could be solved to find the height of the rectangular prism?

Ⓐ $374h = 1,500$

Ⓑ $28h = 1,500$

Ⓒ $748h = 1,500$

Ⓓ $56h = 1,500$

7. Which expression represents the sum of 59 and x?

Ⓐ $59 + x$

Ⓑ $59 \div x$

Ⓒ $59x$

Ⓓ $59 - x$

8. Which number has more than two factors?

Ⓐ 19

Ⓑ 23

Ⓒ 25

Ⓓ 29

9. Which of the following statements about rational numbers is **not** correct?

Ⓐ All whole numbers are also rational numbers.

Ⓑ All integers are also rational numbers.

Ⓒ All rational numbers can be written in the form $\frac{a}{b}$.

Ⓓ Rational numbers cannot be negative.

Mini-Tasks

10. Lisa bought a tank for her hermit crab. The tank can hold 1,331 cubic inches of water and includes a top. The base of the aquarium is a square. The height of the aquarium is 11 inches.

a. What is the length of each side of the base of the tank?

_____

b. What shape is Lisa's tank?

_____

c. Draw a net of the tank.

d. What is the surface area of the tank?

_____

11. Chuck is making a map of his neighborhood. Each grid unit represents one city block. He uses the following coordinates, with north being the direction of the positive *y*-axis.

Library: $(-5, 5)$
Chuck's house: $(-5, -3)$
City Hall: $(3, -3)$

a. Plot each point on the coordinate grid below.

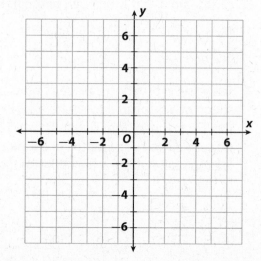

b. How far does Chuck live from the library and from City Hall?

_____

c. Chuck decided to add the post office to his map. The post office is 6 blocks east of the library. What are the coordinates of the post office? Plot the post office on the coordinate grid.

_____

d. If you connect the points on the map, what shape do you make?

_____

e. What is the area of the shape in **d**? Use square blocks as the unit.

_____

Measurement and Data

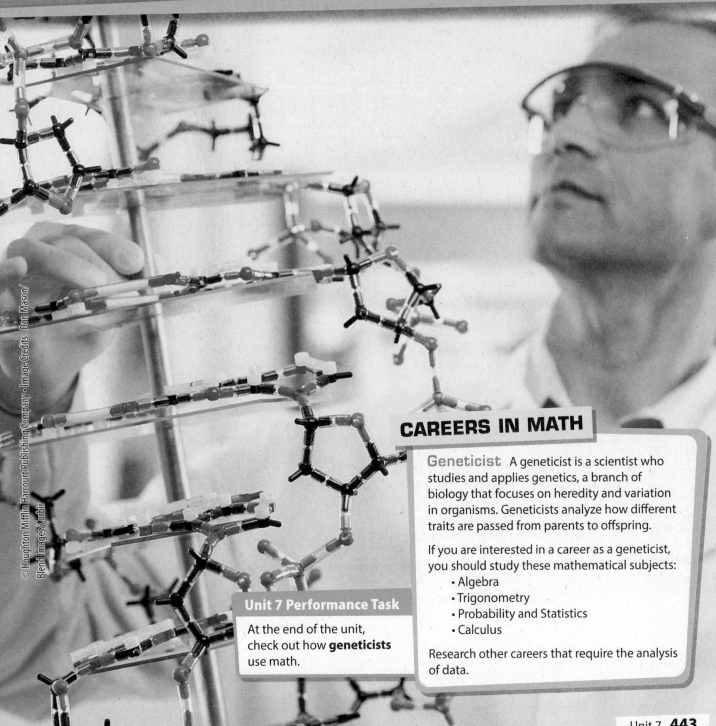

CAREERS IN MATH

Geneticist A geneticist is a scientist who studies and applies genetics, a branch of biology that focuses on heredity and variation in organisms. Geneticists analyze how different traits are passed from parents to offspring.

If you are interested in a career as a geneticist, you should study these mathematical subjects:
- Algebra
- Trigonometry
- Probability and Statistics
- Calculus

Research other careers that require the analysis of data.

Unit 7 Performance Task

At the end of the unit, check out how **geneticists** use math.

© Houghton Mifflin Harcourt Publishing Company • Image Credits: Don Mason/Blend Images/Corbis

Vocabulary Preview

Use the puzzle to preview key vocabulary from this unit. Unscramble the circled letters to answer the riddle at the bottom of the page.

1. **OBX LOTP**

2. **TOD TOLP**

3. **HOSTIARMG**

4. **NIADEM**

5. **PEPRU LAETURQI**

6. **NAME LATESBOL ANITVODIE**

1. A display that shows how the values in a data set are distributed. (Lesson 16.3)
2. A display in which each piece of data is represented by a dot above the number line. (Lesson 16.4)
3. A type of bar graph whose bars represent frequencies of numerical data within intervals. (Lesson 16.5)
4. The middle value of an ordered data set. (Lesson 16.1)
5. The median of the upper half of the data in a box plot. (Lesson 16.3)
6. The mean distance between each data value and the mean of the data set. (Lesson 16.2)

Q: What is a math teacher's favorite dessert?

A: __ __ __ __ __ __ __ __ __ __
__ __ __ __ __ __ __ __ __!

Displaying, Analyzing, and Summarizing Data

? ESSENTIAL QUESTION

How can you solve real-world problems by displaying, analyzing, and summarizing data?

Real-World Video

Biologists collect data on different animals. They can describe the data using measures of center or spread, and by displaying the data in plots or graphs, they may see trends related to the animal population.

⊙ my.hrw.com

GO DIGITAL

my.hrw.com

my.hrw.com

Go digital with your write-in student edition, accessible on any device.

Math On the Spot

Scan with your smart phone to jump directly to the online edition, video tutor, and more.

Animated Math

Interactively explore key concepts to see how math works.

Personal Math Trainer

Get immediate feedback and help as you work through practice sets.

Reading Start-Up

© Houghton Mifflin Harcourt Publishing Company

Vocabulary

Review Words

average *(promedio)*
data *(datos)*
survey *(encuesta)*

Preview Words

box plot *(diagrama de caja)*
categorical data *(datos categóricos)*
dot plot *(diagrama de puntos)*
histogram *(histograma)*
interquartile range *(rango entre cuartiles)*
lower quartile *(cuartil inferior)*
✔ mean *(media)*
mean absolute deviation (MAD) *(desviación absoluta media, (DAM))*
✔ median *(mediana)*
measure of center *(medida central)*
measure of spread *(medida de dispersión)*
✔ mode *(moda)*
range *(rango)*
statistical question *(pregunta estadística)*
upper quartile *(cuartil superior)*

Visualize Vocabulary

Use the review words to complete the chart.

Introduction to Statistics		
Definition	**Example**	**Review word**
A group of facts	The grades of all of the students in a school	
A tool used to gather information from individuals	A questionnaire given to all students to find the number of hours each student spends studying in 1 week	
A value that summarizes a set of unequal values, found by addition and division	Results of the survey show that students typically spend 5 hours a week studying	

Understand Vocabulary

Complete the sentences using the preview words.

1. The average of a data set is the _____.

2. The _____ is the middle value of a data set.

3. The number or category that occurs most frequently in a data set is

    the _____.

Active Reading

Layered Book Before beginning the module, create a layered book to help you learn the concepts in this module. Label each flap with lesson titles from this module. As you study each lesson, write important ideas, such as vocabulary and formulas under the appropriate flap. Refer to your finished layered book as you work on exercises from this module.

Are YOU Ready?

Complete these exercises to review skills you will need for this module.

Remainders

EXAMPLE

$$\begin{array}{r} 7.25 \\ 12\overline{)87.00} \\ 84 \\ \hline 30 \\ -24 \\ \hline 60 \\ -60 \\ \hline 0 \end{array}$$

Write a decimal point and a zero in the dividend.

Place a decimal point in the quotient.

Add more zeros to the dividend if necessary.

Find the quotient. Write the remainder as a decimal.

1. $15\overline{)42}$ _____ **2.** $75\overline{)93}$ _____ **3.** $52\overline{)91}$ _____ **4.** $24\overline{)57}$ _____

Read Bar Graphs

EXAMPLE   How many goals did Alec score?

The first bar shows how many goals Alec scored.

The bar extends to a height of 5.

Alec scored 5 goals.

5. How many goals did Dion score? _____

6. Which two players together scored the same number of goals as Jeff? _____

7. How many fewer goals than Cesar did Alec score? _____

Are YOU Ready? *(cont'd)*

Complete these exercises to review skills you will need for this module.

Remainders

8. There are 16 ounces in a pound. Christine says that a 50-ounce bag of rice weighs exactly 3 pounds. Is she correct? Use long division to show why or why not. If she is not correct, use a decimal to write the amount of rice in pounds.

Read Bar Graphs

9. The bar graph shows the number of cases of water a grocer ordered each week. Each case contains 24 bottles of water.

   a. How many bottles of water were ordered in Week 1?

   b. How many more bottles of water were ordered in Week 3 than in the previous week? Show your work.

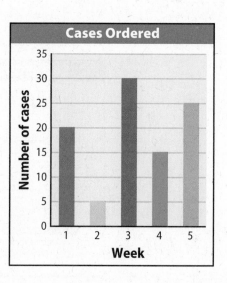

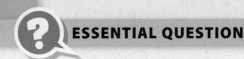

LESSON 16.1 Measures of Center

6.7.16.1

Students will use measures of center to describe a data set.

? ESSENTIAL QUESTION

How can you use measures of center to describe a data set?

EXPLORE ACTIVITY 1

Finding the Mean

A **measure of center** is a single number used to describe a set of numeric data. A measure of center describes a typical value from the data set.

One measure of center is the *mean*. The **mean**, or average, of a data set is the sum of the data values divided by the number of data values in the set.

Tami surveyed five of her friends to find out how many brothers and sisters they have. Her results are shown in the table.

Number of Siblings				
Amy	Ben	Cal	Don	Eva
2	3	1	1	3

A Model each person's response as a group of counters.

B Now rearrange the counters so that each group has the same number of counters.

Each group now has _____ counter(s). This value is the mean. This model demonstrates how the mean "evens out" the data values.

C Use numbers to calculate the mean.

The sum of the data values is $2 + 3 + \boxed{} + \boxed{} + \boxed{} = \boxed{}$.

How many data values are in the set? _____

$$\text{Mean} = \frac{\text{sum of data values}}{\text{number of data values}} = \frac{\boxed{}}{\boxed{}} = \boxed{}$$

Math Talk

Mathematical Processes

Suppose you have a data set in which all of the values are 2. What is the mean?

Reflect

1. Can the mean be greater than the greatest value in a data set? Why or why not?

_____

_____

_____

_____

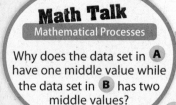

Math On the Spot

⊙ my.hrw.com

Finding the Median

Another measure of center is the *median*. The **median** represents the middle value of an ordered data set.

EXAMPLE 1 Real World

A A coach records the distances that some cross-country team members ran last week. Find the median.

Write the data values in order from least to greatest.

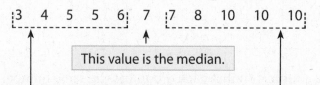

The median is 7.

Math Talk

Mathematical Processes

Why does the data set in **A** have one middle value while the data set in **B** has two middle values?

Distances Run	
Cara	3 mi
Rob	5 mi
Maria	7 mi
Olivia	10 mi
Paul	10 mi
Chris	4 mi
Amir	7 mi
Iris	5 mi
Alex	8 mi
Tara	10 mi
Ned	6 mi

B Find the median of these test scores: 87, 90, 77, 83, 99, 94, 93, 90, 85, 83.

Write the data values in order from least to greatest.

77   83   83   85   ⌐87   90⌐   90   93   94   99

This data set has two middle values: 87 and 90.

The median is the average of these two values:

$$\text{Median} = \frac{87 + 90}{2} = 88.5$$

The median is 88.5.

Reflect

2. **What If?** Which units are used for the data in ? If the coach had recorded some distances in kilometers and some in miles, can you still find the median of the data? Explain.

_____

_____

YOUR TURN

3. Charlotte recorded the number of minutes she spent exercising in the past ten days: 12, 4, 5, 6, 8, 7, 9, 8, 2, 1. Find the median of the data.

_____

Personal Math Trainer

Online Assessment and Intervention

⏻ my.hrw.com

EXPLORE ACTIVITY 2 Real World

Comparing the Mean and the Median

The mean and median of a data set may be equal, very close to each other, or very different from each other. For data sets where the mean and median differ greatly, one likely describes the data set better than the other.

The monthly earnings of several teenagers are $200, $320, $275, $250, $750, $350, and $310.

A Find the mean.

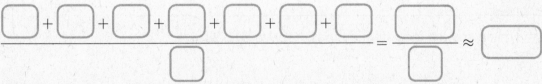

B Write the data values in order from least to greatest and find the median.

_____

C The mean and the median differ by about $_____. Why?

_____

_____

D Which measure of center better describes the typical monthly earnings for this group of teenagers—the mean or the median? Explain.

_____

_____

Reflect

4. **Communicate Mathematical Ideas** Luka's final exam scores for this semester are 70, 72, 99, 72, and 69. Find the mean and median. Which is a better description of Luka's typical exam score? Explain your thinking.

_____

_____

Guided Practice

1. Spencer surveyed five of his friends to find out how many pets they have. His results are shown in the table. What is the mean number of pets? (Explore Activity 1)

Number of Pets				
Lara	**Cody**	**Sam**	**Ella**	**Maria**
3	5	2	4	1

$$\text{Mean} = \frac{\text{sum of data values}}{\text{number of data values}} = \frac{\boxed{}}{\boxed{}} = \boxed{}$$

The mean number of pets is _____

2. The following are the weights, in pounds, of some dogs at a kennel: 36, 45, 29, 39, 51, 49. (Example 1)

   a. Find the median. _____

   b. Suppose one of the weights were given in kilograms. Can you still find the median? Explain.

   _____

3. a. Find the mean and the median of this data set: 9, 6, 5, 3, 28, 6, 4, 7. (Explore Activity 2)

   _____

   b. Which better describes the data set, the mean or the median? Explain.

   _____

   _____

? ESSENTIAL QUESTION CHECK-IN

4. How can you use measures of center to describe a data set?

   _____

   _____

16.1 Independent Practice

Personal Math Trainer

Online Assessment and Intervention

my.hrw.com

Several students in Ashton's class were randomly selected and asked how many text messages they sent yesterday. Their answers were 1, 0, 10, 7, 13, 2, 9, 15, 0, 3.

5. How many students were asked? How do you know?

_____

_____

_____

6. Find the mean and the median for these data.

Mean = _____   Median = _____

The points scored by a basketball team in its last 6 games are shown. Use these data for 7 and 8.

Points Scored					
73	77	85	84	37	115

7. Find the mean score and the median score.

Mean = _____   Median = _____

8. Which measure better describes the typical number of points scored? Explain.

_____

_____

_____

Some people were asked how long it takes them to commute to work. Use the data for 9–11.

9. What units are used for the data? What should you do before finding the mean and median number of minutes?

16 min	5 min
7 min	8 min
14 min	12 min
0.5 hr	1 hr

_____

10. Find the mean and median number of minutes.

Mean = _____   Median = _____

11. Which measure do you think is more typical of the data?

_____

_____

_____

Work Area

12. Critique Reasoning For two weeks, the school librarian recorded the number of library books returned each morning. The data are shown in the dot plot. The librarian found the mean number of books returned each morning.

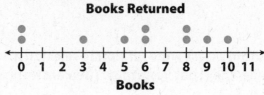

Books Returned

Books

$$\frac{8 + 6 + 10 + 5 + 9 + 8 + 3 + 6}{8} = \frac{55}{8} \approx 6.9$$

Is this the correct mean of this data set? If not, explain and correct the answer.

_____

_____

13. Critical Thinking Lauren's scores on her math tests are 93, 91, 98, 100, 95, 92, and 96. What score could Lauren get on her next math test so that the mean and median remain the same? Explain your answer.

_____

_____

_____

14. Persevere in Problem Solving Yuko wants to take a job selling cars. Since she will get a commission for every car she sells, she finds out the sale price of the last four cars sold at each company.

Company A: $16,000; $20,000; $25,000; $35,000;

Company B: $21,000, $23,000, $36,000, $48,000

a. Find the mean selling price at each company.

_____

b. Find the median selling price at each company.

_____

c. Communicate Mathematical Ideas At either company, Yuko will get paid a commission of 20% of the sale price of each car she sells. Based on the data, where do you recommend she take a job? Why?

_____

_____

_____

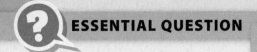

LESSON 16.2 Mean Absolute Deviation

6.7.16.2

Students will determine and use the mean absolute deviation of a set of data points.

? ESSENTIAL QUESTION

How can you determine and use the mean absolute deviation of a set of data points?

EXPLORE ACTIVITY

Understanding Mean Absolute Deviation

A **measure of variability** is a single number used to describe the spread of a data set. It can also be called a measure of spread. One measure of variability is the **mean absolute deviation (MAD)**, which is the mean of the distances between the data values and the mean of the data set.

The data represent the height, in feet, of various buildings. Find the mean absolute deviation for each data set.

A 60, 58, 54, 56, 63, 65, 62, 59, 56, 58

Calculate the mean. Round to the nearest whole number.

Complete the table.

Height (ft)	60	58	54	56	63	65	62	59	56	58
Distance from mean										

Calculate the MAD by finding the mean of the values in the second row of the table. Round to the nearest whole number.

B 46, 47, 56, 48, 46, 52, 57, 52, 45

Find the mean. Round to the nearest whole number.

Complete the table.

Height (ft)	46	47	56	48	46	52	57	52	45
Distance from mean									

Math Talk
Mathematical Processes
What is the difference between a measure of center and a measure of variability?

Calculate the MAD. Round to the nearest whole number.

Reflect

1. **Analyze Relationships** Compare the MADs. How do the MADs describe the distribution of the heights in each group?

_____

_____

Math On the Spot
my.hrw.com

Using Mean Absolute Deviation

The mean absolute deviation can be used to answer statistical questions in the real world. Many of these questions may have implications for the operation of various businesses.

EXAMPLE 1 Real World

A chicken farmer wants her chickens to all have about the same weight. She is trying two types of feed to see which type produces the best results. All the chickens in Pen A are fed Premium Growth feed, and all the chickens in Pen B are fed Maximum Growth feed. The farmer records the weights of the chickens in each pen in the tables below. Which chicken feed produces less variability in weight?

Pen A: Premium Growth Weights (lb)									
5.8	6.1	5.5	6.6	7.3	5.9	6.3	5.7	6.8	7.1

Pen B: Maximum Growth Weights (lb)									
7.7	7.4	5.4	7.8	6.1	5.2	7.5	7.9	6.3	5.6

STEP 1 Find the mean weight of the chickens in each pen. Round your answers to the nearest tenth.

Pen A: $\dfrac{5.8 + 6.1 + 5.5 + 6.6 + 7.3 + 5.9 + 6.3 + 5.7 + 6.8 + 7.1}{10} \approx 6.3$

Pen B: $\dfrac{7.7 + 7.4 + 5.4 + 7.8 + 6.1 + 5.2 + 7.5 + 7.9 + 6.3 + 5.6}{10} \approx 6.7$

Find the distance from the mean for each of the weights.

The distances from the mean for Pen A are the distance of each weight from 6.3 lb.

Pen A: Premium Growth										
Weight (lb)	5.8	6.1	5.5	6.6	7.3	5.9	6.3	5.7	6.8	7.1
Distance from mean	0.5	0.2	0.8	0.3	1.0	0.4	0	0.6	0.5	0.8

The distances from the mean for Pen B are the distance of each weight from 6.7 lb.

Pen B: Maximum Growth										
Weight (lb)	7.7	7.4	5.4	7.8	6.1	5.2	7.5	7.9	6.3	5.6
Distance from mean	1.0	0.7	1.3	1.1	0.6	1.5	0.8	1.2	0.4	1.1

STEP 3 Calculate the MAD for the chickens in each pen. Round your answers to the nearest tenth.

Pen A: $\dfrac{0.5 + 0.2 + 0.8 + 0.3 + 1.0 + 0.4 + 0 + 0.6 + 0.5 + 0.8}{10} \approx 0.5$ lb

Pen B: $\dfrac{1.0 + 0.7 + 1.3 + 1.1 + 0.6 + 1.5 + 0.8 + 1.2 + 0.4 + 1.1}{10} \approx 1.0$ lb

Since Pen A's MAD is less, Premium Growth feed produces less variability in weight.

Math Talk

Mathematical Processes

Will a smaller mean always signal less variability?

YOUR TURN

2. Two waiters at a cafe each served 10 large fruit smoothies. The amount in each large smoothie is shown below. Which waiter's smoothies showed less variability?

Amounts in Waiter A's Large Smoothies (oz)									
19.1	20.1	20.9	19.6	20.9	19.5	19.2	19.4	20.3	20.9

Amounts in Waiter B's Large Smoothies (oz)									
20.1	19.6	20.0	20.5	19.8	20.0	20.1	19.7	19.9	20.4

Animated Math

my.hrw.com

Personal Math Trainer

Online Assessment and Intervention

my.hrw.com

Using a Spreadsheet to Find MAD

Spreadsheets can be used to find the mean absolute deviation of a data set.

EXAMPLE 2

A paper mill is testing two paper-cutting machines. Both are set to produce pieces of paper with a width of 8.5 inches. The actual widths of 8 pieces of paper cut by each machine are shown. Use a spreadsheet to determine which machine has less variability and, thus, does a better job.

Widths of Pieces of Paper Cut by Machine A (in.)							
8.502	8.508	8.499	8.501	8.492	8.511	8.505	8.491

Widths of Pieces of Paper Cut by Machine B (in.)							
8.503	8.501	8.498	8.499	8.498	8.504	8.496	8.502

STEP 1 Enter the data values for Machine A into row 1 of a spreadsheet, using cells A to H.

	A	B	C	D	E	F	G	H
1	8.502	8.508	8.499	8.501	8.492	8.511	8.505	8.491
2								
3								

STEP 2 Enter "mean = " into cell A2 and the formula =AVERAGE(A1:H1) into cell B2.

	A	B	C	D	E	F	G	H
1	8.502	8.508	8.499	8.501	8.492	8.511	8.505	8.491
2	mean =	8.501125						
3								

STEP 3 Enter "MAD = " into cell A3 and the formula =AVEDEV(A1:H1) into cell B3.

	A	B	C	D	E	F	G	H
1	8.502	8.508	8.499	8.501	8.492	8.511	8.505	8.491
2	mean =	8.501125						
3	MAD =	0.005375						

The MAD for Machine A is about 0.0054 in.

STEP 4 Repeat Steps 1–3 with the data values for Machine B.

	A	B	C	D	E	F	G	H
1	8.503	8.501	8.498	8.499	8.498	8.504	8.496	8.502
2	mean =	8.500125						
3	MAD =	0.002375						

The MAD for Machine B is about 0.0024 in.

Machine B has less variability, so it does a better job.

My Notes

3. Two aspirin-making devices are set to make tablets containing 0.35 gram of aspirin. The actual amounts in 8 tablets from each device are shown. Use a spreadsheet to determine which device has less variability.

Amounts of Aspirin in Tablets Made by Device A (g)							
0.353	0.351	0.350	0.352	0.349	0.348	0.350	0.346

Amounts of Aspirin in Tablets Made by Device B (g)							
0.349	0.341	0.347	0.358	0.359	0.354	0.339	0.343

Guided Practice

1. A bus route takes about 45 minutes. The company's goal is a MAD of less than 0.5 minute. One driver's times for 9 runs of the route are shown. Did the bus driver meet the goal? (Explore Activity and Example 1)

Times to Complete Bus Route (min)								
44.2	44.9	46.1	45.8	44.7	45.2	45.1	45.3	44.6

a. Calculate the mean of the bus times. _____

b. Calculate the MAD to the nearest tenth. _____

The bus driver **did / did not** meet the company's goal.

2. Below are a different driver's times on the same route. Find the mean and the MAD using a spreadsheet. Enter the data values into row 1 using cells A to I. Enter "mean =" into cell A2 and "MAD =" into cell A3. (Example 2)

Times to Complete Bus Route (min)								
44.4	43.8	45.6	45.9	44.1	45.6	44.0	44.9	45.8

The mean is _____ minutes, and the MAD is _____ minutes.

This time, the bus driver **did / did not** meet the company's goal.

ESSENTIAL QUESTION CHECK-IN

3. What is the mean absolute deviation and what does it tell you about data sets?

_____

_____

16.2 Independent Practice

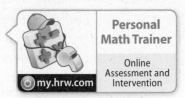

Personal
Math Trainer

Online
Assessment and
Intervention

my.hrw.com

Frank wants to know how many people live in each household in his town. He conducts a random survey of 10 people and asks how many people live in their household. His results are shown in the table.

Number of People per Household									
1	6	2	4	4	3	5	5	2	8

4. Calculate the mean number of people per household. _____

5. Calculate the MAD of the number of people per household. _____

6. What conclusions can you draw about the "typical" number of people in each household? Explain.

_____

_____

_____

_____

Teachers are being trained to standardize the scores they give to students' essays. The same essay was scored by 10 different teachers at the beginning and at the end of their training. The results are shown in the tables.

Scores for Essay at Beginning of Teachers' Training									
76	81	85	79	89	86	84	80	88	79

Scores for Essay at End of Teachers' Training									
79	82	84	81	77	85	82	80	78	83

7. Calculate the MADs for the teachers' scores. Did the teachers make progress in standardizing their scores?

_____

_____

_____

8. What If? What would it mean if the teachers had a MAD of 0?

_____

_____

The annual rainfall for Austin, Texas, and San Antonio, Texas, in each of the years from 2002 to 2011 are shown in the tables. Use the data for 9–11.

Annual Rainfall for Austin, Texas (in.)									
36.00	21.41	52.27	22.33	34.70	46.95	16.07	31.38	37.76	19.68

Annual Rainfall for San Antonio, Texas (in.)									
46.27	28.45	45.32	16.54	21.34	47.25	13.76	30.69	37.39	17.58

9. Use a spreadsheet to find the mean for the two cities' annual rainfalls. In which city does it rain more in a year, on average?

_____

_____

_____

10. Use your spreadsheet to find the MADs. Use the MADs to compare the distribution of annual rainfall for the two cities.

_____

_____

_____

11. **Make a Conjecture** Does the information allow you to predict how the future amounts of rainfall for the two cities will compare? Explain.

_____

_____

_____

12. **Critical Thinking** The life spans of 10 adult mayflies have a mean of 4 hours and a MAD of 2 hours. Fill in the table with possible values for the life spans. You can use the same value more than once.

Life Spans of Ten Mayflies (h)									

Can any one of the 10 mayflies in the group live for 1 full day? Justify your answer.

_____

_____

_____

Work Area

13. Multistep In a spreadsheet, before entering any data values, first enter "mean =" into cell A2 and the formula =AVERAGE(A1:J1) into cell B2. Next, enter "MAD =" into cell A3 and the formula =AVEDEV(A1:J1) into cell B3. You should see #DIV/0! in cell B2 and #NUM! in cell B3 as shown. Now do the following:

	A	B
1		
2	mean =	#DIV/0!
3	MAD =	#NUM!

a. Enter "1" into cell A1. What do you get for the mean and the MAD of the data set? Explain why this makes sense.

_____

_____

_____

b. Enter "2" into cell B1. What do you get for the mean and the MAD of the data set this time? Explain why this makes sense.

_____

_____

_____

c. Enter the numbers 3 through 10 into cells C1 to J1 and watch the mean and the MAD change. Do they increase, decrease, or stay the same? Explain why this makes sense.

_____

_____

_____

14. Make a Conjecture Each of the values in a data set is increased by 10. Does this affect the MAD of the data set? Why or why not?

_____

_____

_____

15. What If? Suppose a data set contains all whole numbers. Would the MAD for the data set also be a whole number? Explain.

_____

_____

_____

16.3 Box Plots

6.7.16.3

Students will use a box plot and measures of spread to describe a data set.

ESSENTIAL QUESTION

How can you use a box plot and measures of spread to describe a data set?

EXPLORE ACTIVITY Real World

Math On the Spot

my.hrw.com

Using a Box Plot

A **box plot** is a display that shows how the values in a data set are distributed, or spread out.

To make a box plot, first find five values for the data set:

- the least value
- the **lower quartile** — the median of the lower half of the data
- the median
- the **upper quartile** — the median of the upper half of the data
- the greatest value

Animated
Math

my.hrw.com

EXAMPLE 1 The heights of several students are shown. Make a box plot for the data.

Students' Heights (in.)					
60	58	54	56	63	61
65	61	62	59	56	58

STEP 1 Order the data and find the needed values.

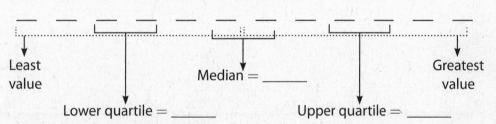

Least value

Median = _____

Greatest value

Lower quartile = _____

Upper quartile = _____

STEP 2 Draw the box plot.

Draw a number line that includes all the data values.

On the number line, draw dots above the least value, the lower quartile, the median, the upper quartile, and the greatest value.

Draw a segment connecting the least value to the lower quartile.

Draw a box whose ends pass through the lower and upper quartiles. Draw a vertical segment through the median.

Draw a segment connecting the upper quartile to the greatest value.

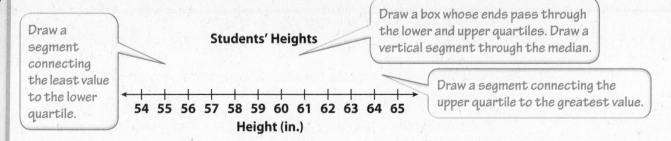

Students' Heights

54 55 56 57 58 59 60 61 62 63 64 65
Height (in.)

Reflect

1. In the example, what percent of the data values are included in the box portion? What percent are included in each of the "whiskers" on the

ends of the box? _____

YOUR TURN

2. The daily high temperatures for some days last month are shown. Make a box plot of the data.

Daily High Temperatures (°F)

85	78	92	88	78	84
80	94	89	75	79	83

Personal Math Trainer

Online Assessment and Intervention

⏻ my.hrw.com

<!-- number line 70 74 78 82 86 90 94 98 -->

70   74   78   82   86   90   94   98

Daily High Temperatures, °F

Math On the Spot

⏻ my.hrw.com

Finding the Interquartile Range

A **measure of spread** is a single number that describes the spread of a data set. One measure of spread is the *interquartile range*. The **interquartile range (IQR)** is the difference of the upper quartile and the lower quartile.

EXAMPLE 2 Real World

The box plots compare the ages of dancers in two different dance troupes.

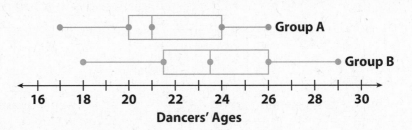

● Group A

● Group B

16   18   20   22   24   26   28   30

Dancers' Ages

A Find the IQR for each set of data.

Group A: IQR = Upper quartile − Lower quartile

$$= \quad 24 \quad - \quad 20 \quad = \quad 4$$

Group B: IQR = Upper quartile − Lower quartile

$$= \quad 26 \quad - \quad 21.5 \quad = \quad 4.5$$

B Compare the IQRs. How do the IQRs describe the distribution of the ages in each group?

The IQR of group B is slightly greater than the IQR of group A. The ages in the middle half of group B are slightly more spread out than in group A.

YOUR TURN

3. The box plots compare the weekly earnings of two groups of salespeople from different clothing stores. Find and compare the IQRs of the box plots.

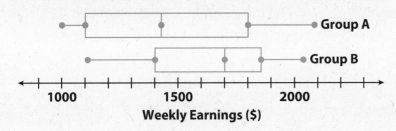

Group A

Group B

Weekly Earnings ($)

_____

_____

_____

Finding the Range

Another measure that describes the spread of a set of data is the *range*. The **range** is the difference of the greatest value and the least value in a set of data.

EXAMPLE 3

The data sets show the ages of the players on two professional baseball teams. Find the range of each set of data.

Team A	36, 27, 28, 31, 39, 39, 28, 29, 24, 29, 30, 31, 29, 29, 28, 29, 31, 29, 32, 25, 37, 21, 26, 33, 29
Team B	25, 25, 26, 30, 27, 24, 29, 21, 27, 28, 26, 27, 25, 31, 22, 23, 29, 28, 25, 26, 28, 30, 23, 28, 29

STEP 1 Arrange the data sets in order from least to greatest.

Team A: 21, 24, 25, 26, 27, 28, 28, 28, 29, 29, 29, 29, 29, 29, 29, 30, 31, 31, 31, 32, 33, 36, 37, 39, 39

Team B: 21, 22, 23, 23, 24, 25, 25, 25, 25, 26, 26, 26, 27, 27, 27, 28, 28, 28, 28, 29, 29, 29, 30, 30, 31

STEP 2 Find the range of the data. Subtract the least value from the greatest value in each data set.

Team A: $39 - 21 = 18$

Team B: $31 - 21 = 10$

The range of ages for team A is 18 years, while the range of ages for team B is 10 years.

Math Talk

Mathematical Processes

How can you find the range of a set of data represented by a box plot?

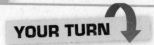

4. Find the range of each set of data. Which city's data has a greater range?

Average Monthly High Temperature (°F)	
Miami, FL	76, 78, 80, 83, 87, 90, 91, 91, 89, 86, 82, 78, 84
Chicago, IL	31, 35, 47, 59, 70, 80, 84, 82, 75, 62, 48, 35, 59

_____

Guided Practice

The RBIs (runs batted in) for 15 players from the 2010 Seattle Mariners are shown. Use this data set for 1–7.

Mariners' RBIs
15 51 35 25 58 33 64
43 33 29 14 13 11 4 10

1. Order the data from least to greatest. (Explore Activity Example 1)

_____

2. Find the median. (Explore Activity Example 1) _____

3. Find the lower quartile. (Explore Activity Example 1) _____

4. Find the upper quartile. (Explore Activity Example 1) _____

5. Make a box plot for the data. (Explore Activity Example 1)

```
←|||||||||||||||||||||||||||||||||||||||||||||||||||||||||||||||||||||||→
  0   5  10  15  20  25  30  35  40  45  50  55  60  65  70  75  80
```

6. Find the IQR. (Example 2) _____

7. Find the range. (Example 3) _____

? ESSENTIAL QUESTION CHECK-IN

8. How is the range of a set of data different from the IQR?

_____

_____

_____

_____

16.3 Independent Practice

For 9–12, use the data set of the heights of several different students.

Students' Heights (in.)
46 47 48 48 56 48
46 52 57 52 45

9. Draw a box plot of the data.

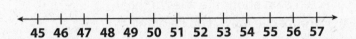

10. How many students are included in the data set? _____

11. What method could have been used to collect the data?

_____

12. **Represent Real-World Problems** What other data could you collect from the students to create a box plot? Provide several examples with units of measurement, if applicable.

_____

For 13–16, use the box plots of the total precipitation for the same group of cities for the months of January and June.

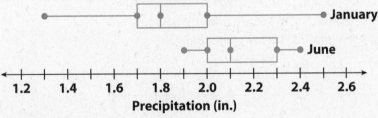

13. Calculate the IQR for each month.

January = _____ inches   June = _____ inches

14. Calculate the range for each month.

January = _____ inches   June = _____ inches

15. Compare the IQRs. What can you conclude about the two data sets?

_____

_____

16. Compare the ranges. What can you conclude about the two data sets?

_____

Work Area

17. **Analyze Relationships** Can two box plots have the same range and IQR and yet represent completely different data? Explain.

_____

_____

_____

_____

18. **Multiple Representations** Matthew collected data about the ages of the actors in two different community theater groups. He drew a box plot for one of the sets of data.

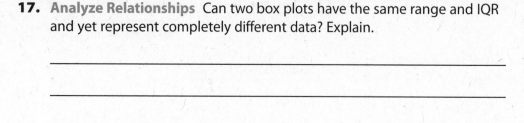

Ages of Actors in the Southside Players

Ages of Actors in the Northside Players	71, 62, 63, 21, 63, 39, 25, 26, 30

a. Find the median, range, and IQR for each set of data.

Theater Group	Median	Range	IQR
Northside Players			
Southside Players			

b. Suppose you were to draw a second box plot for the Northside Players using the same number line as for the Southside Players. Which box plot would be longer overall? Which would have the longest box portion?

_____

_____

_____

c. **Critique Reasoning** Mandy assumes that because nine data values are shown for the Northside Players, nine data values were used to make the box plot for the Southside Players. Explain why this is not necessarily true.

_____

_____

_____

_____

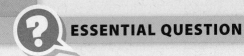

LESSON 16.4 Dot Plots and Data Distribution

6.7.16.4
Students will summarize and display numeric data.

? ESSENTIAL QUESTION

How can you summarize and display numeric data?

EXPLORE ACTIVITY

Variable Data and Statistical Questions

The question "How much does a typical cat weigh?" is an example of a statistical question. A **statistical question** is a question that has many different, or variable, answers.

A Decide whether each of the situations below could yield variable data.

1. Your sister wants to know the typical weight for an adult cat.

   _____

2. You want to know how tall your friend is. _____

3. You want to know how far your house is from school. _____

4. A car owner wants to know how much money people usually pay

   for a new tire. _____

5. How many students were in line for lunch at the cafeteria today

   at 12:30? _____

B For which of the situations in part **A** can you write a statistical question? Write questions for these situations.

_____

_____

Reflect

1. Choose one of the questions you wrote in part **B**. How might you find answers to this question? What units would you use for the answers?

_____

_____

_____

Math On the Spot

⏱ my.hrw.com

Making a Dot Plot

Statistical questions are answered by collecting and analyzing data. One way to understand a set of data is to make a visual display. A **dot plot** is a visual display in which each piece of data is represented by a dot above a number line. A dot plot shows the frequency of each data value.

EXAMPLE 1

A baseball team manager records the number of runs scored by the team in each game for several weeks. Use the data to make a dot plot.

> The team usually scores between 0 and 7 runs in a game, but in one game they scored 11 runs.

1, 3, 1, 7, 2, 0, 11, 2, 2, 3, 1, 3, 4, 2, 2, 4, 5, 2, 6

STEP 1 Make a number line.

Data values range from 0 to 11, so use a scale from 0 to 11.

STEP 2 Draw a dot above the number line for each data value.

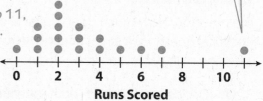

Reflect

2. How many games did the team play during the season? How can you tell from looking at the dot plot?

_____

_____

3. At how many games did the team score 2 runs or fewer? How do you know?

_____

_____

Personal Math Trainer

Online Assessment and Intervention

⏱ my.hrw.com

YOUR TURN

4. A different baseball team scores the following numbers of runs in its games for several weeks:
4, 4, 6, 1, 2, 4, 1, 2, 5, 3, 3, 5, 4, 2

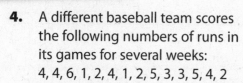

Runs Scored

Use the data to make a dot plot. Tell how many games the team played, and identify the data value with the greatest frequency.

_____

_____

Interpreting a Dot Plot

A dot plot can give you a visual picture of the spread, center, and shape of a data distribution.

You can describe the spread of a data set by identifying the least and greatest values. You can also look for **outliers** which are data values that are either much greater or much less than the other data values.

You can describe the center and shape of a data set in terms of *peaks, clusters,* or *symmetry*. A symmetric distribution has approximately the same number of data values on either side of the center.

EXAMPLE 2

Describe the spread, center, and shape of each data distribution.

A The data values are spread out from 3 to 7 with no outliers.

The data has a cluster from 3 to 7 with one peak at 5, which is the center of the distribution.

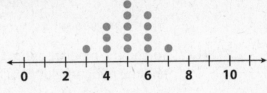

The distribution is symmetric. The data values are clustered around the center of the distribution.

B The data values are spread out from 1 to 9. The data value 1 appears to be an outlier.

The data has a cluster from 6 to 9 with one peak at 9, which is the greatest value in the data set.

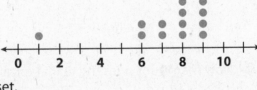

The distribution is not symmetric. The data values are clustered at one end of the distribution.

My Notes

YOUR TURN

5. Describe the spread, center, and shape of the data distribution from Example 1.

_____

_____

_____

_____

Personal Math Trainer

Online Assessment and Intervention

my.hrw.com

Finding Measures from a Dot Plot

You can also find and calculate measures of center and spread from a dot plot.

EXAMPLE 3

The dot plot shows the number of runs scored by a baseball team in each game for several weeks from Example 1.

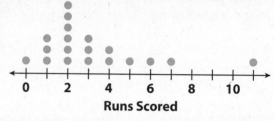

Runs Scored

A Find the mean, median, and range of the data.

> **STEP 1** To find the mean, find the sum of the data values and divide by the number of data values.
>
> $$\frac{1(0) + 3(1) + 6(2) + 3(3) + 2(4) + 1(5) + 1(6) + 1(7) + 1(11)}{19} = \frac{61}{19} \approx 3.2$$
>
> The mean is about 3.2.

> **STEP 2** To find the median, count the dots from left to right until you find the middle value. You may need to find the mean of two middle values.
>
> The median is 2.

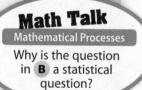

Math Talk

Mathematical Processes

Why is the question in **B** a statistical question?

> **STEP 3** To find the range, read the least and greatest values from the dot plot. Subtract the least value from the greatest.
>
> $11 - 0 = 11$
>
> The range is 11.

B How many runs does the team typically score in a game? Explain.

The mean number of runs is 3.2. The median number of runs is 2.

The shape of the dot plot suggests that the outlier 11 may be affecting these measures of center. To see if that is the case, find the mean and median without including the outlier. Compare these values with the original values.

> **STEP 1** Find the mean without including the outlier.
>
> $$\frac{1(0) + 3(1) + 6(2) + 3(3) + 2(4) + 1(5) + 1(6) + 1(7)}{18} = \frac{50}{18} \approx 2.8$$
>
> Without the outlier, the mean is 2.8, which is less than the original mean of 3.2.

> **STEP 2** Find the median without including the outlier.
>
> Counting from left to right, the median is still 2.

Given that it is not affected by the outlier, the median may be more typical of the data. The team typically scores two runs per game.

6. Find the mean, median, and range of the data from Your Turn question 4. What is the typical number of runs the team scores in a game? Justify your answer.

_____

_____

_____

Personal Math Trainer

Online Assessment and Intervention

⏱ my.hrw.com

Guided Practice

Tell whether the situation could yield variable data. If possible, write a statistical question. (Explore Activity)

1. The town council members want to know how much recyclable trash a typical household in town generates each week.

_____

_____

Kate asked some friends how many movies they saw last winter. Use her data for 2–4.

Movies Seen Last Winter
0, 1, 1, 2, 2, 3, 3, 3, 4, 4, 4, 4, 5, 5, 5, 5, 6, 6, 7, 7, 7, 8, 8, 9, 9, 17

2. Make a dot plot of the data. (Example 1)

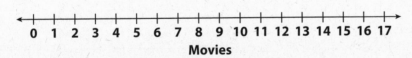

3. Find the mean, median, and range of the data. (Example 3)

_____

4. Describe the spread, center, and shape of the data. (Example 2)

_____

_____

? ESSENTIAL QUESTION CHECK-IN

5. What are some measures of center and spread that you can find from a dot plot? How can making a dot plot help you visualize a data distribution?

_____

_____

16.4 Independent Practice

Personal Math Trainer

Online Assessment and Intervention

my.hrw.com

6. Vocabulary Describe how a statistical question yields an answer with variability. Give an example.

_____

_____

_____

For 7–10, determine whether the question is a statistical question. If it is a statistical question, identify the units for the answer.

7. An antique collector wants to know the age of a particular chair in a shop.

_____

8. How tall do the people in your immediate and extended family tend to be?

9. How tall is Sam?

_____

10. How much did your classmates typically spend on music downloads last year?

_____

For 11–14, use the following data. The data give the number of days of precipitation per month during one year in a city.

12   10   11   9   9   10   12   9   8   7   9   10

11. Make a dot plot of the data.

⟵—+—+—+—+—+—+—+—+—+—+—+—+—+—⟶

12. What does each dot represent? How many months are represented?

_____

_____

13. Describe the shape, center, and spread of the data distribution. Are there any outliers?

_____

_____

_____

14. Find the mean, median, and range of the data.

_____

_____

15. What If? During one month there were 7 days of precipitation. What if there had only been 3 days of precipitation that month? How would that change the measures of center?

_____

_____

_____

_____

For 16–20, use the dot plot of the number of cars sold at a car dealership per week during the first half of the year.

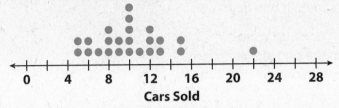

Cars Sold

16. Find the mean, median, and range.

Mean = _____   Median = _____

Range = _____

17. The owner of the car dealership decides to treat the value 22 as an outlier. Which measure of center or spread is affected the most if the owner removes this outlier? Explain.

_____

_____

_____

18. How many cars are sold in a typical week at the dealership? Explain.

_____

_____

19. Write an expression that represents the total number of cars sold during the first half of the year.

_____

_____

20. Describe the spread, center, and shape of the data distribution.

_____

_____

_____

_____

21. Vocabulary Explain how you can tell the frequency of a data value by looking at a dot plot.

_____

_____

For 22–26 use the following data. The data give the number of runs scored by opponents of the Boston Red Sox in June 2010.

4, 4, 9, 0, 2, 4, 1, 2, 11, 8, 2, 2, 5, 3, 2, 5, 6, 4, 0

22. Make a dot plot for the data.

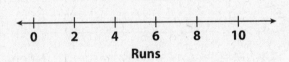

Runs

23. How many games did the Boston Red Sox play in June 2010? Explain.

_____

_____

24. Which data value in your dot plot has the greatest frequency? Explain what that frequency means for this data.

_____

_____

_____

25. Find the mean, median, and range of the data.

_____

_____

26. What is a statistical question that you could answer using the dot plot? Answer your question and justify your response.

_____

_____

_____

_____

_____

27. A pediatrician records the ages of the patients seen in one day:
1, 2, 5, 7, 9, 17, 13, 16, 18, 12, 3, 5, 1.

    a. **Explain the Error** Assuming that some of the patients are infants who are less than 1 year old, what information did the pediatrician forget to write down?

    _____

    b. **Critical Thinking** Can you make a dot plot of the pediatrician's data? Can you find the mean, median, and range? Why or why not?

    _____

    _____

    _____

28. **Multistep** A nurse measured a patient's heart rate at different times over several days.

Heart Rate (beats per minute)
86, 87, 89, 87, 86, 88, 90,
85, 82, 86, 83, 85, 84, 86

    a. Make a dot plot.

    b. Describe the shape, center, and spread of the data. Then find the mean, median, range, and IQR for the data.

    _____

    _____

    _____

    _____

    c. **What If?** The nurse collected the data when the patient was resting. How might the dot plot and the measures change if the nurse collects the data when the patient is exercising?

    _____

    _____

16.5 Histograms

6.7.16.5
Students will display data in a histogram.

? ESSENTIAL QUESTION

How can you display data in a histogram?

EXPLORE ACTIVITY

Grouping Data in Intervals

The members of the high-school basketball team practice free throws. Each player attempts 50 free throws. The number of free throws made by each player is listed below.

25, 29, 29, 30, 33, 34, 35, 35, 36, 39, 42, 44

A Use a dot plot to represent the data.

```
←+—+—+—+—+—+—+—+—+—+—+—+—+—+—+—+—+—+—+—+—+→
  25 26 27 28 29 30 31 32 33 34 35 36 37 38 39 40 41 42 43 44 45
```

B On your dot plot, circle the dots that are in each interval of the frequency table below. Then complete the frequency table.

Interval	Frequency
20–29	
30–39	
40–49	

> Enter the number of data values for the interval 30–39.

C Analyze the data. How were the data collected? How many data values are there? What are the mean, median, range, and IQR of the data?

_____

_____

_____

_____

Reflect

1. Can you use the dot plot to find the mean and the median of the data? Can you use the frequency table? Why or why not?

    _____

    _____

    _____

    _____

2. How do you find the number of data values in a data set from a dot plot? How can you find the number of data values from a frequency table?

    _____

Using a Histogram

A **histogram** is a type of bar graph whose bars represent the frequencies of numeric data within intervals.

EXAMPLE 1

A birdwatcher counts and records the number of birds at a birdfeeder every morning at 9:00 for several days.

12, 3, 8, 1, 1, 6, 10, 14, 3, 6, 2, 1, 3, 2, 7

Make a histogram of the data.

STEP 1 Make a frequency table.

Divide the data into equal-sized intervals of 4. Make a frequency table.

Interval	Frequency
1–4	8
5–8	4
9–12	2
13–16	1

Math Talk

Mathematical Processes

How does the histogram show the total number of days the birdwatcher counted birds?

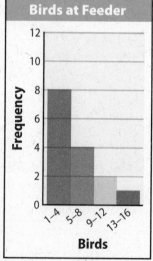

Birds at Feeder

STEP 2 Make a histogram.

The intervals are listed along the horizontal axis. The vertical axis shows the frequencies. For each interval, draw a bar to show the number of days in that interval. The bars should have equal widths. They should touch but not overlap.

Reflect

3. What If? Suppose the birdwatcher continues his observation for three more days and collects these new data values: 5, 18, and 2. How could you change the histogram to include the data?

_____

_____

_____

YOUR TURN

4. Kim has started rating each movie she sees using a scale of 1 to 10 on an online site. Here are her ratings so far:

6, 9, 8, 5, 7, 4, 8, 8, 3, 7, 8, 7, 5, 1, 10

Make a histogram of the data.

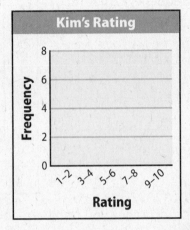

Kim's Rating

Personal Math Trainer

Online Assessment and Intervention

my.hrw.com

Analyzing a Histogram

By grouping data in intervals, a histogram gives a picture of the distribution of a data set.

Math On the Spot

my.hrw.com

EXAMPLE 2 Real World

Use the histogram from Example 1. What are some conclusions about the data that can you make from the shape of the distribution?

The highest bar is for the interval 1–4, which means that on more than half the days (8 out of 15), the birdwatcher saw only 1–4 birds. The bars decrease in height from left to right, showing that it was more likely for the birdwatcher to see a small number of birds rather than a large number on any given day.

YOUR TURN

5. Use your histogram from Your Turn 4. What are some conclusions you can make about Kim's movie ratings from the shape of the distribution?

_____

_____

Personal Math Trainer

Online Assessment and Intervention

my.hrw.com

1. Wendy kept track of the number of text messages she sent each day for three weeks. Complete the frequency table.
   (Explore Activity)

   0, 5, 5, 7, 11, 12, 15, 20, 22, 24, 25,
   25, 27, 27, 29, 29, 32, 33, 34, 35, 35

Interval	Frequency
0–9	

Ed counted the number of seats available in each cafe in his town. Use his data for 2–3.

18, 20, 22, 26, 10, 12, 16, 18, 7, 8

2. Complete the frequency table and the histogram. (Example 1)

Interval	Frequency
1–7	
8–14	
15–21	
22–28	

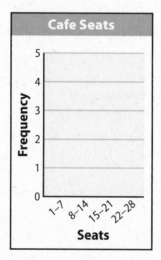

Cafe Seats

3. What are some conclusions you can make about the distribution of the data? (Example 2)

_____

_____

_____

_____

4. How can you display data in a histogram?

_____

_____

_____

16.5 Independent Practice

Personal Math Trainer

my.hrw.com

Online Assessment and Intervention

An amusement park employee records the ages of the people who ride the new roller coaster during a fifteen–minute period.

Ages of riders: 47, 16, 16, 35, 45, 43, 11, 29, 31, 50, 23, 18, 18, 20, 29, 17, 18, 48, 56, 24, 18, 21, 38, 12, 23.

5. Complete the frequency table. Then make a histogram of the data.

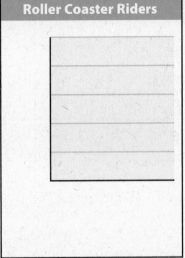

Roller Coaster Riders

Interval	Frequency
10–19	

6. Describe two things you know about the riders who are represented by the data.

_____

_____

_____

7. **Multiple Representations** West Middle School has classes of many different sizes during first period. The number of students in each class is shown.

9, 23, 18, 14, 20, 26, 14, 18, 18, 12, 8, 13, 21, 22, 28, 10, 7, 19, 24, 20

a. Hank made a histogram using intervals of 6–10, 11–15, and so on. How many bars did his histogram

have? What was the height of the highest bar? _____

b. Lisa made a histogram using intervals of 0–9, 10–19, and so on. How many bars did her histogram have?

What was the height of the highest bar? _____

c. Besides a histogram, what are some other ways you could display these data?

_____

8. **Communicate Mathematical Ideas** Can you find the mean or median of a set of data from a histogram? Explain.

_____

_____

9. **Multistep** A theater owner keeps track of how many people come to see movies on 21 different Saturdays.

Saturday Moviegoers

Interval	Frequency
60–69	1
70–79	3
80–89	10
90–99	7

Saturday Moviegoers

a. Use the data to make a histogram.

b. **Make a Prediction** The theater owner asks, "How many moviegoers come to the theater on a typical Saturday?" What would you tell the theater owner? Use your histogram to support your answer.

_____

_____

_____

_____

c. **Communicate Mathematical Ideas** Is the theater owner's question a statistical question? Why or why not?

_____

10. **Explain the Error** Irina says she can find the range of a set of data from a histogram. Is she correct? Justify your answer.

_____

_____

_____

Ready to Go On?

Personal Math Trainer
Online Assessment and Intervention
my.hrw.com

16.1 Measures of Center

1. Find the mean and median of these data: 2, 5, 9, 11, 17, 19. _____

16.2 Mean Absolute Deviation

2. Find the distance of each data value in Exercise 1 from the mean. Then find the

mean absolute deviation of the data. _____

16.3 Box Plots

3. Make a box plot for the data set.

| 36 | 42 | 44 | 52 | 61 | 70 | 78 |

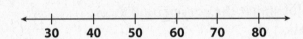

16.4 Dot Plots and Data Distribution

A baseball team scored the following number of runs over a 10-game period:
6, 6, 8, 5, 4, 6, 4, 3, 8, 4

4. Make a dot plot for the data.

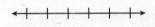

5. Find the mean, median, and range.

_____

_____

16.5 Histograms

6. Make a histogram for the data set.

23	45	62	19
48	10	39	54
39	16	48	12
25	32	18	4

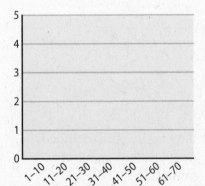

? ESSENTIAL QUESTION

7. How can you represent and summarize data in a dot plot?

_____

_____

Assessment Readiness

Personal
Math Trainer

Online
Assessment and
Intervention

my.hrw.com

Selected Response

1. What is the interquartile range of the data represented by the box plot shown below?

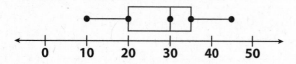

Ⓐ 15 Ⓒ 35

Ⓑ 20 Ⓓ 40

The dot plot shows the ages of quiz show contestants.

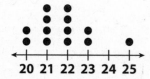

2. What is the median of the data?

Ⓐ 21 Ⓒ 22

Ⓑ 21.5 Ⓓ 25

3. Which inequalities describe the possible ages of the contestants in the dot plot?

Ⓐ $a > 20$ and $a < 25$

Ⓑ $a \geq 20$ and $a \leq 25$

Ⓒ $a < 20$ and $a > 25$

Ⓓ $a \leq 20$ and $a \geq 25$

4. Suppose a new data value, 30, is included in the dot plot. Which statement describes the effect on the median?

Ⓐ The median would increase.

Ⓑ The median would decrease.

Ⓒ The median would stay the same.

Ⓓ The median would equal the mean.

5. Andrea recorded the points she scored in her last eight basketball games. What is the mean absolute deviation of the scores?

28, 32, 47, 16, 40, 35, 38, 54

Ⓐ 8.5 Ⓒ 17.75

Ⓑ 36.25 Ⓓ 38

Mini-Task

6. The frequency table shows data about how many tickets were sold by students.

Tickets Sold	Frequency
0–9	2
10–19	4
20–29	3
30–39	1

a. Use the frequency table to make a histogram.

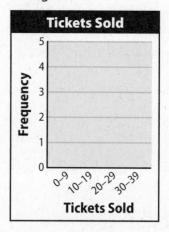

b. How many students sold tickets?

_____

c. What percent of the students sold 20 or more tickets?

_____

MODULE 16 Displaying, Analyzing, and Summarizing Data

© Houghton Mifflin Harcourt Publishing Company

Key Vocabulary

box plot *(diagrama de caja)*
categorical data *(datos categóricos)*
dot plot *(diagrama de puntos)*
histogram *(histograma)*
interquartile range *(rango entre cuartiles)*
lower quartile *(cuartil inferior)*
mean *(media)*
mean absolute deviation (MAD) *(desviación absoluta media, (DAM))*
measure of center *(medida central)*
measure of spread *(medida de dispersión)*
median *(mediana)*
mode *(moda)*
range *(rango)*
statistical question *(pregunta estadística)*
upper quartile *(cuartil superior)*

? ESSENTIAL QUESTION

How can you solve real-world problems by displaying, analyzing, and summarizing data?

EXAMPLE 1

The ages of Thomas's neighbors are shown.

Ages of Thomas's Neighbors
30, 48, 31, 45, 42, 32, 32, 38, 34, 50, 49, 48

Make a box plot of the data.

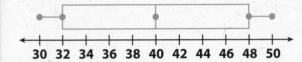

30   31   <u>32   32</u>   34   <u>38   42</u>   45   <u>48   48</u>   49   50

Lower quartile = 32   Median = 40   Upper quartile = 48

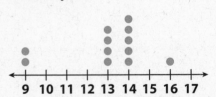

30 32 34 36 38 40 42 44 46 48 50

EXAMPLE 2

Find the mean, median, and range of the data shown on the dot plot.

The mean is 13. $\dfrac{2(9) + 4(13) + 5(14) + 16}{12} = 13$

The median is 13.5.   9, 9, 13, 13, 13, <u>13, 14</u>, 14, 14, 14, 14, 16

The range is 7. $16 - 9 = 7$

9 10 11 12 13 14 15 16 17

EXAMPLE 3

Find the mean absolute deviation (MAD) of the data in Example 2. Round to the nearest tenth.

The MAD is the mean distance of each of the 12 data points from the mean, 13.

$$\frac{4 + 4 + 0 + 0 + 0 + 0 + 1 + 1 + 1 + 1 + 1 + 3}{12} = \frac{16}{12} \approx 1.3$$

The mean absolute deviation is approximately 1.3.

EXERCISES

1. The number of goals for the 13 players on a soccer team are 4, 9, 0, 1, 1, 2, 0, 0, 2, 8, 8, 3, 1. Find the median, lower quartile, and upper quartile. Then make a box plot for the data. (Lesson 16.3) _____

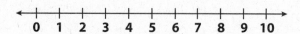

2. The coach recorded the time it took 14 students to run a mile. The times are as follows: 9:23, 8:15, 9:23, 9:01, 6:45, 6:55, 7:20, 9:14, 6:21, 7:12, 7:34, 6:10, 9:15, 9:18. (Lesson 16.5)

Use the data to complete the frequency table. Then use the table to make a histogram.

Interval	Frequency
6–6:59	

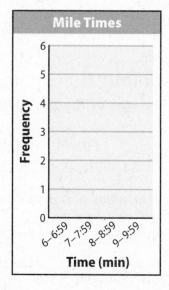

3. Find the mean and mean absolute deviation of the set of data. Round to the nearest hundredth. (Lesson 16.2)

Distance per day (mi) driven by Juan						
12	9	7	7	11	10	7

Mean: _____   Mean absolute deviation: _____

Unit 7 Performance Tasks

1. **CAREERS IN MATH** Geneticist Kinesha collects data about the heights of students in her science class. What measures of center and variation are appropriate for the data? Which of the data displays that you learned about in this unit could Keisha use to display the data? Which could be used to show the measures of center and variation you named? Explain.

_____

_____

_____

Selected Response

1. Over 6 days, Jim jogged 6.5 miles, 5 miles, 3 miles, 2 miles, 3.5 miles, and 4 miles. What is the mean distance that Jim jogged?

Ⓐ 3.75 miles   Ⓒ 4.5 miles

Ⓑ 4 miles   Ⓓ 6.5 miles

Use the data set below for 2–3.

26	30	45	43	26
14	28	33	56	29

2. What is the mean of the data set?

Ⓐ 14   Ⓒ 33

Ⓑ 26   Ⓓ 46

3. What is the mean absolute deviation?

Ⓐ 2

Ⓑ 4

Ⓒ 6

Ⓓ 9

4. The ages of the volunteers at a local food bank are shown below.

34, 25, 24, 50, 18, 46, 43, 36, 32

What is the median of this set of data?

Ⓐ 32   Ⓒ 34

Ⓑ 33.1   Ⓓ 50

5. Which expression shows the prime factorization of 120?

Ⓐ $2^3 \times 3 \times 5$

Ⓑ $2 \times 3 \times 5$

Ⓒ 10^{12}

Ⓓ $2 \times 5 \times 12$

6. The dot plot shows the number of participants in each age group in a science fair.

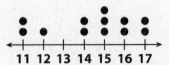

Which of the following is **not** supported by the dot plot?

Ⓐ The range is 6.

Ⓑ The mean of the ages is about 14.4.

Ⓒ The mode of the ages is 13.

Ⓓ The median of the ages is 15.

7. Sarita recorded the distances she ran for 5 days: 5 miles, 4 miles, 5.5 miles, 4.5 miles, and 5.5 miles. What is the mean distance Sarita ran?

Ⓐ 4.9 miles

Ⓑ 5 miles

Ⓒ 5.1 miles

Ⓓ 5.5 miles

8. On a map of the city, 1 centimeter represents 2.5 miles. What distance on the map would represent 20 miles?

Ⓐ 6 centimeters

Ⓑ 8 centimeters

Ⓒ 12 centimeters

Ⓓ 18 centimeters

9. The ratio of the number of male lions to female lions in the animal reserve is 21:20. If there are 123 lions in the animal reserve, how many of the lions are female?

Ⓐ 40   Ⓒ 60

Ⓑ 50   Ⓓ 70

Mini-Tasks

10. The students in Ms. Lorenzo's class collected the following numbers of bottle caps:

10, 20, 40, 50, 30, 10, 60, 10, 20
40, 30, 30, 50, 70, 50, 70, 60, 30

  a. Make a dot plot for the data.

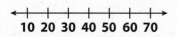

    10 20 30 40 50 60 70

  b. What is the median?

    _____

  c. What is the mean?

    _____

11. The heights in inches of 8 students are 50, 53, 52, 68, 54, 49, 55, and 51.

  a. What is the mean of the students' heights?

    _____

  b. Is there an outlier in the data set? If so, which number is the outlier?

    _____

  c. What is the mean height if the outlier is removed from the data?

    _____

Read a graph or diagram as closely as you read the actual test question. These visual aids contain important information.

12. The data show the latest math test scores in Mr. White's class.

98	76	76	85	43
90	85	76	98	100
75	84	95	87	98
100	57	92	67	73
56	97	100	75	100

  a. Draw a histogram of the data.

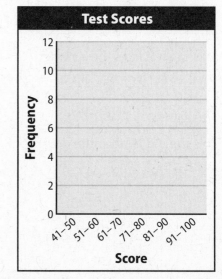

  b. What is the outlier? Would removing the outlier change how the chart looks?

    _____

    _____

    _____

The Number System

CONVENTION CENTER

MUSEUM of S

CAREERS IN MATH

Urban Planner An urban planner creates plans for urban, suburban, and rural communities and makes recommendations about locations for infrastructure, such as buildings, roads, and sewer and water pipes. Urban planners perform cost-benefit analysis of projects, use measurement and geometry when they design the layout of infrastructure, and use statistics and mathematical models to predict the growth and future needs of a population.

If you are interested in a career as an urban planner, you should study these mathematical subjects:
- Algebra
- Geometry
- Trigonometry
- Statistics

Research other careers that require using measurement, geometry, and mathematical modeling.

Unit 8 Performance Task

At the end of the unit, check out how **urban planners** use math.

Vocabulary Preview

Use the puzzle to preview key vocabulary from this unit. Unscramble the circled letters within found words to answer the riddle at the bottom of the page.

1. NIOARLTA MURNEB

2. GREITEN

3. PIRGENAET CMSEADIL

4. EADITIVD SENEIRV

5. TIIRANGTNEM SAELIDMC

1. Any number that can be written as a ratio of two integers. (Lesson 17.1)
2. A member of the set of whole numbers and their opposites. (Lesson 17.1)
3. Decimals in which one or more digits repeat infinitely. (Lesson 17.1)
4. The opposite of any number. (Lesson 17.3)
5. Decimals that have a finite number of digits. (Lesson 1.71)

Q: Why were the two fractions able to settle their differences peacefully?

A: They were both __ __ __ __ __ __ __!

Adding and Subtracting Integers

? ESSENTIAL QUESTION

How can you use addition and subtraction of integers to solve real-world problems?

Real-World Video

Death Valley contains the lowest point in North America, elevation −282 feet. The top of Mt. McKinley, elevation 20,320 feet, is the highest point in North America. To find the difference between these elevations, you can subtract integers.

ⓞ my.hrw.com

GO DIGITAL
my.hrw.com

my.hrw.com

Go digital with your write-in student edition, accessible on any device.

Math On the Spot

Scan with your smart phone to jump directly to the online edition, video tutor, and more.

Animated Math

Interactively explore key concepts to see how math works.

Personal Math Trainer

Get immediate feedback and help as you work through practice sets.

Reading Start-Up

© Houghton Mifflin Harcourt Publishing Company

Vocabulary

Review Words
- difference *(diferencia)*
- integers *(enteros)*
- ✔ negative number *(número negativo)*
- ✔ opposites *(opuestos)*
- ✔ positive number *(número positivo)*
- sum *(suma)*
- ✔ whole number *(número entero)*

Preview Words
- absolute value *(valor absoluto)*
- additive inverse *(inverso aditivo)*
- expression *(expresión)*
- model *(modelo)*

Visualize Vocabulary

Use the ✔ words to fill in the ovals on the graphic. You may put more than one word in each oval.

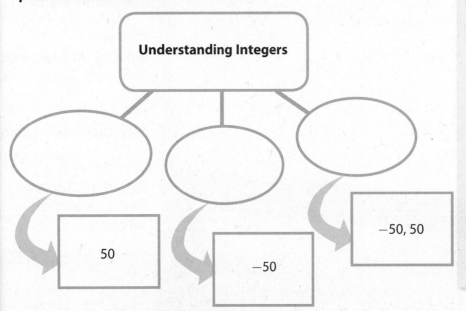

Understanding Integers

50

−50

−50, 50

Understand Vocabulary

Complete the sentences using the preview words.

1. The _____ of a number gives its distance from zero.

2. The sum of a number and its _____ is zero.

Active Reading

Booklet Before beginning the module, create a booklet to help you learn the concepts in this module. Write the main idea of each lesson on each page of the booklet. As you study each lesson, write important details that support the main idea, such as vocabulary and processes. Refer to your finished booklet as you work on assignments and study for tests.

Are YOU Ready?

Complete these exercises to review skills you will need for this module.

Understand Integers

EXAMPLE   A diver descended 20 meters.

$$-20$$

Decide whether the integer is positive or negative:
descended → negative
Write the integer.

Write an integer to represent each situation.

1. an elevator ride down 27 stories

2. a $700 profit

3. 46 degrees below zero

4. a gain of 12 yards

_____   _____   _____   _____

Whole Number Operations

EXAMPLE   245 − 28

$$\begin{array}{r} \overset{3\ 15}{2\cancel{4}\cancel{5}} \\ -\ 2\ 8 \\ \hline 2\ 1\ 7 \end{array}$$

245 − 28 = 217

Think:
8 > 5
Regroup 1 ten as 10 ones.
1 ten + 5 ones = 15 ones
Subtract: 15 − 8 = 7

Find the sum or difference.

5. $\begin{array}{r} 183 \\ +\ 78 \\ \hline \end{array}$

6. $\begin{array}{r} 677 \\ -288 \\ \hline \end{array}$

7. $\begin{array}{r} 1,188 \\ +\ 902 \\ \hline \end{array}$

8. $\begin{array}{r} 2,647 \\ -1,885 \\ \hline \end{array}$

Locate Points on a Number Line

EXAMPLE

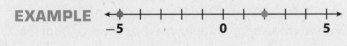

Graph +2 by starting at 0 and counting 2 units to the *right*.
Graph −5 by starting at 0 and counting 5 units to the *left*.

Graph each number on the number line.

9. 7   **10.** −4   **11.** −9   **12.** 4

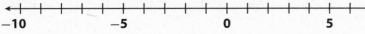

Complete these exercises to review skills you will need for this module.

Understand Integers

13. Parvana records the transactions for her bank account for the week. On Monday, she made a deposit of $45. On Tuesday, she used her debit card to pay $18 for a new shirt. On Thursday, she withdrew $7 from an ATM. Write an integer to represent each of Parvana's bank transactions.

Whole Number Operations

14. Lonnie made 1,200 dog collars to sell at the craft market. The table shows the number of collars he sold at the market over three weekends. How many collars does he have left? Show your work.

Lonnie's Dog Collars	
Weekend	**Number sold**
1	357
2	418
3	306

Locate Points on a Number Line

15. On a winter day, the temperature in degrees Fahrenheit was six degrees below zero at sunrise, four degrees at noon, and three degrees below zero at sunset. Graph each temperature on the number line. Explain how you chose each point.

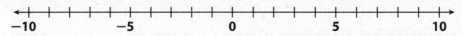

Adding Integers with the Same Sign

How do you add integers with the same sign?

EXPLORE ACTIVITY 1

Modeling Sums of Integers with the Same Sign

You can use colored counters to add positive integers and to add negative integers.

○ = 1
● = −1

Model with two-color counters.

A $3 + 4$

3 positive counters ○ ○ ○
4 positive counters ○ ○ ○ ○ } total number of counters

How many counters are there in total? _____

What is the sum and how do you find it?

_____

_____

B $-5 + (-3)$

5 negative counters ● ● ● ● ●
3 negative counters ● ● ● } total number of counters

How many counters are there in total? _____

Since the counters are negative integers, what is the sum? _____

Math Talk
Mathematical Processes

What does the color of each row of counters represent?

Reflect

1. **Communicate Mathematical Ideas** When adding two numbers with the same sign, what sign do you use for the sum?

_____

Adding on a Number Line

Positive and negative numbers can be represented by arrows on a number line. For instance, the arrow shown is for 4. The arrow is 4 units long and points in the positive direction. An arrow for −4 would be 4 units long and point in the negative direction.

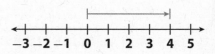

The temperature was 2 °F below zero. The temperature drops by 5 °F. What is the temperature now?

A What is the initial temperature written as an integer?

_____

B Draw the arrow for the initial temperature on the number line.

C A drop in temperature of 5° is like adding −5° to the temperature.

To add −5, start at the tip of your first arrow, and draw an arrow representing −5. A single arrow from the start of your first arrow to the end of your second represents the sum.

D What is the temperature written as an integer?

_____

The temperature is _____

| above / below | zero.

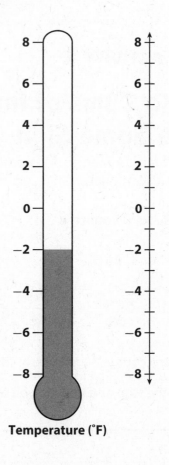

Temperature (°F)

Reflect

2. Draw Conclusions What is the length of the resulting arrow when you add two arrows pointing in the negative direction?

_____

3. What If? Suppose the temperature is 1 °F and rises by 3 °F. Explain how to use the number line to find the new temperature. Then make a conclusion similar to the one you made in Question 2.

_____

_____

_____

Adding Integers with a Common Sign

To add integers with the same sign, add the absolute values of the integers and use the sign of the integers for the sum.

Math On the Spot
my.hrw.com

EXAMPLE 1

Add $-7 + (-6)$.　　　The signs of both integers are the same.

STEP 1　Find the absolute values.

$|-7| = 7$　$|-6| = 6$　The absolute value is always positive or zero.

STEP 2　Find the sum of the absolute values: $7 + 6 = 13$

STEP 3　Use the sign of the integers to write the sum.

$-7 + (-6) = -13$　The sign of each integer is negative.

Math Talk
Mathematical Processes

Can you use the same procedure you use to find the sum of two negative integers to find the sum of two *positive* numbers? Explain.

Reflect

4. **Communicate Mathematical Ideas** Does the Commutative Property of Addition apply when you add two negative integers? Explain.

_____

_____

5. **Critical Thinking** Choose any two negative integers. Is the sum of the integers less than or greater than the value of either of the integers? Will this be true no matter which integers you choose? Explain.

_____

_____

_____

_____

YOUR TURN

Find each sum.

6. $-8 + (-1) = $ _____

7. $-3 + (-7) = $ _____

8. $-48 + (-12) = $ _____

9. $-32 + (-38) = $ _____

10. $109 + 191 = $ _____

11. $-40 + (-105) = $ _____

12. $-150 + (-1500) = $ _____

13. $-200 + (-800) = $ _____

Personal Math Trainer

Online Assessment and Intervention

my.hrw.com

Find each sum. (Explore Activity 1)

1. $-5 + (-1)$

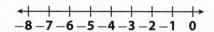

    a. How many counters are there? _____

    b. Do the counters represent positive or

       negative numbers? _____

    c. $-5 + (-1) =$ _____

2. $-2 + (-7)$

    a. How many counters are there? _____

    b. Do the counters represent positive or

       negative numbers? _____

    c. $-2 + (-7) =$ _____

Model each addition problem on the number line to find each sum.
(Explore Activity 2)

3. $-5 + (-2) =$ _____

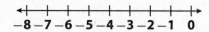

5. $-3 + (-4) =$ _____

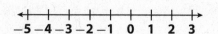

7. $-2 + (-2) =$ _____

4. $-1 + (-3) =$ _____

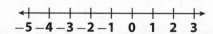

6. $-4 + (-1) =$ _____

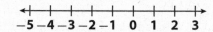

8. $-6 + (-8) =$ _____

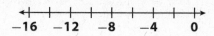

Find each sum. (Example 1)

9. $-5 + (-4) =$ _____

11. $-9 + (-1) =$ _____

13. $-52 + (-48) =$ _____

15. $-4 + (-5) + (-6) =$ _____

10. $-1 + (-10) =$ _____

12. $-90 + (-20) =$ _____

14. $5 + 198 =$ _____

16. $-50 + (-175) + (-345) =$ _____

? ESSENTIAL QUESTION CHECK-IN

17. How do you add integers with the same sign?

_____

_____

17.1 Independent Practice

18. **Represent Real-World Problems** Jane and Sarah both dive down from the surface of a pool. Jane first dives down 5 feet, and then dives down 3 more feet. Sarah first dives down 3 feet, and then dives down 5 more feet.

a. **Multiple Representations** Use the number line to model the equation $-5 + (-3) = -3 + (-5)$.

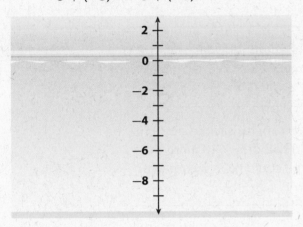

b. Does the order in which you add two integers with the same sign affect the sum? Explain.

_____

_____

c. Interpret the sum in context.

_____

_____

19. A golfer has the following scores for a four-day tournament.

Day	1	2	3	4
Score	−3	−1	−5	−2

What was the golfer's total score for the tournament?

_____

20. A football team loses 3 yards on one play and 6 yards on another play. Write a sum of negative integers to represent this situation. Find the sum and explain how it is related to the problem.

_____

_____

21. When the quarterback is sacked, the team loses yards. In one game, the quarterback was sacked four times. What was the total sack yardage?

Sack	1	2	3	4
Sack yardage	−14	−5	−12	−23

_____

22. **Multistep** The temperature in Jonestown and Cooperville was the same at 1:00. By 2:00, the temperature in Jonestown dropped 10 degrees, and the temperature in Cooperville dropped 6 degrees. By 3:00, the temperature in Jonestown dropped 8 more degrees, and the temperature in Cooperville dropped 2 more degrees.

a. Write and evaluate a sum to model the change to the temperature in Jonestown since 1:00.

_____

b. Write and evaluate a sum to model the change to the temperature in Cooperville since 1:00.

_____

c. Where is it colder at 3:00, Jonestown or Cooperville? Explain your reasoning.

_____

_____

23. Represent Real-World Problems Julio is playing a trivia game. On his first turn, he lost 100 points. On his second turn, he lost 75 points. On his third turn, he lost 85 points. Write a sum of three negative integers that models the change to Julio's score after his first three turns.

_____

 **FOCUS ON HIGHER ORDER THINKING**

Work Area

24. Multistep On Monday, Jan made withdrawals of $25, $45, and $75 from her savings account. On the same day, her twin sister Julie made withdrawals of $35, $55, and $65 from *her* savings account.

a. Write a sum of negative integers to show Jan's withdrawals on Monday. Find the total amount Jan withdrew.

_____

b. Write a sum of negative integers to show Julie's withdrawals on Monday. Find the total amount Julie withdrew.

_____

c. Julie and Jan's brother also withdrew money from his savings account on Monday. He made three withdrawals and withdrew $10 more than Julie did. What are three possible amounts he could have withdrawn?

_____

25. Communicate Mathematical Ideas Why might you want to use the Commutative Property to change the order of the integers in the following sum before adding?

$$-80 + (-173) + (-20)$$

_____

_____

26. Critique Reasoning The absolute value of the sum of two different integers with the same sign is 8. Pat says there are three pairs of integers that match this description. Do you agree? Explain.

_____

_____

_____

_____

© Houghton Mifflin Harcourt Publishing Company

Adding Integers with Different Signs

7.1.1.2
Students will add integers with different signs.

? **ESSENTIAL QUESTION**

How do you add integers with different signs?

EXPLORE ACTIVITY 1

Adding on a Number Line

When you add integers with different signs on a number line, one of the arrows "cancels out" at least part of the other. What remains is the sum.

The 1 unit remaining on the arrow pointing in the positive direction indicates that the sum is 1.

The 1 unit remaining on the arrow pointing in the negative direction indicates that the sum is -1.

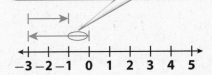

$3 + (-2) = 1$ $-3 + 2 = -1$

Model each sum on a number line.

A Use a model to find the sum: $4 + (-3) = $ _____

Start at 0. Draw the arrow for 4. Then, starting from directly above the tip of the arrow for 4, draw the arrow for -3.

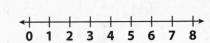

B Use a model to find the sum: $-7 + 5 = $ _____

Start at _____. Draw the arrow for _____.

Then, starting at _____, draw the arrow for _____.

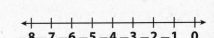

C Use a model to find the sum: $6 + (-6) = $ _____

Start at _____. Draw the arrow for _____.

Then, starting at _____, draw the arrow for _____.

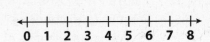

Reflect

1. **Make a Prediction** Predict the sum $-2 + 2$. Explain your prediction and check it using the number line.

_____

_____

Modeling Sums of Integers with Different Signs

You can use colored counters to model adding integers with different signs. When you add a positive integer (yellow counter) and a negative integer (red counter), the result is 0. One red and one yellow counter form a *zero pair*.

$1 + (-1) = 0$

Model and find each sum using counters. Part A is modeled for you. For Part B, follow the steps to model and find the sum using counters.

A Model $3 + (-2)$.

Start with 3 positive counters to represent 3.

Add 2 negative counters to represent adding -2.

Form zero pairs.

What is left when you remove the zero pairs?

_____ counter

Find the sum: $3 + (-2) =$ _____

> The value of a zero pair is 0. Adding or subtracting 0 to any number does not change its value.

B Model $-6 + 3$.

Start with _____ counters to represent _____.

Add _____ counters to represent adding _____.

Form zero pairs.

What is left when you remove the zero pairs?

_____ counters

Find the sum: $-6 + 3 =$ _____

Reflect

2. Make a Prediction Kyle models a sum of two integers. He uses more negative (red) counters than positive (yellow) counters. What do you predict about the sign of the sum? Explain.

_____

_____

YOUR TURN

Model and find each sum using counters.

3. $5 + (-1)$ _____

4. $4 + (-6)$ _____

5. $1 + (-7)$ _____

6. $3 + (-4)$ _____

Adding Integers

You have learned how to add integers with the same signs and how to add integers with different signs. The table below summarizes the rules for adding integers.

	Adding Integers	Examples
Same Signs	Add the absolute values of the integers. Use the common sign for the sum.	$3 + 5 = 8$ $-2 + (-7) = -9$
Different Signs	Subtract the lesser absolute value from the greater absolute value. Use the sign of the integer with the greater absolute value for the sum.	$3 + (-5) = -2$ $-10 + 1 = -9$
Inverse Property of Addition	The opposite of any number is called its **additive inverse.** The sum of a number and its additive inverse is 0.	$4 + (-4) = 0$ $-11 + 11 = 0$

EXAMPLE 1

Find each sum.

A $-11 + 6$

$|-11| - |6| = 5$ Subtract the lesser absolute value from the greater.

$-11 + 6 = -5$ Use the sign of the number with the greater absolute value.

B $(-37) + 37$

$(-37) + 37 = 0$ Inverse Property of Addition

Math Talk
Mathematical Processes

Describe a real-world situation involving integers in which opposite quantities combine to make 0.

YOUR TURN

Find each sum.

7. $-51 + 23 =$ _____

8. $10 + (-18) =$ _____

9. $13 + (-13) =$ _____

10. $25 + (-26) =$ _____

© Houghton Mifflin Harcourt Publishing Company

Use a number line to find each sum. (Explore Activity 1)

1. $7 + (-5) =$ _____

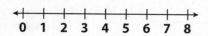

2. $-2 + 7 =$ _____

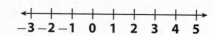

3. $-8 + 3 =$ _____

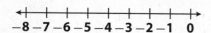

4. $1 + (-4) =$ _____

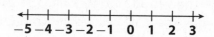

Circle the zero pairs in each model. Find the sum. (Explore Activity 2)

5. $-4 + 5 =$ _____

6. $-6 + 6 =$ _____

7. $2 + (-5) =$ _____

8. $-3 + 7 =$ _____

Find each sum. (Example 1)

9. $-8 + 14 =$ _____

10. $7 + (-5) =$ _____

11. $5 + (-21) =$ _____

12. $14 + (-14) =$ _____

13. $0 + (-5) =$ _____

14. $32 + (-8) =$ _____

? ESSENTIAL QUESTION CHECK-IN

15. Describe how to find the sums $-4 + 2$ and $-4 + (-2)$ on a number line.

_____

_____

_____

17.2 Independent Practice

Find each sum.

16. $-15 + 71 = $ _____

17. $-53 + 45 = $ _____

18. $-79 + 79 = $ _____

19. $-25 + 50 = $ _____

20. $18 + (-32) = $ _____

21. $5 + (-100) = $ _____

22. $-12 + 8 + 7 = $ _____

23. $-8 + (-2) + 3 = $ _____

24. $15 + (-15) + 200 = $ _____

25. $-500 + (-600) + 1200 = $ _____

26. A football team gained 9 yards on one play and then lost 22 yards on the next. Write a sum of integers to find the overall change in field position. Explain your answer.

_____

27. A soccer team is having a car wash. The team spent $55 on supplies and earned $275, including tips. The team's profit is the amount the team made after paying for supplies. Write a sum of integers that represents the team's profit.

_____

28. Write and solve a problem involving a number and its opposite using the illustration shown. Identify any properties you use.

_____

_____

_____

_____

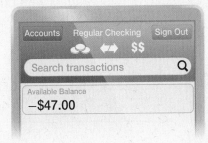

29. The sum of two integers with different signs is 8. Give two possible pairs of integers that fit this description.

_____

30. **Multistep** Bart and Sam played a game in which each player earns or loses points in each turn. A player's total score after two turns is the sum of his points earned or lost. The player with the greater score after two turns wins. Bart earned 123 points and lost 180 points. Sam earned 185 points and lost 255 points. Which person won the game? Explain.

_____

_____

Work Area

31. Critical Thinking Explain how you could use a number line to show that $-4 + 3$ and $3 + (-4)$ have the same value. Which property of addition states that these sums are equivalent?

_____

_____

_____

_____

32. Represent Real-World Problems Jim is standing beside a pool. He drops a weight from 4 feet above the surface of the water in the pool. The weight travels a total distance of 12 feet down before landing on the bottom of the pool. Explain how you can write a sum of integers to find the depth of the water.

_____

_____

_____

_____

33. Communicate Mathematical Ideas You are using counters to model the sum of two integers with different signs. Under what conditions will the model represent a positive sum?

_____

_____

_____

_____

34. Analyze Relationships You know that the sum of -5 and another integer is a positive integer. What can you conclude about the sign of the other integer? What can you conclude about the value of the other integer? Explain.

_____

_____

_____

_____

17.3 Subtracting Integers

7.1.1.3
Students will subtract integers.

? **ESSENTIAL QUESTION**

How do you subtract integers?

EXPLORE ACTIVITY 1

Modeling Integer Subtraction

You can use counters to find the difference of two integers. In some cases, you may need to add zero pairs.

$1 + (-1) = 0$

Model and find each difference using counters.

A Model $-4 - (-3)$.

Start with 4 negative counters to represent -4.

Take away 3 negative counters to represent subtracting -3.

What is left? _____

Find the difference: $-4 - (-3) =$ _____

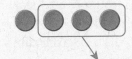

B Model $6 - (-3)$.

Start with 6 positive counters to represent 6.

You need to take away 3 negative counters, so add 3 zero pairs.

Take away 3 negative counters to represent subtracting -3.

What is left? _____

Find the difference: $6 - (-3) =$ _____

C Model $-2 - (-5)$.

Start with _____ counters.

You need to take away _____ counters, so add _____ zero pairs.

Take away _____ counters.

What is left? _____

Find the difference: $-2 - (-5) =$ _____

Reflect

1. **Communicate Mathematical Ideas** Suppose you want to model the difference $-4 - 7$. Do you need to add zero pairs? If so, why? How many should you add? What is the difference?

_____

_____

_____

Subtracting on a Number Line

You can think about modeling the difference $5 - 3$ on a horizontal number line by starting at 0 and moving 5 units to the right, then moving 3 units to the left. Notice that you model the sum $5 + (-3)$ in the same way. Subtracting 3 is the same as adding its opposite, -3.

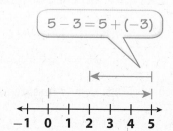

You can use the fact that subtracting a number is the same as adding its opposite to find a difference of two integers.

Find each difference on a number line.

A Find $-1 - 5$ on a number line.

Rewrite subtraction as addition of the opposite.

$-1 - 5 = -1 +$ _____

Start at _____. Draw the arrow for _____.

Then, starting at _____, draw the arrow for _____.

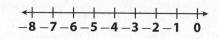

The difference is _____.

B Find $-7 - (-3)$.

Rewrite subtraction as addition of the opposite.

$-7 - (-3) = -7 +$ _____

Start at _____. Draw the arrow for _____.

Then, starting at _____, draw the arrow for _____.

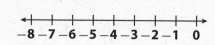

The difference is _____.

Reflect

2. **Communicate Mathematical Ideas** Describe how to find $5 - (-8)$ on a number line. If you found the difference using counters, would you get the same result? Explain.

_____

_____

_____

_____

_____

Subtracting Integers by Adding the Opposite

You can use the fact that subtracting an integer is the same as adding its opposite to solve problems.

Math On the Spot

⏻ my.hrw.com

EXAMPLE 1

The temperature on Monday was $-5\,°C$. By Tuesday the temperature rose to $-2\,°C$. Find the change in temperature.

Animated Math

⏻ my.hrw.com

STEP 1 Write a subtraction expression.

final temperature − Monday's temperature = change in temperature

$-2\,°C - (-5\,°C)$

STEP 2 Find the difference.

$-2 - (-5) = -2 + 5$ *To subtract −5, add its opposite, 5.*

$-2 + 5 = 3$ *Use the rule for adding integers.*

The temperature increased by $3\,°C$.

> **Math Talk**
> Mathematical Processes
>
> Why does it make sense that the change in temperature is a positive number?

Reflect

3. **What If?** In Example 1, the temperature rose by $3\,°C$. Suppose it fell from $-2\,°C$ to $-10\,°C$. Predict whether the change in temperature would be positive or negative. Then subtract to find the change.

_____

_____

YOUR TURN

Find each difference.

4. $-7 - 2 =$ _____

5. $-1 - (-3) =$ _____

6. $3 - 5 =$ _____

7. $-8 - (-4) =$ _____

Guided Practice

Explain how to find each difference using counters. (Explore Activity 1)

1. $5 - 8 =$ _____

_____

_____

_____

2. $-5 - (-3) =$ _____

_____

_____

_____

Use a number line to find each difference. (Explore Activity 2)

3. $-4 - 5 = -4 +$ _____ $=$ _____

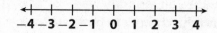

$$-9\ -8\ -7\ -6\ -5\ -4\ -3\ -2\ -1\quad 0$$

4. $1 - 4 = 1 +$ _____ $=$ _____

$$-4\ -3\ -2\ -1\quad 0\quad 1\quad 2\quad 3\quad 4$$

Solve. (Example 1)

5. $8 - 11 =$ _____

6. $-3 - (-5) =$ _____

7. $15 - 21 =$ _____

8. $-17 - 1 =$ _____

9. $0 - (-5) =$ _____

10. $1 - (-18) =$ _____

11. $15 - 1 =$ _____

12. $-3 - (-45) =$ _____

13. $19 - (-19) =$ _____

14. $-87 - (-87) =$ _____

? ESSENTIAL QUESTION CHECK-IN

15. How do you subtract an integer from another integer without using a number line or counters? Give an example.

_____

_____

17.3 Independent Practice

16. Theo had a balance of −$4 in his savings account. After making a deposit, he has $25 in his account. What is the overall change to his account?

_____

17. As shown, Suzi starts her hike at an elevation below sea level. When she reaches the end of the hike, she is still below sea level at −127 feet. What was the change in elevation from the beginning of Suzi's hike to the end of the hike?

Current Elevation: −225 feet

_____

18. The record high January temperature in Austin, Texas, is 90 °F. The record low January temperature is −2 °F. Find the difference between the high and low temperatures.

_____

19. Cheyenne is playing a board game. Her score was −275 at the start of her turn, and at the end of her turn her score was −425. What was the change in Cheyenne's score from the start of her turn to the end of her turn?

_____

20. A scientist conducts three experiments in which she records the temperature of some gases that are being heated. The table shows the initial temperature and the final temperature for each gas.

Gas	Initial Temperature	Final Temperature
A	−21 °C	−8 °C
B	−12 °C	12 °C
C	−19 °C	−15 °C

a. Write a difference of integers to find the overall temperature change for each gas.

Gas A: _____

_____

Gas B: _____

_____

Gas C: _____

_____

b. **What If?** Suppose the scientist performs an experiment in which she cools the three gases. Will the changes in temperature be positive or negative for this experiment? Why?

_____

_____

_____

_____

_____

_____

_____

21. Analyze Relationships For two months, Nell feeds her cat Diet Chow brand cat food. Then for the next two months, she feeds her cat Kitty Diet brand cat food. The table shows the cat's change in weight over 4 months.

	Cat's Weight Change (oz)
Diet Chow, Month 1	−8
Diet Chow, Month 2	−18
Kitty Diet, Month 3	3
Kitty Diet, Month 4	−19

Which brand of cat food resulted in the greatest weight loss for Nell's cat? Explain.

_____

_____

 FOCUS ON HIGHER ORDER THINKING

22. Represent Real-World Problems Write and solve a word problem that can be modeled by the difference −4 − 10.

_____

_____

_____

23. Explain the Error When Tom found the difference −11 − (−4), he got −15. What might Tom have done wrong?

_____

_____

_____

24. Draw Conclusions When you subtract one negative integer from another, will your answer be greater than or less than the integer you started with? Explain your reasoning and give an example.

_____

_____

_____

_____

25. Look for a Pattern Find the next three terms in the pattern 9, 4, −1, −6, −11, ... Then describe the pattern.

_____

© Houghton Mifflin Harcourt Publishing Company

Work Area

Applying Addition and Subtraction of Integers

? ESSENTIAL QUESTION

How do you solve multistep problems involving addition and subtraction of integers?

EXPLORE ACTIVITY 1 Real World

Solving a Multistep Problem

You can use what you know about adding and subtracting integers to solve a multistep problem.

Math On the Spot
my.hrw.com

EXAMPLE 1 **A seal is swimming in the ocean 5 feet below sea level. It dives down 12 feet to catch some fish. Then, the seal swims 8 feet up toward the surface with its catch. What is the seal's final elevation relative to sea level?**

STEP 1 Write an expression.

The seal starts at 5 feet below the surface, so its initial position is −5 feet. It swims 12 feet down, and then 8 feet up.

Starts	−	Distance down	+	Distance up
−5	−	_____	+	_____

STEP 2 Add or subtract from left to right to find the value of the expression.

$-5 - 12 + 8 =$ _____ $+ 8 =$ _____

This is reasonable because the seal swam farther down than up.

The seal's final elevation is _____ feet   **above / below**   sea level.

YOUR TURN

1. Anna is in a cave 40 feet below the cave entrance. She descends 13 feet, then ascends 18 feet. Write and evaluate an expression to find her new position relative to the cave entrance.

_____

Personal Math Trainer
Online Assessment and Intervention
my.hrw.com

Applying Properties to Solve Problems

You can use properties of addition to solve problems involving integers.

EXAMPLE 2 Problem Solving

Irene has a checking account. On Monday she writes a $160 check for groceries. Then she deposits $125. Finally she writes another check for $40. What was the total change in the amount in Irene's account?

 Analyze Information

When Irene deposits money, she adds that amount to the account. When she writes a check, that money is deducted from the account.

 Formulate a Plan

Use a positive integer for the amount Irene added to the account. Use negative integers for the checks she wrote. Find the sum.

$$-160 + 125 + (-40)$$

 Solve

Add the amounts to find the total change in the account. Use properties of addition to simplify calculations.

$$-160 + 125 + (-40) = -160 + (-40) + 125 \quad \text{Commutative Property}$$
$$= -200 + 125 \quad \text{Associative Property}$$
$$= -75$$

The amount in the account decreased by $75.

Justify and Evaluate

Irene's account has $75 less than it did before Monday. This is reasonable because she wrote checks for $200 but only deposited $125.

Reflect

2. **Communicative Mathematical Ideas** Describe a different way to find the change in Irene's account.

_____

_____

YOUR TURN

3. Alex wrote checks on Tuesday for $35 and $45. He also made a deposit in his checking account of $180. Find the overall change in the amount in his checking account.

_____

Comparing Values of Expressions

Sometimes you may want to compare values obtained by adding and subtracting integers.

Math On the Spot
my.hrw.com

EXAMPLE 3 Problem Solving

The Tigers, a football team, must gain 10 yards in the next four plays to keep possession of the ball. The Tigers lose 12 yards, gain 5 yards, lose 8 yards, and gain 14 yards. Do the Tigers maintain possession of the ball?

 Analyze Information

When the team gains yards, add that distance.

When the team loses yards, subtract that distance.

If the total change in yards is greater than or equal to 10, the team keeps possession of the ball.

 Formulate a Plan

$-12 + 5 - 8 + 14$

 Solve

$-12 + 5 - 8 + 14$

$-12 + 5 + (-8) + 14$ To subtract, add the opposite.

$-12 + (-8) + 5 + 14$ Commutative Property

$(-12 + (-8)) + (5 + 14)$ Associative Property

$-20 + 19 = -1$

$-1 < 10$ Compare to 10 yards

The Tigers gained less than 10 yards, so they do not maintain possession.

> **Math Talk**
> Mathematical Processes
>
> What does it mean that the football team had a total of −1 yard over four plays?

 Justify and Evaluate

The football team gained 19 yards and lost 20 yards for a total of −1 yard.

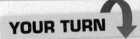

4. Jim and Carla are scuba diving. Jim started out 10 feet below the surface. He descended 18 feet, rose 5 feet, and descended 12 more feet. Then he rested. Carla started out at the surface. She descended 20 feet, rose 5 feet, and descended another 18 feet. Then she rested. Which person rested at a greater depth? Explain.

_____

_____

> **Personal Math Trainer**
> Online Assessment and Intervention
> my.hrw.com

Write an expression. Then find the value of the expression.
(Explore Activity Example 1 and Example 2)

1. Tomas works as an underwater photographer. He starts at a position that is 15 feet below sea level. He rises 9 feet, then descends 12 feet to take a photo of a coral reef. Write and evaluate an expression to find his position relative to sea level when he took the photo.

   _____

2. The temperature on a winter night was −23 °F. The temperature rose by 5 °F when the sun came up. When the sun set again, the temperature dropped by 7 °F. Write and evaluate an expression to find the temperature after the sun set.

   _____

3. Jose earned 50 points in a video game. He lost 40 points, earned 87 points, then lost 30 more points. Write and evaluate an expression to find his final score in the video game.

   _____

Find the value of each expression. (Example 2)

4. $-6 + 15 + 15 = $ _____

5. $9 - 4 - 17 = $ _____

6. $50 - 42 + 10 = $ _____

7. $6 + 13 + 7 - 5 = $ _____

8. $65 + 43 - 11 = $ _____

9. $-35 - 14 + 45 + 31 = $ _____

Determine which expression has a greater value. (Example 3)

10. $-12 + 6 - 4$ or $-34 - 3 + 39$

    _____

11. $21 - 3 + 8$ or $-14 + 31 - 6$

    _____

? ESSENTIAL QUESTION CHECK-IN

12. Explain how you can find the value of the expression $-5 + 12 + 10 - 7$.

    _____

    _____

17.4 Independent Practice

Personal Math Trainer

my.hrw.com

Online Assessment and Intervention

13. Sports Cameron is playing 9 holes of golf. He needs to score a total of at most 15 over par on the last four holes to beat his best golf score. On the last four holes, he scores 5 over par, 1 under par, 6 over par, and 1 under par.

a. Write and find the value of an expression that gives Cameron's score for 4 holes of golf.

_____

b. Is Cameron's score on the last four holes over or under par?

_____

c. Did Cameron beat his best golf score?

_____

14. Herman is standing on a ladder that is partly in a hole. He starts out on a rung that is 6 feet under ground, climbs up 14 feet, then climbs down 11 feet. What is Herman's final position, relative to ground level?

_____

15. Explain the Error Jerome tries to find the value of the expression $3 - 6 + 5$ by first applying the Commutative Property. He rewrites the expression as $3 - 5 + 6$. Explain what is wrong with Jerome's approach.

_____

_____

_____

_____

16. Lee and Barry play a trivia game in which questions are worth different numbers of points. If a question is answered correctly, a player earns points. If a question is answered incorrectly, the player loses points. Lee currently has -350 points.

a. Before the game ends, Lee answers a 275-point question correctly, a 70-point question correctly, and a 50-point question incorrectly. Write and find the value of an expression to find Lee's final score.

_____

b. Barry's final score is 45. Which player had the greater final score?

_____

17. Multistep Rob collects data about how many customers enter and leave a store every hour. He records a positive number for customers entering the store each hour and a negative number for customers leaving the store each hour.

	Entering	Leaving
1:00 to 2:00	30	-12
2:00 to 3:00	14	-8
3:00 to 4:00	18	-30

a. During which hour did more customers leave than arrive?

_____

b. There were 75 customers in the store at 1:00. The store must be emptied of customers when it closes at 5:00. How many customers must leave the store between 4:00 and 5:00?

_____

The table shows the changes in the values of two friends' savings accounts since the previous month.

	June	July	August
Carla	−18	22	−53
Leta	−17	−22	18

18. Carla had $100 in her account in May. How much money does she have in her account in August?

_____

19. Leta had $45 in her account in May. How much money does she have in her account in August?

_____

20. **Analyze Relationships** Whose account had the greatest decrease in value from May to August?

_____

FOCUS ON HIGHER ORDER THINKING

Work Area

21. **Represent Real-World Problems** Write and solve a word problem that matches the diagram shown.

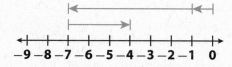

_____

_____

_____

22. **Critical Thinking** Mary has $10 in savings. She owes her parents $50. She does some chores and her parents pay her $12. She also gets $25 for her birthday from her grandmother. Does Mary have enough money to pay her parents what she owes them? If not, how much more money does she need? Explain.

_____

_____

23. **Draw Conclusions** An expression involves subtracting two numbers from a given number. Under what circumstances will the value of the expression be negative? Give an example.

_____

_____

_____

_____

Ready to Go On?

Personal Math Trainer

Online Assessment and Intervention

my.hrw.com

17.1 Adding Integers with the Same Sign

Add.

1. $-8 + (-6)$ _____

2. $-4 + (-7)$ _____

3. $-9 + (-12)$ _____

17.2 Adding Integers with Different Signs

Add.

4. $5 + (-2)$ _____

5. $-8 + 4$ _____

6. $15 + (-8)$ _____

17.3 Subtracting Integers

Subtract.

7. $2 - 9$ _____

8. $-3 - (-4)$ _____

9. $11 - (-12)$ _____

17.4 Applying Addition and Subtraction of Integers

10. A bus makes a stop at 2:30, letting off 15 people and letting on 9. The bus makes another stop ten minutes later to let off 4 more people. How many more or fewer people are on the bus after the second stop compared to the number of people on the bus before the 2:30 stop?

_____

11. Cate and Elena were playing a card game. The stack of cards in the middle had 24 cards in it to begin with. Cate added 8 cards to the stack. Elena then took 12 cards from the stack. Finally, Cate took 9 cards from the stack. How many cards were left in the stack? _____

 ESSENTIAL QUESTION

12. Write and solve a word problem that can be modeled by addition of two negative integers.

_____

_____

_____

Assessment Readiness

Personal
Math Trainer

Online
Assessment and
Intervention

my.hrw.com

Selected Response

1. Which expression has the same value as $-3 + (-5)$?

Ⓐ $-3 - (-5)$

Ⓑ $-3 + 5$

Ⓒ $-5 + (-3)$

Ⓓ $-5 - (-3)$

2. A diver's elevation is -30 feet relative to sea level. She dives down 12 feet. What is her elevation after the dive?

Ⓐ 12 feet

Ⓑ 18 feet

Ⓒ -30 feet

Ⓓ -42 feet

3. Which number line models the expression $-3 + 5$?

Ⓐ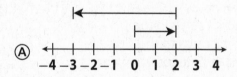

Ⓑ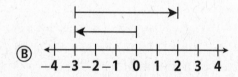

Ⓒ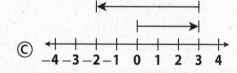

Ⓓ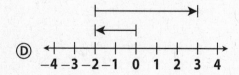

4. Which number can you add to 5 to get a sum of 0?

Ⓐ -10 Ⓒ 0

Ⓑ -5 Ⓓ 5

5. The temperature in the morning was $-3\,°F$. The temperature dropped 11 degrees by night. What was the temperature at night?

Ⓐ $-14\,°F$

Ⓑ $-8\,°F$

Ⓒ $8\,°F$

Ⓓ $14\,°F$

6. Which of the following expressions has the greatest value?

Ⓐ $3 - 7 + (-10)$

Ⓑ $3 + 7 - (-10)$

Ⓒ $3 - 7 - (-10)$

Ⓓ $3 + 7 + (-10)$

Mini-Task

7. At the end of one day, the value of a share of a certain stock was $12. Over the next three days, the change in the value of the share was $-$1$, then, $-$1$, and then $3.

a. Write an expression that describes the situation.

_____

b. Evaluate the expression. _____

c. What does your answer to part **b** mean in the context of the problem?

_____

_____

© Houghton Mifflin Harcourt Publishing Company

Multiplying and Dividing Integers

? **ESSENTIAL QUESTION**

How can you use multiplication and division of integers to solve real-world problems?

Real-World Video

The giant panda is an endangered animal. For some endangered species, the population has made a steady decline. This can be represented by multiplying integers with different signs.

⏻ my.hrw.com

GO DIGITAL

my.hrw.com

my.hrw.com

Go digital with your write-in student edition, accessible on any device.

Math On the Spot

Scan with your smart phone to jump directly to the online edition, video tutor, and more.

X²

Animated Math

Interactively explore key concepts to see how math works.

Personal Math Trainer

Get immediate feedback and help as you work through practice sets.

Reading Start-Up

Visualize Vocabulary

Use the ✔ words to complete the chart. You may put more than one word in each box.

÷, or put into equal groups		×, or repeated addition

Multiplying and Dividing Whole Numbers

$4 \times 1 = 4$		$32 \div 4 = 8$

Vocabulary

Review Words

- ✔ divide (*dividir*)
- ✔ dividend (*dividendo*)
- ✔ divisor (*divisor*)
  - integers (*enteros*)
- ✔ multiply (*multiplicar*)
  - negative number (*número negativo*)
  - operation (*operación*)
  - opposites (*opuestos*)
  - positive number (*número positivo*)
- ✔ product (*producto*)
- ✔ quotient (*cociente*)

Understand Vocabulary

Complete the sentences using the review words.

1. A _____ is a number that is less than 0. A _____ is a number that is greater than 0.

2. Division problems have three parts. The part you want to divide into groups is called the _____. The number that is divided into another number is called the _____. The answer to a division problem is called the _____.

3. _____ are all whole numbers and their opposites.

Active Reading

Double-Door Fold Create a double-door fold to help you understand the concepts in this module. Label one flap "Multiplying Integers" and the other flap "Dividing Integers." As you study each lesson, write important ideas under the appropriate flap. Include information that will help you remember the concepts later when you look back at your notes.

Are YOU Ready?

Complete these exercises to review skills you will need for this module.

Multiplication Facts

> **EXAMPLES**
> $7 \times 9 = \blacksquare$
> $7 \times 9 = 63$
> $12 \times 10 = \blacksquare$
> $12 \times 10 = 120$
>
> Use patterns. When you multiply 9 by a number 1 through 9, the digits of the product add up to 9. $6 + 3 = 9$
>
> Products of 10 end in 0.

Multiply.

1. 9×3 _____ **2.** 7×10 _____ **3.** 9×8 _____ **4.** 15×10 _____

5. 6×9 _____ **6.** 10×23 _____ **7.** 9×9 _____ **8.** 10×20 _____

Division Facts

> **EXAMPLE**
> $48 \div 6 = \blacksquare$
> $48 \div 6 = 8$
>
> Think: 6 times what number equals 48?
> $6 \times 8 = 48$
> So, $48 \div 6 = 8$

Divide.

9. $54 \div 9$ _____ **10.** $42 \div 6$ _____ **11.** $24 \div 3$ _____ **12.** $64 \div 8$ _____

13. $90 \div 10$ _____ **14.** $56 \div 7$ _____ **15.** $81 \div 9$ _____ **16.** $110 \div 11$ _____

Order of Operations

> **EXAMPLE**
> $32 - 2(10 - 7)^2$
> $32 - 2(3)^2$
> $32 - 2(9)$
> $32 - 18$
> 14
>
> To evaluate, first operate within parentheses.
> Next, simplify exponents.
> Then multiply and divide from left to right.
> Finally add and subtract from left to right.

Evaluate each expression.

17. $12 + 8 \div 2$ _____ **18.** $15 - (4 + 3) \times 2$ _____ **19.** $18 - (8 - 5)^2$ _____

20. $6 + 7 \times 3 - 5$ _____ **21.** $9 + (2^2 + 3)^2 \times 2$ _____ **22.** $6 + 5 - 4 \times 3 \div 2$ _____

Complete these exercises to review skills you will need for this module.

Multiplication Facts

23. A chef ordered 400 pounds of potatoes in same-sized bags. Which expressions show the number of bags and number of pounds of potatoes per bag the chef may have ordered? Choose all that apply.

Ⓐ 80×5 Ⓑ 10×40 Ⓒ 20×2 Ⓓ 20×20 Ⓔ 50×80

Division Facts

24. Josh has 36 postcards from national parks he visited. He wants to put them in a binder. Each page in the binder holds 4 postcards. How many pages does he need for the binder? Explain.

Order of Operations

25. A coach bought 3 soccer balls on sale. They normally sell for $26 each. They were on sale for $7 off the original price. The total tax on the balls was $4. The expression $4 + 3(26 - 7)$ can be used to find the total amount the coach paid. Tell why the expression represents the total amount paid. Then explain how to use the order of operations to find the total amount the coach paid for the soccer balls.

18.1 Multiplying Integers

7.1.2.1
Students will multiply integers.

? ESSENTIAL QUESTION

How do you multiply integers?

EXPLORE ACTIVITY 1

Multiplying Integers Using a Number Line

You can use a number line to see what happens when you multiply a positive number by a negative number.

A Henry made three withdrawals of $2 each from his savings account. What was the change in his balance?

Find 3(−2).

To show −2, you would draw an arrow from 0 to _____ .

3(−2) means (_____) + (_____) + (_____).

To show 3(−2), you would draw the sum equivalent to 3(−2).

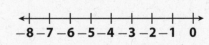

The result is _____.

The change in Henry's balance was _____.

B Lisa plays a video game in which she loses points. She loses 3 points 2 times. What is her score?

Find 2(−3).

2(−3) means (_____) + (_____).
Show this on the number line.

Lisa has a score of _____.

Reflect

1. What do you notice about the product of two integers with different signs?

_____

_____

Modeling Integer Multiplication

Counters representing positive and negative numbers
can help you understand how to find the product of
two negative integers.

○ = +1
● = −1

Find the product of −3 and −4.

Write (−3)(−4) as −3(−4), which means the *opposite* of 3(−4).

STEP 1 Use negative counters to model 3(−4).

3 groups of −4

STEP 2 Make the same model using positive counters to
find the *opposite* of 3(−4).

The *opposite* of
3 groups of −4

STEP 3 Translate the model into a mathematical expression:

(−3)(−4) = _____

The product of −3 and −4 is _____.

Reflect

2. What do you notice about the sign of the product of two negative
integers?

_____

3. **Make a Conjecture** What can you conclude about the sign of the
product of two integers with the same sign?

_____

_____

_____

_____

Multiplying Integers

The product of two integers with opposite signs is negative. The product of two integers with the same sign is positive. The product of 0 and any other integer is 0.

Math On the Spot
my.hrw.com

EXAMPLE 1

A Multiply: (13)(−3).

STEP 1 Determine the sign of the product.

13 is positive and −3 is negative. Since the numbers have opposite signs, the product will be negative.

STEP 2 Find the absolute values of the numbers and multiply them.

$|13| = 13 \qquad |−3| = 3$

$13 \times 3 = 39$

STEP 3 Assign the correct sign to the product.

$13(−3) = −39$ The product is −39.

Animated Math
my.hrw.com

B Multiply: (−5)(−8).

STEP 1 Determine the sign of the product.

−5 is negative and −8 is negative. Since the numbers have the same sign, the product will be positive.

STEP 2 Find the absolute values of the numbers and multiply them.

$|−5| = 5 \qquad |−8| = 8$

$5 \times 8 = 40$

STEP 3 Assign the correct sign to the product.

$(−5)(−8) = 40$ The product is 40.

C Multiply: (−10)(0).

$(−10)(0) = 0$ One of the factors is 0, so the product is 0.

Math Talk
Mathematical Processes

Compare the rules for finding the product of a number and zero and finding the sum of a number and 0.

© Houghton Mifflin Harcourt Publishing Company

YOUR TURN

Find each product.

4. −3(5) _____

5. (−10)(−2) _____

6. 7(−6) _____

7. 0(−22) _____

8. (−15)(−3) _____

9. 8(4) _____

Personal Math Trainer

Online Assessment and Intervention

my.hrw.com

Guided Practice

Find each product. (Explore Activity 2 and Example 1)

1. $-1(9)$ _____

2. $14(-2)$ _____

3. $(-9)(-6)$ _____

4. $(-2)(50)$ _____

5. $(-4)(15)$ _____

6. $-18(0)$ _____

7. $(-7)(-7)$ _____

8. $-15(9)$ _____

9. $(8)(-12)$ _____

10. $-3(-100)$ _____

11. $0(-153)$ _____

12. $-6(32)$ _____

Solve. Show your work.

13. Flora made 7 withdrawals of $75 each from her bank account. What was the overall change in her account? (Example 1)

_____

14. A football team lost 5 yards on each of 3 plays. Explain how you could use a number line to find the team's change in field position after the 3 plays. Then find and interpret the change in position. (Explore Activity 1)

_____

_____

15. The temperature dropped 2 °F every hour for 6 hours. What was the total number of degrees the temperature changed in the 6 hours? (Explore Activity 1)

_____

16. The price of one share of Acme Company declined $5 per day for 4 days in a row. Find and interpret the total change in the price of one share after the 4 days. (Explore Activity 1)

_____

17. A mountain climber climbed down a cliff 50 feet at a time. He did this 5 times in one day. What was the overall change in his elevation? (Explore Activity 1)

_____

ESSENTIAL QUESTION CHECK-IN

18. Explain the process for finding the product of two integers.

_____

_____

_____

528 Unit 8

© Houghton Mifflin Harcourt Publishing Company

18.1 Independent Practice

19. Critique Reasoning Lisa used a number line to model −2(3). Does her number line make sense? Explain why or why not.

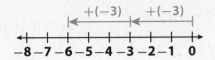

+(−3) +(−3)

−8 −7 −6 −5 −4 −3 −2 −1 0

_____

_____

_____

20. Represent Real-World Problems Mike got on an elevator and went down 3 floors. He meant to go to a lower level, so he stayed on the elevator and went down 3 more floors. How many floors did Mike go down altogether?

_____

Solve. Show your work.

21. When Brooke buys lunch at the cafeteria, money is withdrawn from a lunch account. The table shows amounts withdrawn in one week. By how much did the amount in Brooke's lunch account change by the end of that week?

Lunch Account			
Week 1	**Lunch**	**Cost**	**Balance**
			$28
Monday	Pizza	$4	
Tuesday	Fish Tacos	$4	
Wednesday	Spaghetti	$4	
Thursday	Sandwich	$4	
Friday	Chicken	$4	

_____

22. Adam is scuba diving. He descends 5 feet below sea level. He descends the same distance 4 more times. What is Adam's final elevation?

_____

_____

23. The price of jeans was reduced $6 per week for 7 weeks. By how much did the price of the jeans change over the 7 weeks?

_____

_____

24. Casey uses some of his savings on batting practice. The cost of renting a batting cage for 1 hour is $6. He rents a cage for 9 hours in each of two months. What is the change in Casey's savings after two months?

_____

_____

_____

25. Volunteers at Sam's school use some of the student council's savings for a special project. They buy 7 backpacks for $8 each and fill each backpack with paper and pens that cost $5. By how much did the student council's savings change because of this project?

_____

_____

_____

26. Communicate Mathematical Ideas Describe a real-world situation that can be represented by the product 8(−20). Then find the product and explain what the product means in terms of the real-world situation.

_____

_____

_____

27. What If? The rules for multiplying two integers can be extended to a product of 3 or more integers. Find the following products by using the Associative Property to multiply 2 numbers at a time.

a. 3(3)(−3) _____   **b.** 3(−3)(−3) _____   **c.** −3(−3)(−3) _____

d. 3(3)(3)(−3) _____   **e.** 3(3)(−3)(−3) _____   **f.** 3(−3)(−3)(−3) _____

g. Make a Conjecture Based on your results, complete the following statements:

When a product of integers has an odd number of negative factors,

then the sign of the product is _____.

When a product of integers has an even number of negative factors,

then the sign of the product is _____.

H.O.T. FOCUS ON HIGHER ORDER THINKING

Work Area

28. Multiple Representations The product of three integers is −3. Determine all of the possible values for the three factors.

_____

29. Analyze Relationships When is the product of two nonzero integers less than or equal to both of the two factors?

_____

_____

30. Justify Reasoning The sign of the product of two integers with the same sign is positive. What is the sign of the product of three integers with the same sign? Explain your thinking.

_____

_____

_____

_____

LESSON

18.2 Dividing Integers

7.1.2.2

Students will divide integers.

ESSENTIAL QUESTION

How do you divide integers?

EXPLORE ACTIVITY (Real World)

A diver needs to descend to a depth of 100 feet. She wants to do it in 5 equal stages. Describe how she should travel at each stage.

A Use the number line at the right to help describe how the diver should travel at each of the 5 stages.

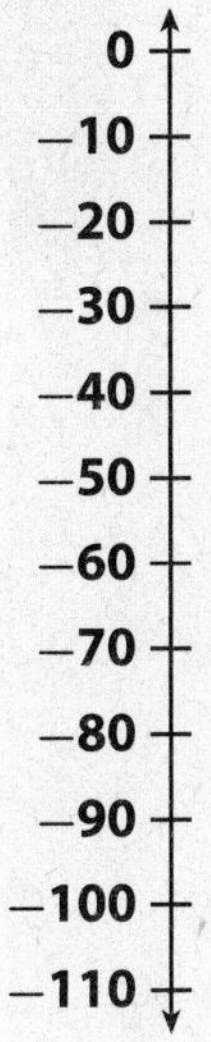
0
−10
−20
−30
−40
−50
−60
−70
−80
−90
−100
−110

____

B To solve this problem, you can set up a division problem: $\frac{-100}{\square} = ?$

C Rewrite the division problem as a multiplication problem.
Think: Some number multiplied by 5 equals −100.

________ $\times\ ? = -100$

D Remember the rules for integer multiplication. If the product is negative, one of the factors must be negative. Since ________ is positive, the unknown factor must be **positive / negative.**

E You know that $5 \times$ ______ $= 100$. So, using the rules for integer multiplication you can say that $5 \times$ ________ $= -100$.

The diver should descend ________ feet at each stage.

F Use the process you just learned to find each of the quotients below.

$\frac{14}{-7} =$ ______ $\frac{-36}{-9} =$ ______ $\frac{-55}{11} =$ ______ $\frac{-45}{-5} =$ ______

Reflect

1. Make a Conjecture Make a conjecture about the quotient of two integers with different signs. Make a conjecture about the quotient of two integers with the same sign.

____

____

Dividing Integers

You used the relationship between multiplication and division to make conjectures about the signs of quotients of integers. As with multiplication, the quotient of two integers with different signs is negative, and the quotient of two integers with the same sign is positive.

You can use multiplication to understand why division by zero is not possible. Think about the division problem below and its related multiplication problem.

$$5 \div 0 = ? \qquad 0 \times ? = 5$$

The multiplication sentence says that there is some number times 0 that equals 5. You already know that 0 times any number equals 0. This means division by 0 is not possible, so we say that division by 0 is undefined.

My Notes

EXAMPLE 1

A Divide: $24 \div (-3)$

STEP 1 Determine the sign of the quotient.

24 is positive and −3 is negative. Since the numbers have opposite signs, the quotient will be negative.

STEP 2 Divide.

$$24 \div (-3) = -8$$

B Divide: $-6 \div (-2)$

STEP 1 Determine the sign of the quotient.

−6 is negative and −2 is negative. Since the numbers have the same sign, the quotient will be positive.

STEP 2 Divide: $-6 \div (-2) = 3$

C Divide: $0 \div (-9)$

STEP 1 Determine the sign of the quotient.

The dividend is 0 and the divisor is not 0. So, the quotient is 0.

STEP 2 Divide: $0 \div (-9) = 0$

YOUR TURN

Find each quotient.

2. $0 \div (-6)$ _____

3. $38 \div (-19)$ _____

4. $-13 \div (-1)$ _____

Using Integer Division to Solve Problems

You can use integer division to solve real-world problems. For some problems, you may need to perform more than one step. Be sure to check that the sign of the quotient makes sense for the situation.

Math On the Spot

⏻ my.hrw.com

EXAMPLE 2

Jake answers questions in two different online Olympic trivia quizzes. In each quiz, he loses points when he gives an incorrect answer. The table shows the score for each wrong answer in each quiz and Jake's total score for wrong answers in each quiz. In which quiz did he have more wrong answers?

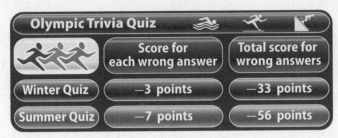

Olympic Trivia Quiz	Score for each wrong answer	Total score for wrong answers
Winter Quiz	−3 points	−33 points
Summer Quiz	−7 points	−56 points

STEP 1 Find the number of incorrect answers Jake gave in the winter quiz.

$-33 \div (-3) = 11$ *Divide the total score for wrong answers by the score for each wrong answer.*

STEP 2 Find the number of incorrect answers Jake gave in the summer quiz.

$-56 \div (-7) = 8$ *Divide the total score for wrong answers by the score for each wrong answer.*

STEP 3 Compare the numbers of wrong answers.

$11 > 8$, so Jake had more wrong answers in the winter quiz.

Math Talk
Mathematical Processes

What is the sign of each quotient in Steps 1 and 2? Why does this make sense for the situation?

YOUR TURN

5. A penalty in Meteor-Mania is −5 seconds. A penalty in Cosmic Calamity is −7 seconds. Yolanda had penalties totaling −25 seconds in a game of Meteor-Mania and −35 seconds in a game of Cosmic Calamity. In which game did Yolanda receive more penalties? Justify your answer.

_____

_____

_____

Personal Math Trainer

Online Assessment and Intervention

⏻ my.hrw.com

Find each quotient. (Example 1)

1. $\dfrac{-14}{2}$ _____

2. $21 \div (-3)$ _____

3. $\dfrac{26}{-13}$ _____

4. $0 \div (-4)$ _____

5. $\dfrac{-45}{-5}$ _____

6. $-30 \div (10)$ _____

7. $\dfrac{-11}{-1}$ _____

8. $-31 \div (-31)$ _____

9. $\dfrac{0}{-7}$ _____

10. $\dfrac{-121}{-11}$ _____

11. $84 \div (-7)$ _____

12. $\dfrac{500}{-25}$ _____

13. $-6 \div (0)$ _____

14. $\dfrac{-63}{-21}$ _____

Write a division expression for each problem. Then find the value of the expression. (Example 2)

15. Clark made four of his truck payments late and was fined four late fees. The total change to his savings from late fees was −$40. How much was one late fee?

_____

16. Jan received −22 points on her exam. She got 11 questions wrong out of 50 questions. How much was Jan penalized for each wrong answer?

_____

17. Allen's score in a video game was changed by −75 points because he missed some targets. He got −15 points for each missed target. How many targets did he miss?

_____

18. Louisa's savings change by −$9 each time she goes bowling. In all, it changed by −$99 during the summer. How many times did she go bowling in the summer?

_____

? ESSENTIAL QUESTION CHECK-IN

19. How is the process of dividing integers similar to the process of multiplying integers?

_____

_____

_____

18.2 Independent Practice

Personal Math Trainer

my.hrw.com

Online Assessment and Intervention

20. Walter buys a bus pass for $30. Every time he rides the bus, money is deducted from the value of the pass. He rode 12 times and $24 was deducted from the value of the pass. How much does each bus ride cost? _____

21. **Analyze Relationships** Elisa withdrew $20 at a time from her bank account and withdrew a total of $140. Francis withdrew $45 at a time from his bank account and withdrew a total of $270. Who made the greater number of withdrawals? Justify your answer.

_____

_____

_____

22. **Multistep** At 7 p.m. last night, the temperature was 10°F. At 7 a.m. the next morning, the temperature was −2°F.

   a. By how much did the temperature change from 7 p.m. to 7 a.m.?

_____

   b. The temperature changed by a steady amount overnight. By how much did it change each hour?

_____

_____

23. **Analyze Relationships** Nola hiked down a trail at a steady rate for 10 minutes. Her change in elevation was −200 feet. Then she continued to hike down for another 20 minutes at a different rate. Her change in elevation for this part of the hike was −300 feet. During which portion of the hike did she walk down at a faster rate? Explain your reasoning.

_____

_____

_____

24. Write a real world description to fit the expression −50 ÷ 5.

_____

_____

_____

25. Communicate Mathematical Ideas Two integers, a and b, have different signs. The absolute value of integer a is divisible by the absolute value of integer b. Find two integers that fit this description. Then decide if the product of the integers is greater than or less than the quotient of the integers. Show your work.

_____

_____

_____

Determine if each statement is true or false. Justify your answer.

26. For any two nonzero integers, the product and quotient have the same sign.

_____

_____

_____

27. Any nonzero integer divided by 0 equals 0.

_____

_____

H.O.T. FOCUS ON HIGHER ORDER THINKING

28. Multi-step A perfect score on a test with 25 questions is 100. Each question is worth the same number of points.

   a. How many points is each question on the test worth? _____

   b. Fred got a score of 84 on the test. Write a division sentence using negative numbers where the quotient represents the number of questions Fred answered incorrectly.

                                       _____

29. Persevere in Problem Solving Colleen divided integer a by -3 and got 8. Then she divided 8 by integer b and got -4. Find the quotient of integer a and integer b. _____

30. Justify Reasoning The quotient of two negative integers results in an integer. How does the value of the quotient compare to the value of the original two integers? Explain.

_____

_____

_____

Work Area

LESSON
18.3 Applying Integer Operations

7.1.2.3
Students will use integer operations to solve real-world problems.

? ESSENTIAL QUESTION

How can you use integer operations to solve real-world problems?

EXPLORE ACTIVITY Problem Solving

Using the Order of Operations with Integers

The order of operations applies to integer operations as well as positive number operations. Perform multiplication and division first, and then addition and subtraction. Work from left to right in the expression.

Math On the Spot

⏵ my.hrw.com

EXAMPLE 1 **Hannah made four withdrawals of $20 from her checking account. She also wrote a check for $215. By how much did the amount in her checking account change?**

 Analyze Information

You need to find the total *change* in Hannah's account. Since withdrawals and writing a check represent a decrease in her account, use negative numbers to represent these amounts.

 Formulate a Plan

Write a product to represent the four withdrawals.

$$-20 + (-20) + (-20) + (-20) = 4\left(\boxed{}\right)$$

Add −215 to represent the check that Hannah wrote.

$$4\left(\boxed{}\right) + \left(\boxed{}\right)$$

 Solve

Evaluate the expression to find by how much the amount in the account changed.

Multiply first. Then add.

$$4(-20) - (215) = \boxed{} + (-215) = \boxed{}$$

The amount in the account ⟨ **increased / decreased** ⟩ by $ _____ .

 Justify and Evaluate

The value −295 represents a decrease of 295 dollars. This makes sense, since withdrawals and writing checks remove money from the checking account.

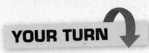

YOUR TURN

1. Reggie lost 3 spaceships in level 3 of a video game. He lost 30 points for each spaceship. When he completed level 3, he earned a bonus of 200 points. By how much did his score change?

_____

_____

2. Simplify: $-6(13) - 21$ _____

Personal Math Trainer

Online Assessment and Intervention

my.hrw.com

Math On the Spot

my.hrw.com

Using Negative Integers to Represent Quantities

You can use positive and negative integers to solve problems involving amounts that increase or decrease. Sometimes you may need to use more than one operation.

EXAMPLE 2

Three brothers each have their own savings. They borrow $72 from their parents for concert tickets. Each brother must pay back an equal share of this amount. Also, the youngest brother owes his parents $15. By how much will the youngest brother's savings change after he pays his parents?

STEP 1 Determine the signs of the values and the operations you will use. Write an expression.

Since the money is being paid back, it will *decrease* the amount in each brother's savings. Use -72 and -15.

Since an *equal share* of the $72 will be paid back, use division to determine 3 equal parts of -72. Then add -15 to one of these equal parts.

Change to youngest brother's savings $= (-72) \div 3 + (-15)$

STEP 2 Evaluate the expression.

$(-72) \div 3 + (-15) = -24 + (-15)$ Divide.

$= -39$ Add.

The youngest brother's savings will decrease by $39.

Math Talk

Mathematical Processes

Suppose the youngest brother has $60 in savings. How much will he have left after he pays his parents what he owes?

Reflect

3. **What If?** Suppose there were four brothers in Example 2. How much would the youngest brother need to pay?

_____

YOUR TURN

Simplify each expression.

4. $(-12) \div 6 + 2$ _____

5. $-87 \div (-3) - 9$ _____

6. $40 \div (-5) + 30$ _____

7. $-39 \div 3 - 15$ _____

Comparing Values of Expressions

Often, problem situations require making comparisons between two values.
Use integer operations to calculate values. Then compare the values.

EXAMPLE 3 Real World

Jill and Tony play a board game in which they move counters along a board. Jill moves her counter back 3 spaces four times, and then moves her counter forward 6 spaces. Tony moves his counter back 2 spaces three times, and then moves his counter forward 3 spaces one time. Find each player's overall change in position. Who moved farther?

STEP 1 Find each player's overall change in position.

Jill: $4(-3) + 6 = -12 + 6 = -6$ *Jill moves back 6 spaces.*

Tony: $3(-2) + 3 = -6 + 3 = -3$ *Tony moves back 3 spaces.*

STEP 2 Compare the numbers of spaces moved by the players.

$|-6| > |-3|$ *Compare absolute values.*

Jill moves farther back than Tony.

> ### Math Talk
> #### Mathematical Processes
>
> Why do you compare absolute values in Step 2?

YOUR TURN

8. Amber and Will are in line together to buy tickets. Amber moves back by 3 places three times to talk to friends. She then is invited to move 5 places up in line. Will moved back by 4 places twice, and then moved up in line by 3 places. Overall, who moved farther back in line?

_____

Evaluate each expression. Circle the expression with the greater value.

9. $(-10) \div 2 - 2 =$ _____

$(-28) \div 4 + 1 =$ _____

10. $42 \div (-3) + 9 =$ _____

$(-36) \div 9 - 2 =$ _____

Evaluate each expression. (Explore Activity Example 1)

1. $-6(-5) + 12$ _____

2. $3(-6) - 3$ _____

3. $-2(8) + 7$ _____

4. $4(-13) + 20$ _____

5. $(-4)(0) - 4$ _____

6. $-3(-5) - 16$ _____

Write an expression to represent the situation. Evaluate the expression and answer the question. (Example 2)

7. Bella pays 7 payments of $5 each to a game store. She returns one game and receives $20 back. What is the change to the amount of money she has?

_____

8. Ron lost 10 points seven times playing a video game. He then lost an additional 100 points for going over the time limit. What was the total change in his score?

_____

9. Ned took a test with 25 questions. He lost 4 points for each of the 6 questions he got wrong and earned an additional 10 points for answering a bonus question correctly. How many points did Ned receive or lose overall?

_____

10. Mr. Harris has some money in his wallet. He pays the babysitter $12 an hour for 4 hours of babysitting. His wife gives him $10, and he puts the money in his wallet. By how much does the amount in his wallet change?

_____

Compare the values of the two expressions using $<, =,$ **or** $>$. (Example 3)

11. $-3(-2) + 3$ _____ $3(-4) + 9$

12. $-8(-2) - 20$ _____ $3(-2) + 2$

13. $-7(5) - 9$ _____ $-3(20) + 10$

14. $-16(0) - 3$ _____ $-8(-2) - 3$

? ESSENTIAL QUESTION CHECK-IN

15. When you solve a problem involving money, what can a negative answer represent?

_____

_____

_____

18.3 Independent Practice

Personal Math Trainer

Online Assessment and Intervention

my.hrw.com

Evaluate each expression.

16. $-12(-3) + 7$ _____

17. $-42 \div (-6) + 5 - 8$ _____

18. $10(-60) - 18$ _____

19. $(-11)(-7) + 5 - 82$ _____

20. $35 \div (-7) + 6$ _____

21. $-13(-2) - 16 - 8$ _____

22. Multistep Lily and Rose are playing a game. In the game, each player starts with 0 points and the player with the most points at the end wins. Lily gains 5 points two times, loses 12 points, and then gains 3 points. Rose loses 3 points two times, loses 1 point, gains 6 points, and then gains 7 points.

    a. Write and evaluate an expression to find Lily's score.

    _____

    b. Write and evaluate an expression to find Rose's score.

    _____

    c. Who won the game?

    _____

Write an expression from the description. Then evaluate the expression.

23. 8 less than the product of 5 and -4

_____

24. 9 more than the quotient of -36 and -4.

_____

25. Multistep Arleen has a gift card for a local lawn and garden store. She uses the gift card to rent a tiller for 4 days. It costs $35 per day to rent the tiller. She also buys a rake for $9.

    a. Find the change to the value on her gift card.

    _____

    b. The original amount on the gift card was $200. Does Arleen have enough left on the card to buy a wheelbarrow for $50? Explain.

    _____

    _____

26. Carlos made up a game where, in a deck of cards, the red cards (hearts and diamonds) are negative and the black cards (spades and clubs) are positive. All face cards are worth 10 points, and number cards are worth their value.

a. Samantha has a king of hearts, a jack of diamonds, and a 3 of spades. Write an expression to find the value of her cards.

_____

b. Warren has a 7 of clubs, a 2 of spades, and a 7 of hearts. Write an expression to find the value of his cards.

_____

c. If the greater score wins, who won?

_____

d. If a player always gets three cards, describe two different ways to receive a score of 7.

_____

_____

 FOCUS ON HIGHER ORDER THINKING

27. Represent Real-World Problems Write a problem that the expression $3(-7) - 10 + 25 = -6$ could represent.

_____

_____

_____

28. Critique Reasoning Jim found the quotient of two integers and got a positive integer. He added another integer to the quotient and got a positive integer. His sister Kim says that all the integers Jim used to get this result must be positive. Do you agree? Explain.

_____

_____

_____

29. Persevere in Problem Solving Lisa is standing on a dock beside a lake. She drops a rock from her hand into the lake. After the rock hits the surface of the lake, the rock's distance from the lake's surface changes at a rate of -5 inches per second. If Lisa holds her hand 5 feet above the lake's surface, how far from Lisa's hand is the rock 4 seconds after it hits the surface?

_____

Work Area

Ready to Go On?

Personal Math Trainer
Online Assessment and Intervention
⏻ my.hrw.com

18.1 Multiplying Integers

Find each product.

1. $(-2)(3)$ _____

2. $(-5)(-7)$ _____

3. $(8)(-11)$ _____

4. $(-3)(2)(-2)$ _____

5. The temperature dropped $3\,°C$ every hour for 5 hours. Write an integer that represents the change in temperature. _____

18.2 Dividing Integers

Find each quotient.

6. $\frac{-63}{7}$ _____

7. $\frac{-15}{-3}$ _____

8. $0 \div (-15)$ _____

9. $96 \div (-12)$ _____

10. An elephant at the zoo lost 24 pounds over 6 months. The elephant lost the same amount of weight each month. Write an integer that represents the change in the elephant's weight each month. _____

18.3 Applying Integer Operations

Evaluate each expression.

11. $(-4)(5) + 8$ _____

12. $(-3)(-6) - 7$ _____

13. $-27 \div 9 - 11$ _____

14. $\frac{-24}{-3} - (-2)$ _____

? ESSENTIAL QUESTION

15. Write and solve a real-world problem that can be represented by the expression $(-3)(5) + 10$.

_____

_____

_____

_____

Assessment Readiness

Personal Math Trainer

Online Assessment and Intervention

my.hrw.com

Selected Response

1. A diver is at an elevation of −18 feet relative to sea level. The diver descends to an undersea cave that is 4 times as far from the surface. What is the elevation of the cave?

   Ⓐ −72 feet

   Ⓑ −22 feet

   Ⓒ −18 feet

   Ⓓ −14 feet

2. The football team lost 4 yards on 2 plays in a row. Which of the following could represent the change in field position?

   Ⓐ −12 yards

   Ⓑ −8 yards

   Ⓒ −6 yards

   Ⓓ −2 yards

3. Clayton climbed down 50 meters. He climbed down in 10-meter intervals. In how many intervals did Clayton make his climb?

   Ⓐ 5

   Ⓑ 10

   Ⓒ 40

   Ⓓ 500

4. Which expression results in a negative answer?

   Ⓐ a negative number divided by a negative number

   Ⓑ a positive number divided by a negative number

   Ⓒ a negative number multiplied by a negative number

   Ⓓ a positive number multiplied by a positive number

5. Clara played a video game before she left the house to go on a walk. She started with 0 points, lost 6 points 3 times, won 4 points, and then lost 2 points. How many points did she have when she left the house to go on the walk?

   Ⓐ −20   Ⓒ 12

   Ⓑ −16   Ⓓ 20

6. Which expression is equal to 0?

   Ⓐ $\frac{-24}{6} - 4$

   Ⓑ $\frac{-24}{-6} + 4$

   Ⓒ $\frac{24}{6} + 4$

   Ⓓ $\frac{-24}{-6} - 4$

Mini-Task

7. Rochelle and Denae started with the same amount of money in their bank accounts. Rochelle made three withdrawals of $25 and then wrote a $100 check. Denae deposited $5 and then wrote a $200 check.

   a. Find the total change in the amount of money in Rochelle's account.

   _____

   b. Find the total change in the amount of money in Denae's account.

   _____

   c. Compare the amounts of money the two women have in their accounts now.

   _____

   _____

   _____

Rational Numbers

ESSENTIAL QUESTION

How can you use rational numbers to solve real-world problems?

Real-World Video

In many competitive sports, scores are given as decimals. For some events, the judges' scores are averaged to give the athlete's final score.

my.hrw.com

GO DIGITAL

my.hrw.com

my.hrw.com

Go digital with your write-in student edition, accessible on any device.

Math On the Spot

Scan with your smart phone to jump directly to the online edition, video tutor, and more.

Animated Math

Interactively explore key concepts to see how math works.

Personal Math Trainer

Get immediate feedback and help as you work through practice sets.

Reading Start-Up

Visualize Vocabulary

Use the ✔ words to complete the graphic. You can put more than one word in each section of the triangle.

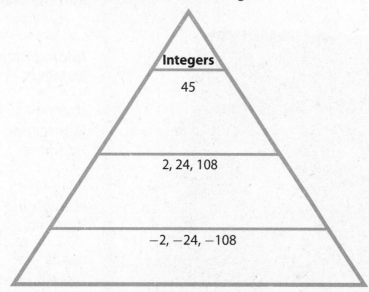

Integers

45

2, 24, 108

−2, −24, −108

Vocabulary

Review Words

   integers *(enteros)*

✔ negative numbers
   (números negativos)

   pattern *(patrón)*

✔ positive numbers
   (números positivos)

✔ whole numbers *(números
   enteros)*

Preview Words

   additive inverse *(inverso
   aditivo)*

   opposite *(opuesto)*

   rational number *(número
   racional)*

   repeating decimal
   (decimal periódico)

   terminating decimal
   (decimal finito)

Understand Vocabulary

Complete the sentences using the preview words.

1. A decimal number for which the decimals come to an end is a

   _____ decimal.

2. The _____ , or _____, of a number is the
same distance from 0 on a number line as the original number, but on
the other side of 0.

Active Reading

Layered Book Before beginning the module,
create a layered book to help you learn the concepts
in this module. At the top of the first flap, write the
title of the module, "Rational Numbers." Label the
other flaps "Adding," "Subtracting," "Multiplying,"
and "Dividing." As you study each lesson, write
important ideas, such as vocabulary and processes,
on the appropriate flap.

Are YOU Ready?

Complete these exercises to review skills you will need for this module.

Multiply Fractions

EXAMPLE $\frac{3}{8} \times \frac{4}{9}$ $\frac{3}{8} \times \frac{4}{9} = \frac{\cancel{3}^1}{\cancel{8}_2} \times \frac{\cancel{4}^1}{\cancel{9}_3}$ Divide by the common factors.

$= \frac{1}{6}$ Simplify.

Multiply. Write the product in simplest form.

1. $\frac{9}{14} \times \frac{7}{6}$ _____ **2.** $\frac{3}{5} \times \frac{4}{7}$ _____ **3.** $\frac{11}{8} \times \frac{10}{33}$ _____ **4.** $\frac{4}{9} \times 3$ _____

Operations with Fractions

EXAMPLE $\frac{2}{5} \div \frac{7}{10} = \frac{2}{5} \times \frac{10}{7}$ Multiply by the reciprocal of the divisor.

$= \frac{2}{\cancel{5}_1} \times \frac{\cancel{10}^2}{7}$ Divide by the common factors.

$= \frac{4}{7}$ Simplify.

Divide.

5. $\frac{1}{2} \div \frac{1}{4}$ _____ **6.** $\frac{3}{8} \div \frac{13}{16}$ _____ **7.** $\frac{2}{5} \div \frac{14}{15}$ _____ **8.** $\frac{4}{9} \div \frac{16}{27}$ _____

9. $\frac{3}{5} \div \frac{5}{6}$ _____ **10.** $\frac{1}{4} \div \frac{23}{24}$ _____ **11.** $6 \div \frac{3}{5}$ _____ **12.** $\frac{4}{5} \div 10$ _____

Order of Operations

EXAMPLE $50 - 3(3 + 1)^2$ To evaluate, first operate within parentheses.

$50 - 3(4)^2$ Next simplify exponents.

$50 - 3(16)$ Then multiply and divide from left to right.

$50 - 48$ Finally add and subtract from left to right.

2

Evaluate each expression.

13. $21 - 6 \div 3$ ____ **14.** $18 + (7 - 4) \times 3$ ____ **15.** $5 + (8 - 3)^2$ ____

16. $9 + 18 \div 3 + 10$ ____ **17.** $60 - (3 - 1)^4 \times 3$ ____ **18.** $10 - 16 \div 4 \times 2 + 6$ ____

Complete these exercises to review skills you will need for this module.

Multiply Fractions

19. Brittany has a wooden plank that is $\frac{3}{4}$ foot long. She paints $\frac{2}{5}$ of the plank with yellow paint. How long is the part of the plank that is painted yellow? Show your work.

Operations with Fractions

20. To find the quotient $4 \div \frac{2}{5}$, Kim wrote the following. What was his error?

$$4 \div \frac{2}{5} = \frac{1}{4} \times \frac{2}{5}$$

$$= \frac{1}{\underset{2}{\cancel{4}}} \times \frac{\overset{1}{\cancel{2}}}{5}$$

$$= \frac{1}{10}$$

Order of Operations

21. Zooey says the expressions $6 + (7 + 2)^2$ and $6 + 7^2 + 2^2$ have the same value. Trey says the expressions do **not** have the same value. Who is correct? How do you know?

LESSON
19.1

7.1.3.1
Students will convert a
rational number to a decimal.

Rational Numbers and Decimals

ESSENTIAL QUESTION

How can you convert a rational number to a decimal?

EXPLORE ACTIVITY

Describing Decimal Forms of Rational Numbers

A **rational number** is a number that can be written as a ratio of two integers a and b, where b is not zero. For example, $\frac{4}{7}$ is a rational number, as is 0.37 because it can be written as the fraction $\frac{37}{100}$.

A Use a calculator to find the equivalent decimal form of each fraction. Remember that numbers that repeat can be written as 0.333… or $0.\overline{3}$.

Fraction	$\frac{1}{4}$	$\frac{5}{8}$	$\frac{2}{3}$	$\frac{2}{9}$	$\frac{12}{5}$		
Decimal Equivalent						0.2	0.875

B Now find the corresponding fraction of the decimal equivalents given in the last two columns in the table. Write the fractions in simplest form.

C **Conjecture** What do you notice about the digits after the decimal point in the decimal forms of the fractions? Compare notes with your neighbor and refine your conjecture if necessary.

_____

Reflect

1. Consider the decimal 0.101001000100001000001…. Do you think this decimal represents a rational number? Why or why not?

_____

_____

2. Do you think a negative sign affects whether or not a number is a rational number? Use $-\frac{8}{5}$ as an example.

_____

_____

3. Do you think a mixed number is a rational number? Explain.

_____

_____

_____

Writing Rational Numbers as Decimals

You can convert a rational number to a decimal using long division. Some decimals are **terminating decimals** because the decimals come to an end. Other decimals are **repeating decimals** because one or more digits repeat infinitely.

EXAMPLE 1

Write each rational number as a decimal.

 $\frac{5}{16}$

Divide 5 by 16.
Add a zero after the decimal point.
Subtract 48 from 50.
Use the grid to help you complete the long division.

Add zeros in the dividend and continue dividing until the remainder is 0.

The decimal equivalent of $\frac{5}{16}$ is 0.3125.

```
        0. 3 1 2 5
  1 6 ) 5. 0 0 0 0
      - 4 8
          2 0
        - 1 6
            4 0
          - 3 2
              8 0
            - 8 0
                0
```

 $\frac{13}{33}$

Divide 13 by 33.
Add a zero after the decimal point.
Subtract 99 from 130.
Use the grid to help you complete the long division.

You can stop dividing once you discover a repeating pattern in the quotient.

Write the quotient with its repeating pattern and indicate that the repeating numbers continue.

The decimal equivalent of $\frac{13}{33}$ is 0.3939…, or $0.\overline{39}$.

```
          0. 3 9 3 9
  3 3 ) 1 3. 0 0 0 0
        - 9 9
          3 1 0
        - 2 9 7
            1 3 0
          -   9 9
              3 1 0
            - 2 9 7
                1 3
```

> ### Math Talk
> **Mathematical Processes**
>
> Do you think that decimals that have repeating patterns always have the same number of digits in their pattern? Explain.

Write each rational number as a decimal.

4. $\frac{4}{7}$ _____   5. $\frac{1}{3}$ _____   6. $\frac{9}{20}$ _____

Math On the Spot

⏱ my.hrw.com

Writing Mixed Numbers as Decimals

You can convert a mixed number to a decimal by rewriting the fractional part of the number as a decimal.

EXAMPLE 2 Real World

My Notes

Shawn rode his bike $6\frac{3}{4}$ miles to the science museum. Write $6\frac{3}{4}$ as a decimal.

STEP 1 Rewrite the fractional part of the number as a decimal.

$$\begin{array}{r} 0.75 \\ 4\overline{)3.00} \\ -28 \\ \hline 20 \\ -20 \\ \hline 0 \end{array}$$

Divide the numerator by the denominator.

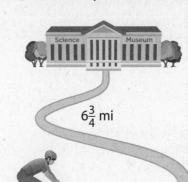

$6\frac{3}{4}$ mi

STEP 2 Rewrite the mixed number as the sum of the whole part and the decimal part.

$$6\frac{3}{4} = 6 + \frac{3}{4}$$
$$= 6 + 0.75$$
$$= 6.75$$

7. Yvonne made $2\frac{3}{4}$ quarts of punch. Write $2\frac{3}{4}$ as a decimal. $2\frac{3}{4} =$ _____

Is the decimal equivalent a terminating or repeating decimal?

_____

8. Yvonne bought a watermelon that weighed $7\frac{1}{3}$ pounds. Write $7\frac{1}{3}$ as

a decimal. $7\frac{1}{3} =$ _____

Is the decimal equivalent a terminating or repeating decimal?

_____

Personal Math Trainer

Online Assessment and Intervention

⏱ my.hrw.com

Write each rational number as a decimal. Then tell whether each decimal is a terminating or a repeating decimal. (Explore Activity and Example 1)

1. $\frac{3}{5} =$ _____

2. $\frac{89}{100} =$ _____

3. $\frac{4}{12} =$ _____

4. $\frac{25}{99} =$ _____

5. $\frac{7}{9} =$ _____

6. $\frac{9}{25} =$ _____

7. $\frac{1}{25} =$ _____

8. $\frac{25}{176} =$ _____

9. $\frac{12}{1,000} =$ _____

Write each mixed number as a decimal. (Example 2)

10. $11\frac{1}{6} =$ _____

11. $2\frac{9}{10} =$ _____

12. $8\frac{23}{100} =$ _____

13. $7\frac{3}{15} =$ _____

14. $54\frac{3}{11} =$ _____

15. $3\frac{1}{18} =$ _____

16. Maggie bought $3\frac{2}{3}$ lb of apples to make some apple pies. What is the weight of the apples written as a decimal? (Example 2)

$3\frac{2}{3} =$ _____

17. Harry's dog weighs $12\frac{7}{8}$ pounds. What is the weight of Harry's dog written as a decimal? (Example 2)

$12\frac{7}{8} =$ _____

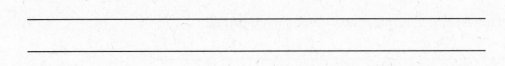 **ESSENTIAL QUESTION CHECK-IN**

18. Tom is trying to write $\frac{3}{47}$ as a decimal. He used long division and divided until he got the quotient 0.0638297872, at which point he stopped. Since the decimal doesn't seem to terminate or repeat, he concluded that $\frac{3}{47}$ is not rational. Do you agree or disagree? Why?

_____

_____

_____

_____

19.1 Independent Practice

Personal Math Trainer

my.hrw.com

Online Assessment and Intervention

Use the table for 19–23. Write each ratio in the form $\frac{a}{b}$ and then as a decimal. Tell whether each decimal is a terminating or a repeating decimal.

Team Sports	
Sport	**Number of Players**
Baseball	9
Basketball	5
Football	11
Hockey	6
Lacrosse	10
Polo	4
Rugby	15
Soccer	11

19. basketball players to football players

_____

20. hockey players to lacrosse players

_____

21. polo players to football players

_____

22. lacrosse players to rugby players

_____

23. football players to soccer players

_____

24. **Look for a Pattern** Beth said that the ratio of the number of players in any sport to the number of players on a lacrosse team must always be a terminating decimal. Do you agree or disagree? Why?

_____

_____

_____

_____

25. Yvonne bought $4\frac{7}{8}$ yards of material to make a dress.

a. What is $4\frac{7}{8}$ written as an improper fraction? _____

b. What is $4\frac{7}{8}$ written as a decimal? _____

c. **Communicate Mathematical Ideas** If Yvonne wanted to make 3 dresses that use $4\frac{7}{8}$ yd of fabric each, explain how she could use estimation to make sure she has enough fabric for all of them.

_____

_____

_____

26. Vocabulary A rational number can be written as the ratio of one

_____ to another and can be represented by a repeating

or _____ decimal.

27. Problem Solving Marcus is $5\frac{7}{24}$ feet tall. Ben is $5\frac{5}{16}$ feet tall. Which of the two boys is taller? Justify your answer.

_____

28. Represent Real-World Problems If one store is selling $\frac{3}{4}$ of a bushel of apples for $9, and another store is selling $\frac{2}{3}$ of a bushel of apples for $9, which store has the better deal? Explain your answer.

_____

_____

_____

_____

H.O.T. FOCUS ON HIGHER ORDER THINKING

29. Analyze Relationships You are given a fraction in simplest form. The numerator is not zero. When you write the fraction as a decimal, it is a repeating decimal. Which numbers from 1 to 10 could be the denominator?

_____

_____

30. Communicate Mathematical Ideas Julie got 21 of the 23 questions on her math test correct. She got 29 of the 32 questions on her science test correct. On which test did she get a higher score? Can you compare the fractions $\frac{21}{23}$ and $\frac{29}{32}$ by comparing 29 and 21? Explain. How can Julie compare her scores?

_____

_____

_____

_____

31. Look for a Pattern Look at the decimal 0.121122111222.... If the pattern continues, is this a repeating decimal? Explain.

_____

_____

_____

ESSENTIAL QUESTION

How can you add rational numbers?

EXPLORE ACTIVITY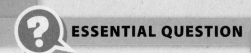

Adding Rational Numbers with the Same Sign

Previously, you used an arrow for each addend to add integers on a number line. You can also use a point for the first addend and movement in a positive or negative direction to represent adding the second addend.

Math On the Spot
my.hrw.com

EXAMPLE 1 Use a number line to solve each problem.

A Malachi hikes for 2.5 miles and stops for lunch. Then he hikes for 1.5 more miles. How many miles did he hike altogether?

> **STEP 1** Use positive numbers to represent the distance Malachi hiked.

> **STEP 2** Find 2.5 + _____.

> **STEP 3** Start at _____.

Move right on a horizontal number line to add a positive number. Move left to add a negative number.

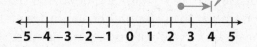
$$-5\ -4\ -3\ -2\ -1\ \ 0\ \ 1\ \ 2\ \ 3\ \ 4\ \ 5$$

> **STEP 4** The second addend is *positive*. Move 1.5 units to the _____.

> The result is _____. Malachi hiked _____ miles.

B Kyle pours out $\frac{3}{4}$ liter of liquid from a beaker. Then he pours out another $\frac{1}{2}$ liter of liquid. What is the overall change in the amount of liquid in the beaker?

> **STEP 1** Use negative numbers to represent the amount of change each time Kyle pours liquid from the beaker.

> **STEP 2** Find ⬜ + ⬜ .

> **STEP 3** Start at _____.

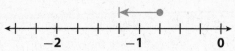
$$-2 \qquad\quad -1 \qquad\quad 0$$

> **STEP 4** The second addend is negative. Move $\left|-\frac{1}{2}\right| = \frac{1}{2}$ unit to the left.

> The result is _____.

> The amount of liquid in the beaker has decreased by _____ liters.

Reflect

1. What do you notice about the signs of the sums and the signs of the addends in parts Ⓐ and Ⓑ?

_____

_____

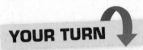

YOUR TURN

Use a number line to find each sum.

2. $3 + 1\frac{1}{2} =$ _____

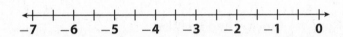

0   1   2   3   4   5

3. $-2.5 + (-4.5) =$ _____

−7   −6   −5   −4   −3   −2   −1   0

Personal Math Trainer

Online Assessment and Intervention

my.hrw.com

Math On the Spot

my.hrw.com

Adding Rational Numbers with Different Signs

You can also use a number line to add rational numbers with different signs. You start at the first number and move in the positive or negative direction by the absolute value of the second number, according to its sign.

EXAMPLE 2 Real World

Ⓐ **During the day, the temperature increases by 4.5 degrees. At night, the temperature decreases by 7.5 degrees. What is the overall change in temperature?**

STEP 1 Use a positive number to represent the increase in temperature and a negative number to represent a decrease in temperature.

STEP 2 Find $4.5 + (-7.5)$.

STEP 3 Start at 4.5.

−5 −4 −3 −2 −1   0   1   2   3   4   5

STEP 4 Move $|-7.5| = 7.5$ units to the *left* because the second addend is *negative*.

The result is −3.

The temperature decreased by 3 degrees overall.

Math Talk

Mathematical Processes

How can you tell that the answer is reasonable?

B Ernesto writes a check for $2.50. Then he deposits $6 in his checking account. What is the overall increase or decrease in the account balance?

STEP 1 Use a positive number to represent a deposit and a negative number to represent a withdrawal or a check.

STEP 2 Find $-2.5 + 6$.

STEP 3 Start at -2.5.

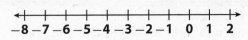
$$-5\ -4\ -3\ -2\ -1\quad 0\quad 1\quad 2\quad 3\quad 4\quad 5$$

STEP 4 Move $|6| = 6$ units to the *right* because the second addend is *positive*.

The result is 3.5. The account balance will increase by $3.50.

Reflect

4. Do $-3 + 2$ and $2 + (-3)$ have the same sum? Does it matter if the negative number is the first addend or the second addend?

_____

_____

_____

5. **Make a Conjecture** To add integers with different signs, you subtract the lesser absolute value from the greater absolute value and use the sign of the integer with the greater absolute value. Make a conjecture about adding any two rational numbers that have different signs. Explain using parts **A** and **B**.

_____

_____

_____

_____

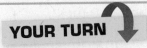
YOUR TURN

Use a number line to find each sum.

6. $-8 + 5 =$ _____
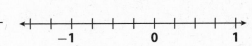
$$-8\ -7\ -6\ -5\ -4\ -3\ -2\ -1\quad 0\quad 1\quad 2$$

7. $\frac{1}{2} + \left(-\frac{3}{4}\right) =$ _____
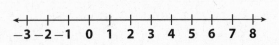
$$-1\qquad\qquad 0\qquad\qquad 1$$

8. $-1 + 7 =$ _____
$$-3\ -2\ -1\quad 0\quad 1\quad 2\quad 3\quad 4\quad 5\quad 6\quad 7\quad 8$$

© Houghton Mifflin Harcourt Publishing Company

Animated Math

my.hrw.com

My Notes

Personal Math Trainer

Online Assessment and Intervention

my.hrw.com

Additive Inverses of Rational Numbers

The opposite, or additive inverse, of a number is the same distance from 0 on a number line as the original number, but on the other side of 0. Recall the Inverse Property of Addition from your work with integers: The sum of a number and its additive inverse is 0. Zero is its own additive inverse.

EXAMPLE 3

A A football team loses 3.5 yards on its first play. On the next play, it gains 3.5 yards. What is the overall increase or decrease in yards?

STEP 1 Use a positive number to represent the gain in yards and a negative number to represent the loss in yards.

STEP 2 Find $-3.5 + 3.5$.

STEP 3 Start at -3.5.

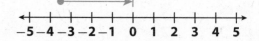

STEP 4 Move $|3.5| = 3.5$ units to the *right*, because the second addend is *positive*.

The result is 0. This means the overall change is 0 yards.

B Kendrick adds $\frac{3}{4}$ cup of broth to a pot. Then he removes $\frac{3}{4}$ cup. What is the overall increase or decrease in the amount of broth in the pot?

STEP 1 Use a positive number to represent broth added to the pot and a negative number to represent broth removed from the pot.

STEP 2 Find $\frac{3}{4} + \left(-\frac{3}{4}\right)$.

STEP 3 Start at $\frac{3}{4}$.

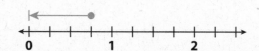

STEP 4 Move $\left|-\frac{3}{4}\right| = \frac{3}{4}$ units to the *left* because the second addend is *negative*.

The result is 0. This means the overall change is 0 cups.

My Notes

YOUR TURN

Use a number line to find each sum.

9. $2\frac{1}{2} + \left(-2\frac{1}{2}\right) = $ _____

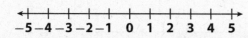

10. $-4.5 + 4.5 = $ _____

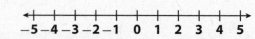

Adding Rational Numbers Using Rules

As you have seen in this lesson, the rules for adding integers also apply to adding rational numbers that are not integers.

Same signs: Add the absolute value of the numbers. Use the common sign for the sum.

Different signs: Subtract the lesser absolute value from the greater absolute value. Use the sign of the number with the greater absolute value.

Math On the Spot
⏱ my.hrw.com

EXAMPLE 4

Tina spent $5.25 on craft supplies to make friendship bracelets. She made $3.75 on Monday. On Tuesday, she sold an additional $4.50 worth of bracelets. What was Tina's overall profit or loss?

STEP 1 Use *negative* numbers to represent the amount Tina *spent* and *positive* numbers to represent the money Tina *earned*.

> Profit means the difference between income and costs is positive.

STEP 2 Find $-5.25 + 3.75 + 4.50$.

STEP 3 Group numbers with the same sign.

$-5.25 + (3.75 + 4.50)$ Associative Property of Addition

STEP 4 $-5.25 + 8.25$ Add the numbers inside the parentheses.

Find the difference of the absolute values: $8.25 - 5.25$.

3 Use the sign of the number with the greater absolute value. The sum is positive.

Tina earned a profit of $3.00.

YOUR TURN

Find each sum.

11. $-1.5 + 3.5 + 2 =$ _____

12. $3\frac{1}{4} + (-2) + \left(-2\frac{1}{4}\right) =$ _____

13. $-2.75 + (-3.25) + 5 =$ _____

14. $15 + 8 + (-3) =$ _____

Personal Math Trainer
Online Assessment and Intervention
⏱ my.hrw.com

Use a number line to find each sum. (Explore Activity Example 1 and Example 2)

1. $-3 + (-1.5) =$ _____

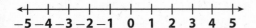

2. $1.5 + 3.5 =$ _____

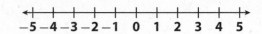

3. $\frac{1}{4} + \frac{1}{2} =$ _____

4. $-1\frac{1}{2} + \left(-1\frac{1}{2}\right) =$ _____

5. $3 + (-5) =$ _____

6. $-1.5 + 4 =$ _____

7. Victor borrowed $21.50 from his mother to go to the theater. A week later, he paid her $21.50 back. How much does he still owe her? (Example 3)

_____

8. Sandra used her debit card to buy lunch for $8.74 on Monday. On Tuesday, she deposited $8.74 back into her account. What is the overall increase or decrease in her bank account? (Example 3)

_____

Find each sum without using a number line. (Example 4)

9. $2.75 + (-2) + (-5.25) =$ _____

10. $-3 + \left(1\frac{1}{2}\right) + \left(2\frac{1}{2}\right) =$ _____

11. $-12.4 + 9.2 + 1 =$ _____

12. $-12 + 8 + 13 =$ _____

13. $4.5 + (-12) + (-4.5) =$ _____

14. $\frac{1}{4} + \left(-\frac{3}{4}\right) =$ _____

15. $-4\frac{1}{2} + 2 =$ _____

16. $-8 + \left(-1\frac{1}{8}\right) =$ _____

? ESSENTIAL QUESTION CHECK-IN

17. How can you use a number line to find the sum of -4 and 6?

_____

_____

19.2 Independent Practice

Personal Math Trainer

Online Assessment and Intervention

my.hrw.com

18. Samuel walks forward 19 steps. He represents this movement with a positive 19. How would he represent the opposite of this number?   _____

19. Julia spends $2.25 on gas for her lawn mower. She earns $15.00 mowing her neighbor's yard. What is Julia's profit?   _____

20. A submarine submerged at a depth of -35.25 meters dives an additional 8.5 meters. What is the new depth of the submarine?   _____

21. Renee hiked for $4\frac{3}{4}$ miles. After resting, Renee hiked back along the same route for $3\frac{1}{4}$ miles. How many more miles does Renee need to hike to return to the place where she started?   _____

22. **Geography** The average elevation of the city of New Orleans, Louisiana, is 0.5 m below sea level. The highest point in Louisiana is Driskill Mountain at about 163.5 m higher than New Orleans. How high is Driskill Mountain?   _____

23. **Problem Solving** A contestant on a game show has 30 points. She answers a question correctly to win 15 points. Then she answers a question incorrectly and loses 25 points. What is the contestant's final score?

_____

Financial Literacy **Use the table for 24–26. Kameh owns a bakery. He recorded the bakery income and expenses in a table.**

Month	Income ($)	Expenses ($)
January	1,205	1,290.60
February	1,183	1,345.44
March	1,664	1,664.00
June	2,413	2,106.23
July	2,260	1,958.50
August	2,183	1,845.12

24. In which months were the expenses greater than the income? Name the month and find how much money

was lost. _____

25. In which months was the income greater than the expenses? Name the months and find how much money was gained.

_____

26. **Communicate Mathematical Ideas** If the bakery started with an extra $250 from the profits in December, describe how to use the information in the table to figure out the profit or loss of money at the bakery by the end of August. Then calculate the profit or loss.

_____

_____

_____

27. Vocabulary −2.9 is the _____ of 2.9.

28. The basketball coach made up a game to play where each player takes 10 shots at the basket. For every basket made, the player gains 10 points. For every basket missed, the player loses 15 points.

   a. The player with the highest score sank 7 baskets and missed 3. What was the highest score?

   _____

   b. The player with the lowest score sank 2 baskets and missed 8. What was the lowest score?

   _____

   c. Write an expression using addition to find the score for a player who sank 5 baskets and missed 5 baskets. Interpret the result.

   _____

   _____

 **FOCUS ON HIGHER ORDER THINKING**

29. Represent Real-World Problems Write and solve a real-world addition problem involving the sum of a rational number and its additive inverse.

_____

_____

30. Communicate Mathematical Ideas Explain the different ways it is possible to add two rational numbers and get a negative number.

_____

_____

_____

31. Explain the Error A student evaluated $-4 + x$ for $x = -9\frac{1}{2}$ and got an answer of $5\frac{1}{2}$. What might the student have done wrong?

_____

_____

32. Draw Conclusions How can you use mental math and the Inverse Property of Addition to find the sum $[5.5 + (-2.3)] + (-5.5 + 2.3)$?

_____

_____

? **ESSENTIAL QUESTION**

How do you subtract rational numbers?

EXPLORE ACTIVITY

Subtracting Positive Rational Numbers

Recall that, on a horizontal number line, the positive direction is to the right, and the negative direction is to the left. On a vertical number line, the positive direction is up, and the negative direction is down.

You can use subtraction of a positive number to represent a decrease. To subtract a positive rational number on a number line, start at the first number and move in the negative direction.

Math On the Spot
my.hrw.com

EXAMPLE 1 **The temperature on a thermometer on Monday was 3.5 °C. The temperature on Thursday was 5.25 degrees less than the temperature on Monday. What was the temperature on Thursday?**

Subtract to find the temperature on Thursday.

STEP 1 Find $3.5 -$ _____.

STEP 2 Start at _____.

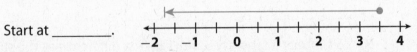

STEP 3 You are subtracting a positive number. Move $|5.25| = 5.25$ units

to the _____.

The result is _____. The temperature on Thursday was _____ °C.

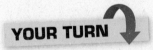

Use a number line to find each difference.

1. $-6.5 - 2 =$ _____

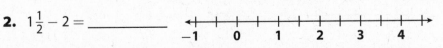

2. $1\frac{1}{2} - 2 =$ _____

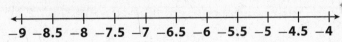

3. $-2.25 - 5.5 =$ _____

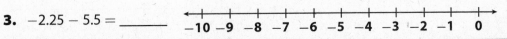

Personal Math Trainer

Online Assessment and Intervention

my.hrw.com

© Houghton Mifflin Harcourt Publishing Company

Subtracting Negative Rational Numbers

Subtracting a positive rational number is represented on a number line by movement in the *negative* direction. Subtracting a negative rational number is represented by movement in the opposite or *positive* direction.

EXAMPLE 2

During the hottest week of the summer, the water level of the Muskrat River was $\frac{5}{6}$ foot below normal. The following week, the level was $\frac{1}{3}$ foot below normal. What was the overall change in the water level?

Subtract to find the difference in water levels.

STEP 1 Find $-\frac{1}{3} - \left(-\frac{5}{6}\right)$.

STEP 2 Start at $-\frac{1}{3}$.

STEP 3 Move $\left|-\frac{5}{6}\right| = \frac{5}{6}$ unit up because you are subtracting a *negative* number.

The result is $\frac{1}{2}$.

So, the water level increased by $\frac{1}{2}$ foot.

Math Talk

Mathematical Processes

How do you know the correct order for subtracting the numbers?

Reflect

4. Work with other students to compare addition of negative numbers on a number line to subtraction of negative numbers on a number line.

_____

_____

5. To subtract integers, you rewrote the difference as the sum of the first integer and the opposite of the second, and used the rules for adding integers. Apply the same method to the Activity and the Example. What do you notice?

_____

_____

YOUR TURN

Use a number line to find each difference.

6. $0.25 - (-1.50) =$ _____

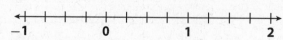

7. $-\frac{1}{2} - \left(-\frac{3}{4}\right) =$ _____

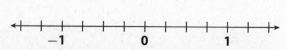

Adding the Opposite

Joe is diving $2\frac{1}{2}$ feet below sea level. He decides to descend $7\frac{1}{2}$ more feet. How many feet below sea level is he?

STEP 1   Use negative numbers to represent the number of feet below sea level.

STEP 2   Find $-2\frac{1}{2} - 7\frac{1}{2}$.

STEP 3   Start at $-2\frac{1}{2}$.

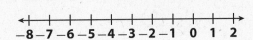

STEP 4   Move $\left|7\frac{1}{2}\right| = 7\frac{1}{2}$ units to the _____

because you are subtracting a _____ number.

The result is -10.

Joe is _____ sea level.

> You move left on a horizontal number line to add a negative number. You move the same direction to subtract a positive number.

Reflect

8. Use a number line to find each difference or sum.

    a. $-3 - 3 =$ _____

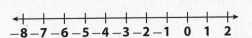

    b. $-3 + (-3) =$ _____

9. **Make a Conjecture** Work with other students to make a conjecture about how to change a subtraction problem into an addition problem.

_____

_____

_____

> **Math Talk**
> Mathematical Processes
>
> Compare the results from **8a** and **8b**.

Adding the Opposite

To subtract a number, add its opposite. This can also be written as $p - q = p + (-q)$.

You can use this property to subtract rational numbers. Rewrite subtracting a number as adding its opposite, or additive inverse.

EXPLORE ACTIVITY 3 Real World

Finding the Distance Between Two Numbers

A cave explorer climbed from an elevation of −11 meters to an elevation of −5 meters. What vertical distance did the explorer climb?

There are two ways to find the vertical distance.

A Graph the numbers _____ and _____ as points on the number line to represent the elevations. Count the number of units between them.

The explorer climbed _____ meters.

This means that the vertical distance between

−11 meters and −5 meters is _____ meters.

B Find the difference between the two elevations and use absolute value to find the distance.

$-11 - (-5) =$ _____

Take the absolute value of the difference because distance traveled is always a nonnegative number.

$|-11 - (-5)| =$ _____

The vertical distance is _____ meters.

```
 0
−1
−2
−3
−4
−5
−6
−7
−8
−9
−10
−11
```

Reflect

10. Does it matter which way you subtract the values when finding distance? Explain.

_____

_____

11. Would the same methods work if both the numbers were positive? What if one of the numbers were positive and the other negative?

_____

Distance Between Two Numbers

The distance between two values a and b on a number line is represented by the absolute value of the difference of a and b.

Distance between a and $b = |a - b|$ or $|b - a|$.

© Houghton Mifflin Harcourt Publishing Company • Image Credits: Robbie Shone/Aurora Photos/Alamy

Use a number line to find each difference.
(Explore Activity Example 1, Example 2, and Explore Activity 3)

1. $5 - (-8) =$ _____

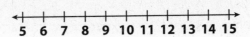

2. $-3\frac{1}{2} - 4\frac{1}{2} =$ _____

3. $-7 - 4 =$ _____

4. $-0.5 - 3.5 =$ _____

Find each difference. (Explore Activity 2)

5. $-14 - 22 =$ _____

6. $-12.5 - (-4.8) =$ _____

7. $\frac{1}{3} - \left(-\frac{2}{3}\right) =$ _____

8. $65 - (-14) =$ _____

9. $-\frac{2}{9} - (-3) =$ _____

10. $24\frac{3}{8} - \left(-54\frac{1}{8}\right) =$ _____

11. A girl is snorkeling 1 meter below sea level and then dives down another 0.5 meter. How far below sea level is the girl? (Explore Activity 2) _____

12. The first play of a football game resulted in a loss of $12\frac{1}{2}$ yards. Then a penalty resulted in another loss of 5 yards. What is the total loss or gain? (Explore Activity 2) _____

13. A climber starts descending from 533 feet above sea level and keeps going until she reaches 10 feet below sea level. How many feet did she descend? (Explore Activity 2) _____

14. Write two absolute-value expressions for the distance between -7 and 5 on a number line. Then give the distance between the numbers. (Explore Activity 3) _____

? ESSENTIAL QUESTION CHECK-IN

15. Mandy is trying to subtract $4 - 12$, and she has asked you for help. How would you explain the process of solving the problem to Mandy, using a number line?

_____

_____

_____

19.3 Independent Practice

Personal
Math Trainer
Online
Assessment and
Intervention

16. Science At the beginning of a laboratory experiment, the temperature of a substance is $-12.6\,°C$. During the experiment, the temperature of the substance decreases $7.5\,°C$. What is the final temperature of the substance?

_____

17. A diver went 25.65 feet below the surface of the ocean, and then 16.5 feet further down, he then rose 12.45 feet. Write and solve an expression to find the diver's new depth.

_____

_____

18. A city known for its temperature extremes started the day at -5 degrees Fahrenheit. The temperature increased by 78 degrees Fahrenheit by midday, and then dropped 32 degrees by nightfall.

a. What expression can you write to find the temperature at nightfall?   _____

b. What expression can you write to describe the overall change in temperature? *Hint*: Do not include the temperature at the beginning of the day since you only want to know about how much the temperature changed.   _____

c. What is the final temperature at nightfall? What is the overall change in temperature?   _____

19. Financial Literacy On Monday, your bank account balance was $-\$12.58$. Because you didn't realize this, you wrote a check for $30.72 for groceries.

a. What is the new balance in your checking account?   _____

b. The bank charges a $25 fee for paying a check on a negative balance. What is the balance in your checking account after this fee?   _____

c. How much money do you need to deposit to bring your account balance back up to $0 after the fee?   _____

Astronomy Use the table for problems 20–21.

20. How much deeper is the deepest canyon on Mars than the deepest canyon on Venus?

_____

Elevations on Planets		
	Lowest (ft)	Highest (ft)
Earth	−36,198	29,035
Mars	−26,000	70,000
Venus	−9,500	35,000

21. **Persevere in Problem Solving** What is the difference between Earth's highest mountain and its deepest ocean canyon? What is the difference between Mars's highest mountain and its deepest canyon? Which difference is greater? How much greater is it?

_____

22. Pamela is making the legs for a three-legged stool from two pieces of scrap wood. The lengths of the two pieces of wood are $36\frac{5}{8}$ inches and $21\frac{1}{8}$ inches. Each leg is $16\frac{1}{2}$ inches long.

a. Pamela cuts one leg from each piece of wood. Write and evaluate two expressions to show how much of each piece of wood is left over.

_____

b. Will Pamela have enough wood for a third leg? Explain.

_____

_____

23. Jeremy is practicing some tricks on his skateboard. One trick takes him forward 5 feet, then he flips around and moves backward 7.2 feet, and then he moves forward again for 2.2 feet.

a. What expression could be used to find how far Jeremy is from his starting position when he finishes the trick?

_____

b. How far from his starting point is he when he finishes the trick? Explain.

_____

24. Tavia, Mitch, and Kate are playing a game. Players gain or lose points each round. The players' scores at the end of the first two rounds are shown in the table.

a. How far apart are Mitch's and Tavia's scores after Round 1?

	Round 1	Round 2
Kate	$2\frac{1}{2}$	$-\frac{3}{4}$
Mitch	$-1\frac{3}{4}$	$1\frac{1}{2}$
Tavia	$-\frac{1}{2}$	$3\frac{3}{4}$

_____

b. Find the change in Kate's score from Round 1 to Round 2.

_____

c. When you subtract to find the answers in parts **a** and **b**, does the order of the numbers matter? Explain your reasoning.

_____

_____

_____

25. Look for a Pattern Show how you could use the Commutative Property to simplify the evaluation of the expression $-\frac{7}{16} - \frac{1}{4} - \frac{5}{16}$.

_____

_____

_____

26. Problem Solving The temperatures for five days in Kaktovik, Alaska, are given below.

$-19.6\,°F$, $-22.5\,°F$, $-20.9\,°F$, $-19.5\,°F$, $-22.4\,°F$

Temperatures for the following week are expected to be twelve degrees lower every day. What are the highest and lowest temperatures expected for the corresponding 5 days next week?

_____

_____

27. Make a Conjecture Must the difference between two rational numbers be a rational number? Explain.

_____

_____

_____

_____

_____

_____

28. Look for a Pattern Evan said that the difference between two negative numbers must be negative. Was he right? Use examples to illustrate your answer.

_____

_____

_____

_____

Identifying Operations

7.1.GF.3.3

Students will decide whether to model a real-world situation with addition or subtraction.

? ESSENTIAL QUESTION

How do you decide whether to model a real-world situation with addition or subtraction?

EXPLORE ACTIVITY

Applying Subtraction

A lab technician is studying the effect of storage temperatures on samples. Write and evaluate an expression for each situation using the rules for adding and subtracting rational numbers. Then explain the value in context.

A Sample A is stored at 1.25 °C. The technician lowers the temperature by 2.5 °C. What is the resulting temperature?

- The temperature is *decreasing*. Subtract the amount of change from the original temperature.

$1.25 - \boxed{}$

- Rewrite the expression as addition of the opposite.

$1.25 - \boxed{} = 1.25 + \left(\boxed{}\right)$

- The signs are different, so subtract the lesser absolute value from the greater absolute value.

$\left|\boxed{}\right| - |1.25| = \boxed{} - 1.25$

$= \boxed{}$

- Use the sign of the number with the greater absolute value.

$1.25 - 2.5 = \boxed{}$

The resulting temperature is _____ °C, which is 1.25 degrees below 0 degrees Celsius.

$\xleftarrow{\qquad} \;|{-}3\;\;{-}2\;\;{-}1\;\;\;0\;\;\;1\;\;\;2\;\;\;3\;\;\rightarrow$

B The coldest temperature the lab technician used was −2.25 °C. The warmest temperature was 1.25 °C. What was the range in temperature?

- Find the absolute value of the difference between the two temperatures.

$\left|1.25 - \left(\boxed{}\right)\right|$

- Rewrite the expression as addition of the opposite.

$\left|1.25 - \left(\boxed{}\right)\right| = \left|1.25 + \left(\boxed{}\right)\right|$

- Evaluate the new expression.

$= \boxed{}$

The value _____ means that the range in temperature was _____ °C.

$\xleftarrow{\qquad} \;{-}3\;\;{-}2\;\;{-}1\;\;\;0\;\;\;1\;\;\;2\;\;\;3\;\;\rightarrow$

Match each situation to an expression. Then answer the question.

  A $-15.5 + 12.5$ **B** $-15.5 - 12.5$ **C** $|-15.5 - 12.5|$

1. The temperature started at -15.5 °F and fell 12.5 °F. What was the temperature then?

_____

2. A boater is at an elevation of 12.5 meters, directly above a diver at an elevation of -15.5 meters. How far apart are they?

_____

3. Jo has a $-\$15.50$ balance on a credit card and pays $\$12.50$. What is her new balance?

_____

Write and evaluate an expression for each situation using the rules for adding and subtracting rational numbers. Explain the value in context.

4. *Par* is the number of strokes an experienced golfer should need to complete a hole on a golf course, or the entire course. Par is represented by 0. Scores below par are negative and scores over par are positive.

  a. Hannah scored -3 on the first hole and 5 on the next. What was her total?

_____

  b. Edwin scored -2 on the first hole. His total for that hole and the next was 1. What was his score on the second hole?

_____

_____

  c. Rachel scored 4 on the first hole. How many points apart were Rachel's and Hannah's scores on the first hole?

_____

_____

5. In an aquarium, a betta and a danio swim one above the other. The betta's elevation is $-8\frac{1}{4}$ inches. The danio's is $-16\frac{3}{4}$ inches.

  a. How far apart are the fish?

_____

  b. Suppose the betta swam to the danio's elevation. What would be the change in the betta's elevation?

_____

_____

Multiplying Rational Numbers

7.1.3.4
Students will multiply rational numbers.

? ESSENTIAL QUESTION

How do you multiply rational numbers?

EXPLORE ACTIVITY Real World

Math On the Spot
my.hrw.com

Multiplying Rational Numbers with Different Signs

The rules for the signs of products of rational numbers with different signs are summarized below. Let p and q be rational numbers.

Products of Rational Numbers

Sign of Factor p	Sign of Factor q	Sign of Product pq
+	−	−
−	+	−

You can also use the fact that multiplication is repeated addition.

EXAMPLE 1 Gina hiked down a canyon and stopped each time she descended $\frac{1}{2}$ mile to rest. She hiked a total of 4 sections. What is her overall change in elevation?

STEP 1 Use a negative number for the change in elevation.

STEP 2 Find $4\left(\boxed{} \right)$.

STEP 3 Start at 0. Move $\frac{1}{2}$ unit to the _____ 4 times.

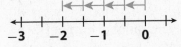

The result is _____. The overall change is _____ miles.

Check: Use the rules for multiplying rational numbers.

A negative times a positive is _____. $4\left(-\frac{1}{2}\right) = -\dfrac{\boxed{}}{2}$

$= \rule{1cm}{0.4pt}$ ✓

Personal Math Trainer

Online Assessment and Intervention

my.hrw.com

YOUR TURN

1. Use a number line to find $2(-3.5)$. _____

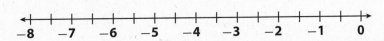

Multiplying Rational Numbers with the Same Sign

The rules for the signs of products with the same signs are summarized below.

Products of Rational Numbers

Sign of Factor *p*	Sign of Factor *q*	Sign of Product *pq*
+	+	+
−	−	+

You can also use a number line to find the product of rational numbers with the same signs.

My Notes

EXAMPLE 2

Multiply −2(−3.5).

STEP 1 First, find the product 2(−3.5).

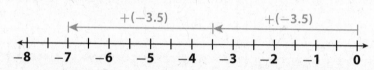

STEP 2 Start at 0. Move 3.5 units to the left two times.

STEP 3 The result is −7.

STEP 4 This shows that 2 groups of −3.5 equals −7.

So, −2 groups of −3.5 must equal the *opposite* of −7.

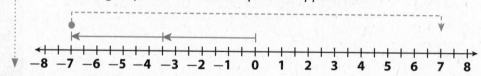

STEP 5 −2(−3.5) = 7

Check: Use the rules for multiplying rational numbers.

−2(−3.5) = 7   *A negative times a negative equals a positive.*

Personal Math Trainer

Online Assessment and Intervention

my.hrw.com

YOUR TURN

2. Find −3(−1.25). _____

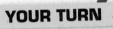

Multiplying More Than Two Rational Numbers

If you multiply three or more rational numbers, you can use a pattern to find the sign of the product.

Math On the Spot

my.hrw.com

EXAMPLE 3

Multiply $\left(-\dfrac{2}{3}\right)\left(-\dfrac{1}{2}\right)\left(-\dfrac{3}{5}\right)$.

STEP 1 First, find the product of the first two factors. Both factors are negative, so their product will be positive.

STEP 2 $\left(-\dfrac{2}{3}\right)\left(-\dfrac{1}{2}\right) = +\left(\dfrac{\cancel{2}}{3} \cdot \dfrac{1}{\cancel{2}}\right)$

$= \dfrac{1}{3}$

STEP 3 Now, multiply the result, which is positive, by the third factor, which is negative. The product will be negative.

STEP 4 $\dfrac{1}{3}\left(-\dfrac{3}{5}\right) = \dfrac{1}{\cancel{3}}\left(-\dfrac{\cancel{3}}{5}\right)$

STEP 5 $\left(-\dfrac{2}{3}\right)\left(-\dfrac{1}{2}\right)\left(-\dfrac{3}{5}\right) = -\dfrac{1}{5}$

Reflect

3. **Look for a Pattern** You know that the product of two negative numbers is positive, and the product of three negative numbers is negative. Write a rule for finding the sign of the product of n negative numbers.

_____

_____

_____

> **Math Talk**
> **Mathematical Processes**
> Suppose you find the product of several rational numbers, one of which is zero. What can you say about the product?

YOUR TURN

Find each product.

4. $\left(-\dfrac{3}{4}\right)\left(-\dfrac{4}{7}\right)\left(-\dfrac{2}{3}\right)$ _____

5. $\left(-\dfrac{2}{3}\right)\left(-\dfrac{3}{4}\right)\left(\dfrac{4}{5}\right)$ _____

6. $\left(\dfrac{2}{3}\right)\left(-\dfrac{9}{10}\right)\left(\dfrac{5}{6}\right)$ _____

Personal Math Trainer

Online Assessment and Intervention

my.hrw.com

Use a number line to find each product. (Explore Activity Example 1 and Example 2)

1. $5\left(-\frac{2}{3}\right) =$ _____

2. $3\left(-\frac{1}{4}\right) =$ _____

3. $-3\left(-\frac{4}{7}\right) =$ _____

4. $-\frac{3}{4}(-4) =$ _____

5. $4(-3) =$ _____

6. $-1.8(5) =$ _____

7. $-2\,(-3.4) =$ _____

8. $0.54(8) =$ _____

9. $-5(-1.2) =$ _____

10. $-2.4(3) =$ _____

Multiply. (Example 3)

11. $\frac{1}{2} \times \frac{2}{3} \times \frac{3}{4} = \boxed{} \times \frac{3}{4} =$ _____

12. $-\frac{4}{7}\left(-\frac{3}{5}\right)\left(-\frac{7}{3}\right) = \left(\boxed{}\right) \times \left(-\frac{7}{3}\right) =$ _____

13. $-\frac{1}{8} \times 5 \times \frac{2}{3} =$ _____

14. $-\frac{2}{3}\left(\frac{1}{2}\right)\left(-\frac{6}{7}\right) =$ _____

15. The price of one share of Acme Company stock declined $3.50 per day for 4 days in a row. What was the overall change in the price of one share? (Explore Activity Example 1)

_____

16. In one day, 18 people each withdrew $100 from an ATM machine. What was the overall change in the amount of money in the ATM machine? (Explore Activity Example 1)

_____

? ESSENTIAL QUESTION CHECK-IN

17. Explain how you can find the sign of the product of two or more rational numbers.

_____

_____

_____

19.4 Independent Practice

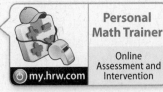

Personal Math Trainer

Online Assessment and Intervention

my.hrw.com

18. Financial Literacy Sandy has $200 in her bank account.

a. If she writes 6 checks for $19.98 each, what expression describes the change in her bank account?

_____

b. What is her account balance after the checks are cashed? Show your work.

_____

19. Communicating Mathematical Ideas Explain, in words, how to find the product of $-4(-1.5)$ using a number line. Where do you end up?

_____

_____

_____

_____

20. Greg sets his watch for the correct time. Exactly one week later, he finds that his watch has lost $3\frac{1}{4}$ minutes. It loses time at the same rate for a total of 8 weeks. Write a multiplication expression that describes the situation. Find the product and explain how it is related to the problem.

_____

_____

21. A submarine dives below the surface, heading downward in three moves. If each move downward was 325 feet, where is the submarine after it is finished diving?

_____

_____

22. Multistep For home economics class, Sandra has 5 cups of flour. She made 3 batches of cookies that each used 1.5 cups of flour. Write and solve an expression to find the amount of flour Sandra has left after making the 3 batches of cookies.

_____

_____

23. Critique Reasoning In class, Matthew stated, "I think that a negative is like an opposite. That is why multiplying a negative times a negative equals a positive. The opposite of negative is positive, so it is just like multiplying the opposite of a negative twice, which is two positives." Do you agree or disagree with his reasoning? What would you say in response to him?

_____

_____

_____

_____

_____

_____

_____

_____

24. Kaitlin is on a long car trip. Every time she stops to buy gas, she loses 15 minutes of travel time. If she has to stop 5 times, how late will she be getting to her destination?

_____

_____

25. The table shows the scoring system for quarterbacks in Jeremy's fantasy football league. In one game, Jeremy's quarterback had 2 touchdown passes, 16 complete passes, 7 incomplete passes, and 2 interceptions. How many total points did Jeremy's quarterback score?

Quarterback Scoring	
Action	**Points**
Touchdown pass	6
Complete pass	0.5
Incomplete pass	−0.5
Interception	−1.5

_____

 **FOCUS ON HIGHER ORDER THINKING**

Work Area

26. Represent Real-World Problems The ground temperature at Brigham Airport is 12°C. The temperature decreases by 6.8 °C for every increase of 1 kilometer above the ground. What is the temperature outside a plane flying at an altitude of 5 kilometers above Brigham Airport?

_____

27. Identify Patterns The product of four numbers, *a*, *b*, *c*, and *d*, is a negative number. The table shows one combination of positive and negative signs of the four numbers that could produce a negative product. Complete the table to show the seven other possible combinations.

a	*b*	*c*	*d*
+	+	+	−

28. Reason Abstractly Find two integers whose sum is −7 and whose product is 12. Explain how you found the numbers.

_____

_____

_____

_____

Dividing Rational Numbers

? ESSENTIAL QUESTION

How do you divide rational numbers?

EXPLORE ACTIVITY

Placement of Negative Signs in Quotients

Quotients can have negative signs in different places.

Let p and q be rational numbers.

Quotients of Rational Numbers

Sign of Dividend p	Sign of Divisor q	Sign of Quotient $\frac{p}{q}$
+	−	−
−	+	−
+	+	+
−	−	+

Are the rational numbers $\frac{12}{-4}$, $\frac{-12}{4}$, and $-\left(\frac{12}{4}\right)$ equivalent?

A Find each quotient. Then use the rules in the table to make sure the sign of the quotient is correct.

$\frac{12}{-4} = $ _____ $\frac{-12}{4} = $ _____ $-\left(\frac{12}{4}\right) = $ _____

B What do you notice about each quotient?

_____

C The rational numbers ☐ **are / are not** ☐ equivalent.

D **Conjecture** Explain how the placement of the negative sign in the rational number affects the sign of the quotients.

_____

_____

E If p and q are rational numbers and q is not zero, what do you know about $-\left(\frac{p}{q}\right)$, $\frac{-p}{q}$, and $\frac{p}{-q}$?

_____

Reflect

Write two equivalent expressions for each quotient.

1. $\frac{14}{-7}$ _____ , _____

2. $\frac{-32}{-8}$ _____ , _____

Math On the Spot

my.hrw.com

Quotients of Rational Numbers

The rules for dividing rational numbers are the same as the rules for dividing integers.

EXAMPLE 1

Over 5 months, Carlos wrote 5 checks for a total of $323.75 to pay for his cable TV service. His cable bill is the same amount each month. What was the change in Carlos's bank account each month to pay for cable?

Find the quotient: $\frac{-323.75}{5}$

Math Talk

Mathematical Processes

Describe another real-world problem that you solve by dividing a negative decimal by a positive number.

STEP 1 Use a negative number to represent the withdrawal from his account each month.

STEP 2 Find $\frac{-323.75}{5}$.

STEP 3 Determine the sign of the quotient.

The quotient will be negative because the signs are different.

STEP 4 Divide.

$$\frac{-323.75}{5} = -64.75$$

Carlos withdrew $64.75 each month to pay for cable TV.

Personal Math Trainer

Online Assessment and Intervention

my.hrw.com

YOUR TURN

Find each quotient.

3. $\frac{2.8}{-4} =$ _____

4. $\frac{-6.64}{-0.4} =$ _____

5. $-\frac{5.5}{0.5} =$ _____

6. A diver descended 42.56 feet in 11.2 minutes. What was the diver's average change in elevation per minute?

_____

© Houghton Mifflin Harcourt Publishing Company

Complex Fractions

A **complex fraction** is a fraction that has a fraction in its numerator, denominator, or both.

$$\frac{\frac{a}{b}}{\frac{c}{d}} = \frac{a}{b} \div \frac{c}{d}$$

EXAMPLE 2 Real World

A Find $\dfrac{\frac{7}{10}}{-\frac{1}{5}}$.

STEP 1 Determine the sign of the quotient.
The quotient will be negative because the signs are different.

STEP 2 Write the complex fraction as division: $\dfrac{\frac{7}{10}}{-\frac{1}{5}} = \frac{7}{10} \div -\frac{1}{5}$

STEP 3 Rewrite using multiplication: $\frac{7}{10} \times \left(-\frac{5}{1}\right)$ *Multiply by the reciprocal.*

STEP 4 $\frac{7}{10} \times \left(-\frac{5}{1}\right) = -\frac{35}{10}$ *Multiply.*

$\qquad\qquad = -\frac{7}{2}$ *Simplify.*

$\qquad \dfrac{\frac{7}{10}}{-\frac{1}{5}} = -\frac{7}{2}$

B Maya wants to divide a $\frac{3}{4}$-pound box of trail mix into small bags. Each bag will hold $\frac{1}{12}$ pound of trail mix. How many bags of trail mix can Maya fill?

STEP 1 Find $\dfrac{\frac{3}{4}}{\frac{1}{12}}$.

STEP 2 Determine the sign of the quotient.
The quotient will be positive because the signs are the same.

STEP 3 Write the complex fraction as division: $\dfrac{\frac{3}{4}}{\frac{1}{12}} = \frac{3}{4} \div \frac{1}{12}$.

STEP 4 Rewrite using multiplication: $\frac{3}{4} \times \frac{12}{1}$.   *Multiply by the reciprocal.*

STEP 5 $\frac{3}{4} \times \frac{12}{1} = \frac{36}{4} = 9$ *Multiply.*

$\qquad \dfrac{\frac{3}{4}}{\frac{1}{12}} = 9$ *Simplify.*

Maya can fill 9 bags of trail mix.

YOUR TURN

7. $\dfrac{-\frac{5}{8}}{\frac{6}{7}} = $ _____

8. $\dfrac{-\frac{5}{12}}{\frac{2}{3}} = $ _____

9. $\dfrac{-\frac{4}{5}}{\frac{1}{2}} = $ _____

Find each quotient. (Explore Activities Example 1, and Example 2)

1. $\dfrac{0.72}{-0.9} = $ _____

2. $\left(\dfrac{-\frac{1}{5}}{\frac{7}{5}} \right) = $ _____

3. $\dfrac{56}{-7} = $ _____

4. $\dfrac{251}{4} \div \left(-\dfrac{3}{8} \right) = $ _____

5. $\dfrac{75}{-\frac{1}{5}} = $ _____

6. $\dfrac{-91}{-13} = $ _____

7. $\dfrac{-\frac{3}{7}}{\frac{9}{4}} = $ _____

8. $-\dfrac{12}{0.03} = $ _____

9. A water pail in your backyard has a small hole in it. You notice that it has drained a total of 3.5 liters in 4 days. What is the average change in water volume each day? (Example 1)

   _____

10. The price of one share of ABC Company declined a total of $45.75 in 5 days. What was the average change of the price of one share per day? (Example 1)

    _____

11. To avoid a storm, a passenger-jet pilot descended 0.44 mile in 0.8 minute. What was the plane's average change of altitude per minute? (Example 2)

    _____

? ESSENTIAL QUESTION CHECK-IN

12. Explain how you would find the sign of the quotient $\dfrac{32 \div (-2)}{-16 \div 4}$.

    _____

    _____

    _____

    _____

    _____

    _____

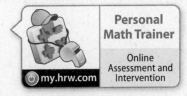

Personal
Math Trainer

my.hrw.com

Online
Assessment and
Intervention

19.5 Independent Practice

13. $\dfrac{\frac{5}{2}}{-\frac{2}{8}} =$ _____

14. $5\frac{1}{3} \div \left(-1\frac{1}{2}\right) =$ _____

15. $\dfrac{-120}{-6} =$ _____

16. $\dfrac{\frac{4}{5}}{-\frac{2}{3}} =$ _____

17. $1.03 \div (-10.3) =$ _____

18. $\dfrac{-0.4}{80} =$ _____

19. $1 \div \dfrac{9}{5} =$ _____

20. $\dfrac{\frac{-1}{4}}{\frac{23}{24}} =$ _____

21. $\dfrac{-10.35}{-2.3} =$ _____

22. Alex usually runs for 21 hours a week, training for a marathon. If he is unable to run for 3 days, describe how to find out how many hours of training time he loses, and write the appropriate integer to describe how it affects his time.

_____

_____

_____

_____

_____

_____

23. The running back for the Bulldogs football team carried the ball 9 times for a total loss of $15\frac{3}{4}$ yards. Find the average change in field position on each run.

_____

24. The 6:00 a.m. temperatures for four consecutive days in the town of Lincoln were $-12.1\,°C$, $-7.8\,°C$, $-14.3\,°C$, and $-7.2\,°C$. What was the average 6:00 a.m. temperature for the four days?

_____

25. **Multistep** A seafood restaurant claims an increase of $1,750.00 over its average profit during a week where it introduced a special of baked clams.

a. If this is true, how much extra profit did it receive per day?

_____

b. If it had, instead, lost $150 per day, how much money would it have lost for the week?

_____

c. If its total loss was $490 for the week, what was its average daily change?

_____

26. A hot air balloon descended 99.6 meters in 12 seconds. What was the balloon's average rate of descent in meters per second?

_____

27. Sanderson is having trouble with his assignment. His shown work is as follows:

$$\frac{-\frac{3}{4}}{\frac{4}{3}} = -\frac{3}{4} \times \frac{4}{3} = -\frac{12}{12} = -1$$

However, his answer does not match the answer that his teacher gives him. What is Sanderson's mistake? Find the correct answer.

_____

_____

_____

_____

28. **Science** Beginning in 1996, a glacier lost an average of 3.7 meters of thickness each year. Find the total change in its thickness by the end of 2012.

_____

H.O.T. **FOCUS ON HIGHER ORDER THINKING**

29. **Represent Real-World Problems** Describe a real-world situation that can be represented by the quotient $-85 \div 15$. Then find the quotient and explain what the quotient means in terms of the real-world situation.

_____

_____

_____

_____

30. **Construct an Argument** Divide 5 by 4. Is your answer a rational number? Explain.

_____

_____

_____

31. **Critical Thinking** Should the quotient of an integer divided by a nonzero integer always be a rational number? Why or why not?

_____

_____

_____

Applying Properties to Numerical Expressions

7.1.GF.3.5
Students will justify their steps when solving mathematical and real-world problems.

? ESSENTIAL QUESTION

How can you justify your steps when solving mathematical and real-world problems?

EXPLORE ACTIVITY 1

Justifying That $(-1)(-1) = 1$

You can use properties of operations along with the order of operations to simplify expressions. When you solve a mathematical or real-world problem, you can use these properties and rules to justify that a step is valid.

Justify or complete each step to show that $(-1)(-1) = 1$.

$$(-1)(0) = 0 \qquad \text{Multiplication Property of _____}$$

$$(-1)(-1 + 1) = 0 \qquad \text{_____}$$

$$(-1)(-1) + (-1)(1) = 0 \qquad \text{_____}$$

$$(-1)(-1) + \boxed{} = 0 \qquad \text{Identity Property of _____}$$

$$(-1)(-1) + (-1) + \boxed{} = 0 + \boxed{} \qquad \text{Addition Property of Equality}$$

$$(-1)(-1) + (-1 + 1) = 0 + 1 \qquad \text{_____}$$

$$(-1)(-1) + \boxed{} = 0 + 1 \qquad \text{_____ Property of Addition}$$

$$(-1)(-1) = \boxed{} \qquad \text{_____ Property of Addition}$$

Reflect

1. How do you know which property justifies the first step?

_____

_____

2. How do you know which number to add to both sides of the equation in the step involving the Addition Property of Equality?

_____

_____

_____

EXPLORE ACTIVITY 2

Applying Properties Strategically

The value of shares of stock varies as the price per share changes. Claire bought 8 shares of stock for $5.65 per share. The price increased $1.26 per share by midday and then decreased $0.65 per share by day's end. What was the total value of Claire's shares at the end of the day? Did they gain or lose value during the day? Justify your steps.

A The ⬚original / final⬚ value of Claire's shares is equal to 8(5.65).

B The midday ⬚gain / loss⬚ in the value of her shares is equal to 8(1.26).

C The end-of-day loss in the value of ⬚one of / all of⬚ her shares is equal to 8(−0.65).

D Add the expressions. Simplify the sum and justify each step.

8(5.65) + 8(1.26) + 8(−0.65)

8(5.65 + 1.26 + (−0.65))

8(⬚_____⬚ + ⬚_____⬚ + (−0.65))   _____
                                          Commutative Property of Addition

8(1.26 + [5.65 + (−0.65)])   _____

8(1.26 + ⬚___⬚)   Add.

8(6.26)   _____

⬚_____⬚   Multiply.

E The value of Claire's 8 shares at the end of the day was _____. She paid _____ for the 8 shares, so they ⬚gained / lost⬚ value during the day.

Reflect

3. Interpret the expression 1.26 + (−0.65) in terms of the situation. Using the expression, represent the total change in value of the shares over the day if Claire had bought 20 shares. Interpret the change.

_____

_____

4. Write and evaluate an expression to show what the change in value per share would be if Claire's 8 shares were worth $43.20 instead of $50.08 at the end of the day. Interpret the result.

_____

_____

© Houghton Mifflin Harcourt Publishing Company

Simplify each expression. Justify each step.

1. $\left(-\dfrac{5}{2}\right)\left(-\dfrac{2}{5}\right)$ _____

2. $-132.59 + 0$ _____

3. $201.75 + (-201.75)$ _____

4. $\dfrac{1}{3}(1)$ _____

5. $3.6(2.5) + 3.6(-2.5)$

6. $\left(\dfrac{2}{3}\right)\left(-\dfrac{4}{3}\right)\left(\dfrac{3}{2}\right)$

7. $3\left(\dfrac{2}{3} + \left(-\dfrac{1}{3}\right)\right) + \dfrac{1}{2}(-4 + 2)$

Write an expression involving negative rational numbers to represent each situation. Evaluate the expression and explain the value in the context of the problem.

8. Experts say that when you buy a new car, the value decreases 9% when you drive the car off the lot. The Millers paid $28,456 for a new car. How does the value of the car change after they drive it off the lot?

_____

9. A bottle contains 68 teaspoons of solution. The solution drops out of the bottle at a constant rate during a 102-minute experiment. The bottle is completely empty just as the experiment ends. At what rate does the number of teaspoons of solution in the bottle change?

_____

_____

10. In golf, *par* on a hole is the number of strokes an experienced golfer should need to complete the hole. Par is represented by 0, scores under par are negative, and scores over par are positive. The table shows Michelle's scores and the number of times in an 18-hole game she got each score. Her game score is the sum of her scores for each hole. What was her game score?

Score	Number
−2	2
−1	3
0	12
+1	1

_____

_____

11. Ka'me and four friends go to a water park. Admission is $31.50 per person. Ka'me uses a coupon for $5 off each ticket for up to 4 people. Abby and Allen write expressions to represent the total amount Ka'me and his friends pay for admission.

Abby: $4(31.50 + (-5.00)) + 31.50$ **Allen:** $5(31.50) + 4(-5.00)$

Rewrite Abby's expression to show it is equal to Allen's expression. Justify each step.

Estimation Strategies

7.1.GR.3.6

Students will use mental math and estimation to assess the reasonableness of calculations.

? ESSENTIAL QUESTION

How can you use mental math and estimation to assess the reasonableness of calculations?

EXPLORE ACTIVITY

Compatible Numbers

You can use rounding, compatible numbers, and other strategies to help you estimate. *Compatible numbers* are numbers that make a calculation easier to do with mental math.

A Estimate the product using rounding and compatible numbers.

Round 92 and use a compatible fraction.
$$\frac{11}{30} \times 92 \approx \frac{\boxed{}}{\boxed{}} \times \boxed{} = \boxed{}$$

B The answer to Part A is an **overestimate / underestimate** because both

factors were **rounded up / rounded down** .

C Estimate the sum using the front-end and adjust strategy.

$3 + \boxed{} + 1 + \boxed{} = \$ \boxed{}$ Add the front-end digits.

$3.18
5.59
0.95
1.37
+2.79

$0.18 + \boxed{} \approx \$1$

$0.37 + \boxed{} \approx \$1$ Adjust by grouping cents amounts into dollars.

$\boxed{} \approx \$1$

$\boxed{} + 3 = \$ \boxed{}$ Add the results.

D Is the answer to Part C an *overestimate* or an *underestimate*? Explain.

_____

Reflect

1. **What if?** How would Parts C and D change if $3.18 changed to $3.46?

_____

_____

Reasonable Estimates

Estimation is helpful when you don't need an exact answer or when you want to check that an answer is reasonable. In a multistep problem, it might make sense to overestimate in some steps and underestimate in others.

EXAMPLE 1

Manuel earns a salary of $35,000 per year. He pays an income tax rate of 12%. He budgeted his weekly income after taxes to be $592.31. Use estimation to confirm that his budget is reasonable.

STEP 1 Use a compatible percent to estimate Manuel's annual income tax. 12% is close to 10%, so mentally multiply by 0.10 to estimate the tax.

$35,000 \times 0.10 = 3,500$ *$3,500 is an underestimate of the annual tax.*

STEP 2 Estimate how much of his annual income Manuel will keep after taxes. Since $3,500 is an underestimate, round up to the leading digit ($4,000) and subtract using mental math.

$35,000 - 4,000 = 31,000$ *He keeps about $31,000 per year.*

STEP 3 Estimate Manuel's weekly income, after taxes. There are 52 weeks in a year. So use 50 as the divisor and 30,000 as a compatible dividend.

$30,000 \div 50 = 600$ *His weekly after-tax income is about $600.*

Manuel's answer is reasonable, because $592.31 is close to $600.

Practice

1. Marta uses the expression $92 − 0.15($92) to find the sale price of an item and gets the answer $78.20. Show how to find an underestimate and an overestimate to explain why her answer is reasonable.

   _____

   _____

   _____

2. A club is planning a banquet. The club spends $60 for each table of 8 guests (dinner included). The club also spends $46 on decorations, $225 on a DJ, $150 on a photographer, and $760 for the hall. The club expects about 150 people to attend. Explain how to estimate the total cost.

   _____

   _____

   _____

Applying Rational Number Operations

7.1.3.6
Students will use different forms of rational numbers and strategically choose tools to solve problems.

? ESSENTIAL QUESTION

How do you use different forms of rational numbers and strategically choose tools to solve problems?

EXPLORE ACTIVITY (Real World)

Math On the Spot
⏻ my.hrw.com

Assessing Reasonableness of Answers

Even when you understand how to solve a problem, you might make a careless solving error. You should always check your answer to make sure that it is reasonable.

EXAMPLE 1 Jon is hanging a picture. He wants to center it horizontally on the wall. The picture is $32\frac{1}{2}$ inches long, and the wall is $120\frac{3}{4}$ inches long. How far from each edge of the wall should he place the picture?

STEP 1 Find the total length of the wall not covered by the picture.

Subtract the whole number parts. Then subtract the fractional parts.

$$120\frac{3}{4} - 32\frac{1}{2} = \boxed{} \boxed{}$$

120$\frac{3}{4}$ in.

32$\frac{1}{2}$ in.

STEP 2 Find the length of the wall on each side of the picture.

Multiply by $\frac{1}{2}$.

$$\frac{1}{2}\left(\boxed{}\right) = \boxed{} \boxed{}$$

Jon should place the picture _____ inches from each edge of the wall.

STEP 3 Check the answer for reasonableness.

The wall is about 120 inches long. The picture is about 30 inches long. The length of wall space left for *both* sides of the picture is about $120 - 30 = 90$ inches. The length left for *each* side is about $\frac{1}{2}(90) = 45$ inches.

The answer is reasonable because it is close to the estimate.

YOUR TURN

1. A 30-minute TV program consists of three commercials, each $2\frac{1}{2}$ minutes long, and four equal-length entertainment segments. How long is each entertainment segment? _____

Personal Math Trainer
Online Assessment and Intervention
⏻ my.hrw.com

Using Rational Numbers in Any Form

You have solved problems using integers, positive and negative fractions, and positive and negative decimals. A single problem may involve rational numbers in two or more of those forms.

EXAMPLE 2 *Problem Solving*

Alana uses $1\frac{1}{4}$ cups of flour for each batch of blueberry muffins she makes. She has a 5-pound bag of flour that cost $4.49 and contains seventy-six $\frac{1}{4}$-cup servings. How many batches can Alana make if she uses all the flour? How much does the flour for one batch cost?

Muffins
1¼ cups all purpose flour
¾ cup white sugar
½ teaspoon salt
2 teaspoons baking powder
⅓ cup vegetable oil
1 egg
⅕ cup milk
1 cup fresh blueberries

 Analyze Information

Identify the important information.

- Each batch uses $1\frac{1}{4}$ cups of flour.
- Seventy-six $\frac{1}{4}$-cup servings of flour cost $4.49.

 Formulate a Plan

Use logical reasoning to solve the problem. Find the number of cups of flour that Alana has. Use that information to find the number of batches she can make. Use that information to find the cost of flour for each batch.

 Solve

Number of cups of flour in bag:

$$76 \text{ servings} \times \frac{1}{4} \text{ cup per serving} = 19 \text{ cups}$$

Number of batches Alana can make:

> Write $1\frac{1}{4}$ as a decimal.

$$\text{total cups of flour} \div \frac{\text{cups of flour}}{\text{batch}} = 19 \text{ cups} \div \frac{1.25 \text{ cups}}{1 \text{ batch}}$$
$$= 19 \div 1.25$$
$$= 15.2$$

Alana cannot make 0.2 batch. The recipe calls for one egg, and she cannot divide one egg into tenths. So, she can make 15 batches.

Cost of flour for each batch: $4.49 \div 15 = 0.299, or about $0.30.

 Justify and Evaluate

A bag contains about 80 quarter cups, or about 20 cups. Each batch uses about 1 cup of flour, so there is enough flour for about 20 batches. A bag costs about $5.00, so the flour for each batch costs about $5.00 \div 20 = 0.25. The answers are close to the estimates, so the answers are reasonable.

2. A 4-pound bag of sugar contains 454 one-teaspoon servings and costs $3.49. A batch of muffins uses $\frac{3}{4}$ cup of sugar. How many batches can you make if you use all the sugar? What is the cost of sugar for each batch? (1 cup = 48 teaspoons) _____

Using Tools Strategically

A wide variety of tools are available to help you solve problems. Rulers, models, calculators, protractors, and software are some of the tools you can use in addition to paper and pencil. Choosing tools wisely can help you solve problems and increase your understanding of mathematical concepts.

Math On the Spot

⊕ my.hrw.com

EXAMPLE 3 (Real World)

The depth of Golden Trout Lake has been decreasing in recent years. Two years ago, the depth of the lake was 186.73 meters. Since then the depth has been changing at an average rate of $-1\frac{3}{4}\%$ per year. What is the depth of the lake today?

STEP 1 Convert the percent to a decimal.

$-1\frac{3}{4}\% = -1.75\%$ *Write the fraction as a decimal.*

$\qquad\ \ = -0.0175$ *Move the decimal point two places left.*

STEP 2 Find the depth of the lake after one year. Use a calculator to simplify the computations.

$186.73 \times (-0.0175) \approx -3.27$ meters   *Find the change in depth.*

$186.73 - 3.27 = 183.46$ meters   *Find the new depth.*

STEP 3 Find the depth of the lake after two years.

$183.46 \times (-0.0175) \approx -3.21$ meters   *Find the change in depth.*

$183.46 - 3.21 = 180.25$ meters   *Find the new depth.*

STEP 4 Check the answer for reasonableness.

The original depth was about 190 meters. The depth changed by about -2% per year. Because $(-0.02)(190) = -3.8$, the depth changed by about -4 meters per year or about -8 meters over two years. So, the new depth was about 182 meters. The answer is close to the estimate, so it is reasonable.

Math Talk

Mathematical Processes

How could you write a single expression for calculating the depth after 1 year? after 2 years?

© Houghton Mifflin Harcourt Publishing Company

YOUR TURN

3. Three years ago, Jolene bought $750 worth of stock in a software company. Since then the value of her purchase has been increasing at an average rate of $12\frac{3}{5}$% per year. How much is the stock worth now? _____

Guided Practice

1. Mike hiked to Big Bear Lake in 4.5 hours at an average rate of $3\frac{1}{5}$ miles per hour. Pedro hiked the same distance at a rate of $3\frac{3}{5}$ miles per hour. How long did it take Pedro to reach the lake? *(Explore Activity Example 1 and Example 2)*

    STEP 1 Find the distance Mike hiked.

    4.5 h × ⬚ miles per hour = ⬚ miles

    STEP 2 Find Pedro's time to hike the same distance.

    ⬚ miles ÷ ⬚ miles per hour = ⬚ hours

2. Until this year, Greenville had averaged 25.68 inches of rainfall per year for more than a century. This year's total rainfall showed a change of $-2\frac{3}{8}$% with respect to the previous average. How much rain fell this year? *(Example 3)*

    STEP 1 Use a calculator to find this year's decrease to the nearest hundredth.

    ⬚ inches × ⬚ ≈ ⬚ inches

    STEP 2 Find this year's total rainfall.

    ⬚ inches − ⬚ inches ≈ ⬚ inches

? ESSENTIAL QUESTION CHECK-IN

3. Why is it important to consider using tools when you are solving a problem?

    _____

    _____

    _____

19.6 Independent Practice

Personal Math Trainer

Online Assessment and Intervention

my.hrw.com

Solve, using appropriate tools.

4. Three rock climbers started a climb with each person carrying 7.8 kilograms of climbing equipment. A fourth climber with no equipment joined the group. The group divided the total weight of climbing equipment equally among the four climbers. How much

did each climber carry? _____

5. Foster is centering a photo that is $3\frac{1}{2}$ inches wide on a scrapbook page that is 12 inches wide. How far from each side of the page

should he put the picture? _____

6. Diane serves breakfast to two groups of children at a daycare center. One box of Oaties contains 12 cups of cereal. She needs $\frac{1}{3}$ cup for each younger child and $\frac{3}{4}$ cup for each older child. Today's group includes 11 younger children and 10 older children. Is one box of Oaties enough for everyone?

Explain. _____

7. The figure shows how the yard lines on a football field are numbered. The goal lines are labeled G. A referee was standing on a certain yard line as the first quarter ended. He walked $41\frac{3}{4}$ yards to a yard line with the same number as the one he had just left. How far was the referee from the nearest goal

line? _____

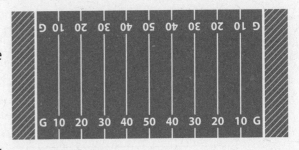

In 8–10, a teacher gave a test with 50 questions, each worth the same number of points. Donovan got 39 out of 50 questions right. Marci's score was 10 percentage points higher than Donovan's.

8. What was Marci's score? Explain.

_____

_____

9. How many more questions did Marci answer correctly? Explain.

_____

_____

10. Explain how you can check your answers for reasonableness.

_____

_____

_____

For 11–13, use the expression $1.43 \times \left(-\frac{19}{37}\right)$.

11. Critique Reasoning Jamie says the value of the expression is close to −0.75. Does Jamie's estimate seem reasonable? Explain.

_____

12. Find the product. Explain your method.

_____

_____

13. Does your answer to Exercise 12 justify your answer to Exercise 11?

_____

 **FOCUS ON HIGHER ORDER THINKING**

14. Persevere in Problem Solving A scuba diver dove from the surface of the ocean to an elevation of $-79\frac{9}{10}$ feet at a rate of −18.8 feet per minute. After spending 12.75 minutes at that elevation, the diver ascended to an elevation of $-28\frac{9}{10}$ feet. The total time for the dive so far was $19\frac{1}{8}$ minutes. What was the rate of change in the diver's elevation during the ascent? _____

15. Analyze Relationships Describe two ways you could evaluate 37% of the sum of $27\frac{3}{5}$ and 15.9. Tell which method you would use and why.

_____

_____

_____

_____

_____

16. Represent Real-World Problems Describe a real-world problem you could solve with the help of a yardstick and a calculator.

_____

_____

_____

_____

_____

Work Area

Fraction Challenge

INSTRUCTIONS

Playing the Game

STEP 1 Have one student in your group shuffle the game cards and then place them face-down in a draw pile. Each game card shows a different positive or negative fraction.

STEP 2 Take turns drawing two cards from the draw pile. Wait to turn your cards over until all players, including the shuffler, have drawn two cards.

STEP 3 Look at your two fractions and the target value for the round on the scorecard shown below. Choose the operation (addition, subtraction, multiplication, or division) to perform on your fractions, in either order, that gets you as close as possible to the target value.

Write your expression and its simplified value on your scorecard.

Round	Target	Expression	Result	Points
1	Greatest number			
2	Least number			
3	Closest to 1			
4	Closest to 0			
5	Closest to −1			
			Total:	

Compare results with the other players in your group. Whoever is closest to the target value for the round receives 5 points. The other players receive 4, 3, and 2 points as their results get farther from the target.

For a tie, both players receive the same number of points, and the next point value is skipped, as shown below.

Player 1

Round	Target	Expression	Result	Points
5	Closest to −1	$-\frac{5}{4} - \left(-\frac{1}{2}\right)$	$-\frac{3}{4}$	5

Both players get 5 points because they are closest to and equally distant from −1.

Player 2

Round	Target	Expression	Result	Points
5	Closest to −1	$-\frac{5}{8} \times \frac{2}{1}$	$-1\frac{1}{4}$	5

No player gets 4 points. The next closest players get 3 points and 2 points, respectively.

Player 3

Round	Target	Expression	Result	Points
5	Closest to −1	$-\frac{3}{8} - \frac{1}{6}$	$-\frac{13}{24}$	3

Player 4

Round	Target	Expression	Result	Points
5	Closest to −1	$-\frac{5}{6} \div \frac{8}{3}$	$-\frac{5}{16}$	2

STEP 5 Place your used game cards in a discard pile.

STEP 6 Repeat steps 2–5 for each round until the scorecard is filled in.

Winning the Game

The winner is the player with the most points. The maximum score per round is 5 points. So after 5 rounds, the player with the score closest to 25 points wins.

Player 1

Round	Target	Expression	Result	Points
5	Closest to −1	$-\frac{5}{4} - \left(-\frac{1}{2}\right)$	$-\frac{3}{4}$	5
			Total:	24

Ready to Go On?

19.1 Rational Numbers and Decimals

Write each mixed number as a decimal.

1. $4\frac{1}{5}$ _____

2. $12\frac{14}{15}$ _____

3. $5\frac{5}{32}$ _____

19.2 Adding Rational Numbers

Find each sum.

4. $4.5 + 7.1 =$ _____

5. $5\frac{1}{6} + \left(-3\frac{5}{6}\right) =$ _____

19.3 Subtracting Rational Numbers

Find each difference.

6. $-\frac{1}{8} - \left(6\frac{7}{8}\right) =$ _____

7. $14.2 - (-4.9) =$ _____

19.4 Multiplying Rational Numbers

Multiply.

8. $-4\left(\frac{7}{10}\right) =$ _____

9. $-3.2(-5.6)(4) =$ _____

19.5 Dividing Rational Numbers

Find each quotient.

10. $-\frac{19}{2} \div \frac{38}{7} =$ _____

11. $\frac{-32.01}{-3.3} =$ _____

19.6 Applying Rational Number Operations

12. Luis bought stock at $83.60. The next day, the price increased $15.35. This new price changed by $-4\frac{3}{4}\%$ the following day. What was the final stock price? Is your answer reasonable? Explain.

_____

_____

? **ESSENTIAL QUESTION**

13. How can you use negative numbers to represent real-world problems?

_____

_____

Selected Response

1. What is $-7\frac{5}{12}$ written as a decimal?

- Ⓐ -7.25
- Ⓑ $-7.333\ldots$
- Ⓒ $-7.41666\ldots$
- Ⓓ -7.512

2. Glenda began the day with a golf score of -6 and ended with a score of -10. Which statement represents her golf score for that day?

- Ⓐ $-6 - (-10) = 4$
- Ⓑ $-10 - (-6) = -4$
- Ⓒ $-6 + (-10) = -16$
- Ⓓ $-10 + (-6) = -16$

3. A submersible vessel at an elevation of -95 feet descends to 5 times that elevation. What is the vessel's new elevation?

- Ⓐ -475 ft
- Ⓒ 19 ft
- Ⓑ -19 ft
- Ⓓ 475 ft

4. The temperature at 7 P.M. at a weather station in Minnesota was $-5\,°F$. The temperature began changing at the rate of $-2.5\,°F$ per hour. What was the temperature at 10 P.M.?

- Ⓐ $-15\,°F$
- Ⓒ $2.5\,°F$
- Ⓑ $-12.5\,°F$
- Ⓓ $5\,°F$

5. What is the sum of -2.16 and -1.75?

- Ⓐ 0.41
- Ⓒ -0.41
- Ⓑ 3.91
- Ⓓ -3.91

6. On Sunday, the wind chill temperature reached $-36\,°F$. On Monday, the wind chill temperature only reached $\frac{1}{4}$ of Sunday's wind chill temperature. What was the lowest wind chill temperature on Monday?

- Ⓐ $-9\,°F$
- Ⓒ $-40\,°F$
- Ⓑ $-36\frac{1}{4}\,°F$
- Ⓓ $-144\,°F$

7. The level of a lake was 8 inches below normal. It decreased $1\frac{1}{4}$ inches in June and $2\frac{3}{8}$ inches more in July. What was the new level with respect to the normal level?

- Ⓐ $-11\frac{5}{8}$ in.
- Ⓒ $-9\frac{1}{8}$ in.
- Ⓑ $-10\frac{5}{8}$ in.
- Ⓓ $-5\frac{3}{8}$ in.

Mini-Task

8. The average annual rainfall for a town is 43.2 inches.

a. What is the average *monthly* rainfall?

_____

b. The difference of a given month's rainfall from the average monthly rainfall is called the *deviation*. What is the deviation for each month shown?

Town's Rainfall in Last Three Months			
Month	May	June	July
Rain (in.)	$2\frac{3}{5}$	$\frac{7}{8}$	$4\frac{1}{4}$

_____

c. The average monthly rainfall for the previous 9 months was 4 inches. Did the town exceed its average annual rainfall? If so, by how much?

_____

MODULE 17 — Adding and Subtracting Integers

? ESSENTIAL QUESTION

How can you use addition and subtraction of integers to solve real-world problems?

EXAMPLE 1

Add.

A. $-8 + (-7)$ The signs of both integers are the same.

    $8 + 7 = 15$ Find the sum of the absolute values.

    $-8 + (-7) = -15$ Use the sign of integers to write the sum.

B. $-5 + 11$ The signs of the integers are different.

    $|11| - |-5| = 6$ Greater absolute value – lesser absolute value.

    $-5 + 11 = 6$ 11 has the greater absolute value, so the sum is positive.

EXAMPLE 2

The temperature Tuesday afternoon was 3 °C. Tuesday night, the temperature was −6 °C. Find the change in temperature.

Find the difference $-6 - 3$.

Rewrite as $-6 + (-3)$.   −3 is the opposite of 3.

$-6 + (-3) = -9$

The temperature decreased 9 °C.

EXERCISES

Add. (Lessons 17.1, 17.2)

1. $-10 + (-5)$ _____

2. $9 + (-20)$ _____

3. $-13 + 32$ _____

Subtract. (Lesson 17.3)

4. $-12 - 5$ _____

5. $25 - (-4)$ _____

6. $-3 - (-40)$ _____

7. Antoine has $13 in his checking account. He buys some school supplies and ends up with $5 in his account. What was the overall change in Antoine's account? (Lesson 17.4) _____

Multiplying and Dividing Integers

? ESSENTIAL QUESTION

How can you use multiplication and division of integers to solve real-world problems?

EXAMPLE 1

Multiply.

A. $(13)(-3)$

Find the sign of the product. The numbers have different signs, so the product will be negative. Multiply the absolute values. Assign the correct sign to the product.

$$13(-3) = -39$$

B. $(-5)(-8)$

Find the sign of the product. The numbers have the same sign, so the product will be positive. Multiply the absolute values. Assign the correct sign to the product.

$$(-5)(-8) = 40$$

EXAMPLE 2

Christine received -25 points on her exam for 5 wrong answers. How many points did Christine receive for each wrong answer?

Divide -25 by 5.

The signs are different.

$-25 \div 5 = -5$ *The quotient is negative.*

Christine received -5 points for each wrong answer.

EXAMPLE 3

Simplify: $15 + (-3) \times 8$

Multiply first.

$15 + (-24)$

Add.

-9

EXERCISES

Multiply or divide. (Lessons 18.1, 18.2)

1. $-9 \times (-5)$ _____

2. $0 \times (-10)$ _____

3. $12 \times (-4)$ _____

4. $-32 \div 8$ _____

5. $-9 \div (-1)$ _____

6. $-56 \div 8$ _____

Simplify. (Lesson 18.3)

7. $-14 \div 2 - 3$ _____

8. $8 + (-20) \times 3$ _____

9. $36 \div (-6) \times -15$ _____

10. Tony bought 3 packs of pencils for $4 each and a pencil box for $7. Mario bought 4 binders for $6 each and used a coupon for $6 off. Write and evaluate expressions to find who spent more money. (Lesson 18.3)

_____

Rational Numbers

Key Vocabulary

rational number (*número racional*)

repeating decimal (*decimal periódico*)

terminating decimal (*decimal finito*)

? ESSENTIAL QUESTION

How can you use rational numbers to solve real-world problems?

EXAMPLE 1

Eddie walked $1\frac{2}{3}$ miles on a hiking trail. Write $1\frac{2}{3}$ as a decimal. Use the decimal to classify $1\frac{2}{3}$ according to the number group(s) to which it belongs.

$1\frac{2}{3} = \frac{5}{3}$ Write $1\frac{2}{3}$ as an improper fraction.

$$\begin{array}{r} 1.66 \\ 3)\overline{5.00} \\ -3 \\ \hline 20 \\ -18 \\ \hline 20 \\ -18 \\ \hline 2 \end{array}$$

Divide the numerator by the denominator.

The decimal equivalent of $1\frac{2}{3}$ is 1.66…, or $1.\overline{6}$. It is a repeating decimal, and therefore can be classified as a rational number.

EXAMPLE 2

Find each sum or difference.

A. $-2 + 4.5$

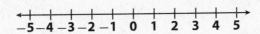

Start at -2 and move 4.5 units to the right: $-2 + 4.5 = 2.5$.

B. $-\frac{2}{5} - \left(-\frac{4}{5}\right)$

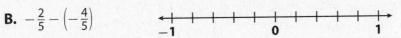

Start at $-\frac{2}{5}$. Move $\left|-\frac{4}{5}\right| = \frac{4}{5}$ unit to the right because you are subtracting a negative number: $-\frac{2}{5} - \left(-\frac{4}{5}\right) = \frac{2}{5}$.

EXAMPLE 3

Find the product: $3\left(-\frac{1}{6}\right)\left(-\frac{2}{5}\right)$.

$3\left(-\frac{1}{6}\right) = -\frac{1}{2}$ Find the product of the first two factors. One is positive and one is negative, so the product is negative.

$-\frac{1}{2}\left(-\frac{2}{5}\right) = \frac{1}{5}$ Multiply the result by the third factor. Both are negative, so the product is positive.

$3\left(-\frac{1}{6}\right)\left(-\frac{2}{5}\right) = \frac{1}{5}$

EXAMPLE 4

Find the quotient: $\frac{15.2}{-2}$.

$\frac{15.2}{-2} = -7.6$ *The quotient is negative because the signs are different.*

EXAMPLE 5

A lake's level dropped an average of $3\frac{4}{5}$ inches per day for 21 days. A heavy rain then raised the level 8.25 feet, after which it dropped $9\frac{1}{2}$ inches per day for 4 days. Jayden says that overall, the lake level changed about $-1\frac{1}{2}$ feet. Is this answer reasonable?

Yes; the lake drops about 4 inches, or $\frac{1}{3}$ foot, per day for 21 days, rises about 8 feet, then falls about $\frac{3}{4}$ foot for 4 days:
$-\frac{1}{3}(21) + 8 - \frac{3}{4}(4) = -7 + 8 - 3 = -2$ feet.

EXERCISES

Write each mixed number as a whole number or decimal. Classify each number according to the group(s) to which it belongs: rational numbers, integers, or whole numbers. (Lesson 19.1)

1. $\frac{3}{4}$ _____ **2.** $\frac{8}{2}$ _____

3. $\frac{11}{3}$ _____ **4.** $\frac{5}{2}$ _____

Find each sum or difference. (Lessons 19.2, 19.3)

5. $-5 + 9.5$ _____ **6.** $\frac{1}{6} + \left(-\frac{5}{6}\right)$ _____ **7.** $-0.5 + (-8.5)$ _____

8. $-3 - (-8)$ _____ **9.** $5.6 - (-3.1)$ _____ **10.** $3\frac{1}{2} - 2\frac{1}{4}$ _____

Find each product or quotient. (Lessons 19.4, 19.5)

11. $-9 \times (-5)$ _____ **12.** $0 \times (-7)$ _____ **13.** -8×8 _____

14. $\frac{-56}{8}$ _____ **15.** $\frac{-130}{-5}$ _____ **16.** $\frac{34.5}{1.5}$ _____

17. $-\frac{2}{5}\left(-\frac{1}{2}\right)\left(-\frac{5}{6}\right)$ _____ **18.** $\left(\frac{1}{5}\right)\left(-\frac{5}{7}\right)\left(\frac{3}{4}\right)$ _____

19. Lei withdrew $50 from her bank account every day for a week. What was the change in her account in that week?

_____

20. Dan is cutting 4.75 foot lengths of twine from a 240 foot spool of twine. He needs to cut 42 lengths, and says that 40.5 feet of twine will remain. Show that this is reasonable.

_____

1. **CAREERS IN MATH** | **Urban Planner** Armand is an urban planner, and he has proposed a site for a new town library. The site is between City Hall and the post office on Main Street.

City Hall ●————————— Library site ●————————————— Post office ●

The distance between City Hall and the post office is $6\frac{1}{2}$ miles. City Hall is $1\frac{1}{4}$ miles closer to the library site than it is to the post office.

   a. Write $6\frac{1}{2}$ miles and $1\frac{1}{4}$ miles as decimals.

   _____

   b. Let d represent the distance from City Hall to the library site. Write an expression for the distance from the library site to the post office.

   _____

   c. Write an equation that represents the following statement: The distance from City Hall to the library site plus the distance from the library site to the post office is equal to the distance from City Hall to the post office.

   _____

   d. Solve your equation from part **c** to determine the distance from City Hall to the library site, and the distance from the post office to the library site.

   _____

   _____

2. Sumaya is reading a book with 288 pages. She has already read 90 pages. She plans to read 20 more pages each day until she finishes the book.

   a. Sumaya writes the equation $378 = -20d$ to find the number of days she will need to finish the book. Identify the errors that Sumaya made.

   _____

   _____

   b. Write and solve an equation to determine how many days Sumaya will need to finish the book. In your answer, count part of a day as a full day. Show that your answer is reasonable.

   _____

   _____

c. Estimate how many days you would need to read a book about the same length as Sumaya's book. What information did you use to find the estimate?

_____

_____

_____

3. Jackson works as a veterinary technician and earns $12.20 per hour.

a. Jackson normally works 40 hours a week. In a normal week, what is his total pay before taxes and other deductions?

_____

b. Last week, Jackson was ill and missed some work. His total pay before deductions was $372.10. Write and solve an equation to find the number of hours Jackson worked.

_____

c. Jackson records his hours each day on a time sheet. Last week when he was ill, his time sheet was incomplete. How many hours are missing? Show your work. Then show that your answer is reasonable.

Mon	Tues	Wed	Thurs	Fri
8	$7\frac{1}{4}$	$8\frac{1}{2}$		

_____

_____

_____

d. When Jackson works more than 40 hours in a week, he earns 1.5 times his normal hourly rate for each of the extra hours. Jackson worked 43 hours one week. What was his total pay before deductions? Justify your answer.

_____

_____

e. What is a reasonable range for Jackson's expected yearly pay before deductions? Describe any assumptions you made in finding your answer.

_____

_____

_____

Selected Response

1. What is $-6\frac{9}{16}$ written as a decimal?

- (A) -6.625
- (B) -6.5625
- (C) -6.4375
- (D) -6.125

2. Working together, 6 friends pick $14\frac{2}{5}$ pounds of pecans at a pecan farm. They divide the pecans equally among themselves. How many pounds does each friend get?

- (A) $20\frac{2}{5}$ pounds
- (B) $8\frac{2}{5}$ pounds
- (C) $2\frac{3}{5}$ pounds
- (D) $2\frac{2}{5}$ pounds

3. What is the value of $(-3.25)(-1.56)$?

- (A) -5.85
- (B) -5.07
- (C) 5.07
- (D) 5.85

4. Mrs. Rodriguez is going to use $6\frac{1}{3}$ yards of material to make two dresses. The larger dress requires $3\frac{2}{3}$ yards of material. How much material will Mrs. Rodriguez have left to use on the smaller dress?

- (A) $1\frac{2}{3}$ yards
- (B) $2\frac{1}{3}$ yards
- (C) $2\frac{2}{3}$ yards
- (D) $3\frac{1}{3}$ yards

5. Jaime had $37 in his bank account on Sunday. The table shows his account activity for the next four days. What was the balance in Jaime's account after his deposit on Thursday?

Jamie's Bank Account		
Day	Deposit	Withdrawal
Monday	$17.42	none
Tuesday	none	$-$12.60
Wednesday	none	$-$9.62
Thursday	$62.29	none

- (A) $57.49
- (B) $59.65
- (C) $94.49
- (D) $138.93

6. A used motorcycle is on sale for $3,600. Erik makes an offer equal to $\frac{3}{4}$ of this price. How much does Erik offer for the motorcycle?

- (A) $4,800
- (B) $2,700
- (C) $2,400
- (D) $900

7. Ruby ate $\frac{1}{3}$ of a pizza, and Angie ate $\frac{1}{5}$ of the pizza. How much of the pizza did they eat in all?

- (A) $\frac{1}{15}$ of the pizza
- (B) $\frac{1}{8}$ of the pizza
- (C) $\frac{3}{8}$ of the pizza
- (D) $\frac{8}{15}$ of the pizza

8. Winslow buys 1.2 pounds of bananas. The bananas cost $1.29 per pound. To the nearest cent, how much does Winslow pay for the bananas?

Ⓐ $1.08

Ⓑ $1.20

Ⓒ $1.55

Ⓓ $2.49

9. The temperature was −10 °F and dropped by 16 °F. Which statement represents the resulting temperature in degrees Fahrenheit?

Ⓐ −10 − (−16) = −6

Ⓑ −10 − 16 = −26

Ⓒ 10 − (−16) = 26

Ⓓ −10 + 16 = 6

10. A scuba diver at a depth of −12 ft (12 ft below sea level), dives down to a coral reef that is 3.5 times the diver's original depth. What is the diver's new depth?

Ⓐ −420 ft

Ⓑ −42 ft

Ⓒ 42 ft

Ⓓ about 3.4 ft

11. The school Spirit Club spent $320.82 on food and took in $643.59 selling the food. How much did the Spirit Club make?

Ⓐ −$322.77

Ⓑ −$964.41

Ⓒ $322.77

Ⓓ $964.41

12. Lila graphed the points −2 and 2 on a number line. What does the distance between these two points represent?

Ⓐ the sum of −2 and 2

Ⓑ the difference of 2 and −2

Ⓒ the difference of −2 and 2

Ⓓ the product of −2 and 2

Some answer choices, called distracters, may seem correct because they are based on common errors.

13. What is a reasonable estimate of $-3\frac{4}{5} + (-5.25)$ and the actual value?

Ⓐ $-4 + (-5) = -9; -9\frac{1}{20}$

Ⓑ $-3 + (-5) = -8; -8\frac{1}{20}$

Ⓒ $-4 + (-5) = -1; -8\frac{9}{20}$

Ⓓ $-3 + (-5) = 8; 8\frac{1}{20}$

Mini-Task

14. Juanita is watering her lawn using the water stored in her rainwater tank. The water level in the tank drops $\frac{1}{3}$ inch every 10 minutes she waters.

a. What is the change in the tank's water level after 1 hour?

_____

b. What is the expected change in the tank's water level after 2.25 hours?

_____

c. If the tank's water level is 4 feet, how many days can Juanita water if she waters for 15 minutes each day?

_____

Ratios and Proportional Relationships

MODULE 20
Rates and Proportionality

MODULE 21
Proportions and Percents

CAREERS IN MATH

Bicycle Tour Operator A bike tour operator organizes cycling trips for tourists all over the world. Bike tour operators use math to calculate expenses, determine rates, and compute payroll information for their employees. If tours include travel in another country, operators must understand how to calculate currency exchange rates.

If you are interested in a career as a bicycle tour operator, you should study these mathematical subjects:
- Basic Math
- Business Math

Research other careers that require the understanding of business mathematics.

Unit 9 Performance Task

At the end of the unit, check out how **bicycle tour operators** use math.

© Houghton Mifflin Harcourt Publishing Company • Image Credits: KAREN BLEIER/AFP/Getty Images

Vocabulary Preview

Use the puzzle to preview key vocabulary from this unit. Unscramble the circled letters within found words to answer the riddle at the bottom of the page.

1. A relationship between two quantities in which the rate of change or the ratio of one quantity to the other is constant. (Lesson 20.3)

⎯◯⎯ ⎯◯⎯ ⎯⎯ ⎯⎯ ⎯⎯ ⎯⎯ ⎯⎯ ⎯⎯

◯⎯ ⎯⎯ ⎯◯⎯ ⎯⎯ ⎯⎯ ⎯⎯ ⎯⎯

2. Describes how much a quantity decreases in comparison to the original amount. (Lesson 21.1) ⎯⎯ ⎯⎯ ⎯◯⎯ ⎯⎯ ⎯⎯ ⎯⎯ ⎯⎯

⎯⎯ ⎯⎯ ⎯⎯ ⎯⎯ ⎯⎯ ⎯⎯ ⎯⎯

3. A fixed percent of the principal. (Lesson 21.3)

⎯⎯ ⎯⎯ ⎯⎯ ⎯◯⎯ ⎯⎯   ⎯⎯ ⎯⎯ ⎯⎯ ⎯◯⎯ ⎯⎯

4. The quantity *k* in a relationship described by an equation of the form *y = kx*. (Lesson 20.3)

⎯⎯ ⎯◯⎯ ⎯⎯ ⎯⎯ ⎯⎯ ⎯⎯ ⎯⎯   ⎯⎯ ⎯⎯

⎯⎯ ⎯⎯ ⎯⎯ ⎯⎯ ⎯⎯ ⎯◯⎯ ⎯⎯ ⎯⎯

5. A ratio that compares the amount of change in the dependent variable to the amount of change in the independent variable. (Lesson 20.2)

⎯◯⎯ ⎯⎯   ⎯◯⎯ ⎯⎯   ⎯⎯ ⎯⎯ ⎯⎯ ⎯⎯ ⎯⎯

Q: What did the athlete order when he needed a huge helping of mashed potatoes?

A: ⎯⎯ ⎯⎯ ⎯⎯ ⎯⎯ - ⎯⎯ ⎯⎯ ⎯⎯ ⎯⎯ ⎯⎯ ⎯⎯ ⎯⎯ !

Rates and Proportionality

ESSENTIAL QUESTION

How can you use rates and proportionality to solve real-world problems?

Real-World Video

You can use rates to describe lots of real-world situations. A cyclist can compute rates such as miles per hour or rotations per minute.

my.hrw.com

© Houghton Mifflin Harcourt Publishing Company • Image Credits: ©OSO Media/ Alamy Images

GO DIGITAL
my.hrw.com

my.hrw.com

Go digital with your write-in student edition, accessible on any device.

Math On the Spot

Scan with your smart phone to jump directly to the online edition, video tutor, and more.

Animated Math

Interactively explore key concepts to see how math works.

Personal Math Trainer

Get immediate feedback and help as you work through practice sets.

Reading Start-Up

© Houghton Mifflin Harcourt Publishing Company

Visualize Vocabulary

Use the ✔ words to complete the graphic. You can put more than one word in each bubble.

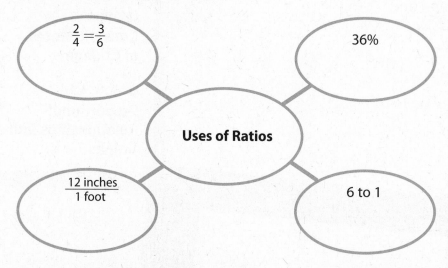

$\frac{2}{4} = \frac{3}{6}$

36%

Uses of Ratios

$\frac{12 \text{ inches}}{1 \text{ foot}}$

6 to 1

Vocabulary

Review Words

constant (*constante*)
✔ conversion factor (*factor de conversión*)
✔ equivalent ratios (*razones equivalentes*)
✔ percent (*porcentaje*)
rate (*tasa*)
✔ ratio (*razón*)

Preview Words

complex fraction (*fracción compleja*)
constant of proportionality (*constante de proporcionalidad*)
proportion (*proporción*)
proportional relationship (*relación proporcional*)
rate of change (*tasa de cambio*)
unit rates (*tasas unitarias*)

Understand Vocabulary

Match the term on the left to the definition on the right.

1. rate of change
2. proportion
3. unit rate

A. Statement that two rates or ratios are equivalent.

B. A rate that describes how one quantity changes in relation to another quantity.

C. Rate in which the second quantity is one unit.

Active Reading

Three-Panel Flip Chart Before beginning the module, create a three-panel flip chart to help you organize what you learn. Label each flap with one of the lesson titles from this module. As you study each lesson, write important ideas like vocabulary, properties, and formulas under the appropriate flap.

Are YOU Ready?

Complete these exercises to review skills you will need for this module.

Operations with Fractions

EXAMPLE $\frac{3}{10} \div \frac{5}{8} = \frac{3}{10} \times \frac{8}{5}$ Multiply by the reciprocal of the divisor.

$= \frac{3}{10_5} \times \frac{8^4}{5}$ Divide by the common factors.

$= \frac{12}{25}$ Simplify.

Divide.

1. $\frac{3}{4} \div \frac{4}{5}$ _____

2. $\frac{5}{9} \div \frac{10}{11}$ _____

3. $\frac{3}{8} \div \frac{1}{2}$ _____

4. $\frac{16}{21} \div \frac{8}{9}$ _____

Ordered Pairs

EXAMPLE

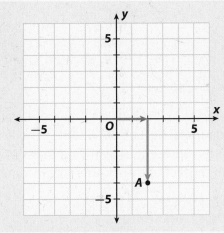

To write the ordered pair for A, start at the origin.
Move 2 units right.
Then move 4 units down.
The ordered pair for point A is $(2, -4)$.

Write the ordered pair for each point.

5. B _____

6. C _____

7. D _____

8. E _____

9. F _____

10. G _____

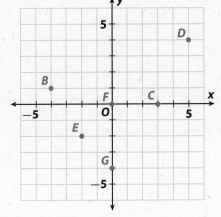

Complete these exercises to review skills you will need for this module.

Operations with Fractions

11. A track is $\frac{3}{4}$ mile long. The track is measured in units called furlongs. One furlong is equivalent to $\frac{1}{8}$ mile. How long is the track in furlongs? Show your work.

12. Which is greater: $\frac{1}{2} \div \frac{7}{10}$ or $\frac{1}{2} \div \frac{7}{8}$? How do you know?

Ordered Pairs

13. The origin on the coordinate grid represents Lincoln Middle School. Dora, Pedro, Naomi, and Rajeev live at the points represented by their initials. Write the ordered pair for each student's home with respect to the location of Lincoln Middle School.

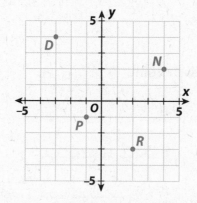

20.1 Unit Rates

7.2.4.1

Students will find and use unit rates.

? ESSENTIAL QUESTION

How do you find and use unit rates?

EXPLORE ACTIVITY

Exploring Rates

Commonly used rates like miles per hour make it easy to understand and compare rates.

Jeff hikes $\frac{1}{2}$ mile every 15 minutes, or $\frac{1}{4}$ hour. Lisa hikes $\frac{1}{3}$ mile every 10 minutes, or $\frac{1}{6}$ hour. How far do they each hike in 1 hour? 2 hours?

A Use the bar diagram to help you determine how many miles Jeff hikes. How many $\frac{1}{4}$ -hours are in 1 hour? How far does Jeff hike in 1 hour?

? miles

| $\frac{1}{4}$ hour | $\frac{1}{4}$ hour | $\frac{1}{4}$ hour | $\frac{1}{4}$ hour |

$\frac{1}{2}$ mile

_____

B Complete the table for Jeff's hike.

Distance (mi)	$\frac{1}{2}$				
Time (h)	$\frac{1}{4}$	$\frac{1}{2}$	$\frac{3}{4}$	1	2

C Complete the bar diagram to help you determine how far Lisa hikes. How many miles does she hike in 1 hour?

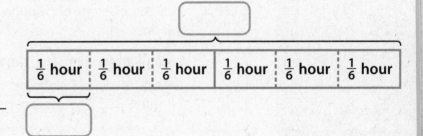

| $\frac{1}{6}$ hour | $\frac{1}{6}$ hour | $\frac{1}{6}$ hour | $\frac{1}{6}$ hour | $\frac{1}{6}$ hour | $\frac{1}{6}$ hour |

_____

D Complete the table for Lisa's hike.

Distance (mi)	$\frac{1}{3}$				
Time (h)	$\frac{1}{6}$	$\frac{1}{3}$	$\frac{1}{2}$	1	2

Reflect

1. How did you find Jeff's distance for $\frac{3}{4}$ hour?

_____

2. Which hiker walks farther in one hour? Which is faster?

_____

Math On the Spot

⏻ my.hrw.com

Finding Unit Rates

A rate is a comparison of two quantities that have different units, such as miles and hours. Rates are often expressed as **unit rates**, that is, with a denominator of 1 unit.

$$\frac{60 \text{ miles} \div 2}{2 \text{ hours} \div 2} = \frac{30 \text{ miles}}{1 \text{ hour}} \quad \text{This means 30 miles per hour.}$$

When the two quantities being compared in the rate are both fractions, the rate is expressed as a *complex fraction*. A **complex fraction** is a fraction that has a fraction in its numerator, denominator, or both.

$$\frac{\frac{a}{b}}{\frac{c}{d}} = \frac{a}{b} \div \frac{c}{d}$$

EXAMPLE 1

While remodeling her kitchen, Angela is repainting. She estimates that she paints 55 square feet every half-hour. How many square feet does Angela paint per hour?

STEP 1 Determine the units of the rate.

The rate is **area in square feet** per **time in hours**.

STEP 2 Find Angela's rate of painting in area painted per time.

area painted: 55 sq ft **time:** $\frac{1}{2}$ hour

$$\frac{\text{area painted}}{\text{time}} = \frac{55 \text{ square feet}}{\frac{1}{2} \text{ hour}}$$

> The fraction represents area in square feet per time in hours.

STEP 3 Find Angela's unit rate of painting in square feet per hour.

$$\frac{55}{\frac{1}{2}} = 55 \div \frac{1}{2} \qquad \textit{Rewrite the fraction as division.}$$

$$= \frac{55}{1} \times \frac{2}{1} \qquad \textit{Multiply by the reciprocal.}$$

$$= \frac{110 \text{ square feet}}{1 \text{ hour}} \qquad \textit{The unit rate has a denominator of 1.}$$

Angela paints 110 square feet per hour.

YOUR TURN

3. Paige mows $\frac{1}{6}$ acre in $\frac{1}{4}$ hour. How many acres does Paige mow per hour?

_____

4. Greta uses 3 ounces of pasta to make $\frac{3}{4}$ of a serving of pasta. How many ounces of pasta are there per serving?_____

Using Unit Rates

You can use unit rates to simplify rates and ratios that appear complicated, such as those containing fractions in both the numerator and denominator.

EXAMPLE 2 Real World

Two pools are leaking. After 15 minutes, pool A has leaked $\frac{2}{3}$ gallon. After 20 minutes, pool B has leaked $\frac{3}{4}$ gallon. Which pool is leaking faster?

My Notes

STEP 1 Find the rate in volume (gallons) per time (hours) at which each pool is leaking. First convert minutes to hours.

Pool A

$$\frac{\frac{2}{3}\text{ gal}}{15\text{ min}} = \frac{\frac{2}{3}\text{ gal}}{\frac{1}{4}\text{ h}}$$

> 15 min = $\frac{1}{4}$ h

Pool B

$$\frac{\frac{3}{4}\text{ gal}}{20\text{ min}} = \frac{\frac{3}{4}\text{ gal}}{\frac{1}{3}\text{ h}}$$

> 20 min = $\frac{1}{3}$ h

STEP 2 To find the unit rates, first rewrite the fractions.

Pool A

$$\frac{\frac{2}{3}\text{ gal}}{\frac{1}{4}\text{ h}} = \frac{2}{3} \div \frac{1}{4}$$

Pool B

$$\frac{\frac{3}{4}\text{ gal}}{\frac{1}{3}\text{ h}} = \frac{3}{4} \div \frac{1}{3}$$

STEP 3 To divide, multiply by the reciprocal.

Pool A

$$\frac{2}{3} \div \frac{1}{4} = \frac{2}{3} \times \frac{4}{1}$$
$$= \frac{8}{3}, \text{ or } 2\frac{2}{3} \text{ gal per h}$$

Pool B

$$\frac{3}{4} \div \frac{1}{3} = \frac{3}{4} \times \frac{3}{1}$$
$$= \frac{9}{4}, \text{ or } 2\frac{1}{4} \text{ gal per h}$$

STEP 4 Compare the unit rates.

Pool A   Pool B

$$2\frac{2}{3} \ > \ 2\frac{1}{4}$$

So, Pool A is leaking faster.

Math Talk
Mathematical Processes

How do you compare mixed numbers?

YOUR TURN

5. Jaylan makes limeade using $\frac{3}{4}$ cup water for every $\frac{1}{5}$ cup lime juice. Wanchen makes limeade using $\frac{2}{3}$ cup water for every $\frac{1}{6}$ cup lime juice. Find the unit rates of water (cups) per lime juice (cups). Whose limeade has a weaker lime flavor? Explain.

_____

_____

_____

_____

Guided Practice

1. Brandon enters bike races. He bikes $8\frac{1}{2}$ miles every $\frac{1}{2}$ hour. Complete the table to find how far Brandon bikes for each time interval. (Explore Activity)

Distance (mi)	$8\frac{1}{2}$				
Time (h)	$\frac{1}{2}$	1	$1\frac{1}{2}$	2	$2\frac{1}{2}$

Find each unit rate. (Example 1)

2. Julio walks $3\frac{1}{2}$ miles in $1\frac{1}{4}$ hours.

_____

3. Kenny reads $\frac{5}{8}$ page in $\frac{2}{3}$ minute.

_____

4. A garden snail moves $\frac{1}{6}$ foot in $\frac{1}{3}$ hour.

_____

5. A machine covers $\frac{5}{8}$ square foot in $\frac{1}{4}$ hour.

_____

Find each unit rate. Determine which is lower. (Example 2)

6. Brand A: 240 mg sodium for $\frac{1}{3}$ pickle or Brand B: 325 mg sodium for $\frac{1}{2}$ pickle

_____

_____

7. Ingredient C: $\frac{1}{4}$ cup for $\frac{2}{3}$ serving or Ingredient D: $\frac{1}{3}$ cup for $\frac{3}{4}$ serving

_____

_____

ESSENTIAL QUESTION CHECK-IN

8. How can you find a unit rate when given a rate?

_____

_____

20.1 Independent Practice

Personal Math Trainer

Online Assessment and Intervention

my.hrw.com

9. The information for two pay-as-you-go cell phone companies is given.

On Call	Talk Time
3.5 hours: $10	$\frac{1}{2}$ hour: $1.25

a. What is the unit rate in dollars per hour for each company?

_____

_____

b. Analyze Relationships Which company offers the best deal? Explain your answer.

_____

_____

c. What If? Another company offers a rate of $0.05 per minute. How would you find the unit rate per hour?

_____

_____

d. Draw Conclusions Is the rate in part **c** a better deal than On Call or Talk Time? Explain.

_____

_____

10. **Represent Real-World Problems** Your teacher asks you to find a recipe that includes two ingredients with a ratio of $\frac{\frac{1}{2} \text{ cup}}{\frac{1}{8} \text{ cup}}$.

a. Give an example of two ingredients in a recipe that would meet this requirement.

_____

_____

_____

b. If you needed to triple the recipe, would the ratio change? Explain.

_____

_____

_____

_____

c. What is the unit rate of the two ingredients in part **a**?

_____

_____

11. A radio station requires DJs to play 2 commercials for every 10 songs they play. What is the unit rate of songs to commercials?

_____

12. **Multistep** Terrance and Jesse are training for a long-distance race. Terrance trains at a rate of 6 miles every half hour, and Jesse trains at a rate of 2 miles every 15 minutes.

a. What is the unit rate in miles per hour for each runner?

_____

b. How long will each person take to run a total of 50 miles at the given rates?

_____

_____

c. Sandra runs at a rate of 8 miles in 45 minutes. How does her unit rate compare to Terrance's and to Jesse's?

_____

_____

13. Analyze Relationships Eli takes a typing test and types all 300 words in $\frac{1}{10}$ hour. He takes the test a second time and types the words in $\frac{1}{12}$ hour. Was he faster or slower on the second attempt? Explain.

_____

_____

Work Area

14. Justify Reasoning An online retailer sells two packages of protein bars.

Package	10-pack of 2.1 ounce bars	12-pack of 1.4 ounce bars
Cost ($)	15.37	.15.35

a. Which package has the better price per bar?

_____

_____

_____

b. Which package has the better price per ounce?

_____

_____

_____

c. Which package do you think is a better buy? Justify your reasoning.

_____

_____

15. Check for Reasonableness A painter painted about half a room in half a day. Coley estimated the painter would paint 7 rooms in 7 days. Is Coley's estimate reasonable? Explain.

_____

_____

16. Communicate Mathematical Ideas If you know the rate of a water leak in gallons per hour, how can you find the number of hours it takes for 1 gallon to leak out? Justify your answer.

_____

_____

_____

ESSENTIAL QUESTION

How can you identify and represent proportional relationships?

EXPLORE ACTIVITY Real World

Discovering Proportional Relationships

The bar diagram shows how far one tortoise walks on land over time.

A Use the bar diagram to determine how many inches the tortoise travels in the third second.

_____

10.5 in.

| 1 sec | 1 sec | 1 sec |

3.5 in.   3.5 in.   ?

B Complete the table, assuming that the tortoise continues at a steady pace.

Time (sec)	1	2	3	4	5
Distance (in.)			10.5		

C For each column of the table, write a rate that compares the distance and the time. Put distance in the numerator and time in the denominator. Divide to write the rate as a decimal.

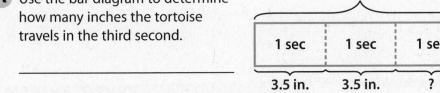

D What do you notice about the decimal forms of the rates?

_____

E Use a unit rate to describe how the distance the tortoise travels is related to time.

_____

Reflect

1. Suppose the tortoise travels for 12 seconds at the same rate. Explain how you could find the distance the tortoise travels.

_____

2. Explain why the tortoise's walking rate could be called *constant*.

_____

Math On the Spot

my.hrw.com

Proportional Relationships

A **proportion** is a statement that two rates or ratios are equivalent. For example, $\frac{6 \text{ mi}}{2 \text{ h}} = \frac{3 \text{ mi}}{1 \text{ h}}$, or $\frac{2}{4} = \frac{1}{2}$.

A **proportional relationship** between two quantities is one in which the ratio of one quantity to the other is constant. A **rate of change** is a rate that describes how one quantity changes in relation to another quantity. In a proportional relationship, the rate of change is constant.

Proportional relationships are often described using words such as *per* or *for each*. For example, the rate $\frac{\$1.25}{1 \text{ pound}}$ could be described as $1.25 per pound or $1.25 for each pound.

EXAMPLE 1

Callie earns money by dog sitting. Based on the table, is the relationship between the amount Callie earns and the number of days a proportional relationship?

Number of Days	1	2	3	4	5
Amount Earned ($)	16	32	48	64	80

STEP 1 Write the rates.

$\dfrac{\text{Amount earned}}{\text{Number of days}} = \dfrac{\$16}{1 \text{ day}}$ *Put the amount earned in the numerator and the number of days in the denominator.*

$\dfrac{\$32}{2 \text{ days}} = \dfrac{\$16}{1 \text{ day}}$

$\dfrac{\$48}{3 \text{ days}} = \dfrac{\$16}{1 \text{ day}}$ *Each rate is equal to $\dfrac{\$16}{1 \text{ day}}$, or $16 per day.*

$\dfrac{\$64}{4 \text{ days}} = \dfrac{\$16}{1 \text{ day}}$

$\dfrac{\$80}{5 \text{ days}} = \dfrac{\$16}{1 \text{ day}}$

STEP 2 Compare the rates. The rates are all equal. This means the rate is constant, so the relationship is proportional.

The constant rate of change is $16 per day.

My Notes

Math Talk

Mathematical Processes

How can you use the constant rate to find how much Callie earns for 10 days of dog sitting?

YOUR TURN

3. The table shows the distance Allison drove on one day of her vacation. Is the relationship between the distance and the time a proportional relationship? Did she drive at a constant speed? Explain.

Time (h)	1	2	3	4	5
Distance (mi)	65	120	195	220	300

Writing an Equation for a Proportional Relationship

If there is a proportional relationship between x and y, you can describe that relationship using the equation $y = kx$. The variable x is the independent variable and y is the dependent variable. The variable k is called the **constant of proportionality**, and it represents the constant rate of change or constant ratio between x and y. The value of k is represented by the equation $k = \frac{y}{x}$.

Math On the Spot

my.hrw.com

EXAMPLE 2

Two pounds of the cashews shown cost \$19, and 8 pounds cost \$76. Show that the relationship between the number of pounds of cashews and the cost is a proportional relationship. Then write an equation for the relationship. Describe the proportional relationship in words.

STEP 1 Make a table relating cost in dollars to pounds.

Number of Pounds	2	3	8
Cost (\$)	19	28.50	76

STEP 2 Write the rates as fractions. Put the dependent variable, cost, in the numerator. Then write each rate as a decimal.

$$\frac{\text{Cost}}{\text{Number of Pounds}} \rightarrow \quad \frac{19}{2} = 9.50 \qquad \frac{28.50}{3} = 9.50 \qquad \frac{76}{8} = 9.50$$

The rates are all equal to \$9.50 per pound. They are constant, so the relationship is proportional. The constant rate of change is \$9.50 per pound.

STEP 3 To write an equation, first tell what the variables represent.

- Let x represent the number of pounds of cashews.
- Let y represent the cost in dollars.
- Use the decimal form of the constant rate of change as the constant of proportionality.

The equation for the relationship is $y = 9.5x$.

The cost is \$9.50 per pound.

Math Talk
Mathematical Processes

How can you use your equation to find the cost of 6 pounds of cashews?

YOUR TURN

4. The table shows the number of adults required for a given number of students for a school field trip. Show that the relationship between the number of adults and the number of students is a proportional relationship. Then write an equation for the relationship.

Number of students	12	36	60
Number of adults	1	3	5

_____

_____

Guided Practice

1. The table shows the relationship between the age and height of a student. Use unit rates to determine if the relationship is a proportional relationship. (Explore Activity and Example 1)

Age (years)	6	7	8	9
Height (inches)	48	49	52	54

$\dfrac{\text{Height}}{\text{Age}}$:

The relationship ⟨ **is/ is not** ⟩ proportional.

Find the constant of proportionality *k*. Then write an equation for the relationship between *x* and *y*. (Example 2)

2.

x	2	4	6	8
y	10	20	30	40

_____

3.

x	8	16	24	32
y	2	4	6	8

_____

? ESSENTIAL QUESTION CHECK-IN

4. How can you represent a proportional relationship using an equation?

_____

_____

20.2 Independent Practice

Personal Math Trainer

my.hrw.com

Online Assessment and Intervention

Information on three car-rental companies is given.

5. Write an equation that gives the cost y of renting a car for x days from Rent-All. _____

6. What is the cost per day of renting a car from A-1? _____

7. **Analyze Relationships** Which company offers the best deal? Why?

_____

_____

Rent-All				
Days	3	4	5	6
Total Cost ($)	55.50	74.00	92.50	111.00

A-1 Rentals	**Car Town**
The cost y of renting a car for x days is $10.99 for each half day.	The cost of renting a car from us is just $19.25 per day!

8. **Critique Reasoning** A skydiver jumps out of an airplane. After 0.8 second, she has fallen 100 feet. After 3.1 seconds, she has fallen 500 feet. Emtiaz says that the skydiver should fall about 187.5 feet in 1.5 seconds. Is his answer reasonable? Explain.

_____

_____

_____

Steven earns extra money babysitting. He charges $31.25 for 5 hours and $50 for 8 hours.

9. Explain why the relationship between how much Steven charges and time is a proportional relationship.

_____

10. **Interpret the Answer** Explain what the constant rate of change means in the context.

_____

11. Write an equation to represent the relationship. Tell what the variables represent.

_____

_____

12. How much would Steven charge for 3 hours? _____

A submarine dives 300 feet every 2 minutes, and 6,750 feet every 45 minutes.

13. Find the constant rate at which the submarine dives. Give your answer in feet per minute and in feet per hour.

_____

14. Let x represent the time of the dive. Let y represent the depth of the submarine. Write an equation for the proportional relationship using the rate in feet per minute.

_____

15. Draw Conclusions If you wanted to find the depth of a submarine during a dive, would it be more reasonable to use an equation with the rate in feet per minute or feet per hour? Explain your reasoning.

_____

 FOCUS ON HIGHER ORDER THINKING

16. Critique Reasoning Jack is 12 and his sister Sophia is 16. Jack says that the relationship between his age and Sophia's is proportional and the constant of proportionality is $\frac{12}{16}$. Do you agree? Explain.

_____

_____

17. Make a Conjecture There is a proportional relationship between your distance from a thunderstorm and the time from when you see lightning until you hear thunder. If that time is 9 seconds, the storm is about 3 kilometers away. If that time doubles, do you think the distance also doubles? Justify your reasoning.

_____

_____

18. Communicate Mathematical Ideas Luke's turkey chili recipe calls for 1.5 pounds of ground turkey for every 6 servings. How many servings can he make if he has 5 pounds of ground turkey? Show your work.

_____

_____

_____

_____

Work Area

LESSON
20.3

7.2.4.3
Students will use graphs
to represent and analyze
proportional relationships.

Proportional Relationships and Graphs

How can you use graphs to represent and analyze proportional relationships?

EXPLORE ACTIVITY Real World

Graphing Proportional Relationships

You can use a graph to explore proportional relationships.

The equation $y = 5x$ represents the relationship between the number of gallons of water used (y) and the number of minutes (x) for most showerheads manufactured before 1994.

A Explain why the relationship is proportional. Describe the relationship in words.

_____

_____

B Complete the table.

> Substitute 2 for x in the equation $y = 5x$ and evaluate to find water used in 2 minutes.

Time (min)	1	2	3		10
Water Used (gal)	5			35	

C Write the data in the table as ordered pairs (time, water used).

(1, 5), (2, ___), (3, ___), (__ , 35), (10, ___)

D Plot the ordered pairs.

E If the showerhead is used for 0 minutes, how many gallons of water will be used? What ordered pair represents this situation? What is

this location called? _____

F If the showerhead is used for 1 minute, how many gallons of water will be used? What ordered pair represents this situation? Why is this ordered pair significant?

_____

G **Draw Conclusions** If you continued the table to include 23 minutes, would the point (23, 125) be on this graph? Why or why not?

_____

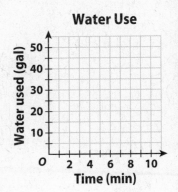

Water Use

Identifying Proportional Relationships

In addition to using a table to determine if a relationship is proportional, you also can use a graph. A relationship is a proportional relationship if its graph is a straight line through the origin.

EXAMPLE 1

The table shows the relationship between the amount charged by a house cleaning company ($) and the amount of time worked (hours). Is the relationship a proportional relationship? Explain.

Time (h)	1	2	3	5	8
Total cost ($)	45	90	135	225	360

STEP 1 Write the data in the table as ordered pairs (time, cost).

(1, 45), (2, 90), (3, 135), (5, 225), (8, 360)

STEP 2 Graph the ordered pairs.

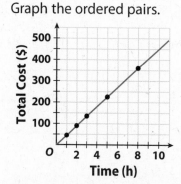

Place time on the x-axis and total cost on the y-axis.

Plot each point.

Notice that the points are on a line.

The graph is a line that goes through the origin.

The relationship is proportional. The point (1, 45) on the graph shows that the constant of proportionality (unit rate) is $45 per hour.

The housecleaning company charges $45 per hour.

Math Talk
Mathematical Processes

How does the table show a proportional relationship?

YOUR TURN

1. Jared rents bowling shoes for $6 and pays $5 per bowling game. Is the relationship a proportional relationship? Explain.

Games	1	2	3	4
Total Cost ($)	11	16	21	26

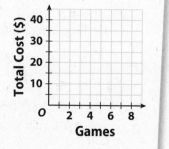

_____

_____

Math On the Spot
my.hrw.com

Animated Math
my.hrw.com

Personal Math Trainer

Online Assessment and Intervention

my.hrw.com

Analyzing Graphs

Recall that you can describe a proportional relationship with the equation $y = kx$. The constant of proportionality k tells you how steep the graph of the relationship is. The greater the absolute value of k, the steeper the line.

Math On the Spot
my.hrw.com

EXAMPLE 2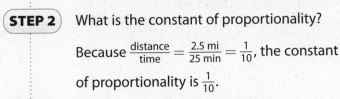

The graph shows the relationship between time in minutes and the number of miles Damon runs. Write an equation for this relationship.

STEP 1 Choose a point on the graph and tell what the point represents.

The point (25, 2.5) represents the distance (2.5 miles) that Damon runs in 25 minutes.

STEP 2 What is the constant of proportionality?

Because $\frac{\text{distance}}{\text{time}} = \frac{2.5 \text{ mi}}{25 \text{ min}} = \frac{1}{10}$, the constant of proportionality is $\frac{1}{10}$.

STEP 3 Write an equation in the form $y = kx$.

$$y = \frac{1}{10}x$$

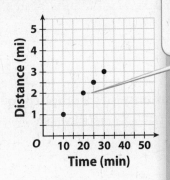

> The points appear to form a line through the origin so the relationship is proportional.

Reflect

2. What do the points (0, 0) and $(1, \frac{1}{10})$ on the graph tell you?

_____

3. **What If?** Suppose you drew a graph representing the relationship $y = \frac{1}{8}x$ between time in minutes and the number of miles Esther runs. How would the graph compare to the one for Damon? Explain.

_____

4. Use your equation to find how far Damon runs in 40 minutes. How much time would it take him to run 7.5 miles? _____

Math Talk
Mathematical Processes

What is the meaning of the point on the graph in Exercise 5 with x-coordinate 1?

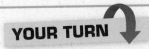

5. The graph shows the relationship between the distance a bicyclist travels and the time in hours.

   a. What does the point (4, 60) represent?

   _____

   b. What is the constant of proportionality? _____

   c. Write an equation in the form $y = kx$ for this relationship. _____

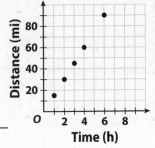

Personal Math Trainer
Online Assessment and Intervention
my.hrw.com

For each situation, tell whether the relationship is a proportional relationship. Explain why or why not. If it is, identify the unit rate. (Explore Activity)

1. The table shows the number of pages a student reads in various amounts of time.

Time (h)	3	5	9	10
Pages	195	325	585	650

_____

_____

2. The double number line diagram shows the rate at which a babysitter is paid.

Dollars 0 $15 $30 $45 $60

Hours 0   2   4   6   8

_____

_____

Tell whether the relationship is a proportional relationship. Explain why or why not. (Explore Activity and Example 1)

3.
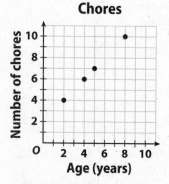
Chores

_____

_____

4.
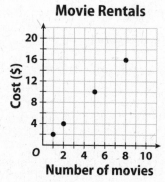
Movie Rentals

_____

_____

Write an equation of the form $y = kx$ for the relationship shown in each graph. (Example 2)

5.
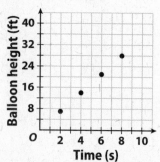

_____

6.
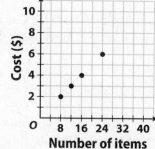

_____

© Houghton Mifflin Harcourt Publishing Company

? ESSENTIAL QUESTION CHECK-IN

7. How does a graph show a proportional relationship?

_____

20.3 Independent Practice

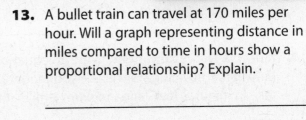

For Exercises 8–12, the graph shows the relationship between time and distance run by two horses.

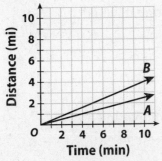

8. Explain the meaning of the point (0, 0).

_____

_____

9. How long does it take each horse to run a mile?

_____

_____

10. Multiple Representations Write an equation for the relationship between time and distance for each horse.

_____

11. Draw Conclusions At the given rates, how far would each horse run in 12 minutes?

_____

_____

12. Analyze Relationships Draw a line on the graph representing a horse that runs faster than horses A and B.

_____

_____

13. A bullet train can travel at 170 miles per hour. Will a graph representing distance in miles compared to time in hours show a proportional relationship? Explain.

_____

_____

_____

_____

14. Critical Thinking For the equations $y = 3.5x$ and $y = 25x + 40.50$, x represents time in hours and y represents cost in dollars. Which equation is **not** the equation of a proportional relationship? Explain.

_____

_____

_____

15. Multiple Representations Bargain DVDs cost $5 each at Mega Movie.

a. Graph the proportional relationship that gives the cost y in dollars of buying x bargain DVDs.

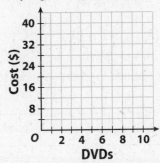

b. Give an ordered pair on the graph and explain its meaning in the real world context.

_____

_____

The graph shows the relationship between distance and time as Glenda swims.

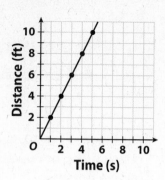

16. How far did Glenda swim in 4 seconds? _____

17. Communicate Mathematical Ideas Is this a proportional relationship? Explain your reasoning.

_____

18. Multiple Representations Write an equation that shows the relationship between time and distance. Use your equation to find how long it would take in minutes for Glenda to swim $\frac{1}{2}$ mile at this rate. _____

 **FOCUS ON HIGHER ORDER THINKING**

19. Make a Conjecture If you know that a relationship is proportional and are given one ordered pair that is not (0, 0), how can you find another pair?

_____

_____

_____

_____

The tables show the distance traveled by three cars.

Car 1	
Time (h)	Distance (mi)
0	0
2	120
3	180
5	300
6	360

Car 2	
Time (h)	Distance (mi)
0	0
5	200
10	400
15	600
20	800

Car 3	
Time (h)	Distance (mi)
0	0
1	65
2	85
3	105
4	125

20. Communicate Mathematical Ideas Which car is not traveling at a constant speed? Explain your reasoning.

_____

_____

21. Make a Conjecture Car 4 is traveling at twice the rate of speed of car 2. How will the table values for car 4 compare to the table values for car 2?

_____

_____

_____

Work Area

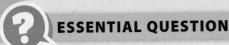
7.2.GF.4.3
Students will tell whether a relationship between two quantities is or is not proportional.

Assessing Proportionality

? **ESSENTIAL QUESTION**

How can you tell whether a relationship between two quantities is or is not proportional?

EXPLORE ACTIVITY

Examining Relationships

You can use logical reasoning and facts about proportional relationships to decide whether a relationship between two quantities is proportional.

Examine each relationship to tell whether it is proportional. Explain. If it is proportional, find the constant of proportionality.

A **Max and Meena volunteered to clean windows in a community center. Each student worked at the same rate. Together, the 2 students finished the job in 3 hours.**

If the relationship were proportional, doubling the number of students

would _____ the number of hours to finish the job, to keep the ratio of time to students constant. However, common sense indicates that if twice as many people work on the same job at the same rate, it

will take _____ the time.

The relationship | **is / is not** | proportional.

B **The Tranhs pay a $40 entry fee at a theme park and $5.00 for every book of tickets for rides. The graph shows the relationship between the number of books of tickets and the total cost of entry and tickets.**

Total Cost

Although the points lie on a line, the graph does not

go through the _____ , therefore you can tell that

the relationship | **is / is not** | proportional.

Reflect

1. In Part A, what fraction of the job does each student complete in an hour? _____

2. In Part B, is the relationship between the cost of tickets and the number of books of tickets proportional? If so, what is the constant of proportionality? _____

© Houghton Mifflin Harcourt Publishing Company

For Exercises 1–4, examine each relationship to tell whether it is proportional. Explain. If it is proportional, find the constant of proportionality.

1. The table below shows the number of pies Ned baked and the number of apples used.

Pies	5	7	8	10
Apples	22	35	48	50

_____

_____

2. The table indicates the amount of water for cooking different amounts of one type of pasta.

Packages	$\frac{1}{3}$	$\frac{1}{2}$	1
Water (qt)	2	3	5

_____

_____

3. The diagram shows the number of pages of a book Eleanor read during the 45 minutes between the end of school and her music lesson, during another 1.25 hours before dinner, and during another half hour before bed.

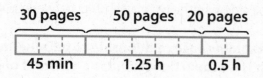

_____

_____

4. An apartment manager needs to hire workers to paint 50 apartments. Suppose they all paint at the same rate. The relationship between the number of workers x and the number of days y it takes to complete the job is given by the equation $y = \frac{300}{x}$.

_____

5. **Critical Thinking** The graph shows the relationship between your earnings y and the time x you spend mowing the lawn.

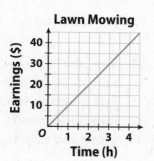

a. Is the relationship between time spent mowing and earnings proportional? Explain. If so, write an equation in the form $y = kx$ for the relationship.

_____

b. Suppose you triple the number of hours spent mowing. Will the number of dollars triple? Explain.

_____

_____

_____

c. Suppose you increase your mowing time by 3 hours. Will your pay increase by $3? Explain.

_____

Proportional or Not Proportional?

That Is the Question

INSTRUCTIONS

STEP 1 Working with a partner, read one game card at a time and decide if the relationship on the card is proportional or not. Relationships are represented using tables, equations, graphs, verbal descriptions, or diagrams. You are not expected to write equations for relationships.

STEP 2 Separate the cards into a group labeled *Proportional* and a group labeled *Not Proportional*.

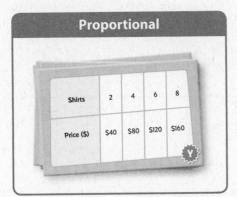

Proportional

Shirts	2	4	6	8
Price ($)	$40	$80	$120	$160

Y

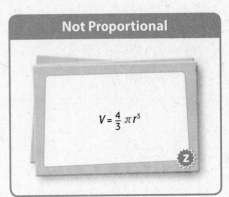

Not Proportional

$$V = \frac{4}{3}\pi r^3$$

Z

STEP 3 For the cards in the proportional group, write the card letters in alphabetical order in the first column of the table on the next page.

Card Letter	Independent Variable	Dependent Variable	Constant of Proportionality
Y	Number of shirts	Price ($)	20

STEP 4 Complete the remaining columns of the table for each card. You should complete the Independent Variable and Dependent Variable columns with the variable or the name of the quantity, and you should include units if applicable.

Card Letter	Independent Variable	Dependent Variable	Constant of Proportionality

Work Area

Match the Proportional Relationships

© Houghton Mifflin Harcourt Publishing Company

INSTRUCTIONS

Playing the Game

STEP 1 Have one student in your group shuffle the game cards. Each card uses a table, equation, graph, or verbal description to portray a proportional relationship. Arrange the cards face-down in a 4-by-4 grid.

STEP 2 Take turns. When it is your turn, turn two cards face-up in their places in the grid.

Strawberries are on sale for $1.25 per pound.

Pounds	1	1.6	2	5
Cost ($)	1.25	2.00	2.50	6.25

STEP 3 If the two cards demonstrate the same proportional relationship, remove them from the grid and keep the matching pair. If the two cards do not demonstrate the same proportional relationship, turn the cards back face-down in their original positions. This ends your turn whether or not you turn over a matching pair.

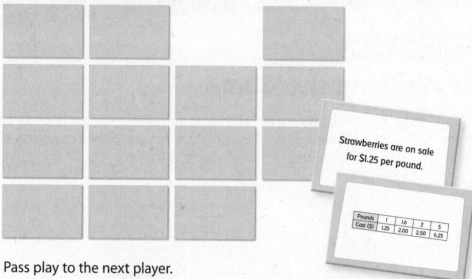

Strawberries are on sale for $1.25 per pound.

Pounds	1	1.6	2	5
Cost ($)	1.25	2.00	2.50	6.25

STEP 4 Pass play to the next player.

STEP 5 The game ends when players have collected all of the pairs. (There will be no cards left over.)

 Winning the Game

The student with the most pairs of relationship cards when the game ends is the winner.

Ready to Go On?

Personal Math Trainer

Online Assessment and Intervention

⏻ my.hrw.com

20.1 Unit Rates

Find each unit rate. Round to the nearest hundredth, if necessary.

1. $140 for 18 ft² _____

2. 14 lb for $2.99 _____

Circle the better deal in each pair. Then give the unit rate for the better deal.

3. $\frac{\$56}{25 \, gal}$ or $\frac{\$32.05}{15 \, gal}$ _____

4. $\frac{\$160}{5 \, g}$ or $\frac{\$315}{9 \, g}$ _____

20.2 Constant Rates of Change

5. The table shows the amount of money Tyler earns for mowing lawns. Is the relationship a proportional relationship? Why or why not?

Number of Lawns	1	2	3	4
Amount Earned ($)	15	30	48	64

_____

6. On a recent day, 8 euros were worth $9 and 24 euros were worth $27. Write an equation of the form $y = kx$ to show the relationship between the number of euros and the value in dollars.

_____ , where y is dollars and x is euros

20.3 Proportional Relationships and Graphs

7. The graph shows the number of servings in different amounts of frozen yogurt listed on a carton. Write an equation that gives the number of servings y in x pints.

_____

Frozen Yogurt

8. A refreshment stand makes 2 large servings of frozen yogurt from 3 pints. Add the line to the graph and write its equation.

_____

? ESSENTIAL QUESTION

9. How can you use rates to determine whether a situation is a proportional relationship?

_____

_____

Assessment Readiness

Personal Math Trainer

Online Assessment and Intervention

my.hrw.com

Selected Response

1. Kori spent $46.20 on 12 gallons of gasoline. What was the price per gallon?

   Ⓐ $8. 35   Ⓒ $2.59

   Ⓑ $3.85   Ⓓ $0.26

2. A rabbit can run short distances at a rate of 35 miles per hour. A fox can run short distances at a rate of 21 miles per half hour. Which animal is faster, and by how much?

   Ⓐ The rabbit; 7 miles per hour

   Ⓑ The fox; 7 miles per hour

   Ⓒ The rabbit; 14 miles per hour

   Ⓓ The fox; 14 miles per hour

3. A pet survey found that the ratio of dogs to cats is $\frac{2}{5}$. Which proportion shows the number of dogs if the number of cats is 140?

   Ⓐ $\dfrac{2 \text{ dogs}}{5 \text{ cats}} = \dfrac{140 \text{ dogs}}{350 \text{ cats}}$

   Ⓑ $\dfrac{2 \text{ dogs}}{5 \text{ cats}} = \dfrac{140 \text{ cats}}{350 \text{ dogs}}$

   Ⓒ $\dfrac{2 \text{ dogs}}{5 \text{ cats}} = \dfrac{28 \text{ dogs}}{140 \text{ cats}}$

   Ⓓ $\dfrac{2 \text{ dogs}}{5 \text{ cats}} = \dfrac{56 \text{ dogs}}{140 \text{ cats}}$

4. What is the cost of 2 kilograms of flour if 3 kilograms cost $4.86 and the unit price for each package of flour is the same?

   Ⓐ $0.81   Ⓒ $3.24

   Ⓑ $2.86   Ⓓ $9.72

5. One gallon of paint covers about 450 square feet. How many square feet will 1.5 gallons of paint cover?

   Ⓐ 300 ft²   Ⓒ 675 ft²

   Ⓑ 451.5 ft²   Ⓓ 900 ft²

6. The graph shows the relationship between the late fines the library charges and the number of days late.

   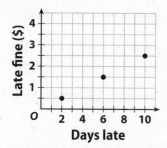

   What is an equation for the relationship?

   Ⓐ $y = 0.25x$ Ⓒ $y = 0.50x$

   Ⓑ $y = 0.40x$ Ⓓ $y = 0.75x$

Mini-Task

7. School is 2 miles from home along a straight road. The table shows your distance from home as you walk home at a constant rate.

Time (min)	10	20	30
Distance from home (mi)	1.5	1	0.5

   a. Is the relationship in the table proportional?

   _____

   b. Find your distance from school for each time in the table.

   _____

   c. Write an equation representing the relationship between the distance from school and time walking.

   _____

Proportions and Percent

? ESSENTIAL QUESTION

How can you use proportional relationships and percent to solve real-world problems?

Real-World Video

A store may have a sale with deep discounts on some items. They can still make a profit because they first markup the wholesale price by as much as 400%, then markdown the retail price.

⏻ my.hrw.com

GO DIGITAL
my.hrw.com

my.hrw.com

Go digital with your write-in student edition, accessible on any device.

Math On the Spot

Scan with your smart phone to jump directly to the online edition, video tutor, and more.

Animated Math

Interactively explore key concepts to see how math works.

Personal Math Trainer

Get immediate feedback and help as you work through practice sets.

Reading Start-Up

Visualize Vocabulary

Use the ✔ words to complete the triangle. Write the review word that fits the description in each section of the triangle.

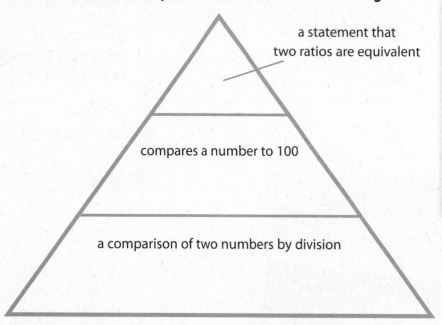

a statement that two ratios are equivalent

compares a number to 100

a comparison of two numbers by division

Understand Vocabulary

Complete the sentences using the preview words.

1. A fixed percent of the principal is _____.

2. The original amount of money deposited or borrowed is the _____.

3. A _____ is the amount of increase divided by the original amount.

Active Reading

Tri-Fold Before beginning the module, create a tri-fold to help you learn the concepts and vocabulary in this module. Fold the paper into three sections. Label the columns "What I Know," "What I Need to Know," and "What I Learned." Complete the first two columns before you read. After studying the module, complete the third.

Are YOU Ready?

Complete these exercises to review skills you will need for this module.

Personal Math Trainer

Online Assessment and Intervention

my.hrw.com

Percents and Decimals

EXAMPLE

$147\% = 100\% + 47\%$ Write the percent as the sum of 1 whole and a percent remainder.

$= \frac{100}{100} + \frac{47}{100}$ Write the percents as fractions.

$= 1 + 0.47$ Write the fractions as decimals.

$= 1.47$ Simplify.

Write each percent as a decimal.

1. 22% _____   **2.** 75% _____   **3.** 6% _____   **4.** 189% _____

Write each decimal as a percent.

5. 0.59 _____   **6.** 0.98 _____   **7.** 0.02 _____   **8.** 1.33 _____

Find the Percent of a Number

EXAMPLE

30% of 45 = ?

$30\% = 0.30$ Write the percent as a decimal.

$\begin{array}{r} 45 \\ \times\,0.3 \\ \hline 13.5 \end{array}$ Multiply.

Find the percent of each number.

9. 50% of 64 _____   **10.** 7% of 30 _____   **11.** 15% of 160 _____

12. 32% of 62 _____   **13.** 120% of 4 _____   **14.** 6% of 1,000 _____

Complete these exercises to review skills you will need for this module.

Percents and Decimals

15. A company's profits this year were 128% of last year's profits. Drew recorded this year's profits as 12.8 times last year's profits. What mistake, if any, did Drew make?

16. Carlos puts 0.3 of his monthly income into savings. What percent of his monthly income is **not** put into savings? How do you know?

Find the Percent of a Number

17. In a school with 300 students, 18% of the students take violin lessons, and 6% of the students take clarinet lessons.

  a. Find the number of students who take each type of lesson.

  b. How many more students take violin lessons than take clarinet lessons?

18. A jacket costs $45. The sales tax on the jacket is 6%. Julia has $48. Does she have enough money to buy the jacket? Explain.

PERCENTO%!

INSTRUCTIONS

Playing the Game

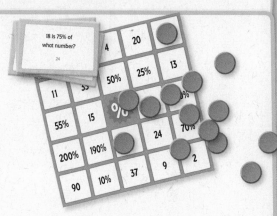

STEP 1 One student is the caller. This student gets the caller cards. Each caller card contains a percent problem and its answer.

STEP 2 Each player gets a *Percento!* board and 20–25 counters. The center is a free space. Players should cover the center square before play begins.

STEP 3 On each turn, the caller reads aloud a problem to the players. The caller does not read the answer.

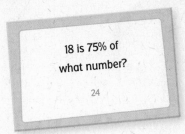

18 is 75% of
what number?

24

STEP 4 The players solve the problem read by the caller. Then they find the answer on their *Percento!* board and cover that square.

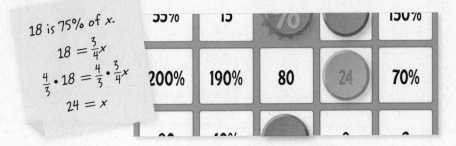

STEP 5 The caller places the cards that have been read in a discard pile.

Winning the Game

A player who covers five squares in a row horizontally, vertically, or diagonally says, "Percento!" The caller uses the cards in the discard pile to check that this player has calculated correctly. If so, that player is the winner. If not, play continues until someone else says, "Percento!"

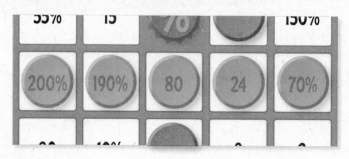

Percent Increase and Decrease

? ESSENTIAL QUESTION

How do you use percents to describe change?

EXPLORE ACTIVITY

Finding Percent Increase

Percents can be used to describe how an amount changes.

$$\text{Percent Change} = \frac{\text{Amount of Change}}{\text{Original Amount}}$$

The change may be an increase or a decrease. **Percent increase** describes how much a quantity increases in comparison to the original amount.

EXAMPLE 1 Amber got a raise, and her hourly wage increased from $8 to $9.50. What is the percent increase?

STEP 1 Find the amount of change.

Amount of Change = Greater Value − Lesser Value

Substitute values. = [ ] − [ ]

Subtract. = [ ]

STEP 2 Find the percent increase. Round to the nearest percent.

$$\text{Percent Change} = \frac{\text{Amount of Change}}{\text{Original Amount}}$$

Substitute values. = $\dfrac{[\quad]}{8.00}$

Divide. = _____

Write as a percent and round. ≈ _____

Reflect

1. What does a 100% increase mean?

_____

_____

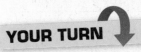

2. The price of a pair of shoes increases from $52 to $64. What is the percent increase to the nearest percent? _____

Personal Math Trainer
Online Assessment and Intervention
⏻ my.hrw.com

Math On the Spot
⏻ my.hrw.com

Finding Percent Decrease

When the change in the amount decreases, you can use a similar approach to find percent decrease. **Percent decrease** describes how much a quantity decreases in comparison to the original amount.

EXAMPLE 2

David moved from a house that is 89 miles away from his workplace to a house that is 51 miles away from his workplace. What is the percent decrease in the distance from his home to his workplace?

STEP 1 Find the amount of change.

Amount of Change = Greater Value − Lesser Value

$= 89 - 51$ *Substitute values.*

$= 38$ *Subtract.*

STEP 2 Find the percent decrease. Round to the nearest percent.

$$\text{Percent Change} = \frac{\text{Amount of Change}}{\text{Original Amount}}$$

$= \frac{38}{89}$ *Substitute values.*

≈ 0.427 *Divide.*

$= 43\%$ *Write as a percent and round.*

Math Talk

Mathematical Processes

How can you use the benchmark fractions $\frac{1}{3}$ and $\frac{1}{2}$ to check that the answer is reasonable?

Reflect

3. Critique Reasoning David considered moving even closer to his workplace. He claims that if he had done so, the percent of decrease would have been more than 100%. Is David correct? Explain your reasoning.

_____

_____

_____

Personal Math Trainer

Online Assessment and Intervention

my.hrw.com

YOUR TURN

4. The number of students in a chess club decreased from 18 to 12. What is the percent decrease? Round to the nearest percent. _____

5. Officer Brimberry wrote 16 tickets for traffic violations last week, but only 10 tickets this week. What is the percent decrease? _____

© Houghton Mifflin Harcourt Publishing Company

Using Percent of Change

Given an original amount and a percent increase or decrease, you can use the percent of change to find the new amount.

Math On the Spot
my.hrw.com

EXAMPLE 3

The grizzly bear population in Yellowstone National Park in 1970 was about 270. Over the next 35 years, it increased by about 115%. What was the population in 2005?

STEP 1 Find the amount of change.

$1.15 \times 270 = 310.5$ Find 115% of 270. Write 115% as a decimal.

≈ 311 Round to the nearest whole number.

STEP 2 Find the new amount.

New Amount = Original Amount + Amount of Change

$= 270 + 311$ Substitute values.

$= 581$ Add.

Add the amount of change because the population increased.

The population in 2005 was about 581 grizzly bears.

Reflect

6. Why will the percent of change always be represented by a positive number?

_____

_____

_____

7. Draw Conclusions If an amount of $100 in a savings account increases by 10%, then increases by 10% again, is that the same as increasing by 20%? Explain.

_____

_____

_____

YOUR TURN

A TV has an original price of $499. Find the new price after the given percent of change.

8. 10% increase _____

9. 30% decrease _____

Personal Math Trainer

Online Assessment and Intervention

my.hrw.com

Guided Practice

Find each percent increase. Round to the nearest percent. (Explore Activity Example 1)

1. From $5 to $8 _____

2. From 20 students to 30 students _____

3. From 86 books to 150 books _____

4. From $3.49 to $3.89 _____

5. From 13 friends to 14 friends _____

6. From 5 miles to 16 miles _____

7. Nathan usually drinks 36 ounces of water per day. He read that he should drink 64 ounces of water per day. If he starts drinking 64 ounces, what is the percent increase? Round to the nearest percent.
(Explore Activity Example 1)   _____

Find each percent decrease. Round to the nearest percent. (Example 2)

8. From $80 to $64 _____

9. From 95°F to 68°F _____

10. From 90 points to 45 points _____

11. From 145 pounds to 132 pounds _____

12. From 64 photos to 21 photos _____

13. From 16 bagels to 0 bagels _____

14. Over the summer, Jackie played video games 3 hours per day. When school began in the fall, she was only allowed to play video games for half an hour per day. What is the percent decrease? Round to the nearest percent. (Example 2)   _____

Find the new amount given the original amount and the percent of change. (Example 3)

15. $9; 10% increase _____

16. 48 cookies; 25% decrease _____

17. 340 pages; 20% decrease _____

18. 28 members; 50% increase _____

19. $29,000; 4% decrease _____

20. 810 songs; 130% increase _____

21. Adam currently runs about 20 miles per week, and he wants to increase his weekly mileage by 30%. How many miles will Adam run per week? (Example 3)   _____

? ESSENTIAL QUESTION CHECK-IN

22. What process do you use to find the percent change of a quantity?

_____

_____

21.1 Independent Practice

Personal
Math Trainer

Online
Assessment and
Intervention

my.hrw.com

23. Complete the table.

Item	Original Price	New Price	Percent Change	Increase or Decrease
Bike	$110	$96		
Scooter	$45	$56		
Tennis Racket	$79		5%	Increase
Skis	$580		25%	Decrease

24. **Multiple Representations** The bar graph shows the number of hurricanes in the Atlantic Basin from 2006–2011.

a. Find the amount of change and the percent of decrease in the number of hurricanes from 2008 to 2009 and from 2010 to 2011. Compare the amounts of change and percents of decrease.

_____

_____

_____

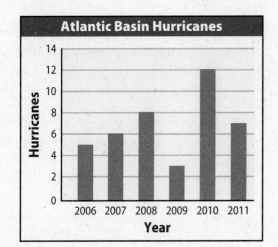

b. Between which two years was the percent of change the greatest? What was the percent of change during that period?

_____

25. **Represent Real-World Problems** Cheese sticks that were previously priced at "5 for $1" are now "4 for $1". Find each percent of change and show your work.

a. Find the percent decrease in the number of cheese sticks you can buy for $1.

_____

b. Find the percent increase in the price per cheese stick.

_____

_____

26. Percent error calculations are used to determine how close to the true values, or how accurate, experimental values really are. The formula is similar to finding percent of change.

$$\text{Percent Error} = \frac{|\text{Experimental Value} - \text{True Value}|}{\text{True Value}} \times 100$$

In chemistry class, Charlie records the volume of a liquid as 13.3 milliliters. The true volume is 13.6 milliliters. What is his percent error? Round to the

nearest percent. _____

 FOCUS ON HIGHER ORDER THINKING

27. Look for a Pattern Leroi and Sylvia both put $1,000 in a savings account. Leroi decides he will put in an additional $100 each month. Sylvia decides to put in an additional 10% of the amount in the account each month.

a. Who has more money after the first additional deposit? Explain.

_____

_____

b. Who has more money after the second additional deposit? Explain.

_____

_____

c. How do you think the amounts in the two accounts will compare after a year?

_____

_____

28. Critical Thinking Suppose an amount increases by 50%, then decreases by 50%. Will the amount after the decrease be the same as the original amount? Explain your reasoning.

_____

_____

_____

29. Look for a Pattern Ariel deposited $600 into a bank account. Each Friday she will withdraw 10% of the money in the account to spend. Ariel thinks her account will be empty after 10 withdrawals. Do you agree? Explain.

_____

_____

Work Area

© Houghton Mifflin Harcourt Publishing Company

LESSON
21.2

7.2.5.2
Students will rewrite expressions to help solve markup and markdown problems.

Rewriting Percent Expressions

? ESSENTIAL QUESTION

How can you rewrite expressions to help you solve markup and markdown problems?

EXPLORE ACTIVITY (Real World)

Math On the Spot
⏻ my.hrw.com

Calculating Markups

A *markup* is one kind of percent increase. You can use a bar model to represent the *retail price* of an item, that is, the total price including the markup.

EXAMPLE 1 To make a profit, stores mark up the prices on the items they sell. A store manager buys skateboards from a supplier for *s* dollars. What is the retail price for skateboards that the manager buys for $35 and $56 after a 42% markup?

STEP 1 Draw a bar for the cost of the skateboard *s*.

Then draw a bar that shows the markup: _____% of *s*, or 0.42*s*.

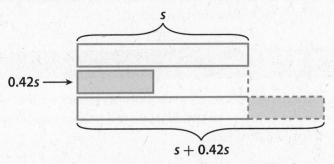

These bars together represent the cost plus the markup, $s +$ _____.

STEP 2 Retail price = Original cost + Markup

$$= \quad s \quad + \quad 0.42s$$
$$= \quad 1s \quad + \quad 0.42s \quad \text{Identity Property of Multiplication}$$
$$= \quad \underline{\hspace{2cm}} \quad \text{Distributive Property}$$

STEP 3 Use the expression to find the retail price of each skateboard.

$s = \$35 \longrightarrow$ Retail price $= 1.42(\$35) \quad = \boxed{}$

$s = \$56 \longrightarrow$ Retail price $= 1.42\left(\$\boxed{}\right) = \boxed{}$

Reflect

1. Write an equation showing that the relationship between the supplier price, *s*, and the retail price, *r*, is proportional. What is the constant of proportionality?

_____

YOUR TURN

2. Rick buys remote control cars to resell. He applies a markup of 10%.

   a. Write two expressions that represent the retail price of the cars.

   _____

   b. If Rick buys a remote control car for $28.00, what is his selling price?

   _____

3. An exclusive clothing boutique triples the price of the items it purchases for resale.

   a. What is the boutique's markup percent? _____

   b. Write two expressions that represent the retail price of the clothes.

   _____

Personal Math Trainer

Online Assessment and Intervention

⊙ my.hrw.com

Math On the Spot

⊙ my.hrw.com

Calculating Markdowns

An example of a percent decrease is a *discount*, or *markdown*. A price after a markdown may be called a sale price. You can also use a bar model to represent the price of an item including the markdown.

EXAMPLE 2

A discount store marks down all of its holiday merchandise by 20% off the regular selling price. Find the discounted price of decorations that regularly sell for $16 and $23.

Animated Math

⊙ my.hrw.com

STEP 1 Use a bar model.

Draw a bar for the regular price p.

Then draw a bar that shows the discount: 20% of p, or $0.2p$.

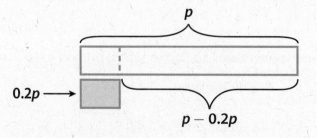

The difference between these two bars represents the price minus the discount, $p - 0.2p$.

STEP 2   Sale price = Original price − Markdown

$$= \quad p \quad - \quad 0.2p$$

$$= \quad 1p \quad - \quad 0.2p \qquad \text{Identity Property of Multiplication}$$

$$= \quad 0.8p \qquad \text{Distributive Property}$$

Math Talk

Mathematical Processes

How do the expressions $1p - 0.2p$ and $0.8p$ for the sale price shed light on the problem?

STEP 3   Use the expression to find the sale price of each decoration.

$p = \$16 \longrightarrow$ Retail price $= 0.8(\$16) = \$12.80$

$p = \$23 \longrightarrow$ Retail price $= 0.8(\$23) = \$18.40$

Reflect

4. Analyze Relationships Is the relationship between the original price p and the retail price r proportional? Justify your answers.

_____

_____

YOUR TURN

5. A bicycle shop marks down each bicycle's selling price b by 24% for a holiday sale.

a. Draw a bar model to represent the problem.

b. What is a single term expression for the sale price? _____

6. Jane sells pillows. For a sale, she marks them down 5%.

a. Write two expressions that represent the sale price of the pillows.

_____

b. If the original price of a pillow is $15.00, what is the sale price?

_____

Personal Math Trainer

Online Assessment and Intervention

my.hrw.com

© Houghton Mifflin Harcourt Publishing Company

1. Dana buys dress shirts from a clothing manufacturer for *s* dollars each, and then sells the dress shirts in her retail clothing store at a 35% markup. (Explore Activity Example 1)

   a. Write the markup using a decimal. _____

   b. Write an expression for the retail price of the dress shirt. _____

   c. What is the retail price of a dress shirt that Dana purchased for $32.00? _____

   d. How much was added to the original price of the dress shirt? _____

List the markup and retail price of each item. Round to two decimal places when necessary. (Explore Activity Example 1)

	Item	Price	Markup %	Markup	Retail Price
2.	Hat	$18	15%		
3.	Book	$22.50	42%		
4.	Shirt	$33.75	75%		
5.	Shoes	$74.99	33%		
6.	Clock	$48.60	100%		
7.	Painting	$185.00	125%		

Find the sale price of each item. Round to two decimal places when necessary. (Example 2)

8. Original price: $45.00; Markdown: 22%

   _____

9. Original price: $89.00; Markdown: 33%

   _____

10. Original price: $23.99; Markdown: 44%

    _____

11. Original price: $279.99, Markdown: 75%

    _____

? ESSENTIAL QUESTION CHECK-IN

12. How can you determine the sale price if you are given the regular price and the percent of markdown?

    _____

    _____

21.2 Independent Practice

Personal Math Trainer

Online Assessment and Intervention

my.hrw.com

13. A bookstore manager marks down the price of older hardcover books, which originally sell for *b* dollars, by 46%.

a. Write the markdown using a decimal. _____

b. Write an expression for the sale price of the hardcover book.

_____

c. What is the sale price of a hardcover book for which the original retail price was $29.00? _____

d. If you buy the book in part **c**, how much do you save by paying the sale price? _____

14. Raquela's coworker made price tags for several items that are to be marked down by 35%. Match each Regular Price to the correct Sale Price, if possible. Not all sales tags match an item.

Regular Price $3.29	Regular Price $4.19	Regular Price $2.79	Regular Price $3.09	Regular Price $3.77

Sale Price $2.01	Sale Price $2.45	Sale Price $1.15	Sale Price $2.72	Sale Price $2.24

15. Communicate Mathematical Ideas For each situation, give an example that includes the original price and final price after markup or markdown.

a. A markdown that is greater than 99% but less than 100%

_____

b. A markdown that is less than 1%

_____

c. A markup that is more than 200%

_____

16. Represent Real-World Problems Harold works at a men's clothing store, which marks up its retail clothing by 27%. The store purchases pants for $74.00, suit jackets for $325.00, and dress shirts for $48.00. How much will Harold charge a customer for two pairs of pants, three dress shirts, and a suit jacket? Use estimation to explain why your answer is reasonable.

_____

_____

17. Analyze Relationships Your family needs a set of 4 tires. Which of the following deals would you prefer? Explain.

(I) Buy 3, get one free   **(II)** 20% off   **(III)** $\frac{1}{4}$ off

_____

_____

 **FOCUS ON HIGHER ORDER THINKING**

18. Critique Reasoning Margo purchases bulk teas from a warehouse and marks up those prices by 20% for retail sale. When teas go unsold for more than two months, Margo marks down the retail price by 20%. She says that she is *breaking even*, that is, she is getting the same price for the tea that she paid for it. Is she correct? Explain.

_____

_____

_____

19. Problem Solving Grady marks down some $2.49 pens to $1.99 for a week and then marks them back up to $2.49. Find the percent of increase and the percent of decrease to the nearest tenth. Are the percents of change the same for both price changes? If not, which is a greater change?

_____

_____

20. Persevere in Problem Solving At Danielle's clothing boutique, if an item does not sell for eight weeks, she marks it down by 15%. If it remains unsold after that, she marks it down an additional 5% each week until she can no longer make a profit. Then she donates it to charity.

Rafael wants to buy a coat originally priced $150, but he can't afford more than $110. If Danielle paid $100 for the coat, during which week(s) could Rafael buy the coat within his budget? Justify your answer.

_____

_____

Work Area

Applications of Percent

© Houghton Mifflin Harcourt Publishing Company

ESSENTIAL QUESTION

How do you use percents to solve problems?

EXPLORE ACTIVITY

Finding an Original or Final Amount

Sales tax, which is the tax on the sale of an item or service, is a percent of the purchase price that is collected by the seller. The relationship between an original amount and the amount after a percent change is a proportional relationship. For a given sales tax rate, you can use proportional reasoning to find the total cost if you know the price, or the price if you know the total cost.

EXAMPLE 1 **Marcus bought a varsity jacket. The total cost, including an 8% sales tax, was $86.40. What was the price p of the jacket?**

You can draw a bar model to visualize the problem.

Because 100% is not evenly divisible by 8%, you can more easily use a proportion or an equation to solve the problem.

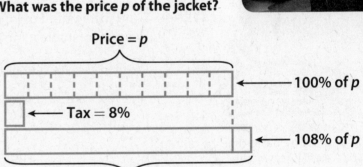

Method 1 Use a proportion comparing ratios of price to total cost.

percent　**dollars**

$$\frac{100}{108} = \frac{p}{\boxed{}}$$

$$86.40 \times \frac{100}{108} = 86.40 \times \frac{p}{86.40}$$

$$\frac{\boxed{}}{108} = p$$

$$\boxed{} = p$$

Method 2 Use an equation relating price and total cost.

Total Cost = 108% of Price

$$\boxed{} = 1.08p$$

$$\frac{86.40}{1.08} = \frac{1.08p}{1.08}$$

$$\boxed{} = p$$

The price of the jacket, before sales tax, was $_____.

Check: If the jacket's price is $80, the total cost with tax is

$$1.08(80) = \$\boxed{}.$$

Math On the Spot
my.hrw.com

YOUR TURN

Personal Math Trainer

Online Assessment and Intervention

my.hrw.com

1. Sharon wants to buy a shirt that costs $20. The sales tax is 5%. How much is the sales tax? What is her total cost for the shirt? _____

Math On the Spot

my.hrw.com

Finding Simple Interest

When you deposit money in a savings account, your money usually earns interest. When you borrow money, you must pay back the original amount of the loan plus interest. **Simple interest** is a fixed percent of the *principal*. The **principal** is the original amount of money deposited or borrowed.

EXAMPLE 2 Real World

Terry deposits $200 into a bank account that earns 3% simple interest per year. What is the total amount in the account after 2 years?

STEP 1 Find the amount of interest earned in one year. Then calculate the amount of interest for 2 years.

Write 3% as a decimal: 0.03

Interest Rate × Initial Deposit = Interest for 1 year

0.03 × $200 = $6

Interest for 1 year × 2 years = Interest for 2 years

$6 × 2 = $12

Math Talk

Mathematical Processes

Is interest *I* earned on $200 proportional to time *t* in years? If so, write the equation.

STEP 2 Add the interest for 2 years to the initial deposit to find the total amount in his account after 2 years.

Initial deposit + Interest for 2 years = Total

$200 + $12 = $212

The total amount in the account after 2 years is $212.

Reflect

2. Write an equation relating the total amount *a* in Terry's account to the number of years, *t*. Is the relationship proportional? Explain.

_____

3. Commission and interest problems have some similarities. A salesperson receives a percent of the selling price of the item(s) sold, called a commission. Nadia earns a salary of $3,300 per month selling furniture, plus a 3.25% commission. Calculate Nadia's total earnings in a month when her sales totaled $29,600. Show your work.

_____

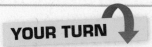

YOUR TURN

4. Ariane borrows $400 on a 4-year loan. She is charged 5% simple interest per year. How much interest is she charged for 4 years? What is the total amount she has to pay back? _____

Using Multiple Percents

Some situations require applying more than one percent to a problem. For example, when you dine at a restaurant, you might pay a tax on the meal, and pay a tip to the wait staff. The tip is usually paid on the amount before tax. When you pay tax on a sale item, you pay tax only on the discounted price.

 EXAMPLE 3 Problem Solving

The Maxwell family goes out for dinner, and the price of the meal is $60. The sales tax on the meal is 7%, and they also want to leave a 15% tip. What is the total cost of the meal?

Analyze Information

Identify the important information.

- The bill for the meal is $60.
- The sales tax is 7%, or 0.07.
- The tip is 15%, or 0.15.

The total cost will be the sum of the bill for the meal, the sales tax, and the tip.

Formulate a Plan

Calculate the sales tax separately, then calculate the tip, and then add the products to the bill for the meal to find the total.

 Solve

Sales tax: $0.07 \times \$60 = \$4.20$ Tip: $0.15 \times \$60 = \$9.00$

Meal + Sales tax + Tip = Total cost

$60 + $4.20 + $9 = $73.20

The total cost is $73.20.

Math Talk
Mathematical Processes

Write an equation and a proportion you could use to find the total cost c given the price p.

 Justify and Evaluate

Estimate the sales tax and tip. Sales tax is about 10% plus 15% for tip gives 25%. Find 25% of the bill: $0.25 \times \$60 = \$15$. Add this to the bill: $60 + $15 = $75. The total cost should be about $75.

YOUR TURN

5. Samuel orders four DVDs from an online music store. Each DVD costs $9.99. He has a 20% discount code, and sales tax is 6.75%. What is the total cost of his order?

_____

Guided Practice

1. 5% of $30 = _____

2. 15% of $70 = _____

3. 0.4% of $100 = _____

4. 150% of $22 = _____

5. 1% of $80 = _____

6. 200% of $5 = _____

7. Brandon buys a radio for $43.99 in a state where the sales tax is 7%. (Explore Activity Example 1)

   a. How much does he pay in taxes? _____

   b. What is the total Brandon pays for the radio? _____

8. Luisa received $108 for a necklace she sold on an online auction. The auction site took a fee of 10% of the selling price. What was the selling price of the necklace? (Explore Activity Example 1) _____

9. Joe borrowed $2,000 from the bank at a rate of 7% simple interest per year. How much interest did he pay in 5 years? (Example 2) _____

10. Sonia works at a sporting goods store. She earns $415 per week plus a 5.25% commission on her sales. One week, her sales are $2,200. What is her total income for the week? (Example 2) _____

11. Martin finds a shirt on sale for 10% off at a department store. The original price was $20. Martin must also pay 8.5% sales tax. (Example 3)

    a. How much is the shirt before taxes are applied? _____

    b. How much is the shirt after taxes are applied? _____

12. Teresa's restaurant bill comes to $29.99 before tax. If the sales tax is 6.25% and she tips the waiter 20%, what is the total cost of the meal? (Example 3) _____

? ESSENTIAL QUESTION CHECK-IN

13. How can you determine the total cost of an item including tax if you know the price of the item and the tax rate?

_____

_____

21.3 Independent Practice

Personal Math Trainer

Online Assessment and Intervention

my.hrw.com

14. Emily takes her friend Darren out to eat for his birthday. She pays a total of $45, which includes a 20% tip. There is no tax. Find the cost of the meals before the tip.

_____

15. The Jayden family eats at a restaurant that is having a 15% discount promotion. Their meal costs $78.65 before the discount, and they leave a 20% tip. If the tip applies to the cost of the meal before the discount, what is the total cost of the meal?

_____

16. A jeweler buys a ring from a jewelry maker for $125. He marks up the price by 135% for sale in his store. What is the selling price of the ring with 7.5% sales tax?

_____

17. Luis wants to buy a skateboard that usually sells for $79.99. All merchandise is discounted by 12%. What is the total cost of the skateboard if Luis has to pay a state sales tax of 6.75%?

_____

18. Kedar earns a monthly salary of $2,200 plus a 3.75% commission on the amount of his sales at a men's clothing store. What would he earn this month if he sold $4,500 in clothing? Round to the nearest cent.

_____

19. Danielle earns a 7.25% commission on everything she sells at the electronics store where she works. She also earns a base salary of $750 per week. What were her sales last week if her total earnings for the week were $1,076.25?

_____

20. Francois earns a weekly salary of $475 plus a 5.5% commission on sales at a gift shop. How much would he earn in a week if he sold $700 in goods? Round to the nearest cent.

_____

21. Sandra is 4 feet tall. Pablo is 10% taller than Sandra, and Michaela is 8% taller than Pablo.

   a. Explain how to find Michaela's height with the given information.

   _____

   _____

   _____

   _____

   _____

   _____

   b. What is Michaela's approximate height in feet and inches?

   _____

22. Troy is buying a car that costs $15,000. He plans to get a 5-year loan to pay for it. He can get a loan for $15,000 or he can pay $3,000 from his savings and get a loan for the rest. The savings account pays 2% simple interest per year. The simple interest rate for the loan is 0.5% per year.

   a. How much interest over a 5-year period will Troy receive on his $3,000 if he does not withdraw that money from his savings account? _____

   b. How much more interest will he pay to borrow $15,000 than $12,000? Why is the $15,000 option reasonable?

   _____

© Houghton Mifflin Harcourt Publishing Company

23. Multistep Eric downloads the coupon shown and goes shopping at Gadgets Galore, where he buys a digital camera for $95 and an extra battery for $15.99.

   a. What is the total cost if the coupon is applied to the digital camera?

   _____

   b. What is the total cost if the coupon is applied to the extra battery?

   _____

   c. To which item should Eric apply the discount? Explain.

   _____

   d. Eric has to pay 8% sales tax after the coupon is applied. How much is his total bill?

   _____

24. Kim takes some furniture to a consignment store. The store sells used items and takes a fee of 20% of the selling price. The remaining percent of the selling price goes to the seller, Kim.

   a. What percent of the selling price p is the amount the seller gets?

   _____

   b. Kim receives a check from the consignment store for $592. What was the selling price of the furniture?

   _____

 **FOCUS ON HIGHER ORDER THINKING**

Work Area

25. Analyze Relationships Marcus can choose between a monthly salary of $1,500 plus 5.5% of sales or $2,400 plus 3% of sales. He expects sales between $5,000 and $10,000 a month. Which salary option should he choose? Explain.

_____

_____

_____

26. Multistep In chemistry class, Bob recorded the volume of a liquid as 13.2 mL. The true volume was 13.7 mL. Use the formula to find the percent error of Bob's measurement to the nearest tenth of a percent.

$$\text{Percent Error} = \frac{|\text{Experimental Value} - \text{True Value}|}{\text{True Value}} \times 100$$

_____

Ready to Go On?

Personal Math Trainer

Online Assessment and Intervention

my.hrw.com

21.1 Percent Increase and Decrease

Find the percent change from the first value to the second.

1. 36; 63 _____

2. 50; 35 _____

3. 40; 72 _____

4. 92; 69 _____

21.2 Markup and Markdown

Use the original price and the markdown or markup to find the retail price.

5. Original price: $60; Markup: 15%; Retail price: _____

6. Original price: $32; Markup: 12.5%; Retail price: _____

7. Original price: $50; Markdown: 22%; Retail price: _____

8. Original price: $125; Markdown: 30%; Retail price: _____

21.3 Applications of Percent

9. Mae Ling earns a weekly salary of $325 plus a 6.5% commission on sales at a gift shop. How much would she make in a work week if she sold $4,800 worth of merchandise? _____

10. Ramon earns $1,735 each month and pays $53.10 for electricity. To the nearest tenth of a percent, what percent of Ramon's earnings are spent on electricity each month? _____

11. James, Priya, and Siobhan work in a grocery store. James makes $7.00 per hour. Priya makes 20% more than James, and Siobhan makes 5% less than Priya. How much does Siobhan make per hour? _____

12. The Hu family goes out for lunch, and the price of the meal is $45. The sales tax on the meal is 6%, and the family also leaves a 20% tip on the pre-tax amount. What is the total cost of the meal? _____

? ESSENTIAL QUESTION

13. Give three examples of how percents are used in the real-world. Tell whether each situation represents a percent increase or a percent decrease.

_____

_____

Assessment Readiness

Personal Math Trainer

Online Assessment and Intervention

my.hrw.com

Selected Response

1. Zalmon walks $\frac{3}{4}$ of a mile in $\frac{3}{10}$ of an hour. What is his speed in miles per hour?

Ⓐ 0.225 miles per hour

Ⓑ 2.3 miles per hour

Ⓒ 2.5 miles per hour

Ⓓ 2.6 miles per hour

2. Find the percent change from 70 to 56.

Ⓐ 20% decrease   Ⓒ 25% decrease

Ⓑ 20% increase   Ⓓ 25% increase

3. The rainfall total this year was 10.2 inches, which is 20% less than last year's rainfall total. What was last year's rainfall total?

Ⓐ 8.16 inches   Ⓒ 12.75 inches

Ⓑ 12.24 inches   Ⓓ 20.4 inches

4. A pair of basketball shoes was originally priced at $80, but was marked up 37.5%. What was the retail price of the shoes?

Ⓐ $50   Ⓒ $110

Ⓑ $83   Ⓓ $130

5. The sales tax rate in Jan's town is 7.5%. If she buys 3 lamps for $23.59 each and a sofa for $769.99, how much sales tax does she owe?

Ⓐ $58.85   Ⓒ $67.26

Ⓑ $63.06   Ⓓ $71.46

6. The day after a national holiday, decorations were marked down 40%. Before the holiday, a patriotic banner cost $5.75. How much did the banner cost after the holiday?

Ⓐ $1.15   Ⓒ $3.45

Ⓑ $2.30   Ⓓ $8.05

7. Dustin makes $2,330 each month and pays $840 for rent. To the nearest tenth of a percent, what percent of Dustin's earnings are spent on rent?

Ⓐ 84.0%   Ⓒ 56.4%

Ⓑ 63.9%   Ⓓ 36.1%

8. A scuba diver is positioned at −30 feet. How many feet will she have to rise to change her position to −12 feet?

Ⓐ −42 ft   Ⓒ 18 ft

Ⓑ −18 ft   Ⓓ 42 ft

9. A bank offers an annual simple interest rate of 8% on home improvement loans. Tobias borrowed $17,000 over a period of 2 years. How much did he repay altogether?

Ⓐ $1,360   Ⓒ $18,360

Ⓑ $2,720   Ⓓ $19,720

Mini-Task

10. The granola Summer buys used to cost $6.00 per pound, but it has been marked up 15%.

a. How much did it cost Summer to buy 2.6 pounds of granola at the old price?

_____

b. How much does it cost her to buy 2.6 pounds of granola at the new price?

_____

c. Suppose Summer buys 3.5 pounds of granola. How much more does it cost at the new price than at the old price?

_____

MODULE 20 ▸ Rates and Proportionality

Key Vocabulary
complex fraction *(fracción compleja)*

constant of proportionality *(constante de proporcionalidad)*

proportion *(proporción)*

proportional relationship *(relación proporcional)*

rate of change *(tasa de cambio)*

unit rate *(tasa unitaria)*

? ESSENTIAL QUESTION

How can you use rates and proportionality to solve real-world problems?

EXAMPLE 1

A store sells onions by the pound. Is the relationship between the cost of an amount of onions and the number of pounds proportional? If so, write an equation for the relationship, and represent the relationship on a graph.

Number of pounds	2	5	6
Cost ($)	3.00	7.50	9.00

Write the rates.

$$\frac{cost}{number\ of\ pounds} : \frac{\$3.00}{2\ pounds} = \frac{\$1.50}{1\ pound}$$

$$\frac{\$7.50}{5\ pounds} = \frac{\$1.50}{1\ pound}$$

$$\frac{\$9.00}{6\ pounds} = \frac{\$1.50}{1\ pound}$$

The rates are constant, so the relationship is proportional.

The constant rate of change is $1.50 per pound, so the constant of proportionality is 1.5. Let x represent the number of pounds and y represent the cost.

The equation for the relationship is $y = 1.5x$.

Plot the ordered pairs (pounds, cost): (2, 3), (5, 7.5), and (6, 9).

Connect the points with a line.

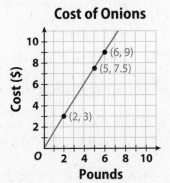

Cost of Onions

EXERCISES

1. Steve uses $\frac{8}{9}$ gallon of paint to paint 4 identical birdhouses. How many gallons of paint does he use for each birdhouse?

    (Lesson 20.1) _____

2. Ron walks 0.5 mile on the track in 10 minutes. Stevie walks 0.25 mile on the track in 6 minutes. Find the unit rate for each walker in miles per hour. Who is the faster walker?

    (Lesson 20.1) _____

    _____

3. The table below shows the proportional relationship between Juan's pay and the hours he works. Complete the table. Plot the data and connect the points with a line. (Lessons 20.2, 20.3)

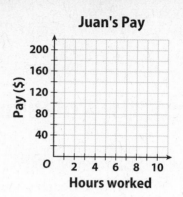

Juan's Pay

Hours worked	2		5	6
Pay ($)	40	80		

Proportions and Percent

Key Vocabulary

percent decrease *(porcentaje de disminución)*

percent increase *(porcentaje de aumento)*

principal *(capital)*

simple interest *(interés simple)*

? **ESSENTIAL QUESTION**

How can you use proportions and percent to solve real-world problems?

EXAMPLE 1

Donata had a 25-minute commute from home to work. Her company moved, and now her commute to work is 33 minutes long. Does this situation represent an increase or a decrease? Find the percent increase or decrease in her commute to work.

This situation represents an increase. Find the percent increase.

amount of change = greater value − lesser value

$33 - 25 = 8$

$$\text{percent increase} = \frac{\text{amount of change}}{\text{original amount}}$$

$\frac{8}{25} = 0.32 = 32\%$

Donata's commute increased by 32%.

1. Michelle purchased 25 audio files in January. In February she purchased 40 audio files. Find the percent increase. (Lesson 21.1) _____

2. Sam's dog weighs 72 pounds. The vet suggests that for the dog's health, its weight should decrease by 12.5 percent. According to the vet, what is a healthy weight for the dog? (Lesson 21.1) _____

3. The original price of a barbecue grill is $79.50. The grill is marked down 15%. What is the sale price of the grill? (Lesson 21.2) _____

4. A sporting goods store marks up the cost *s* of soccer balls by 250%. Write an expression that represents the retail cost of the soccer balls. The store buys soccer balls for $5.00 each. What is the retail price of the soccer balls? (Lesson 21.2) _____

1. **CAREERS IN MATH** Bicycle Tour Operator Viktor is a bike tour operator and needs to replace two of his touring bikes. He orders two bikes from the sporting goods store for a total of $2,000 and pays using his credit card. When the bill arrives, he reads the following information:

> **Balance:** $2,000
> **Annual interest rate:** 14.9%
> **Minimum payment due:** $40
> **Late fee:** $10 if payment not received by 3/1/2013

a. To keep his good credit, Viktor promptly sends in a minimum payment of $40. When the next bill arrives, it looks a lot like the previous bill.

> Balance: $1,984.34
> Annual interest rate: 14.9%
> Minimum payment due: $40
> Late fee: $10 if payment not received by 4/1/2013

Explain how the credit card company calculated the new balance. Notice that the given interest rate is annual, but the payment is monthly.

_____

_____

_____

b. Viktor was upset about the new bill, so he decided to send in $150 for his April payment. The minimum payment on his bill is calculated as 2% of the balance (rounded to the nearest dollar) or $20, whichever is greater. Fill out the details for Viktor's new bill.

> **Balance:** _____
>
> **Annual interest rate:** _____
>
> **Minimum payment due:** _____
>
> **Late fee: $10 if payment not received by** _____

c. Viktor's bank offers a credit card with an introductory annual interest rate of 9.9%. He can transfer his current balance for a fee of $40. After one year, the rate will return to the bank's normal rate, which is 13.9%. The bank charges a late fee of $15. Give two reasons why Viktor should transfer the balance, and two reasons why he should not.

_____

_____

_____

_____

2. *Acceleration* is the rate at which the velocity of an object changes. Students in a science class study the acceleration of an object due to gravity. They perform an experiment in which they drop a ball from a balcony and measure the ball's velocity in meters per second at various times as it falls toward the ground. The table shows their measurements.

Time (s)	Velocity (m/s)	Acceleration(m/s²)
0.00	0.00	—
0.05	0.49	
0.09	0.89	
0.14	1.37	

a. When velocity is measured in meters per second, acceleration is measured in *meters per second* per *second*, or *meters per second squared* (written m/s²). Complete the third column of the table by finding the ratio of the change in velocity to the change in time from one row to the next.

b. Describe what you notice about the acceleration ratio in your table.

_____

c. What is the average acceleration?

_____

d. What does your answer to part **c** suggest about the rate of change in velocity over time for this situation?

_____

e. Many things affect the acceleration due to gravity on Earth, including altitude, latitude, tides, and local gravity variations. Suppose that the accepted acceleration due to gravity in your location is 9.803 m/s². Use the formula below to find the percent error of the average acceleration due to gravity for this experiment. Give your answer to the nearest thousandth of a percent.

$$\frac{|\text{Experimental Value} - \text{True Value}|}{\text{True Value}} \times 100$$

_____

f. Make a conjecture about a possible source of error in this experiment.

_____

Assessment Readiness

Personal
Math Trainer

Online
Assessment and
Intervention

my.hrw.com

Selected Response

1. If the relationship between distance y in feet and time x in seconds is proportional, which rate is represented by $\frac{y}{x} = 0.6$?

   Ⓐ 3 feet in 5 s

   Ⓑ 3 feet in 9 s

   Ⓒ 10 feet in 6 s

   Ⓓ 18 feet in 3 s

2. The Baghrams make regular monthly deposits in a savings account. The graph shows the relationship between the number x of months and the amount y in dollars in the account.

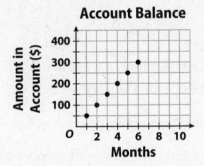

Account Balance

What is the equation for the deposit?

   Ⓐ $\frac{y}{x} = \$25$/month

   Ⓑ $\frac{y}{x} = \$40$/month

   Ⓒ $\frac{y}{x} = \$50$/month

   Ⓓ $\frac{y}{x} = \$75$/month

Read graphs and diagrams carefully. Look at the labels for important information.

3. What is the decimal form of $-4\frac{7}{8}$?

   Ⓐ -4.9375

   Ⓑ -4.875

   Ⓒ -4.75

   Ⓓ -4.625

4. Find the percent change from 72 to 90.

   Ⓐ 20% decrease

   Ⓑ 20% increase

   Ⓒ 25% decrease

   Ⓓ 25% increase

5. A store had a sale on art supplies. The price p of each item was marked down 60%. Which expression represents the new price?

   Ⓐ $0.4p$ Ⓒ $1.4p$

   Ⓑ $0.6p$ Ⓓ $1.6p$

6. Clarke borrows $16,000 to buy a car. He pays simple interest at an annual rate of 6% over a period of 3.5 years. How much does he pay altogether?

   Ⓐ $18,800

   Ⓑ $19,360

   Ⓒ $19,920

   Ⓓ $20,480

7. To which set or sets does the number 37 belong?

   Ⓐ integers only

   Ⓑ rational numbers only

   Ⓒ integers and rational numbers only

   Ⓓ whole numbers, integers, and rational numbers

8. In which equation is the constant of proportionality 5?

Ⓐ $x = 5y$

Ⓑ $y = 5x$

Ⓒ $y = x + 5$

Ⓓ $y = 5 - x$

9. Suri charges by the day to walk a dog. She charges $6.25 for 5 days and $8.75 for 7 days. Which equation represents this relationship?

Ⓐ $y = 7x$

Ⓑ $y = 5x$

Ⓒ $y = 2.50x$

Ⓓ $y = 1.25x$

10. Randy walks $\frac{1}{2}$ mile in each $\frac{1}{5}$ hour. How far will Randy walk in one hour?

Ⓐ $\frac{1}{2}$ miles

Ⓑ 2 miles

Ⓒ $2\frac{1}{2}$ miles

Ⓓ 5 miles

11. On a trip to Spain, Sheila bought a piece of jewelry that cost $56.75. She paid for it with her credit card, which charges a foreign transaction fee of 3%. How much was the foreign transaction fee?

Ⓐ $0.17

Ⓑ $1.07

Ⓒ $1.70

Ⓓ $17.00

12. A baker is looking for a recipe that has the lowest unit rate for flour per batch of muffins. Which recipe should she use?

Ⓐ $\frac{1}{2}$ cup flour for $\frac{2}{3}$ batch

Ⓑ $\frac{2}{3}$ cup flour for $\frac{1}{2}$ batch

Ⓒ $\frac{3}{4}$ cup flour for $\frac{2}{3}$ batch

Ⓓ $\frac{1}{3}$ cup flour for $\frac{1}{4}$ batch

Mini-Task

13. Kevin was able to type 2 pages in 5 minutes, 3 pages in 7.5 minutes, and 5 pages in 12.5 minutes.

a. Make a table of the data.

b. Graph the relationship between the number of pages typed and the number of minutes.

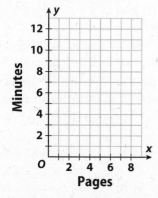

c. Describe how you know this is a proportional relationship.

_____

_____

_____

_____

d. Explain how to use the graph to find the unit rate.

_____

_____

_____

_____

_____

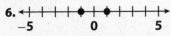

UNIT 1 Selected Answers

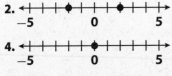

LESSON 1.1

Your Turn

6.

−5   0   5

8. −10 **9.** 5 **10.** 0 **11.** 6

Guided Practice

2.
−5   0   5

4.
−5   0   5

5. −4 **6.** 11 **7.** −3 **8.** 3 **9.** 0
10. −22

Independent Practice

13. 17 **15.** 2 **17.** 12 **19a.** gain
b. Tino **c.** Tino and Luis **d.** −6
e. No; −6 pound change means
Frankie lost 6 pounds. **21.** 4 units
23. 14 units **25.** −9; it is 9 units
away from 0 on a number line, and
6 is only 6 units away from 0.

LESSON 1.2

Your Turn

2. 4, 2, 0, −3, −5, −6

−6   0   4

3. 9, 8, 5, 2, 0, −1, −6, −10
4. < **5.** < **6.** >
7. −2 > −18; −18 < −2
8. −39 < 39; 39 > −39

Guided Practice

1b. A **c.** B **2.** −9, −6, −3, 0, 1, 4, 8
3. −65, −13, −7, 7, 34, 55, 62
4. −17 > −22; −22 < −17 **5.** <
6. < **7.** > **8.** > **9.** > **10.** < **11.** <
12. > **13a.** −3 < 2 **b.** 0 > −4

Independent Practice

15b. E. Simpson **17.** 167 > −65
19b. −5, −2, 2, 4, 7 **21.** 377 > 249
23. Argentina **25.** No; −12 °F <
−3 °F, so it was getting colder
outside. **27.** −10, −3, 5, 16 and
−3, 5, −10, 16

LESSON 1.3

Your Turn

4. The temperature at night
reached 13 °F below zero.
5. 12 **6.** 91 **7.** 55 **8.** 0 **9.** 88 **10.** 1

Guided Practice

1. negative **2a.** −$10; it is a fee, so
it represents a change of −$10 in
the amount of money Ryan has.
b. | −10 | = 10

−10   0

3a. more than 100 **b.** less than
Leo **c.** more than 50

Independent Practice

5. The first week his balance
changed by +$80. The second
week his balance changed by
−$85. **7b.** April **9a.** −5, 4, −1, 3,
−2 **b.** The spinner landing on red
results in a change of −$5 to
Lisa's amount of money. **13.** No;
−| −4 | = −4, and | −(−4) | =
| 4 | = 4.

LESSON 2.1

Your Turn

3. 7 **4.** 4 **5.** 8 teams; 4 girls,
5 boys

Guided Practice

1. Common factors: 1, 2, 4, 8;
Possible numbers of vests: 1, 2, 4,
8; GCF = 8; greatest number of
vests = 8 **2.** 9; 9; 4; 9; 5; 9; 4; 5
3. 15; 15; 5; 15; 6; 15; 5; 6

Independent Practice

5. 1, 2, 3, 4, 6, 12 **7.** 1, 3, 13, 39
9. 8 **11.** 5 **13.** 1 **15.** 12 **17.** 4
19. 1, 2, 4, or 8 shelves
21. 6 groups; 2 coaches and 7
players **23.** 8 × (7 + 8) = 8 × 15
25. 6 × (5 + 9) = 6 × 14
27. 11 × (5 + 6) 11 × 11
29. 5 × (8 + 5) 8 × 13

31. 1 is a factor of all whole
numbers. Some pairs of whole
numbers have no common
factors other than 1. For example,
7 and 16 have no common factors
other than 1. **33.** Find the factors
of all three numbers, and take the
greatest factor that is common to
all three. For example, for the GCF
of 6, 9, and 12, the factors of 6 are
1, 2, 3, and 6; the factors of 9 are 1,
3, and 9; and the factors of 12 are
1, 2, 3, 4, 6, and 12. So, the GCF is 3.

LESSON 2.2

Your Turn

2. 36; 4, 8, 12, 16, 20, 24, 28, 32,
36, 40; 9, 18, 27, 36, 45, 54, 63, 72,
81, 90

Guided Practice

1. 36th and 72nd visits; 36th visit

Independent Practice

3. 56 **5.** 60 **7.** 48 **9.** 45
11a. February 15 **b.** No; there are
only 28 or 29 days in February,
and the next common multiple
of 3 and 5 is 30. **13.** 40 **15.** 120
17. The LCM is the greater of the
two numbers. **19.** 5 and 12.

LESSON 3.1

Your Turn

3. $\frac{-15}{1}$ **4.** $\frac{31}{100}$ **5.** $\frac{41}{9}$ **6.** $\frac{62}{1}$
9. rational numbers **10.** rational
numbers **11.** integers and
rational numbers **12.** whole
numbers, integers, and rational
numbers

Guided Practice

1a. 4 rolls of ribbon divided evenly among the 5 friends. $4 \div 5$.
b. $\frac{4}{5}$ roll **2.** $\frac{7}{10}$ **3.** $\frac{-29}{1}$ **4.** $\frac{25}{3}$
5. integers, rational numbers
6. rational numbers

Independent Practice

11. $\frac{22}{5}$, or $4.40 **13.** Venn **15.** $\frac{35}{2}$, rational numbers **17.** $\frac{8}{15}$ cup

LESSON 3.2

Your Turn

2. -7, 3.5, -2.25, and $-9\frac{1}{3}$. **4.** 4.5
5. $1\frac{1}{2}$ **6.** 4 **7.** $3\frac{1}{4}$

Guided Practice

1.
2.
3.
4.

5. -3.78 **6.** $7\frac{5}{12}$ **7.** 0 **8.** -4.2
9. -12.1 **10.** -2.6 **11.** They are the same distance from 0 on the number line. **12.** 5.23 **13.** $4\frac{2}{11}$
14. 0 **15.** $6\frac{3}{5}$ **16.** 2.12 **17.** 8.2

Independent Practice

19a. Girardi $85.23, Lewis $-$20.44, Stein $116.33, Yuan $-$13.50, Wenner $9.85
b. Wenner **c.** Stein **23.** to the left
25a. $-25,344$ ft **b.** -5 and -4
c.

LESSON 3.3

Your Turn

3. 0.15, $\frac{3}{5}$, $\frac{7}{10}$, 0.85 **5.** -1.8, -1.25, 1, $1\frac{2}{5}$, $1\frac{9}{10}$

Guided Practice

1. $\frac{3}{5}$ **2.** 0.25 **3.** $\frac{9}{10}$ **4.** $\frac{1}{10}$ **5.** 0.3
6. $1\frac{2}{5}$ **7.** 0.8 **8.** $\frac{2}{5}$ **9.** 0.75
10. $\frac{1}{5}$, 0.4, $\frac{1}{2}$, 0.75 **11.** $12\frac{3}{4}$, 12.7, $12\frac{3}{5}$

12. 2.3, 2.6, $2\frac{4}{5}$ **13.** $\frac{5}{48}$, $\frac{3}{16}$, 0.5, 0.75
14. $\frac{1}{5}$, 0.35, $\frac{12}{25}$, 0.5, $\frac{4}{5}$ **15.** $-\frac{3}{4}$, $-\frac{7}{10}$, $\frac{3}{4}$, $\frac{8}{10}$ **16.** -0.65, $-\frac{3}{8}$, $\frac{5}{16}$, $\frac{2}{4}$ **17.** $-2\frac{4}{5}$, -2.6, -2.3 **18.** -0.72, $-\frac{5}{8}$, -0.6, $-\frac{7}{12}$
19. 1.2, $1\frac{1}{3}$, 1.45, $1\frac{1}{2}$ **20.** -0.35, -0.3, 0.5, 0.55

Independent Practice

23a. $6\frac{1}{6}$, 5.5, $4\frac{3}{8}$, 4.3, $\frac{15}{4}$ **b.** Claire, Peter, Brenda, and Jim; Micah
c. Yes; the smallest donation is $\frac{15}{4}$ pounds. $\frac{1}{2}$ is equal to $\frac{2}{4}$ pound. $\frac{15}{4} + \frac{2}{4} = \frac{17}{4} = 4\frac{1}{4} = 4.25$ pounds, which is enough to win a free movie coupon.

UNIT 2 Selected Answers

LESSON 4.1

Your Turn

1. $\frac{1}{10}$ **2.** $\frac{7}{12}$ **3.** $\frac{2}{7}$ **4.** $\frac{8}{35}$ **5.** $\frac{4}{15}$ **6.** $\frac{1}{7}$
8. 15 **9.** 12 **10.** $\frac{8}{3}$ **11.** $\frac{7}{2}$ **12.** $25\frac{9}{10}$
13. 23 **15.** $\frac{11}{21}$ **16.** $\frac{4}{15}$ **17.** $\frac{1}{24}$
18. $1\frac{11}{20}$ **19.** $6\frac{13}{15}$ **20.** $3\frac{1}{42}$

Guided Practice

1. $\frac{5}{16}$ **2.** $\frac{1}{3}$ **3.** $\frac{3}{20}$ **4.** 38 **5.** $\frac{3}{4}$ **6.** 6
7. 3 **8.** 16 **9.** 24 **10.** 15 **11.** $\frac{7}{12}$
12. $\frac{7}{15}$ **13.** $\frac{1}{5}$ **14.** $\frac{24}{35}$ **15.** $3\frac{19}{24}$
16. $5\frac{19}{45}$

Independent Practice

19a. 10 pounds **b.** 5 more bags
21a. oranges = $1\frac{1}{2}$, apples = $1\frac{4}{5}$,
blueberries = $\frac{3}{4}$ cup, peaches = 2
b. Sample answer: If you triple
3, it becomes 9. If you triple $\frac{1}{2}$, it
becomes $1\frac{1}{2}$. Add $9 + 1\frac{1}{2} = 10\frac{1}{2}$.
23a. $22\frac{1}{2}$ minutes **b.** Yes, there
is enough time; 15 min for the
teacher's introduction + 15 min
for students to get ready +
$22\frac{1}{2}$ min for speeches = $52\frac{1}{2}$ min
25. Cameron divided a factor in
one of the numerators by the GCF
but did not divide a factor in one
of the denominators by the GCF.
He should have simplified $\frac{4}{9}$ to $\frac{4}{3}$
and multiplied $\frac{1}{7}$ and $\frac{4}{3}$ to find the
product $\frac{4}{21}$.

LESSON 4.2

Your Turn

5. $\frac{8}{7}$ **6.** $\frac{1}{9}$ **7.** 11 **10.** $2\frac{1}{4}$ **11.** $1\frac{1}{2}$

Guided Practice

1. $\frac{5}{2}$ **2.** 9 **3.** $\frac{3}{10}$ **4.** $\frac{4}{5}$ **5.** $\frac{3}{8}$ **6.** $1\frac{1}{4}$

Independent Practice

9. 4 runners will be needed.
11. $\frac{1}{10}$ pound **13.** 9 bags
15. 8 **17.** 2; $\frac{1}{12}$ meter
19. Greater than $\frac{1}{2}$ **21.** Robyn

LESSON 4.3

Your Turn

6. 9; $10\frac{1}{2} \div 1\frac{1}{4} = 8\frac{2}{5}$; She will need
9 containers. **8.** $4\frac{1}{2}$ meters
9. $3\frac{1}{4}$ yards

Guided Practice

1. 17; 17; 4; 3; $5\frac{2}{3}$ **2.** 3; 9; 3; 4; 9; $\frac{2}{3}$
3. $3\frac{5}{9}$ **4.** $2\frac{4}{5}$ **5.** $3\frac{1}{3}$ **6.** 4 **7.** $26 \div 5\frac{1}{2}$;
The width is $4\frac{8}{11}$ feet. **8.** $230 \div 12\frac{1}{2}$;
$18\frac{2}{5}$ feet

Independent Practice

13a. No **b.** $\frac{11}{20}$ of a cup; $5\frac{1}{2}$ cups ÷
10 people $= \frac{11}{2} \times \frac{1}{10} = \frac{11}{20}$
c. She would need $7\frac{1}{2}$ cups total,
so she would need 2 more cups
of trail mix. **15.** yes because the
height is $4\frac{1}{4}$ feet **17.** $5\frac{1}{4}$ feet
19. He used the reciprocal of $\frac{3}{4}$
instead of the reciprocal of $2\frac{3}{4}$.

LESSON 4.4

Your Turn

1. 10

Guided Practice

1. 13

Independent Practice

3. $8 per hour
5. 40 appointments
7. 93 pieces **9.** $1\frac{5}{24}$ gallons
11. Sample answer: A person
taking a test averages $\frac{3}{8}$ minute
to read a question and $\frac{5}{6}$ minute
to answer the question. It takes
the person 29 minutes to answer
all of the questions. How many
questions are on the test?
24 questions

LESSON 5.1

Your Turn

3. 109 **4.** 587 **7.** 231 R21
8. 46 R16 **9.** 105 bags; 3 rocks
left over

Guided Practice

1. 30,000; 500; 60 **2.** 96 **3.** 89
4. 98 R7 **5.** 42 **6.** 61 **7.** 94 R15
8. 24 R9 **9.** 127 **10.** 81 R28
11. 300 items **12.** 32 seats
13. 85 boxes

Independent Practice

15. 268 **17.** 209
19. 86 R39 **21.** 587
23. 67 rows; $8,450 \div 125 =$
67 R75 so he will have 67 full rows
and one partial row of 75 trees.
25. 69 people **29.** Multiply the
quotient and the divisor, then add
the remainder to the product. If
the division was done correctly,
the result will equal the dividend.
31. No; 78,114 is about 80,000 and
192 is about 200; $80,000 \div 200 =$
400, and 40 isn't close to 400.
33. More; the whole amount is
divided into smaller portions, so
there will be more bags; since 25
is half of 50, they will have twice
as many bags.

LESSON 5.2

Your Turn

5. 0.69 **6.** 0.939 **7.** 7.85 **8.** 21.15

Guided Practice

1. 0.91 **2.** 0.78 **3.** 62.35
4. 37.11 **5.** 3.955 **6.** 2.57
7. 11.949 **8.** 1.806 **9.** 30.1
10. 65.841 **11.** 23.356
12. 7.35 **13.** 37.68 **14.** 72.25
15. 31.25 feet **16.** $11.36

UNIT 2 Selected Answers *(cont'd)*

Independent Practice
19. 5.495 **21.** 63.022
23. 11.949 **25.** 6.408
27. Jahmya; $0.54 more
29. $1.53 **31a.** 27.78 minutes
b. 32.22 minutes
33. Sample answer: The sum
$2.55 + (3.72 + 1.45) =$
$2.55 + 5.17 = 7.72$. Using the
Commutative Property, the
sum can be written as $2.55 +$
$(1.45 + 3.72) = 7.72$, and using
the Associative Property, the
sum can be written as $(2.55 + 1.45) +$
$3.72 = 7.72$.

LESSON 5.3

Your Turn
3. 1; 1; 6300; 12600; 192.78; 2
4. 2; 2; 5856; 39040; 4.4896; 4
5. 49980; 428400; 48.4092
6. 8043; 22980; 919200; 95.0223
7. 38.75

Guided Practice
1. 0.28

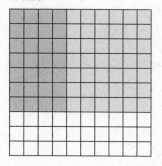

2. 2.64

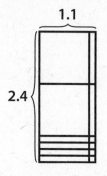

3. 0.0108 **4.** 130.055 **5.** 0.1152
6. 2,021.175 **7.** 14.858 **8.** 2.48292
9. 23.63 **10.** 173.90 **11.** 29.21
12. 1.06

Independent Practice
15. 14 inches **17.** $342 **19.** $15.50
21. $23.58 **23.** 20.425 miles
25. 14.125 miles **27.** 3.48 is
closer to 3 and 7.33 is closer to 7;
$3 \times 7 = 21$ **29.** The 22-karat gold
statue; 24.549 ounces

LESSON 5.4

Your Turn
3. 1.95 **4.** 0.92 **5.** 8.5 **6.** 18

Guided Practice
1. 7.375 **2.** 3.31 **3.** 7 **4.** 0.15
5. 77 **6.** 2.65 **7.** 33.16 **8.** 1.95
9. 19 **10.** 0.3 **11.** 6.2 **12.** 405
13. 250 **14.** 11.8 **15.** 0.8 pound
16. 3.5 pounds **17.** 18.1 seconds
18. 18 **19.** $2.73 per gallon
20. 20 inches

Independent Practice
23. $8.50 **25a.** 10 movies
27. beef **29a.** 0.42 **b.** 0.25
c. 0.15 **31.** 42 **33.** 20 weeks

LESSON 5.5

Your Turn
2. He paid $\frac{29}{2} \times \frac{3}{5} = 8\frac{7}{10}$ dollars or
$14.5 \times 0.6 = 8.70

Guided Practice
1. $134\frac{1}{2}$ miles **2.** $397.80

Independent Practice
3. $3\frac{1}{2}$ gallons **5.** 2 batteries
7. $5.88; No. They earned $7.84
on Wednesday. $7.84 - 5.88 = 1.96$,
so they don't have enough money.
9. 3 games **13.** 35.

 **Selected Answers**

MODULE 6

LESSON 6.1

Your Turn

5. 3 : 1; 3 to 1; $\frac{3}{1}$ **6.** 8 : 3; 8 to 3; $\frac{8}{3}$
7. 1 : 1; 1 to 1; $\frac{1}{1}$ **8.** $\frac{4}{5}, \frac{16}{20}, \frac{12}{15}$ **9.** $\frac{10}{4}$, $\frac{15}{6}, \frac{20}{8}$

Guided Practice

1. 1 to 5 **2.** 5; 3 **3.** 5; 25
4. 60 pets **5.** 2 to 5; 2 : 5; $\frac{2}{5}$
6. 5 to 12; 5 : 12; $\frac{5}{12}$
7. Sample answer: $\frac{5}{6}, \frac{20}{24}, \frac{25}{30}$
8. Sample answer: $\frac{7}{1}, \frac{21}{3}, \frac{28}{4}$
9. Sample answer: $\frac{8}{14}, \frac{12}{21}, \frac{16}{28}$

Independent Practice

11. 2 to 6, 3 to 9, 4 to 12
13. 16 roses and 24 carnations
15. 20; her current ratio of movie posters to band posters is 120 : 100. If she sells 24 movie posters, she will have 96 left. 120 : 100 = 96 : 80, so she should sell 20 movie posters. **17a.** 18 **b.** 12
19. 3 : 2; 30 girls and 20 boys
21. Tina multiplied 6 by 6 to get 36 and 8 by 8 to get 64. She should have multiplied both terms by the same number.

LESSON 6.2

Your Turn

3. 12
4. 45 minutes, $\frac{27 \text{ minutes} \div 3}{3 \text{ miles} \div 3} = \frac{9 \text{ minutes}}{1 \text{ mile}}$. The unit rate is 9 minutes per mile. $\frac{9 \text{ minutes} \times 5}{1 \text{ mile} \times 5} = \frac{45 \text{ minutes}}{5 \text{ miles}}$

Guided Practice

1. 0.21; 0.19 **2.** family size **3.** $48
4. 16 **5.** 72 **6.** 300 calories **7.** $6

Independent Practice

9. $12.50 per lawn **11.** Alastair
13a. 5 minutes; 7 balloons
b. $1\frac{2}{5}$ balloons per minute
c. 14 balloons

15. $10.50
17. There are 12 inches in 1 foot, and 2.54 × 12 = 30.48 centimeters per foot; there are 3 feet per yard, so 30.48 cm × 3 = 91.44 centimeters per yard.
19. The unit costs are $1.10 per pound for a 1-pound bag, $0.99 per pound for a 2-pound bag, and $0.95 per pound for a 3-pound bag. The unit cost decreases as the quantity of sugar increases.

LESSON 6.3

Your Turn

1. Anna: $\frac{2}{5}$ cup; Bailey: $\frac{3}{8}$ cup; ratio of concentrate to total cups of lemonade is 2 to 5 for Anna and 3 to 8 for Bailey. So, Anna has $\frac{2}{5}$ cup of concentrate in 1 cup of lemonade, and Bailey has $\frac{3}{8}$ cup. **2.** No, the ratios are not equivalent. $\frac{2 \times 4}{3 \times 4} = \frac{8}{12}$ $\frac{8}{12} > \frac{7}{12}$

Guided Practice

1b. $\frac{5}{6} > \frac{4}{6}$; No Celeste is not using the correct ratio of apples to oranges **2.** No; Neha used the greater ratio of bananas to oranges. **3.** Tim can read 140 words in 5 minutes.
4. On average, the cafeteria sells 120 drinks per hour.

Independent Practice

7. $63 **9.** 175 miles
11. 6 pounds; 19 apples
13. approximately 22 inches
17. All of the rates should be equivalent to each other. One way to check that they are equivalent is to divide the top term by the bottom term. All of the quotients will be equal if the rates are all correct.

MODULE 7

LESSON 7.1

Your Turn

3.

Time (min)	2	3	3.5	5	6.5
Water used (gal)	8	12	14	20	26

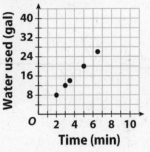

Guided Practice

1. $\frac{6}{12} = \frac{9}{18} = \frac{21}{42} = \frac{27}{54}$
2.

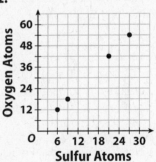

3. $\frac{2}{4} = \frac{4}{8} = \frac{7}{14} = \frac{8}{16}$
4.

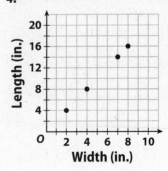

5.

Boxes	5	8	10
Candles	60	96	120

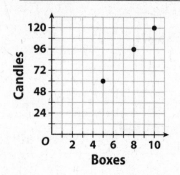

Independent Practice

7. $\dfrac{\text{money collected}}{\text{sweatshirts sold}} = \dfrac{\$60}{3 \text{ sweatshirts}} = \dfrac{\$20}{1 \text{ sweatshirt}} = \$20$ per sweatshirt sold **11.** $480 **13.** 330 mi

LESSON 7.2

Your Turn
1. 10 cheese pizzas
2. 108 minutes **3.** 50 miles

Guided Practice
1. 6; 6; 18 **2.** 2; 2; 2 **3.** $45
4. 18 inches tall **5.** 60 seconds
6. 13 measures **7.** 40 minutes
8. 26 paychecks **9.** 24 kilometers

Independent Practice
11a. 1 inch = 12 miles **b.** 24 miles
13a. 60 seats **b.** 150 seats
15. 45 ft **17.** Ira **19.** No, the caterpillar's unit rate should be 5 feet per minute.
21a. b. 80 minutes

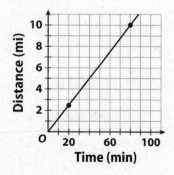

LESSON 7.3

Your Turn
2. 72 inches **3.** 2.5 meters

Guided Practice
1. 3 **2.** 48 **3.** 32 cups
4. 12,000 pounds
5. 500 meters **6.** 3,500 grams
7. 1,750 mg **8.** 2.7 cm
9. 6 pounds **10.** 10 miles

Independent Practice
13. 126; 10.5; 3.5 **15.** The large size **17.** 3 kilometers
19a. between 7 tons and 8 tons **b.** No **21.** You get the original number.

LESSON 7.4

Your Turn
2. 5.676 **3.** 4.27 **4.** 9 **5.** 7.40
7. 64.55

Guided Practice
1. 8.05; 5 miles; 1.61 km **2.** 18.95; 5 gallons; 3.79 L **3.** 30.48 **4.** 1.816
5. 18.28 **6.** 339.6 **7.** 4.73 **8.** 437.64
9. 2.64 **10.** 450 **11.** 64.96 **12.** 6,211

Independent Practice
15. one inch **17.** one mile
19. one liter **21.** 4 liters **23.** 22.7 kg **25.** 2-liter juice bottle **27.** 2.75 pounds **29a.** Yes; Two half-gallon containers will hold one gallon, which is about 3.79 liters. **b.** No; A gallon jug can hold 3.79 liters, so a half-gallon jug would hold half of that, which is only 1.895 liters.
33. Multiply the number of pounds by 0.454; 3.8 kg

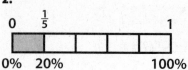

LESSON 8.1

Your Turn
2. 90% **3.** 40% **4.** about $\frac{2}{3}$

Guided Practice
1. 4; 4; 36; 36%
2.

0   $\frac{1}{5}$ 1

0% 20%   100%

3. 10; 60% **4.** 1: 50% **5.** 1; 80%
6. about $\frac{2}{5}$

Independent Practice
9. 55 **11.** $\frac{9}{10} = 90\%$, $\frac{4}{5} = 80\%$, $\frac{17}{20} = 85\%$, 80%, 85%, 90%
13. 30% of your minutes are used up **17.** No

LESSON 8.2

Your Turn
1. $\frac{3}{20}$, 0.15 **2.** $\frac{12}{25}$, 0.48 **3.** $\frac{4}{5}$, 0.8
4. $\frac{3}{4}$, 0.75 **5.** $\frac{9}{25}$, 0.36 **6.** $\frac{2}{5}$, 0.4
8. 0.36, 36% **9.** 0.875, 87.5%

Guided Practice
1. $\frac{3}{25}$; 0.12 **2.** 53%, $\frac{53}{100}$ **3.** 107%; $\frac{107}{100}$, $1\frac{7}{100}$ **4.** 0.35; 35% **5.** 0.375; 37.5%

Independent Practice
7. $\frac{18}{25}$, 0.72 **9.** $\frac{500}{100}$, $\frac{5}{1} = \frac{5}{1}$, 5 **11.** $\frac{37}{100}$, 0.37 **13.** 0.625, 62.5% **15.** 3.5, 350% **17.** $\frac{68}{80} = \frac{17}{20}$, 85%; 0.85
19. 6 **23.** 1, 100%, 1

LESSON 8.3

Your Turn
5. 19 **6.** 81 **7.** 45 **9.** 76%
11. 20 **12.** 500

Guided Practice
1. 240 televisions are high definition. **2.** 65; 200; 130
3. ×; 900; 9; 9 **4.** 21; 100; 300; 7%
5. 9; 300

Independent Practice
7. 48 tiles **9.** 8 pages **11.** 252 friends **13.** 20 **15.** 70 **17.** 1,400
19. 40 **21.** 20 **23.** 9 **25.** $500
27. $30 **29.** $175 **31.** $\frac{25}{100} = \frac{?}{50}$; 25% of 50 is 12.5.

MODULE 9

LESSON 9.1

Your Turn

2. 4^3 **3.** 6^1 **4.** $\left(\frac{1}{8}\right)^2$ **5.** 5^6 **6.** 81
7. 1 **8.** $\frac{8}{125}$ **9.** 144

Guided Practice

2. 6^3 **3.** 10^7 **4.** $\left(\frac{3}{4}\right)^5$ **5.** $\left(\frac{7}{9}\right)^8$ **6.** 512
7. 2,401 **8.** 1,000 **9.** $\frac{1}{16}$ **10.** $\frac{1}{27}$
11. $\frac{36}{49}$ **12.** 0.64 **13.** 0.125
14. 1.21 **15.** 1 **16.** 12 **17.** 1
18. 169 **19.** $\frac{4}{25}$ **20.** 0.81

Independent Practice

23. 3 **25.** 3 **27.** 1 **29.** 2 **31.** 4
33. 3 **35.** 8 **37.** 9 **39.** 3^4 pages, or
81 pages **41.** 2^6 dollars, or $64
47. 2^6, 4^3, and 8^2

LESSON 9.2

1. 1, 3, 7, 21 **2.** 1, 37 **3.** 1, 2, 3, 6, 7,
14, 21, 42 **4.** 1, 2, 3, 5, 6, 10, 15, 30

Guided Practice

1. 1, 2, 3, 6, 9, 18 **2.** 1, 2, 4, 13, 26,
52 **4.** $2 \cdot 3 \cdot 67$ **5.** $2^2 \cdot 3^2$ **6.** 2^5
7. $3 \cdot 3 \cdot 3$ or 3^3

Independent Practice

9. 1×12; 2×6; 3×4
13. $2^3 \cdot 3^2 \cdot 7$ **15.** $2 \cdot 5 \cdot 23$
19. prime factorization of $27 = 3^3$

LESSON 9.3

Your Turn

2. 1,222 **3.** 170 **5.** 125 **6.** 15
7. 0

Guided Practice

1. $3 \times 2^2 = 12$ angelfish **2.** 16; 64;
76; 13 **3.** 3; 9; 54; 62 **4.** 6; 36; 9;
108; 101 **5.** 2; 8; 4; 32; 10

Independent Practice

7. 19 **9.** 15 **11.** 39
15a. $3 \times 2 \times 2 \times 2 \times 2 = 3 \times 2^4$
b. $3 \times 2^4 - 7 = 3 \times 16 - 7 =$
$48 - 7 = 41$ butterflies

17a. $6^2 + 2 \times 6 + 24 = 72$ square
inches **b.** 8 in. by 9 in.
19. $8 \times 4 - (2 \times 3 + 8) \div 2$

MODULE 10

LESSON 10.1

Your Turn

1. $7n$ **2.** $4 - y$ **3.** $x + 13$
4. Sample answer: the quotient of
x and 12 **5.** Sample answer:
10 multiplied by y **6.** Sample
answer: c plus 3
7.

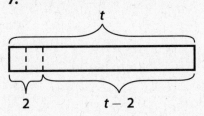

8.

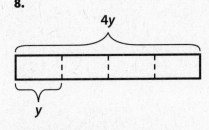

9. No; the expressions are not
equivalent. **10.** $\frac{d}{4}$

Guided Practice

1. $y - 3$ **2.** $2p$ **3.** Sample answer:
12 added to y **4.** Sample answer:
10 divided into p
5.

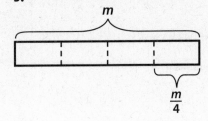

6.

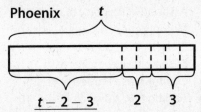

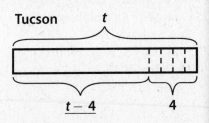

7. No **8.** $24c$

Independent Practice

11. $\frac{n}{8}$ **13.** $b + 14$ **15.** $a - 16$
17. $3w$ **19.** $\frac{13}{z}$ **21.** $w - 8$
23. Sample answer: 83 added to m
25. Sample answer: t minus 29
27. Sample answer: the product
of 11 and x **29.** Sample answer:
k less than 5 **31.** $8w$ **33a.** $3d$
b. $3g$ **c.** In Mia's expression, the
numeral is the number of gallons
and variable is the cost per gallon;
in Bob's, the numeral is the
cost per gallon and the variable
is the number of gallons he
buys. **41.** $55h$ **43a.** $\frac{s}{2}$
b. $\frac{s}{2} - 1$ shoes

LESSON 10.2

Your Turn

1. 32 **2.** 4.7 **3.** 3 **4.** 18 **5.** 18
6. 55 **7.** 6 **8.** 39 **9.** 17
10. 24; 8 **11.** 420

Guided Practice

1. 16 **2.** 6 **3.** 2 **4.** 10.5 **5.** $2\frac{1}{18}$
6. 50 **7a.** $12x + 5$ **b.** 3; 36; 41;
$41 **8a.** $2w + 2l$ **b.** 7; 5; 10; 24;
24 feet

Independent Practice

11. 42 **15.** $2(x^2)$; $2(64) =$
128 square feet

LESSON 10.3

Your Turn

3. Sample answer: $a(bc)$; Associative Property of Multiplication **4.** Sample answer: $(3 + 4)y$; Distributive Property **5.** Sample answer: 7×6; Commutative Property of Addition **6.** $2(3x - 5) = 6x - 10$; not equivalent **7.** $2 - 2 + 5x = 5x$; equivalent **8.** Jamal bought $2x + 8$ stickers. $2(4 + x) = 8 + 2x = 2x + 8$; yes **9.** $5y$ **10.** $10x^2 - 4$ **11.** $2a^5 + 5b$ **12.** $8m + 2 + 4n$

Guided Practice

2. not equivalent **3.** Sample answer: ba; Commutative Prop. of Mult. **4.** Sample answer: $5(3x) - 5(2)$; Distributive Prop. **5.** not equivalent **6.** not equivalent **7.** $44y$ **8.** $2x$

Independent Practice

11. Sample answer: $13 + x$; Commutative Prop. of Addition **13.** Sample answer: $(2 + a) + b$; Associative Prop. of Addition **15.** $2x^4$ **17.** $13b - 10$ **19.** $4y + 10$ **21.** $15y^2 - 6$ **23.** $0.5x^4 + 10.5$ **25.** $3x + 12 + x$ is equivalent to $4(3 + x)$. **27.** $(46 + 38 + 29)g + (29 + 27 + 17)s + (29 + 23 + 19)b$; $113g + 73s + 71b$ **29.** $36.4 + 4x$ in. **31.** $3x^2 - 4x + 7$; It does not have any like terms.

UNIT 5 Selected Answers

MODULE 11

LESSON 11.1

Your Turn

1. yes **2.** no **3.** yes **4.** no
5. $f + 9 = 38$ **6.** $17n = 102$
7. $c - 3 = 12$ **8.** $2h = 8$
10. Sample equation: $x + 24 = 62$; $38

Guided Practice

1. no; 14; 5 **2.** yes; 52; 4 **3.** yes
4. yes **5.** no **6.** yes **7.** no
8. yes **9.** no **10.** no **11.** yes
12. no **13.** $8r = 256$ **14.** Sample answer: $\frac{f}{2} = 5$ **15.** Sample equation: $8x = 208$; $26
16. Sample equation: $x + 24 = 92$; $68\,°F$

Independent Practice

19. $x + 8 = 31$; 23 pounds
21. Sample answer: $4x = 20$; Yes: $20 \div x = 4$ or $x = 20 \div 4$
23a. $29 - 13 = x$; $13 + x = 29$; the distance between Hadley and Greenville. **b.** Yes; 16 is a solution of the equations in a. **25.** Both equations are correct. Another correct equation is $44 - 7 = x$.
27. Yes, because $4 + f = 12$ means there are 8 flute players, and 8 is twice 4. **29.** Yes

LESSON 11.2

Your Turn

4. 3.5

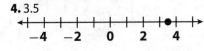

5. $\frac{5}{4}$, or $1\frac{1}{4}$

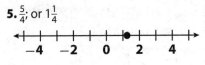

6. $x + 65 = 90$; $x = 25°$
7. $x + 42 = 90$; $x = 48°$

Guided Practice

1a. number of guests who left when the party ended. **c.** 11 **2.** 5

3. 1.5

4. 4.5 **5.** 40 **6.** $\frac{5}{4}$ **7.** $x + 45 = 180$; $x = 135°$ **8.** $x = 275$

Independent Practice

11. Sample answer: $14 = b - 12$; $b = 26$ **13.** Sample answer: $x + 8 = 37$; 29 compact cars **15.** Sample answer: $m - 123.45 = 36.55$; $160 **17.** $c = 2.50$ **19a.** $1.49 + a = 2.99$; $2.49 + r = 3.99$ **b.** Both a and r are equal to $1.50, so the discount is the same.

LESSON 11.3

Your Turn

2. 7

3. 9

4. Sample answer: $\frac{x}{5} = 9$; $x = 45$; Roberto gave away $45 - 9 = 36$ cards. **5.** $x = 35$

Guided Practice

1a. number of miles run each day **b.** 5; x; 15 **c.** 3 **2.** 9

3. 8

4. $24 = 6w$; $w = 4$ inches; length is 2 inches longer than the width
5. Sample problem: The area of a rectangle is 45 cm², and the length is 15 cm. What is the width?; $w = 3$

Independent Practice

7. $\frac{c}{28} = 3$; 84 cookies **9.** $4k = 44$; 11 books **11.** $3.5d = 14$; 4 days
13. $\frac{w}{4} = 14$; 56 minutes **17.** 81
19. 31 inches

LESSON 11.4

Your Turn

3.

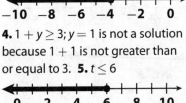

4. $1 + y \geq 3$; $y = 1$ is not a solution because $1 + 1$ is not greater than or equal to 3. **5.** $t \leq 6$

6. $w > 2$

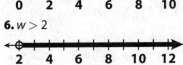

Guided Practice

1. 3, 1

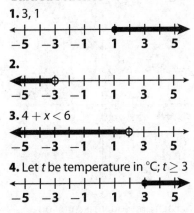

2.

3. $4 + x < 6$

4. Let t be temperature in $°C$; $t \geq 3$

Independent Practice

7.

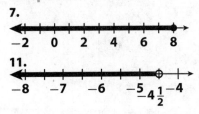

11.

13. $x \leq -3$ **15.** $x \geq -3.5$
19. $g > 150$

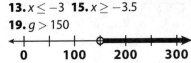

© Houghton Mifflin Harcourt Publishing Company

LESSON 12.1

Your Turn

4. $G(4, -4)$; IV; $E(-2, 4)$; II
5. $F(3, 2)$; I; $H(-1, -3)$; III
6–10.

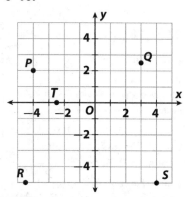

11. Ted $(-20, -20)$, Ned $(-20, 30)$

Guided Practice

1. left; up; $(-5, 1)$; II **2.** 2; 3; $(2, -3)$; IV
3–4.

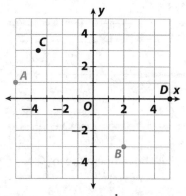

5. Each grid square is $\frac{1}{2}$ unit on a side.
6–7.

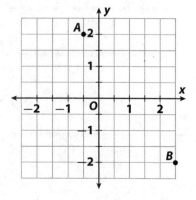

Independent Practice

11. Sam is 3 km south and 7 km east of the theater.
13. $(-3, 0.5)$ **15.** $W(-0.75, -1.0)$

LESSON 12.2

Your Turn

8. Sample answer: Bridget's grandmother gave her a collection of 15 perfume bottles. Bridget adds one bottle per week to the collection. The independent variable is the number of weeks. The dependent variable is the number of perfume bottles in her collection. The value of y is always 15 units greater than the value of x.
9. Sample answer: Colin created a website to sell T-shirts that are printed with funny slogans. He makes $16 per T-shirt. The independent variable is the number of T-shirts he sells, and the dependent variable is his profit in dollars. As the independent variable increases by 1, the dependent variable increases by 16. **10.** Sample answer: Tickets to the school musical cost $3 each. The independent variable is the number of tickets purchased, and the dependent variable is the total cost. The value of y is always 3 times the value of x.

Guided Practice

1. Time is the independent variable and cost is the dependent variable.
2a.

Time x (h)	0	1	2	2
Distance y (mi)	0	60	120	180

b. Time is the independent variable and distance is the dependent variable. **c.** The value of y is always 60 times the value of x. **3.** The value of the dependent variable is 5 times the value of the independent variable.

Independent Practice

7a. number of markers **b.** number of gift bags **c.** The relationship is multiplicative because y increases by a factor of 5 as x increases by 1.
d. The number of glitter markers is 5 times the number of gift bags.

LESSON 12.3

Your Turn

2. $y = x - 2$ **3.** $y = 2.5x$ **4.** $y = x + 5$
5. $y = 2x$ **6.** $k = r + 5$; 57 years old

Guided Practice

1. $y = x - 4$ **2.** $y = 4x$ **3.** $y = x + 3$
4. $y = \frac{x}{6}$
5. $c = 1.35n$; $33.75

Independent Practice

9. The y-value is $\frac{1}{4}$ of the x-value.
11a. $e = 8.25h$ **b.** $206.25 = 8.25h$; $25 = h$; 25 hours **13.** Not possible; there is no consistent pattern between the y-values and corresponding x-values.
15. No

LESSON 12.4

Your Turn

4.

x	$x + 2.5 = y$	(x, y)
0	$0 + 2.5 = 2.5$	$(0, 2.5)$
1	$1 + 2.5 = 3.5$	$(1, 3.5)$
2	$2 + 2.5 = 4.5$	$(2, 4.5)$
3	$3 + 2.5 = 5.5$	$(3, 5.5)$

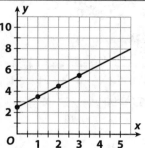

Guided Practice

1. $y = 3x$

Hours worked	Lawns mowed
0	0
1	3
2	6
3	9

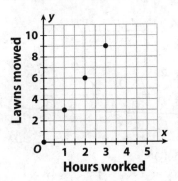

2.

x	0	1	2	3
y	0	1.5	3	4.5

3.

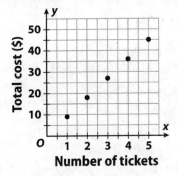

Independent Practice

5.

Additional hours	0	5	10	15	20
Total hours	20	25	30	35	40

7. 20 hours; when 0 additional hours are worked, the total is 20 hours.

9.

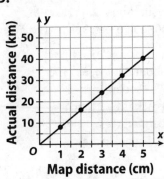

11a.

Number of tickets, x	1	2	3	4	5
Total cost ($), y	9	18	27	36	45

b. Dependent: total cost; independent: number of tickets

MODULE 13

LESSON 13.1

Your Turn

2. 366 **3.** 210 **4.** 66.5 **5.** 90 **6.** 165

Guided Practice

1. 13; 9; 117 **2.** 14; 9; 15; 168
3. 18; 11; 99

Independent Practice

5. 84 cm² **7.** 936 in² **9.** 72 m²
11. 8.25 ft² **13.** 1,620 in² **15.** 57 ft²
17. 9 in. and 15 in.

LESSON 13.2

Your Turn

3. 59.5 in² **5.** 12 ft²

Guided Practice

1. 14; 8; 56 **2.** 12; 30; 80

Independent Practice

5. 240 ft² **7.** 288 ft² **9.** 71.5 in²
11. 20 ft² **13.** Monica forgot to
multiply by $\frac{1}{2}$. The area of the
fabric is 45 in². **17a.** 6 in. **b.** 1 in.
and 36 in., 2 in. and 18 in., 3 in. and
12 in., 4 in. and 9 in.

LESSON 13.3

Your Turn

1. 8 in. **3.** 4 ft **4.** 8 pallets

Guided Practice

1. $70 = \frac{1}{2}\left(8\frac{3}{4}\right)b$; 16 in. **2.** $791 =$
$\frac{1}{2}h(26.5 + 30)$; 28 centimeters
3. area; $A = 42(28) = 1,176$ ft²;
number of gallons of paint;
$n = 1,176 \div 350 = 3.36$; 4

Independent Practice

5. $5\frac{1}{2}$ ft **7.** 1.2 cm **9.** 16 in. and
8 in. **11.** 128 patches **13a.** 702 ft²
b. 1,458 ft² **c.** 486 ft² **15a.** $3\frac{1}{2}$ yd
b. $10\frac{2}{3}$ yd²

LESSON 13.4

Your Turn

3. 44 square meters
4. 567 square inches
5. $3,348

Guided Practice

1. $\frac{1}{8}$ square unit **2.** 112 **3.** 196
4. 240 square feet; 3 cans of paint

Independent Practice

7a. about 60% **b.** $321.75
9a. 73.5 square inches
b. 21 inches by 21 inches
c. 8 banners; yes
11. 50 square inches

MODULE 14

LESSON 14.1

Your Turn

3. 9 units **4.** 5 units
5. 0.8 hours, or 48 minutes

Guided Practice

1. (5, 2) **2.** (6, 8) **3.** $|5| + |-2| =$
$5 + 2 = 7$ **4.** $|5| - |1| = 5 - 1 = 4$
5. 2 units **6.** 3 units
5–6.

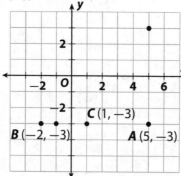

7. 5 blocks
8. 21 minutes; 4.5 minutes

Independent Practice

11. Place another point on the
other side of the y-axis the same
distance from the y-axis as point
A; (−1.5, −2.5); 3 units
13. (7, −3); 14 units **15.** (−2.4, −1);
4.8 units **17.** 3 hours

LESSON 14.2

Your Turn

2. 30 blocks **3.** 32 square units

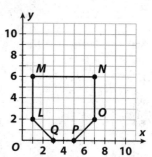

Guided Practice

1. square

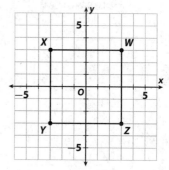

2. 6; 24 **3.** 36 square yards
4. L; 24 square inches

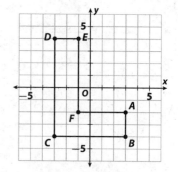

Independent Practice

7a. hexagon **b.** 18 units
c. trapezoid; 15 units
11. The octagon is a regular
octagon, so all the sides will have
the same length as the side whose
endpoints are given. Since that
side length $= |4| - |1| = 3$ units,
the perimeter of the octagon is
$8(3) = 24$ units.

MODULE 15

LESSON 15.1

Your Turn
4. 896 in² **6.** $7.92

Guided Practice
1. 1; 4 **2.** 36; 48; 84
3a. 248 square inches
b. 24,800 square inches **c.** 2 cans

Independent Practice
5. 272 in² **7.** 80 tiles
9. rectangular pyramid; triangular prism **11.** Sample answer: Decide whether the figure is a prism or a pyramid, and what the shapes of the bases and faces are. Make a net of the figure, and label the dimensions. Use appropriate area formulas to find the areas of the faces, and then find the sum of the areas.

LESSON 15.2

Your Turn
2. 75 cubic inches
3. $55\frac{1}{8}$ cubic inches
4. $393\frac{3}{4}$ cubic meters

Guided Practice
1. 2 **2.** 8
3. 10; 3.2; 5; 160 cubic meters
4. $7\frac{1}{4}$; 4; 29; 232 cubic meters
5. 277.5 cubic feet
6. $526\frac{1}{2}$ cubic inches
7. 357 cubic inches
9. 110.25 cubic inches
11. A: 120 in³; B: 960 in³; 8 times as great **13.** 58.5 cubic inches
15. $2\frac{47}{64}$ cubic feet
17. $\frac{1}{8}$ m; find a fraction that, when multiplied by itself 3 times, equals $\frac{1}{512}$ **19.** Both are correct.

LESSON 15.3

Your Turn
2. $\frac{5}{2}$ ft or $2\frac{1}{2}$ ft **3.** 1.5 feet

Guided Practice
1. 6,336 = 16(18)w; w = 22 cm
2. V = 72 in³; 4 inches

Independent Practice
3. 12.4 inches
5. 6 centimeters
7. Volume: 2,000 mm³; weight: 1 ounce **9.** 1 inch; 25%
11. 42.9; 4.3; 30.0.

UNIT 7 Selected Answers

MODULE 16

LESSON 16.1

Your Turn

3. median = 6.5 minutes

Guided Practice

1. 15; 5; 3; 3 **2a.** 42 **b.** No **3a.** mean: 8.5; median: 6 **b.** The median; sample answer: the median is closer to most of the data values than the mean is.

Independent Practice

5. Ten students were asked, because there are 10 data values in the list. **7.** 78.5; 80.5 **9.** Minutes and hours; convert all times to minutes. **11.** Median; it is closer to most of the data values; the data value for 1 hr (60 min) raises the mean. **13.** 95

LESSON 16.2

Your Turn

2. The MAD for Waiter A is 0.6 oz, and for Waiter B is 0.2 oz, so Barista B's smoothies showed less variability. **3.** A: MAD ≈ 0.0017; B: MAD ≈ 0.0063; A has less variability.

Guided Practice

1. did
a. 45.1 min
b. 0.4 min
2. 44.9; 0.733333; did not

Independent Practice

5. 1.6 people
7. The MAD at the beginning was about 3.7, and at the end it was about 2.1, so they made progress.
9. The mean for Austin is 31.855 in., and for San Antonio is 30.459 in.; Austin.
13a. mean = 1, MAD = 0; Because 1 is the only data value, it is the

mean of the data set and does not deviate from the mean.
b. mean = 1.5, MAD = 0.5; 1 + 2 = 3, and 3 ÷ 2 = 1.5. Also, both 1 and 2 are 0.5 away from 1.5.
c. Increase; the values are getting larger, so the mean increases, and they are getting more spread out, so the MAD increases.

LESSON 16.3

Your Turn

3. Group A IQR = $700. Group B IQR = $450. Group A's IQR is greater, so the salaries in the middle 50% for group A are more spread out than those for group B.
4. Miami = 15, Chicago = 53; Chicago

Guided Practice

1. 4; 10; 11; 13; 14; 15; 25; 29; 33; 33; 35; 43; 51; 58; 64 **2.** 29 **3.** 13
4. 43 **6.** 30 **7.** 60

Independent Practice

11. Sample answer: Students could have measured each others' heights. **13.** 0.3; 0.3 **15.** The IQRs are the same. The spreads of the middle 50% of the data values are the same for the two data sets. **17.** Yes

LESSON 16.4

Your Turn

4. 14 games; the value with the greatest frequency is 4; there were 4 games in which the team scored 4 runs. **5.** spread: 0 to 11. 11 appears to be an outlier. The data has a cluster from 0 to 7 with one peak at 2. The distribution is not symmetric because the data is not clustered around the center of the distribution. **6.** Mean: about 3.3, median: 3.5, range: 5; sample

answer: between 3 and 4 runs. The mean and median are close in value, and there are no outliers.

Guided Practice

1. Variable data **3.** Mean: about 5.2; median = 5; range = 17.
4. spread: 0 to 17. 17 appears to be an outlier. The distribution is not symmetric.

Independent Practice

7. not statistical **9.** not statistical
11.

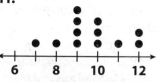

Days of Precipitation

15. The mean would change to about 9.3; the median would stay at 9.5; the range would change to 9 days. **19.** 5(2) + 6(2) + 7 + 8(3) + 9(2) + 10(5) + 11 + 12(3) + 13(2) + 15(2) + 22
21. Count the number of dots above a data value. **23.** 19; Each dot represents one game. **25.** Mean: about 3.9 runs; median: 4 runs; range: 11 runs **27a.** the units for the ages (years, months, weeks) **b.** No

LESSON 16.5

Your Turn

4.

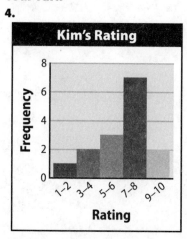

5. Sample answer: Kim gave ratings of 7 or 8 to 7 of 15 movies. She gave ratings of 9 or 10 to 2 of 15 movies.

Guided Practice

1.

Interval	Frequency
0–9	4
10–19	3
20–29	9
30–39	5

2. 1; 3; 4; 2

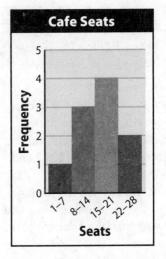

3. Sample answer: Only one cafe has less than 7 seats available. The bars increase in height until they reach the interval for 15–21 seats, and then they decrease in height, showing that most cafes have 21 or fewer seats.

5.

Interval	Frequency
10–19	9
20–29	7
30–39	3
40–49	4
50–59	2

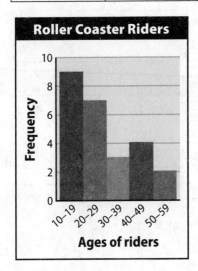

7a. 6 **b.** 3 bars; 9
c. box plot, dot plot

9. a.

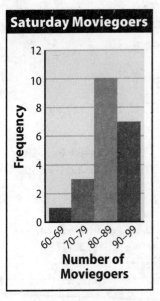

UNIT 8 Selected Answers

MODULE 17

LESSON 17.1

Your Turn

6. −9 **7.** −10 **8.** −60 **9.** −70 **10.** 300 **11.** −145 **12.** −1,650 **13.** −1,000

Guided Practice

1a. 6 **b.** negative **c.** −6 **2a.** 9 **b.** negative **c.** −9 **3.** −7

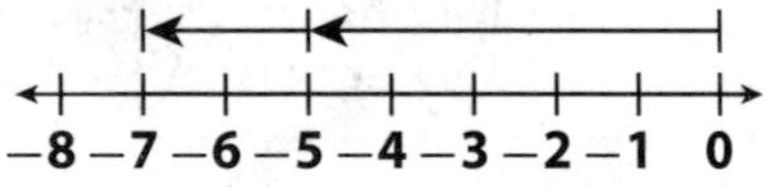

4. −4

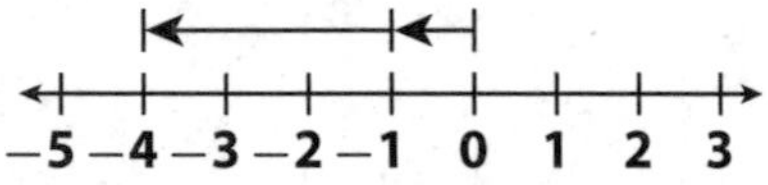

5. −7

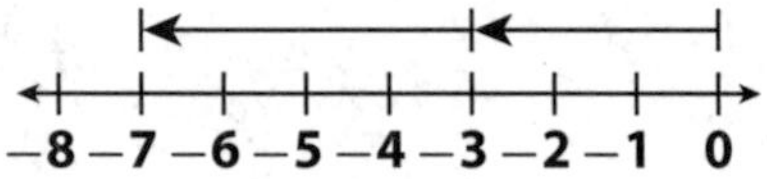

6. −5

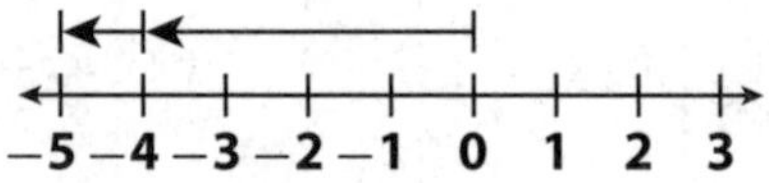

7. −4

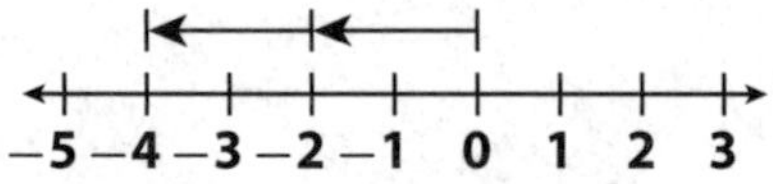

8. −14

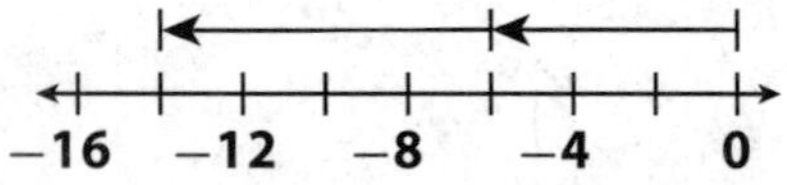

9. −9 **10.** −11 **11.** −10 **12.** −110 **13.** −100 **14.** 203 **15.** −15 **16.** −570

Independent Practice

19. −11 **21.** −54 yards **23.** $-100 + (-75) + (-85) = -260$

LESSON 17.2

Your Turn

3. 4 **4.** −2 **5.** −6 **6.** −1 **7.** −28 **8.** −8 **9.** 0 **10.** −1

Guided Practice

1. 2

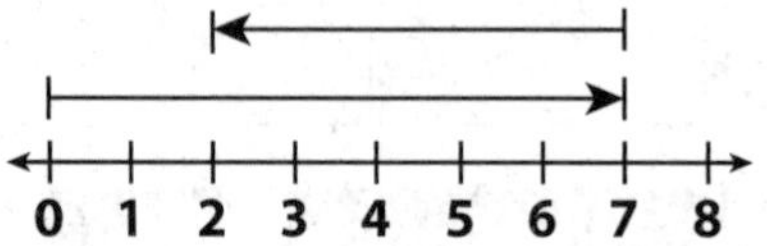

2. 5

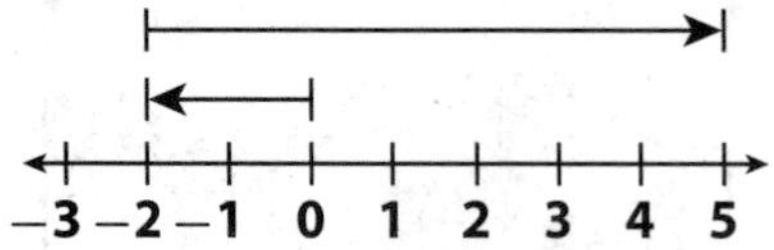

3. −5

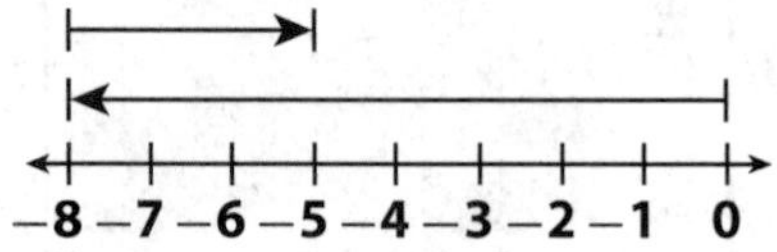

4. −3

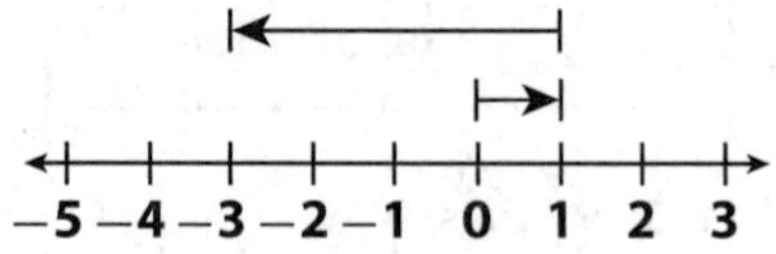

5. 1 **6.** 0 **7.** −3 **8.** 4 **9.** 6 **10.** 2 **11.** −16 **12.** 0 **13.** −5 **14.** 24

Independent Practice

17. −8 **19.** 25 **21.** −95 **23.** −7 **25.** 100 **27.** $-55 + 275 = 220$. The team's profit was $220.

LESSON 17.3

Your Turn

4. −9 **5.** 2 **6.** −2 **7.** −4

Guided Practice

1. −3 **2.** −2 **3.** (−5); −9 **4.** (−4); −3 **5.** −3 **6.** 2 **7.** −6 **8.** −18 **9.** 5 **10.** 19 **11.** 14 **12.** 42 **13.** 38 **14.** 0

Independent Practice

17. $-127 - (-225) = 98$ feet **19.** −150 points **21.** Diet Chow **25.** −16, −21, −26

LESSON 17.4

Your Turn

1. $-40 - 13 + 18$; −35; 35 feet below the cave entrance **3.** $-35 + (-45) + 180 = 100$; $100 increase **4.** Jim

Guided Practice

1. $-15 + 9 - 12 = -18$; 18 feet below sea level **2.** $-23 + 5 - 7 = -25$; −25 °F **3.** $50 - 40 + 87 - 30 = 67$ **4.** 24 **5.** −12 **6.** 18 **7.** 21 **8.** 97 **9.** 27 **10.** $(-12 + 6 - 4) < (-34 - 3 + 39)$ **11.** $(21 - 3 + 8) > (-14 + 31 - 6)$

Independent Practice

13a. $5 - 1 + 6 - 1 = 9$ **b.** over par **c.** yes **15.** The Commutative Property does not apply to subtraction. $3 - 6 + 5 = 2$ and $3 - 5 + 6 = 4$ **17a.** 3:00 to 4:00 **b.** 87 **19.** $24 **23.** The sum of the other two numbers must be greater than the value of the first number.

MODULE 18

LESSON 18.1

Your Turn

4. −15 **5.** 20 **6.** −42 **7.** 0 **8.** 45 **9.** 32

Guided Practice

1. −9 **2.** −28 **3.** 54 **4.** −100 **5.** −60 **6.** 0 **7.** 49 **8.** −135 **9.** −96 **10.** 300 **11.** 0 **12.** −192 **13.** $7(-75) = -525$; −$525 **14.** Show 3(−5) on a number line as $(-5) + (-5) + (-5)$; $3(-5) = -15$; −15 yards; the team lost 15 yards. **15.** $6(-2) = -12$; −12 °F **16.** $4(-5) = -20$; −$20; the share price decreased by $20 in 4 days. **17.** $5(-50) = -250$; −250 feet

Independent Practice

19. No **21.** 5(−4) = −20; $20 decrease **23.** 7(−6) = −42; the cost of the jeans decreased by $42 over the 7 weeks. **25.** 7(−8) = −56; 7(−5) = −35; −56 + (−35) = −91. The savings decreased by $91. **27a.** −27 **b.** 27 **c.** −27 **d.** −81 **e.** 81 **f.** −81 **g.** negative; positive

LESSON 18.2

Your Turn

2. 0 **3.** −2 **4.** 13 **5.** Yolanda received the same number of penalties in each game, 5; −25 ÷ (−5) = 5 and −35 ÷ (−7) = 5.

Guided Practice

1. −7 **2.** −7 **3.** −2 **4.** 0 **5.** 9 **6.** −3 **7.** 11 **8.** 1 **9.** 0 **10.** 11 **11.** −12 **12.** −20 **13.** undefined **14.** 3 **15.** −40 ÷ (4) = −10; $10 **16.** −22 ÷ (11) = −2; 2 points **17.** −75 ÷ (−15) = 5; 5 targets **18.** −99 ÷ (−9) = 11; 11 times

Independent Practice

21. Elisa; Elisa made −140 ÷ (−20) = 7 withdrawals; Francis made −270 ÷ (−45) = 6 withdrawals, and 7 > 6. **23.** the first part **27.** False; division by 0 is undefined for any dividend. **29.** 12

LESSON 18.3

Your Turn

1. Reggie earned 110 points; 3(−30) + 200 = −90 + 200 = 110. **2.** −78 − 21 = −99 **4.** 0 **5.** 20 **6.** 22 **7.** −28 **8.** Will **9.** −7; −6; (−28) ÷ 4 + 1 **10.** −5; −6; 42 ÷ (−3) + 9

Guided Practice

1. 42 **2.** −21 **3.** −9 **4.** −32 **5.** −4 **6.** −1 **7.** 7(−5) + 20 = −15; 15 dollars less **8.** 7(−10) + (−100) = −170; 170 fewer points **9.** 6(−4) + 10 = −14; lost 14 points **10.** 4(−12) + 10 = −38;

$38 less **11.** > **12.** = **13.** > **14.** <

Independent Practice

17. 4 **19.** 0 **21.** 2 **23.** 5(−4) − 8 = −28 **25a.** 4(−35) − 9 = −149; $149 less **b.** Yes **29.** 80 inches

LESSON 19.1

Your Turn

4. 0.571428… **5.** 0.333… **6.** 0.45 **7.** 2.75; terminating decimal **8.** 7.333…; repeating decimal

Guided Practice

1. 0.6; terminating **2.** 0.89; terminating **3.** 0.333…; repeating **4.** 0.2525…; repeating **5.** 0.7777…; repeating **6.** 0.36; terminating **7.** 0.04; terminating **8.** 0.14204545…; repeating **9.** 0.012; terminating **10.** 11.166… **11.** 2.9 **12.** 8.23 **13.** 7.2 **14.** 54.2727… **15.** 3.0555… **16.** 3.666… **17.** 12.875

Independent Practice

19. $\frac{5}{11}$; 0.4545…; repeating **21.** $\frac{4}{11}$; 0.3636…; repeating **23.** $\frac{11}{11}$; 1; terminating **25a.** $\frac{39}{8}$ **b.** 4.875 **27.** Ben is taller because 5.3125 > 5.2916…. **29.** When the denominator is 3, 6, 7, or 9, the result will be a repeating decimal. **31.** No; although the digits follow a pattern, the same combination of digits do not repeat.

LESSON 19.2

Your Turn

2. $4\frac{1}{2}$

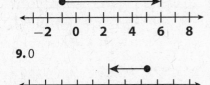

3. −7

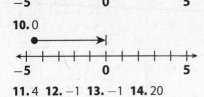

---

6. −3

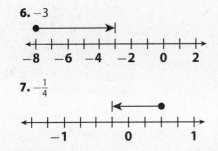

7. $-\frac{1}{4}$

8. 6

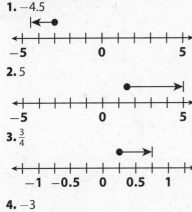

9. 0

10. 0

11. 4 **12.** −1 **13.** −1 **14.** 20

Guided Practice

1. −4.5

2. 5

3. $\frac{3}{4}$

4. −3

5. −2

6. 2.5

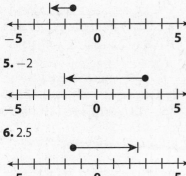

7. $0 **8.** $0 **9.** −4.5 **10.** 1 **11.** −2.2 **12.** 9 **13.** −12 **14.** $-\frac{1}{2}$ **15.** $-2\frac{1}{2}$ **16.** $-9\frac{1}{8}$

Independent Practice

19. $12.75 **21.** $1\frac{1}{2}$ miles **23.** $30 + 15 + (-25) = 20$; the final score is 20 points **25.** June: $306.77, July: $301.50, Aug: $337.88 **27.** opposite or additive inverse

LESSON 19.3

Your Turn

1. -8.5

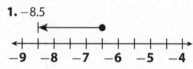

2. $-\frac{1}{2}$

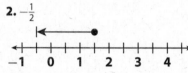

3. -7.75

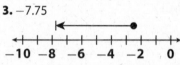

6. 1.75

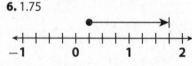

7. $\frac{1}{4}$

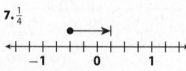

Guided Practice

1. 13

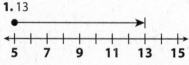

2. -8

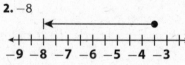

3. -11

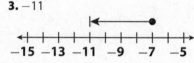

4. -4

5. -36 **6.** -7.7 **7.** 1 **8.** 79
9. $2\frac{7}{9}$ **10.** $78\frac{1}{2}$ **11.** 1.5 meters
12. $17\frac{1}{2}$ yard loss **13.** 543 feet
14. $|-7 - 5|$, or $|5 - (-7)|$; 12

Independent Practice

17. $-25.65 - 16.5 + 12.45$; -29.7 ft; the diver is 29.7 ft below the surface. **19a.** $-\$43.30$
b. $-\$68.30$ **c.** $\$68.30$
21. 65,233 ft; 96,000 ft; 96,000 ft (Mars); 30,767 ft
23a. $5 - 7.2 + 2.2$ **b.** He is exactly where he started because $5 - 7.2 + 2.2 = 0$.

LESSON 19.4

Your Turn

1. -7

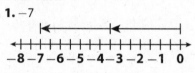

2. 3.75

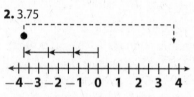

4. $-\frac{2}{7}$ **5.** $\frac{2}{5}$ **6.** $-\frac{1}{2}$

Guided Practice

1. $-3\frac{1}{3}$

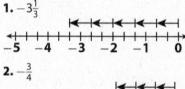

2. $-\frac{3}{4}$

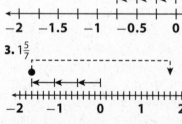

3. $1\frac{5}{7}$

4. 3

5. -12 **6.** -9 **7.** 6.8 **8.** 4.32
9. 6 **10.** -7.2 **11.** $\frac{1}{3}, \frac{1}{4}$ **12.** $\frac{12}{35}, -\frac{4}{5}$
13. $-\frac{5}{12}$ **14.** $\frac{2}{7}$ **15.** $4(-3.50) = -14$; The share price decreased by $14.
16. $18(-100) = -1,800$; The money in the ATM decreased by $1,800.

Independent Practice

21. The submarine would be 975 feet below sea level, or -975 feet. **25.** 13.5 points

LESSON 19.5

Your Turn

3. -0.7 **4.** 16.6 **5.** -11
6. -3.8 feet per minute **7.** $\frac{35}{48}$
8. $-\frac{5}{8}$ **9.** $-1\frac{3}{5}$

Guided Practice

1. -0.8 **2.** $-\frac{1}{7}$ **3.** -8 **4.** $-\frac{502}{3}$
5. -375 **6.** 7 **7.** $-\frac{4}{21}$ **8.** -400
9. -0.875 liter per day
10. $-45.75 \div 5 = -9.15$; $-\$9.15$ per day, on average **11.** -0.55 mile per minute

Independent Practice

13. -20 **15.** 20 **17.** -0.1
19. $\frac{5}{9}$ **21.** 4.5 **23.** $-1\frac{3}{4}$ yards
25a. $250 per day **b.** $1,050 per day **c.** $-\$70$ **31.** Yes, since an integer divided by an integer is a ratio of two integers and the denominator is not zero, the number is rational by definition.

LESSON 19.6

Your Turn

1. $5\frac{5}{8}$ min **2.** 12 batches; $0.29 per batch **3.** $1,070.72

Guided Practice

1. Step 1: $3\frac{1}{5}$ or 3.2 mi/h, 14.4 mi; Step 2: 14.4 mi, $3\frac{3}{5}$ or 3.6 mi/h, 4 h
2. Step 1: 25.68 in., -0.02375 in, -0.61 in.; Step 2: 25.68 in., 0.61 in., 25.07 in.

Independent Practice

5. $4\frac{1}{4}$ in. **7.** $29\frac{1}{8}$ yd
9. 5 more; $88\% = \frac{88}{100} = \frac{44}{50}$
11. Yes, because the product is negative and about half of 1.5.
13. Sample answer: Yes; $-0.7343 \approx -0.75$ **15.** Sample answer: (1) Convert the fraction to a decimal and find the sum of 27.6 and 15.9, then multiply the result by 0.37. (2) Convert the fraction, then use the Distributive Property. Multiply both 27.6 and 15.9 by 0.37, then add the products. The first method; there are fewer steps and so fewer chances to make errors.

 **UNIT 9** Selected Answers

MODULE 20

LESSON 20.1

Your Turn

3. $\frac{1}{6} \div \frac{1}{4} = \frac{1}{6} \times \frac{4}{1} = \frac{4}{6} = \frac{2}{3}; \frac{2}{3}$ acre per hour **4.** 4 ounces **5.** Jaylon's unit rate is $3\frac{3}{4}$ cups of water per cup of lime juice. Wanchen's unit rate is 4 cups of water per cup of lime juice. Wanchen's limeade has a weaker lime flavor because $4 > 3\frac{3}{4}$ and the limeade with a greater ratio of water to lime juice will have a weaker flavor.

Guided Practice

2. $2\frac{4}{5}$ miles per hour **3.** $\frac{15}{16}$ page per minute **4.** $\frac{1}{2}$ foot per hour **5.** $2\frac{1}{2}$ square feet per hour **6.** Brand A: 720 mg/pickle, Brand B: 650 mg/pickle; Brand B **7.** C: $\frac{3}{8}$ cup/serving, D: $\frac{4}{9}$ cup/serving; Ingredient C

Independent Practice

9a. On Call: about $2.86 per hour; Talk Time: $2.50 per hour **b.** Talk Time; their rate per hour is lower. **c.** Multiply 0.05 times 60 because there are 60 minutes in 1 hour. **d.** The unit rate is $3 per hour, so it is not a better deal. **11.** $\frac{5 \text{ songs}}{1 \text{ commercial}}$ **13.** Faster; he typed 50 words per minute in his first attempt and 60 words per minute in his second attempt.

LESSON 20.2

Your Turn

3. No; the rates are not equal because her speed changed. **4.** Each rate is equal to $\frac{1 \text{ adult}}{12 \text{ students}}$. The relationship is proportional; $a = \frac{1}{12}s$.

Guided Practice

1. 8; $\frac{49}{7} = 7; \frac{52}{8} = 6.5; \frac{54}{9} = 6$; the relationship is not proportional.

2. $k = 5$; $y = 5x$ **3.** $k = \frac{1}{4}$; $y = \frac{1}{4}x$

Independent Practice

5. $y = 18.50x$ **7.** Rent—All has the best deal because it has the lowest rate per day ($18.50). **9.** The rates have the same unit rate, $6.25 per hour. **11.** x is the number of hours Steven babysits, and y is the amount he charges; the equation is $y = 6.25x$. **13.** 150 feet per minute; 9,000 feet per hour **15.** Feet per minute

LESSON 20.3

Your Turn

1. No; A line drawn through the points does not go through the origin.

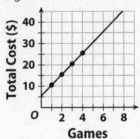

5a. The bicyclist rides 60 miles in 4 hours. **b.** 15 **c.** $y = 15x$

Guided Practice

1. proportional; pages is always 65 times the number of hours; 65 pages/hour. **2.** proportional; earnings are always 7.5 times the number of hours; $7.50/hour. **3.** not proportional; the line will not pass through the origin. **4.** proportional; the line will pass through the origin. **5.** $y = 3.5x$ **6.** $y = \frac{1}{4}x$

Independent Practice

9. Horse A takes about 4 minutes. Horse B takes about 2.5 minutes. **11.** Horse A: $y = 3$ miles; Horse B: $y = 4\frac{4}{5}$ miles **13.** Yes; A graph of miles traveled compared to number of hours will

form a line that passes through the origin.

15a.

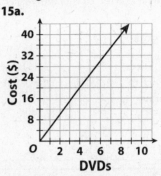

b. Sample answer: (4, 20); 4 DVDs cost $20. **17.** Yes. The graph is a line that passes through the origin. **21.** If the values in the "Time" column are the same, each value in the "Distance" column for Car 4 will be twice the corresponding value for Car 2.

MODULE 21

LESSON 21.1

Your Turn

2. 23% **4.** 33% **5.** 37.5% **8.** $548.90 **9.** $349.30

Guided Practice

1. 60% **2.** 50% **3.** 74% **4.** 11% **5.** 8% **6.** 220% **7.** 78% **8.** 20% **9.** 28% **10.** 50% **11.** 9% **12.** 67% **13.** 100% **14.** 83% **15.** $9.90 **16.** 36 cookies **17.** 272 pages **18.** 42 members **19.** $27,840 **20.** 1,863 songs **21.** 26 miles

Independent Practice

25a. Amount of change = 1; percent decrease = $\frac{1}{5}$ = 20% **27a.** They have the same. $1,000 + $100 = $1,100 and $1,000 + 10\%($1,000) = $1,100. **b.** Sylvia has more. Leroi has $1,100 + $100 = $1,200, and Sylvia has $1,100 + 10\%($1,100) = $1,210.

29. No. The first withdrawal is $60. Each withdrawal after that is less than $60 because it is 10% of the remaining balance. There will be money left after 10 withdrawals.

LESSON 21.2

Your Turn

2a. $1c + 0.1c$; $1.1c$ **b.** $30.80
3a. 200% **b.** $1c + 2c$; $3c$
5a.

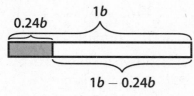

b. $0.76b$ **6a.** $1p - 0.05p$, $0.95p$
b. $14.25

Guided Practice

1a. $0.35s$ **b.** $1s + 0.35s$ or $1.35s$
c. $43.20 **d.** $11.20 **2.** $2.70;
$20.70 **3.** $9.45; $31.95 **4.** $25.31;
$59.06 **5.** $24.75; $99.74 **6.** $48.60;
$97.20 **7.** $231.25; $416.25 **8.** $35.10
9. $59.63 **10.** $13.43 **11.** $70.00

Independent Practice

13a. $0.46b$ **b.** $1b - 0.46b$ or $0.54b$
c. $15.66 **d.** $13.34 **17.** Either buy 3, get one free or $\frac{1}{4}$ off. Either case would result in a discount of 25%, which is better than 20%.
19. No; first change: 20.1% decrease; second change: 25.1% increase. The second percent change is greater.

LESSON 21.3

Your Turn

1. $1; $21 **3.** $4,262; total $=$ $3,300 + 0.0325(29,600) = 3,300 + 962 = 4,262$ **5.** $34.13

Guided Practice

1. $1.50 **2.** $10.50 **3.** $0.40 **4.** $33
5. $0.80 **6.** $10 **7a.** $3.08 **b.** $47.07
8. $120 **9.** $700 **10.** $530.50
11a. $18 **b.** $19.53 **12.** $37.86

Independent Practice

15. $82.58 **17.** $75.14 **19.** $4,500
21a. Multiply Sandra's height by 0.10 and add the product to 4 to get Pablo's height. Then multiply Pablo's height by 0.08 and add the product to Pablo's height to get Michaela's height. **b.** about 4 feet 9 inches **23a.** $101.49
b. $109.39 **c.** Digital camera; he can save $8. **d.** $109.61

Glossary/Glosario

ENGLISH	SPANISH	EXAMPLES
absolute value The distance of a number from zero on a number line; shown by | |.	**valor absoluto** Distancia a la que está un número de 0 en una recta numérica. El símbolo del valor absoluto es | |.	$\|-5\| = 5$
acute angle An angle that measures greater than 0° and less than 90°.	**ángulo agudo** Ángulo que mide más do 0° y menos de 90°.	
acute triangle A triangle with all angles measuring less than 90°.	**triángulo acutángulo** Triángulo en el que todos los ángulos miden menos de 90°.	
addend A number added to one or more other numbers to form a sum.	**sumando** Número que se suma a uno o más números para formar una suma.	In the expression $4 + 6 + 7$, the numbers 4, 6, and 7 are addends.
Addition Property of Opposites The property that states that the sum of a number and its opposite equals zero.	**Propiedad de la suma de los opuestos** Propiedad que establece que la suma de un número y su opuesto es cero.	$12 + (-12) = 0$
additive inverse The opposite of a number.	**inverso aditivo** El opuesto de un número.	-4 is the additive inverse of 4.
adjacent angles Angles in the same plane that have a common vertex and a common side.	**ángulos adyacentes** Ángulos en el mismo plano que comparten un vértice y un lado.	$\angle 1$ and $\angle 2$ are adjacent angles.
algebraic expression An expression that contains at least one variable.	**expresión algebraica** Expresión que contiene al menos una variable.	$x + 8$ $4(m - b)$
algebraic inequality An inequality that contains at least one variable.	**desigualdad algebraica** Desigualdad que contiene al menos una variable.	$x + 3 > 10$ $5a > b + 3$
alternate exterior angles For two lines intersected by a transversal, a pair of angles that lie on opposite sides of the transversal and outside the other two lines.	**ángulos alternos externos** Dadas dos rectas cortadas por una transversal, par de ángulos no adyacentes ubicados en los lados opuestos de la transversal y fuera de las otras dos rectas.	$\angle 4$ and $\angle 5$ are alternate exterior angles.

alternate interior angles For two lines intersected by a transversal, a pair of nonadjacent angles that lie on opposite sides of the transversal and between the other two lines.

ángulos alternos internos Dadas dos rectas cortadas por una transversal, par de ángulos no adyacentes ubicados en los lados opuestos de la transversal y entre las otras dos rectas.

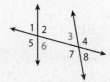

∠3 and ∠6 are alternate interior angles.

angle A figure formed by two rays with a common endpoint called the vertex.

ángulo Figura formada por dos rayos con un extremo común llamado vértice.

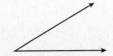

area The number of square units needed to cover a given surface.

área El número de unidades cuadradas que se necesitan para cubrir una superficie dada.

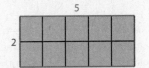

The area is 10 square units.

arithmetic sequence A sequence in which the terms change by the same amount each time.

sucesión aritmética Una sucesión en la que los términos cambian la misma cantidad cada vez.

The sequence 2, 5, 8, 11, 14 . . . is an arthmetic sequence.

Associative Property of Addition The property that states that for three or more numbers, their sum is always the same, regardless of their grouping.

Propiedad asociativa de la suma Propiedad que establece que agrupar tres o más números en cualquier orden siempre da como resultado la misma suma.

$2 + 3 + 8 = (2 + 3) + 8 = 2 + (3 + 8)$

Associative Property of Multiplication The property that states that for three or more numbers, their product is always the same, regardless of their grouping.

Propiedad asociativa de la multiplicación Propiedad que establece que agrupar tres o más números en cualquier orden siempre da como resultado el mismo producto.

$2 \cdot 3 \cdot 8 = (2 \cdot 3) \cdot 8 = 2 \cdot (3 \cdot 8)$

asymmetrical Not identical on either side of a central line; not symmetrical.

asimétrico Que no es idéntico a ambos lados de una línea central; no simétrico.

average The sum of the items in a set of data divided by the number of items in the set; also called *mean*.

promedio La suma de los elementos de un conjunto de datos dividida entre el número de elementos del conjunto. También se le llama *media*.

Data set: 4, 6, 7, 8, 10

Average: $\frac{4 + 6 + 7 + 8 + 10}{5} =$ $\frac{35}{5} = 7$

axes The two perpendicular lines of a coordinate plane that intersect at the origin. singular: axis

ejes Las dos rectas numéricas perpendiculares del plano cartesiano que se intersecan en el origen.

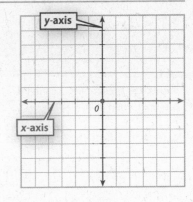

Glossary/Glosario

B

bar graph A graph that uses vertical or horizontal bars to display data.

gráfica de barras Gráfica en la que se usan barras verticales u horizontales para presentar datos.

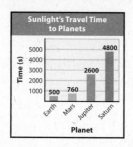

base (in numeration) When a number is raised to a power, the number that is used as a factor is the base.

base (en numeración) Cuando un número es elevado a una potencia, el número que se usa como factor es la base.

$3^5 = 3 \cdot 3 \cdot 3 \cdot 3 \cdot 3$; 3 is the base.

base (of a polygon or three-dimensional figure) A side of a polygon; a face of a three-dimensional figure by which the figure is measured or classified.

base (de un polígono o figura tridimensional) Lado de un polígono; la cara de una figura tridimensional, a partir de la cual se mide o se clasifica la figura.

bases of   bases of
a cylinder   a prism

base of   base of
a cone   a pyramid

bisect To divide into two congruent parts.

trazar una bisectriz Dividir en dos partes congruentes.

box plot A graph that shows how data are distributed by using the median, quartiles, least value, and greatest value; also called a box-and-whisker plot.

gráfica de caja Gráfica para demostrar la distribución de datos utilizando la mediana, los cuartiles y los valores menos y más grande; también llamado gráfica de mediana y rango.

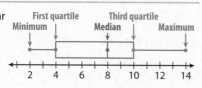

break (graph) A zigzag on a horizontal or vertical scale of a graph that indicates that some of the numbers on the scale have been omitted.

discontinuidad (gráfica) Zig-zag en la escala horizontal o vertical de una gráfica que indica la omisión de algunos de los números de la escala.

C

capacity The amount a container can hold when filled.

capacidad Cantidad que cabe en un recipiente cuando se llena.

categorical data Data that consists of nonnumeric information.

datos categóricos Datos que constan de información no numérica.

Glossary/Glosario

Celsius A metric scale for measuring temperature in which 0°C is the freezing point of water and 100°C is the boiling point of water; also called *centigrade*.

Celsius Escala métrica para medir la temperatura, en la que 0° C es el punto de congelación del agua y 100° C es el punto de ebullición. También se llama *centígrado*.

center (of a circle) The point inside a circle that is the same distance from all the points on the circle.

centro (de un círculo) Punto interior de un círculo que se encuentra a la misma distancia de todos los puntos de la circunferencia.

center (of rotation) The point about which a figure is rotated.

centro (de una rotación) Punto alrededor del cual se hace girar una figura.

checking account An account at a financial institution that allows for withdrawals and deposits.

cuenta corriente Una cuenta en una institución financiera que permite para retiros y depósitos.

chord A line segment whose endpoints lie on a circle.

cuerda Segmento cuyos extremos se encuentran en un círculo.

circle The set of all points in a plane that are the same distance from a given point called the center.

círculo Conjunto de todos los puntos en un plano que se encuentran a la misma distancia de un punto dado llamado centro.

circle graph A graph that uses sections of a circle to compare parts to the whole and parts to other parts.

gráfica circular Gráfica que usa secciones de un círculo para comparar partes con el todo y con otras partes.

circumference The distance around a circle.

circunferencia Distancia alrededor de un círculo.

clockwise A circular movement in the direction shown.

en el sentido de las manecillas del reloj Movimiento circular en la dirección que se indica.

Glossary/Glosario

ENGLISH	SPANISH	EXAMPLES
clustering A method used to estimate a sum when all addends are close to the same value.	**agrupación** Método que se usa para estimar una suma cuando todos los sumandos se aproximan al mismo valor.	27, 29, 24, and 23 all cluster around 25.
coefficient The number that is multiplied by the variable in an algebraic expression.	**coeficiente** Número que se multiplica por la variable en una expresión algebraica.	5 is the coefficient in $5b$.
combination An arrangement of items or events in which order does not matter.	**combinación** Agrupación de objetos o sucesos en la cual el orden no es importante.	For objects A, B, C, and D, there are 6 different combinations of 2 objects: AB, AC, AD, BC, BD, CD.
common denominator A denominator that is the same in two or more fractions.	**denominador común** Denominador que es común a dos o más fracciones.	The common denominator of $\frac{5}{8}$ and $\frac{2}{8}$ is 8.
common factor A number that is a factor of two or more numbers.	**factor común** Número que es factor de dos o más números.	8 is a common factor of 16 and 40.
common multiple A number that is a multiple of each of two or more numbers.	**múltiplo común** Un número que es múltiplo de dos o más números.	15 is a common multiple of 3 and 5.
Commutative Property of Addition The property that states that two or more numbers can be added in any order without changing the sum.	**Propiedad conmutativa de la suma** Propiedad que establece que sumar dos o más números en cualquier orden no altera la suma.	$8 + 20 = 20 + 8$
Commutative Property of Multiplication The property that states that two or more numbers can be multiplied in any order without changing the product.	**Propiedad conmutativa de la multiplicación** Propiedad que establece que multiplicar dos o más números en cualquier orden no altera el producto.	$6 \cdot 12 = 12 \cdot 6$
compatible numbers Numbers that are close to the given numbers that make estimation or mental calculation easier.	**números compatibles** Números que están cerca de los números dados y hacen más fácil la estimación o el cálculo mental.	To estimate $7{,}957 + 5{,}009$, use the compatible numbers 8,000 and 5,000: $8{,}000 + 5{,}000 = 13{,}000$.
compensation When a number in a problem is close to another number that is easier to calculate with, the easier number is used to find the answer. Then the answer is adjusted by adding to it or subtracting from it.	**compensación** Cuando un número de un problema está cerca de otro con el que es más fácil hacer cálculos, se usa el número más fácil para hallar la respuesta. Luego, se ajusta la respuesta sumando o restando.	
complement The set of all outcomes that are not the event.	**complemento** La serie de resultados que no están en el suceso.	When rolling a number cube, the complement of rolling a 3 is rolling a 1, 2, 4, 5, or 6.

ENGLISH	SPANISH	EXAMPLES
complementary angles Two angles whose measures add to 90°.	**ángulos complementarios** Dos ángulos cuyas medidas suman 90°.	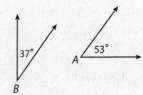 The complement of a 53° angle is a 37° angle.
complex fraction A fraction that contains one or more fractions in the numerator, the denominator, or both.	**fracción compleja** Fracción que contiene una o más fracciones en el numerador, en el denominador, o en ambos.	
composite number A number greater than 1 that has more than two whole-number factors.	**número compuesto** Número mayor que 1 que tiene más de dos factores que son números cabales.	4, 6, 8, and 9 are composite numbers.
compound inequality A combination of more than one inequality.	**desigualdad compuesta** Combinación de dos o más desigualdades.	$-2 \leq x < 10$
cone A three-dimensional figure with one vertex and one circular base.	**cono** Figura tridimensional con un vértice y una base circular.	
congruent Having the same size and shape.	**congruentes** Que tienen la misma forma y el mismo tamaño.	
congruent angles Angles that have the same measure.	**ángulos congruentes** Ángulos que tienen la misma medida.	m $\angle ABC$ = m $\angle DEF$
congruent figures Two figures whose corresponding sides and angles are congruent.	**figuras congruentes** Figuras que tienen el mismo tamaño y forma.	
congruent line segments Two line segments that have the same length.	**segmentos congruentes** Dos segmentos que tienen la misma longitud.	
conjecture A statement that is believed to be true.	**conjetura** Enunciado que se supone verdadero.	
constant A value that does not change.	**constante** Valor que no cambia.	$3, 0, \pi$

constant of proportionality A constant ratio of two variables related proportionally.

constante de proporcionalidad Razón constante de dos variables que están relacionadas en forma proporcional.

coordinate grid A grid formed by the intersection of horizontal and vertical lines that is used to locate points.

cuadrícula de coordenadas cuadrícula formada por la intersección de líneas horizontales y líneas verticales que se usan por localizar puntos.

coordinate plane A plane formed by the intersection of a horizontal number line called the *x*-axis and a vertical number line called the *y*-axis.

plano cartesiano Plano formado por la intersección de una recta numérica horizontal llamada eje *x* y otra vertical llamada eje *y*.

coordinates The numbers of an ordered pair that locate a point on a coordinate graph.

coordenadas Los números de un par ordenado que ubican un punto en una gráfica de coordenadas.

The coordinates of *B* are (−2, 3).

correspondence The relationship between two or more objects that are matched.

correspondencia La relación entre dos o más objetos que coinciden.

corresponding angles (for lines) Angles in the same position formed when a third line intersects two lines.

ángulos correspondientes (en líneas) Ángulos en la misma posición formados cuando una tercera línea interseca dos líneas.

∠1 and ∠3 are corresponding angles.

corresponding angles (in polygons) Angles in the same relative position in polygons with an equal number of sides.

ángulos correspondientes (en polígonos) Ángulos que se ubican en la misma posición relativa en polígonos que tienen el mismo número de lados.

∠*A* and ∠*D* are corresponding angles.

corresponding sides Sides in the same relative position in polygons with an equal number of sides.

lados correspondientes Lados que se ubican en la misma posición relativa en polígonos que tienen el mismo número de lados.

$\overline{AB}$ and $\overline{DE}$ are corresponding sides.

counterclockwise A circular movement in the direction shown.

en sentido contrario a las manecillas del reloj Movimiento circular en la dirección que se indica.

ENGLISH	SPANISH	EXAMPLES
credit card A plastic card issued by a financial company allowing a customer to buy goods or services on credit.	**tarjeta de crédito** Tarjeta de pago plástica que un cliente puede utilizar para comprar bienes o servicios. El cliente puede pagar por las compras a plazos, pero pagará intereses en el saldo restante.	
credit history Information about how a consumer has borrowed and repaid debt.	**historia crediticia** Información del buen manejo de dinero y pago de cuentas por parte de un cliente.	
credit report A report containing detailed information on a person's credit history.	**informe crediticio** Informe que recopilan las agencias acerca de la historia crediticia de un cliente y que ayuda a los prestamistas a decidir si dan dinero a crédito a los clientes.	
credit score A number based on information in a consumer's credit report that measures an individual's creditworthiness.	**calificación crediticia** Número basado en información de un informe crediticio de un cliente. Se usa para predecir la posibilidad de que una persona se retrase en hacer pagos o que no pague una deuda.	
cross product The product of numbers on the diagonal when comparing two ratios.	**producto cruzado** El producto de los números multiplicados en diagonal cuando se comparan dos razones.	For the proportion $\frac{2}{3} = \frac{4}{6}$, the cross products are $2 \cdot 6 = 12$ and $3 \cdot 4 = 12$.
cube (geometric figure) A rectangular prism with six congruent square faces.	**cubo (figura geométrica)** Prisma rectangular con seis caras cuadradas congruentes.	
cube (in numeration) A number raised to the third power.	**cubo (en numeración)** Número elevado a la tercera potencia.	$5^3 = 5 \cdot 5 \cdot 5 = 125$
cumulative frequency The frequency of all data values that are less than or equal to a given value.	**frecuencia acumulativa** Muestra el total acumulado de las frecuencias.	
customary system The measurement system often used in the United States.	**sistema usual de medidas** El sistema de medidas que se usa comúnmente en Estados Unidos.	inches, feet, miles, ounces, pounds, tons, cups, quarts, gallons
cylinder A three-dimensional figure with two parallel, congruent circular bases connected by a curved lateral surface.	**cilindro** Figura tridimensional con dos bases circulares paralelas y congruentes, unidas por una superficie lateral curva.	

debit card An electronic card issued by a financial institution that allows a customer to access their account to withdraw cash or pay for goods and services

tarjeta de débito Tarjeta de pago plástica que un cliente puede usar para pagar por bienes o servicios. El dinero se retira inmediatamente de la cuenta corriente o de ahorros del cliente.

---

degree The unit of measure for angles or temperature.

grado Unidad de medida para ángulos y temperaturas.

---

denominator The bottom number of a fraction that tells how many equal parts are in the whole.

denominador Número de abajo en una fracción que indica en cuántas partes iguales se divide el entero.

$$\frac{3}{4} \longleftarrow \text{denominator}$$

---

dependent events Events for which the outcome of one event affects the probability of the other.

sucesos dependientes Dos sucesos son dependientes si el resultado de uno afecta la probabilidad del otro.

A bag contains 3 red marbles and 2 blue marbles. Drawing a red marble and then drawing a blue marble without replacing the first marble is an example of dependent events.

---

dependent variable The output of a function; a variable whose value depends on the value of the input, or independent variable.

variable dependiente Salida de una función; variable cuyo valor depende del valor de la entrada, o variable independiente.

For $y = 2x + 1$, y is the dependent variable: input: x output: y.

---

diagonal A line segment that connects two nonadjacent vertices of a polygon.

diagonal Segmento de recta que une dos vértices no adyacentes de un polígono.

---

diameter A line segment that passes through the center of a circle and has endpoints on the circle, or the length of that segment.

diámetro Segmento de recta que pasa por el centro de un círculo y tiene sus extremos en la circunferencia, o bien la longitud de ese segmento.

---

difference The result when one number is subtracted from another.

diferencia El resultado de restar un número de otro.

---

dimension The length, width, or height of a figure.

dimensión Longitud, ancho o altura de una figura.

---

discount The amount by which the original price is reduced.

descuento Cantidad que se resta del precio original de un artículo.

Distributive Property The property that states if you multiply a sum by a number, you will get the same result if you multiply each addend by that number and then add the products.

Propiedad distributiva Propiedad que establece que, si multiplicas una suma por un número, obtendrás el mismo resultado que si multiplicas cada sumando por ese número y luego sumas los productos.

$5(20 + 1) = 5 \cdot 20 + 5 \cdot 1$

Glossary/Glosario

ENGLISH	SPANISH	EXAMPLES
dividend The number to be divided in a division problem.	**dividendo** Número que se divide en un problema de división.	In $8 \div 4 = 2$, 8 is the dividend.
divisible Can be divided by a number without leaving a remainder.	**divisible** Que se puede dividir entre un número sin dejar residuo.	18 is divisible by 3.
divisor The number you are dividing by in a division problem.	**divisor** El número entre el que se divide en un problema de división.	In $8 \div 4 = 2$, 4 is the divisor.
dot plot A visual display in which each piece of data is represented by a dot above a number line.	**diagrama de puntos** Despliegue visual en que cada dato se representa con un punto sobre una recta numérica.	
double-bar graph A bar graph that compares two related sets of data.	**gráfica de doble barra** Gráfica de barras que compara dos conjuntos de datos relacionados.	
double-line graph A graph that shows how two related sets of data change over time.	**gráfica de doble línea** Gráfica lineal que muestra cómo cambian con el tiempo dos conjuntos de datos relacionados.	

E

edge The line segment along which two faces of a polyhedron intersect.	**arista** Segmento de recta donde se intersecan dos caras de un poliedro.	Edge
elements The words, numbers, or objects in a set.	**elementos** Palabras, números u objetos que forman un conjunto.	Elements of A: 1, 2, 3, 4
empty set A set that has no elements.	**conjunto vacío** Un conjunto que no tiene elementos.	
endpoint A point at the end of a line segment or ray.	**extremo** Un punto ubicado al final de un segmento de recta o rayo.	
equally likely Outcomes that have the same probability.	**igualmente probables** Resultados que tienen la misma probabilidad de ocurrir.	When you toss a coin, the outcomes "heads" and "tails" are equally likely.

ENGLISH	SPANISH	EXAMPLES
equation A mathematical sentence that shows that two expressions are equivalent.	**ecuación** Enunciado matemático que indica que dos expresiones son equivalentes.	$x + 4 = 7$ $6 + 1 = 10 - 3$
equilateral triangle A triangle with three congruent sides.	**triángulo equilátero** Triángulo con tres lados congruentes.	
equivalent Having the same value.	**equivalentes** Que tienen el mismo valor.	
equivalent expression Equivalent expressions have the same value for all values of the variables.	**expresión equivalente** Las expresiones equivalentes tienen el mismo valor para todos los valores de las variables.	$4x + 5x$ and $9x$ are equivalent expressions.
equivalent fractions Fractions that name the same amount or part.	**fracciones equivalentes** Fracciones que representan la misma cantidad o parte.	$\frac{1}{2}$ and $\frac{2}{4}$ are equivalent fractions.
equivalent ratios Ratios that name the same comparison.	**razones equivalentes** Razones que representan la misma comparación.	$\frac{1}{2}$ and $\frac{2}{4}$ are equivalent ratios.
estimate (n) An answer that is close to the exact answer and is found by rounding or other methods.	**estimación** Una solución aproximada a la respuesta exacta que se halla mediante el redondeo u otros métodos.	
estimate (v) To find an answer close to the exact answer by rounding or other methods.	**estimar** Hallar una solución aproximada a la respuesta exacta mediante el redondeo u otros métodos.	
evaluate To find the value of a numerical or algebraic expression.	**evaluar** Hallar el valor de una expresión numérica o algebraica.	Evaluate $2x + 7$ for $x = 3$. $2x + 7$ $2(3) + 7$ $6 + 7$ 13
even number A whole number that is divisible by two.	**número par** Un número cabal que es divisible entre dos.	
event An outcome or set of outcomes of an experiment or situation.	**suceso** Un resultado o una serie de resultados de un experimento o una situación.	
expanded form A number written as the sum of the values of its digits.	**forma desarrollada** Número escrito como suma de los valores de sus dígitos.	236,536 written in expanded form is $200,000 + 30,000 + 6,000 + 500 + 30 + 6$.
experiment In probability, any activity based on chance.	**experimento** En probabilidad, cualquier actividad basada en la posibilidad.	Tossing a coin 10 times and noting the number of "heads"

Glossary/Glosario

ENGLISH	SPANISH	EXAMPLES
experimental probability The ratio of the number of times an event occurs to the total number of trials, or times that the activity is performed.	**probabilidad experimental** Razón del número de veces que ocurre un suceso al número total de pruebas o al número de veces que se realiza el experimento.	Kendra attempted 27 free throws and made 16 of them. Her experimental probability of making a free throw is $\frac{\text{number made}}{\text{number attempted}} = \frac{16}{27} \approx 0.59$.
exponent The number that indicates how many times the base is used as a factor.	**exponente** Número que indica cuántas veces se usa la base como factor.	$2^3 = 2 \cdot 2 \cdot 2 = 8$; 3 is the exponent.
exponential form A number is in exponential form when it is written with a base and an exponent.	**forma exponencial** Cuando se escribe un número con una base y un exponente, está en forma exponencial.	4^2 is the exponential form for $4 \cdot 4$.
expression A mathematical phrase that contains operations, numbers, and/or variables.	**expresión** Enunciado matemático que contiene operaciones, números y/o variables.	$6x + 1$

F

ENGLISH	SPANISH	EXAMPLES
face A flat surface of a polyhedron.	**cara** Lado plano de un poliedro.	
factor A number that is multiplied by another number to get a product.	**factor** Número que se multiplica por otro para hallar un producto.	7 is a factor of 21 since $7 \cdot 3 = 21$.
factor tree A diagram showing how a whole number breaks down into its prime factors.	**árbol de factores** Diagrama que muestra cómo se descompone un número cabal en sus factores primos.	12 / \\ 3 · 4 / \\ 2 · 2 $12 = 3 \cdot 2 \cdot 2$
Fahrenheit A temperature scale in which 32 °F is the freezing point of water and 212 °F is the boiling point of water.	**Fahrenheit** Escala de temperatura en la que 32 °F es el punto de congelación del agua y 212 °F es el punto de ebullición.	
fair When all outcomes of an experiment are equally likely, the experiment is said to be fair.	**justo** Se dice de un experimento donde todos los resultados posibles son igualmente probables.	When tossing a fair coin, heads and tails are equally likely. Each has a probability of $\frac{1}{2}$.
formula A rule showing relationships among quantities.	**fórmula** Regla que muestra relaciones entre cantidades.	$A = \ell w$ is the formula for the area of a rectangle.
fraction A number in the form $\frac{a}{b}$, where $b \neq 0$.	**fracción** Número escrito en la forma $\frac{a}{b}$, donde $b \neq 0$.	
frequency The number of times a data value occurs.	**frecuencia** Cantidad de veces que aparece el valor en un conjunto de datos.	In the data set 5, 6, 7, 8, 6, the data value 6 has a frequency of 2.

frequency table A table that lists items together according to the number of times, or frequency, that the items occur.

tabla de frecuencia Una tabla en la que se organizan los datos de acuerdo con el número de veces que aparece cada valor (o la frecuencia).

Data set: 1, 1, 2, 2, 3, 4, 5, 5, 5, 6, 6
Frequency table:

Date	Frequency
1	2
2	2
3	1
4	1
5	3
6	2

front-end estimation An estimating technique in which the front digits of the addends are added.

estimación por partes Técnica en la que se suman sólo los números enteros de los sumandos y luego se ajusta la suma para tener una estimación mas exacta.

Estimate $25.05 + 14.671$ with the sum $25 + 14 = 39$. The actual value is 39 or greater.

function An input-output relationship that has exactly one output for each input.

función Relación de entrada-salida en la que a cada valor de entrada corresponde un valor de salida.

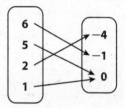

function table A table of ordered pairs that represent solutions of a function.

tabla de funciónes Tabla de pares ordenados que representan soluciones de una función.

x	3	4	5	6
y	7	9	11	13

grants Money awarded to students that does not need to be repaid.

beca Dinero que se otorga a estudiantes y el cual no se necesita devolver.

graph of an equation A graph of the set of ordered pairs that are solutions of the equation.

gráfica de una ecuación Gráfica del conjunto de pares ordenados que son soluciones de la ecuación.

greatest common factor (GCF) The largest common factor of two or more given numbers.

máximo común divisor (MCD) El mayor de los factores comunes compartidos por dos o más números dados.

The GCF of 27 and 45 is 9.

height In a triangle or quadrilateral, the perpendicular distance from the base to the opposite vertex or side. In a prism or cylinder, the perpendicular distance between the bases.

altura En un triángulo o cuadrilátero, la distancia perpendicular desde la base de la figura al vértice o lado opuesto. En un prisma o cilindro, la distancia perpendicular entre las bases.

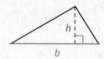

ENGLISH	SPANISH	EXAMPLES
heptagon A seven-sided polygon.	**heptágono** Polígono de siete lados.	
hexagon A six-sided polygon.	**hexágono** Polígono de seis lados.	
histogram A bar graph that shows the frequency of data within equal intervals.	**histograma** Gráfica de barras que muestra la frecuencia de los datos en intervalos iguales.	
hypotenuse In a right triangle, the side opposite the right angle.	**hipotenusa** En un triángulo rectángulo, el lado opuesto al ángulo recto.	

I

Identity Property of Addition The property that states the sum of zero and any number is that number.	**Propiedad de identidad de la suma** Propiedad que establece que la suma de cero y cualquier número es ese número.	$7 + 0 = 7$ $-9 + 0 = -9$
Identity Property of Multiplication The property that states that the product of 1 and any number is that number.	**Propiedad de identidad de la multiplicación** Propiedad que establece que el producto de 1 y cualquier número es ese número.	$5 \times 1 = 5$ $-8 \times 1 = -8$
improper fraction A fraction in which the numerator is greater than or equal to the denominator.	**fracción impropia** Fracción cuyo numerador es mayor que o igual al denominador.	$\frac{5}{5}$ $\frac{7}{3}$
independent variable The input of a function; a variable whose value determines the value of the output, or dependent variable.	**variable independiente** Entrada de una función; variable cuyo valor determina el valor de la salida, o variable dependiente.	For $y = 2x + 1$, x is the dependent variable. Input: x output: y
indirect measurement The technique of using similar figures and proportions to find a measure.	**medición indirecta** La técnica de usar figuras semejantes y proporciones para hallar una medida.	
inequality A mathematical sentence that shows the relationship between quantities that are not equal.	**desigualdad** Enunciado matemático que muestra una relación entre cantidades que no son iguales.	$5 < 8$ $5x + 2 \geq 12$

ENGLISH	SPANISH	EXAMPLES
input The value substituted into an expression or function.	**valor de entrada** Valor que se usa para sustituir una variable en una expresión o función.	For the rule $y = 6x$, the input 4 produces an output of 24.
integer A member of the set of whole numbers and their opposites.	**entero** Un miembro del conjunto de los números cabales y sus opuestos.	$\ldots -3, -2, -1, 0, 1, 2, 3, \ldots$
interest The amount of money charged for borrowing or using money, or the amount of money earned by saving money.	**interés** Cantidad de dinero que se cobra por el préstamo o uso del dinero, o la cantidad que se gana al ahorrar dinero.	
interquartile range (IQR) The difference of the third (upper) and first (lower) quartiles in a data set, representing the middle half of the data.	**rango intercuartil (RIC)** Diferencia entre el tercer cuartil (superior) y el primer cuartil (inferior) de un conjunto de datos, que representa la mitad central de los datos.	Lower half Upper half 18, (23,) 28, 29, (36,) 42 First quartile Third quartile Interquartile range: $36 - 23 = 13$
intersecting lines Lines that cross at exactly one point.	**rectas secantes** Líneas que se cruzan en un solo punto.	m n
intersection (sets) The set of elements common to two or more sets.	**intersección (de conjuntos)** Conjunto de elementos comunes a dos o más conjuntos.	
interval The space between marked values on a number line or the scale of a graph.	**intervalo** El espacio entre los valores marcados en una recta numérica o en la escala de una gráfica.	
inverse operations Operations that undo each other: addition and subtraction, or multiplication and division.	**operaciones inversas** Operaciones que se cancelan mutuamente: suma y resta, o multiplicación y división.	
isosceles triangle A triangle with at least two congruent sides.	**triángulo isósceles** Triángulo que tiene al menos dos lados congruentes.	

L

lateral surface In a cylinder, the curved surface connecting the circular bases; in a cone, the curved surface that is not a base.	**superficie lateral** En un cilindro, superficie curva que une las bases circulares; en un cono, la superficie curva que no es la base.	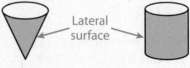 Lateral surface
least common denominator (LCD) The least common multiple of two or more denominators.	**mínimo común denominador (m.c.d.)** El mínimo común múltiplo de dos o más denominadores.	The LCD of $\frac{3}{4}$ and $\frac{5}{6}$ is 12.

ENGLISH	SPANISH	EXAMPLES
least common multiple (LCM) The smallest number, other than zero, that is a multiple of two or more given numbers.	**mínimo común múltiplo (m.c.m.)** El menor de los múltiplos (distinto de cero) de dos o más números.	The LCM of 10 and 18 is 90.
like fractions Fractions that have the same denominator.	**fracciones semejantes** Fracciones que tienen el mismo denominador.	$\frac{5}{12}$ and $\frac{3}{12}$ are like fractions.
like terms Terms with the same variables raised to the same exponents.	**términos semejantes** Términos con las mismas variables elevadas a los mismos exponentes.	$3a^2b^2$ and $7a^2b^2$
line A straight path that has no thickness and extends forever.	**recta** Trayectoria recta que no tiene ningún grueso y que se extiende por siempre.	$\longleftrightarrow \; \ell$
line graph A graph that uses line segments to show how data changes.	**gráfica lineal** Gráfica que muestra cómo cambian los datos mediante segmentos de recta.	 Marlon's Video Game Scores
line plot A number line with marks or dots that show frequency.	**diagrama de puntos** Recta numérica con marcas o puntos que indican la frecuencia.	 Number of Pets
line of reflection A line that a figure is flipped across to create a mirror image of the original figure.	**línea de reflexión** Línea sobre la cual se invierte una figura para crear una imagen reflejada de la figura original.	 Line of reflection
line of symmetry The imaginary "mirror" in line symmetry.	**eje de simetría** El espejo imaginario en la simetría axial.	
line segment A part of a line between two endpoints.	**segmento de recta** Parte de una línea con dos extremos.	 $A \quad\quad B$
line symmetry A figure has line symmetry if one-half is a mirror image of the other half.	**simetría axial** Una figura tiene simetría axial si una de sus mitades es la imagen reflejada de la otra.	

Glossary/Glosario

linear equation An equation whose solutions form a straight line on a coordinate plane.

ecuación lineal Ecuación en la que las soluciones forman una línea recta en un plano cartesiano.

$y = 2x + 1$

M

mean The sum of the items in a set of data divided by the number of items in the set; also called *average*.

media La suma de todos los elementos de un conjunto de datos dividida entre el número de elementos del conjunto.

Data set: 4, 6, 7, 8, 10

Mean: $\frac{4+6+7+8+10}{5} = \frac{35}{5} = 7$

mean absolute deviation (MAD) The mean distance between each data value and the mean of the data set.

desviación absoluta media (DAM) Distancia media entre cada dato y la media del conjunto de datos.

measure of center A measure used to describe the middle of a data set. Also called measure of central tendency.

medida central Medida que se usa para describir el centro de un conjunto de datos; la media, la mediana y la moda son medidas centrales. También se conocen como medidas de tendencia central.

measure of spread A measure that describes how far apart the data are distributed.

medida de dispersión Medida que describe la separación en una distribución de datos.

median The middle number or the mean (average) of the two middle numbers in an ordered set of data.

mediana El número intermedio o la media (el promedio) de los dos números intermedios en un conjunto ordenado de datos.

Data set: 4, 6, 7, 8, 10
Median: 7

metric system A decimal system of weights and measures that is used universally in science and commonly throughout the world.

sistema métrico Sistema decimal de pesos y medidas empleado universalmente en las ciencias y por lo general en todo el mundo.

centimeters, meters, kilometers, grams, kilograms, milliliters, liters

midpoint The point that divides a line segment into two congruent line segments.

punto medio El punto que divide un segmento de recta en dos segmentos de recta congruentes.

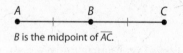

B is the midpoint of $\overline{AC}$.

mixed number A number made up of a whole number that is not zero and a fraction.

número mixto Número compuesto por un número cabal distinto de cero y una fracción.

$5\frac{1}{8}$

mode The number or numbers that occur most frequently in a set of data; when all numbers occur with the same frequency, we say there is no mode.

moda Número o números más frecuentes en un conjunto de datos; si todos los números aparecen con la misma frecuencia, no hay moda.

Data set: 3, 5, 8, 8, 10
Mode: 8

multiple The product of a number and any nonzero whole number.

múltiplo El producto de un número y cualquier número cabal distinto de cero es un múltiplo de ese número.

ENGLISH	SPANISH	EXAMPLES
Multiplication Property of Zero The property that states that the product of any number and 0 is 0.	**Propiedad de multiplicación del cero** Propiedad que establece que el producto de cualquier número y 0 es 0.	$6 \times 0 = 0$ $-5 \times 0 = 0$
multiplicative inverse One of two numbers whose product is 1.	**inverso multiplicativo** Uno de dos números cuyo producto es igual a 1.	The multiplicative inverse of $\frac{3}{4}$ is $\frac{4}{3}$.

ENGLISH	SPANISH	EXAMPLES
negative number A number less than zero.	**número negativo** Número menor que cero.	-2 is a negative number. 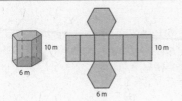
net An arrangement of two-dimensional figures that can be folded to form a polyhedron.	**plantilla** Arreglo de figuras bidimensionales que se doblan para formar un poliedro.	
numerator The top number of a fraction that tells how many parts of a whole are being considered.	**numerador** El número de arriba de una fracción; indica cuántas partes de un entero se consideran.	$\frac{3}{4}$ ← numerator
numerical expression An expression that contains only numbers and operations.	**expresión numérica** Expresión que incluye sólo números y operaciones.	$(2 \cdot 3) + 1$

ENGLISH	SPANISH	EXAMPLES
obtuse angle An angle whose measure is greater than 90° but less than 180°.	**ángulo obtuso** Ángulo que mide más de 90° y menos de 180°.	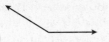
obtuse triangle A triangle containing one obtuse angle.	**triángulo obtusángulo** Triángulo que tiene un ángulo obtuso.	
odd number A whole number that is not divisible by two.	**número impar** Un número cabal que no es divisible entre dos.	
opposites Two numbers that are an equal distance from zero on a number line; also called additive inverse.	**opuestos** Dos números que están a la misma distancia de cero en una recta numérica. También se llaman *inversos aditivos*.	5 and -5 are opposites. 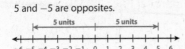

order of operations A rule for evaluating expressions: first perform the operations in parentheses, then compute powers and roots, then perform all multiplication and division from left to right, and then perform all addition and subtraction from left to right.

orden de las operaciones Regla para evaluar expresiones: primero se resuelven las operaciones entre paréntesis, luego se hallan las potencias y raíces, después todas las multiplicaciones y divisiones de izquierda a derecha y, por último, todas las sumas y restas de izquierda a derecha.

$$3^2 - 12 \div 4 \quad \text{Evaluate the power.}$$
$$9 - 12 \div 4 \quad \text{Divide.}$$
$$9 - 3 \quad \text{Subtract.}$$
$$6$$

ordered pair A pair of numbers that can be used to locate a point on a coordinate plane.

par ordenado Par de números que sirven para ubicar un punto en un plano cartesiano.

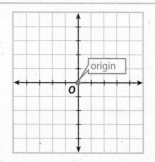

The coordinates of B are $(-2, 3)$.

origin The point where the *x*-axis and *y*-axis intersect on the coordinate plane; (0, 0).

origen Punto de intersección entre el eje *x* y el eje *y* en un plano cartesiano: (0, 0).

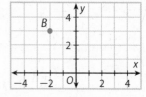

outcome A possible result of a probability experiment.

resultado Posible resultado de un experimento de probabilidad.

When rolling a number cube, the possible outcomes are 1, 2, 3, 4, 5, and 6.

outlier A value much greater or much less than the others in a data set.

valor atípico Un valor mucho mayor o menor que los demás valores de un conjunto de datos.

output The value that results from the substitution of a given input into an expression or function.

valor de salida Valor que resulta después de sustituir un valor de entrada determinado en una expresión o función.

For the rule $y = 6x$, the input 4 produces an output of 24.

overestimate An estimate that is greater than the exact answer.

estimación alta Estimación mayor que la respuesta exacta.

100 is an overestimate for the sum $23 + 24 + 21 + 22$.

P

parallel lines Lines in a plane that do not intersect.

rectas paralelas Líneas que se encuentran en el mismo plano pero que nunca se intersecan.

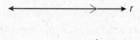

Glossary/Glosario

ENGLISH	SPANISH	EXAMPLES
parallelogram A quadrilateral with two pairs of parallel sides.	**paralelogramo** Cuadrilátero con dos pares de lados paralelos.	
pentagon A five-sided polygon.	**pentágono** Polígono de cinco lados.	
percent A ratio comparing a number to 100.	**porcentaje** Razón que compara un número con el número 100.	$45\% = \frac{45}{100}$
percent of decrease A percent change describing a decrease in a quantity.	**porcentaje de disminución** Porcentaje de cambio en que una cantidad disminuye.	An item that costs $8 is marked down to $6. The amount of the decrease is $2, and the percent of decrease is $\frac{2}{8} = 0.25 = 25\%$.
percent of increase A percent change describing an increase in a quantity.	**porcentaje de incremento** Porcentaje de cambio en que una cantidad aumenta.	The price of an item increases from $8 to $12. The amount of the increase is $4, and the percent of increase is $\frac{4}{8} = 0.5 = 50\%$.
perfect square A square of a whole number.	**cuadrado perfecto** El cuadrado de un número cabal.	$5^2 = 25$, so 25 is a perfect square.
perimeter The distance around a polygon.	**perímetro** Distancia alrededor de un polígono.	perimeter = 48 ft
permutation An arrangement of items or events in which order is important.	**permutación** Arreglo de objetos o sucesos en el que el orden es importante.	For objects *A*, *B*, and *C*, there are 6 different permutations: *ABC*, *ACB*, *BAC*, *BCA*, *CAB*, *CBA*.
perpendicular bisector A line that intersects a segment at its midpoint and is perpendicular to the segment.	**mediatriz** Línea que cruza un segmento en su punto medio y es perpendicular al segmento.	ℓ is the perpendicular bisector of $\overline{AB}$.
perpendicular lines Lines that intersect to form right angles.	**rectas perpendiculares** Líneas que al intersecarse forman ángulos rectos.	
pi (π) The ratio of the circumference of a circle to the length of its diameter; $\pi \approx 3.14$ or $\frac{22}{7}$.	**pi (π)** Razón de la circunferencia de un círculo a la longitud de su diámetro; $\pi < 3.14$ ó $\frac{22}{7}$	

ENGLISH	SPANISH	EXAMPLES
plane A flat surface that has no thickness and extends forever.	**plano** Superficie plana que no tiene ningún grueso y que se extiende por siempre.	plane *R* or plane *ABC*
point An exact location that has no size.	**punto** Ubicación exacta que no tiene ningún tamaño.	*P* • point *P*
polygon A closed plane figure formed by three or more line segments that intersect only at their endpoints.	**polígono** Figura plana cerrada, formada por tres o más segmentos de recta que se intersecan sólo en sus extremos.	
polyhedron A three-dimensional figure in which all the surfaces or faces are polygons.	**poliedro** Figura tridimensional cuyas superficies o caras tienen forma de polígonos.	
population The whole group being surveyed.	**población** El grupo completo que es objeto de estudio.	In a survey about eating habits of middle school students, the population is all middle school students.
positive number A number greater than zero.	**número positivo** Número mayor que cero.	2 is a positive number.
power A number produced by raising a base to an exponent.	**potencia** Número que resulta al elevar una base a un exponente.	$2^3 = 8$, so 2 to the 3rd power is 8.
prediction A guess about something that will happen in the future.	**predicción** Pronóstico sobre algo que puede ocurrir en el futuro.	
prime factorization A number written as the product of its prime factors.	**descomposición en factores primos** Un número escrito como el producto de sus factores primos.	$10 = 2 \cdot 5$ $24 = 2^3 \cdot 3$
prime number A whole number greater than 1 that has exactly two factors, itself and 1.	**número primo** Número cabal mayor que 1 que sólo es divisible entre 1 y él mismo.	5 is prime because its only factors are 5 and 1.
principal The initial amount of money borrowed or saved.	**capital** Cantidad inicial de dinero depositada o recibida en préstamo.	
prism A polyhedron that has two congruent, polygon-shaped bases and other faces that are all rectangles.	**prisma** Poliedro con dos bases congruentes con forma de polígono y caras con forma de rectángulos.	

Glossary/Glosario

ENGLISH	SPANISH	EXAMPLES
probability A number from 0 to 1 (or 0% to 100%) that describes how likely an event is to occur.	**probabilidad** Un número entre 0 y 1 (ó 0% y 100%) que describe qué tan probable es un suceso.	A bag contains 3 red marbles and 4 blue marbles. The probability of randomly choosing a red marble is $\frac{3}{7}$.
product The result when two or more numbers are multiplied.	**producto** Resultado de multiplicar dos o más números.	The product of 4 and 8 is 32.
proper fraction A fraction in which the numerator is less than the denominator.	**fracción propia** Fracción en la que el numerador es menor que el denominador.	$\frac{3}{4}, \frac{1}{13}, \frac{7}{8}$
proportion An equation that states that two ratios are equivalent.	**proporción** Ecuación que establece que dos razones son equivalentes.	$\frac{2}{3} = \frac{4}{6}$
proportional relationship A relationship between two quantities in which the ratio of one quantity to the other quantity is constant.	**relación proporcional** Relación entre dos cantidades en que la razón de una cantidad a la otra es constante.	
protractor A tool for measuring angles.	**transportador** Instrumento para medir ángulos.	
pyramid A polyhedron with a polygon base and triangular sides that all meet at a common vertex.	**pirámide** Poliedro cuya base es un polígono; tiene caras triangulares que se juntan en un vértice común.	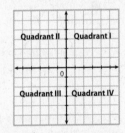

Q

quadrant The x- and y-axes divide the coordinate plane into four regions. Each region is called a quadrant.	**cuadrante** El eje x y el eje y dividen el plano cartesiano en cuatro regiones. Cada región recibe el nombre de cuadrante.	
quartile Three values, one of which is the median, that divide a data set into fourths.	**cuartil** Cada uno de tres valores, uno de los cuales es la mediana, que dividen en cuartos un conjunto de datos.	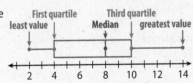
quotient The result when one number is divided by another.	**cociente** Resultado de dividir un número entre otro.	In $8 \div 4 = 2$, 2 is the quotient.

Glossary/Glosario

radius A line segment with one endpoint at the center of a circle and the other endpoint on the circle, or the length of that segment.

radio Segmento de recta con un extremo en el centro de un círculo y el otro en la circunferencia, o bien la longitud de ese segmento.

range In statistics, the difference between the greatest and least values in a data set.

rango (en estadística) Diferencia entre los valores máximo y mínimo de un conjunto de datos.

rate A ratio that compares two quantities measured in different units.

tasa Una razón que compara dos cantidades medidas en diferentes unidades.

rate of change A ratio that compares the difference between two output values to the difference between the corresponding input values.

tasa de cambio Razón que compara la diferencia entre dos salidas con la diferencia entre dos entrados.

The cost of mailing a letter increased from 22 cents in 1985 to 25 cents in 1988. The rate of change was
$$\frac{25 - 22}{1988 - 1985} = \frac{3}{3}$$
$$= 1 \text{ cent per year.}$$

rate of interest The percent charged or earned on an amount of money; see *simple interest*.

tasa de interés Porcentaje que se cobra por una cantidad de dinero prestada o que se gana por una cantidad de dinero ahorrada; ver *interés simple*.

ratio A comparison of two quantities by division.

razón Comparación de dos cantidades mediante una división.

12 to 25, 12:25, $\frac{12}{25}$

rational number A number that can be expressed as a ratio of two integers and can be written in the form $\frac{a}{b}$, where a and b are integers and $b \neq 0$.

número racional Número que se puede escribir como una razón de dos enteros y se puede expresar como $\frac{a}{b}$, donde a y b son números enteros y $b \neq 0$.

3, 1.75, $0.\overline{3}$, $-\frac{2}{3}$, 0

ray A part of a line that starts at one endpoint and extends forever in one direction.

rayo Parte de una línea que comienza en un extremo y se extiende siempre en una dirección.

D

reciprocal One of two numbers whose product is 1.

recíproco Uno de dos números cuyo producto es igual a 1.

The reciprocal of $\frac{2}{3}$ is $\frac{3}{2}$.

rectangle A parallelogram with four right angles.

rectángulo Paralelogramo con cuatro ángulos rectos.

rectangular prism A polyhedron whose bases are rectangles and whose other faces are rectangles.

prisma rectangular Poliedro cuyas bases son rectángulos y cuyas caras tienen forma de rectángulos.

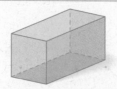

ENGLISH	SPANISH	EXAMPLES

reflection A transformation of a figure that flips the figure across a line.

reflexión Transformación que ocurre cuando se invierte una figura sobre una línea.

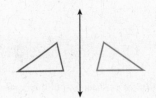

---

regular polygon A polygon with congruent sides and angles.

polígono regular Polígono con lados y ángulos congruentes.

---

relative frequency The ratio of the number of times an event or data value occurs and the total number of events or data values.

frecuencia relativa La razón del número de veces que ocurre un evento o dato (frecuencia) al total del número de eventos o datos.

---

repeating decimal A decimal in which one or more digits repeat infinitely.

decimal periódico Decimal en el que uno o más dígitos se repiten infinitamente.

$0.75757575\ldots = 0.\overline{75}$

---

rhombus A parallelogram with all sides congruent.

rombo Paralelogramo en el que todos los lados son congruentes.

---

right angle An angle that measures 90°.

ángulo recto Ángulo que mide exactamente 90°.

---

right triangle A triangle containing a right angle.

triángulo rectángulo Triángulo que tiene un ángulo recto.

---

rotation A transformation in which a figure is turned around a point.

rotación Transformación que ocurre cuando una figura gira alrededor de un punto.

---

rotational symmetry A figure that can be rotated about a point by an angle less than 360° so that the image coincides with the preimage has rotational symmetry.

simetría de rotación Una figura que puede rotarse alrededor de un punto en un ángulo menor de 360° de forma tal que la imagen coincide con la imagen original que tenga simetría de rotación.

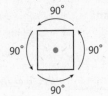

---

rounding Replacing a number with an estimate of that number to a given place value.

redondear Sustituir un número por una estimación de ese número hasta cierto valor posicional.

2,354 rounded to the nearest thousand is 2,000; 2,354 rounded to the nearest 100 is 2,400.

Glossary/Glosario

sales tax A percent of the cost of an item which is charged by governments to raise money.

impuesto sobre la venta Porcentaje del costo de un artículo que los gobiernos cobran para recaudar fondos.

sample A part of a group being surveyed.

muestra Parte de un grupo que es objeto de estudio.

In a survey about eating habits of middle school math students, a sample is a survey of 100 randomly chosen students.

sample space All possible outcomes of an experiment.

espacio muestral Conjunto de todos los resultados posibles de un experimento.

When rolling a number cube, the sample space is 1, 2, 3, 4, 5, 6.

scale The ratio between two sets of measurements.

escala La razón entre dos conjuntos de medidas.

1 cm: 5 mi

scale drawing A drawing that uses a scale to make an object proportionally smaller than or larger than the real object.

dibujo a escala Dibujo en el que se usa una escala para que un objeto se vea proporcionalmente mayor o menor que el objeto real al que representa.

A blueprint is an example of a scale drawing.

scale model A proportional model of a three-dimensional object.

modelo a escala Modelo proporcional de un objeto tridimensional.

scalene triangle A triangle with no congruent sides.

triángulo escaleno Triángulo que no tiene lados congruentes.

scholarship A monetary award to a student to support their education.

becas Dinero que se otorga a los estudiantes en base a logros.

scientific notation A method of writing very large or very small numbers by using powers of 10.

notación científica Método que se usa para escribir números muy grandes o muy pequeños mediante potencias de 10.

$12{,}560{,}000{,}000{,}000 = 1.256 \times 10^{13}$

segment A part of a line made of two endpoints and all points between them.

segmento Parte de una línea que consiste en dos extremos y todos los puntos entre éstos.

A ———————— B

sequence An ordered list of numbers.

sucesión Lista ordenada de números.

2, 4, 6, 8, 10, . . .

set A group of items.

conjunto Un grupo de elementos.

side A line bounding a geometric figure; one of the faces forming the outside of an object.

lado Línea que delimita las figuras geométricas; una de las caras que forman la parte exterior de un objeto.

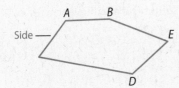

---

significant figures The figures used to express the precision of a measurement.

dígitos significativos Dígitos usados para expresar la precisión de una medida.

---

similar Figures with the same shape but not necessarily the same size are similar.

semejantes Figuras que tienen la misma forma, pero no necesariamente el mismo tamaño.

---

simple event An event consisting of only one outcome.

suceso simple Suceso que tiene sólo un resultado.

In the experiment of rolling a number cube, the event consisting of the outcome 3 is a simple event.

---

simple interest A fixed percent of the principal. It is found using the formula $I = Prt$, where P represents the principal, r the rate of interest, and t the time.

interés simple Un porcentaje fijo del capital. Se calcula con la fórmula $I = Cit$, donde C representa el capital, i, la tasa de interés y t, el tiempo.

---

simplest form (of a fraction) A fraction is in simplest form when the numerator and denominator have no common factors other than 1.

mínima expresión (de una fracción) Una fracción está en su mínima expresión cuando el numerador y el denominador no tienen más factor común que 1.

Fraction: $\frac{8}{12}$
Simplest form: $\frac{2}{3}$

---

simplify To write a fraction or expression in simplest form.

simplificar Escribir una fracción o expresión numérica en su mínima expresión.

---

simulation A model of an experiment, often one that would be too difficult or too time-consuming to actually perform.

simulación Representación de un experimento, por lo regular de uno cuya realización sería demasiado difícil o llevaría mucho tiempo.

---

skew lines Lines that lie in different planes that are neither parallel nor intersecting.

líneas oblicuas Líneas que se encuentran en planos distintos, por eso no se intersecan ni son paralelas.

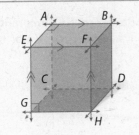

---

slope The constant rate of change of a line.

pendiente La tasa de cambio constante de una línea.

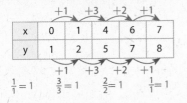

ENGLISH	SPANISH	EXAMPLES
solid figure A three-dimensional figure.	**cuerpo geométrico** Figura tridimensional.	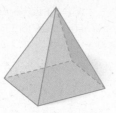
solution of an equation A value or values that make an equation true.	**solución de una ecuación** Valor o valores que hacen verdadera una ecuación.	Equation: $x + 2 = 6$ Solution: $x = 4$
solution of an inequality A value or values that make an inequality true.	**solución de una desigualdad** Valor o valores que hacen verdadera una desigualdad.	Inequality: $x + 3 \geq 10$ Solution set: $x \geq 7$
solution set The set of values that make a statement true.	**conjunto solución** Conjunto de valores que hacen verdadero un enunciado.	Inequality: $x + 3 \geq 5$ Solution set: $x \geq 2$
solve To find an answer or a solution.	**resolver** Hallar una respuesta o solución.	
square (geometry) A rectangle with four congruent sides.	**cuadrado (en geometría)** Rectángulo con cuatro lados congruentes.	
square (numeration) A number raised to the second power.	**cuadrado (en numeración)** Número elevado a la segunda potencia.	In 5^2, the number 5 is squared.
square number A number that is the product of a whole number and itself.	**cuadrado de un número** El producto de un número cabal multiplicado por sí mismo.	25 is a square number since $5^2 = 25$.
square root A number that is multiplied by itself to form a product is called a square root of that product.	**raíz cuadrada** El número que se multiplica por sí mismo para formar un producto se denomina la raíz cuadrada de ese producto.	$16 = 4 \cdot 4$ and $16 = -4 \cdot -4$, so 4 and -4 are square roots of 16.
standard form (in numeration) A number written using digits.	**forma estándar** Una forma de escribir números por medio de dígitos.	Five thousand, two hundred ten in standard form is 5,210.
statistical question A question that has many different, or variable, answers.	**pregunta estadística** Pregunta con muchas respuestas o variables diferentes.	

Glossary/Glosario

straight angle An angle that measures 180°.

ángulo llano Ángulo que mide exactamente 180°.

---

subset A set contained within another set.

subconjunto Conjunto que pertenece a otro conjunto.

---

substitute To replace a variable with a number or another expression in an algebraic expression.

sustituir Reemplazar una variable por un número u otra expresión en una expresión algebraica.

---

sum The result when two or more numbers are added.

suma Resultado de sumar dos o más números.

---

supplementary angles Two angles whose measures have a sum of 180°.

ángulos suplementarios Dos ángulos cuyas medidas suman 180°.

30° 150°

---

surface area The sum of the areas of the faces, or surfaces, of a three-dimensional figure.

área total Suma de las áreas de las caras, o superficies, de una figura tridimensional.

12 cm

6 cm

8 cm

Surface area = 2(8)(12) + 2(8)(6) + 2(12)(6) = 432cm^2

T

term (in an expression) The parts of an expression that are added or subtracted.

término (en una expresión) Las partes de una expresión que se suman o se restan.

$3x^2 +$ $6x -$ 8

↑   ↑   ↑

Term   Term   Term

---

terminating decimal A decimal number that ends, or terminates.

decimal finito Decimal con un número determinado de posiciones decimales.

6.75

---

tessellation A repeating pattern of plane figures that completely covers a plane with no gaps or overlaps.

teselado Patrón repetido de figuras planas que cubren totalmente un plano sin superponerse ni dejar huecos.

---

theoretical probability The ratio of the number of ways an event can occur to the total number of equally likely outcomes.

probabilidad teórica Razón del número de las maneras que puede ocurrir un suceso al número total de resultados igualmente probables.

When rolling a number cube, the theoretical probability of rolling a 4 is $\frac{1}{6}$.

---

tip The amount of money added to a bill for service; usually a percent of the bill.

propina Cantidad que se agrega al total de una factura por servicios. Por lo general, es un porcentaje del total de la factura.

transformation A change in the size or position of a figure.

transformación Cambio en el tamaño o la posición de una figura.

translation A movement (slide) of a figure along a straight line.

traslación Desplazamiento de una figura a lo largo de una línea recta.

trapezoid A quadrilateral with at least one pair of parallel sides.

trapecio Cuadrilátero con al menos un par de lados paralelos.

tree diagram A branching diagram that shows all possible combinations or outcomes of an event.

diagrama de árbol Diagrama ramificado que muestra todas las posibles combinaciones o resultados de un suceso.

trial Each repetition or observation of an experiment.

prueba Cada repetición u observación de un experimento.

In the experiment of rolling a number cube, each roll is one trial.

triangle A three-sided polygon.

triángulo Polígono de tres lados.

Triangle Sum Theorem The theorem that states that the measures of the angles in a triangle add to 180°.

Teorema de la suma del triángulo Teorema que establece que las medidas de los ángulos de un triángulo suman 180°.

triangular prism A polyhedron whose bases are triangles and whose other faces are rectangles.

prisma triangular Poliedro cuyas bases son triángulos y cuyas demás caras tienen forma de rectángulos.

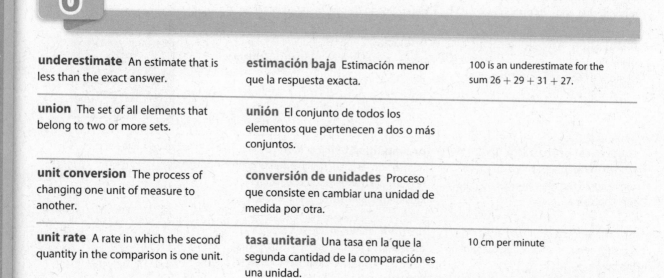

U

underestimate An estimate that is less than the exact answer.

estimación baja Estimación menor que la respuesta exacta.

100 is an underestimate for the sum $26 + 29 + 31 + 27$.

union The set of all elements that belong to two or more sets.

unión El conjunto de todos los elementos que pertenecen a dos o más conjuntos.

unit conversion The process of changing one unit of measure to another.

conversión de unidades Proceso que consiste en cambiar una unidad de medida por otra.

unit rate A rate in which the second quantity in the comparison is one unit.

tasa unitaria Una tasa en la que la segunda cantidad de la comparación es una unidad.

10 cm per minute

Glossary/Glosario

ENGLISH	SPANISH	EXAMPLES
unlike fractions Fractions with different denominators.	**fracciones distintas** Fracciones con distinto denominador.	$\frac{3}{4}$ and $\frac{1}{2}$ are unlike fractions.

ENGLISH	SPANISH	EXAMPLES
variable A symbol used to represent a quantity that can change.	**variable** Símbolo que representa una cantidad que puede cambiar.	In the expression $2x + 3$, x is the variable.
variation (variability) The spread of values in a set of data.	**variación (variabilidad)** Amplitud de los valores de un conjunto de datos.	The data set {1, 5, 7, 10, 25} has greater variation than the data set {8, 8, 9, 9, 9}.
Venn diagram A diagram that is used to show relationships between sets.	**diagrama de Venn** Diagrama que muestra las relaciones entre conjuntos.	
vertex (vertices) On an angle or polygon, the point where two sides intersect.	**vértice (vértices)** En un ángulo o polígono, el punto de intersección de dos lados.	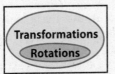 A is the vertex of $\angle CAB$.
vertical angles A pair of opposite congruent angles formed by intersecting lines.	**ángulos opuestos por el vértice** Par de ángulos opuestos congruentes formados por líneas secantes.	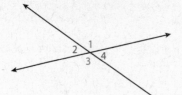 $\angle 1$ and $\angle 3$ are vertical angles. $\angle 2$ and $\angle 4$ are vertical angles.
volume The number of cubic units needed to fill a given space.	**volumen** Número de unidades cúbicas que se necesitan para llenar un espacio.	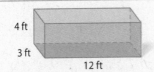 Volume $= 3 \cdot 4 \cdot 12 = 144$ ft³

ENGLISH	SPANISH	EXAMPLES
work-study program A program in which students are able to work at jobs on campus to make money to pay their college tuition.	**programas de trabajo y estudio** Programas que permiten a los estudiantes universitarios trabajar a medio tiempo y así ganar dinero para las matrículas universitarias y los gastos.	

Glossary/Glosario

x-axis The horizontal axis on a coordinate plane.

eje x El eje horizontal del plano cartesiano.

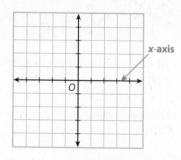

x-coordinate The first number in an ordered pair; it tells the distance to move right or left from the origin, (0, 0).

coordenada x El primer número en un par ordenado; indica la distancia que debes avanzar hacia la izquierda o hacia la derecha desde el origen, (0, 0).

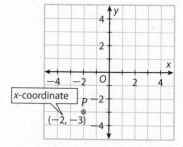

y-axis The vertical axis on a coordinate plane.

eje y El eje vertical del plano cartesiano.

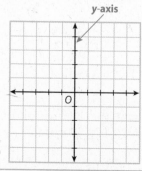

y-coordinate The second number in an ordered pair; it tells the distance to move up or down from the origin, (0, 0).

coordenada y El segundo número en un par ordenado; indica la distancia que debes avanzar hacia arriba o hacia abajo desde el origen, (0, 0).

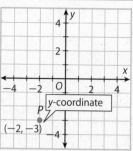

zero pair A number and its opposite, which add to 0.

par nulo Un número y su opuesto, que sumados dan 0.

18 and -18

Index

Index

Index

Index

of percents using grids, 203
of perimeter using grids, 408
positive and negative numbers, 9
rational numbers, 60
rational numbers and absolute values, 55
rational numbers and opposites, 54
relationships between rational numbers, integers, and whole numbers, 49, 50
to represent ratios, 149
sums of integers with different signs, 502–503
sums of integers with the same sign, 495

models, strategic use of, 485

money. *See* Financial literacy

Moon, 103, 111

Multiple Representations, 8, 12, 17, 47, 58, 91, 100, 113, 117, 125, 134, 154, 156, 184, 207, 210, 214, 247, 282, 302, 356, 376, 434, 468, 481, 499, 530, 621, 622, 633

multiples, 37, 38
common, 38
least common, 37–40, 81–82

multiplication
algebraic expressions for, 261
associative property of, 277
commutative property of, 277, 571
of decimals, 119–122
of equations, 313
to find equivalent ratios, 151
of fractions, 80–81
two fractions, 79–80
using GCF in, 79–82
whole numbers and fractions, 80–81
identity property of, 277
in order of operations, 249
of integers, 525–526
prime factorization and, 244
of rational numbers, 571–576
with different signs, 571–572
with the same sign, 572–573
three or more numbers, 573–574
using number lines, 571–574
repeated, 237. *See also* exponents
as repeated addition, 571
rewriting division problems as, 579

Multistep, 51, 57, 83, 95, 123, 134, 153, 159, 165, 183, 190, 208, 222, 253, 267, 268, 310, 318, 343, 349, 356, 376, 381, 382, 387, 394, 434, 462, 475, 476, 482, 499, 500, 505, 517, 535, 541, 575, 581, 609, 646

multistep equations, 606–608, 613–614
for simple interest, **642**
using multiple percents, **643**

multistep problems, with fractions and mixed numbers, 97–100
multistep equations, 606–608, 613–614

music, 83

rational numbers, 549
adding, 555–559
dividing, 577–582
multiplying, 571–574
subtracting, 564, 568

nets, 419
and surface area, 419–424
of prisms, 421
of pyramids, 420
using, 419

New Orleans, Louisiana, 562

number lines
absolute value and, 19–20
distance on, 566–567
double, 163
equivalent fractions and decimals on, 59, 60, 132
elevation and, 513, 531
inequalities and, 15, 319–321
integers on, 9–10
adding, 496, 501–502
multiplying, 525
subtracting, 508
opposites on, 9, 54
ordering integers on, 14
positive and negative numbers on, 7, 9, 13, 14
rational numbers on, 6, 54, 61
adding, 555–560
multiplying, 571–574
subtracting, 563–567
representing rates on, 163
solving equations using, 305, 312, 313

numbers
additive inverse of, 558–559, 562
exponents representing, 237–242
finding distance between, 566
mixed, 74
dividing, 91–93
multistep problems with fractions and, 97–100
negative, 2, 7, 13–14, 20–21
positive, 7, 13–15
prime, 32
rational. *See* rational numbers
whole. *See* whole numbers

numerator, 606

numerical expressions
defined, 250
simplifying, 250–253

occupations. *See* careers

octagons, 407, 412

operations, 261
with fractions
GCF in multiplying fractions, 79–82
LCM in adding and subtracting fractions, 81–82
word problems with, 97–100
with integers, 495–520, 525–544
interpret in context, 513–518, 537–542, 570A–570B, 582B, 582D, 583–588

for multistep problems, 97
order of, 97, 98, 249–254
with rational numbers, 131–134, 495–544, 583–588
converting fractions and decimals, 132
interpreting word problems, 131–132
See also individual operations

opposites, 6, 8, 277, 558, 575
evaluating expressions and, 270–271
on a number line, 9, 54

ordered pairs, 407, 617, 618

order of operations, 97, 98, 249–254
defined, 232
exponents with grouping symbols, 251
in simplifying numerical expressions, 250–253
using, 249–250

origin, 292, 331, 617, 618

ounces, 191, 195

outliers, 471

P

parallelograms, 371, 389, 394, 409

parentheses, order of operations and, 97, 249, 251

patterns
in multiplying rational numbers, 573, 576
in ratios, 553
in repeated multiplication, 237
in repeating decimals, 550, 554
in simplifying expressions, 570

peaks, 471

pentagons, 412

percent bars, 204

percents, 202, 203
applications of, 641–646
benchmarks and proportional reasoning and, 204–205
defined, 628
error, 634
fractions and, 204
markup and markdown, 635–640
modeling equivalencies with decimals and fractions, 210
percent decrease, 600, 628, 630–634, 642–644
percent increase, 628, 629, 631–640
rewriting expressions of, 641–646
rounding, 632, 638
simple interest, 642
solving problems involving, 215–219
using grids to model, 203
using multiple percents, 643
writing as decimals and fractions, 209
writing fractions as, 211–212

percent decrease, 600, 628, 630-634
markdowns, 642–644

percent increase, 628, 629, 631-634
markups, 641–646

Performance Tasks, 70, 140, 228, 288, 362, 440, 486, 595–596

perimeter
of hexagons, 411
of polygons in coordinate plane, 408

Index

tips, 643–645, 647
tons, 433
trapezoids, 372–373, 384
    area of, 394
    perimeter of, 411
triangles
    area of, 377–380, 383, 389–392, 394, 412
    on coordinate plane, 407
    problem solving using area of, 383
triangular prisms, 422–424
triangular pyramids, 420
tri–folds, 45, 171
two–panel flip charts, 29, 147, 399

Understand Vocabulary, 29, 45, 77, 105, 147,
    171, 201, 235, 259, 295, 329, 369, 399, 417,
    447, 493, 523, 547, 603, 627
unit cost, 156
unit price, 156
unit rates, 148, 156, 172
    calculating, 156–157, 605–610
    problem solving with, 157–158
    solving proportions with, 180
    using to convert units, 186–187
units
    converting using conversion factors, 187–188
    using models to convert, 185
    using proportions and unit rates to convert,
        186–187
Unpacking the Standards, 6, 30, 46, 78, 106,
    148, 172, 202, 236, 260, 296, 330, 370, 400,
    418, 448, 494, 524, 548, 604, 628
upper quartile, 463

variability
    mean absolute deviation, 455–462
    measure of, 455
variable data, statistical questions and, 469
variables, 261
    defined, 232
    in equations with proportional relationships,
        613
    independent and dependent in tables and
        graphs, 337–341

    writing equations from tables and, 346–347
Venn diagrams, 2, 49
Venus, 568
vertices, 407
    of polygons, 407, 409, 410
    of triangles, 412
Video Tutor. *See* Math on the Spot
Visualize Vocabulary, 5, 29, 45, 77, 105, 147,
    171, 201, 235, 259, 295, 329, 369, 399, 417,
    447, 493, 523, 547, 603, 627
vocabulary, 22, 29, 36, 39, 45, 51, 77, 105, 112,
    171, 301, 329, 334, 349, 399, 411, 423, 554, 562
    Understand Vocabulary, 29, 45, 77, 105, 147,
        171, 201, 235, 259, 295, 329, 369, 399, 417,
        447, 493, 523, 547, 603, 627
    Visualize Vocabulary, 5, 29, 45, 77, 105, 147,
        171, 201, 235, 259, 295, 329, 369, 399,
        417, 447, 493, 523, 547, 603, 627
    Vocabulary Preview, 2, 74, 144, 232, 292, 366,
        444, 490, 600
Vocabulary Preview, 2, 74, 144, 232, 292, 366,
    444, 490, 600
volume
    of cubes, 425–426, 428
    of rectangular prisms, 425–434
    solving equations for, 431–434

weight, measurements of, 186
What If?, 12, 31, 91, 117, 118, 134, 154, 159, 177,
    195, 244, 268, 282, 307, 345, 382, 451, 460,
    462, 475, 476, 479, 511, 530, 538, 609, 619
What's the Error?, 193
whole numbers
    division
        of decimals by whole numbers, 126
        of multi–digit whole numbers, 107–112
    greatest common factor of, 31–36
    least common multiple, 37–40
    multiplying fractions and, 80–81
    Venn diagram of, 49
width, volume and, 426–434
word problems
    expressions representing, 134
    with fractions and mixed numbers, 97–100
    interpreting, 131–134

x–axis, 331, 401, 404
x–coordinate, 331

yards, 191, 194–196, 410
Yellowstone National Park, 631
y–axis, 401, 404
y–coordinate, 331

zero
    absolute value and, 6
    as additive inverse, 558
    as an exponent, 239
    division by, 532
    as placeholder, 114, 115
    points on axes and, 332
    in products of rational numbers, 563
    properties of operations and, 277

Index

ASSESSMENT REFERENCE SHEET

TABLE OF MEASURES

Length

1 inch = 2.54 centimeters

1 meter ≈ 39.37 inches

1 mile = 5,280 feet

1 mile = 1,760 yards

1 mile ≈ 1.609 kilometers

1 kilometer ≈ 0.62 mile

Mass/Weight

1 pound = 16 ounces

1 pound ≈ 0.454 kilogram

1 kilogram ≈ 2.2 pounds

1 ton = 2,000 pounds

Capacity

1 cup = 8 fluid ounces

1 pint = 2 cups

1 quart = 2 pints

1 gallon = 4 quarts

1 gallon ≈ 3.785 liters

1 liter ≈ 0.264 gallon

1 liter = 1000 cubic centimeters

FORMULAS

Area

Parallelogram	$A = bh$
Circle	$A = \pi r^2$
Triangle	$A = \frac{1}{2} bh$

Volume

General Prisms	$V = Bh$
Cylinder	$V = \pi r^2 h$
Sphere	$V = \frac{4}{3} \pi r^3$
Cone	$V = \frac{1}{3} \pi r^2 h$

Circumference

Circle	$C = \pi d$ or $C = 2\pi r$

Other

Pythagorean Theorem	$a^2 + b^2 = c^2$